ACCOUNTING THEORY

To Dimitra

Ahmed Riahi-Belkaoui

University of Illinois at Chicago Illinois, USA

Fifth Edition

ACCOUNTING THEORY

Australia • Canada • Mexico • Singapore • Spain • United Kingdom • United States

THOMSON
TM

Accounting Theory: Fifth Edition

Copyright © Thomson Learning 2004
The Thomson logo is a registered trademark used herein under licence.

For more information, contact Thomson Learning, High Holborn House,
50–51 Bedford Row, London WC1R 4LR or visit us on the World Wide Web at:
http://www.thomsonlearning.co.uk

British Library Cataloguing-in-Publication Data
A catalogue record for this book is available from the British Library

ISBN 1-84480-029-6

Typeset by Saxon Graphics Ltd, Derby
Printed in Great Britain by TJ International, Padstow, Cornwall

Contents

Edinburgh Napier University
Information Services / Library

Customer name: SHUO WANG
Customer ID: *********3608

Title: Socio-economic accounting /
ID: 38042000754941
Due: 24/04/2017 23:59:00 BST

Title: Accounting theory /
ID: 38042007642513
Due: 24/04/2017 23:59:00 BST

Total items: 2
27/03/2017   15:46
Overdue: 0
Hold requests: 0

Thank you for using Self Service Loan &
Return
Your loan will renew automatically for up to
12 weeks (books) or 4 weeks (most other
items), if the title is not Requested
Keep up to date through LibrarySearch /
My Library Card, and your weekly Library
Activity Update
We welcome your Feedback
Email: Library@Napier.ac.uk
Phone: 0131 455 3500

Preface

A single generally accepted accounting theory does not exist at this time. Several attempts have been made to formulate such a theory. Starting with different assumptions and using different methodologies, the various attempts have resulted in different frameworks for financial reporting standards.

The construction of an accounting theory requires the justification or refutation of existing accounting practices. Under the traditional approach, construction and verification of a theory were considered virtually synonymous. In the past ten years, however, a new approach that employs a distinct verification process has emerged. The underlying objective of both approaches is the same: to develop a conceptual framework for what accountants do or are expected to be doing. A coherent system of objectives and assumptions is necessary for the promulgation of consistent standards that define the nature, function, and scope of financial statements and the techniques for producing them. In other words, the standard-setting process must be guided by a generally accepted accounting theory.

Constructing and verifying an accounting theory consists of defining and selecting the objectives of accounting and financial statements and delineating the elements of financial statements, the attributes of these elements, and the appropriate unit of measure to be used. Given the diversity of assumptions within the accounting environment, writers, researchers, and practitioners have tackled the task of theory construction in various ways. The result has been a state of continual crisis or revolution within accounting, in which (1) various accounting paradigms, or models, have competed for primacy, (2) vested interests groups have argued for the domination of their particular paradigms and resultant theories, and (3) a gradual politicization of the standard-setting process has taken place.

Accounting Theory, Fifth Edition is intended for junior, senior, and graduate courses in financial accounting, financial accounting theory, seminars in asset valuation and income determination, and contemporary issues in accounting. The textbook should be helpful to those who wish to study for professional accounting examinations and to those who wish to keep up to date with current accounting research and education.

Accounting Theory, Fifth Edition consist of 16 chapters. Chapter 1 describes the history and development of accounting. Chapter 2 covers the nature and uses of accounting. Chapter 3 covers the elements and structure of a theory. Chapter 4 describes the traditional approaches to the formulation of an accounting theory. Chapter 5 elaborates on the regulatory approaches to accounting theory. Chapter 6 discusses the development of a conceptual framework for financial accounting. Chapter 7 identifies and explains the theoretical structure of accounting. Chapter 8 covers the issues of fairness, disclosure and future trends in accounting. Chapter 9 looks at the research perspective in accounting. Chapter 10 presents a philosophical and scientific view of accounting as a multiparadigmatic science. Chapter 11 presents the event and behavioral approaches to the formulation of an accounting theory. Chapter 12 examines the predictive approaches to the formulation of an accounting theory. Chapter 13 presents the positive approach to the formulation of an accounting theory and covers the issues of income smoothing and earnings management. Chapter 14 commences the examination of the asset valuation/income determination issue by focusing on current-value accounting. Chapter 15 presents general price-level accounting as an alternative accounting approach. Finally, Chapter 16 offers a synthesis of the asset valuation and income determination models; a clear differentiation is made between the attributes to be measured and the unit of measurement used.

Acknowledgments

I wish to express appreciation to the offices of the American Institute of Certified Public Accountant (AICPA), the Financial Accounting Standard Board (FASB), the American Accounting Association and the Editor of *Accounting, Organizations and Society* for their kind permission to reprint some of their material.

FASB Statement No. 5, *Recognition and Measurement in Financial Statements of Business Enterprises*, is copyrighted by the Financial Accounting Standard Board, 401 Merritt 7, P.O. Box 5116, Norwalk, Connecticut 06856–5116, USA. Portions are reprinted with permission. Complete copies of this document are available from the FASB.

I am indebted to numerous people for their help in reviewing the manuscript for the fifth edition. Literally scores of changes have been made in the fifth edition as a result of comments and suggestions received from anonymous reviewers of the manuscript at various stages.

I wish to thank Vijay Kamdar and Maninder Bhuller of the University of Illinois at Chicago for their cheerful and intelligent assistance. I also thank them for their continuous and intelligent support. Finally, Fiona Freel and Annette Abel of Thomson Learning are to be congratulated for a professional job.

The history and development of accounting

1.1 Introduction

The importance of accounting has always needed some strong defense. Witness the following quotation:

> I have tried to remove the stigma attached to accounting by showing that in its origin it is respectable, nay, even academic: that despite its present disrepute it has from time to time attracted the attention of men of unquestioned intellectual attainment; that it justifies itself in that it has arisen to meet a social need. Its functions are to locate responsibility, to prevent fraud, to guide industry, to determine equities, to solve the all essential conundrum of business: "What are my profits?"; to facilitate the government in its fiscal operations, to guide the business manager in the attempt to secure efficiency. Are not these efforts worthy of any man's attention? And so I close this paper with quotations from men whom all must respect: Scott, the romanticist,

declared the profession of accounting "respectable"; Goethe, the universal genius, speaks of bookkeeping as 'one of the fairest inventions of the human mind' and Cayley, scientist beyond question, even more significantly declared "Bookkeeping is one of the two perfect sciences." With these I rest the defense of my houn' dog.[1]

The study of the history and development of accounting is very important to an understanding and appreciation of present and future practices, as well as of the institutional structure of the discipline. This chapter presents the important facets of the history and development of accounting that should be known by every serious student of the accounting discipline.

1.2 Evolution of double-entry bookkeeping

1.2.1 Early history of accounting

Various attempts have been made to locate the place and time of birth of the double-entry system, resulting in various scenarios.[2] Most of the scenarios recognize the presence of some form of record-keeping in most civilizations dating back to about 3000 BC. Included are the Chaldean-Babylonian, Assyrian and Sumerian civilizations, the producers of the first organized government in the world, some of the oldest written languages, and the oldest surviving business records; the Egyptian civilizations, where scribes formed the "pivots on which the whole machinery of the treasury and the other departments turned",[3] the Chinese civilization, with government accounting playing a key and sophisticated role during the Chao Dynasty (1122–256 BC); the Greek civilization, where Zenon, a manager of the great estate of Appolonius, introduced in 256 BC an elaborate system of responsibility accounting;[4] and the Roman civilization, with laws requiring taxpayers to prepare statements of their financial positions, and with civil rights depending on the level of property declared by the citizens.[5] The presence of these forms of bookkeeping in the ancient world has been attributed to various factors, including the invention of writing, the introduction of Arabic numerals and of the decimal system, the diffusion of knowledge of algebra, the presence of inexpensive writing material, the rise of literacy, and the existence of a standard medium of exchange. In fact, A.C. Littleton lists seven preconditions for the emergence of systematic bookkeeping:

> *The Art of Writing*, since bookkeeping is first of all a record; *Arithmetic*, since the mechanical aspect of bookkeeping consists of a sequence of simple computations; *Private Property*, since bookkeeping is concerned only with recording the facts about property and property rights; *Money* (i.e., incompleted transactions), since there would be little impulse to make any record whatever if all exchanges were completed on the spot; *Commerce*, since a merely local trade would never have created enough pressure (volume of business) to stimulate men to coordinate diverse ideas into a system; *Capital*, since without capital commerce would be trivial and credit would be inconceivable.[6]

Each of the ancient civilizations mentioned earlier included these prerequisites, explaining the presence of some form of bookkeeping.

What is still missing is a scenario of the history of accounting from the isolated pieces of information in early bookkeeping treatises. One plausible scenario goes as follows:

> Were we to trace this important science [accounting] back to its original, we would be naturally led to ascribe the first invention to the first considerable merchants; and

there are none who have a fairer claim to precedency in point in time than those of Arabia. The Egyptians, who for many ages made a glorious appearance in the commercial world, derived their first notions of trade from their intercourse with these ingenious people; and, of consequence, from them likewise they must have received their first form of accountantship, which in the natural way of trade, was communicated to all the cities on the Mediterranean. When the western empire had been over-run by the Barbarians, and all the countries of which it had been composed, took that opportunity of asserting their own independency, commerce filed quickly after liberty; and immediately Italy, which had formerly been the court of the Universe, became the seat of trade, to which the ruin of the eastern empire by the Turks, into whose genius or constitution the arts of commerce never entered, did not a little contribute. The business of exchange, by which the Lombards connected all the trading cities of Europe, likewise introduced their method of keeping accounts, by double entry; whence, at this day, it gets the name of Italian book-keeping.[7]

This Italian bookkeeping prospered, with the development of the commercial republics of Italy and the use of the double-entry bookkeeping method in the fourteenth century. The first double-entry books known to exist are those of Massari of Genoa, dating back from the year 1340.[8] This double-entry bookkeeping preceded Pacioli by some two hundred years. Raymond de Rover describes the early development of accounting in Italy as follows:

> The great achievement of the Italian merchants, roughly between 1250 and 1400, was to fuse all these heterogeneous elements into an integrated system of classification in which the pigeon holes were called accounts and which rested on the principle of dual entries for all transactions. One should not, however, assume that balancing the books was a primary objective of medieval accounting. On the contrary; in Italy at least, the merchants had begun by 1400 to use accounting as a tool of management control. To be sure, they were not so far advanced as we are today and they were even far from realizing all the potentialities of double-entry bookkeeping. Nevertheless, they had made a start by developing the rudiments of cost accounting by introducing reserves and other modes of adjustments, such as accruals and deferred items, and by giving attentions to the audit of balance sheets. Only in the analysis of financial statements did the merchants of that time make a little progress.[9]

It is also fair to mention that a rudimentary form of double-entry accounting existed among the ancient Incas in 1577.

1.2.2 Luca Pacioli's contribution

Luca Pacioli, a Franciscan friar, is generally associated with the introduction of double-entry bookkeeping. In 1494 he published his book, *Summa de Arithmetica Geometria, Proportioni et Proportionalita* which included two chapters – *de Computis et Scripturis* – describing double-entry bookkeeping. His treatise reflected the practices of Venice at the time, which became known as "the Method of Venice" or "the Italian method". Therefore, he did not invent double-entry bookkeeping, but described what was being practiced at the time. He stated that the purpose of bookkeeping was "to give the trader without delay information as to his assets and liabilities".[10] Debit (adebeo) and credit (credito) were used for the entries to secure a double-entry. He said, "All entries ... have to be double entries, that is, if you make one creditor, you must make someone debtor."[11] Three books are used: a memorandum, a journal and a ledger. The entries are quite descriptive. Pacioli suggested that "not only was the name of the buyer or seller recorded, as well as the description of the goods with its weight, size or measurement, and price, but the terms of payment were also shown" and "wherever cash was received or disbursed, the record was shown of the kind of currency and its converted value…"[12]. At the same time, given the short duration of business ventures, Pacioli advised the computation of a periodic profit and the closing of the books. The following advice is given:

> It is always good to close the books each year, especially if you are in a partnership with others. Frequent accounting makes for long friendship.[13]

Pacioli's book was translated into several languages, contributing to the spread in popularity of the Italian method. It is interesting to note that Pacioli counted Leonardo Da Vinci as a friend. Da Vinci even collaborated with Pacioli on the "Divine Proportione" book for which Pacioli provided the text and Da Vinci the illustrations.

1.2.3 Development of double-entry bookkeeping

The "Italian method" spread throughout Europe in the sixteenth and seventeenth centuries, later acquiring new characteristics and developments, to become what we know as the double-entry model. In an effort to show that the double-entry model has evolved in ways that closely resemble the descriptions of normal science, Cushing outlines a series of developments.[14] They include the following:

1. Around the sixteenth century a few changes were made in bookkeeping techniques. Noticeable changes were the introduction of specific journals for the recording of different types of transactions. According to Yamey:

   > This involved the use of specialized subsidiary books, for example, for recording cash transactions, bills transactions or particular types of expenditures. The purpose was to keep detail out of the journal and also the ledger, so as to avoid filling them up too quickly. … It seems to have been fairly common practice to have had at least a separate cash book, with periodic postings of totals to the cash account in the ledger, with or without a summarized entry in the journal.[15]

2. The sixteenth and seventeenth centuries saw the evolution of the practice of period financial statements.[16] In addition, the seventeenth and eighteenth centuries saw the evolution of the personification of all accounts and transactions, in an effort to rationalize debit and credit rules that are applied to impersonal and abstract accounts.[17]

3. The application of the double-entry system was extended to other types of organizations. According to Peragallo:

   > In the second cycle, extending from 1559 to 1795, a new element appeared – the critique of bookkeeping. This is also the period when double-entry extended its field of application to other types of organizations, such as monasteries and the state. With the critique and the widening sphere of bookkeeping, began theoretical research into the subject.[18]

4. The seventeenth century saw the use of separate inventory accounts for different types of goods. According to Yamey:

   > … various goods accounts together with other goods on consignment accounts, goods in partnership ("company") accounts, and voyage accounts may make up a large part of a ledger. And one would look in vain for a single collective trading account, in which the results of all buying-and-selling

activity are brought together for a period, preparatory to transfer to the general profit-and-loss account. One must conclude that many merchants found it useful to have many separate goods accounts, even where there was no question of accounting to partners or principals for the disposal of their goods.[19]

5. Beginning with the East India Company in the seventeenth century and continuing with the growth of the corporation following the industrial revolution, accounting acquires a better status, characterized by the need for cost accounting, and a reliance on concepts of continuity, periodicity and accrual.[20]

6. The methods of treating fixed assets evolved by the eighteenth century. According to Yamey:

> First, the asset is carried forward at original cost, the difference between "revenue" payments and receipts (e.g., house repairs and rents received), which generally were entered in the asset account, being transferred to the profit-and-loss account at balancing date. Second, the asset account, containing entries for original outlay and other expenditures and receipts (including receipts from the sales of part of the asset) is closed at balancing date and the difference between total debits and total credits is carried forward as the account balance. There is no debit or credit to the profit-and-loss account. Third, the asset is revalued, upwards or downwards, at balancing date; the revised value is carried forward in the account and the balancing difference (including the gain or loss on revaluation) is carried to profit-and-loss account.[21]

7. Up to the early nineteenth century, depreciating property was accounted for as unsold merchandise. In the last half of the nineteenth century, depreciation in the railroad industry was considered unnecessary unless the property was deemed to be in improper working condition. While still not heavily used, there is evidence, provided by Saliero in 1915, of the existence of the following depreciation methods: straight line, reducing method, sinking fund and annuity methods, and unit cost method.[22] It is only following the 1930s that depreciation charges became more common.[23]

8. Cost accounting emerged in the nineteenth century as a product of the industrial revolution. It originated in fifteenth-century textile factories. D.R. Scott noted the consequences of factory developments in *The Cultural Significance of Accounts*:

> Before the industrial revolution, accounting was mainly a record of the external relations of one business unit with other business units, a record of relations determined in the market. But with the advent of large-scale productive operations ... necessity arose for more emphasis upon the accounting for interests within the competitive unit and upon the use of accounting records as a means of administrative control over the enterprise. ... The appearance of cost accounting in manufacturing ... is [an] example.[24]

The records of early nineteenth-century textile mills and of giant manufacturing firms are used to support two hypotheses:

(a) The first hypothesis is that the increased use of fixed assets prompted the development of industrial cost accounting.[25,26]

(b) The second hypothesis is that changes in the way economic activity was organized, not just changes in the temporal structure of their costs, prompted the development of internal cost accounting procedures in the nineteenth century.[27]

9. The latter half of the nineteenth century saw the development of techniques of accounting for prepayments and accruals, to allow the computation of periodic profit.[28]

10. The latter nineteenth and twentieth centuries saw the development of funds statements.[29]

11. The twentieth century saw the development of accounting methods for complex issues, ranging from the computation of earnings per share, accounting for business computations, accounting for inflation, long-term leases and pensions, to the crucial problem of accounting for the new products of financial engineering.

1.3 The development of accounting principles in the USA

Various groups in the USA, implementing a mix of approaches, have subjected accounting theory and principles to a constant reexamination and critical analysis. Four phases of this process may be identified. In the first phase (1900–33) management had complete control over the selection of financial information disclosed in annual reports; in the second (1933–59) and third phases (1959–73) the professional bodies played a significant role in developing principles; and in the fourth phase, which continues to the present, the Financial Accounting Standards Board (FASB) and various pressure groups are moving toward a politicization of accounting.

1.3.1 Management contribution phase (1900–33)

The influence of management in the formulation of accounting principles arose from the increasing number of shareholders and the dominant economic role played by industrial corporations after 1900. The diffusion of stock ownership gave management complete control over the format and content of accounting disclosures. The intervention of management may be characterized best by ad hoc solutions to urgent problems and controversies. The consequences of the dependence on management initiative include:

1. Given the pragmatic character of the solutions adopted, most accounting techniques lacked theoretical support.

2. The focus was on the determination of taxable income and the minimization of income taxes.

3. The techniques adopted were motivated by the desire to smooth earnings.

4. Complex problems were avoided and expedient solutions were adopted.

5. Different firms adopted different accounting techniques for the same problem.[30]

This situation generated dissatisfaction during the 1920s. Two men, William Z. Ripley and J.M.B. Hoxley, were particularly outspoken in arguing for an improvement in standards of financial reporting.[31] Similarly Adolph A. Berle and Gardiner C. Means pointed to corporate wealth and the power of industrial corporations, and called for the protection of investors.[32]

The main players of the time were a professional association of accountants, The American Institute of Accountants (AIA), which in 1917 established a Board of Examiners to create a uniform CPA examination, and The New York Stock Exchange, which from 1900 required all corporations applying for listing to agree to publish annual financial statements. A theoretical and controversial debate of the period was the question of accounting for interest costs. The FASB's Discussion Memorandum on "Accounting for Interest Costs" traces the background of the "interest as a cost" controversy:

Towards the end of the nineteenth century, the issue of accounting for interest arose as part of a large concern with developing realistic product costs to serve as a basis for establishing selling prices and measuring manufacturing efficiency. The increasing complexity of business, the increasing reliance on machinery and the consequent need to invest large amounts of capital for long periods of time greatly increased the amount of overhead. The inclusion of overhead in product cost therefore became a major accounting issue.[33]

The position of the AIA at the request of the Federal Trade Commission (FTC) was that "no selling costs, interest charges or administrative expenses are included in the factory overhead costs".[34] Opposition to the Institute's position was met by the statement in a report that "the inclusion in production cost of interest is unsound in theory and wrong, not to say absurd, in practice".[35] The opposition lost, as the Institute yielded to the call for uniform accounting practices by the FTC and a "horrifying" call by its chairman, Edward N. Hurley, that "consideration might be given to the possibility of developing a register of public accountants whose audit certificates would be acceptable to the Commission and the [Federal Reserve] Board".[36] It is interesting to note, however, that the dispute on accounting for interest costs was viewed later by Previts and Merino as a conflict between the entity and proprietary theories.[37]

Another important event of the era was the growing effect on accounting theory of taxation of business income. While the Revenue Act of 1913 provided for the calculation of taxable income on the basis of cash receipts and disbursements, the 1918 Act was the first to recognize the role of accounting procedures in the determination of taxable income. As stated in Section 212(b) of this act:

> The net income shall be computed upon the basis of the taxpayer's annual accounting period (fiscal year or calendar year, as the case may be) in accordance with the method of accounting regularly employed in keeping the books of such taxpayer; but if no such method of accounting has been so employed, or if the method employed does not reflect the income, the computation shall be made upon such basis and in such manner as in the opinion of the Commissioner does clearly reflect the income.

It set the stage for the beginning of a harmonization between tax accounting and financial accounting.

1.3.2 Institution contribution phase (1933–59)

This phase was marked by the creation and the increasing role of institutions in the development of accounting principles. It included the creation of the Securities and Exchange Commission (SEC); the approval by the AIA of "broad principles"; and the new role of the Committee on Accounting Procedures. Each is reviewed below.

1. In 1934 Congress created the SEC to administer various federal investment laws, including the Securities Act of 1933 that regulates the issuance of securities in the interstate markets and the Securities Act of 1934 that regulates the trading of securities. With regard to its role in the development of accounting principles, Section 13(b) of the 1934 Securities Exchange Act provides that:

> The commission may prescribe, in regards to reports pursuant (*sic*) to this title, the form or forms in which the required information shall be set forth, the items or details to be shown in the balance sheet and the earnings statement and the methods to be followed in the preparation of reports, in the appraisal or

valuation of assets and liabilities, in the determination of depreciation and depletion, in the differentiation of recurring and nonrecurring income. ...

To make things clear, on April 25, 1938 the SEC sent a definitive message that unless the profession established a standards-setting body, the SEC would use its mandate and develop accounting principles. Witness the following statement from Accounting Series Release (ASR) No. 4:

> In cases where financial statements filed with the Commission ... are prepared in accordance with accounting principles for which there is no substantial authoritative support, such financial statements will be presumed to be misleading or inaccurate despite disclosures contained in the certificate of the accountant or in footnotes to the statements provided the matters are material. In cases where there is a difference of opinion between the Commission and the registrant as to the proper principles of accounting to be followed, disclosure will be accepted in lieu of correction of the financial statements themselves only if the points involved are such that there is substantial authoritative support for the practices followed by the registrant and the position of the Commission has not previously been expressed in rules, regulations, or other official releases of the Commission, including the published opinions of its chief accountant.[38]

It set the stage for the role of the SEC as a creative irritant in the development of accounting principles in the USA.

2. Following the publication by Ripley of an article criticizing reporting techniques as deceptive, George O. May, an Englishman, proposed that the American Institute of Certified Public Accountants (AICPA) begin a cooperative effort with the stock exchange so that:

> ... standards might be established for balance-sheets and income accounts which would be welcomed by many corporation executives and accountants who desire to be guided by the best practice, if they can be assured what that practice is.[39]

As a result, the AICPA's Special Committee in cooperation with the Stock Exchange suggested the following general solution to the NYSE Committee:

> The more practical alternative would be to leave every corporation free to choose its own methods of accounting within ... very broad limits ... but require disclosure of the methods employed and consistency in their application from year to year. ...[40]

In addition, the Committee proposed the first formal attempt to develop generally accepted accounting techniques. Known as May's "board principles", they include the following:

(a) That income accounts should not include unrealized profit, and expenses ordinarily chargeable against income should not be charged instead against unrealized profit.

(b) That capital surplus (additional paid-in capital) should not be charged with amounts chargeable ordinarily to income.

(c) That earned surplus (or retained earnings) of a subsidiary company created prior to acquisition was not part of the consolidated earned surplus of the parent.

(d) That dividends on treasury stock may not be credited to the company's income.

(e) That amounts receivable from officers, employees, and affiliated companies should be shown separately.

A good evaluation of this joint effort goes as follows:

> The recommendations [all aspects of the original NYSE/AICPA document] were not fully implemented, but the basic concept which permitted each corporation to choose those methods and procedures which were most appropriate for its own financial statements within the basic framework of "accepted accounting principles" became the focal point of the development of principles in the United States.[41]

3. Following the SEC's issuance of ASR No. 4, which challenged the profession to provide "substantial authoritative support" for accepted accounting principles, and the increasing criticism from the newly created American Accounting Association and its members, the Institute decided in 1938 to empower the Committee on Accounting Procedure (CAP) to issue pronouncements. CAP issued twelve Accounting Research Bulletins (ARBs) during the 1938–9 period alone, and continued doing so during the war years. The post-war period was one of intense activity for the CAP, with the issuance of eighteen ARBs from 1946 to 1953, with a strategy of eliminating questionable and suspect accounting practices, and focusing on particular reporting problems, including accounting for the effects of price-level changes, and recommending the current operating performance concept in ARB 32. In spite of these efforts, the period 1957 to 1959 was marked with an intensive criticism of the CAP for various reasons, including failure to give adequate hearings to financial executives and accounting practitioners; failure to work on unpopular issues; failure to develop a comprehensive statement of basic accounting principles;[42] and crossing swords several times with the SEC, which was displeased by the CAP's preference for the "current-operating performance" conception of income statement and by the failure of the CAP to limit the alternatives available to management.[43]

1.3.3 Professional contribution phase (1959–73)

The discontent with the CAP was best expressed by the then president of the AICPA, Alvin R. Jennings, with the question "how successful have we been in narrowing areas of difference and inconsistency in the preparation and presentation of financial information?".[44] A Special Committee on Research Program set up in 1957 and 1958 proposed the dissolution of the CAP and its research department.[45] The AICPA accepted the recommendations of the committee and established in 1959 the Accounting Principles Board and the Accounting Research Division with the mission to advance the written expression of what constitutes generally accepted accounting principles. The Accounting Research Division proceeded with the publication of a rigorously argued position that depended on deductive reasoning.

The APB also issued various Opinions dealing with controversial issues, amounting to 31 Opinions between 1959 and 1973. The American Accounting Association also participated in the process through several research studies and attempts to develop an integrated statement of basic accounting theory. The efforts were not always successful. The APB found itself embattled and criticized for:

- limited, controversial or ad hoc opinion, including APB 8 on pension accounting, APB 11 on income tax allocation, and APBs 2 and 4 on investment tax credit; and
- failing to solve problems of accounting for business combinations and goodwill.

The suspected link of the profession to the APB did not help. The intervention of professional associations and agencies in the formulation of an accounting theory was spurred on by efforts to eliminate undesirable techniques and to codify acceptable techniques. Again, dependence on such association and agencies has not been without consequences, which include the following:

1. The association and agencies did not rely on any established theoretical framework.
2. The authority of the statements was not clear-cut.
3. The existence of alternative treatments allowed flexibility in the choice of accounting techniques.

The dissatisfactions with the results of professional intervention, as expressed in the writing of Briloff, were quite effective in bringing to the attention of the general public the accounting abuses that dominated certain annual reports.[46]

1.3.4 Politicization phase (1973–present)

The limitations of both professional associations and management in formulating an accounting theory led to the adoption of a more deductive approach as well as to the politicization of the standard-setting process – a situation created by the generally accepted view that accounting numbers affect economic behavior and, consequently, that accounting rules should be established in the political arena. In the same view, Horngren states:

> The setting of accounting standards is as much a product of political action as flawless logic or empirical findings. Why? Because the setting of standards is a social decision. Standards place restrictions on behavior; therefore, they must be accepted by the affected parties. Acceptance may be forced or voluntary or some of both. In a democratic society, getting acceptance is an exceedingly complicated process that requires skillful marketing in a political arena.[47]

Since its inception, the FASB has adopted a deductive and a quasi-political approach to the formulation of accounting principles. The FASB's conduct is better marked, first, by an effort to develop a theoretical framework or accounting constitution, and second, by the emergence of various interest groups, the contribution of which is required for the "general" acceptance of new standards. The standard-setting process therefore has a political aspect. The following statement by the FASB indicates its awareness of this new situation:

> The process of setting accounting standards can be described as democratic because, like all rule-making bodies, the Board's right to make rules depends ultimately on the consent of the ruled. But because standards setting required some perspective, it would not be appropriate to establish a standard based solely on a canvass of the constituents. Similarly, the process can be described as legislative because it must be deliberative and because all views must be heard. But the standard setters are expected to represent the entire constituency as a whole and not be representatives of a specific constituent group. The process can be described as political because there is an educational effort involved in getting a new standard accepted. But it is not political in the sense that an accommodation is required to get a statement issued.[48]

That the process of formulating accounting standards is becoming political is better expressed by a report released by the Senate Subcommittee on Report, Accounting, and Management, entitled *The Accounting Establishment*. Known as the "Metcalf Report", it charged that the "Big Eight" accounting firms monopolize the auditing of large corporations and control the standard-setting process. The relationship of the major organizations suggests the "Big Eight" and the AICPA have control over accounting standards approved by the SEC. After emphasizing the need for the federal government to ensure that publicly owned corporations are properly accountable to the public, the report made the following recommendations aimed at enhancing corporate accountability:

1. Congress should exercise stronger oversight of accounting practices promulgated or approved by the federal government, and more leadership in establishing proper goals and policies. …

2. Congress should establish comprehensive accounting objectives for the federal government to guide agencies and departments in performing their responsibilities. … A comprehensive set of federal accounting objectives should encompass such goals as uniformity, consistency, clarity, accuracy, simplicity, meaningful presentation, and fairness in application. In addition, Congress should establish specific policies abolishing such "creative accounting" techniques as percentage of completion income recognition, inflation accounting, "normalized" accounting and other potentially misleading accounting methods. …

3. Congress should amend the federal securities laws to restore the right of damaged individuals to use independent auditors for negligence under the fraud provisions of the securities laws. …

4. Congress should consider methods of increasing competition among accounting firms for selection as independent auditors for major corporations. …

5. The federal government should establish financial accounting standards for publicly owned corporations. …

6. The federal government should establish auditing standards used by independent auditors to certify the accuracy of corporate financial statements and supporting records. …

7. The federal government should itself periodically inspect the works of independent auditors for publicly-owned corporations. …

8. The federal government should restore public confidence in the actual independence of auditors who certify the accuracy of corporate financial statements under the federal securities laws by promulgating and enforcing strict standards of conduct for such auditors. …

9. The federal government should require the nation's fifteen largest accounting firms to report basic operational and financial reports annually. …

10. The federal government should define the responsibilities of the independent auditors so that they clearly meet the expectations of the Congress, the public and courts of law. …

11. The federal government should establish financial accounting standards, cost accounting standards, auditing standards, and other accounting practices in meetings open to the public. …

12. The federal government should act to relieve excessive concentration in the supply of auditing and accounting services to major publicly owned corporations. …

13. The federal government should retain accounting firms which act as independent auditors only to perform auditing and accounting services. …

14. The Securities and Exchange Commission should treat all independent auditors equally in disciplinary and enforcement proceedings under the federal security laws. …

15. The Membership of the Cost Accounting Standards Board should not be dominated by representatives of the industry and accounting firms which may have vested interests in the standards established by the Board. …

16. Federal employees should not serve on committees of the American Institute Certified Public Accountants or similar organizations that are assigned directly or indirectly to influence accounting policies and procedures of the federal government. …[49]

The "Metcalf Report" is only an example of the various studies of the accounting profession triggered by the political nature of the process of formulating accounting standards. The Appendix in this chapter presents the major studies of the accounting profession from 1972 to 1995.

1.4 Accounting and capitalism

Accounting and capitalism have been linked by some economic historians with the general claim that double-entry bookkeeping has been vital to the development and evolution of capitalism. Max Weber emphasizes the argument as follows:

> The modern rational organization of capitalistic enterprise would not have been possible without two other important factors in its development: the separation of business from the household … and, closely connected with it, rational bookkeeping.[50]

This thesis was best expanded by Sombart as follows:

> One cannot imagine what capitalism would be without double-entry bookkeeping: the two phenomena are connected as intimately as form and content. One cannot say whether capitalism created double-entry bookkeeping as a tool in its expansion; or perhaps, conversely, double-entry bookkeeping created capitalism.[51]

This link between accounting and capitalism became known as the Sombart thesis or argument. It argues that the transformation of assets into abstract values and the quantitative expression of the results of business activities, systematic accounting in the form of double-entry bookkeeping made it possible firstly, for the capitalistic entrepreneur to plan, conduct and measure the impact of his/her activities; and secondly, for a separation of owners and the business itself, thus allowing the growth of the corporation. The following four reasons are generally advanced to explain the role of double-entry in the economic expansion following the close of the Middle Ages:

1. *Double-entry contributed to a new attitude toward economic life.* The old medieval goal of substance was replaced by the capitalistic goal of profits. The spirit of acquisition was promoted and encouraged. Double-entry bookkeeping was imbued with the search for profits. The goals of the enterprise could be placed in a specific form and the concept of capital was made possible.

2. *This new spirit of acquisition was aided and propelled by the refinement of economic calculations.* The use of an integrated system of interrelated accounts made it possible for the entrepreneur to pursue profits rationally. Rationalization could now be based on a rigorous calculation. Present economic status could be readily determined and rational plans for future operations could be developed.

3. *This new rationalism was further enhanced by systematic organization.* Systematic bookkeeping promotes order in the accounts and organization in the firm. Its very duality provides for a check on accuracy, and its mechanization and objectivity contribute to an orderly and continued recording of business affairs. It is a unique system of classification.

4. *Double-entry bookkeeping permits a separation of ownership and management and thereby promotes the growth of the large joint stock company.* By permitting a

distinction between business and personal assets it makes possible the autonomous existence of the enterprise. Its standardized techniques make it a means of communication readily understood by many rather than by just the owner-manager and his bookkeeping.[52]

The thesis is not surprising. It is derived from a general conclusion at that time that trade was the natural consequence of the adoption of double-entry bookkeeping. Whether or not double-entry in systematic accounting was indispensable for the success of commercial enterprises is not easy to determine.[53] While it is possible to find general statements made about the urgency of keeping books, historical evidence provided by Yamey indicates that businessmen in the sixteenth through eighteenth centuries did not use double-entry bookkeeping to keep track of profits and capital, but simply as a record of transactions.[54] He states:

> ... double-entry system does little more than provide a framework into which accounting data can be fitted and within which the data can be arranged, grouped and regrouped. The system does not itself determine the range of data to be included in a particular setting, nor impose a particular pattern of internal ordering and re-ordering of data.[55]

He also makes the points that:

- double-entry bookkeeping is not necessary for determining profits and capital,
- double-entry bookkeeping is only useful for routine problems, and
- it is not necessarily useful for selection from the opportunities available to the businessmen.

The differences of views between Sombart and Yamey lie basically "on the interpretation of the significance of early double-entry techniques and the use to which early double-entry records were put".[56] Accordingly, Winjum tried to give an interpretation that contradicts Yamey's, by providing evidence as early as the sixteenth century where profit and loss determination was an important facet of double-entry bookkeeping. He concludes as follows:

> Sombart was correct in directing attention to the relationship between accounting and the use of capitalism. The system of double-entry bookkeeping does have the capability of making a positive contribution towards economic growth. Although the ability of double-entry to reveal the success or failure of a business enterprise for a specific period of time was not valued by the early English merchants, double-entry's capacity to accumulate data on individual operating activities, combined with its ability to bring order to the affairs and accounts of these merchants, stimulated and rationalized the economic activities of the early English merchants.[57]

1.5 Relevance of accounting history

Accounting history is important to accounting pedagogy, policy and practice. It makes it possible to "better ... understand our present and to forecast or control our future".[58] Accounting history may be narrated by relating episodes of accounting history in a particular, specific, non-analytic manner, "with descriptions of theories of knowledge, the unique work of individuals, their systems of values and the criticisms of their related works,[59] or interpretational by providing explanations of these episodes.[60] A good definition of accounting history follows:

> Accounting history is the study of the evolution in accounting thought, practices and institutions in response to changes in the environment and societal needs. It also considers the effect that this evolution has worked on the environment.[61]

It is a study of the heritage of accounting and its contribution to accounting pedagogy, policy and perspective.

With regard to pedagogy, accounting history can be very helpful to a better understanding and appreciation of the field of accounting and its evolution as a social science. A good rationale for the relevance of history in pedagogy goes as follows:

> First, a profession based on traditions built over many centuries should educate its members to appreciate their intellectual heritage. Second, the import of advances in thought, of major contributions to the literature, and of crucial positive studies may be lost, fragmented, or inadequately recognized in the longer term unless they are documented and incorporated by scholars who have historical skills. Third, without access to analyses and interpretations of historical developments in accounting thought and practice, today's empiricists risk basing their investigations upon incomplete or unjustified claims about the past.[62]

With regard to policy perspective, accounting history is instrumental to a better understanding of the accounting problems and their institutional contexts as well as the formulation of public policy.

With regard to accounting practice, accounting history could provide a better assessment of the existing practices by a comparison with the methods used in the past.

The relevance of accounting history to accounting practice, policy and pedagogy call for more accounting history inquiry. The subject matter of this historical research will include such areas as biography, institutional history, development of thought, general history, critical history, taxonomic and bibliographic databases, and historiography.[63] These are defined in Exhibit 1.1. They constitute an ideal tool for a historiography of accounting and promise to provide important knowledge to a better conduct of accounting research, practice and policy.

1.6 International accounting issues

1.6.1 Definitions of international accounting

There is definitely a confusion in the literature about the meaning of international accounting, evidenced by the various definitions encompassing different scopes. A useful clarification of these definitions was provided by Weirich *et al.*, by their identifying three major concepts:

1. parent–foreign subsidiary accounting or accounting for subsidiaries;
2. comparative or international accounting;
3. universal or world accounting.[64]

The concept of *universal or world accounting* is by far the largest in scope. It directs international accounting to the formulation and study of a universally accepted set of accounting principles. It aims for a complete standardization of accounting principles internationally. The definition adopted by Weirich *et al.* is as follows:

Area	Principal aspects
Biography	Influence of key individuals on accounting concepts, practice, and institutions
Institutional history	Traditions of the accounting profession and organizations. Considers influence on the social, economic, and political environments; source of data for explanatory research in other accounting history subjects
Development of thought	Identifies and explicates conceptual foundations and individuals and institutions related thereto. Traces and models conceptual development; impact of schools of thought on practice and other disciplines and institutions
General history	Macro perspective of accounting development; traditional and/or national emphasis; develops specific areas (e.g. cost accounting)
Critical history	Adopts a perspective inclined toward criticism in examining the role of an historical factor in the context of conflicting social, political, economic and institutional interaction
Database – taxonomies and bibliographies	Source of primary information; support for contemporary and historical research
Historiography	The structure of historical research; evaluates accounting history research; perspective on methods for conducting and interpreting accounting history research

Source: Gary John Privets, Lee D. Parker, and Edward N. Coffman, "An Accounting Historiography: Subject Matter and Methodology", *Abacus* (Accounting Foundation, September, 1990), p. 142.

Exhibit 1.1 Historical research subject matter

World Accounting. In the framework of this concept, international accounting is considered to be a universal system that could be adopted in all countries. A world-wide set of generally accepted accounting principles (GAAP), such as the set maintained in the United States, would be established. Practices and principles would be developed which were applicable to all countries. This concept would be the ultimate goal of an international system.[65]

While very commendable, this goal is unlikely to be achieved in the near future, and may be safely characterized as highly idealistic by some, and even utopian by others. Pessimistic attitudes are based on the many obstacles to a complete standardization of accounting principles.

The concept of comparative or international accounting directs international accounting to a study and understanding of national differences in accounting. It involves:

(a) an awareness of the international diversity in corporate accounting and reporting practices;

(b) understanding of the accounting principles and practices of individual countries; and

(c) ability to assess the impact of diverse accounting practices on financial reporting.[66]

There is a general consensus in accounting literature that the term "international accounting" refers to comparative accounting principles. The definition is:

> *International Accounting.* A second major concept of the term "international accounting" involves a descriptive and informative approach. Under this concept, international accounting includes all varieties of principles, methods and standards of accounting of *all* countries. This concept includes a set of generally accepted accounting principles established for each country, thereby requiring the accountant to be multiple principle conscious when studying international accounting. ... No universal or perfect set of principles would be expected to be established. A collection of all principles, methods and standards of all countries would be considered as the international accounting system. These variations result because of differing geographic, social, economic, political and legal influences.[67]

The concept of *parent–foreign subsidiary* accounting, or *accounting for foreign subsidiaries*, is by far the oldest and narrowest in scope. It reduces international accounting to the process of consolidating the accounts of the parent company and its subsidiaries and translating foreign currency into local currency. The definition is:

> *Accounting for Foreign Subsidiaries.* The third major concept that may be applied to international accounting refers to the accounting practices of a parent company and a foreign subsidiary: A reference to a particular country or domicile is needed under the concept for effective internal financial reporting. The accountant is concerned mainly with the translation and adjustment of the subsidiary's financial statement. Different accounting problems arise and different accounting principles are to be followed depending upon which country is used as a reference for translation and adjustment purposes.[68]

The advent of new international accounting paradigms expanded the framework to include new notions of international accounting. As a result, an exhaustive list of international accounting concepts and theories was provided by Amenkhienan to include the following:

1. universal or world theory;
2. multinational theory;
3. comparative theory;
4. international transactions theory;
5. translation theory.[69]

These theories imply respectively:

1. a universal concept being nurtured by the pragmatists who believe that the solutions to the problems raised in internal reporting lie in worldwide uniformity in accounting;
2. a multinational concept which suggests that international accounting includes all the varieties of principles, standards, and practices of all countries;
3. a comparative concept which suggests an analytical classification of national accounting systems, as has been done in the other social sciences such as economics, politics and laws;
4. an international concept built around accounting information needed in international trade and international investment decisions;
5. a translation concept which is used to characterize accounting for parent companies and foreign subsidiaries.[70]

Each of these theories provides some grounds for the development of a conceptual framework for international accounting. While arguments can be made for the desirability of one theory over the others, the first three – universal, multinational, and comparative – have generated better followings than the other two. The debate lies between those favoring uniformity leading to a universal theory, those favoring standardization leading to a multinational theory, and those favoring analysis of different national accounting systems leading to a comparative theory.

The comparative accounting literature includes various attempts to classify the accounting patterns in the world of accounting in different historical "zones of accounting influences". A good explanation for the various zones of accounting influence is that the accounting objectives, standards, policies and techniques result from environmental factors in each country; if these environmental factors differ significantly between countries, it would be expected that the major accounting concepts and practices in use in various countries would also differ: It is generally accepted in international accounting that accounting objectives, standards, policies and techniques reflect the particular environment of the standard-setting body. The environmental conditions likely to affect the determination of accounting standards include the following:

1. cultural relativism, whereby accounting concepts in any given country are as unique as any other cultural traits;[71]

2. linguistic relativism, whereby accounting as a language with its lexical and grammatical characteristics will affect the linguistic and nonlinguistic behavior of users;[72]

3. political and civil relativism, whereby accounting concepts in any given country rest on the political and civil context of that country;

4. economic and demographic relativism, whereby accounting concepts in any given country rest on the economic and demographic context of that country;

5. legal and tax relativism, whereby accounting concepts in any given country rest on the legal and tax base of that country.[73]

1.6.2 Harmonization of accounting standards

The nature of harmonization of accounting standards

Harmonization has for a long time been erroneously associated with complete standardization. It is in effect different from standardization. Wilson presents this useful distinction:

> The term harmonization as opposed to standardization implies a reconciliation of different points of view. This is a more practical and conciliatory approach than standardization, particularly when standardization means that the procedures of one country should be adopted by all others. Harmonization becomes a matter of better communication of information in a form that can be interpreted and understood internationally.[74]

This definition of harmonization is more realistic and has a greater likelihood of being accepted than standardization. Every host country has its own sets of rules, philosophies, and objectives at the national level, aimed at protecting or controlling the national resources. This aspect of nationalism gives rise to particular rules and measures which ultimately affect a country's accounting system. Harmonization consists of recognizing these national idiosyncrasies and attempting to reconcile them with other countries' objectives as a first step. The second step is to correct or eliminate some of these barriers, in order to achieve an acceptable degree of harmonization.

Merits of harmonization

There are various advantages to harmonization. First, for many countries, there are still no adequate codified standards of accounting and auditing. Internationally accepted standards not only would eliminate the set-up costs for those countries but would allow them to immediately become part of the mainstream of accepted international accounting standards. Some of this work is already being accomplished by the major accounting firms in their international practice. For example, Macrae states:

> Each of these forms of course has only been able to set and enforce the standards for its own organization, but combined, they determine the standards followed in a substantial portion of international audit engagements.[75]

Second, the growing internationalization of the world's economies and the increasing interdependency of nations in terms of international trade and investment flows is a major argument for some form of internationally accepted standards of accounting and auditing. Such internationalization will also facilitate international transactions, pricing and resource allocation decisions, and may render the international financial markets more efficient.

Third, the need for companies to raise outside capital, given the insufficiency of retained earnings to finance projects and the availability of foreign loans, has increased the need for accounting harmonization. In effect, suppliers of capital, here and abroad, tend to rely on financial reports to make the best investment and loan decisions, and tend to show preference for comparable reporting.

Limits to harmonization

Current trends seem to indicate that there is little chance of ever achieving international harmonization. The following arguments are usually advanced to justify this pessimistic attitude. First, tax collections in all countries are one of the greatest sources of demand for accounting services. Because tax-collection systems vary internationally, it can be easily expected that it will lead to a diversity in the accounting principles and systems used internationally. Seidler states:

> Since tax collection systems vary widely between countries, and since governments show little sign of desiring to harmonize tax systems (except in the collection of maximum amounts from multinational corporations), there is little reason to expect that this barrier to international accounting harmonization will disappear.[76]

Second, accounting policies are known to be fashioned sometimes to achieve either political or economic goals compatible with the economic or political system espoused by a given country. Since there is little hope of having a single political or economic system internationally, it can be expected that the differences in political and economic systems will continue to act as a barrier to international accounting harmonization.

Third, some of the obstacles to international harmonization are created by accountants themselves through strict national licensing requirements. An extreme example occurred in 1976, when the French profession required foreign accountants practicing in France to sit for an oral examination. As a result of the French experience, the EEC became involved with the qualifications of auditors. The first published version of the draft Eighth Directive created several restraints on the ability of foreign accountants to practice in the EEC member countries. Consider the following paragraphs from the first version of the draft of the Eighth Directive:

The partners, members, persons responsible for management, administration, direction or supervision of such professional companies or associations who do not personally fulfill the Directive (i.e., non-EEC qualified accountants) shall exercise no influence over the statutory audits carried out under the auspices of such approved professional companies or associations.

The law shall, in particular, ensure:

- that the above-mentioned persons may not participate in the appointment or removal of auditors and that they may not issue to the latter any instructions regarding the carrying out of audits …
- that the confidentiality of audit reports produced by the auditors and all documents relating thereto are protected and that these are withheld from the knowledge of the above-mentioned persons.

1.7 Conclusions

This chapter has presented the important facets of the history and development of accounting. The historical evolution of accounting provides clues and explanations for most of the important events that shaped the rise of double-entry bookkeeping and the development of modern accounting. It increases the ability of people interested in the accounting discipline to make judgments on a broader and more informed basis. It allows us to relate the past to what is practiced and to what ought to be practiced, in other words a link between the historical state and both the positive and normative state, a link that supports the view of history as a cultural product acquired within the full context of social, political, economic, and temporal environments.

Appendix 1.A – Major studies of the accounting profession from 1972 through 1995

Study/Date/Members	Background
1. *Establishing Financial Accounting Standards*, Report of the Study on Establishment of Accounting Principles (Wheat Committee), AICPA, March 1972 Francis M. Wheat, Chairman John C. Biegler Arnold I. Levine Wallace E. Olson Thomas C. Pryor Roger B. Smith David Solomons	In March 1971, the AICPA appointed the Wheat Committee to study the establishment of accounting principles and make recommendations for improving that process. The Committee was formed in response to the wave of criticism on corporate financial reporting during the mid-1960s arising from the rapid expansion of accounting firms, the development of increasingly complex and innovative business practices, and the corporate merger movement. The Wheat Committee concluded that there needed to be a substantial change in the structure for establishing financial accounting standards to insure public confidence in the way financial information is reported. The Wheat Committee recommended creating a Financial Accounting Foundation, a Financial Accounting Standards Board, and a Financial Accounting Standards Advisory Council.
2. *Objectives of Financial Statements*, Report of the Study Group on the	In April 1971, the AICPA appointed the Trueblood Committee to provide a statement of basic objectives that

Study/Date/Members	Background
Objectives of Financial Statements (Trueblood Committee), AICPA, October 1973 Robert M. Trueblood, Chairman Richard M. Cyert Sidney Davidson James Don Edwards Oscar S. Gellein C. Reed Parker Andrew J. Reinhart Howard O. Wagner Frank T. Weston	would be responsive and relevant to the needs of users. Previously issued objectives, while appropriate, were stated in relatively abstract terms, which offered little practical guidance in the preparation of financial statements. The Committee's conclusions followed a fundamental concept that financial statements should aid economic decision-making, and it emphasized the needs of outside users rather than the operating of business managers. The Committee also stated that accounting concepts should serve the goals of both private and public sectors of the economy. The work of the Trueblood Committee laid the fundamental groundwork for the Financial Board's (FASB) Accounting Standards work during the 1970s on establishing a conceptual framework for accounting.
3. *The Adequacy of Auditing Standards Procedures Currently Applied in the Examination of Financial Statements*, Report of the Special Committee on Equity Funding, AICPA, February 1975 Martin L. Stone, Chairman J.T. Arenberg, Jr. Leo E. Burger Robert C. Holsen A.E. Mackay	In May 1973, the AICPA appointed the Special Committee on Equity Funding to study whether the Equity Funding collapse in 1973 suggested a need for changes in generally accepted auditing standards. The Committee concluded that, except for certain observations relating to the confirmation of insurance in force and auditing related party transactions, generally accepted auditing standards were adequate and there were no changes called for in the procedures commonly used by auditors.
4. *Federal Regulation and Regulatory Reform*, Report by the Subcommittee on Oversight and Investigations of the Committee on Interstate and Foreign Commerce, U.S. House of Representatives (Moss Subcommittee), October 1976 John E. Moss, Chairman Richard L. Ottinger Robert (Bob) Krueger James M. Collins Norman F. Lent Anthony Toby Moffett Matthew J. Rinaldo Jim Santini W. Henson Moore W.S. (Bill) Stuckey, Jr. Samuel L. Devine James H. Scheuer Henry A. Waxman Philip R. Sharp Andrew Maguire Harley O. Staggers	In April 1975, the Moss Subcommittee undertook a comprehensive study of federal regulatory agencies that included an assessment of the independence, performance, and economic effects of the activities of regulatory agencies under the Subcommittee's jurisdiction. This study was prompted by attacks on federal regulation and the Subcommittee's obligation to measure the performance of agencies it created. The study attempted to determine the true problems of regulation, their nature and extent, and, if needed, possible remedies. The study found that all organizations investigated suffered a critical defect – an insufficient response to the public they were created to serve. The Subcommittee's recommendations related mostly to actions the SEC could take to improve the corporate governance function. Several recommendations involved corporate boards of directors and/or their audit committees and the evaluation and reporting on corporate internal control systems.

Study/Date/Members	Background
5. *The Accounting Establishment*, a Staff Study prepared by the Subcommittee on Reports, Accounting, and Management of the Committee on Government Operations, U.S. Senate (Metcalf Subcommittee), March 1977 Lee Metcalf, Chairman John L. McClellan Bill Brock Edmund S. Muskie Charles H. Percy Sam Nunn Lowell P Weicker, Jr. John Glenn	The Metcalf Subcommittee staff began this study in 1975 to provide the Congress and the public with an understanding of the various private organizations and federal agencies involved in establishing and administering accounting practices which have substantial impact on federal policies and programs, as well as private economic decisions. The study was precipitated by continual revelations of previously unreported wrongdoing by major corporations, as well as a series of corporate failures and financial difficulties which had come to light. The staff study's recommendations dealt with the issues of setting accounting and auditing standards, auditor independence, and audit quality.
6. *The Structure of Establishing Financial Accounting Standards*, Report of the Structure Committee, the Financial Accounting Foundation, April 1977 Russel E. Palmer, Chairman J.O. Edwards James Don Edwards Walter P. Stern Alva O. Way John C. Whitehead	In 1976, the Board of Trustees of the Financial Accounting Foundation (FAF) asked the Structure Committee to perform a comprehensive review of the operations of FASB and the Financial Accounting Standards Advisory Council (FASAC) and recommend any changes needed in their size, composition, and functions. This review was undertaken for a number of reasons, one of them being the unusually vocal criticism of FASB. The Structure Committee concluded that the process of setting accounting standards should remain in the private sector, and FASB is the right body to discharge that responsibility. The Committee's report contains recommendations concerning the structure of FASB's constituency relationships, the organizational structure of FASB and staff, the process of issuing a statement, and the structure of FASB's communications.
7. *Improving the Accountability of Publicly Owned Corporations and their Auditors*, Report of the Subcommittee on Reports, Accounting, and Management of the Committee on Governmental Affairs, U.S. Senate (Metcalf Subcommittee), November 1977 Lee Metcalf, Chairman Henry M. Jackson John C. Danforth Charles H. Percy	In 1975, the Metcalf Subcommittee began an inquiry into various accounting practices and responsibilities of the federal government. The study was initiated because of concerns over the activities and accountability of publicly owned corporations arising from a series of unexpected corporate failures and disclosures of widespread questionable and illegal acts by management. The report summarizes the Subcommittee's views regarding the way in which existing accounting and financial reporting practices should be improved to benefit the public. The Subcommittee's recommendations included actions needed to improve/ensure audit quality, auditor independence, and the detection and reporting of illegal acts.
8. *The Commission on Auditors' Responsibilities: Report, Conclusions and Recommendations* (Cohen Commission), AICPA, 1978 Manuel F. Cohen, Chairman Lee J. Seidler	In 1974, the AICPA appointed the Cohen Commission to develop conclusions and recommendations on the appropriate responsibilities of independent auditors. The Commission was tasked to consider whether a generally perceived gap between what the public expects or needs and what auditors can and should reasonably expect to accomplish actually existed. If such a gap existed, the

Study/Date/Members	Background
Walter S. Holmes, Jr. LeRoy Layton William C. Norby Kenneth W. Stringer John J. van Benten	Commission was to determine how the disparity could be resolved. The Cohen Commission found that a significant gap did exist between the performance of auditors and the expectations of users of financial statements, and traced the gap to the accounting profession's failure to react and evolve quickly enough to changes in the American business. Its conclusions and recommendations address auditor independence, education, auditor communications, responsibilities for the detection of fraud, quality control mechanisms, and a broader audit function beyond the financial statements.
9. *Report of the Special Committee of the AICPA to Study the Structure of the Auditing Standards Executive Committee* (Oliphant Committee), AICPA, May 1978 Walter J. Oliphant, Chairman Ivan O. Bull Philip L. Delliese Samuel A. Derieux Louis M. Kessler	In June 1977, the AICPA appointed the Oliphant Committee to study the structure within the AICPA for developing auditing standards to determine what changes, if any, were necessary to improve the process. The AICPA appointed this Committee in response to concerns over the Cohen Commission's recommendations relating to setting auditing standards. The Committee concluded that there were steps that could be taken to improve the effectiveness of setting auditing standards. Accordingly, the Oliphant Committee proposed that the Auditing Standards Executive Committee (AudSEC) be reconstituted within the AICPA as the AICPA Auditing Standards Board (ASB) and made several recommendations pertaining to the mission and structure of this new board.
10. *Scope of Services By CPA Firms*, Report of the Public Oversight Board of the SEC Practice Section, Division for CPA Firms, AICPA, March 1979 John J. McCloy, Chairman Ray Garrett, Jr. William L. Cary John D. Harper Arthur M. Wood	In July 1978, the Public Oversight Board (POB) reported on its views with respect to the scope of services for member firms of the SEC practice section. The Executive Committee of the SEC Practice Section requested the POB's views in response to questions concerning whether engaging in management advisory services (MAS) for audit clients creates a conflict of interest. In general, the POB concluded that maintenance of independence should be the only limitation on scope of services and that independence be assessed after giving consideration to potential benefits derived from furnishing various services. The POB recommended reliance on existing programs and procedures and suggested that adherence to the portions of the existing MAS Professional Standards and the Code of Professional Ethics dealing with independence be made a condition of membership in the SEC Practice Section.
11. *Interim Review of the FASB and FASAC*, Report of the Structure Committee, Financial Accounting Foundation, May 1979 J.O. Edwards, Chairman William H. Dougherty, Jr. Richard S. Hickok Harvey Kapnick Walter P. Stern John C. Whitehead	In 1979, the Structure Committee of the FAF undertook an interim review of FASB and FASAC to follow up on progress made by FASB and FASAC Foundation, responding to the Committee's findings from its 1977 review (see number 6 above). The Committee reported that both FASB and FASAC have initiated desirable changes to the standard-setting process going beyond the Committee's 1977 report recommendations. The Committee's interim report suggests areas for further improvement, including increasing public awareness, reaching out to all major constituents, experimenting with FASAC committees, improving utilization of task forces, and enhancing the quality of staff.

Study/Date/Members	Background
12. *Operating Efficiency of the FASB*, Report of the Structure Committee, Financial Accounting Foundation, August 1982 Charles G. Steele, Chairman Kenneth S. Axelson William H. Dougherty, Jr. Paul J. Dunphy Thomas L. Holton Warren J. Robertson Hyman Weinberg	In 1982, the Structure Committee of the FAF undertook a review of the efficiency of FASB. This review was conducted in line with the bylaws of FAF, which require a periodic review of the basic structure of establishing and improving standards of financial accounting. The Structure Committee's overall conclusion was that FASB was operating efficiently and effectively, that is, appropriate standard-setting systems were in place and functioning well. The Committee's recommendations call for improved relationships and communications with constituencies, increased responses on FASB products, accelerated progress on certain concepts statements, and timely guidance for questions concerning implementation of standards and for emerging issues.
13. *Report of the Special Review Committee*, Financial Accounting Foundation, 1985 R. Leslie Ellis, Chairman Charles T. Horngren Thomas L. Holton John H. Poelker John F. Ruffle	In January 1985, the Board of Trustees of the FAF initiated actions to assess the extent and nature of concerns about the standards-setting process and to begin simultaneously a study of the composition of FASB and criteria for selection of its members. These actions were taken in response to concerns expressed by certain constituents about the composition and operations of FASB. The work of the Special Review Committee of the FAF concluded that there is strong widespread support for FASB and its operations, and there is very little evidence of deep dissatisfaction in any segment of the constituency. However, the Committee found some concerns with the qualifications of the FASB Chairman and members, the composition of FASB, the process of selecting members, the lengthy time frame imposed by FASB's due process, and inhibitions on free exchange of ideas caused by the "sunshine rule". The Committee made several recommendations to address these concerns.
14. *Challenge and Opportunity for the Accounting Profession*: *Strengthening the Public's Confidence,* the Price Waterhouse Proposals, 1985 Joseph E. Connor, Chairman	In 1985, in response to what it termed a "twin crisis in credibility and liability" (emanating from a succession of spectacular business failures that were seen as audit failures), Price Waterhouse developed a program of action to enhance the credibility and viability of the accounting profession. The principal components of this program include: expanding auditing standards to reduce the risk that management fraud will go undetected, enhancing self-regulation, and seeking equity in civil liability.
15. *Restructuring Professional Standards To Achieve Professional Excellence in a Changing Environment*, Report of the Special Committee on Standards of Professional Conduct for Certified Public Accountants (Anderson Committee), April 1986 George D. Anderson, Chairman Robert L. Bunting Joseph P. Cummings	In October 1983, the AICPA appointed the Anderson Committee to study the relevance and effectiveness of professional standards in today's environment. The AICPA initiated the study in response to concerns over the profession's ability to serve the public interest and retain public confidence in a rapidly changing environment. The Committee concluded that some legitimate concerns had been raised about certified public accountants' behavior and commitment to quality and reached a strong consensus that the accounting profession must make substantial reforms in the way it achieves adherence to its standards. The Committee's report contains sweeping

Study/Date/Members	Background
James Don Edwards Robert C. Ellyson Francis A. Humphries Richard Kasten James Kurtz Bernard Z. Lee Herman J. Lowe Archie E. MacKay William L. Raby Frank S. Sato Ralph Saul John P. Thomas Kathryn D. Wriston	revisions to the AICPA's Code of Professional Ethics and substantial reforms in the way adherence to professional standards is achieved.
16. *The Future Relevance, Reliability, and Credibility of Financial Information*, Recommendations to to the AICPA Board of Directors by seven major accounting firms (Big 7), April 1986 J. Michael Cook, Deloitte Haskins & Sells William L. Gladstone, Arthur Young Ray J. Groves, Ernst & Whinney Larry D. Homer, Peat, Marwick, Mitchell & Co. Edward A. Kangas, Touche Ross & Co. Duane R. Kullberg, Arthur Andersen & Co. Peter R. Scanlon, Coopers & Lybrand	In 1986, the heads of seven major accounting firms submitted recommendations to the AICPA Board of Directors to improve the relevance, reliability, and credibility of financial information. The firms' initiative was prompted by the swift pace and impact of changing business and economic conditions and the firms' recognition of the accounting profession's obligation to assure the utility of audited financial statements. The firms' recommendations addressed the need for more information on risks and uncertainties in financial reporting, auditor independence, peer review, an enhanced ASB, and other issues.
17. *Financial Reporting and the Role of Independent Auditors*, Statement of Charles A. Bowsher, Comptroller General of the United States, June 1986	In June 1986, GAO participated in a congressional hearing, before the Subcommittee on Oversight and Investigations of the House Committee on Energy and Commerce, on financial reporting, the role of independent auditors, and the SEC's oversight of the accounting profession. The hearing was part of a series of hearings prompted by alleged audit failures. At that hearing, GAO testified that the public expects improvements in the areas of early warning disclosures, fraud detection, compliance with laws and regulations, internal controls, and peer review. GAO encouraged the accounting profession and the SEC to take action in these areas.
18. *Report of the Task Force on Risks and Uncertainties*, AICPA, July 1987 Arthur Siegel, Chairman James R. Colford John D. Collins Phillip W. Crawford Richard Dieter John E. Ellingsen Rosemary E. McGovern Rudolph W. Schattke Roger W. Trupin	In 1985, the AICPA established the Task Force on Risks and Uncertainties to consider ways to improve disclosure about the risks and uncertainties that faced business enterprises in light of the volatile business environment of the 1980s. The Task Force concluded that a business enterprise should disclose more information about the risks and uncertainties facing it as of the date of the financial reports. The Task Force's recommendations focused primarily on increased disclosures of significant risks and uncertainties that stem from the necessary use of estimates in the preparation of financial statements and from significant concentrations in aspects of the entity's operations.

Study/Date/Members	Background
19. *Report of the National Commission on Fraudulent Financial Reporting* (Treadway Commission), October 1987 James C. Treadway, Jr., Chairman William M. Batten William S. Kanaga Hugh L. Marsh, Jr. Thomas L. Storrs Donald H. Trautlein	The Treadway Commission, formed in 1985, was a private-sector initiative jointly sponsored by the AICPA, the American Accounting Association, the Financial Executives Institute, the Institute of Internal Auditors, and the National Association of Accountants. The Commission was created to identify the causal factors that can lead to fraudulent financial reporting and steps to reduce its incidence. The Commission's conclusions highlighted the need for improvements in areas including corporate reporting on internal controls, the establishment of independent audit committees, auditor detection and reporting of fraud, and steps needed to help ensure audit quality. The Treadway Commission's report contained numerous recommendations to deter fraudulent financial reporting which were addressed to the management of public companies, independent public accountants, the SEC and other regulatory agencies, and educators.
20. *Letter to the Honorable Fernand J. St Germain, Chairman, Committee on Banking, Finance and Urban Affairs,* House of Representatives, GAO, (B229444) August 1988	GAO's 1988 letter to the Chairman discusses items that GAO believed should be addressed in any legislation to provide new securities powers to banks. Specifically, GAO felt that two further items should be added to the proposed legislation (Depository Institutions Act of 1988) to ensure that safeguards are in place and are functioning properly to ensure the safety and soundness of the nation's banks. The first item addresses the need for a requirement for independent financial audits of banks and bank holding companies that have a securities affiliate including requiring a financial audit of the securities affiliate. The second item addresses internal control and compliance reporting by management and the independent auditor.
21. *The Structure for Establishing Financial Accounting Standards,* the Report of the Financial Accounting Foundation's Committee to Review Structure for Financial Accounting Standards, January 1989 Thomas L. Holton, Chairman R. Leslie Ellis Robert E. Frazer Ray J. Groves Charles T. Horngren Robert A. Mellin J. Ronald Morgan Earle E. Morris, Jr. John E. Poelker Edus H. Warren, Jr.	In January 1988, the FAF's Committee to Review Structure for Financial Accounting Standards was appointed to review the structure and operations of FASB and FASAC, as required by FAF's bylaws. The Committee concluded that despite the concerns expressed by the business community and public accounting profession about certain aspects of FASB activities, the make-up, organization, and operations of FASB are basically sound. The Committee's report, however, does include several recommendations to strengthen FASB.
22. *CPA Audit Quality: Failures of CPA Audits To Identify and Report Significant Savings and Loan Problems* (GAO/AFMD-89–45) February 1989	Prompted by the savings and loan (S&L) crisis of the 1980s, the Committee on Banking, Finance and Urban Affairs, House of Representatives, asked GAO to review the quality of audits of S&Ls in the Dallas Federal Home Loan Bank

Study/Date/Members	Background
	District. GAO concluded that, for 6 of 11 failed S&Ls in its review, CPAs did not adequately audit and/or report the S&L's financial or internal control problems in accordance with professional standards. GAO recommended that the AICPA provide improved guidance for ensuring that S&L audits are performed in a quality manner by (1) revising the AICPA industry audit guide for savings and loan associations and (2) communicating results presented in this GAO report to all AICPA members.
23. *CPA Audit Quality: Status of Actions Taken To Improve Auditing and Financial Reporting of Public Companies* (GAO/AFMD-89–38) March 1989	In 1987, the Chairman, Oversight and Investigations Subcommittee, House Committee on Energy and Commerce, asked that GAO review the implementation of the changes to improve auditing and financial reporting of public companies and that GAO identify related recommendations which would require legislative or regulatory actions in order to be implemented. This request was sparked by the well-publicized business failures which raised questions about the effectiveness of the independent audit of public companies and the SEC's oversight of the public accounting profession. GAO concluded that the public accounting profession and others have taken positive actions to address concerns about audit quality and the accuracy and reliability of financial disclosures of public companies. However, the report notes that actions remain to be taken. GAO made recommendations to the SEC and the AICPA regarding additional steps needed to improve audit quality and financial disclosures.
24. *Bank Failures: Independent Audits Needed to Strengthen Internal Control and Bank Management* (GAO/AFMD-89–25) May 1989	To address concerns about the steadily increasing number of failures of insured banks, GAO undertook a review to summarize data on internal weaknesses and environmental factors which bank examiners cited for insured banks which failed in 1987, to determine the extent to which insider abuse and fraud were present in 1987 failed banks and to identify potential areas of concern. GAO found that serious internal control weaknesses contributed significantly to virtually all the bank failures in 1987. GAO also found that only about a third of the banks that failed in 1987 had audits by independent public accountants. GAO recommended that each insured bank have an annual independent audit and provide auditor reports on internal controls and compliance with laws and regulations.
25. *Thrift Failures: Costly Failures Resulted from Regulatory Violations and Unsafe Practices* (GAO/AFMD-89–62) June 1989	In response to a large number of thrift failures and the resulting thrift industry crisis, GAO initiated a review to provide perspective on factors that characterized those thrift failures that have caused some of the larger losses to the Federal Savings and Loan Insurance Corporation, and especially to determine whether violations of federal laws or regulations, related unsafe practices, and fraud and insider abuse were present. GAO found indications of fraud or insider abuse at all the failed thrifts in GAO's sample. GAO recommended that the Congress pass legislation that among other things, would require management and auditor

Study/Date/Members	Background
	reporting to the federal regulator on internal controls and on compliance with laws and regulations in order to reduce thrifts' vulnerability to fraud and insider abuse.
26. *Prevention, Detection, and Reporting Financial Irregularities*, Statement of Charles A. Bowsher, Comptroller General of the United States (GAO/T-AFMD-90–27) August 1990	In 1990, the Comptroller General testified before the Subcommittee on Telecommunications and Finance, House Committee on Energy and Commerce, on GAO's support of proposed amendments to the 1934 act to strengthen both management and auditor responsibilities for detecting and reporting irregularities. GAO made recommendations concerning management and auditor responsibilities for internal controls and compliance with laws and regulations, the need to strengthen audit requirements, methods of responding to audit discoveries, and the jurisdiction of the SEC. GAO also made suggestions concerning audit committees, peer reviews, notification of auditor changes, and sharing reports and information with independent public accountants concerning regulators' knowledge of potential mismanagement, fraud, or abuse by companies.
27. *Failed Banks: Accounting and Auditing Reforms Urgently Needed* (GAO/AFMD-91–43) April 1991	GAO analyzed 1988 and 1989 bank failures to identify the impact of accounting and internal control weaknesses on those failures and the critical need for reforms to minimize future losses to the Bank Insurance Fund and the taxpayer. GAO initiated this review to address congressional and public concerns that the external reports prepared by banks, both annual financial statements and call reports, did not always alert users to the troubled financial condition of banks in a timely manner. GAO concluded that accounting rules for recognizing losses were seriously flawed, impeding early warning of troubled banks, and that internal control weaknesses were a major cause of bank failures. GAO made several recommendations concerning an early warning system, the role of the audit committees, the independent auditor's review of the quarterly financial reports, and auditor's communications with regulators regarding internal control weaknesses and noncompliance with laws and regulations.
28. *Letter to the Honorable Ron Wyden, House of Representatives*, GAO (B-240516) May 1, 1991	As requested, the Comptroller General provided GAO's views on how internal controls could be strengthened to further protect investors and limit the government's exposure to major losses, such as the massive bailout of the savings and loans sector during the 1980s and its severe economic consequences for investors and government alike. This request was made in response to fundamental questions concerning corporate accountability, the effectiveness of corporate governance and regulation, and the adequacy of audit requirements. GAO's letter highlights the severity of internal control weaknesses and outlines the type of legislative remedies required, such as greater reporting on internal controls, stronger roles for audit committees, and direct reporting of illegal acts.

Study/Date/Members	Background
29. *Audit Committees: Legislation Needed to Strengthen Bank Oversight* (GAO/AFMD-92–19) October 1991	This GAO report examines the extent to which audit committees of large banks had the independence, expertise, and information needed to properly carry out their functions and provides further support for earlier GAO recommendations. GAO undertook this review as a result of the record number of failing banks during the 1980s. The study found that many audit committees lacked the independence, expertise, and information necessary to properly oversee bank operations. The report reiterates recommendations made by GAO in an April 1991 report on failed banks (see number 27 above) which calls for legislation concerning audit committee requirements; internal control reporting by management; and internal control reporting, compliance reporting, and reporting on quarterly data by the independent auditor.
30. *Employee Benefits: Improved Plan Reporting and CPA Audits Can Increase Protection Under ERISA* (GAO/AFMD-92–14) April 1992	The Chairmen of the House Subcommittee on Oversight and the House Subcommittee on Labor–Management Relations requested that GAO identify problems in the performance of employee benefit plan audits. This request resulted from significant deficiencies in audits of private employee benefit plans as identified by the Department of Labor's Office of Inspector General in November 1989. GAO's review of a sample of plan audits also found serious audit weaknesses, many of which stemmed from a lack of auditor knowledge about special considerations associated with auditing employee benefit plans. GAO recommended, among other things, that the AICPA improve its audit guide concerning audits of employee benefit plans and that the AICPA communicate to its membership the results of investigations of deficient plan audits.
31. *In the Public Interest; Issues Confronting the Accounting Profession*, a special report by the Public Oversight Board of the SEC Practice Section, AICPA, March 1993 A.A. Sommer, Jr., Chairman Robert K. Mautz, Vice Chairman Melvin R. Laird Paul W. McCracken Robert F. Froehlke	The POB issued this report in response to a request from representatives of a number of accounting firms that the POB consider whether it could support the accounting profession's efforts to obtain relief from what the profession believed to be an excessive burden of litigation. The POB concluded that the litigation risks confronting the profession pose serious dangers to its ability to perform its assigned role in society. The POB also addressed some of the criticisms pertaining to the profession's performance. The POB's report contains 25 recommended actions to enhance the usefulness and reliability of financial statements; strengthen the performance and professionalism of the public accounting profession, including the ability of auditors to detect fraud and irregularities; and improve self-regulation.
32. *Meeting the Financial Reporting Needs of the Future: A Public Commitment From the Public Accounting Profession*, AICPA Board of Directors, June 1993	In June 1993, the Board of Directors of the AICPA issued a policy statement which details the steps necessary to improve the value of financial information and the public's confidence in it. The policy statement describes how public confidence in the financial reporting system has been shaken in recent years by highly publicized business failures and includes actions the Board believes are needed

Study/Date/Members	Background
	to solidify the public trust in the financial reporting system. The statement identifies five principal goals for reform concerning the prevention and detection of fraud, the utility of financial reporting, the independence and objectivity of independent auditors, unwarranted litigation, and strengthening the accounting profession's disciplinary system.
33. *Financial Reporting in the 1990s and Beyond*, Association for Investment Management and Research (AIMR), November 1993 Peter H. Knutson	AIMR's report sets forth the position of investment advisors and financial analysts on the universe of financial reporting as it affects analysis today and into the next century. The report explains the function of financial analysis, its sources and uses of information, and speaks to the trends that are expected to change practices in both analysis and accounting during the next decade or more. AIMR's conclusions and recommendations call for a substantial expansion in the quality and quantity of financial information now being reported. AIMR also recommends increased participation by financial statement users in the accounting standard-setting process.
34. *Staff Report on Auditor independence*, report prepared by the Office of the Chief Accountant, Securities and Exchange Commission, March 1994	This SEC staff report responds to the March 18, 1993, request from Congressman Edward J. Markey, Chairman of the Subcommittee on Telecommunications and Finance of the House Committee on Energy and Commerce, that the SEC study the need for, and any impediments to, the independence of public accountants in performing their responsibilities under the federal securities laws. This request was made in consideration of a proposed bill to make the auditing profession more accountable to the investing public. The SEC's report provides background information on the issue of auditor independence, discusses the Commission's independence rule and related interpretations and pronouncements of the AICPA and other nations' independence requirements, and discusses recent and certain current proposals regarding independence issues. The report concluded that the combination of the extensive systems of independence requirements issued by the Commission and the AICPA, coupled with the Commission's active enforcement program, provide investors reasonable safeguards against loss due to the conduct of audits by accountants that lack independence from their audit clients. Therefore, the SEC concluded that no further legislation or rules or regulations were necessary at that time with respect to auditor independence.
35. *Financial Derivatives: Actions Needed To Protect the Financial System* (GAO/GGD-94–133) May 1994	In response to congressional requests, GAO undertook a review of derivative products to determine among other things whether existing accounting rules resulted in financial reports that provided market participants and investors adequate information about firms' use of derivatives. This review was sparked by congressional efforts to better anticipate and prevent future financial crises. GAO found that accounting standards for derivatives were incomplete and inconsistent and have not kept pace

Study/Date/Members	Background
	with business practices. GAO made recommendations to FASB and the SEC concerning the development and issuance of accounting and disclosure requirements for derivatives, the adoption of market value accounting for all financial instruments, and the requirements for independent audit committees and internal control reporting for SEC registrants that are major end users of derivatives.
36. *Strengthening the Professionalism of the Independent Auditor*, Public Oversight Board Advisory Panel on Auditor Independence (Kirk Panel), September 1994 Donald J. Kirk, Chairman George D. Anderson Ralph S. Saul	In February 1994, the POB appointed the Kirk Panel to (1) assess the working relationship among the SEC, FASB, the auditing profession, and the business community and (2) identify and evaluate steps to bolster the objectivity, independence, and professionalism of the auditing firms. The Kirk Panel was appointed in response to a January 11, 1994, speech, given by Walter Schuetze, the Chief Accountant of the SEC, which questioned the independence of auditors. The Panel concluded that at this time there is no need for additional rules, regulations, or legislation dealing with auditor independence. However, the Panel made several suggestions to strengthen auditor independence, to bring auditing into the mainstream of corporate governance, and to restore auditing to its important role in our society. These suggestions cover issues such as auditor independence; more involvement of the boards of directors and audit committees with the independent auditor; the relationships between the accounting profession, standard setters, and the SEC; and litigation reform.
37. *Improving Business Reporting – A Customer Focus: Meeting the Information Needs of Investors and Creditors*, Comprehensive Report of the Special Committee on Financial Reporting (Jenkins Committee), AICPA, 1994 Edmund L. Jenkins, Chairman Gregory J. Jonas, Executive Director Michael H. Sutton, Vice Chairman Lonnie Arnett Raymond J. Bromark Edmund Coulson Robert K. Elliott Larry Grinstead William W. Holder Robert L. Israeloff Gaylen N. Larson Joseph D. Lhotka James C. Meehan Harold L. Monk, Jr. Edward F Rockman Harry N. Winograd	In 1991, the AICPA Board of Directors formed the Jenkins Committee to address concerns about the relevance and usefulness of business reporting. The Committee's charge was to recommend (1) the nature of information that should be made available to others by management and (2) the extent to which auditors should report on the various elements of that information. The Committee concluded that a lot is right with today's business reporting in that it generally provides users with essential information that heavily influences their decisions. In particular, financial statements are viewed as an excellent framework for capturing and organizing financial information. However, many users are strongly critical of certain aspects of today's reporting. Accordingly, the Committee made recommendations to standard setters, the Congress, regulators, and the accounting profession to improve the types of information in business reporting, to improve financial statements and related disclosures, to improve auditor involvement with business reporting, and to facilitate change in business reporting.

Source: United States General Accounting Office; The Accounting Profession. Appendices to Major Issues: Progress and Concerns (Washington, DC: United States General Accounting Office, September 1996), pp. 6–15.

Notes

1. Rand Hatfield, "A Historical Defense of Bookkeeping", *The Journal of Accounting* (April, 1924), p. 753.

2. Yamey, B.S., "Early Views on the Origins and Development of Book-keeping and Accounting", *Accounting and Business Research* (Special Accounting History Issue, 1980), pp. 81–92.

3. Woolf, A.H., *A Short History of Accounting and Accountants* (London: Gee and Coy, 1912), p. 6.

4. Hain, H.P., "Accounting Control in the Zenon Papyri", *The Accounting Review* (October, 1966), pp. 700–2.

5. Penndorf, B., "The Relation of Taxation to the History of the Balance Sheet", *The Accounting Review* (December, 1930), p. 244.

6. Littleton, A.C., *Accounting Evolution to 1900* (New York: American Institute Publishing Company, 1933; reprinted by Russell and Russell, NY, 1966), p. 12.

7. Yamey, B.S., "Early Views on the Origins and Development of Book-keeping and Accounting", op. cit., p. 244.

8. Peragallo, Edward, *Origin and Evolution of Double Entry Bookkeeping* (New York: American Institute Publishing Co., 1938).

9. De Rover, Raymond, "The Development of Accounting Prior to Luca Pacioli According to the Account Books of Medieval Merchants", in A.C. Littleton and B.S. Yamey (eds.), *Studies in History of Accounting* (Homewood, IL: Richard D. Irwin, Inc., 1956).

10. Green, Wilmer L., *History and Survey of Accountancy* (New York: Standard Text Press, 1930), p. 91.

11. Geijsbeek, J., *Ancient Double-Entry Bookkeeping* (Houston: Lawrence, KS: Scholars Book Co.,1976), p. 25.

12. Green, Wilmer L., *History and Survey of Accountancy*, op. cit., p. 8.

13. Geijsbeek, J., *Ancient Double-Entry Bookkeeping*, op. cit., p. 67.

14. Cushing, Barry E., "A Kuhnian Interpretation of the Historical Evolution of Accounting", *The Accounting Historians Journal* (December, 1985), p. 17.

15. Yamey, B.S., "Some Topics in the History of Financial Accounting in England, 1550–1900", in W.T. Baxter and S. Davidson (eds.), *Studies in Accounting* (London: The Institute of Chartered Accountants in England and Wales, 1977), p. 18.

16. Littleton, A.C., *Accounting Evolution* to 1900, op. cit., pp. 123–40.

17. Ibid., p. 49.

18. Peragallo, Edward, *Origin and Evolution of Double Entry Bookkeeping*, op. cit., p. 54.

19. Yamey, B.S., "Some Topics in the History of Financial Accounting in England, 1550–1900", op. cit., p. 19.

20. Chatfield, Michael, *A History of Accounting Thought* (Hinsdale, IL: The Dryden Press, 1974), Chapters 7–8.

21. Yamey, B.S., "Some Topics in the History of Financial Accounting in England, 1550–1900", op. cit., p. 23.

22. Saliero, Earl A., *Principles of Depreciation* (New York: The Ronald Press, 1915), pp. 134–74.

23. Hatfield, Henry Rand, *Accounting, Its Principles and Problems* (New York: D. Appleton & Co., 1927), p. 140.

24. Scott, D.R., *The Cultural Significance of Accounts* (New York: Henry Holt and Company, 1931), p. 143.

25. Garner, S.E., *Evolution of Cost Accounting to 1925* (Tuscaloosa, AL: University of Alabama Press, 1954), p. 28.

26. Chatfield, Michael, *A History of Accounting Thought*, op. cit.

27. Johnson, H. Thomas, "Toward a New Understanding of Nineteenth-Century Cost Accounting", *The Accounting Review* (January, 1969), pp. 124–36.

28. Yamey, B.S., "Some Topics in the History of Financial Accounting in England, 1550–1900", op. cit., pp. 24–5.

29. Rosen, L.S., and DeCoster, Don T., "Funds' Statements: A Historical Perspective", *The Accounting Review* (January, 1969), pp. 124–36.

30. Skinner, R.M., *Accounting Principles: A Canadian Study* (Toronto: Canadian Institute of Chartered Accountants, 1973), p. 314.

31. Ripley, W.Z., *Alain Street and Wall Street* (Boston: Little and Brown, 1927) and *Railroads, Finance and Organization* (New York: Longmans, Green and Co., 1915); Hoxley, J.M.B., "Accounting for Investors", *Journal of Accountancy* (October, 1930), pp. 251–81.

32. Berle, Adolph A., and Means, Gardiner C., *The Modern Corporation and Private Property* (New York: Macmillan, 1933).

33. Financial Accounting Standards Board, "Accounting for Interest Costs", *Dissertation Memorandum* (FASB 1977), para. 174.

34. "Uniform Accounts", *Federal Reserve Bulletin* (April 1, 1917), p. 267.

35. "Report of the Special Committee on Interest in Relation to Cost", *1918 Yearbook of the American Institute of Accountants* (AIA, 1918), p. 112.

36. Carey, John L., *The Rise of the Accounting Profession: From Technician to Professional: 1896–1936* (New York: American Institute of Certified Public Accountants, 1969).

37. Previts, Gary John, and Merino, Barbara D., *A History of Accounting in America* (New York: The Ronald Press, 1979).

38. Securities Exchange Commission, "Administrative Policy on Financial Statements", *Accounting Securities Release No. 4.* (Securities and Exchange Commission, 1938), p. 5.

39. May, George O., "Corporate Publicity and the Auditor", *The Journal of Accountancy* (November, 1926), p. 324.

40. American Institute of Accountants, *Audits of Corporate Accountants* (New York: American Institute of Certified Public Accountants, 1934), p. 9.

41. Storey, Reed K., *The Search for Accounting Principles – Today's Problems in Perspective* (New York: AICPA, 1964), p. 12.

42. Spacek, Leonard, *Business Success Requires an Understanding of Unsolved Problem, Accounting and Financial Reporting* (Arthur Andersen & Co., 1959).

43. Storey, Reed K., *The Search for Accounting Principles – Today's Problems in Perspective*, op. cit., pp. 48–51.

44. Jennings, Alvin R., "Present-Day Challenges in Financial Reporting", *The Journal of Accountancy* (January, 1958), p. 2534.

45. "Report to Council of the Special Committee on Research Program", *The Journal Accountancy* (January, 1958), pp. 62–8.

46. Briloff, Abraham J., *Unaccountable Accounting* (New York: Harper and Row, 1972).

47. Horngren, Charles T., "The Marketing of Accounting Standards", *The Journal of Accountancy* (October, 1973), p. 61.

48. Structure Committee, *The Structure of Establishing Financial Accounting Standard* (Stamford, CT: Financial Accounting Foundation, April 1977), p. 15.

49. US Senate Committee on Government Operations, Subcommittee on Reports, Accounting and Management, summary of *The Accounting Establishment, A Staff Study* (New York National Association of Accountants, December 1976), pp. 20–4.

50. Andreski, S. (ed.), *Max Weber on Capitalism, Bureaucracy and Religion* (London: George Allen, 1983), p. 26.

51. Sombart, Werner, *Der Moderne Kapitalismus* (Munich: Dunker and Hurnblot, 1919), Vol. l, p. 118.

52. Winjum, James O., "Accounting and the Rise of Capitalism: An Accountant's View", *Journal of Accounting Research* (Autumn, 1971), pp. 336–7.

53. Yamey, B.S., "Scientific Bookkeeping and the Rise of Capitalism", *The Economic History Review* (1, 1949), pp. 99–113.

54. Yamey, B.S., "Accounting and Rise of Capitalism: Further Notes on a Theme by Sombart", *Journal of Accounting Research* (Autumn, 1964), pp. 47–136.

55. Ibid., p. 177.

56. Yamey, B.S., "Introduction", in A.C. Littleton and B. Yamey (eds.), *Studies in the History of Accounting* (Homewood, IL: Richard D. Irwin, Inc., 1956), p. 9.

57. Winjum, James O., "Accounting and the Rise of Capitalism: An Accountant's View", op. cit., p. 350.

58. Haskins, C.W., *Business Education and Accountancy*, E.A. Cleveland (ed.) (Harper and Brothers, 1904, reprinted by Arno Press, New York, 1978), p. 141.

59. Previts, G.J., Parker, L.D., and Coffman, E.N., "An Accounting Historiography: Subject Matter and Methodology", *Abacus* (September, 1990).

60. Degler, L.N., "Should Historians Be Skeptical about Using Psychological Methods?", *The Chronicle of Higher Education* (27, May, 1987).

61. Committee on Accounting History Report of the Committee, *The Accounting Review* (Supplement to Vol. XLV, 1920), p. 53.

62. Previts, G.J., Parker, L.D., and Coffman, E.N., "Accounting History: Definition and Relevance", *Abacus* (26, 1, 1990), pp. 3–4.

63. Previts, G.J., "Methods and Meanings of Historical Interpretation for Accounting", *The Accounting Historians' Notebook* (Fall, 1984).

64. Weirich, T.R., Avery, C.G., and Anderson, H.R., "International Accounting: Varying Definitions", *International Journal of Accounting Education and Research* (Fall, 1971), pp. 79–87.

65. Ibid.

66. Qureshi, M., "Pragmatic and Academic Bases of International Accounting", *Management International Review* (2, 1979), p. 62.

67. Ibid.

68. Ibid.

69. Amenkhienan, F.E., *Accounting in the Developing Countries: A Framework for Standard Setting* (Ann Arbor, MI: UMI Research Press, 1986), p. 20.

70. Ibid., p. 20.

71. Belkaoui, Ahmed, "Cultural Studies and Accounting Research", Report of the Cultural Studies and Accounting Research Committee, *Advances in International Accounting* (4, 1991).

72. Belkaoui, Ahmed, "Language and Accounting", *Journal of Accounting Literature* (8, 1989).

73. Belkaoui, Ahmed, "Economic Political and Civil Indicators and Reporting and Disclosure Adequacy", *Journal of Accounting and Public Policy* (2, 1983).

74. Wilson, J.A., "The Need for Standardization of International Accounting", *Touche Ross Tempo* (Winter, 1969), p. 40.

75. Macrae, E.W., "Impediments to a Free International Market in Accounting and the Effects on International Accounting Firms", in *The International World of Accounting Challenges and Opportunities*, J.C. Burton (ed.) (New York: Arthur Young, 1981), p. 150.

76. Seidler, Lee J., "Technical Issues in International Accounting", in S. Choi (ed.), *Multinational Accounting: A Research Framework for the Eighties* (Ann Arbor, MI: UMI Research Press, 1981), p. 41.

References

The development of accounting principles in the USA

Blough, Carmen, "Development of Accounting Principles in the United States", *Berkeley Symposium on the Foundation of Financial Accounting* (Los Angeles: University of California, 1967), pp. 1–14.

Chatfield, Michael, *A History of Accounting Thought* (Hinsdale, IL: Dryden Press, 1974).

Moonitz, Maurice, "Three Contributions to the Development of Accounting Principles Prior to 1930", *Journal of Accounting Research* (Spring, 1970), pp. 145–55.

Previts, Gary John, and Merino, Barbara D., *A History of Accounting in America* (New York: The Ronald Press, 1979).

Storey, Reed K., *The Search for Accounting Principles – Today's Problems in Perspective* (New York: American Institute of Certified Public Accountants, 1964).

Accounting and capitalism

Sombart, Werner, *The Quintessence of Capitalism* (New York: Dutton & Co., 1915).

Winjum, James O., "Accounting and the Rise of Capitalism: An Accountant's View", *Journal of Accounting Research* (Autumn, 1971), pp. 333–50.

Yamey, B.S., "Scientific Bookkeeping and the Rise of Capitalism", *The Economic History Review* (1, 1949), pp. 99–113.

Yamey, B.S., "Accounting and the Rise of Capitalism: Further Notes on a Theme of Sombart", *Journal of Accounting Research* (Autumn, 1964), pp. 117–35.

Relevance of accounting history

American Accounting Association, "Committee on Accounting History", *The Accounting Review* (Supplement to Vol. XLV, 1970).

Cushing, B.E., "A Kuhnian Interpretation of the Historical Evolution of Accounting", *The Accounting Historian's Journal* (December, 1989), pp. 1–41.

Degos, Jean-Guy; *Histoire de la Comptabilité* (Paris: Presses Universitaires de France, 1998).

Parker, L.D., "The Classical Model of Control in the Accounting Literature", *The Accounting Historians' Journal* (Spring, 1986a).

Parker, L.D., "Henry Fayol, Accounting and Control: An Environmental Reflection", *The Accounting Historians' Notebook* (Spring, 1986b).

Parker, L.D., *Developing Control Concepts in the Twentieth Century* (New York: Garland Press, 1986).

Parker, R.H., *Bibliographies for Accounting Historians* (New York: Arno Press, 1980).

Parker, R.H., "The Study of Accounting History", in A. Hopwood and M. Bromwich (eds.), *Essays in British Accounting Research* (London: Pitman, 1981).

Parker, R.H., *The Developments of the Accountancy Profession in Britain to the Early Twentieth Century* (Monograph No. 5, The Academy of Accounting Historians, 1986).

Peloubet, M.E., "The Imprint of Personalities on the Accounting Profession", *Fifty Years of Service, 1898–1948* (New Jersey Society of Certified Public Accountants, 1948).

Peragallo, E., *Origin and Evolution of Double Entry Bookkeeping* (New York: American Institute Publishing Company, 1938).

Peragallo, E., "Development of the Compound Entry in the Fifteenth Century Ledger of Jachomo Badoer, A Venetian Merchant", *The Accounting Review* (January, 1983).

Previts, Gary John, Parker, Lee D., and Coffman, Edward N., "Accounting History: Definition and Relevance", *Abacus* (26, 1, 1990), pp. 1–13.

Previts, G.J., "The SEC and Its Chief Accountants: Historical Impressions", *Journal of Accountancy* (August, 1978).

Previts, G.J., *A Critical Evaluation of Comparative Financial Accounting Thought in America, 1901 to 1920* (New York: Arno Press, 1980).

Previts, G.J., "Methods and Meanings of Historical Interpretations for Accountancy", *The Accounting Historians' Notebook* (Fall, 1984).

Previts, G.J., *The Scope of CPA Services: A Study of the Development of the Concept of Independence and the Profession's Role in Society* (New York: John Wiley, 1985).

Previts, G.J., and Merino, B.D., *A History of Accounting in America: An Historical Interpretation of the Cultural Significance of Accounting* (New York: The Ronald Press, 1979).

Evolution of double-entry bookkeeping

Cushing, B.E., "A Kuhnian Interpretation of the Historical Evolution of Accounting", *The Accounting Historians' Journal* (December, 1985), pp. 1–41.

Garner, S.P., *Evolution of Cost Accounting to 1925* (Tuscaloosa, AL: University of Alabama Press, 1954).

Geijsbeek, J., *Ancient Double-Entry Bookkeeping* (Houston, TX: New York: Scholars Book Co., 1974).

Johnson, H.T., "Towards a New Understanding of Nineteenth Century Cost Accounting", *The Accounting Review* (July, 1981), pp. 510–18.

Littleton, A.C., *Accounting Evolution to 1900* (New York: America Institute Publishing Co. Inc., 1933).

Peragallo, E., *Origin and Evolution of Double Entry Bookkeeping* (New York: AICPA, 1938).

International accounting

Amenkhienan, E.R., *Accounting in the Developing Countries: A Framework for Standard Setting* (Ann Arbor, MI: UMI Research Press, 1986).

Bursten, R.J., "The Evolution of Accounting in Developing Countries", *International Journal of Accounting Education and Research* (Fall, 1978).

Choi, F.D.S., and Bavishi, V.B., "Diversity in Multinational Accounting", *Financial Executive* (August, 1988), pp. 46–9.

Cooke, T.E., and Wallace, R.S.O., "Financial Disclosure Regulation and Its Environment: A Review and Further Analysis", *Journal of Accounting and Public Policy* (9, 1990), 79–110.

Enthoven, A.J.H., *Accounting Education in Economic Development Management* (Amsterdam: North Holland, 1981).

Riahi-Belkaoui, Ahmed, *International Accounting* (Westport, CT: Greenwood Publishing Group, 1985).

Riahi-Belkaoui, Ahmed, *The New Environment in International Accounting: Issues and Practices* (Westport, CT: Greenwood Publishing Group, 1987), p. 220.

Riahi-Belkaoui, Ahmed, *Judgment in International Accounting* (Westport, CT: Greenwood Publishing Group, 1990).

Riahi-Belkaoui, Ahmed, *Multinational Management Accounting* (Westport, CT: Greenwood Publishing Group, 1991).

Riahi-Belkaoui, Ahmed, *Multinational Financial Accounting* (Westport, CT: Greenwood Publishing Group, 1991).

Riahi-Belkaoui, Ahmed, *Value Added Reporting: The Lessons for the US* (Westport, CT: Greenwood Publishing Group, 1992), p. 165.

Riahi-Belkaoui, Ahmed, *Accounting for the Developing Countries* (Westport, CT: Greenwood Publishing Group, 1994).

Riahi-Belkaoui, Ahmed, *International and Multinational Accounting* (London: Dryden Press, 1994).

Riahi-Belkaoui, Ahmed, *The Linguistic Shaping of Accounting* (Westport, CT: Greenwood Press, 1995).

Riahi-Belkaoui, Ahmed, *Performance Results in Value Added Reporting* (Westport, CT: Greenwood Publishing, 1996).

Riahi-Belkaoui, Ahmed, *Multinationality and Financial Performance* (Westport, CT: Greenwood Publishing, 1996).

Riahi-Belkaoui, Ahmed, *Disclosure Adequacy: Nature and Determinants* (Westport, CT: Greenwood Publishing, 1997).

Riahi-Belkaoui, Ahmed, *Significant Current Issues in International Taxation* (Westport, CT: Greenwood Publishing, 1998).

Riahi-Belkaoui, Ahmed, *The Nature, Estimation and Management of Political Risk* (Westport, CT: Greenwood Publishing, 1998).

Riahi-Belkaoui, Ahmed, *Performance Results of Multinationality* (Westport, CT: Greenwood Publishing, 1999).

Riahi-Belkaoui, Ahmed, *Value Added Reporting and Research* (Westport, CT: Greenwood Publishing, 1999).

The nature and uses of accounting

2

One hears different definitions of accounting, encounters different debates about whether it is an art or a science, and so many who are puzzled or confused about its role. This chapter intends to bring some answers and restore some order to these issues concerning the nature of accounting, its links to management, its reliance on double-entry accounting and generally accepted accounting principles. This order, however, brings more questions about its uses, as evidenced by the frequency of accounting changes and the evidence of earnings management: such is the relative complexity of the nature and uses of accounting that this chapter introduces.

2.1 Definitions and role of accounting

2.1.1 Definitions of accounting

The Committee on Terminology of the American Institute of Certified Public Accountants defined accounting as follows:

> Accounting is the art of recording, classifying, and summarizing in a significant manner and in terms of money, transactions and events which are, in part at least, of a financial character, and interpreting the results thereof.[1]

The scope of accounting from the above definition appears limited. A broader perspective is offered by the following definition of accounting as:

> The process of identifying, measuring, and communicating economic information to permit informed judgments and decisions by users of the information.[2]

More recently, accounting has been defined with reference to the concept of quantitative information:

> Accounting is a service activity. Its function is to provide quantitative information, primarily financial in nature about economic entities that is intended to be useful in making economic decisions, in making resolved choices among alternative courses of action.[3]

These definitions refer to accounting as either an "art" or a "service activity" and imply that accounting encompasses a body of techniques that is deemed useful for certain fields. *The Handbook of Accounting* identifies the following fields in which accounting is useful: financial reporting; tax determination and planning; independent audits; data processing and information systems; cost and management accounting; national income accounting; and management consulting. Since then the list has expanded to include interesting new developments such as international accounting, behavioral accounting, socio-economic accounting, governmental accounting, not-for-profit accounting, and third world accounting, to name only a few. In fact, research as well as practice have taken accounting to new frontiers, making accounting a full-fledged science.

For example, in addition to the traditional audit services, accountants can provide a lot of services related to the quality of the information. Known as assurances services, they are independent professional services aimed at improving the quality of information, or its content, for decision-making. The enterprise supplies to and receives information from four sources.

1. To the capital suppliers, it provides (a) financial statements, (b) press releases, (c) analysts' meetings and (d) fact books. From the suppliers, it receives information about (a) truth in lending, (b) undertaking in securities offering and (c) financial capacity.

2. To the customers and suppliers, it provides information about product/services quality and receives information about credit worthiness and customer qualifications.

3. To the community in general, it receives information about (a) tax policy/regulation, (b) employment requirements, (c) air/water quality and (d) environmental restrictions and provides information about (a) environmental effects, (b) employment effects and (c) tax returns.

4. To talent, it receives information about (a) credentials/competencies, (b) employment policies, (c) compensation and (d) job-related information, and provides information about (a) benefits, (b) employment policies, (c) compensation and (d) job-related information.[4]

All these new services can be facilitated by the accountants' provision of assurance services, aimed at improving the quality of the information. A sample of assurance service possibilities, obtained from a 1997 survey of 21 large CPA firms, includes:

1. assessment of ethics-related risks and vulnerabilities;
2. controls over and risk related to investments;
3. adequacy of controls and policies for derivatives;
4. information systems security reviews;
5. assessment of risk of accumulation, distribution and storage of digital information;
6. fraud and illegal acts risk assessment;
7. management/board salary benchmarking;
8. internal audit quality assurance;
9. adequacy of billing system compared to competitors;
10. advertising rates to be paid vs. those charged;
11. customer satisfaction surveys – reports/validations;
12. review of compliance with investment policy;
13. compliance with trading policies and procedures;
14. compliance with royalty agreements (entertainment);
15. identification of critical items to monitor;
16. examination of software specifications;
17. ISO 9000 certification;
18. examination of hardware benchmark test results;
19. newspaper circulation audits:
20. annual environmental report;
21. audit of milestones in long-term incentive plans;
22. compliance with industry standards for additives test labs;
23. verification of contributions under incentive plan;
24. verification of construction costs for incentive grant.[5]

These assurance services are crucial to the CPA firm given the forces impacting the problem. These forces include:

1. the decline of students and young people electing to join the CPA profession;
2. a borderless world with a marketplace demanding more complex, real-time advice and presenting unlimited opportunities for CPAs to expand their skills, competencies, and services;

3. technological advances that are reshaping lifestyles, work patterns, educational experiences, and communication styles and techniques and rewriting the "rules of business", leaving far behind those who will not harness it and effectively integrate it;

4. pressure to transform finance from scorekeeper to business partner, capable of delivering value to the organization and of helping to create a sustainable competitive advantage;

5. market value shifts with a market decline of the profession's cornerstone service: accounting, auditing, and tax preparation;

6. leadership imperative requiring new insights, new skills and extraordinary ability in the world of commerce that is global, technological, instantaneous, and increasingly critical;

7. technology displacement where the transitional, essential skills of the CPAs are being replaced by new and numerous technologies;

8. the rise of non-CPA competitors that are not bound by the problems of codes of standards and ethics.[6]

2.1.2 Accounting: an art or a science?

The accounting literature developed at one point in time a long-drawn-out debate of whether accounting is a science.[7] Those who argue that accounting is an art or a trade suggest that the accounting skills necessary to be a good tradesman should be taught and that a "legalistic" approach to accounting is warranted. The advocates of accounting as a science suggest instead the teaching of the accounting model of measurements to give the accounting students more conceptual insight into what conventional accrual accounting is attempting to do to meet the general objectives of serving users' needs; and to provoke critical thought about the field and the dynamics of change in accounting.[8] How accounting is taught, as a trade or as a science, will affect the views of the field and the preparedness of those students electing to major in accounting and ultimately to join the ranks of the accounting profession. Theory, in both the normative and positive sense, and the science of accounting, placed at the front and not only at the back of the curriculum, may help the students to understand accounting practices better, to be prepared for changes in these practices, and ultimately to make better policy decisions. This last argument fits perfectly to the now widely held view that accounting is a full-fledged social science. This argument was eloquently made by Mautz as follows:

> Accounting deals with enterprises, which are certainly social groups; it is concerned with transactions and other economic events which have social consequences and influence social relationships; it produces knowledge that is useful and meaningful to human beings engaged in activities having social implications; it is primarily mental in nature. On the basis of the guidelines available, accounting is a social science.[9]

The view of accounting as a social science permeates the atmosphere of the academic and research environment in accounting, creating a schism in the department and profession. There is ample evidence supporting a schism between the practice and academic accounting communities, characterized mainly by a lack of common interests.[10] This is evidenced by the following responses to an AICPA survey of Institute members in education:

● "the most important problem facing CPAs in education is the fact that academe has become too divorced from the accounting profession",

- "much of the accounting research currently conducted bears no relevance to 'real world' accounting", and
- "educators often lack interactions with practitioners".[11]

2.1.3 The virtues and role of accounting

The virtues of accounting practice include:

- *honesty* of the accountant in general and the auditor in particular,
- *concern for the economic status of others* in the form of stewardship and accountability,
- *sensitivity to the value of cooperation and conflict* by preempting conflicts and producing a kind of enforced cooperation through the use of management accounting techniques,
- *communicative character of accounting* by telling about economic experiences through accounting discourse, and
- *dissemination of economic information* by providing economic information for decision making.[12]

But the realization of these virtues is sometimes stalled by the obstacles of:

- *the dominance of external rewards* threatening auditor independence,
- *the corrupting power of institutions*, and
- *the failure to distinguish between virtues and laws.*[13]

The role of accounting is to produce information about the economic *behavior* resulting from a firm's activities within its environment. The result is best represented by what the FASB calls "the information spectrum." It is shown in Exhibit 2.1 and is composed of the financial statements, the notes to the financial statements, other means of financial reporting and other information. Only the financial statements, including the notes thereto, of a firm are audited in the sense that an auditor has exercised independent judgment to attest to the fact that these statements fairly represent the firm's position and performance in accordance with generally accepted accounting principles.

Prakash and Rappaport provide an interesting frame of reference, based on information flows, that shows the role of accounting in providing the kind of information that ties together the managerial processes and links the firms to its environment.[14] This frame of reference is shown in Exhibit 2.2. It shows the internal structure of the firm as composed of five informational processes – planning, decision-making, implementation-cum-observation, data structuring, and performance evaluation. They all interlink in such a way as to provide necessary information to management. It also shows the various informational links of the firm to its environment, allowing (a) factor and product markets coupling, (b) external evaluation compliance, and (c) economic feedback and regulatory compliance. The soundness of this frame of reference is its ability to show:

> … that the firm, in functioning as a system within the parameters determined by its environment, itself functions as an element in a higher level system, namely the economy, wherein it interacts and interrelates with other elements and so takes part in the process of determining the very parameters within which it must function internally.[15]

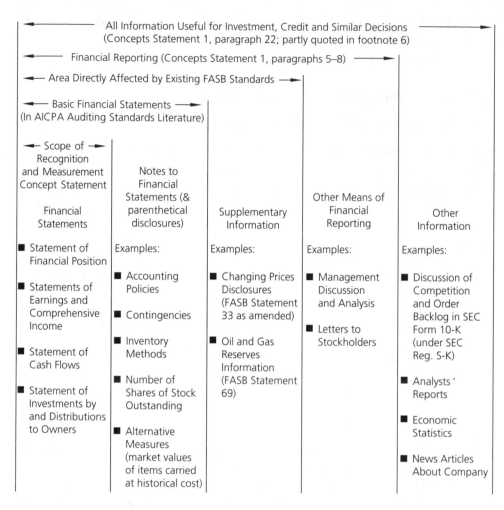

Source: FASB Statement of Financial Accounting Concepts No. 5, Recognition and Measurement in Financial Statements of Business Enterprises (December, 1984), p. 5. Reprinted with permission.

Exhibit 2.1   Information spectrum

2.2 Measurement in accounting

2.2.1 Nature of measurement in accounting

It is generally considered that accounting is a measurement as well as a communication discipline. By measurement is meant "the assignment of numerals to objects or events according to rules".[16] The first step in accounting is to identify and select these objects, activities or events and their attributes that are deemed relevant to users before actual measurement takes place. Naturally, limitations of availability of data as well as specific characteristics of the environment, like uncertainty, lack of objectivity and verifiability, may create constraints to measurement. Notwithstanding these constraints, measurement in accounting traditionally involves the assignment of numerical values to objects, events or their attributes in such a way as to insure easy aggregation or disaggregation of the data. Where measurement is inadequate or infeasible, nonquantifiable or nonmonetary information may be provided in the footnotes.

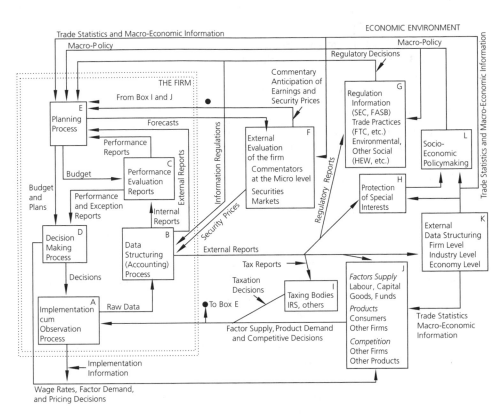

Source: Prem Prakash and Alfred Rappaport, "Informational Interdependencies: System Structure Induced by Accounting Information", *The Accounting Review* (October, 1975), p. 727. Reprinted with permission.

Exhibit 2.2   System structure induced by accounting information

2.2.2 Types of measures

Various types of measures are possible in accounting:

1. Accounting measures can be either direct or indirect. Direct or primary measures are actual measures of an object or its attributes. Indirect or secondary measures are derived indirectly by an algebraic transformation of a set of numbers that themselves represent direct measures of some objects or attributes. These objects or attributes are the *intrinsic objects* of an indirect measure. The unit cost of production that is derived by dividing the total production by the volume of production is an indirect or secondary measure. Most measures used in accounting are indirect measures resulting from some transformation. It is the degree of transformation that provides the distinction between what is perceived as a direct or an indirect measure, and defines the source of the measurement error. Thus, a measurement error would occur either in (a) the original primary quantification or (b) the transformation process.[17]

2. With respect to decision time dimension, accounting measures can be classified as a past measure, a present measure, or a future measure to refer respectively to a measure of a past, present or future event.

3. To refer to whether the accounting object or its attribute measures belong to a past, present or future event relative to the time at which measurement is made, the accounting measures can be classified as a retrospective measure, a contemporary measure, or a prospective measure. This makes it possible to have:

(a) three kinds of past measures: retrospective past measures, contemporary past measures and prospective past measures;

(b) two kinds of present measures: contemporary present measures and prospective present measures;

(c) all future measures to be prospective.[18]

4. Measurements can be either:

(a) fundamental measurements where the number can be assigned to the property by reference to natural laws, and do not rely on the measurement of any other variables;

(b) derived measurements which rely on the measurement of two or more quantities and depend on the existence of a verified empirical theory linking the given property to other properties.

5. Measurements can be either (a) made when confirmed empirical theories may be used to support their existence; or (b) made by fiat, based on arbitrary definition. Most accounting measurements are measurements by fiat, although a scientific approach to accounting theory construction and verification attempts to provide the necessary empirical testing, and thereby reduce and even eliminate some of the arbitrariness in definition and measurement of accounting concepts. Mattessich states:

> [measurement by fiat] is the least desirable since it depends greatly on the intuition of the experimenter and offers frequently too large a number of definitional possibilities or alternatives. We might measure the value of an asset by its purchase price (historic cost basis), by its discounted expected net revenues, by the potential of its liquidation yield, or many other variations and confirmations. There neither exists at present the possibilities to infer accounting values through "natural laws" (i.e., by fundamental measurement) nor through a combination of two or more fundamental measures that result in derived measurement. Most of the economic and accounting measures belong in the category of measurement by fiat, which is reflected in a certain definitional arbitrariness of our discipline.[19]

2.2.3 Types of scales

Every measurement is made on a scale. Scales can be described in general terms as nominal, ordinal, interval or ratio.

A nominal scale assists in the determination of equality, like the numberings of footballers. It is a simple classification or labeling system like the case of a chart of accounts. The numbers reflect the objects themselves, rather than their properties.

An ordinal scale assists in the determination of greater or lesser, like grades of wool or street numbers. It is an order of preference system. One problem with the ordinal scale is that the differences or intervals between the numbers are not necessarily equal.

An interval scale assists in the determination of the equality of intervals or difference like temperature and time. It assigns equal values to intervals between assigned numbers.

A ratio scale assists in the determination of the equality of ratios, with the additional feature of the existence of a unique origin, a natural zero point, where the distance from it for at least one object is known.

Accounting relies on each of the scale of measurements:

> The nominal scale although basic to the accounting process is neither the only nor the most important scale pertaining to our discipline. The evaluation process – the core of

theoretical accountancy – utilizes the ratio scale; statement analysts primarily work with ordinal scales; and certain aspects of cost accounting can be considered as applying the *interval scale*.[20]

2.3 The rationale behind double-entry accounting

Double-entry accounting achieved its most serious notoriety with Friar Luca Pacioli's treatise on bookkeeping. In one of the five sections of his book *Summa de Arithmetica, Geometria, Proportioni et Proportionalita*, published in 1494, he provided a description of double-entry bookkeeping, known then as "the method of Venice". In its most simple formulation, double-entry is a formulation of "where-got, where-give", a two-dimensional system that permits classification within one set of classes. It calls for a dual classification along a duality principle. This is best defined by Mattessich as:

> The assertion that a transaction or flow has basically two dimensions: an aspect and a counter-aspect (to avoid the terms *input* and *output* which have too concrete a flavor of the term *debit* and *credit* which have too strong a flavor of the technical recording process). More precisely; the principle asserts that *there exists economic events which are isomorphic to a two-dimensional classification of a value within a set of classes* [Author's italics].[21]

Double-entry accounting consists of two kinds: a classificational double-entry accounting and a causal double-entry accounting. Both kinds rely on the equality of debits and credits.

A classificational double-entry accounting is aimed at maintaining the fundamental accounting equation that summarizes the classificational position:

$$\text{Assets} = \text{Liabilities} + \text{Owner's Equity}$$

In this classificational double-entry accounting a debit portrays a classification, while a credit portrays another classification. Two different classifications are made. For example, the purchase of inventory on credit for $20,000 is recorded as:

	Dr	Cr
Inventory	$20,000	
Accounts Payable		$20,000

Two classifications were made by this entry, one based on the new asset acquired and the other based on the new liability incurred; both belong to different sides of the accounting equation.

A causal double-entry bookkeeping describes the cause–effect relationship between an increment and a decrement. The value of an increment (debit) is offset by an equal value of a decrement (credit). For example, the purchase of the same inventory for cash is recorded as:

	Dr	Cr
Inventory	$20,000	
Cash		$20,000

In assessing both kinds of double-entry bookkeeping, we cannot avoid regarding the classificational as merely a special case of multiple-entry bookkeeping, and unlike what Arthur Cayley (1984) thought, it is not absolutely perfect. How about the causal double-entry bookkeeping? Ijiri makes the most eloquent case as follows:

Contrary to classificational double entry, the duality in causal double entry has a much deeper root. In causal double entry, an increment (debit) is matched with a decrement (credit). If we were to add a third element to make it a triple entry, what would this element be? It is hard to conceive of such an element because the duality stems not from a selection of two classifications out of many, as in classificational double entry, but from our perception of change in the resource set as being an addition and subtraction. If the positive is matched with the negative, nothing else is left to be matched unless we introduce additional dimensions to the change.[22]

2.4 Generally accepted accounting principles (GAAP)

2.4.1 The meaning of GAAP

Accounting is practiced within an implicit framework. This framework is known as generally accepted principles. Statement No. 4 of the Accounting Principles Board of the American Institute of Certified Public Accountants (hereafter AICPA) Accounting Principles Board stated that GAAP are noted in "experience, reason, custom, usage, and … practical necessity"[23] and they "…. encompass the convention, rules, and procedures necessary to define accepted accounting practice at a particular time".[24] They are a guide to the accounting profession in the choice of accounting techniques and the preparation of financial statements in a way considered to be good accounting practice. The conventions, rules, and procedures have acquired the special status of being included in GAAP because they have *substantial authoritative support*. The APB referred to this term in Chapter 6 of the APB Statement No. 4:

> In as much as generally accepted accounting principles embody a consensus they depend on notions such as general *acceptance and substantial authoritative support* which are not precisely defined.[25]

One way to give a recognizable meaning to the term "generally accepted" is to describe the conditions under which an accounting method will be deemed as generally accepted. For example, Skinner argues that the accounting method must meet at least one and usually some of the following conditions, to qualify as generally accepted:

- The method will be in actual use in a significant number of cases where the circumstances are suitable.
- The method would have support in the pronouncements of the professional accounting societies, or other authoritative bodies such as the Securities and Exchange Commission in the United States.
- The method would have support in the writing of a number of respected accounting teachers and thinkers.[26]

The literature pertaining to GAAP has expanded in time to include volumes of statements, opinions, and other pronouncements from a variety of authoritative sources. It includes the pronouncements currently in force of the various standard-setting bodies, namely the Financial Accounting Standards Board (FASB) statements of financial accounting standards (SFAS) and the interpretations, along with the Accounting Principles Board (APB) opinions and the American Institute of Certified Public Accountants (AICPA) accounting research bulletins. Other common sources of the GAAP are:

1. AICPA industry audit and accounting guides and statements of positions and AICPA accounting interpretations;

2. other identified publications of the FASB, such as its technical bulletins, and those of its predecessors, such as APB statements;

3. publications of the Securities and Exchange Commission (SEC), such as accounting series releases;

4. recognized and prevalent practices as reflected in the annual AICPA publication *Accounting Trends and Techniques*;

5. AICPA issues papers, FASB concepts statements, textbooks, and articles.

This profusion of sources may be viewed as a hierarchy. Exhibit 2.3 looks at the hierarchy as a four-story house – the house of GAAP. The authoritativeness of accounting guidance rests on the various official positions of the profession and the SEC.

Use of the term "general acceptance" remains a source of confusion, especially in a new situation or when a standard is mandated. As stated by Skinner:

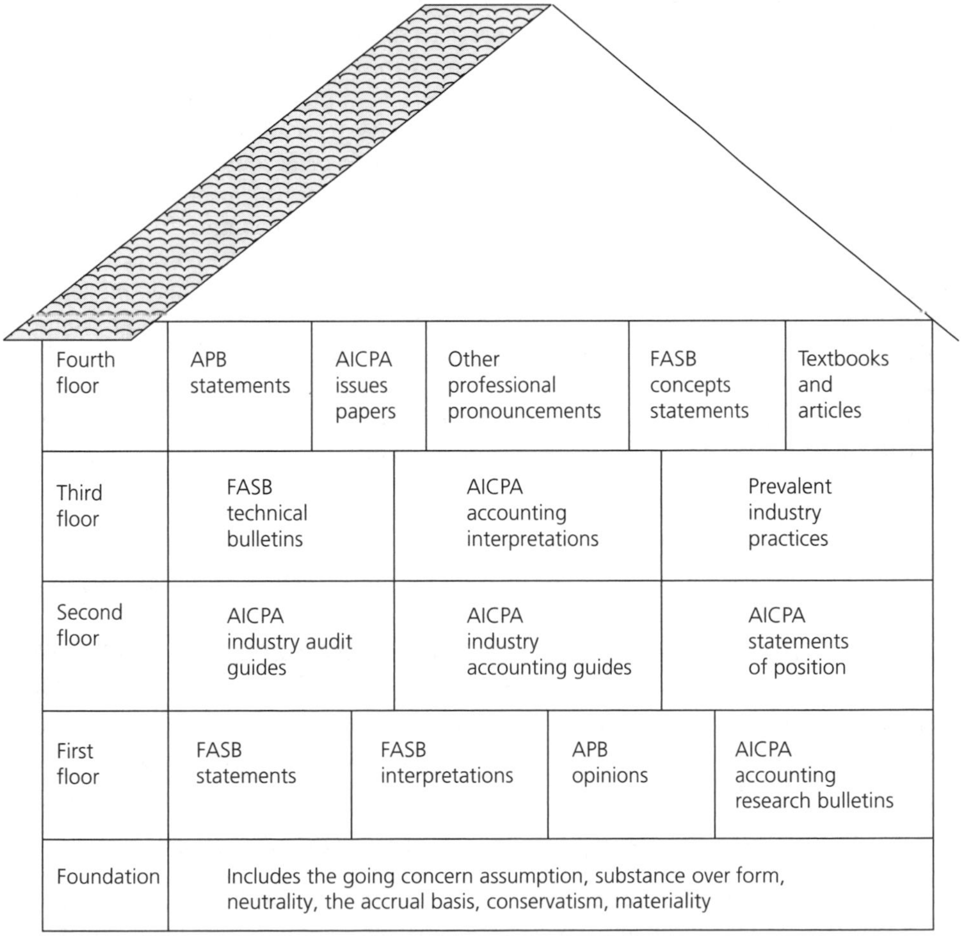

Fourth floor	APB statements	AICPA issues papers	Other professional pronouncements	FASB concepts statements	Textbooks and articles
Third floor	FASB technical bulletins		AICPA accounting interpretations		Prevalent industry practices
Second floor	AICPA industry audit guides		AICPA industry accounting guides		AICPA statements of position
First floor	FASB statements	FASB interpretations	APB opinions		AICPA accounting research bulletins
Foundation	Includes the going concern assumption, substance over form, neutrality, the accrual basis, conservatism, materiality				

Source: Stevin Rubin, "The House of GAAP", *Journal of Accountancy* (June, 1984), p. 123. Reprinted with permission, by the American Institute of Certified Public Accountants, Inc.

Exhibit 2.3 The house of GAAP

In a new situation, obviously there is not generally accepted principle. If different entities adopt different policies, there is no mechanism for judging which is generally accepted. (In practice, it is not impossible that all will be considered generally accepted.) On the other hand, a recommendation of a standard-setting body is automatically deemed generally accepted to the exclusion of other practices, no matter how unpopular the recommendation is.[27]

2.4.2 What should it be? GAAP, Special GAAP, or OCBOA?

There is a change of perception of the GAAPs. They are not seen as being a rigid set of measurement rules. Their numerous applications differ, in fact, depending on the circumstances. On the one hand, we have various and different special GAAPs, such as the GAAPs for governmental organizations, the GAAPs for regulated business enterprises, the GAAPs for non-profit organizations, the GAAPs for investment companies, and the GAAPs for banks. There is even serious debate in favor of a special set of GAAPs for small enterprises. This has been officially adopted by the FASB, which has either given small and closely held businesses some relief from certain financial statement disclosure requirements – like the suspension in 1978 of the requirements to disclose earnings per share and segment information for companies whose securities are not publicly traded – or has distinguished between disclosure that should be required for all enterprises and that which should be required for only certain designated types of enterprise.

There is also more interest in alternatives to the GAAP, basically on financial statements prepared in accordance with other comprehensive bases of accounting (OCBOA). The impulse to switch to the OCBOA came from changes in the tax laws made by the Economic Recovery Act of 1981 and the increasing separation of tax accounting from the GAAP accounting, the increase in the number of partnerships, the subchapter S corporations and other entities that prefer to present tax or cash-basis financial statements, and the tentative conclusions of the AICPA accounting standards overload-study special committee in favor of the increased tax basis of accounting. Guidance to practitioners faced with the OCBOA statements is provided in the 1976 AICPA Statement on Auditing Standards No. 14 *Special Reports*. Of the four types of report identified, one is based on the OCBOA. To be classified as OCBOA, one of the following four criteria must be met:

1. A basis of accounting necessary to meet regulatory requirements. It is basically GAAP for regulated companies.
2. A basis of accounting that may be used for income tax returns. It is basically the tax basis of accounting.
3. A basis of accounting based on cash receipts and disbursements with or without some accrual support. It is basically the cash basis or the modified cash basis of accounting.
4. A basis of accounting resulting from the application of a definite set of criteria. Current-value financial statements or price-level adjusted financial statements are good examples.

The use of the OCBOA statements presents more problems to both users and CPAs:

1. To the users, they may not appear as an acceptable or known alternative to the GAAP. This may be aggravated by the requirement that the auditor's report includes a middle paragraph that: (a) states, or preferably refers to the note to the financial statements which states the basis of presentation of the financial statements on which the auditor is reporting;

(b) refers to the note to the financial statements that describes how the basis of presentation differed from the GAAP and that may state the monetary effect of such differences;

(c) states that the financial statements are not intended to be presented in conformity with the GAAP.

This middle paragraph may be perceived by the less-than-sophisticated user as a qualification by the auditor, rather than an informational statement.

2. To the practitioner, the OCBOA statements may present problems due to the lack of comprehensive guidance similar to the one available for the GAAP statements. To alleviate the situation the AICPA Technical Information Service (TIS), a consultation services department, may be used by an AICPA member to obtain assistance on any accounting or auditing problem by letter or toll-free telephone call.

But what should it be: GAAP, special GAAP, or OCBOA? Those in favor of more uniformity and comparability would argue for the GAAP; those in favor of more flexibility and better avenues to deal with varying circumstances would argue for the special GAAP. Those arguing for unique circumstances or against standards overload would argue for the OCBOA.

2.4.3 Little GAAP vs. big GAAP

Accounting is facing the problem of small businesses being overburdened by administrative and accounting costs in order to comply with irrelevant rules, and the need for relief in the form of exemptions. When one considers that more than one-half of the USA's manufacturing, trade, and retail sales are produced by medium-sized and small businesses that are not listed on the New York or American stock exchanges, the gravity of the problem is further magnified. The question is whether any real difference exists between large and small businesses and among the needs of their respective information users to justify differences in the accounting rules in the form of two GAAPs: a little GAAP for smaller and/or closely held businesses, and a big GAAP for large companies.

Differences between large and small businesses

With respect to the differences between large and small business, the question is to identify those companies for which more relief from existing financial reporting requirements should be made. A definition is needed to distinguish between small and large companies on the basis of the real differences between them. The FASB tentatively defined a small company as follows:

> A company whose operations are relatively small, usually with total revenues of less than $5 million. It typically (a) is owner-managed, (b) has few other owners, if any, (c) has all owners actively involved in the conduct of enterprise affairs except possibly for certain family members, (d) has infrequent transfer of ownership interest, and (e) has a simple capital structure.[28]

It also defined a public company as follows:

> A company (a) whose securities trade in a public market on a stock exchange or in the over-the-counter market or (b) that is required to file financial statements with the Securities and Exchange Commission. A company is also considered a public company if its financial statements are issued in preparation for the sale of any class of securities in a public market.[29]

It follows that a large company is any company that is other than the above-defined small company, and a private company is any company that is other than the above-defined public company. Although these definitions show the real differences between small and large companies and public and private companies, they do not indicate whether the disclosure and reporting relief should be provided to private companies, to small companies, or to private and small companies.

Differences among users of financial statements

With respect to the differences among users, the issues are to identify (a) whether there are real differences between the needs of users of financial statements of public companies and users of financial statements of private companies, and (b) whether there are real differences among users regarding the degree of their reliance on financial statements of private companies as sources of information. Empirical research on both questions presents conflicting evidence. Evidence asserts that financial analysts and public stockholders are the primary users of the financial statements of public companies, whereas owner-managers and creditors are the primary users of financial statements of private companies: it follows that different groups may be perceived to have different information needs. Other evidence, however, asserts that bank loan officers and security analysts have a high degree of similarity of preferences for various types of information that are typically included in the financial statements. It attributed the few instances in which those two groups might have a difference in preference for information to a difference in focus (for example, cash-flow analysis for bankers versus earnings per share for security analysts). This last finding has been the prevalent position of standard-setters when it comes to defining the needs of users. Statement No. 4 of the Accounting Principles Board identified the following different user groups: owners, creditors and suppliers (both present and potential), management, taxing authorities, employees, customers, financial analysts and advisers, stock exchanges, lawyers, regulatory or registration authorities, financial press and reporting agencies, trade associations and labor unions. Although it acknowledged that these groups have different needs, the statement observed that:

> … the problem of ascertaining specialized needs of a large number of users, the cost of attempting to serve those needs on an individual basis, and the confusion that might result from disseminating more than one set of information about the financial results of an enterprise's operation militate against attempting to serve all needs of users with special-purpose reports.

It also identified one of the basic features of financial accounting as the presentation of "general-purpose financial information that is designed to serve the common needs of present and potential owners and creditors". This basic feature of financial accounting is based on the presumption that "a significant number of users need similar information". As we might expect, the FASB adopted similar positions. Its stated objective for financial reporting is to serve the needs of users of financial statements in general and not the particular needs of specific users.

Another indication of the FASB's view was expressed in an FASB exposure draft issued before the issuance of FASB Statement No. 14, *Financial Reporting for segments of a Business Enterprise*:

> The Board believes, however, that there is no fundamental difference in the types of decisions and the decision-making process of those who use the financial statements of smaller or privately held enterprises … Information of the type required to be disclosed by this statement is as important to users of the financial statements of a

large or publicly held enterprise. Accordingly, this statement applies to all financial statements that present financial position or results of operations in conformity with generally accepted accounting principles.

There seems to be awareness by the standard-setters that small and closely held companies are in an economic environment completely different from that of large publicly held companies.

Many, however, will disagree with the APB Statement No. 4 and the FASB positions on the nature of the user and his or her further needs and with most of the empirical findings that there may be no basic differences in the needs of users of financial statements. The intuitive and at the same time accurate view is that principal users of public company financial statements are financial analysts and public stockholders, and financial statements of smaller and/or closely held businesses are usually directed toward owner-managers and bankers and other credit grantors.

Official positions on "Little GAAP"

The need for differential measurement, reporting, and disclosure on the basis of either size (small versus large) or ownership (public versus private) has been a concern of the profession since 1952. The AICPA's accounting standards division began a study of the application of the GAAP to smaller and/or closely held businesses by forming in 1974 the Committee on Generally Accepted Accounting Principles for Smaller and/or Closely Held Businesses (the "little GAAP" Committee). Four basic questions were asked in a discussion paper distributed to more than 20,000 members:

1. Are any differences in the application of the generally accepted accounting principles appropriate?
2. If there were differences in the application of generally accepted accounting principles, on what basis should the different applications be determined?
3. If there were differences in the application of the generally accepted accounting principles, what differences would be appropriate?
4. If there were differences in the application of the generally accepted accounting principles, what impact would this have on the independent CPA?

The "little GAAP" Committee studied the response and concluded generally in its 1976 report that there was strong support within the profession as a whole for reconsideration of existing practices with respect to the application of the generally accepted accounting principles to the financial statements of smaller and/or closely held businesses, and with respect to standards for reports of CPAs on such statements. More specifically, the report (pages 8 and 9) contained the following conclusions and recommendations directly related to the issues being considered:

[Conclusions]

- ... The same measurement principles should be applied in the general purpose financial statements of all entities, because the measurement process should be independent of the nature of users and their interest in the resulting measurements.

- ... The nature of the information disclosed and the extent of detail necessary for any particular disclosure may well vary depending on the needs of users.

- ... [There should be a distinction between] disclosures ... required by the GAAP [and] additional or analytical [disclosure] in the financial statements of all entities.

[Recommendations]

- ... The Financial Accounting Standards Board should develop criteria to distinguish disclosures that should be required by GAAP ... from disclosures that merely provide additional or analytical data ... The criteria should then be used in a formal review of disclosures presently considered to be required by GAAP and should be considered by the Board in any new pronouncements.

- ... The AICPA auditing standards division should reconsider pronouncements concerning a CPA's report on (a) unaudited financial statements, including those accompanied by an "internal use only" disclaimer, (b) financial information presented on prescribed forms, and (c) interim financial statements of smaller and/or closely held businesses.

- ... The Financial Accounting Standards Board should amend APB Opinion No. 15 [*Earnings Per Share*], to require only publicly traded companies ... to disclose earnings-per-share data.

The official reactions to these recommendations were positive. The AICPA created the Accounting and Review Services Committee (ARSC) and gave it the status of a senior committee. Its objective was to reconsider all aspects of AICPA pronouncements applicable to the association of CPAs with unaudited financial statements, a project that is basically small-business oriented. Since then the ARSC has issued statements on standards for accounting and review services (SSARs), which establish and delineate the CPA's involvement with unaudited financial statements of companies. The ultimate result is to give to small businesses the possibility of appearing "unaudited but OK".

The FASB reacted favorably to the report. In 1978 it issued Statement No. 21 *Suspension of the Reporting of Earnings per Share and Segment Information by Nonpublic Enterprises,* which suspends the earnings-per-share and segment disclosures as requirements for reporting by private companies. It also started including in its pronouncements size tests that exempt small and private companies from certain requirements.

The AICPA, however, was not impressed with the FASB efforts. Thus in 1980 the Technical Issues Committee of the AICPA Private Companies Practice Section began a project to identify significant measurement and disclosure requirements of the generally accepted accounting principles that either (a) were not relevant to the financial statements of most small and medium-sized privately owned businesses (private companies) or (b) did not provide benefits to the users of those statements sufficient to justify the costs of applying the principles.

In 1982 the committee issued its report, *Sunset Review of Accounting Principles*. It recommended changing or eliminating eleven accounting and disclosure requirements that the committee believed either should not apply to private companies or do not sufficiently benefit the users of private companies' financial statements to justify their costs. The eleven issues examined were:

1. deferred income taxes;
2. leases;
3. capitalization of interest;
4. imputed interests;
5. compensated balances;
6. business combinations;
7. troubled debt restructuring;

8. research and development costs;
9. discounted operations;
10. tax benefit of operations;
11. investment tax credits.

The ball was once more in the FASB's court. Would it go toward the creation of a "little GAAP", or would it treat the problems faced by small businesses within the standards-overload problem? The more logical approach for the FASB would be to treat the standards-overload problem first, which would alleviate the problems faced by small businesses. Creating a "little GAAP" would be practically and logically unsound. Most of the objections to having two sets of GAAPs are convincing.

Examples of objections are as follows:

1. Improvements in reporting to one group of users should result in improving the reporting to other groups.
2. All companies operate in the same environment, face similar economic conditions, and could have the same types of transactions.
3. Most companies belong to either trade associations or industry groups that typically summarize financial statements of companies in the association or the group, and different accounting requirements for different companies within the same group could distort financial comparisons.
4. Most private companies would eventually become public.

2.5 Accounting policy and changes

Firms need to make choices among the different accounting methods in recording transactions and preparing their financial statements. These choices, as dictated by generally accepted accounting principles, represent the accounting policies of the firm. They are best defined by the Accounting Principles Board in its Opinion 22, *Disclosure of Acceding Policies* (April 1972), paragraph 6:

> The *accounting policies* of a reporting entity are the specific accounting principles and the methods of applying those principles that are judged by the management of the entity to be the most appropriate in the circumstances to present fairly financial position, changes in financial position, and results of operations in accordance with generally accepted accounting principles and that accordingly have been adopted for preparing the financial statements.

Firms also make accounting changes as part of their accounting policies. The general belief is that firms make accounting changes to mask performance problems. The accounting literature explains the changes in accounting principles and estimates in terms of management's desire to reach definite objectives such as income smoothing,[30] or the reduction of agency costs associated with a violation of debt covenants. A summary of existing research results suggests that as the tightness of debt covenant increases, firms are more likely to loosen the tightness of covenant restrictions through appropriate accounting changes.[31] In fact two studies that examined the accounting changes of (a) successful and unsuccessful firms[32] and (b) firms facing or experiencing bond rating changes,[33] provide some evidence consistent with the assertion that managers can modify income through judicious accounting changes.

Accounting regulators have tried to limit management's ability to use accounting changes to increase or decrease net income. Since 1970, APB No. 20 has stipulated that accounting changes should be accounted for as a cumulative effect change, requiring the reporting in the comparative income statements of the cumulative effect of change in the net income of the period of the change as well as the disclosure in the notes of the effect of adopting the new accounting principle on income before extraordinary income and net income (and on rotated per share amounts) of the period change. Similarly, the SEC's Accounting Release No. 177 required that accounting changes be made to more preferable accounting methods, using reasonable business judgment in the choice. While both pronouncements act as a control mechanism, they do not eliminate management's ability to increase and/or decrease income through accounting changes. SEC Chairman Arthur Levitt contended that public companies have used six accounting practices to manage corporate earnings:

1. overstatement of restructuring changes to clean up the balance sheet;
2. classification of a significant portion of the price of an acquired entity as research and development so that the amount can be written off as a one-time charge;
3. creation of large liabilities for future expenses (recorded as part of the accounting for an acquisition) to protect future earnings;
4. use of unrealistic assumptions to estimate liabilities for items such as sales returns, loan losses, and warranty costs so that the over-accrual can be reversed to improve earnings during a subsequent period;
5. intentional inclusion of errors in the company's books and justifying the failure to correct the errors by arguing materiality; and
6. recognition of revenue before the earnings process is complete.[34]

2.6 Designed accounting

Basically, if an interested and inquisitive observer from outside the accounting establishment examines the accounting discipline and the accounting process and output, he/she may be easily tempted to see more of various deliberate attempts to choose accounting techniques and solutions that fit a pre-established goal and picture to be conveyed as representative constructions of realities. This phenomenon may be labeled as designed accounting as it contrasts with a choice of principle-based techniques and solutions, a phenomenon that can be labeled principled accounting. Aspects of designed accounting include different concepts such as: (a) the selective financial misrepresentation hypothesis, (b) income smoothing, (c) earnings management, (d) creative accounting and (e) accounting fraud. They are briefly examined next. A more exhaustive presentation is included in later chapters.

2.6.1 The selective financial misrepresentation hypothesis

Accounting information is basically the accounting surrogate used by decision-makers who can't rely on directly observed events. A manipulation of these surrogates provides decision-makers with the opportunity of sending the kind of signals that shape people's perceptions of managerial performance, which is made possible by arbitrary, complicated and misleading rules. The selective financial misrepresentation hypothesis, as advanced by Revsine,[35] maintains that "The problem is not accidental, but instead results from contrived and flexible reporting rules promulgated by standard setters who have been 'captured' by the intended regulatees and others involved in the financial reporting process."[36] The "capturing" refers to the process where the main objective of regulation, which is the protection of consumers, is reversed to make the regulatees the beneficiaries.[37] The selective financial representation hypothesis is assumed to be across both public and private sectors "since participants in both the sectors are motivated to support standards that selectively misrepresent economic reality when it suits their purpose".[38] It applies to managers, shareholders, auditors and standard-setters.

1. Managers prefer "loose" reporting standards over tight standards because it allows (a) a shifting of income between years more favorable to bonus attainment, (b) impressing the shareholders and (c) protecting their jobs by forestalling takeovers.[39]

2. Shareholders benefit also from the loose standards given that the smoothing of reporting earnings by managers lowers the volatility of reported earnings, lowering the market's perception of default risk and increasing firm value.

3. Auditors may prefer the same reporting rules that distort economic reality for *client harmony*, or rigid rules when they present a convenient shield to hide behind.[40]

4. Standard-setters may favor the self-misrepresentation hypothesis for both self-protection and altruism.

5. Academics may favor the selective misrepresentation hypothesis as it provides them with the opportunity of providing theories and proposals in exchange for more remuneration and prestige.

The situation calls for a change by insulating the standard-setting process from regulatory capture. Revsine suggests the following four-step process:

1. educating the public,
2. improving the process for selecting and monitoring standard-setters,
3. establishing new funding arrangements, and
4. creating independence for the standard-setters.[41]

SEC Chairman Levitt proposed a six-part action plan to address these issues and improve the "reliability and transparency" of financial statements:

• Public companies will be required to make detailed disclosures about the impact of changes in accounting assumptions so that the market can "better understand the nature and effects of the restructuring liabilities and other loss accruals".

• New SEC guidance will emphasize "the need to consider qualitative, not just quantitative factors" when judging materiality.

• AICPA will clarify the rules for auditing purchased research and development and "argue for existing guidance on restructuring, large acquisition write-offs, and revenue recognition practices".

• Additional SEC guidance on revenue recognition may be published. This project will consider the applicability of recently adopted software revenue recognition standards to other industries.

• The FASB will accelerate certain projects that relate to the definition of constructive liability.

• The SEC's Divisions of Enforcement and Corporation Finance will review companies that announce "restructuring liability reserves, major write-offs, or other practices that appear to manage earnings".[42]

2.6.2 Income smoothing

An early definition of income smoothing states that it "moderates year-to-year fluctuations in income by shifting earnings from peak years to less successful periods."[43]

A more recent definition of income smoothing sees the phenomenon as "the process of manipulating the time profile of earnings or earning reports to make the reported income less variable, while not increasing reported earnings over the long-run."[44] Both definitions seem to imply that there is only one form of income smoothing used to dampen fluctuations of earnings towards an expected level of earnings. Of the studies that distinguished between potentially different types of smoothing, the article by Eckel[45] provides the more exhaustive classification of the different types of smooth income streams. The first distinction is made between an intentional or designed smoothing and a natural smoothing. The second distinction is to classify the intentional or designed smoothing with either an artificial smoothing or a real smoothing. These various types of smoothing are explicated next.

Intentional or designed smoothing refers specifically to the deliberate decisions or choices made to dampen earnings fluctuations around a desired level. Therefore intentional or designed smoothing is essentially an accounting smoothing that uses the existing flexibility in generally accepted accounting principles and the choices and combinations available to smooth income. It is therefore and essentially a form of designed accounting.

Natural smoothing, unlike designed smoothing, is a natural product of the income-generating process, rather than the result of actions taken by management. Eckel gives the following example:

> For example, one would expect the income generating process of public utilities to be such that income streams would be naturally smooth.[46]

Designed smoothing may be accomplished by either artificial or real smoothing. Artificial smoothing is the result of resorting to accounting manipulations to smooth income. As stated by Eckel:

> These manipulations do not represent underlying economic events or affect cash flows, but shift costs and/or revenues from one period to another. For example, a firm would increase or decrease reported income smoothing by changing its actuarial assumptions concerning pension costs".[47]

Finally, real smoothing involves the deliberate choice and timing of transactions that can affect cash flows and control underlying economic events. It can be accomplished by choices and timing of purchasing, hiring production, investment, sales, capital budgeting, research and development, advertising and other decisions. It is basically a choice of a business conduct to deliberately alter the cash flows of a corporation towards dampening earnings fluctuations. It can be either an attempt to control economic events or an attempt to construct economic events with the intention of affecting cash flows and smooth earnings. The actions taken by management in real smoothing are intended to alter the firm's production and/or investment decisions at year-end based on the knowledge of how the firm has performed up to the time of the year.[48]

2.6.3 Earnings management

Managers have the flexibility of choosing between the alternative ways to account for transactions as well as choosing between options within the same accounting treatment. This flexibility, which is intended to allow managers to adapt to economic circumstances and portray the correct economic consequences of transactions, can also be used to affect the level of earnings at any particular time with the objective of securing gains for management and the stakeholders. This is the essence of earnings management, which is the ability to "manipulate" the choices available and make the right choices that can achieve a desired level of income. It is another flagrant example of designed accounting.

Various definitions have been offered to explain earnings management as a special form of "designed" rather than "principled" accounting. Schipper sees earnings management as a purposeful intervention in the external reporting process with the intent of obtaining some private gain.[49] This is assumed to be possible through either a selection of accounting methods within GAAP or by applying given methods in particular ways.[50] Schipper also views earnings management from either an economic (or true) income perspective or an informational perspective. The true income perspective assumes (a) the existence of a true economic income which is distributed by a deliberate earnings management and/or by measurement errors embedded in accounting rules and (b) noisy unmanaged earnings acquire through earnings management new properties in terms of amount, bias or variance. The informational perspective assumes (a) earnings is one of the signals used for decisions and judgments, and (b) managers have private information which they can use when they choose elements within GAAP under different sets of contracts which determine their conversation and behavior.[51]

The information perspective is better explicated in the following definition:

> Earnings Management occurs when managers use judgment in financial reporting and in structuring transactions to alter financial reports to either mislead some stakeholders about the underlying economic performance of the company or to influence contractual outcomes that depend on reported accounting numbers.[52]

This definition of Healy and Wahlen focuses on the exercise of judgment in financial report (a) to mislead stakeholders who either do not or cannot do earnings management and (b) to make financial reports more informative to users. There is therefore a good and bad side to earnings management: (a) the bad side is the cost created by misallocation of resources and (b) the good side is the potential improvements in management's credible communication of private information to external stakeholders, improving resource allocation decisions.[53]

2.6.4 Creativity in accounting

Creativity in accounting implies a liberal interpretation of accounting rules allowing choices that may result in a depiction of financial situations that are more or less optimistic than the real situations. It may take different forms depending on the objectives of the preparers of the accounting reports. These forms of creativity in accounting are generally known in practice and in the literature as (a) "big bath" accounting and (b) creative accounting.

1. "Big bath" accounting

"Big bath" accounting refers generally to the steps taken by management to drastically reduce current earnings per share in order to increase future earnings per share. The situation is akin to a choice of income-decreasing procedures that increase the probability of meeting future earnings' targets. As stated by Healy: "if earnings are so low that no matter which accounting procedures are selected target earnings will not be met, managers have incentives to further reduce current earnings by deferring revenues or accelerating write-offs, a strategy known as 'taking a bath'".[54]

The "big bath" procedure may generally follow a change in management, giving an opportunity to new managers to develop a lower income anchor against which they will be evaluated in the future, guaranteeing themselves an initial good performance. [55]

A good description of "big bath" follows:

> Companies are most likely to take a big bath during particular periods. First, when new managers take over, they are tempted to write off the old projects and assets of their predecessors to show strong improvements during the coming years. Second, when a company has a large nonrecurring gain, it might search for large expenses to charge against it. And third, when earnings are particularly weak, management sees an opportunity to shift additional expenses (which will most likely not even be noticed) to the current period. The benefit, naturally, is that the additional current charges mean fewer charges in the future.[56]

Another good definition of "big bath" follows:

> The bath is described as a "clean up" of balance sheet accounts. Assets are written down or written off, and provisions are made for estimated losses and expenses which may be incurred in the future. These actions decrease income or increase losses for the current period while relieving future income of expenses which it would otherwise have had to absorb. In simple terms taking a bath tends to inflate future income by depressing current income.[57]

Most of the evidence in "big bath" accounting is anecdotal and of a journalistic nature. The following three stories give good examples of how "big bath" accounting is used.

1. In December 1990, the Financial Accounting Standard Board issued Statement No. 106, "Employers' accounting for Post Retirement Benefits other than Pensions", to account for health care and other welfare benefits provided to retirees, their spouses, dependents, and beneficiaries. These other welfare benefits refer to life insurance offered outside a pension plan, dental care as well as medical care, eye care, legal and tax services, tuition assistance, daycare, and housing assistance. At the time of the adoption of FASB Statement No. 106, a transitional amount is computed. It is equal to the difference between (1) the accumulated post-retirement benefit obligation (APBO) and (2) the fair value of the plan assets, plus any accrued obligation or less any prepaid cost (asset). Given that most plans were unfunded and most employees were accruing benefits costs for the first time, the transition amounts were material. The choices were either (1) an immediate change to expense for unrecognized past costs as well as recognition of the total unrecognized liability, which will create a major drain on the reported earnings in the year of change, or (2) deferral and amortization of the expense, as well as the recognition of a rapidly increasing liability, which will create a major drain on the earnings for many years.[58] The choice of the first option will constitute a good example of a "big bath" choice. In fact the adoption of FASB No. 106 led (a) IBM to declare a $2.3 billion change, resulting in IBM's first-ever quarterly loss in March 1991, (b) General Electric Co. to declare a $2.7 billion change, and (c) AT&T to absorb a $2.1 billion pre-tax hit for post-retirement benefits in the fourth quarter of 1993.[59]

2. In March 2001, P&G announced that it would take a $1.4 billion charge to reduce its work force by 9 percent, or 9,600 employees. These charges followed a $2.1 billion restructuring effort that started in 1999. Then, in June 2001 the company announced that it would take another charge of $900 million to write off under-performing

assets. This is a good example of a "big bath" approach that seems unending, stretching the definition of one-time expense too liberally.

3. Nortel Networks, which in the year 2000 was a glamour stock, declared a $19.2 billion loss in the second quarter of 2001. The $19.2 billion loss exceeded the annual gross domestic product of El Salvador and approached that of Bolivia. In a year the market value of the company shrank by one-quarter trillion dollars. Of this $19.2 billion loss, $12.3 billion was a write-off Nortel was taking in goodwill on recent acquisitions. The story unfolds as follows: In the year 2000 Nortel went on an acquisition spree, acquiring eleven technology concerns at a time when its own tangible assets were just $167 million. This did not stop Nortel paying an exorbitant $19.7 billion, mostly in shares for the acquisitions, which was equivalent to 118 times the value of these acquired companies. For example, in 2000 Nortel paid Xros $3.2 billion in stock at a time when Xros' tangible assets were $3 million. This "big bath" story is a good example of a management making bad buys and then trying to start again from scratch.

2. Creative accounting

Creative accounting is a term generally used in the popular press to refer to what journalists suspect accountants do to make financial results look much better than they should. This suspicion is prevalent in most countries. It is most acknowledged in the USA by Schilit,[60] in the UK by Griffiths,[61,62] in France by Stolowy[63] and in Australia by Revsine[64] and Craig and Walsh.[65] As a result of this international evidence of the phenomenon, creative accounting has acquired various characterizations and definitions. Descriptions of creative accounting are as follows:

1. Creative accounting represents the means by which is achieved a deviation between accounts which are anything other than an approximation which have their basis in the transactions and events of the year under review and the original starting point.[66]

2. Creative accounting involves manipulation, deceit and misrepresentation.[67]

3. Creative accounting involves an accounting sleight of hand.[68]

4. Creative accounting include activities such as "fiddling the books", "cosmetic reporting", and "window dressing".[69]

5. Creative accounting is the "transformation of financial accounting figures from what they actually are to what preparers desire by taking advantage of the existing rules and/or ignoring some or all of them".[70] It involves both "window dressing" and "off-balance-sheet financing". Window dressing is defined as the arrangement of affairs so that the financial statements give a misleading or unrepresentative impression of the company's financial position.[71] Off-balance-sheet financing is defined as "the funding or refunding of a company's operations in such a way that, under legal requirements and existing accounting conventions, some or all of the finance may not be shown on its balance sheet".[72]

6. Creative accounting was also referred to as the use of accounting gimmicks to boost anemic earnings or to smooth out erratic earnings.[73] This is accomplished by the use of seven major shenanigans defined as follows:

   (a) recording revenue before it is earned;
   (b) creating fictitious revenue;
   (c) boosting profits with non-recurring transactions;
   (d) shifting current expenses to a later period;
   (e) failing to record or disclose liabilities;

(f) shifting current income to a later period;

(g) shifting future expenses to an earlier period.[74]

Shenanigans are defined as follows:

> Unlike obsenity, financial shenanigans are easy to define but more difficult to detect in practice. Financial shenanigans are actions or omissions intended to hide or distort the real financial performance or financial condition of an entity. They range from minor deceptions (such as failing to clearly segregate operating from non operating gains and losses) to more serious misapplications of accounting principles (such as failing to write-off worthless assets; they also include fraudulent behavior, such as the recording of fictitious revenue to overstate the real financial performance).[75]

2.6.5 Fraud in accounting

Fraud has many definitions. It is a crime. The Michigan criminal law states:

> Fraud is a generic term, and embraces all the multifarious means which human ingenuity can devise, which are resorted to by one individual to get advantage over another by false representations. No definite and invariable rule can be laid down as a general proposition in defining fraud, as it includes surprise, trick, cunning and unfair ways by which another is cheated. The only boundaries defining it are those that limit human knavery.[76]

It is the intentional deception of another person by lying and cheating for the purpose of deriving an unjust, personal, social, political, or economic advantage over that person.[77] It is definitively immoral.

Within a business organization fraud can be perpetrated for or against the firm. It is then *corporate fraud*. Management or a person in a position of trust can perpetrate it. It is then a *management fraud* or *white-collar crime*. It may involve the use of an accounting system to portray a false image of the firm. It is then a form of *fraudulent financial reporting*. It may also involve a failure of the auditor to detect errors or misstatements. It is then an *audit failure*. In all these cases – corporate fraud, management fraud, white-collar crime, fraudulent financial reporting, audit failure – the accountant as preparer, auditor, or user stands to suffer heavy losses.

a. Corporate fraud

Corporate frauds or economic crimes are perpetrated generally by officers, executives, and/or profit center managers of public companies to satisfy their short-term economic needs. In fact, it may be the short-term-oriented management style that creates the need for corporate fraud, given the pressure to increase current profitability in the face of few opportunities and the need to take unwise risks with the firm's resources. As confirmed by Jack Bologna:

> Rarely is compensation based on the longer-term growth and development of the firm. As a consequence of this myopic view of performance criteria, the executives and officers of many public companies have a built-in incentive or motivation to play fast and loose with their firm's assets and financial data.[78]

In fact, more than the pressure for short-term profitability, it is economic greed and avarice that blot social values and lead to corporate fraud. Evidence from the Federal Bureau of

Investigation shows that arrests from two categories of corporate fraud have climbed: fraud jumped 75 percent between 1976 and 1986, and embezzlement rose 26 percent.[79] In fact, corporate fraud goes beyond mere fraud and embezzlement.

The situation points to a myriad of activities that may result in corporate fraud. The increase in corporate fraud in the United States and elsewhere is the result of evasion in business ethics.

b. Fraudulent financial reporting

Fraudulent financial reporting is so rampant that a special commission was created to investigate it: the National Commission on Fraudulent Financial Reporting. The commission defined fraudulent financial reporting as "intentional or reckless conduct, whether act or omission, that results in materially misleading financial statements". Such reporting undermines the integrity of financial information and can affect a range of victims: shareholders, creditors, employees, auditors, and even competitors. It is used by firms that are facing economic crises as well as by those motivated by a misguided opportunism.

Common types of fraudulent financial reporting include:

(a) the manipulation, falsification or altering of records or documents;

(b) the suppression or omission of the effects of completed transactions from records of documents;

(c) the recording of transactions without substance;

(d) the misapplication of accounting policies; and

(e) the failure to disclose significant information.

There is a deliberate strategy to deceive by distorting the information and the information records. This results from a number of documented dysfunctional behaviors: smoothing, biasing, focusing, gaming, filtering, and illegal acts. Such behaviors generally occur when managers have a low belief both in the analyzability of information and in the measurability and verifiability of data.[80] Of all these documented dysfunctional behaviors the one most likely to result in fraudulent financial reporting is the occurrence of illegal acts by violation of a private or public law through various type of frauds. One type of fraud is fraud from within the accounting system. Examples include the following:

1. False input scams (creating fake debits)
   (a) False or inflated claims from vendors, suppliers, benefits claimants, and employees, or false refund or allowance claims by customers
   (b) Lapping on receivable payments or customer bank deposits
   (c) Check kiting
   (d) Inventory manipulation and reclassification
       (1) Arbitrary write-ups and write-downs
       (2) Reclassification to lower value, obsolete, damaged, or "sample" status
   (e) Intentional misclassification of expenditures
       (1) Operational expense versus capital expenditures
       (2) Personal expense versus business expense
   (f) Fabrication of sales and cost of sales data
   (g) Misapplication and misappropriation of funds and other corporate assets (theft and embezzlement)
   (h) Computerized input and fraudulent access scams
       (1) Data diddling and manipulation
       (2) Impersonation and impostor terminal

        (3) Scavenging

        (4) Piggybacking

        (5) Wiretapping

        (6) Interception and destruction of input and source documents

        (7) Fabrication of batch or hash totals

        (8) Simulation and modeling fraud (fraudulent parallel systems)

    (i) Forgery, counterfeiting, or altering of source documents, authorizations, computer program documentation, or loan collateral

    (j) Overstating revenues and assets

    (k) Understating expenses and liabilities

    (l) Creating off-line reserves

    (m)Related party transactions

    (n) Spurious assets and hidden liabilities

    (o) "Smoothing" profits

    (p) Destruction, obliteration, and alteration of supporting documents

    (q) Exceeding limits of authority

2. False thruput scams

    (a) Salami slicing, trap doors, Trojan horse, logic

    (b) Designed random error during processing cycle

3. Output scams

    (a) Scavenging through output

    (b) Output destruction, obliteration

    (c) Theft of output reports and logs

    (d) Theft of programs, data files, and systems programming and operations documentation.[81]

It does not always start with an illegal act. Managers are known to choose accounting methods in terms of the economic consequences. Various studies have argued that managerial preferences for accounting methods and procedures may vary, depending on the expected economic consequences of those methods and procedures. It has been well established that the manager's choice of accounting methods may depend on the effect on reported income,[82] the degree of owner versus manager control of the company,[83] and methods of determining managerial bonuses.[84] This effort to use accounting methods to show a good picture of the company becomes more pressing on managers who are facing some form of financial distress, and are in need of showing economic events in the most optimistic way. This may lead to suppressing or delaying the dissemination of negative information.[85,86] The next natural step for these managers is to use fraudulent financial reporting. To hide difficulties and to deceive investors, declining and failing companies have resorted to the following fraudulent reporting practices:

(a) prematurely recognizing income, (b) improperly treated operating leases as sales, (c) inflated inventory by improper application of the Last In-First Out (LIFO) inventory method, (d) included fictitious amounts in inventories, (e) failed to recognize losses through write-offs and allowances, (f) improperly capitalized or deferred costs and expenses, (g) included unusual gains in operating income, (h) overvalued marketable securities, (i) created "sham" year-end transactions to boost reported earnings, and (j) charged their accounting practices to increase earnings without disclosing the changes.[87]

One factor in the increase of fraudulent financial reporting that has escaped scrutiny is the failure of accounting educational institutions to teach ways of detecting fraud and the importance of its detection to the entire financial reporting system. The emphasis in university and CPA examinations is on financial auditing rather than on forensic, fraud, or investigative reporting. J.C. Threadway, Jr., chairman of the National Commission on Fraudulent Financial Reporting, sees it this way:

> If you go back to the accounting literature of the 1920s or earlier, you'll find the detection of fraud mentioned as the objective of an audit much more prominently. Our work to date in looking at the way accounting and auditing are taught today in colleges and business schools indicates that fraud detection is largely ignored. In fact, there are texts currently in use that do not even talk about the detection of fraud.[88]

Because the Securities and Exchange Commission is dedicated to the protection of the interests of investors and the integrity of capital markets, it is concerned that adequate disclosures are provided for the public to allow a better judgment of the situation. One financial disclosure fraud enforcement program called for disclosures in four areas:

1. Liquidity problems, such as (a) decreased inflow of collections from sales to customers, (b) the lack of availability of credit from suppliers, bankers, and others, and (c) the inability to meet maturing obligations when they fall due.
2. Operating trends and factors affecting profits and losses, such as (a) curtailment of operations, (b) decline of orders, (c) increased competition, or (d) cost overruns on major contracts.
3. Material increases in problem loans must be reported by financial institutions.
4. Corporations cannot avoid their disclosure obligations when they approach business decline or failure.

Corporations need to adopt measures to reduce exposure on causes of fraudulent and questionable financial reporting practices. Example of suggestions for the reduction of exposure include:

1. the formulation of desired stands of behavior;
2. the maintenance of an effective system of internal control;
3. the maintenance of effective financial organization with acknowledged responsibility for maintaining good financial reporting practices;
4. the maintenance of an effective internal audit function;
5. having the board of directors play an active role in reviewing financial reporting policies and practices;
6. the monitoring of the capabilities and circumstances of individuals in positions affecting the financial reporting;
7. the promise and use of strong penalties for the violation of guidelines;
8. making sure that the performance targets are realistic; and
9. bewaring of high emphasis on short-term financial performance.[89]

c. White-collar crime

White-collar crime was a concern for Durkheim who was convinced that the "anomie state" of "occupational ethics" was the cause "of the incessant recurrent conflicts, and the multifarious disorders of which the economic world exhibits so sad a spectacle".[90] At the same time, Ross noticed the rise in vulnerability created by the increasingly complex forms of interdependence in society and the exploitations of these vulnerabilities by a new class he called "criminaloid".[91] He argued that a new criminal was at large, one "who picks pockets with a railway rebate, murders with an adulterant instead of a bludgeon, burglarizes with a 'rake-off' instead of a jimmy, cheats with a company prospectus instead of a deck of cards, or scuttles his town instead of his ship".[92] The phrase white-collar crime was originated in Edwin Sutherland's presidential address to the American Sociological Society in December 1939.[93] He defined it as "a crime committed by a person of respectability and high social status in the course of his occupation".[94] A debate followed, with Clinard's defining white-collar crime as restricted only to "illegal activities among business and professional men",[95] and Hartung defining it as "a violation of law regulating business, which is committed for a firm by the firm or its agents in the conduct of its business".[96] Basically, one view of white-collar crime focused on occupation and the other focused on the organization. But in fact it is the worlds of both occupation and organization that are the world of white-collar crime and that constitute what the knife and gun are to street crime.[97] White-collar crimes have not been condemned as vehemently as other common crimes. One reason is that their crime is not to cause physical injury, but to further organizational goals. In fact, individuals were found to consider organizational crimes to be far more serious than those with physical impact.[98] Another reason for the indifference to white-collar crime may be the possibility that members of the general public are themselves committing white-collar crimes on a smaller scale.[99] In addition, the white-collar criminal generally finds support for his behavior in group norms, which places him in a different position from the common criminal. As Aubert explains:

> But what distinguishes the white-collar criminal in this aspect is that his group often has an elaborate and widely accepted ideological rationalization for the offenses, and is a group of great social significance outside the sphere of criminal activity – usually a group with considerable economic and political power.[100]

The white-collar criminal is motivated by social norms, accepted and enforced by groups that indirectly give support to the illegal activity. In a lot of cases the organization itself is committing the white-collar crime, sometimes because it may be the only response to economic demands.

White-collar crime may be characterized by five principal components: (1) intent to commit the crime, (2) disguise of purpose, (3) reliance on the naivete of the victim(s), (4) voluntary victim action to assist the offender, and (5) concealment of the violation.[101] Unlike traditional crime, its objective is to steal kingly sums rather than small sums of money, and its modus operandi is to use technology and mass communications rather than brute force and crude tools. In addition, white-collar crime relies on the ignorance and greed of its victim.[102] It inflicts economic harm, physical harm, and damages to the social fabric.

d. Audit failure

Auditors are expected to detect and correct or reveal any material omissions or misstatements of financial information. When auditors fail to meet these expectations, an audit failure is the inevitable result. It is then the level of audit quality that can avoid the incurrence of audit failures. Audit quality has been defined as the probability that financial statements contain no material omission or misstatements.[103] It has also been defined in terms of audit risk, with high-quality services reflecting lower audit risk.[104] Audit risk was defined as the risk that "the auditor may unknowingly fail to appropriately modify his opinion on financial statements that are materially misstated".[105]

Audit failures do, however, occur and, as a consequence, bring audit firms face to face with costly litigation and loss of reputation, not to mention court-imposed judgments and out-of-court settlements. It is the client's or user's losses that lead to the litigation situation and the potential of payments to the plaintiff. Litigation can be used as an indirect measure of audit quality using an inverse relation – auditors with relatively low (high) litigation offer higher- (lower-) quality audits. This relation was verified in a study that indicated, as expected, that non-Big Eight firms as a group had higher litigation occurrence rates than the Big Eight, and that supported the Big Eight as quality-differentiated auditors.[106]

But not all litigations follow directly from audit failures. In a study that described the role of business failures and management fraud in both legal actions brought against auditors and the settlement of such actions, Palmrose found that (a) nearly half of the cases that alleged audit failures involved business failures or clients with severe financial difficulties, and (b) most lawsuits that involved bankrupt clients also involved management fraud.[107] These findings point to the fact that business failures and management fraud play a great role in the occurrence of audit failures, which calls for the auditor to take a responsible attitude in the detection of fraud, as it may affect the audit quality, the audit risk, and the potential for costly litigations. As stated by Connor:

> Establishing the requirement to identify the conditions underlying fraudulent reporting as an independent objective of the audit process would help to clarify auditor responsibility and increase auditor awareness of this responsibility. Performance of the recommended procedures of management control review and evaluation and fraud risk evaluation would improve the probability of detecting conditions leading to misstated financial statements. The required focus on financial condition would help identify more effectively those entities that would qualify as business failure candidates in the near term.[108]

Although management fraud and business failure may play a great role in audit failures, there are other reasons for such failures. For example, St. Pierre and Anderson's extended analysis of documented audit failures identified three other reasons: (1) error centering on the auditor's interpretation of generally accepted accounting principles; (2) error centering on the auditor's interpretation of generally accepted auditing standards or implementation of generally accepted auditing standards; and (3) error centering on fraud of the auditor.[109]

2.7 Technical and ideological proletarianization of accountants

The first element in the new era conflict is the emergence of new class differences among accountants. Accountants as professional employees in accounting or nonaccounting organizations are considered members of the new class of salaried professionals. They are identified by Bell and other "post industrial" theorists as a major protagonist of the new coming post-industrial society, or as members of the "new working class", "professional-managerial class", "new petty bourgeoisie", or "new class", and are identified by Marxist theorists as a major new actor in contemporary capitalism.[110, 111] There has been a tremendous growth of accountants in the labor force from 22,916 in 1900 (0.08 percent of the labor force) to 1,047,000 in 1980 (1.08 percent of the labor force), a percentage increase from 1900–80 of 4,468.86 percent.[112] It is the highest increase among professionals, surpassing physicians (224.01 percent), lawyers (408.27 percent), architects (750.58 percent), dentists (371.94 percent), engineers (3,717.26 percent), and natural scientists (2,399.17 percent). The US Bureau of Labor Statistics reports that in 1986 there were 1.3 million accountants and auditors, up from 1.1 million in 1983.[113]

This growth of accountants followed the need for more advanced accounting technologies to deal with requirements of a more sophisticated production apparatus. The use of these advanced technologies requires accountants to pool their efforts in small and/or large CPA firms, leading to a decline in opportunities for self-employment in the field and to their dependence on the financial and institutional resources of corporations and the state.

Accountants were reluctant to abandon the idea of an independent economic position; however, increasingly they joined accounting and nonaccounting firms, small and large, corporate or state bureaucracies. In the process they became subject to the authority and control of heteronomous management, and suffered a slow degradation of status and reward. What really resulted from these developments is a proletarianization of accountants, working according to a division of labor conceived and monitored by management, following procedural rules and repertories created by administrative processes and/or fiat. While they still maintain control over their own knowledge base, which gives them some negotiating powers, their contractual employment subordinates them to a heteronomous management who had appropriated power over the total labor process.

The proletarianization of accountants reflected a shift of control toward employers or management and a loss of the creative freedom accountants enjoyed as self-employed professionals. Thus, the change in accounting technology forced a change in the structure of the accounting labor process and put the accountants in a new form of "proletarian class", subordinated, like craftsmen before them, to capitalist management. In the process, as theorized by Marx, they lost control of both the *means* and *ends* of labor, a phenomenon labeled as *technical proletarianization.*[114, 115] It has been speeded up and made easier by the higher degree of specialization and fragmentation imposed on accounting practice, a process of "de-skilling", that is, of rationalizing previously professional tasks into a number of routinized functions requiring little training. An AICPA task force lists 41 activities that describe the six general work categories performed by CPAs in public accounting: engagement management and administration, auditing, tax practice, management advisory services, other professional services, and office and firm administration [AICPA, 1983]. A challenge facing accounting firms over the coming decade will be the need for even more specialization in auditing, tax, and consulting.

In addition to technical proletarianization, the emergence of the "new working class", or "professional managerial class", led also to an *ideological proletarianization*, which refers to the appropriation of control by management for capital, over the goals and social purposes to which work is put.[116] Ideological proletarianization may be more pronounced in accounting due to the general inability of accountants to control organizational policy and the specific goals and purposes of work. The accountant, bound by specialized tasks, has lost control of the nature of the total product and may be indifferent to the outcome of the activities in which he/she is involved. This loss of vision of the total product, its use and disposition allows direct management of labor (i.e., technical proletarianization). In this way, technical and ideological proletarianization feed on each other.

The technical proletarianization of the accountant may lead to the accountant losing the knowledge base as "capital" restructures through management the specification of the product and management restructures the organization of work.

Proletarianization renders the accountant a mere technician of functionaries, separate from the major social, moral, and technological issues of his or her profession. The end and social use of the accountant's labor is institutionally channeled, with little provisions made for his/her interest as a professional and the interest of the clients. Marx discusses a similar transition from independent professional "craftsman" to a de-skilled worker.

These changes have led to a decrease in the number and quality of people going into accounting programs. The accounting profession lacks "glamour", and survey results suggest that accountants come from poorer socioeconomic backgrounds than attorneys and physicians.[117] The director of personnel at one of the Big Eight firms explains as follows: "Part of it is that a number of people find investment banking sexier, more exciting. You can make a big buck a lot quicker."[118] The lack of glamour may force the profession to offer high entry-level salaries.

For now, in answer to the technical and ideological proletarianization, the accountant, as well as other members of the "new working class", may respond by either *ideological desensitization*, a denial or separation of the self from the ideological control of the job, disclaiming either interest or responsibility for the social issues to which their work is put, or *ideological cooperation*, a redefinition of one's goal to make them consistent with institutional imperatives.

In either case – ideological desensitization or ideological cooperation – there is high likelihood of alienation of the accountant from his/her work evidenced by the high level of turnover. About 85 percent of the accounting graduates joining the big CPA firms will leave within ten years for positions in government, industry, education, or smaller CPA firms.[119] Benke and Rhode[120] estimated the replacement cost of each entry-level staff accountant to exceed $20,000 and for one large CPA firm with a turnover of 10,000 employees over a recent ten-year period [Healy, 1976], that price would be $200,000,000 in replacement costs. Other studies reported an increase in the level of turnover.[121] Variables explaining this high turnover were found to be (a) the work environment in the audit department, (b) the co-workers and uncompensated overtime (in the tax department), and (c) professional challenge in the management services department.

Alienation in the domain of work has a fourfold aspect: The person is alienated from the object he/she produces, from the process of production, from him/herself and from the community of his/her fellows. In their alienated condition, the mind-set of accountants, their consciousness, is to a large extent only the reflection of the conditions in which they find themselves and of their position in the process of production. This situation is particularly serious for female accountants. The percentage of female accounting graduates with bachelor's and master's degrees has increased from 28 percent in 1976–7 to 49 percent in 1985–6. Yet, they feel that they do not have the same chance for promotion as men,[122] and they do not earn as much.[123]

2.8 The manufactured consciousness of users

Why don't shareholders and users ask for more and better information? An explanation based on a notion of ideological domination would argue that the socioeconomic hierarchy has been relatively impervious to the information at annual and other meetings. As with the case of any other commodity, the capitalist domination of information can be expressed in three propositions:[124]

1. the class rule of management appropriates the information product they create;
2. such domination is maintained by the state's enforcement of contractual arrangements, protection of property rights, and maintenance of public order; and
3. information tools at the disposition of management, such as annual reports and press releases, allow management to disseminate information useful for the preservation of its interests.[125]

The three propositions amount to three forms of domination: market exploitation, legal coercion, and ideological domination. These forms of domination, although analytically separable, are empirically interdependent. They allow management to convey its beliefs to the users and, in the process, shape their consciousness about the firm. What the users acquire is a *manufactured consciousness* compatible with the expectations of management.[126] Sometimes, in the process leading to the "manufactured consciousness", management may substitute a "false consciousness" through a process researchers have identified with various labels, from income smoothing[127] to mere fraudulent financial reporting.[128]

In manufacturing the consciousness of users through the selective dissemination of information, management may contribute to class brainwashing and collective hypnosis,[129] or social conditioning.[130]

The concern is, therefore, that the user should be better informed, and thus a democratic norm is upheld. The manufacturing of consciousness is an obstacle to the expansion of data that is relevant to the users. The proper task is to announce the truth, expose the error, and identify all the constraints that can impede inquiring, comprehension, and efficient action. This is the proper task of *Ideologiekritik*,[131] a similar approach, labeled the ethical approach to financial accounting, which rests on concepts of fairness, justice, equity and truth.[132] Fairness, as fair, unbiased and impartial presentation, implies that the preparers of accounting information have acted in good faith and used ethical business practices and sound accounting judgment.[133, 134] After questioning the singular reliance on decision usefulness and its association with serious conceptual problems, Paul Williams presented arguments supporting a concept of fairness as a construct necessary to provide accounting problems.[135] Users need to be informed by normative standards that permit the evaluation of "what is". To be fully informed requires at least minimal competence, not only technical, but also moral and empirical. Failure in any of these competencies exposes the user to ideological dominations that are conveyed in the accounting reports by management, eager to maximize its own interests.

A user needs to be informed of the wide dissemination of accounting reports. The general rationale is that accounting reports, when disseminated, can have many readers. A better strategy in line with the attribute of better informing the user is to expose the user to various accounting reports from various sources. That is, not only can an accounting report have many users, but also the act of examining accounting reports takes on a new character: from the activities of reading a single "sacrosanct" accounting report (i.e., the annual report) to that of comparing, cross-referencing, combining, and selecting among different reports and different information. The user then assumes a more active role than the relatively passive one of reading a single report, like the annual report. What may result is a shift of the user's expertise: an expansion of the breadth of knowledge so that the user may acquire a better sense of what is useful and what is not, and an evaluation of the different preparers of accounting information. Subjecting the preparers to questioning, even if publicly, will be the major result of a better informed user. The level of accounting "informedness" is not necessarily limited to "natural" differences of cognitive ability and motivation, but its acquisition is both a consequence and a cause of the effective exercise of political power. The skills, generated by the information, are the essential part of the political arsenal by which *progressive users* may thwart the simple goals of managers to maximize their own wealth and redirect it to goals of maximizing social welfare.

2.9 Ethical perspective in accounting

Accountants find themselves performing tasks daily in an environment governed by a complex set of rules, principles, and practices. In performing their tasks they are asked to take a certain role. A role is best described as follows:

The concept of a role is … one which enters in the sociologist's account of a social interaction. It is needed in describing the repeatable patterns of social relations which are not mere physical facts and which are structured partly by the rules of acceptable behavior in the society in question.[136]

In performing their roles, accountants face formal or legal rules of behavior but also moral elements created by specific situations. By accepting certain roles, accountants accept at the same time the resulting obligations and moral responsibilities of roles, or as F.H. Bradley puts it: "There is nothing than my station and its duties, nor anything higher or more truly beautiful."[137] It implies that there are ethics behind "my station and duties" that need to be accounted for. By ethics is meant the concern with the moral judgments involved in making moral decisions about what is morally right and wrong or morally good and bad. This assumes the existence of moral standards that affect our human well-being,[138] are not established or changed by decisions of authoritative bodies,[139] are intended to override self-interest,[140] and are based on impartial considerations.[141,142]

Various categories of ethical perspectives or modes of ethical thinking are applicable to accounting. They are reviewed next before a discussion of the implementation, teaching, and research of ethics in accounting.

2.9.1 Utilitarian ethics

Utilitarian ethics or utilitarianism as an approach to resolving moral issues is also known as consequentialism. The approach considers an action as being morally right or wrong based solely on the consequences that result from performing it. The right action is the one that brings the best consequences, or the greatest amount of utility.

The implicit assumption is that the costs and benefits of an action are measurable on a common numerical scale and can be added and subtracted from each other.[143] The interests to consider when choosing an action are the nonegoist and altruistic approaches that consider the most utility for all the persons affected by the action.[144]

The advantages of utilitarian ethics are related to:

- *The goal of morality:* "It asserts that morality is important because the performance of right actions leads to the general satisfaction of human desires."[145]

- *The process of moral reasoning:* "The consequentialist at least offers a relatively clear procedure for finding out what is the right thing to do: list the alternatives, ascertain their probable consequences, and evaluate the consequences in light of their implications for everyone affected."[146]

- *Flexibility and exceptions:* "We simply need to recognize the special cases in which there is good reason to believe that the consequences of following the traditional moral rule are worse than the consequences of making an exception."[147]

- *Avoiding rule conflict:* "From the consequentialist perspective, the existence of a conflict in rules is a signal that we are dealing with one of those exceptional circumstances in which we cannot simply follow even the soundest of rules."[148]

The difficulties with utilitarianism relate to:

- *The objection from special obligation*: "It fails to take into account our special moral obligations to people with whom we have a special relation."[149]

- *The objection from rights*: "[It] does not take into account the existence of individual rights in deciding on moral issues."[150]

- *The objection from justice:* "By only paying attention to one factor, the consequentialist has left out other important moral factors, such as justice, that need to be weighed."[151]

In addition, there are serious problems of measurement in the sense that some benefits and costs are interactable to measurement,[152] many benefits and costs of an action cannot be reliably predicted and measured,[153] and there is a lack of clarity on what is to count as a benefit and what as a cost.[154,155]

2.9.2 Deontological ethics

Deontological ethics as an approach to resolving moral issues is also known as rule-based morality. The approach considers an action as morally right if it conforms with a proper moral rule. An action that violates the rule but results in beneficial actions is still considered wrong. The sources of the rule could be either theological in the sense that the actions are stipulated as moral by a religion, or societal in the sense that they are the result of a social consensus as to whether they are right or wrong.

Because of the limitations of these two sources, criteria have been adopted based on either the consequences of adopting a particular set of moral rules, or our supposed faculty of moral intuition.[156] First, this rule consequentialism differs from the act consequentialism adopted by utilitarianism because it states that, in effect, "the rightness of a particular action lies in its conformity with the proper moral rule; the properness of the moral rule, in turn is based on the value of the consequences of it being followed."[157] Second, the intuitionist approach holds that our special faculty of moral intuition tells us which actions have the inherent properties of being morally right.

Rule-based moralists can accommodate most of the weaknesses of utilitarianism. The weaknesses correspond to the strengths of utilitarianism.

2.9.3 The notion of fittingness

Because of the strengths and limitations of both utilitarianism and deontological ethics, a suitable compromise would be ideal.[158] One compromise suggested by W.W. May is to use aspects of both approaches.[159] An alternative to both utilitarianism and deontological ethics is offered by the notion of fittingness. Fittingness, from the ancient Greek concept of *kathokonda*, may be used to evaluate the morality of actions by a reference to whether they are appropriate and proper with the ethos shared by the individual and the society. Martin Heidegger speaks of ethos as comprised of "freely accepted obligations and traditions", of "that which concerns free behavior and attitudes", and of "the shaping of man's historical being".[160] The ethos defines the fitting response, the arena for moral discourse and action. Compared to the other views of ethics the notion of fittingness proposes a dramatic shift. As Calvin Schrag states:

> This shift is a shift away from the primacy of theological inquiry (what is the end of man in terms of his nature-conferred essence?), the primacy of deontological inquiry (what is the unconditional duty of man?) and the primacy of utilitarian inquiry (what is the greatest good for the greatest number?). The question "How does one perform a fitting response?" is, we submit, more originative than inquiry about ends, duties and the good. It is only by addressing this question that ends duties, and the good achieve a context for definition.[161]

The notion of fittingness places the individual in a context of responsibility and responsiveness to the ethos in which are gathered the social and political concerns of the society around him or her. To Reinhold Niebuhr, the fitting action is part of the ethics of responsibility.[162] How others reacted to a previous act and how they will react to a similar act determines a responsible act. The responsible act must interpret the old reactions and fit itself in the new reactions. Fittingness becomes the criteria for evaluating moral choice. As stated again by Schrag: "The language of morality is the language of responsiveness and responsibility and if there is to be talk of 'an ethics' in all this it will need to be an ethics of the fitting response."[163]

2.10 Conclusions

One is left after reading this chapter with a sense of bewilderment that a discipline that appears so mundane and practical to some can be so complex, so ridden with issues and meanings. The definition and uses of accounting leave us with the certain fact that indeed accounting is a social science, a science with practical rules and supporting theories. The reader is assumed to have mastered the practical rules elsewhere. He/she is introduced to the theories of accounting and to the realms of a full-fledged social science that aspires to be at the core of the working of society and the economy.

Notes

1. "Review and Resume", *Accounting Terminology Bulletin No. 1* (New York: American Institute of Certified Public Accountants, 1953), paragraph 5.
2. American Accounting Association, *A Statement of Basic Accounting Theory* (Evanston, IL: American Accounting Association, 1966), p. 1.
3. Accounting Principles Board, *Statement No. 4*, "Basic Concepts and Accounting Principles Underlying Financial Statements of Business Enterprises" (New York: American Institute of Certified Public Accountants, 1970), paragraph 40.
4. Elliot, R.K., and Pallais, Don M., "Assurance Services", *Journal of Accounting* (July, 1997), pp. 56–63.
5. Ibid., p. 63.
6. "CAP Vision", *Future of Accounting* (December, 1990), p. 5.
7. Sterling, R.A., *Toward a Science of Accounting* (Houston: Lawrence, KS: Scholars Book Co., 1979).
8. Burton, John C., "Intermediate Accounting from a User Perspective", in D.L. Jensen (ed.), *The Impact of Ride-Making on Intermediate Financial Accounting Textbooks* (Columbus, OH: College of Administrative Sciences, 1982).
9. Mautz, R.K., "Accounting as a Social Science", *The Accounting Review* (April, 1963), p. 319.
10. Bricker, Robert James, and Previts, Gary John, "The Sociology of Accountancy: A Study of Academic and Practice Community Schisms", *Accounting Horizons* (March, 1990), pp. 1–14.
11. American Institute of Certified Public Accountants: Planning and Research Division, *Education Members Survey* (May, 1989), pp. 102–3.
12. Francis, Jere R., "After Virtue? Accounting as a Moral and Discursive Practice", *Accounting, Auditing and Accountability* (3, 3, 1990), pp. 9–11.
13. Ibid., p. 11.
14. Prakash, Prem, and Rappaport, Alfred, "Informational Interdependencies: System Structure Induced by Accounting Information", *The Accounting Review* (October, 1975), pp. 723–34.

15. Ibid., p. 723.

16. Stevens, S.S., "On the Theory of Scales of Measurement", *Science* (June 7, 1967), p. 677.

17. Committee on Foundations of Accounting Measurement, *Report of the Committee on Foundations of Accounting Measurement, The Accounting Review* (Supplement to Vol. XLVI, 1971), pp. 20–1.

18. Ibid., pp. 27–8.

19. Mattessich, Richard, *Accounting and Analytical Methods* (Homewood, IL: Irwin, 1964), p. 79.

20. Ibid., p. 68.

21. Ibid., p. 26.

22. Ijiri, Yuji, *Theory of Accounting Measurement,* Studies in Accounting Research No. 10 (Sarasota, FL: American Accounting Association, 1975), p. 83.

23. Accounting Principles Board, Statement No. 4, *Basic Concepts and Accounting Principles Underlying Financial Statements of Business Enterprises* (New York: American Institute of Certified Public Accountants, 1970), p. 9084.

24. Ibid., p. 9084.

25. Ibid., footnote to paragraph 137.

26. Skinner, Ross, *Accounting Principles: A Canadian Viewpoint* (Toronto: The Canadian Institute of Chartered Accountants, 1972), p. 26.

27. Skinner, Ross M., *Accounting Standards in Evolution* (New York: Holt, Rhinehart and Winston of Canada, Ltd., 1987), p. 52.

28. Financial Accounting Standards Board, *Financial Reporting by Private and Small Companies* (Stanford, CT, 1981), pp. 3–4.

29. Ibid.

30. Belkaoui, Ahmed, *Accounting and Public Policy* (Westport, CT: Quorum Books, 1985).

31. Christie, A., "Aggregation of Test Statistics: On Evaluation of the Evidence as Contracting and Size Hypotheses", *Journal of Accounting and Economics* (12, 1990).

32. Lilien, S., Mellman, M., and Pastena, V., "Accounting Changes: Successful or Unsuccessful Firms", *The Accounting Review* (October, 1988), pp. 642–51.

33. Belkaoui, A., "The Effect of Bond Ratings on Accounting Changes."

34. "SEC Chairman Discusses Earnings Management", *Deloitte & Touche Review* (October, 12, 1998), p. 1.

35. Revsine, Lawrence, "Selective Financial Misrepresentation Hypothesis", *Accounting Horizons* (December, 1991), pp. 16–27.

36. Ibid., p. 16.

37. Stigler, G.J., "The Theory of Economic Regulation", *Bell Journal of Economics and Management Science* (Spring, 1971), pp. 3–21.

38. Revsine, Lawrence, "The Selective Misrepresentation Hypothesis", op. cit., p. 17.

39. Ibid., p. 17.

40. Ibid., p. 19.

41. Ibid., p. 24.

42. "SEC Chairman Discusses Earnings Management", *Deloitte & Touche Review* (October 12, 1998), p. 1.

43. Copeland, R., "Income Smoothing", *Journal of Accounting Research, Selected Studies* (1968), p. 101.

44. Fudenberg, D., and Tirole, J., "A Theory of Income and Dividend Smoothing Based on Incumbency Rents", *Journal of Political Economy* (1, 1995).

45. Eckel, N., "The Income Smoothing Hypothesis Revisited", *ABACUS* (17, 1981), pp. 28–40.

46. Ibid., p. 28.
47. Ibid., p. 29.
48. Lambert, R.A., "Income Smoothing as Rational Equilibrium Behavior", *The Accounting Review* (59, October, 1989), p. 606.
49. Schipper, K., "Earnings Management", *Accounting Horizons* (December, 1989), p. 92.
50. Ibid., p. 93.
51. Ibid.
52. Healy, Paul N., and Wahlen, James N., "A Review of the Earnings Management Literature and its Implications for Standard Settings", *Accounting Horizons* (13, 1999), p. 368.
53. Ibid., p. 369.
54. Healy, Paul M., "The Effect of Bonus Schemes on Accounting Decisions, *Journal of Accounting and Economics* (7, 1985), p. 86.
55. Moore, N.L., "Management Changes and Discretionary Accounting Decisions", *Journal of Accounting Research* (Spring, 1973), pp. 100–7.
56. Schilit, Howard M., *Financial Shenanigans* (NY: McGraw Hill, 1993), p. 121.
57. Copeland, Ronald M., and Moore, Michael L., "The Financial Bath: Is it Common?" *MSU Business Topics* (Autumn, 1972), p. 63.
58. Kieso, Ronald E., and Weygandt, Jerry J., *Intermediate Accounting* (New York: John Wiley & Sons, Inc., 1998), 9th edn, p. 1126.
59. Ibid., p. 1126.
60. Schilit, H.M., *Financial Shenanigans: How to Detect Accounting Criminals and Fraud in Financial Reports* (New York: McGraw Hill, 1993).
61. Griffiths, I., *Creative Accounting* (London: Irwin, 1996).
62. Griffiths, I., *New Creative Accounting* (London: Macmillan, 1995).
63. Stolowy, Herve, "Comptali Creative", *Encyclopedic de Comptabilite, Controle de bestion et audit* (ed. Bernard Colasse), (Paris: Economica, 2000), pp. 157–8.
64. Revsine, P., "The Corporate AIDS – Funny Financing and Creative Accounting", *Rydges* (November, 1989), pp. 18–20.
65. Craig, R., and Walsh, P., "Adjustments for Extraordinary Items, in Smoothing Reported Profit of Listed Australian Companies: Some Empirical Evidence", *Journal of Business Finance and Accounting* (Spring, 1989), pp. 229–45.
66. Griffiths, I., *New Creative Accounting,* op. cit., pp. vii–viii.
67. Jameson, M., *A Practical Guide to Creative Accounting* (London: Kogan Page, 1988).
68. Pigper, T., *Creative Accounting: The Effectiveness of Financial Reporting in the U.K.* (London: Macmillan, 1994).
69. Mathews, M.R., and Perera, M.H.B., *Accounting Theory and Development* (Melbourne: Nelson, 1996), p. 228.
70. Naser, Kamal H.M., *Creative Financial Accounting: Its Nature and Use* (New York: Prentice-Hall, 1993), p. 2.
71. Ibid., p. 2.
72. Ibid., p. 2.
73. Schilit, Howard M., *Financial Shenanigans*, op. cit., p. ix.
74. Ibid., p. x.
75. Ibid., p. 1.
76. *Michigan Law Review,* ch. 66, sect. 1529.
77. Bologna, Jack, *Corporate Fraud – The Basics of Prevention and Detection* (Boston, MA: Butterworths Publishers, 1984).
78. Ibid., p. 10.
79. "Ethics 101," *U.S. News and World Report* (14 March, 1988), p. 76.

80. National Commission on Fraudulent Financial Reporting, *Report of the National Commission on Fraudulent Financial Reporting* (Washington, DC: April, 1987), p. 2.

81. Bologna, J., *Corporate Fraud: The Basics of Prevention and Detection* (Stoneham, MA: Butterworth Publishers, 1984), p. 63.

82. Lilien, S., and Pastena, V., "Intermethod Comparability: The Case of the Oil and Gas Industry", *The Accounting Review* (July, 1981), pp. 690–703.

83. Dhaliwal, D.S., Salamon, G.L., and Smith, E.D., "The Effect of Owner Versus Management Control on the Choice of Accounting Methods", *Journal of Accounting and Economics I* (1982), pp. 41–53.

84. Healy, P.M., "The Effect of Bonus Schemes on Accounting Decisions", *Journal of Accounting and Economics* (1–3, 1985), pp. 85–107.

85. Schwartz, K.B., "Accounting Changes by Corporations Facing Possible Insolvency," *Journal of Accounting, Auditing and Finance* (Fall, 1982), pp. 32–43.

86. Merchant, Kenneth A., *Fraudulent and Questionable Financial Reporting: A Corporate Perspective* (Morristown, NJ: Financial Executives Research Foundation, 1987), p. 105.

87. Fedders, John M., and Perry, L. Glenn, "Policing Financial Disclosure Fraud: The SEC's Top Priority", *Journal of Accountancy* (July, 1984), p. 59.

88. Lietbag, Bill, "Profile: James C. Treadway, Jr.", *Journal of Accountancy* (September, 1986), p. 80.

89. Merchant, Kenneth, *Fraudulent and Questionable Financial Reporting: A Corporate Perspective* (Morristown, NJ: Financial Executives Research Foundation, 1987), p. 38.

90. Durkheim, Emile, *The Division of Labor of Society,* trans. George Simpson (New York: Free Press, 1964), p. 2.

91. Ross, E.A., *Sins and Society* (Boston, MA: Houghton Mifflin, 1907).

92. Ibid., p. 7.

93. Sutherland, Edwin, "White-Collar Criminality", *American Sociological Review* (5, February, 1940), pp. 110–23.

94. Sutherland, Edwin, *White Collar Crime* (New York: Dryden Press, 1949), p. 9.

95. Clinard, M.B., and Refer, R.F., *Sociology of Deviant Behavior* (New York: Holt, Rinehart and Winston, 1979), p. viii.

96. Hartung, F.E., "White Collar Offenses in the Wholesale Meat Industry in Detroit", *American Journal of Sociology* (56, 1950), p. 25.

97. Wheeler, S., and Rothman, M.L., "The Organization as Weapon in White-Collar Crime", *Michigan Law Review* (June, 1982), pp. 1403–76.

98. Shrager, L.S., and Short, Jr. O.F., "How Serious a Crime? Perceptions of Organizational and Common Crimes", in G. Geis and E. Stotland (eds.), *White-Collar Crime: Theory and Research* (London: Sage, 1980), p. 26.

99. Aubert, V., "White Collar Crime and Social Structure," *American Journal of Sociology* (November, 1952), p. 265.

100. Ibid., p. 266.

101. Edelhertz, H., Stotland, E., Walsh, M., and Weimberg, J., *The Investigation of White Collar Crime: A Manual for Law Enforcement Agencies.* US Department of Justice, LEAA (Washington, DC: Government Printing Office, 1970).

102. Bequai, August, *White-Collar Crime: A 20th Century Crisis* (Lexington, MA: Lexington Books, 1978), p. 13.

103. Palmrose, Zoe-Vonna, "An Analysis of Auditor Litigation and Audit Service Quality", *The Accounting Review* (January, 1988), p. 56.

104. DeAngelo, Linda E., "Auditor Size and Audit Quality," *Journal of Accounting and Economics* (December, 1981), pp. 183–99.

105. American Institute of Certified Public Accountants, *Professional Standards, Vol. I* (New York: AICPA, 1985), SAS no. 47.

106. Palmrose, "Analysis of Auditor Litigation", p. 72.

107. Palmrose, Zoe-Vonna, "Litigation and Independent Auditors: The Role of Business Failures and Management Fraud", *Auditing: A Journal of Practice and Theory* (Spring, 1987), pp. 90–103.

108. Connor, J.E., "Enhancing Public Confidence in the Accounting Profession", *Journal of Accountancy* (July, 1986), p. 83.

109. St. Pierre, K. and Anderson, J., "An Analysis of Audit Failures Based on Documented Legal Cases", *Journal of Accounting, Auditing and Finance* (Fall, 1984), pp. 229–47.

110. Bell, D., *The End of Ideology* (Boston, MA: Free Press, 1961).

111. Ehrenreich, B., and Ehrenreich, J., "The Professional Managerial Class", *Radical America* (11, 1976), pp. 7–31; Poulantzas, N., *Classes in Contemporary Capitalism* (New York: Verso, 1975).

112. Derber, C., "Managing Professionals: Ideological Proletarianization and Mental Labor", *Theory and Society* 11 (1983), pp. 309–41.

113. Kleiman, C., "Scrutiny Hasn't Put Crimp in Auditing", *The Chicago Tribune* (November 29, 1987), Section 8, p. 1.

114. Braverman, H., *Labor and Monopoly Capital* (New York: Monthly Review Press, 1966).

115. Baran, P., and Sweezy, P.I.M., *Monopoly Capital* (New York: Monthly Review Press, 1966).

116. Marglin, S., "What Do Bosses Do?" *Review of Radical and Political Economics* (6, Summer, 1975), pp. 60–112 (7, Spring, 1975), pp. 20–37.

117. Estes, R., "An Intergenerational Comparison of Socioeconomic Status Among CPAs, Attorneys, Engineers and Physicians", in B. Schwartz (ed.), *Advances in Accounting* Vol. 1 (Greenwich, CT: JAI Press, 1984), pp. 1–18.

118. Kleiman, C., "Scrutiny Hasn't Put Crimp in Auditing", *The Chicago Tribune* (November 22, 1987), Section 8, p. 1.

119. Kollaritsch, F.P., "Job Migration Patterns of Accountancy", *Management Accounting* (September, 1968), pp. 52–5.

120. Benke, R.L., Jr., and Rhode, J.G., "Intent to Turnover Among Higher Level Employees in Large CPA Firms", in B. Schwartz (ed.), *Advances in Accounting* Vol. 1 (1984), pp. 157–74.

121. Konstans, C., and Ferris, K., "Female Turnover in Professional Accounting Firms: Some Preliminary Findings", *Michigan CPA* (Winter, 1981), pp. 11–15.

122. Jayson, S., and Williams, K., "Women in Management Accounting: Moving up … slowly", *Management Accounting* (July, 1986), pp. 20–6.

123. Olson, J., and Frieze, I., "Women Accountants – Do They Earn As Much As Men?" *Management Accounting* (July, 1986), pp. 27–31.

124. Simonds, A.E., "On Being Informed", *Theory and Society* (11, 1982), pp. 587–616.

125. Hill, Stephen, and Turner, Bryan S., *The Dominant Ideology Theories* (London: George Allen & Unwin, 1980).

126. Belkaoui, A., *Accounting Theory*, op. cit.

127. Ronen, Joshua, and Sadan, Sincha, *Smoothing Income Numbers Objectives, Means and Implications* (Reading, MA: Addison-Wesley, 1981).

128. National Commission on Fraudulent Financial Reporting, *Report, Exposure Draft*.

129. Therborn, Goran, *The Ideology of Power and the Power of Ideology* (New York: Verso, 1980).

130. Tinker, Tony, *Paper Prophets: A Social Critique of Accounting* (New York: Praeger, 1985).

131. Simonds, A.P., "On Being Informed", op. cit., pp. 587–616.

132. Scott, D.R., "The Basis for Accounting Principles", *The Accounting Review* (December, 1941), pp. 341–9.

133. Patillo, James W., *The Foundations of Financial Accounting* (Baton Rouge, LA: Louisiana State University Press, 1965).

134. Spacek, Leonard, *A Search for Fairness in Financial Reporting to the Public* (Chicago: Arthur Andersen & Co., 1965), pp. 38–77, 349–56.

135. Williams, Paul F., "The Legitimate Concern with Fairness", *Accounting, Organizations and Society* (March, 1987), pp. 169–89.

136. Emmet, D., *Rules, Roles, and Relations* (Boston, MA: Beacon Press, 1966), p. 15.

137. Bradley, F.H., *Ethical Studies* (Indianapolis, IN: Bobbs-Merrill, 1951), p. 136.

138. Hart, H.L.A., *The Concept of Law* (London: Oxford University Press, 1966), pp. 84–5.

139. Baier, Kurt, *The Moral Point of View* (New York: Random House, 1965), pp. 83–90.

140. Scriven, Michael, *Primary Philosophy* (New York: McGraw Hill, 1966), pp. 232–3.

141. Brandts, R.B., *Ethical Theory* (Englewood Cliffs, NJ: Prentice-Hall, 1959), p. 250.

142. Velasquez, Manuel G., *Business Ethics: Concepts and Cases* (Englewood Cliffs, NJ: Prentice-Hall, 1982), pp. 10–11.

143. Sidguiche, Henry, *Methods of Ethics,* 7th edn (Chicago: University of Chicago Press, 1962), p. 413.

144. Mill, John Stuart, *Utilitarianism* (Indianapolis, IN: Bobbs-Merrill, 1957), p. 22.

145. Brady, Baruch, *Ethics and Its Applications* (San Diego, CA: Harcourt, Brace, Jovanovich, 1983), p. 16.

146. Ibid., p. 16.

147. Ibid., p. 17.

148. Ibid., p. 18.

149. Ibid., p. 19.

150. Ibid., p. 19.

151. Ibid., p. 20.

152. Bayles, Michael D., "The Price of Life," *Ethics* (89, 1, October, 1978), pp. 20–34.

153. Moore, G.E., *Principia Ethica*, 5th edn (Cambridge: Cambridge University Press, 1956), p. 146.

154. MacIntyre, A., "Utilitarianism and Cost-Benefit Analysis: An Essay on the Relevance of Moral Philosophy to Bureaucratic Theory," in Kenneth Syre (ed.), *Values in the Electric Power Industry* (Notre Dame, IN: University of Notre Dame Press, 1977).

155. Velasquez, *Business Ethics*, pp. 49–50.

156. Brady, *Ethics and Its Applications*, p. 28.

157. Ibid., p. 28.

158. Ibid., p. 31.

159. May, W.W., "How to Resolve an Ethical Issue," in *Ethics in the Accounting Profession* (New York: Touche Ross, 1985), pp. 32–3.

160. Heidegger, Martin, *An Introduction to Metaphysics*, trans. Ralph Manheim (New York: Doubleday, 1959), p. 13.

161. Schrag, Calvin O., *Communicative Praxis and the Space of Subjectivity* (Bloomington, IN: Indiana University Press, 1986), pp. 203–4.

162. Niebuhr, R., *The Responsible Self* (New York: Harper and Row, 1963), pp. 60–107.

163. Schrag, *Communicative Praxis*, p. 204.

References

Double-entry bookkeeping

Mattessich, Richard, *Accounting and Analytical Methods* (Homewood, IL, 1964).

William, John J., "A New Perspective on the Evolution of Double-Entry Bookkeeping", *The Accounting Historians' Journal* (5, 1, 1978), pp. 29–39.

Measurement in accounting

American Accounting Association, "Report of the Committee on Foundations of Accounting Measurements", *Accounting Review Supplement* (1971), pp. 1–48.

American Accounting Association, "Report of the Committee on Foundations of Accounting Measurements", *Accounting Review Supplement* (1975), pp. 535–73.

Bierman, Harold, "Measurement and Accounting", *The Accounting Review* (July, 1963), pp. 501–7.

Chambers, Raymond J., "Measurement and Misrepresentation", *Management Science* (January, 1960), pp.141–8.

Chambers, Raymond J., "Measurement in Accounting", *Journal of Accounting Research* (Spring, 1965), pp. 32–62.

Chambers, Raymond J., "Asset Measurement and Valuation", *Cost and Management* (March–April, 1971), pp. 30–5.

Chambers, Raymond J., "Measurement and Valuation, Again", *Cost and Management* (July–August, 1971), pp. 12–17.

Chambers, Raymond J., "Measurement in Current Accounting Practices: A Critique", *The Accounting Review* (July, 1972), pp. 488–509.

Devine, Carl T., "Accounting – A System of Measurement Rules", *Essay in Accounting Theory*, Vol. 1, *Studies in Accounting Research* No. 22 (American Accounting Association, 1985), pp. 115–26.

Ijiri, Yuji, *The Foundations of Accounting Measurement: A Mathematical, Economic, and Behavioral Inquiry* (Englewood Cliffs, NJ: Prentice-Hall, 1967).

Ijiri, Yuji, "Theory of Accounting Measurement", *Studies in Accounting Research* No. 10 (American Accounting Association, 1975).

Mattessich, R., "On the Perennial Misunderstanding of Asset Measurement by Means of Present Values", *Cost and Management* (March–April, 1970), pp. 29–31.

Mattessich, R., "On Further Misunderstanding About Asset 'Measurement' and Valuation", *Cost and Management* (March–April, 1971), pp. 36–42.

Mattessich, R., "Asset Measurement and Valuation – A Final Reply to Chambers", *Cost and Management* (July–August, 1971), pp. 18–23.

Mock, Theodore, "Measurement and Accounting Information Criteria", *Studies in Accounting Research* No. 13 (American Accounting Association, 1976).

Vickrey, Don, "Is Accounting a Measurement Discipline?", *The Accounting Review* (October, 1970), pp. 731–42.

Generally accepted accounting principles

Accounting Principles Board, Statement No. 4, *Basic Concepts and Accounting Principles Underlying Financing Statements of Business Enterprises* (New York: American Institute of Certified Public Accountants, 1970).

Alderman, C.W., Guy, D.M., and Meals, D.R., "Other Comprehensive Bases of Accounting: Alternate GAAP?", *The Journal of Accountancy* (August, 1982), pp. 52–62.

Benson, B., "Fitting GAAP to Smaller Business", *The Journal of Accountancy* (February, 1978), pp. 45–51.

Chazen, Charles, and Benson, Benjamin, "Fitting GAAP to Smaller Businesses", *The Journal of Accountancy* (February, 1978), pp. 46–7.

Larson, R.E., and Kelly, T.P, "Differential Measurement in Accounting Standards: The Concept Makes Sense", *The Journal of Accountancy* (November, 1984), pp. 78–86.

Robbins, Barry P., "Perspectives on Tax Basis Financial Statements", *Journal of Accountancy* (August, 1985), pp. 89–100.

Rubin, Steven, "The House of GAAP", *Journal of Accountancy* (June, 1984).

Skinner, Ross, *Accounting Principles: A Canadian Viewpoint* (Toronto: The Canadian Institute of Chartered Accountants, 1972).

Designed accounting

Beidleman, Carl R., "Income Smoothing: The Role of Management", *The Accounting Review* (October, 1973).

DeAngelo, L., "Managerial Competition, Information Costs, and Corporate Conveyance: The Use of Accounting Performance Measures in Proxy Contests", *Journal of Accounting and Economics* (January, 1988), pp. 3–36.

Gordon, M.J., "Postulate, Principles, and Research in Accounting", *The Accounting Review* (April, 1965), pp. 251–63.

Healy, P., "The Effects of Bonus Schemes on Accounting Decisions", *Journal of Accounting and Economics* (April, 1985), pp. 85–107.

Koch, Bruce C., "Income Smoothing: An Experiment", *The Accounting Review* (July, 1981), pp. 574–86.

McNichols, M., and Wilson, G., "Evidence of Earnings Management from the Provision for Bad Debts", *Journal of Accounting* (Supplement, 1998), pp. 1–31.

Accounting: an art or a science?

Beams, Floyd A., "Implications of Pragmatism and Empiricism in Accounting Thought", *The Accounting Review* (April, 1965), pp. 382–8.

Jensen, D.L., *The Impact of Rule-Making on Intermediate Financial Accounting Textbooks* (Columbus, OH: College of Administrative Science, 1982).

Kelly, Arthur C., "Can Corporate Incomes Be Scientifically Ascertained?" *The Accounting Review* (July, 1951), pp. 289–98.

McCowen, George B., "The Accountant as Artist", *The Accounting Review* (April, 1946), pp. 204–11.

Mautz, R.K., "Accounting as a Social Science", *The Accounting Review* (April, 1946), pp. 317–25.

Sterling, R.R., "Toward a Science of Accounting", *Financial Analysts Journal* (September–October, 1975), pp. 28–36.

Sterling, R.R., *Toward a Science of Accounting* (Houston: Lawrence, KS: Scholars Book Co., 1979).

Wilson, D.A., "On the Pedagogy of Financial Accounting", *The Accounting Review* (April, 1979), pp. 396–401.

The elements and structure of an accounting theory

3

Various attempts have been made to build accounting theories aimed at achieving explanation, prediction, and control. Although they are interesting, these new attempts are partial contributions due to the absence of a vigorous thinking structure in the theorizing and the conduct of basic and applied research. The philosophy of science in general and metatheory in particular offer such a thinking structure by providing tools for a science of science or the investigation of investigation. Accordingly, this chapter elaborates on the alternative structures provided by the philosophy of science in general and metatheory in particular for a vigorous appraisal of the methodology of science and the philosophical issues involved in the conduct of accounting research. Broadly, this chapter examines the morphology of a theory, the notion of concepts, the handling of hypotheses, and the context of discovery.

3.1 Notions of a theory

3.1.1 Types of theoretical structures

There is a general confusion between hypothesis, law, and theory. A specific and detailed definition of a theory is provided by Mario Bunge as follows:

In ordinary language and in ordinary metascience "hypothesis," "law," and "theory" are often exchanged and sometimes laws and theories are taken to be the manhood of hypotheses. In advanced science and in contemporary metascience the three terms are usually distinguished: "law" or "law formula" designates a hypothesis of a certain kind – namely, non-singular, non-isolated, referring to a pattern, and corroborated; and "theory" designates a system of hypotheses, among which law formulas are conspicuous – so much so that the core of a theory is a system of law formulas. In order to minimize conclusions we will provisionally adopt the following characterization: A set of scientific hypotheses is a scientific theory if and only if it refers to a given factual subject matter and every member of the set is either an initial assumption (axiom, subsidiary assumption, or datum) or a logical consequence of one or more initial assumptions.[1]

A theory, therefore, includes propositions linking concepts in the form of hypotheses to be tested. The elements included in a theory are concepts, propositions, and hypotheses, linked in a systematic structure to allow explanation and prediction. The systematically related set of propositions forming the hypotheses of a theory are an essential ingredient of a theory. This systematic connection of interrelated hypotheses is obtained through the formalization of a theory, that is, the use of a formal language system that has been axiomatized and appropriately interpreted. The axiomatization consists of transformation rules indicating how statements are combined to deduce other statements in this theory. The interpretation is accomplished by various mechanisms referred to as operational definitions, coordinating definitions, correspondence rules, or epistemic correlations.[2]

How does formal language differ from natural language? Shelby Hunt provided the following response:

Formal language systems differ from natural languages in that they identify all of the primitive elements and they develop a complete "dictionary" which shows how all of the nonprimitive terms are derived from the primitive elements. Further, rather than having the loose and continually evolving formation rules of natural languages, such as English, formed language systems rigorously and exhaustively specify the formation rules delineating the permissible ways to combine elements to form statements.[3]

The degree of formalization of a theory leads to six main types of theoretical structures: deductively complete theories, systematic presuppositions, quasi-deductive theories, theoretical attempts, concatenated theories, and hierarchical theories.[4]

Deductively complete theories possess "a completely formal structure with the axioms fully specified and all steps in the deductive elaboration fully stated".[5] They also have been labeled as *hierarchical theories* and defined as those in which the "component laws are presented as deductions from a small set of basic principles".[6] Systematic presuppositions include formulations that presuppose a body of theory that is either complete or partially complete. *Quasi-deductive theories* are quasi deductive because of the use of inductive logic, an incomplete use of the deductive process, or reliance on relative primitives. *Theoretical attempts* are those systems that can, "without any substantial modification of concept or manipulation, be rendered at least partially into formal structure" or those verbal systems that "cannot be even partially formalized without a substantial modification of the concepts used and clarification of the deductive relationships proposed".[7] *Concatenated theories* are those "whose component laws enter in a network of relations so as to constitute an identifiable configuration or pattern. Most typically, they converge on some central point, each specifying one of the factors which play a part in the phenomenon which the theory is to explain."[8]

3.1.2 Functions and structure of a theory

A theory is identifiable by its structure and the functions it performs. Both the structure and functions of a theory help in meeting the needs of a particular discipline. Although most researchers in the business-related disciplines tended to limit the functions to description and prediction, others, such as John Harvard and Sheth Jagdish, classified the functions into four categories: description, delimitation, generation, and integration.[9] Each of these functions serves as a criterion for the evaluation of the contribution of a theory in meeting the needs of a given discipline.

The *descriptive function* consists of using the constructs or concepts and their relationships so as to provide the best explanation of a given phenomenon and the forces underlying it.

To explain a phenomenon, we give increasingly sophisticated descriptions of it. The need for explanation arises when describing a phenomenon because we wish to answer the question, "Why does the phenomenon occur?" In answering it, we come across hypotheses based on information that surrounds the phenomenon and specifies the conditions of the explanation.[10]

The *delimiting function* consists of selecting the favorite set of events to be explained and assigning a meaning to the formulated abstractions of the descriptive stage. Constraints on or boundaries around speculation and hunches serve that delimiting purpose.

The *generative function* is the ability to generate testable hypotheses, which is the main objective of a theory, or to provide hunches, notions, and ideas from which hypotheses could be developed. What results is a heuristic use of theory. "When a theory is used to stimulate empirical investigation, we speak of using the theory heuristically. Heuristic use of theory, more often than not, is made by analogy or metaphor."[11]

The *integrative function* is the ability to present a coherent and consistent integration of the various concepts and relations of a theory. The structure of a theory is equally important because it determines the functions of that theory. It can be described by certain dimensions: level of abstraction, realism versus idealism, objectivism versus subjectivism, introspection versus extrospection, and level of formality.[12]

The *level of abstraction* consists of simplifying and generalizing concepts and relationships to eliminate less relevant features in explaining the phenomenon. The merit of abstraction is that "the higher the abstraction, the greater the generality in a theory. As such the construct is probably less operational and more hypothetical. However, at the more abstract level, it possesses the power of showing relationships among objects in existence."[13]

The issue of *realism versus idealism* reflects the dilemma facing researchers to adopt either the "idealistic" or "realistic" position. The realist thinks that the world presents one with a structure that one is bound to find. "He believes that whatever he perceives and cognizes really exists 'out there' in the world. Behavioral psychology is based on this type of view."[14] The idealist believes that there is no external world of reality and that the research creates rather than discovers structure. The idealist thinks that living has its advantages and disadvantages:

> The more idealistic type of theoretical structure has the advantage of greater freedom in theorizing, in imaginatively postulating constructs and relations among constructs. It has the disadvantage, however, of removing the theorist from the disciplining effect of fitting his theory to the conventional wisdom about the nature of reality. By distinguishing between intervening variables and hypothetical constructs, we believe that it is possible to achieve the best of both possible worlds.[15]

The issue of *objectivism versus subjectivism* reflects the dilemma facing the researcher regarding whether to view the concepts and propositions objectively, that is, by giving them a common meaning, or subjectively, that is, by given them a unique personal meaning. Objectivism is generally secured by the provision of data subject to measurement in physical terms.

The issue of *introspection versus extrospection* reflects the dilemma facing the researcher regarding whether to formulate theories introspectively, that is, from the perspective of the object of the study, or extrospectively, that is, from his or her perspective as an observer. Behavioral accounting is introspective whereas capital-market-based research is generally extrospective.

The *level of formality* arises from the need in certain situations to provide a formal theory by specifically and uniformly integrating all relevant aspects of a theory – a nomological network of constructs – and in other situations to provide an informal theory characterized by the lack of a clear unifying construct.

3.1.3 Evaluating theories

Although the building of a theory is a worthwhile project, its success depends on its truth and the extent to which it is isomorphic with reality. A theory is evaluated to prove the adequacy of what it proposes. Karl Popper suggested evaluative criteria, namely, internal consistency, logical form, comparison with other theories, and empirical testing.[16] From 70 criteria of "good" theories as induced from the literature, S.C. Dodd selected as most relevant the following 24 evaluative criteria listed by order of importance: (1) verifiability, (2) predictivity, (3) consistency, (4) reliability, (5) accuracy, (6) generality, (7) utility, (8) importance, (9) multipliability, (10) univocality, (11) controllability, (12) standardizability, (13) synergy, (14) parsimony, (15) simplicity, (16) stability, (17) recurrency, (18) translatability, (19) durativity, (20) durability, (21) acquaintancy, (22) popularity, (23) efficacy, and (24) density.[17] Shelby Hunt classified most structures that purport to be a theory under one of the following schemata: theoretical, definitional, classificational, or analytical-conceptual.[18] In evaluating a theory using Hunt's theoretical criteria, there is a need to determine, first, whether the structure contains a systematically related set of statements where *systematically related* refers to the syntactic properties of the structure; second, whether it contains "lawlike generalizations"; and third, whether the structure is empirically testable by yielding hypotheses or predictions that are at least in principle susceptible to empirical testing.

Bunge presented a comprehensive scheme of 20 criteria to evaluate theories, grouped into (1) formal criteria, (2) semantic criteria, (3) epistemological criteria, (4) methodological criteria, and (5) metaphysical criteria.[19] Gerald Zaltman and his associates used the Bunge groupings to develop their own set of 16 criteria. As *formal criteria*, they proposed well-foundedness, internal consistency, independence, and strength. As *semantic criteria*, they proposed linguistic exactness, conceptual unity, empirical interpretability, and representativeness. As *methodological criteria*, they proposed falsifiability and methodological simplicity. As *epistemological criteria*, they proposed confirmation, originality, external consistency, unifying power, heuristic power, and stability. Basically:

(a) Theoretical statements should be well formed (well-foundedness).

(b) Theoretical statements should contain no logical contradictions (internal consistency).

(c) Theoretical statements may include primitive (undefined) concepts and assumptions, which if defined should be mutually independent (independence).

(d) Theoretical statements should be comprehensive (strength).

(e) Theoretical statements should contain no concepts that have *intensional vagueness* (partial indefiniteness of the intension) or *extensional vagueness* (partial determination of the extension of a concept).

(f) Theoretical statements from different disciplines should refer to the same set of phenomena (conceptual units).

(g) Theoretical statements should involve a one-to-one correspondence of symbols to referents (empirical interpretability or univocality).

(h) Theoretical statements should have depth (representativeness).

(i) Theoretical statements should be empirically testable with the possibility of being both confirmed and refitted by the results (falsifiability).

(j) Theoretical statements should not be so complex as to make refutation impossible (methodological simplicity).

(k) Theoretical statements would be true if corroborated (confirmation).

(l) Theoretical statements should be conducive to creativity in formulating hypotheses and empirical tests (originality).

(m) Theoretical statements should be consistent with most of the body of knowledge in other fields as well as its own (external consistency).

(n) Theoretical statements should be able to reach to other unrelated areas (unifying power).

(o) Theoretical statements should be able to generate new research ideas (heuristic power or multiplicability).

(p) Theoretical statements should be flexible enough to accommodate new and non-contradicting evidence (stability).

3.1.4 A general theory versus middle-range theories of accounting

A *theory* is defined as "a set of interrelated constructs (concepts), definitions, and propositions that present a systematic view of the phenomenon by specifying relationships among variables with the purpose of explaining and predicting the phenomena".[20]

It must be recognized at the outset that no comprehensive theory of accounting exists at present. This does not mean that attempts were not made to develop such a general theory. For a long time the idea was deemed possible and generally was triggered in response to the seemingly fragmented accounting research. For example, Richard Mattessich made the point as follows:

> Accounting research during the last fifteen years not only greatly matured but also spread into many directions. The centrifugal force at work in our discipline during the transition period is well manifested in the great variety of modern accounting topics. This force and the dynamics behind it might prove for accounting either lightly beneficial or destructive, depending on how accountants are able to harness it. If the many fugitive parts and pieces of our discipline can be held together and integrated, accounting as an academic discipline will survive, if not it might dissolve and be absorbed by neighboring fields. The present state of accounting research resembles a jigsaw puzzle where some areas slowly grow into meaningful configurations but without yielding the entire picture. Indeed, the individual fragments seem to spread outwards and not towards a common center.[21]

The recent popularity, however, of various and different accounting theories and models is a witness to the lack of popularity of general theorizing and universalistic accounting techniques. A good argument against a general theory of accounting is provided by J.W. Buckley and his associates as follows:

Scholars in other disciplines have not succeeded in encompassing whole bodies of knowledge within a single accepted theory. There is no good reason why accountants should consider themselves unique in this respect. Accounting must be integrated with a wider body of knowledge, and accordingly must meet the tests of the general methodology of the social sciences.[22]

The rise of the fragmented attempts shows the importance of middle-range theories to the field of accounting, where each theory tries to predict and explain only a subset of all accounting phenomena. The attempts also show an agreement with the call for a shift away from the search for a general theory toward the development of theories of the middle range. *Theories of the middle range* have been introduced and defined by Robert Merton as "theories that lie between the minor but necessarily working hypotheses that evolve in abundance during day-to-day research and the all-inclusive systematic efforts to develop a unified theory".[23]

Accounting theories of the middle range result from differences in the way researchers perceive both the "users" of accounting data and the "environments" in which the users and preparers of accounting data are supposed to behave.[24] These divergences led the American Accounting Association's Committee on Concepts and Standards for External Financial Reports to conclude that:

1. No single governing theory of financial accounting is rich enough to encompass the full range of user-environment specifications effectively.

2. There exists in the financial accounting literature not a theory of financial accounting but a collection of theories that can be arranged over the differences in user-environment specifications.[25] Each of these middle-range theories makes its own assumptions about the environment, considers different parameters and variables to be relevant, and leads to different prescriptions for the professional world of accounting. There are at least three ways to construct middle-range theories:

> One approach is to develop more or less specific theories to deal with each particular phenomenon of interest (e.g., communication). ... A second approach is to limit the sample frame of analysis by sorting individuals, groups, or organizations into categories for subsequent analysis. A third strategy is to combine the first two, developing limited range theories concerned with particular phenomena in the context of limited classes of organizations.[26]

3.2 Notions of concepts

3.2.1 Nature and importance of concepts

Concepts are fundamentally important whether in accounting or in other science. "Scientific knowledge is entirely *conceptual*: it consists of systems of concepts interrelated in different ways".[27] Concepts are the main units of a theory, and good theorizing implies good concept formation. Referred to as the *paradox of conceptualization*, it is explained as follows: "The proper concepts are needed to formulate a good theory, but we need a good theory to arrive at proper concepts ... The better our concepts, the better the theory we can formulate with them, and in turn, the better the concepts available for the next, improved theory."[28] Concepts are devised to refer to identifiable characteristics or phenomena. They are different from terms, percepts, or objects. Witness the following quote. "We may therefore think of a set of connections running from sense perceptions *(percepts)*, through mental constructs and images *(concepts)* to linguistic representations *(terms)*. 'Percepts,' 'concepts', and 'terms' cannot be regarded as truly isomorphic. They possess, in some degree, an independent existence."[29] The relation is therefore a continuation starting from the idea or percept, generating a concept designated by terms (*the designation process*) and including few aspects of objects (*the intension process*).[30] The designation process gives rise to definitions, an equivalence relation between the *definiendums*, the term referring to the concept, and the *definiens*, the expression used to define it.

The concept, as referred to by a term, needs now to be interpreted. The interpretation can be (1) *ostensive* by referring the concept to something to which it applies or enumerating objects that are proper interpretations of the concept (*quasi-ostensive interpretation*) or (2) *operational* by referring to properties of the concept. Either type of interpretation raises four aspects of the reference relationship, namely, intension, denotation, connotation, and extension. The confusion between them is clarified as follows:

> The intension of a concept is the list of all the properties it possesses, such as reversibility, demonstrability, complexibility, and so forth. The *denotation* of a concept is the class of objects and events embodying the properties of a concept. Given the denotation, we may be interested in finding out all the properties that are common to all the elements of the denotation. These properties, including those comprised by the concept's intension, constitute the *connotation* of the concept. Finally, we can extend the notion of denotation to all possible objects, past or future, known or unknown, that if they existed would belong to the concept's denotation. We shall call this set the *extension* of a concept.[31]

Concepts come in various types. One distinction is in terms of formal versus nonformal concepts, whereby nonformal concepts, unlike formal ones, refer to some aspect of the real world.[32] Another typology includes observational concepts, theoretical concepts, and disposition concepts. *Observational concepts* are those that possess "certain directly observable characteristics of objects, i.e., properties or relations whose presence or absence in a given case can be intersubjectively ascertained, under suitable circumstances by direct observation" or "whose presence or absence can be ... ascertained".[33]

Theoretical concepts are those playing a special, embedded role in a given theory. Theoretical concepts

> are not introduced by definition or reduction claims based on observables; in fact, they are not introduced by any piecemeal process of assigning meaning to them individually. Rather, the constructs used in theory are introduced jointly, as it were, by setting up a theoretical system formulated in terms of them and giving this system an experiential interpretation, which in turn confers meaning on the theoretical construct.[34]

Disposition concepts refer to a tendency "to display specific reactions ... under certain specifiable circumstances".[35] A behaviorally oriented definition is as follows: "These [concepts] describe the disposition of an object or organism to display a certain characteristic or response, under certain given conditions of stimulation."[36]

3.2.2 The validity of concepts

Although most financial concepts in accounting have been adequately defined, few of them have been validated. The validation of a concept is in fact crucial to its acceptance as a useful concept to be included in a given theory.

Two approaches have been adopted for validation. The first, known as operationism, maintains that only observational concepts are valid. The aim of the operationism is to "emancipate science from any dependency or unverifiable 'metaphysical' commitments".[37] This view was fortunately criticized as too narrow. The second approach focuses on developing measures of concept validity to evaluate the degree to which an instrument can measure the concept under consideration. Zaltman and his associates provided an exhaustive and well-defined list of the types of concept validity encountered in the research literature.[38] They are:

1. Observational validity: The degree to which a concept is reducible to observations.
2. Content validity: The degree to which an operationalization represents the concept about which generalizations are to be made.
3. Criterion-related validity: The degree to which the concept under consideration enables one to predict the value of some other concept that constitutes the criterion.
   (a) Predictive validity: A subtype of criterion-related validity in which the criterion measured is separated in time from the predictor concept.
   (b) Concurrent validity: A subtype criterion-related validity in which the criterion and the predictor concepts are measured at the same time.
4. Construct validity: The extent to which an operationalization measures the concept which it purports to measure.
   (a) Convergent validity: The degree to which two attempts to measure the same concept through maximally different methods are convergent. It is generally represented by the correlation between the two attempts.
   (b) Discriminant validity: The extent to which a concept differs from other concepts.
   (c) Nomological validity: The extent to which predictions based on the concept which an instrument purports to measure are confirmed.
5. Systemic validity: The degree to which a concept enables the integration of previously unconnected concepts and/or the generation of a new conceptual system.
6. Semantic validity: The degree to which a concept has a uniform semantic usage.
7. Control validity: The degree to which a concept is manipulable and capable of influencing other variables of influence.

3.3 The handling of hypotheses

3.3.1 From propositions to hypotheses

The proposition in a theory establishes relation between the concepts of a theory. It is designated by a sentence. It is characterized generally by (1) the number and degree of predicates, that is, the syntactic unit expressing the action performed by or on the state attributed to the subject of the sentence, (2) the degree of generality, that is, the universe of discourse.

Propositions may become hypotheses if they refer to facts that are inexperienced and are at the same time corrigible on the basis of new knowledge.[39] The main characteristic of the hypothesis is empirical testability. The nature of the test depends on whether the propositions are analytic or synthetic. The analytic propositions can be only logically true or false. The synthetic propositions that have empirical significance can be subjected to an empirical test.

A hypothesis is, therefore, a proposition about a relationship whose truth or falsity is yet to be determined by an empirical test. The probability of it being true is accomplished by taking a sample of its logical consequence and confirming that it is true. John O'Shaughnessy recommended the following in formulating hypotheses:

The conditions for the formulation of an hypothesis are that it should explain and be formulated so that consequences can be deduced which are verifiable. Ideally these consequences should be "surprising," as there is always a danger of creating an hypothesis to explain events and their "confirming" the hypothesis by showing that these events are the logical consequences of the hypothesis. One suspects that this circular reasoning is common in social science. There is never any difficulty in devising an hypothesis that explains the present facts but also leads to the prediction and confirmation of what is currently thought unlikely to be true.[40]

3.3.2 The confirmation of hypotheses

The question of whether accounting is a science has never been adequately answered. A good definition of a science, provided by Robert Buzzell, is as follows:

> a classified and systemized body of knowledge, … organized around one or more central theories and a number of general principles, … usually expressed in quantitative terms, … knowledge which permits the prediction and, under some circumstances, the control of future events.[41]

Accounting meets the above criteria. It has a distinct subject matter and includes underlying uniformities and regularities conducive to empirical relationships, authoritative generalizations, concepts, principles, laws, and theories. It definitely can be considered a science. If one subscribes to the unity-of-science argument, a single scientific method is equally applicable to accounting and other sciences. As Carl Hempel observed:

> The thesis of the methodological unity of science states, first of all, that, notwithstanding many differences in their techniques of investigation, all branches of empirical science test and support their statements in basically the same manner, namely by deriving from their implications that can be checked intersubjectively and by performing for those implications the appropriate experimental or observational tests. This, the unity of method thesis holds, is true also of psychology and the social and historical disciplines. In response to the claim that the scholar in these fields, in contrast to the social sciences, often must rely on empathy to establish his assertions, logical-empiricist writers stressed that imaginative identification with a given person often may prove a useful heuristic aid to the investigator who seeks to guess at a hypothesis about that person's beliefs, hopes, fears, and goals. But whether or not a hypothesis they arrived at is factually sound must be determined by reference to objective evidence: the investigator's emphatic experience is logically irrelevant to it.[42]

There is, therefore, a common acceptance by all sciences of a methodology for the justification of knowledge. That methodology rests in determining whether a truth value can, in principle, be assigned to a hypothesis – that is, whether it can be refuted, confirmed, falsified, or verified, respectively. *Confirmation* is the extent to which a hypothesis is capable of being shown to be empirically true, that is, of describing the real world accurately. *Falsification* is the extent to which a hypothesis is capable of being shown to be empirically untrue, that is, of failing to describe the real world accurately. Confirmation of hypotheses does not necessarily imply that they are falsifiable and vice versa. In fact, hypotheses that are naturally grounded in theory can be either purely confirmable, purely refutable, or both confirmable and refutable. *Purely confirmable hypotheses* come from existential statements, that is, statements that propose the existence of some phenomenon. For example, the hypothesis "There are CPAs within public accounting firms who view inflation accounting as useless" is a purely confirmable hypothesis. *Purely refutable hypotheses* come from universal laws, that is, statements that take the form of universal generalized conditionals. An example of such a hypothesis is "All accountants are CPAs". If the hypothesis is stated as "There are accountants who are CPAs", it becomes an existential statement, which is purely confirmable. Therefore, it appears that universal laws are basically negative existential statements that are purely refutable or falsifiable.

Both confirmable and refutable hypotheses come from singular statements, that is, statements that refer only to specific phenomena that are bound in time and space. For example, the hypothesis "All individuals tolerant of ambiguity process more information cues than those who are intolerant of ambiguity" can be both confirmed and refuted. However, there are hypotheses that are neither strictly confirmable nor strictly refutable. They are the hypotheses arising from statistical or tendency laws, that is, statements specifying a "loosely specified" statistical relationship between a phenomenon and a large number of variables. Most accounting hypotheses fall within this category, which makes them neither strictly confirmable nor strictly falsifiable. The market model, the accounting predictive models of economic events, the positive theory of accounting, the human information processing models, and most empirical accounting research fit the description. If the data contradict the hypothesis derived from these theories or models, defenders can always claim different excuses, including contamination of the data or small or biased sample size. The rhetoric of research plays a crucial role in challenging whatever results are provided by the data. Is this a cause for alarm given that statistical laws abound in accounting research? Bunge suggested that this would be a mistake:

> Some die-hard classical determinists claim that stochastic statements do not deserve the name of law and are to be regarded, at their best, as temporary devices. This anachronistic view has no longer currency in physics, chemistry, and certain branches of biology (notably genetics), especially ever since these sciences found that all molar laws in their domains are stochastic laws deducible (at least in principle) from laws concerning single systems in conjunction with definite statistical hypotheses regarding, e.g., the compensation of random deviations. Yet the prejudice against stochastic laws still causes some harm in psychology and sociology, where it serves to attack the stochastic approach without compensating for its loss by a scientific study of individuals.[43]

The refutation or confirmation is done by repeated testimony and new evidences. If adequate repeated testing corroborates a hypothesis, it will average as an empirically universally true generalization or law. Some maintain that because theories are not directly testable, they are not strictly confirmable. Hunt observed that:

> Theories cannot be shown to be conclusively true in an empirical sense. One can only say that certain research hypotheses have been derived from a theory and that these hypotheses have been directly tested. If the hypotheses are confirmed, then this provides empirical support that the theory is, indeed, empirically true; that is, the theory has been empirically corroborated by the confirmation of the research hypotheses. If the hypotheses are rejected by the data, then this provides empirical evidence that a) the theory is false (reality just isn't constructed as the theory suggests), b) errors have been made in the empirical testing procedures, or c) the rejected hypothesis was not properly derived from the theory.[44]

3.3.3 The nature of explanation

Explanation is a vital step in all types of scientific inquiry. Ernest Nagel maintained that "the distinctive aim of the scientific enterprise is to provide systematic and responsibly supported explanations".[45] Explanations, as suggested by Carl Hempel, are answers to the "why" and "what will happen if" questions.[46] Why did users respond to information X? They responded because … Why did bankruptcy take place? Bankruptcy took place because … Accounting researchers are interested in explaining various accounting phenomena. To do so they need to rely on an explanatory model, adequately defined as *"any generalized procedure or structure which purports to represent how phenomena are scientifically explained".*[47] Explanatory models must meet the following requirements.

1. The requirement of *explanatory relevance* means that the explanatory model must somehow show that the phenomenon to be explained was expected given specified circumstances. Explanatory relevance is achieved when "the explanatory information adduced affords grounds for believing that the phenomenon to be explained did, or does, indeed occur. This condition must be met if we are to be entitled to say: That explains it – the phenomenon in question was indeed expected under the circumstances."[48]

2. The requirement of testability means the scientific explanations must be empirically testable. Seven basic models of explanation have been suggested, namely, the deductive-nomological, the probabilistic model, the functional or teleological model, the genetic model, the pattern model, the individual-events model, and the logical empiricist model.

The deductive-nomological model, also referred to as hypothetic-deductive, covering law or simply the deductive, has the following structure:

$$\begin{array}{l} C_1, C_2, C_3, \ldots, C_n \\ ] \text{ Explanans S} \\ \underline{L_1, L_2, L_3, \ldots, L_m} \\ E \text{Explanandum} \end{array}$$

Basically the $C_1, C_2, C_3, \ldots, C_n$ are the characteristics or facts of a particular phenomenon and the $L_1, L_2, L_3, \ldots, L_m$ are the universal deterministic relationships or laws. The characteristics and the laws binding them are the explanans that deductively imply the explanandum. The laws state that every time the characteristics occur, the explanandum E will occur. They have the form: "In all cases when conditions of kind F are realized, conditions of kind G are realized as well."[49] The probabilistic model differs from the deductive-nomological model by relying on probabilistic rather than studying universalistic laws. These statistical laws take the form:

$$P(G, F) = r$$

which means that the probability of G given F is r. The probability may be a mathematical probability, a relative frequency, or a subjective probability. The nature of the explanation is rationally different:

> With a deductive explanation, the explanatory premises would, if true, provide conclusive evidence for the conclusion, constituting a totally sufficient guarantee of the explanatory conclusion. With a probabilistic explanation, the explanatory premises do not provide a guarantee of the conclusion, but merely render it relatively likely.[50]

The probabilistic statements cannot be formally confirmed or disconfirmed In addition, the evidence is not conclusive. As stated by Zaltman and his associates:

> It is also accepted that we cannot deduce from any statistical generalization a statement to the effect that any *particular* event must occur: The explanans of a probabilistic explanation does not logically imply the explanandum; the former gives only a more or less high degree of inductive support or confirmation to the latter. Thus, the truth of the explanans is compatible with the falsehood of the explanandum.[51]

Although various authors have stated that probabilistic explanations are weaker than the deductive ones but are very good when our knowledge is imperfect and should be considered as temporary stopgap measures, others have stressed their importance. For example, consider the following statement by May Broadbeck.

> Without some abstraction or selection from all the possibilities the world presents there can be no science at all. By their very nature scientific laws describe only certain features of the kinds of things or events they hold to be connected. How much can safely be ignored depends upon the way things are ... To say, in consequence, that abstraction is all very well for the physical sciences but will not do for the study of man and society is the counsel of desperation; that is, no solution at all. The social scientist, striving to merit the honorific half of that title, settles for something less than perfection ... The use of the statistical concept [in the physical sciences] makes our ignorance of all the influencing factors a failure in either completeness or closure or, usually, both. Similarly, the social scientist, deliberately selecting for study fewer factors than actually influence the behavior in which he is interested, shifts his goal from predicting individual events or behaviors to predicting the frequency with which this kind of behavior occurs in a large group of individuals possessing the circumscribed number of factors. This is the price. The reward, of course, is that instead of helplessly gazing in dumb wonder at the infinite complexity of man and society, he has knowledge, imperfect rather than perfect to be sure, but knowledge not to be scorned nonetheless, of a probability distribution rather than of individual events. After all, while we might much prefer to know the exact conditions under which cancer develops in a particular person, it is far from valueless to know the factors which are statistically correlated to the frequency of its occurrence.[52]

The *probabilistic model* of explanation has the following structure:

$$b \text{ is } F$$
$$\left.\begin{array}{l} \\ P(G, F) = r \end{array}\right] \text{ The explanans}$$
$$\overline{b \text{ is a } G \text{ The explanandum}}$$

The probabilistic law $P(G, F) = r$ stipulates that given F, the probability of G is r. For example, the probability for a firm having a very high leverage ratio to go bankrupt is high.

$$\frac{\text{XYZ company has a very high leverage ratio}}{\text{XYZ company went bankrupt}}$$

The *functional or teleological-explanation model* answers the "why" question about a phenomenon by referring to particular functions of the phenomenon. In other words, "the 'why' question about a particular event or activity is answered by specifying a goal or end towards the attainment of which the event or activity is a means".[53] Functional explanations are part of the general class of philosophical inquiry known as teleology or the study of purposes. The term *function* can mean (1) the dependence or interdependence between variables, (2) the organic processes ("vital functions") necessary for life and maintenance of species, (3) the recognized use or utility of things, or (4) the contribution that an item makes toward the maintenance of the characteristic of a system.

The *genetic-explanation model* answers the "why" question about a phenomenon by referring to a prior state or a sequence of prior states. Also labeled as *historicist explanation*, it refers to one "in which an *effect* created by causes at some previous period *becomes a cause of that same* effect in succeeding periods".[54]

The *pattern model* of explanation answers the "why" question by fitting the phenomenon into a known pattern. Abraham Kaplan defined and discussed the pattern model:

> Very roughly, [in the pattern model] we know the reason for something when we can fit into a known pattern … something is explained when it is so related to a set of other elements that together they constitute a unified system. We understand something by identifying it as a specific part in an organized whole … in the pattern model we explain by instituting or discovering relations … These relations may be of various different sorts: casual, purposive, mathematical, and perhaps other, basic types, as well as various combinations and derivatives of these. The particular relations that hold constitute a pattern, and an element is explained by being shown to occupy the place that it does occupy in the pattern … The perception that everything is just where it should be to complete the pattern is what gives us the intellectual satisfaction, the sense of closure, all the more satisfying because it was preceded by the tension of ambiguity.[55]

The *individual-events model* answers the "why" question by referring to the individual events as their explananda.

The logical *empiricist model* answers the "why" question by referring not to individual events but to empirical generalizations that subsume and inductively generalize the findings.

Given these types of explanation models, the question becomes one of determining the criteria that help to evaluate explanation. Eugene Meehan offered the following as criteria for judging the "usefulness" of an explanation.

> Four points are particularly important: first, the *scope* of the explanation, the range of events to which it can be applied; second, explanations differ in *precision*, in the accuracy of the expectations they generate and the control procedures they imply; third, explanations differ in *power*, and the amount of control over an empirical situation that they permit; finally, explanations differ in reliability, in the amount of confidence we place on their use.[56]

3.3.4 The nature of prediction

What is the relation of explanation to prediction? Hempel answered the question in terms of the *thesis of structural identity*, or *structural symmetry*: (1) every adequate explanation is potentially a prediction, and (2) every adequate prediction is potentially an explanation.[57] In fact Hempel and P.A. Oppenheim viewed prediction as a special case of explanation. They suggested that the formal structure of explanation applies to prediction with a slight modification.[58] By *prediction* is meant the process "for making deductions from known to unknown events within a conceptually static system".[59] By *scientific prediction* is meant prediction guided by scientific rules. Bunge, in fact, distinguished between scientific predictions and three unscientific predictions, namely, expectation, guess, and prognosis.[60] Prediction may be accomplished by either extrapolation techniques, which predict a variable from itself, or associative techniques, which predict a variable from other variable(s). Some of the criteria identified for an evaluation of prediction include confirmability or refutability, scope, precision, accuracy, and power.[61]

3.4 Context of discovery

This chapter has dealt with the context of participation. However, a more important process preceding justification is the process of discovery. What procedures are used to generate or discover empirical generalizations, laws, or theories? In general, four procedures are used: dreams, Eureka, the deductive approach, and the inductive approach.

Dreams may be one procedure of discovery with an important role in scientific discovery. Hempel referred to how the chemist Kekule discovered the structure of the benzene molecule:

> He had long been trying unsuccessfully to devise a structural formula for the benzene molecule when, one evening in 1865, he found a solution to his problem while he was dozing in front of his fireplace. Gazing into the flame, he seemed to see atoms dancing in snakelike arrays. Suddenly, one of the snakes formed a ring by seizing hold of his own tail and then whirled mockingly before him. Kekule awoke in a flash: he had lit upon the famous and familiar idea of representing the molecular structure of benzene by a hexagonal ring. He spent the rest of the night working out the consequences of this hypothesis.[62]

The *Eureka* route may be one procedure of discovery. Archimedes, finding that the bathwater rose in height when he immersed himself, shouted "Eureka" when he realized that the body immersed in water will be "buoyed up" by a force equal to the weight of the displaced fluid. Newton, with an apple dropping on his head, discovered the universal law of gravitation.

The *deductive approach* is another procedure of discovery. The deductive approach to the construction of any theory begins with basic propositions and proceeds to derive logical conclusions about the subject under consideration. Applied to accounting, the deductive approach begins with basic accounting propositions or premises and proceeds to derive by logical means the accounting principles that serve as guides and bases for the development of accounting techniques. This approach moves from the general (basic propositions about the accounting environment) to the particular (accounting principles first and accounting techniques second). If we assume at this point that the basic propositions about the accounting environment consist of both objectives and postulates, the steps used to derive the deductive approach will include:

1. specifying the objectives of financial statements;
2. selecting the postulates of accounting;
3. deriving the principles of accounting;
4. developing the techniques of accounting.

In a deductively derived accounting theory, therefore, the techniques are related to the principles, postulates, and objectives in such a way that if they are true, the techniques must also be true. The theoretical structure of accounting defined by the sequence of objectives, postulates, principles, and techniques rests on a proper formulation of the objectives of accounting. A proper testing of the resulting theory is also necessary.

The *inductive approach* is also the procedure of discovery. The inductive approach to the construction of a theory begins with observations and measurements and moves towards generalized conclusions. Applied to accounting, the inductive approach begins with observations about the financial information of business enterprises and proceeds to construct generalizations and principles of accounting from these observations on the basis of recurring relationships. Inductive arguments are said to lead from the particular (accounting information depicting recurring relationships) to the general (postulates and principles of accounting). The inductive approach to a theory involves four stages:

1. recording all observations;
2. analyzing and classifying these observations to detect recurring relationships ("likes" and "similarities");
3. inductively deriving generalizations and principles of accounting from observations that depict recurring relationships;
4. testing the generalizations.

Unlike the deductive approach, the truth or falsity of the propositions does not depend on other propositions but must be empirically verified. In induction, the truth of the propositions depends on the observation of sufficient instances of recurring relationships.

Similarly, we may state that accounting propositions that result from inductive inference imply special accounting techniques only with more or less high probability, whereas the accounting propositions that result from deductive inference lead to specific accounting techniques with certainty.

It is interesting that although the deductive approach starts with general propositions, the formulation of the propositions is often accomplished by inductive reasoning, conditioned by the author's knowledge of, and experience with, accounting practice. In other words, the general propositions are formulated through an inductive process, but the principles and techniques are derived by a deductive process.

3.5 Conclusion

The message from this chapter is that accounting research ought to develop a vigorous thinking methodology in both its theorizing and the conduct of basic and applied research. Concepts from philosophy of science and metatheory should prove very helpful as tools for such thinking methodology.

Notes

1. Bunge, Mario, *Scientific Research I: The Search for System* (New York: Springer, 1967), p. 381.
2. Nagel, Ernest, *The Structure of Science* (New York: Harcourt Brace Jovanovich, 1961), p. 93.
3. Hunt, Shelby D., *Marketing Theory: The Philosophy of Marketing Science* (Homewood, IL: Irwin, 1983), p. 233.
4. Harvey, David, *Explanation in Geography* (London: E. Arnold, 1969), pp. 97–9.
5. Ibid., p. 97.
6. Kaplan, A., *The Conduct of Inquiry: Methodology for Behavioral Science* (New York: Chandler, 1964), p. 298.

7. Harvey, *Explanation in Geography*, pp. 98–9.

8. Kaplan, *The Conduct of Inquiry*, p. 298.

9. Howard, John A., and Jagdish, Sheth N., *The Theory of Buyer Behavior* (New York: Wiley, 1969), p. 4.

10. Ibid., p. 5.

11. Ibid., p. 9.

12. Ibid., p. 16.

13. Ibid., p. 17.

14. Ibid., p. 18.

15. Ibid., p. 19.

16. Popper, Karl R., *The Logic of Scientific Discovery* (New York: Harper and Row, 1959), p. 32.

17. Dodd, S.C., "Introducing 'Systemmetrics' for Evaluating Symbolic Systems: Criteria for the Excellence of Scientific Theories", *Systematics* (6, 1968), p. 49.

18. Hunt, Shelby D., "The Morphology of Theory and the General Theory of Marketing", *Journal of Marketing* (35, April, 1971), p. 65.

19. Bunge, *Scientific Research I*, p. 443.

20. Kerlinger, F.N., *Foundations of Behavioral Research* (New York: Holt, Rinehart and Winston, 1964), p. 11.

21. Mattessich, Richard, "Methodological Preconditions and Problems of a General Theory of Accounting," *Accounting Review* (July, 1972), pp. 482–3.

22. Buckley, J.W., Kircher, P., and Mathews, R.D., "Methodology in Accounting Theory", *Accounting Review* (April, 1968), p. 281.

23. Merton, Robert K., *On Theoretical Sociology: Five Essays, Old and New* (New York: Macmillan, 1967), p. 39.

24. Fraser, I.A.M., and Nobes, C.W., "The Assumed Users in Three Accounting Theories", *Accounting and Business Research* (Spring, 1985), pp. 144–7.

25. Statement of *Accounting Theory and Theory Acceptance* (Sarasota, FL: American Accounting Association, 1977), pp. 1–2.

26. Pinder, Craig C., and Moore, Larry F., "The Resurrection of Taxonomy to Aid the Development of Middle-Range Theories of Organizational Behavior," *Administrative Science Quarterly* (March, 1979), pp. 100–1.

27. Bunge, *Scientific Research I*, p. 46.

28. Kaplan, *The Conduct of Inquiry*.

29. Harvey, *Explanation in Geography*, p. 7.

30. Zaltman, Gerald, Pinson, Christian R.A., and Angelman, Reinhard, *Metatheory and Consumer Research* (New York: Holt, Rinehart and Winston, 1973), p. 23.

31. Ibid., p. 32.

32. Bunge, *Scientific Research I*, p. 59.

33. Hempel, Carl G., *Aspects of Scientific Explanation* (New York: Free Press, 1965), p. 22.

34. Ibid., p. 32.

35. Ibid., p. 24.

36. Mandler, G., and Kesser, W., *The Language of Psychology* (New York: Wiley, 1959), p. 115.

37. Nagel, *The Structure of Science*, p. 119.

38. Zaltman, Pinson, and Angelman, *Metatheory and Consumer Research*, p. 44.

39. Bunge, *Scientific Research I*, p. 222.

40. O'Shaughnessy, John, *Inquiry and Decision* (London: Allen & Unwin, 1972), p. 51.

41. Buzzell, Robert D., "Is Marketing a Science?" *Harvard Business Review* (January–February, 1963), p. 37.

42. Hempel, Carl G., "Logical Positivism and the Social Sciences", in Peter Achinstein and Stephen F. Barker (eds.), *Legacy of Logical Positivism* (Baltimore: Johns Hopkins University Press, 1969), p. 191.

43. Bunge, *Scientific Research I*, p. 336.

44. Hunt, Shelby D., *Marketing Theory: The Philosophy of Marketing Science* (Homewood, IL: Irwin, 1983), p. 294.

45. Nagel, *The Structure of Science*, p. 334.

46. Hempel, *Aspects of Scientific Explanation*, p. 334.

47. Hunt, *Marketing Theory*, p. 84.

48. Hempel, *Aspects of Scientific Explanation*, p. 48.

49. Hempel, Carl G., *Philosophy of Natural Science* (Englewood Cliffs, NJ: Prentice-Hall, 1966), p. 55.

50. Rescher, N., *Scientific Explanation* (New York: Free Press, 1970), p. 37.

51. Zaltman, Rinson, and Angelman, *Metatheory and Consumer Research*, p. 132.

52. Broadbeck, M., "Models, Meaning, and Theories", in M. Broadbeck (ed.), *Readings in the Philosophy of the Social Sciences* (New York: Macmillan, 1968), pp. 293–4.

53. Stinchcombe, A.L., *Constructing Social Theories* (New York: Harcourt Brace Jovanovich, 1968), p. 103.

54. Ibid., p. 103.

55. Kaplan, *The Conduct of Inquiry*, pp. 332–5.

56. Meehan, Eugene J., *Explanation in Social Science: A System Paradigm* (Homewood, IL: Dorsey Press, 1968), p. 115.

57. Hempel, *Aspects of Scientific Explanation*, p. 367.

58. Hempel, Carl G., and Oppenheim, P., "Studies in the Logic of Explanation", *Philosophy of Science* (15, 1948), pp. 137–8.

59. Schuessler, R., "Prediction," in D.L. Sills (ed.), *International Encyclopedia of Social Sciences* (New York: Crowell-Collier-Macmillan, 1968).

60. Bunge, M., *Scientific Research II: The Search for Truth* (New York: Springer, 1967), p. 66.

61. Zaltman, Rinson, and Angelman, *Metatheory and Consumer Research*, pp. 160–71.

62. Hempel, *Philosophy of Natural Science*, p. 16.

References

Abell, P., *Model Building in Sociology* (New York: Schoken Books, 1971).

Achinstein, P., *Concepts of Science: A Philosophical Analysis* (Baltimore: Johns Hopkins University Press, 1968).

Bedford, Norton M., and Dopuch, Nicholas, "Research Methodology and Accounting Theory: Another Perspective", *Accounting Review* (July, 1961), pp. 351–61.

Broadbeck, M. (ed.), *Readings in the Philosophy of the Social Sciences* (New York: Macmillan, 1968).

Buckley, J.W., Kircher, P., and Mathews, R.D., "Methodology in Accounting Theory", *Accounting Review* (April, 1968), pp. 274–83.

Bunge, M., *Causality: The Place of the Causal Principle in Modern Science* (New York: Meridian, 1963).

_____, *Metascientific Queries* (Springfield, IL.: Charles C. Thurnay, 1959).

_____, *Scientific Research I: The Search for System* (New York: Springer, 1967).

_____, *Scientific Research II: The Search for Truth* (New York: Springer, 1967).

Campbell, D.T., and Fisk, D.W., "Convergent and Discriminant Validation by the Multi trait-Multimethod Matrix", *Psychological Bulletin* (56, 1959), pp. 81–105.

Caws, P., *The Philosophy of Science: A Systematic Account* (Princeton, NJ: Van Nostrand, 1965).

De Groot, A., *Methodology: Foundation of Influence and Research in the Behavioral Sciences* (The Hague: Mouton, 1969).

Devine, Carl Thomas, "Research Methodology and Accounting Theory Formation", *Accounting Review* (July, 1960), pp. 387–99.

Dodd, S.C., "Introducing Systemmetrics for Evaluating Symbolic Systems: Criteria for the Excellence of Scientific Theories", *Systemmetrics* (6, 1968), pp. 27–45.

Harvey, David, *Explanation in Geography* (London: E. Arnold, 1969).

Hempel, Carl G., *Aspects of Scientific Explanation* (New York: Free Press, 1965).

_____, *Philosophy of Natural Science* (Englewood Cliffs, NJ: Prentice-Hall, 1966).

Hunt, Shelby D., "The Morphology of Theory and the General Theory of Marketing", *Journal of Marketing* (35, April, 1971), pp. 65–8.

Kaplan, A., *The Conduct of Inquiry: Methodology for Behavioral Science* (New York: Chandler, 1964).

Kinnear, T.C., and Taylor, J.R., "Multivariate Methods in Marketing Research: A Further Attempt at Classification", *Journal of Marketing Research* (8, October, 1971).

Mattessich, Richard, "Methodological Preconditions and Problems of a General Theory of Accounting", *Accounting Review* (July, 1972).

Meehan, Eugene J., *Explanation in Social Science: A System Paradigm* (Homewood, IL: Dorsey Press, 1968).

Nagel, Ernest, *The Structure of Science* (New York: Harcourt Brace Jovanovich, 1961).

Popper, K.R., *Conjectures and Refutations: The Growth of Scientific Knowledge* (New York: Harper and Row, 1965).

_____, *The Logic of Scientific Discovery* (New York: Harper and Row, 1959).

_____, *The Logic of Scientific Discovery* (New York: Science Editions, 1961).

Resher, N., *Scientific Explanation* (New York: Free Press, 1970).

Sterling, Robert R., "On Theory Construction and Verification", *Accounting Review* (July, 1970), pp. 444–57.

Stinchcombe, A.L., *Constructing Social Theories* (New York: Harcourt Brace Jovanovich, 1968).

Zaltman, Gerald, Rinson, Christian R.A., and Angelman, Reinhard, *Metatheory and Consumer Research* (New York: Holt, Rinehart and Winston, 1973).

The traditional approaches to the formulation of an accounting theory

4

Various approaches have applied over time to the formulation of an accounting theory. Some of these approaches are known as "traditional" approaches, because they are characterized by the absence of a vigorous process of verification in the attempt to develop an accounting theory. Traditional approaches constitute conventional research rather than new streams of research that rely on traditional reasoning to formulate a conceptual accounting framework. Among these approaches we may distinguish:

1. the non-theoretical approaches;

2. the deductive approach;

3. the inductive approach;

4. the ethical approach;

5. the sociological approach; and

6. the economic approach.

In this chapter, each of these approaches is examined in terms of its contribution to the formulation of an accounting theory, and in terms of its relative advantages for accounting, the differences between theory construction and verification, the nature of an accounting theory, and methodologies for the formulation of an accounting theory.

4.1 The nature of accounting: various images

The Committee on Terminology of the American Institute of Certified Public Accountants originally defined accounting as follows:

> Accounting is the art of recording, classifying, and summarizing, in a significant manner and in terms of money, transactions and events which are, in part at least, of a financial character, and interpreting the results thereof.[1]

More recently, accounting has been defined with reference to the concept of information:

> Accounting is a service activity. Its function is to provide quantitative information, primarily financial in nature, about economic entities that is intended to be useful in making economic decisions, in making reasoned choices among courses of action.[2]

These definitions refer to accounting as either an "art" or a "service activity" and imply that accounting encompasses a body of techniques that is deemed useful for certain fields. *The Handbook of Accounting* identifies the following fields in which accounting is useful: financial reporting; tax determination and planning; independent audits; data processing and information systems; cost and management accounting; national income accounting; and management consulting.[3]

Accountants draw on different images of the accounting process to elaborate different theories of accounting.[4] Before examining the traditional approaches to the formulation of accounting theory, it would be useful to examine some of the images that have shaped developments in financial accounting.

4.1.1 Accounting as an ideology

> Ideologies are world views which, despite their partial and possible crucial insights, prevent us from understanding the society in which we live and the possibility of changing it. They are world views which correspond to the standpoint of classes ...[5]

Accounting has been perceived as an ideological phenomenon – as a means of sustaining and legitimizing the current social, economic, and political arrangements. Karl Marx maintained that accounting perpetrates a form of false consciousness and provides a means for mystifying rather than revealing the true nature of the social relationships that form productive endeavor.[6] Accounting has also been perceived as a myth, symbol, and ritual that permits the creation of a symbolic order within which social agents can interact. Both perceptions are also embodied in the prevalent view of accounting as an instrument of economic rationality and as a tool of a capitalistic system.

The perception of accounting as an instrument of economic rationality is best exemplified by Weber, who defines the formal rationality of economic action as "the extent of quantitative calculation or accounting which is technically possible and which is actually applied".[7] The same point is emphasized well by Heilbroner when he states that:

> Capitalist practice turns the unit of money in a tool of rational cost-profit calculations, of which the towering monument is double-entry bookkeeping … primarily the product of the evolution of economic rationality; the cost-profit calculus, in turn reacts on that rationality; by crystallizing and defining numerically, it powerfully propels the logic of enterprise.[8]

4.1.2 Accounting as a language

Accounting has been perceived as the language of business. It is one means of communicating information about a business.

The perception of accounting as a language is emphasized in most popular accounting textbooks. For example, Ijiri contends that:

> As the language of business, accounting has many things in common with other languages. The various business activities of a firm are reported in accounting statements using accounting language, just as news events are reported in newspapers in the English language. To express an event in accounting not only does one run the risk of being misunderstood but also risks a penalty for misrepresentation, lying or perjury. Comparability of statements is essential to the effective functioning of a language whether it is in English or in Accounting. At the same time, language has to be flexible to adapt to a changing environment.[9]

This perception of accounting as a language is also recognized by the accounting profession, which publishes accounting terminology bulletins. It is acknowledged in the empirical literature, which attempts to measure the communication of accounting concepts.

What makes accounting a language? To answer this question, let us look at the potential parallels between accounting and language. Hawes defines a language as follows:

> Man's symbols are not randomly arranged signs which lead to the conceptualization of isolated and discrete referents. Rather, man's symbols are arranged in a systematic or patterned fashion with certain rules governing their usage. This arrangement of symbols is called a language, and the rules which influence the patterning and usage of the symbols constitute the grammar of the language.[10]

This definition and others indicate that there are two components of a language, namely *symbols and grammatical rules*. Thus, the recognition of accounting as a language rests on the identification of these two components as the two levels of accounting. It may be argued as follows:

1. The *symbols or lexical characteristics* of a language are the "meaningful" units or words identifiable in any language. These symbols are linguistic objects used to identify particular concepts. Symbolic representations do exist in accounting. For

example, McDonald identifies numerals and words and debits and credits as the only symbols accepted and unique to the accounting discipline.[11]

2. The *grammatical rules* of a language refer to the syntactic arrangements in any given language. In accounting, grammatical rules refer to the general set of procedures used that are followed to create all financial data for the business. Jain establishes the following parallel between grammatical rules and accounting rules:

> The CPA (the expert in accounting) certifies the correctness of the application of rules as does an accomplished speaker of a language for the grammatical correctness of the sentence. Accounting rules formalize the inherent structure of a natural language.[12]

Given the existence of these identified components, symbols and grammatical rules accounting may be defined *a priori* as a language.

4.1.3 Accounting as a historical record

Generally, accounting has been viewed as a means of providing the history of an organization and its transactions with its environment. For either the owner or the shareholders of a company, accounting records provide a history of the manager's *stewardship* of the owner's resources. The stewardship concept is basically a feature of the principal–agent relationship, whereby the agent is assumed to safeguard the resources of the principal. The measuring of the stewardship concept has evolved over time. Birnberg distinguishes between four periods:

1. The pure custodial period.
2. The traditional custodial period.
3. The asset-utilization period.
4. The open-ended period.[13]

The first two periods refer to the need for the agent to return the resources intact to the principal by performing minimal tasks to fulfill the custodial function. In these two periods, the disclosure of balance sheet data is considered to be adequate. The third period refers to the need for the agent to provide initiative and insight in using the assets to conform to agreed plans. In addition to the balance sheet, this period requires the acquisition of performance-evaluation data on the effectiveness of the use of the assets. Finally, the open-ended period differs from the asset-utilization period by providing more flexibility in the use of the assets and allowing the agent to chart the course of asset utilization. Birnberg elaborates on this last concept as follows:

> This involves not only the initial direction, but also ascertaining the critical point in time when such directions must be changed. Like strategic control, the stewardship function requires that a significant degree of responsibility be assumed by the servant. The task force is probably characterized by a lack of structure and a significant amount of uncertainty. This suggests that we may find our reporting system to the master caught between the rock and hard place of communication. The need for the detail on one hand and the risk of overload and excessive complexity on the other.[14]

4.1.4 Accounting as current economic reality

Accounting has also been viewed as a means of reflecting current economic reality. The central thesis of advocates of this view is that both balance sheets and income statements should be based on a valuation basis that is more reflective of economic reality than historical costs. The method considered to be most reflective of economic reality focuses on current and future prices rather than on historical prices. The main objective of this image of accounting is the determination of *true income*, a concept that reflects the change in the wealth of the firm over a period of time. Which methods best measure the economic values of assets and liabilities and the related measurement of income is a theoretical and empirical question that has generated the most prolific debate in the accounting literature.

4.1.5 Accounting as an information system

Accounting has always been viewed as an information system. It is assumed to be a process that links an information source or transmitter (usually the accountant), a channel of communication, and a set of receivers (external users). Basically, when considered as a process of communication, accounting can best be defined as "the process of encoding observations in the language of the accounting system, of manipulating the signs and the statements of the system and decoding and transmitting the result".[15] This view of accounting has important conceptual and empirical overtones. First, it assumes that the accounting system is the only formal measurement system in the organization. Second, it raises the possibility of designing an optimal accounting system capable of providing useful information (to the user). The behavior of the sender is important in terms of both the reaction to the information and the use made of the information. Both behaviors are the subject of conceptual and empirical research in the field of behavioral accounting (see Chapter 11). The superiority of the image of accounting as an information system is stated as follows:

> Alternative accounting systems need no longer be justified in terms of their ability to generate "true income" or on the faithfulness with which they represent history. As long as the different users find the information useful, the utility of the system can be established.[16]

4.1.6 Accounting as a commodity

Accounting is also viewed as a commodity that results from an economic activity. It exists because specialized information is in demand and accountants are willing and capable of producing it. As a public commodity, accounting provides ideal ground for regulation, making an impact on public policy and monitoring of all types of contracts between the organization and its environment. The choice of accounting information and/or accounting technique then may have an impact on the welfare of various groups in society. As a result, there is a market for accounting information with its derived demand and supply. This image of accounting as a commodity is having and will continue to have a profound impact on accounting thought and research. For example:

> The emergence of the image of accounting as a commodity again provides a striking example of the manner in which accounting thought reflects its social content. It has arisen in an era of mushrooming regulation and increasing concern with the public interests in a situation of scarce resources and many competing demands. It has provided the rationale for accounting policies which seek to aid the allocation of resources in the service of the public interest.[17]

4.1.7 Accounting as mythology

Accounting may be viewed as mythology or symbolic rituals. It produces myths that are an easy way of understanding the economic world and explaining complex phenomena. Through accounting a complex economic phenomenon is translated for the users in a more simplified and understandable manner, thereby creating more myths than realities. As a result, the collection of accounting information becomes an expected ritual intended to show that intelligent choices are being made and that there is a commitment to the systematic applications of accounting information to decisions. A symbolic use of accounting information becomes a proper managerial behavior. As Martha Feldman and James March stated:

> The gathering of information provides a ritualistic assurance that appropriate attitudes about decision making exist. Within such a scenario of performance, information is not simply a basis for action. It is a representation of competence and a reaffirmation of social virtue. Command of information and information sources enhances competence and inspires confidence. The belief that more information characterizes better decisions engenders a belief that having information, in itself, is good and that a person or organization with more information is better than a person or organization with less. Thus the gathering and use of information in an organization is part of the performance of a decision maker or an organization trying to make intelligent decisions in a situation in which the verification of intelligence is heavily procedural and normative. A good decision maker is one who makes decisions in the way a good decision maker does, and decision makers and organizations establish their legitimacy by their use of information.[18]

Some writers go as far as to claim that they see accounting as a major vehicle for magical practices.[19] Like witchcraft, accounting embraces a system of values that regulates human conduct and explains to humans when things go wrong or right. This view is similar to the view held by Graham Cleverly that the whole accounting and budgeting routine is a sort of religious ceremony – a rain dance.[20] In view of this alleged sad state of accounting, calls are made for a study and understanding of this image of accounting. Trevor Gambling stated:

> No doubt other societies use other devices to the same end, so that a study of what might be called "the anthropology of accountants" would enable us to understand the part accounting plays in our society and maybe even provide insights into less harmful ways of achieving the same results. As it stands, accounting is not a matter of the supernatural, but seems to have something of political activity about it, albeit with a small p! This may seem a strange conclusion, particularly to those readers who are not professionally-trained accountants. One might suppose that accounting was a matter of precision of analysis and balancing the books to the last penny. So it is, but viewed from the situation of a more senior accountant, one sees that it is also a matter of assessing how far data can be pushed to accommodate "political" compromises between collaborators in the enterprise – and still remain in some sense "true and fair." In short the accountant is one of those people who enable a distinctly demoralized modern industrial society to live with itself, by reassuring it that its models and data can pass for "truth." The aura of both reverence and mild dislike which non-accountants feel to surround this curious profession seems very understandable.[21]

Similarly, G.J. Haines, Jr., viewed information as a symbolic representation of reality that an individual decision maker uses to arrive at economic decisions.[22] Basically, accounting converts data into information by processing and invoking data with relevant symbols for the decision maker. The symbolic representation, however, may be a complete or incomplete representation of the decision maker's taste and beliefs with the following consequences:

> If it is complete, he will have encoded all his perceptions satisfactorily and will be willing to delegate his choice problem to the model. If it is incomplete, he will not be willing to delegate his choice to the model, but the model may still be useful to him in predicting changes in his utility occasioned by the various alternatives open to him. An incomplete model is still information according to the definition that has been adopted in this essay, even though it is not perfect information, since it is a symbolic representation that can be used by an individual as an aid to economic decision.[23]

4.1.8 Accounting as rationale

Accounting may be viewed as rationale. It may be used to attach meanings to events and therefore provide a justification for their future occurrence. Given the imprecision and uncertainty surrounding most accounting numbers, accounting may be used as a way of legitimizing their issuance. Accounting, therefore, provides a shield of guarantee or a certification of authority to these numbers and provides a rationale for actions to be based on them. Basically, these are not numbers picked from a hat; they are the legitimate product of accounting to be used to justify particular decisions taken. Rationalization of actions becomes a primary usage of accounting reports. Because organizational decisions, once made, need to be justified, legitimized, and rationalized, accounting provides a useful means of action. The development of the accounting craft followed the need to corroborate organizational actions. This development was characterized by two tendencies: the increasing institutionalization of the craft and the growing objectification and abstraction of accounting knowledge, which provided bases on which one might seek formally to implicate roles that accounting served.[24] The type of rationale that may be provided by accounting depends on the location of organizational uncertainty. Based on a framework introduced by J.D. Thompson and A.A. Tuden, S. Burchell and his associates introduced a framework outlining the various forms of rationalization taken by accounting in the face of uncertainties.[25] The roles of accounting practice may be (as shown in Exhibit 4.1): answer machines providing structured solutions to structured problems; learning machines providing assistance rather than answers; ammunition machines providing arguments for given positions; rationalization machines providing legitimacy and justification to actions that already have been decided upon.

4.1.9 Accounting as imagery

Accounting may be viewed as imagery. It contributes to a creation of a picture or an image of an organization. It acts as a picture of the organization through a selective choice of events and accounts impinging on the organization. The consequence is the creation of a sense of importance attributed to accounting and of a particular conception of organizational reality.[26] A second consequence is that the image created through selective interpretation and representation of events in turn creates a stable and certain environment and basis for decision making. This argument goes as follows:

> Such selective interpretation and representation of events forces enclosure and thus a degree of perceived certainty on the essentially open and uncertain world in which organizations exist. Enclosure and relative certainty allow things to get done, decisions to be made, interactions to take place and outcomes to be evaluated. They enhance a type of learning and provide a stable platform for interpreting "external" events.[27]

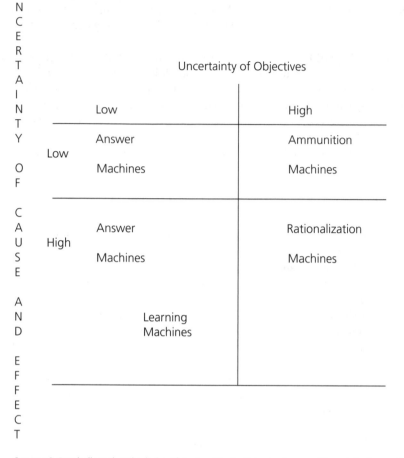

Source: S. Burchell *et al.*, "The Roles of Accounting in Organizations and Society", *Accounting, Organizations, and Society* (June, 1980), p. 14. Reprinted with permission.

Exhibit 4.1 Uncertainty, decision-making, and the roles of accounting practice

Accounting has also been viewed as financial map-making.[28] The complex phenomena are mapped into financial statements. The better the representation of facts, the better the map. The selection of what to be represented may, however, rob the map of its neutrality. As stated by David Solomons:

> Cartographers represent different facts in different ways and match the scale of their maps to their purpose. Every map represents a selection of a small portion of available data, for no map could show physical, political, demographic, climatological, geological, vegetational, and numerous kinds of data and still be intelligible. The need to be selective in the data that one represents does not normally rob the map of its neutrality, although it could.[29]

4.1.10 Accounting as experimentation

Accounting may be viewed as experimentation. It is flexible enough to accommodate various situations, adopt new solutions to new problems, and adapt to the most complex case. Firms can experiment through the use of different accounting data, techniques, reports, or disclosure to fit their particular environment and to adapt to changing circumstances rather than being constrained or fixated by the same conventional approaches. Accounting is experimentation mostly when it is voluntary, innovative, and tentative. It enables one to investigate responses to various accounting options in terms of their usefulness to various constituencies and to ascertain the impact of unlearning previous responses and establishing different behavioral repertoires. As an experiment, accounting allows itself to go through trial and error phases towards a search for the most contingent solution to a given environment and a desired response and behavioral repertoire.

The success of accounting as experimentation rests on the likely response of individuals to data. L.A. Boland and G.A. Newman identified the possible responses of three types of individuals to data, depending upon the theories that the individuals hold concerning what knowledge is and how they should respond to the data; the three types of individuals are the a priorist, the skepticist, and the pessimist.[30] The response of each one determines the success of accounting as experimentation. These responses have been adequately described as follows:

> An *a priorist* would form his tastes and beliefs independently of the data available and would not modify them when new data were revealed. A *skepticist* would have extremely volatile and unstable information unless data were constantly confirming his prior beliefs. A *positivist*, on the other hand, would view data with some objectivity and be willing to modify his tastes or beliefs when new facts come to light.[31]

4.1.11 Accounting as distortion

Because accounting is used to control or influence the actions of both internal and external users, it becomes an ideal target to those seeking to manipulate the nature of the message to be viewed by the user. Four groups of people may affect or be affected by accounting messages: those subjects whose behavior provides data for accounting messages, accountants who prepare the data, accountants who examine the data, and recipients of the data.[32] Each of these groups may then be tempted to engage in dysfunctional rather than normal behavior when it is involved with an accounting message. The dysfunctional behavior involves sending a dishonest or distorted message, that is, "one that managements expect to be interpreted in a manner inconsistent with their actual beliefs about the unobservable attributes of their decisions".[33] The incentives to manipulate the message to be received by the internal or external user stem from the need to ensure or believe that certain messages will yield particular behavior by the internal or external user. This dysfunctional behavior of manipulating data has been labeled as noise.[34] The methods used to distort the information system may be classified in the following six broad categories: smoothing, biasing, focusing, gaming, filtering, and "illegal" acts.[35]

Smoothing involves the process of altering the natural or preplanned flow of data without altering the actual activities of the organization. *Biasing* involves the process of selecting the signal most likely to be acceptable and favorable by the sender. *Focusing* involves the process of either enhancing or degrading certain aspects of the information set. *Gaming* involves the process of selecting activities by the sender so as to cause the desired message to be sent. *Filtering* involves the process of selecting certain favorable aspects of the information set as worthy of communication through overcollection, overrepresentation, aggregation, withholding, or delaying. *Illegal acts* involves the process of falsifying data and hence violating a private or public law.

All these information-manipulation methods and behavior are caused by low beliefs held by the sender in either the analyzability of the situation or the measurability and verifiability of data. Exhibit 4.2 illustrates it.

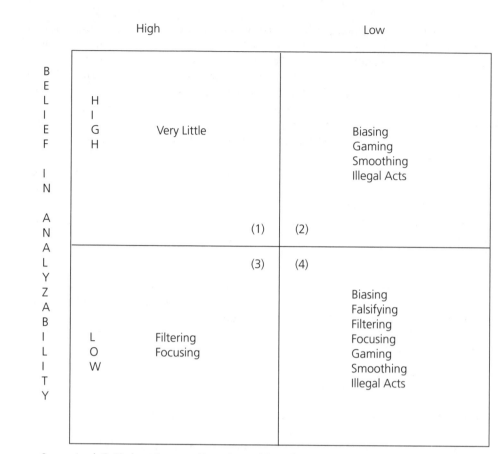

Source: Jacob G. Birnberg, Lawrence Turopolec, and S. Mark Young, "The Organizational Content of Accounting", *Accounting, Organizations, and Society* (July, 1983), p. 125. Reprinted with permission.

Exhibit 4.2   Possible information-manipulation behavior

All of these methods of information manipulation illustrate the belief held by the sender that the information system may convey power to him or her given the ability to affect its output and consequently alter the resource allocation process. M.L. Bariff and J.R. Galbraith have noted that "the design and operation of an organization's information system ... will affect the distribution of intra organizational power".[36] This is equivalent to the old maxim that information is power. It becomes important for organizational members to control the nature of information collected and conveyed and the choice of measures designed into accounting and control systems.

Given these resistances to information systems in general and accounting and control systems in particular, the question is, what would guarantee their easy implementation and effective performance? M. Lynne Markus and Jeffery Pfeffer advanced three hypotheses to explain resistance and system difficulty:

> Accounting and control systems will be implemented easily to the extend that they are (a) consistent with other sources of power in their implications for the distribution of power; (b) consistent with the dominant organizational culture and paradigm in their implications for values and beliefs; and (c) consistent with shared judgment about technical certainty and goal congruence in their assumptions about the degree of certainty about the organization's goals and technology.[37]

4.2 Theory construction and verification

Although accounting is a set of techniques that can be used in specified fields, it is practiced within an implicit *theoretical* framework composed of principles and practices that have been accepted by the profession because of their alleged usefulness and their logic. These "generally accepted accounting principles" guide the accounting profession in the choice of accounting techniques and in the preparation of financial statements in a way considered to be good accounting practice. In response to changing environments, values, and information needs, generally accepted accounting principles are subject to constant reexamination and critical analysis. This is reflected in APB Statement No. 4, which describes the principles as follows:

> Present generally accepted accounting principles are the result of an evolutionary process that can be expected to continue in the future. Changes may occur at any level of generally accepted accounting principles. ... Generally accepted accounting principles change in response to changes in the economic and social conditions, to new knowledge and technology; and to demands of users for more serviceable financial information. The dynamic nature of financial accounting – its ability to change in response to changed conditions – enables it to maintain and increase the usefulness of the information it provides.[38]

Changes in the principles occur mainly as a result of the various attempts to provide solutions to emerging accounting problems and to formulate a theoretical framework for the discipline. Thus, a definite link exists between accounting theory construction attempts either to justify or to refute existing practice. Accounting theory construction stems from the need to provide a rationale for what accountants do or expect to be doing.

The process of accounting theory construction should be completed by theory verification or theory validation. Machlup defines this process as follows:

> Verification in research and analysis may refer to many things, including the correctness of mathematical and logical arguments, the applicability of formulas and equations, the trustworthiness of reports, the authenticity of documents, the genuineness of artifacts or relics, the adequacy of reproductions, translations, and paraphrases, the accuracy of historical and statistical accounts, the corroboration of reported events, the completeness in the enumeration of circumstances in a concrete situation, the reproducibility of experiments, the explanatory or predictive value of generalizations.[39]

This statement implies that theory should be subject to a logical or empirical testing to verify its accuracy. If the theory is mathematically based, the verification should be predicted based on logical consistency. If the theory is based on physical or social phenomena, the verification should be predicted based on logical consistency. If the theory is based on physical or social phenomena, the verification should be predicted based on the relationship between the deduced events and observations in the real world.[40]

Accounting theory, therefore, should be the result of both a process of theory construction and a process of theory verification. A given accounting theory should explain and predict accounting phenomena: when such phenomena occur, they should be regarded as verification of the theory. If a given theory is unable to produce the expected results, it is replaced by a "better" theory.[41] This well-accepted idea in the philosophy of science also applies to, and is accepted in, accounting, as shown by the following statement from the Committee on Accounting Theory and Verification:

Scientific theories provide certain "expectations" or "predictions" about phenomena and, when these expectations occur, they are said to "confirm" the theory. When unexpected results occur, they are considered to be anomalies which eventually require a modification of the theory or the construction of a new theory. The purpose of the new theory or the modified theory is to make the unexpected expected, to convert the anomalous occurrence into an expected and explained occurrence.[42]

To date, this line of thinking has not been strictly followed in accounting. Instead, two approaches have been used. In the traditional approach to accounting theory construction, accounting practice and verification are considered synonymous; in the new approaches to accounting theory construction, attempts are made to logically or empirically verify the theory. In this chapter, we will elaborate on the nature and contribution of the traditional approaches to accounting theory construction. Before we are introduced to the traditional approaches, however, we will examine the nature of an accounting theory and the methodologies adopted for the formulation of an accounting theory. The traditional approaches we will examine are the non-theoretical, pragmatic and authoritarian approach; the deductive approach; the inductive approach; the ethical approach; the sociological approach; the economic approach; and the eclectic approach.

4.3 The nature of an accounting theory

The primary objective of accounting theory is to provide a basis for the prediction and explanation of accounting behavior and events. We assume, as an article of faith, that an accounting theory is possible. A theory is defined as "a set of interrelated constructs (concepts), definitions, and propositions that present a systematic view of phenomena by specifying relations among variables with the purpose of explaining and predicting the phenomena".[43]

It must be recognized at the outset that no comprehensive theory of accounting exists at the present time. Instead, different theories have been and continue to be proposed in the literature. Many of these theories arise from the use of different approaches to the construction of an accounting theory or from the attempt to develop theories of a middle range, rather than one single comprehensive theory. Accounting theories of a middle range result from differences in the way researchers perceive both the "users" of accounting data and the "environments" in which the users and preparers of accounting data are supposed to behave. These divergences led the American Accounting Association's Committee on Concepts and Standards (or External Financial Reports) to conclude that:

1. No single governing theory of financial accounting is rich enough to encompass the full range of user-environment specifications effectively; hence,

2. There exists in the financial accounting literature not a theory of financial accounting but a *collection of theories* which can be arrayed over the differences in user environment specifications.[44]

Despite the presence of accounting theories of a middle range, few authors of these theories have attempted to prove that an accounting theory is possible. Two exceptions deserve our attention.

E.S. Hendriksen used a definition of "theory" that may be applied to accounting. According to *Webster's Third New International Dictionary*, "theory" represents "the coherent set of hypothetical, conceptual, and pragmatic principles forming the general frame of reference for a field of inquiry". Hendriksen therefore defines *accounting theory* as "a set of broad principles that (1) provides a general frame of reference by which accounting practice can be evaluated and (2) guides the development of new practices and procedures".[45] This definition allows us to perceive accounting theory as providing a coherent set of logically derived principles that serve as a frame of reference for evaluating and developing accounting practices.

McDonald argues that a theory must have three elements: (1) encoding of phenomena to symbolic representation, (2) manipulation or combination according to rules, and (3) translation back to real-world phenomena.[46] Each of these theory components is found in accounting. First, accounting employs symbolic representations or symbols; "debit", "credit", and a whole terminology are proper and unique to accounting. Second, accounting employs translation rules; encoding (symbolic representations of economic events and transactions) is a process of translation into and out of symbols. Third, accounting employs rules of manipulation; techniques for the determination of profit may be considered as rules for the manipulation of accounting symbols.

4.4 Methodologies for the formulation of an accounting theory

We have now established that an accounting theory is possible if (1) it constitutes a frame of reference, as suggested by Hendriksen, and (2) it includes three elements: encoding of phenomena to symbolic representation; manipulation or combination according to rules; and translation back to real-world phenomena, as suggested by McDonald.

As in any other discipline, a methodology is required for the formulation of an accounting theory. The divergence of opinions, approaches, and values between accounting practice and accounting research has led to the use of two methodologies. One is descriptive, the other normative.

In the professional world of accounting, the belief is widely held that accounting is an art that cannot be formalized and that the methodology traditionally used in the formulation of an accounting theory is an attempt to justify *what is* by codifying accounting practices. Such a theory is labeled *descriptive accounting* or a *descriptive theory of accounting*.[47]

The descriptive accounting approach has been criticized by proponents of a normative methodology. Normative accounting theory attempts to justify what ought to be, rather than what is. Such a theory is *labeled normative accounting* or a *normative theory of accounting*.[48]

At the risk of oversimplifying, we may assume that, given the complex nature of accounting phenomena and issues, both methodologies may be needed to formulate an accounting theory. The descriptive methodology will attempt to justify some of the accounting practices that are deemed useful, and the normative methodology will attempt to justify some of the accounting practices that ought to be adopted. Among the descriptive theories of accounting are Grady's "Inventory of Generally Accepted Accounting Principles for Business Enterprises", Accounting Principles Board Statement No. 4, and the works of Skinner and Ijiri.[49] Ijiri's book differs from the other attempts to formulate a theory, in that it is not only a descriptive but also an analytic examination of accounting through (1) a mathematical inquiry to examine the logical structure, (2) an economic inquiry to examine what is measured, and (3) a behavioral inquiry to examine how accounting is practiced and used. A distinction is made between two different orientations. One, called *operational accounting*, is aimed at providing useful information for management and investor decisions, especially decisions concerning resource allocation;

the other, called *equity accounting*, is aimed at reconciling the equity of shareholders and other interested parties inside or outside an organization to achieve an equitable distribution of the proceeds or benefits from operations.

Among the normative theories of accounting are the studies by Moonitz, Sprouse and Moonitz, the American Accounting Association's *A Statement of Basic Accounting Theory*, the theory of Edwards and Bell, and the Chambers study.[50] A good review of the descriptive and normative methodologies and of the resulting theories is provided by McDonald and the American Accounting Association's *Statement on Accounting Theory and Theory Acceptance*.[51]

4.5 Approaches to the formulation of an accounting theory

Although there is no single comprehensive theory of accounting, various accounting theories of a middle range have resulted from the use of different approaches. For the sake of clarity, we will limit our discussion in this chapter to the traditional approaches to the formulation of an accounting theory. The traditional approaches are:

1. nontheoretical, practical, or pragmatic (informal);
2. theoretical:

   (a) deductive;
   (b) inductive;
   (c) ethical;
   (d) sociological;
   (e) economic;
   (f) eclectic.

We will examine each of these approaches in the following sections.

4.5.1 Nontheoretical approaches

The nontheoretical approaches are a *pragmatic* (or practical) approach and an *authoritarian* approach.

The *pragmatic approach* consists of the construction of a theory characterized by its conformity to real-world practices that is useful in terms of suggesting practical solutions. According to this approach, accounting techniques and principles should be chosen on the basis of their usefulness to users of accounting information and their relevance to the decision-making process. *Usefulness*, or *utility*, means "that property which fits something to serve or to facilitate its intended purposes".[52]

The *authoritarian approach* to the formulation of an accounting theory, which is employed primarily by professional organizations, consists of issuing pronouncements for the regulation of accounting practices.

Because the authoritarian approach also attempts to provide practical solutions, it is easily identified with the pragmatic approach. Both approaches assume that accounting theory and the resulting accounting techniques must be predicated on the basis of the ultimate uses of financial reports, if accounting is to have a useful function. In other words, a theory without practical consequences is a bad theory.[53]

The use of utility as a criterion for the choice of accounting principles links accounting theory construction to accounting practices, which may explain the lack of enthusiasm generated by the pragmatic approach. In fact, the pragmatic and authoritarian approaches have been largely unsuccessful in reaching satisfactory conclusions in their attempts to construct an accounting theory. For instance, Skinner claims that:

> In essence, the pragmatic approach to the development of accounting principles has been followed by accounting authority in the past, and attempts to reduce conflicting practices have until recently been extremely cautious and tentative. It is apparent on the basis of experience that this approach will never, by itself, come close to solving the problem of conflicts in accepted accounting principles.[54]

Utility is cited as a main objective of accounting by various writers in the literature, including Fremgen and Prince.[55] Mueller also argues that accounting principles should be developed through a pragmatic approach.[56] The practical attempts should not be discarded simply because they are basically nontheoretical. Practical approaches are necessary to any theory with an operational utility. In fact, pragmatic considerations permeate the field of accounting through the generally accepted standard of relevance.[57]

We may also think of the pragmatic approach as including a *theory of accounts*. The approach, which rests on a rationalization of double-entry bookkeeping, was contained in Luca Pacioli's *Summa De Arithmetica, Geometria, Proportioni et Proportionalita*, published in Venice in 1494. Although the *Summa* was a review of the literature of the then-current mathematical technology, it included 36 short chapters on bookkeeping, called *De Computis et Scripturis* (Of Reckonings and Writings).[58]

The theory of accounts approach rationalizes the choice of accounting techniques on the basis of the maintenance of the accounting equations, namely the balance sheet equation and the accounting profit equation.

The balance sheet equation is usually stated as:

Assets = Liabilities + Owner's Equity
The accounting profit equation is usually stated as:
Accounting Profit = Revenues – Costs

These two equations in the theory of accounts approach led to the development of two positions within the standard-setting bodies, namely, a balance-sheet-oriented position and a profit-oriented position. In any case, the theory of accounts approach, like the pragmatic and authoritarian approaches, suffers from the absence of theoretical foundation.

4.5.2 Deductive approach

The deductive approach to the construction of any theory begins with basic propositions and proceeds to derive logical conclusions about the subject under consideration. Applied to accounting, the deductive approach begins with basic accounting propositions or premises and proceeds to derive by logical means accounting principles that serve as guides and bases for the development of accounting techniques. This approach moves from the general (basic propositions about the accounting environment) to the particular (accounting principles first and accounting techniques second). If we assume at this point that the basic propositions about the accounting environment consist of both objectives and postulates, the steps used to derive the deductive approach will include:

1. specifying the objectives of financial statements;
2. selecting the "postulates" of accounting;
3. deriving the "principles" of accounting;
4. developing the "techniques" of accounting.

In a deductively derived accounting theory, therefore, the techniques are related to the principles, postulates, and objectives in such a way that if they are true, the techniques must also be true. The theoretical structure of accounting defined by the sequence of objectives, postulates, principles, and techniques rest on a proper formulation of the objectives of accounting. A proper testing of the resulting theory is also necessary. According to Popper, the testing of deductive theories could be carried out along four lines:

> First, there is the logical comparison of the conclusions among themselves, by which the internal consistency of the system is tested. Secondly, there is the investigation of the logical form of the theory with the object of determining whether it has the character of an empirical or scientific theory, or whether it is, for example, tautological. Thirdly, there is the comparison with other theories, chiefly with the aim of determining whether the theory would constitute a scientific advance should it survive our various tests, and finally, there is the testing of the theory by way of empirical applications of the conclusions which can be derived from it.[59]

The last step is necessary to determine how the theory stands up to the demands of practice. If its predictions are acceptable, then the theory is said to be *verified* or *corroborated* for the time being. If the predictions are not acceptable, then the theory is said to be *falsified.*

Although they do not necessarily adopt the same steps that we have defined for the deductive process, some accounting writers who have dealt primarily with the conceptual underpinnings of accounting may be categorized as "deductive theorists". Such writers as Paton, Canning, Sweeney, MacNeal, Alexander, Edwards and Bell, Moonitz, and Sprouse and Moonitz[60] are deductive theorists. In addition to them, research writers unanimously agree that users should use current price information in their resource allocation decisions. In fact, the search for rigor in the formalization of the structure of accounting theory has led some deductive theorists to resort to the *axiomatic method* found in the writings of Mattessich and Chambers, which involves mathematical, analytic representations and testing.[61]

4.5.3 Inductive approach

The inductive approach to the construction of a theory begins with observations and measurements and moves toward generalized conclusions. Applied to accounting, the inductive approach begins with observations about the financial information of business enterprises and proceeds to construct generalizations and principles of accounting from these observations on the basis of recurring relationships. Inductive arguments are said to lead from the *particular* (accounting information depicting recurring relationships) to the *general* (postulates and principles of accounting). The inductive approach to a theory involves four stages:

1. recording all observations;
2. analysis and classification of these observations to detect recurring relationships ("likes" and "similarities");
3. inductive derivation of generalizations and principles of accounting from observations that depict recurring relationships;
4. testing the generalizations.

Unlike the deductive approach, the truth or falsity of the propositions does not depend on other propositions, but must be empirically verified. In induction, the truth of the propositions depends on the observation of sufficient instances of recurring relationships.

Similarly, we may state that accounting propositions that result from inductive inference imply special accounting techniques only with more or less high probability, whereas the accounting propositions that result from deductive inference lead to specific accounting techniques with certainty.

Some accounting theorists rely on observations of accounting practice to suggest a theoretical framework for accounting. Inductive theorists include Hatfield, Gilman, Littleton, Paton and Littleton, and Ijiri.[62] The understanding objective of most of these authors is to draw theoretical and abstract conclusions from rationalizations of accounting practice. The best defense of the inductive approach is provided by Ijiri in his attempts to generalize the goals implicit in current accounting practice, and to defend the use of historical cost:

> This type of inductive reasoning to derive goals implicit in the behavior of an existing system is not intended to be pro-establishment to promote the maintenance of the status quo. The purpose of such exercise is to highlight where changes are most needed and where they are feasible. Changes suggested as a result of such a study have a much better chance of being actually implemented. Good assumptions in normative models or goals advocated in policy discussions are often stated purely on the basis of one's conviction and preference, rather than on the basis of inductive study of the existing system. This may perhaps be the most crucial reason why so many normative models or policy proposals are not implemented in the real world.[63]

It is interesting to note that although the deductive approach starts with general propositions, the formulation of the propositions is often accomplished by inductive reasoning, conditioned by the author's knowledge of, and experience with, accounting practice. In other words, the general propositions are formulated through an inductive process, but the principles and techniques are derived by a deductive process. Yu suggests that inductive logic may presuppose deductive logic.[64] It is not surprising, therefore, that inductive theorists sometimes interpose deductive reasoning and that deductive theorists sometimes interpose inductive reasoning. It is also interesting to note that when Littleton, an inductive theorist, and Paton, a deductive theorist, collaborate, the results are of a hybrid nature, indicating a compromise between the two approaches.

4.5.4 Ethical approach

The basic core of the ethical approach consists of the concepts of fairness, justice, equity, and truth. Such concepts are D.R. Scott's main criteria for the formulation of an accounting theory.[65] Scott equates "justice" with equitable treatment of all interested parties, "truth" with true and accurate accounting statements without misrepresentation, and "fairness" with fair, unbiased, and impartial presentation. Accountants since Scott have considered these three concepts to be equivalent. Yu, in contrast, perceives only justice and fairness as ethical norms and views truth as a value statement.[66] The "fairness" concept has become implicitly ethical; in general, the "fairness" concept implies that accounting statements have not been subject to undue influence or bias. "Fairness" generally implies that the preparers of accounting information have acted in good faith and employed ethical business practices and sound accounting judgment. "Fairness" is a value statement that is variously applied in accounting. Patillo ranks "fairness" as a basic standard to be used in the evaluation of other standards, because it is the only standard that implies "ethical considerations".[67] Spacek goes one step further in asserting the primacy of the "fairness" concept:

> A discussion of assets, liabilities, revenue, and costs is premature and meaningless until the basic principles that will result in a fair presentation of the facts in the form

of financial accounting and financial reporting are determined. This fairness of accounting and reporting must be for and to people, and these people represent the various segments of our society.[68]

Whatever it may connote, fairness has become one of the basic objectives of accounting. The Committee on Auditing Procedures refers to the criteria of "fairness of presentation" as (1) conformity with generally accepted accounting principles, (2) disclosure, (3) consistency, and (4) comparability.[69] In an unqualified report, the auditor not only states compliance with generally accepted accounting principles and generally accepted auditing standards but also expresses an opinion with the words "present fairly". Thus, the conventional auditor's report reads as follows:

> We have examined the consolidated balance sheet of XYZ, as of June 30, 1998, and consolidated statements of income, retained earnings, and changes in financial position for the year then ended. Our examination was made in accordance with generally accepted auditing standards, and accordingly, included such tests and other procedures as we consider necessary in the circumstances.
>
> In our opinion, these consolidated financial statements present fairly the financial position of the company as of June 30, 1998, and the results of its operations and the changes in financial position for the year then ended in accordance with generally accepted accounting principles applied on a basis consistent with that of the preceding year.

On close examination of this standard auditor's report, we see that the statement "present fairly" is included in addition to the auditor's expressed compliance with generally accepted accounting principles and generally accepted auditing standards. This may be seen as psychologically desirable, because it may increase the user's confidence. On the other hand, it may imply a double standard, because the concept of "fairness" is substituted for the tests of generally accepted accounting principles and generally accepted auditing standards.

"Fairness" is a desirable objective in the construction of an accounting theory if whatever is asserted on its basis is logically or empirically verified and if it is made operational by an adequate definition and identification of its properties.

4.5.5 Sociological approach

The sociological approach to the formulation of an accounting theory emphasizes the social effects of accounting techniques. It is an ethical approach that centers on a broader concept of fairness, *social welfare*. According to the sociological approach, a given accounting principle or technique is evaluated for acceptance on the basis of its reporting effects on all groups in society. Also implicit in this approach is the expectation that accounting data will be useful in making social welfare judgments. To accomplish its objectives, the sociological approach assumes the existence of "established social values" that may be used as criteria for the determination of accounting theory.[70] It may be difficult to identify a strict application of the sociological approach to accounting theory construction, due to the problems associated with determining acceptable "social values" for all people and with identifying the information needs of those who make welfare judgments. We may, however, identify cases in which accounting is expected to serve a useful social role. Belkaoui and Beams and Fertig,[71] among others, refer to the necessity of "internalizing" the social costs and social benefits of the private activities of the business firm. Ladd and Littleton and Zimmerman[72] make several assertions that accounting should serve the public interest and evolve in anticipation of public inputs, minority viewpoints, and even disagreements among groups. Bedford goes one step further by arguing that the maximization of social well-being is related to a measure of income determination that is best for society. Bedford says the measurement of operational income:

> … plays the role of a lubricant, facilitating the functioning of society in an operational sense. Specifically, measured income is used as a computed amount to accomplish objectives necessary for the operation of society.[73]

The sociological approach to the formulation of an accounting theory has contributed to the evolution of a new accounting subdiscipline, known as *socioeconomic accounting*. The main objective of socioeconomic accounting is to encourage the business entities that function in a free-market system to account for the impact of their private production activities on the social environment through measurement, internalization, and disclosure in their financial statements. Over the years, interest in this subdiscipline has increased as a result of the social responsibility trend espoused by organizations, the government, and the public. Social-value-oriented accounting – with its emphasis on "social measurement", its dependence on "social values", and its compliance to a "social-welfare criterion" – will probably play a major role in the future formulation of accounting theory.

4.5.6 Economic approach

The economic approach to the formulation of an accounting theory emphasizes controlling the behavior of macroeconomic indicators that result from the adoption of various accounting techniques. While the ethical approach focuses on a concept of "fairness" and the sociological approach on a concept of "social welfare", the economic approach focuses on a concept of "general economic welfare". According to the approach, the choice of different accounting techniques depends on their impact on the national economic good. Sweden is the usual example of a country that aligns its accounting policies with other macroeconomic policies.[74] More explicitly, the choice of accounting techniques will depend on the particular economic situation. For example, the last in, first out (LIFO) method will be a more attractive accounting technique during periods of continuing inflation than the first in, first out (FIFO) or average cost methods, because LIFO is assumed to produce a lower annual net income by assuming higher, more inflated costs for the goods sold.

The general criteria employed in the macroeconomic approach are firstly, that accounting policies and techniques should reflect "economic reality"[75] and secondly, that the choice of accounting techniques should depend on "economic consequences".[76] "Economic reality" and "economic consequences" are the precise terms being used to argue in favor of the macroeconomic approach.

Until the advent of the Financial Accounting Standards Board, the economic approach and the concept of "economic consequences" were not much used in accounting. The professional bodies were encouraged to resolve any standard-setting controversies within the context of traditional accounting. Few people were concerned with the economic consequences of accounting policies. In one case, the accounting treatment of the investment tax credit generated a debate among the Accounting Principles Board, the industry representative, and the administrations of Presidents Kennedy, Johnson, and Nixon. The government contested the use of the deferral method on the basis that it diluted the incentive effect of an instrument of fiscal policy.[77]

The economic approach and the concepts of "economic consequences" and "economic reality" have been revived since the creation of the Financial Accounting Standards

Board.[78] Most of the questions examined during the short life of the Board have been the subject of a critical examination in terms of the economic consequences of possible recommendations. Some examples are accounting for research and development, self-insurance and catastrophe reserves, development-stage companies, foreign currency fluctuations, leases, the restructuring of troubled debt, inflation accounting and accounting in the petroleum industry.

In setting accounting standards, therefore, the considerations implied by the economic approach are more economic than operational. Although reliance has been on technical accounting considerations in the past, the tenor of the times suggests that standard-setting encompasses social and economic concerns as well. Economic consequence of financial reporting include, among others, (1) wealth distribution, (2) the aggregate level of risk and allocation of risk among individuals, (3) the aggregate consumption and production, (4) the allocation of resources among firms, (5) the use of resources devoted to the production, certification, dissemination, processing, analysis and interpretation of financial information, (6) the use of resources in the development, compliance, enforcement, and litigation of regulations, and (7) the use of resources in the private-sector search for information.[79]

4.6 The eclectic approach to the formulation of an accounting theory

In general, the formulation of an accounting theory and the development of accounting principles have followed an eclectic approach, or a combination of approaches, rather than only one of the approaches presented here. The eclectic approach is mainly the result of numerous attempts by individuals and professional and governmental organizations to participate in the establishment of concepts and principles in accounting. This eclectic approach has given rise to the new approaches being debated in the literature: the regulatory approaches, the behavioral approaches, and the event, predictive, and positive approaches.

4.7 Conclusions

The traditional approach to the formulation of an accounting theory has employed either a normative or a descriptive methodology, a theoretical or a nontheoretical approach, a deductive or an inductive line of reasoning, and has focused on a concept of "fairness", "social welfare", or "economic welfare". The traditional approach has evolved into an eclectic approach and is beginning to be replaced by newer approaches. Whatever approach is chosen, it is important to remember that an accounting theory must be confirmed to be accepted.

Notes

1. Accounting Terminology Bulletin No. 1, *Review and Resume* (New York: American Institute of Certified Public Accountants, 1953), paragraph 9.
2. APB Statement No. 4, *Basic Concepts and Accounting Principles Underlying Financial Statements of Business Enterprises* (New York: American Institute of Certified Public Accountants, 1970), paragraph 40.
3. *The Handbook of Accounting* (Fifth Edition) (New York: American Institute of Certified Public Accountants, 1970), paragraph 9.

4. Davis, S.W, Menon, K., and Morgan, G., "The Images That Have Shaped Accounting Theory", *Accounting, Organizations and Society* (December, 1982), pp. 307–18.

5. Shaw, M., "The Coming Crisis of Radical Sociology", in R. Blackburn (ed.), *Ideology in Social Science* (New York: Fontana, 1972), p. 33.

6. Burchell, S., Clubb, C., Hopwood, A., Hughes, J., and Nahapier, J., "The Roles of Accounting in Organizations and Society", *Accounting, Organizations and Society* (June, 1980), p. 19.

7. Weber, M., *Economy and Society*, Vol. I (New York: Bedminster Press, 1969), p. 85.

8. Heilbroner, R.L., *Business Civilization in Decline* (New York: Penguin Books, 1977). pp. 123–4.

9. Ijiri, Yuji, Accounting Research Study No. 10, "Theory of Accounting Measurement" (Sarasota, FL: American Accounting Association, 1975), p. 14.

10. Hawes, L.C., *Pragmatics of Analoging* (Reading, MA: Addison-Wesley, 1972).

11. McDonald, Daniel L., *Comparative Accounting Theory* (Reading, MA: Addison-Wesley 1972).

12. Jain, Tribhowan N., "Alternative Methods of Accounting and Decision Making: A Psycholinguistic Analysis", *The Accounting Review* (January, 1973), p. 101.

13. Birnberg, J.G., "The Role of Accounting in Financial Disclosure", *Accounting, Organizations and Society* (June, 1980), p. 73.

14. Ibid., p. 74.

15. Chambers, R.J., *Accounting, Evaluation, and Economic Behavior* (Houston, TX: Scholars Book Company, 1974), p. 184.

16. Davis, S.W., Menon, K., and Morgan, G., "The Images That Have Shaped Accounting Theory", op. cit., p. 312.

17. Ibid., p. 313.

18. Feldman, Martha S., and March, James G., "Information in Organizations as Signal and Symbol", *Administrative Science Quarterly* (June, 1981), pp. 177–8.

19. Seed, Alan H. III, "The Rational Abuse of Accounting Information", *Management Accounting* (June, 1970), pp. 9–11; Trevor Gambling, *Societal Accounting* (London: Allen & Unwin, 1974).

20. Cleverly, Graham, *Managers and Magic* (Harmondsworth, Middlesex, England: Pelican, 1973).

21. Gambling, Trevor, "Magic, Accounting, and Morale", *Accounting, Organizations and Society* (Fall ,1977), p. 150.

22. Haines, G.J., Jr., "A Comment on Three Papers in The Effects of Information on Market Behavior", Working Paper (Toronto: University of Toronto, 1977).

23. Thornton, Daniel B., "Information and Institutions in the Capital Market", *Accounting, Organizations and Society* (February, 1980), p. 212.

24. Burchell *et al.*, "The Roles of Accounting in Organizations and Society," p. 7.

25. Thompson, J.D., and Tuden, A.A., "Strategies, Structures, and Processes of Organizational Decision", in J.D. Thompson *et al.* (eds.), *Comparative Studies in Administration* (Pittsburgh: University of Pittsburgh Press, 1959); Burchell *et al.*, "The Roles of Accounting in Organizations and Society", p. 14.

26. Burchell *et al.*, "The Roles of Accounting in Organizations and Society", p. 5.

27. Haines, "Accounting for Accounting", p. 246.

28. Solomons, David, "The Politicization of Accounting", *Journal of Accounting* (November, 1978), pp. 65–72.

29. Ibid., p. 71.

30. Boland, L.A., and Newman, G., *On the Role of Knowledge in Economic Theory*, Discussion Paper 76–5–2 (Vancouver, BC: Simon Fraser University, 1976).

31. Thornton, "Information and Institutions in the Capital Market", p. 213.

32. Green, D., Jr., "Evaluating the Accounting Literature", *Accounting Review* (January, 1978), p. 31.

33. Gonedes, N.J., "Corporate Signaling, External Accounting, and Capital Market Equilibrium: Evidence on Dividends, Income, and Extraordinary Items", *Journal of Accounting Research* (Spring, 1978), p. 31.

34. Shannon, C.E., and Weaver, W., *The Mathematical Theory of Communications* (Urbana: University of Illinois Press, 1949).

35. Birnberg, Jacob G., Turopolic, Lawrence, and Young, S. Mark, "The Organizational Context of Accounting", *Accounting, Organizations and Society* (July, 1983), p. 120.

36. Bariff, M.L., and Galbraith, J.R., "Interorganizational Power Considerations for Designing Information Systems", *Accounting, Organizations and Society* (Fall, 1978), p. 15.

37. Markus, M.L., and Pfeffer, J., "Power and the Design and Implementation of Accounting and Control Systems", *Accounting, Organizations and Society* (July, 1983), p. 105.

38. APB Statement No. 4, paragraphs 208 and 209.

39. Fritz, Machlup, "The Problem of Verification in Economics", *The Southern Economic Journal* (July, 1955), p. 1.

40. "Report of the Committee on Accounting Theory Construction and Verification", *The Accounting Review*, supplement to Vol. 46 (1971), p. 54.

41. Kuhn, Thomas S., "Anomaly and the Emergence of Scientific Discoveries", *The Structure of Scientific Revolution* (Chicago: University of Chicago Press, 1962), pp. 52–65.

42. "Report of the Committee on Accounting Theory Construction and Verification", op. cit., p. 53.

43. Kerlinger, F.N., *Foundations of Behavioral Research* (New York: Holt, Rinehart & Winston, 1964), p. 11.

44. *Statement of Accounting Theory and Theory Acceptance* (Sarasota, FL: American Accounting Association, 1977), pp. 1–2.

45. Hendriksen, E.S., *Accounting Theory*, 3rd edn (Homewood, IL: Richard D. Irwin, 1977), p. 1.

46. McDonald, Daniel L., *Comparative Accounting Theory*, op. cit., pp. 5–8.

47. Ibid., p. 8.

48. Ibid., p. 8.

49. Grady, Paul, Accounting Research Study No. 7, *Inventory of Generally Accepted Accounting Principles for Business Enterprises* (New York: American Institute of Certified Public Accountants, 1965); Skinner, R.M., *Accounting Principles: A Canadian Study* (Toronto: Canadian Institute of Chartered Accountants, 1973); Ijiri, Yuji, *The Foundations of Accounting Measurement: A Mathematical, Economic, and Behavioral Inquiry* (Englewood Cliffs, NJ: Prentice-Hall, 1967).

50. Moonitz, Maurice, *The Basic Postulates of Accounting* (New York: American Institute of Certified Public Accountants, 1961); Sprouse, R.T., and Moonitz, Maurice, Accounting Research Study No. 3, *A Tentative Set of Broad Basic Accounting Principles for Business Enterprises* (New York: American Institute of Certified Public Accountants, 1962); *A Statement of Basic Accounting Theory* (Evanston, IL: American Accounting Association, 1966); Edwards, E.O., and Bell, P.W., *The Theory and Measurement of Business Income* (Berkeley: University of California Press, 1961); Chambers, R.J., *Accounting, Evaluation, and Economic Behavior*, op. cit.

51. McDonald, Daniel L., *Comparative Accounting Theory: Statement of Accounting Theory and Theory Acceptance*, op. cit.

52. Fremgen, James M., "Utility and Accounting Principles", *The Accounting Review* (July, 1967), pp. 457–67.

53. Hendriksen, E.S., *Accounting Theory*, op. cit., p. 23.

54. Skinner, R.M., *Accounting Principles*, op. cit., p. 302.

55. Fremgen, James M., "Utility and Accounting Principles", op. cit.; Prince, T.R., *Extension of the Boundaries of Accounting Theory* (Cincinnati, OH: South-Western, 1973).

56. Mueller, Gerhard G., *International Accounting* (New York: Macmillan, 1967), pp. 27–30.

57. *A Statement of Basic Accounting Theory*, p. 9.

58. Geijsbeek, J.B., *Ancient Double-Entry Bookkeeping: Luca Pacioli's Treatise* (Denver: University of Colorado, 1914).

59. Popper, K.R., *The Logic of Scientific Discovery* (London: Hutchinson, 1959), p. 33.

60. Paton, W.A., *Accounting Theory* (New York: The Ronald Press, 1922); Canning, J.B., *Tax Economics of Accountancy* (New York: The Ronald Press, 1923); Sweeney, Henry W., *Stabilized Accounting* (New York: Hayer & Brothers, 1936); MacNeal, Kenneth, *Truth in Accounting* (Philadelphia: University of Pennsylvania Press, 1939); Alexander, Sidney S., "Income Measurement in a Dynamic Economy", *Five Monographs of Business Income* (New York: American Institute of Certified Public Accountants, 1950); Edwards, E.O., and Bell, P.W., *The Theory and Measurement of Business Income*; Moonitz, Maurice, *The Basic Postulates of Accounting*; Sprouse, R.T., and Moonitz, Maurice, "A Tentative Set of Broad Basic Accounting Principles for Business Enterprises", op. cit.

61. Mattessich, R., *Accounting and Analytical Methods* (Homewood, IL: Richard D. Irwin, 1964); Chambers, R.J., *Accounting, Evaluation, and Economic Behavior*, op. cit.

62. Hatfield, H.R., *Accounting* (New York: D. Appleton & Company, 1927); Gilman, S., *Accounting Concepts of Profit* (New York: The Ronald Press, 1939); Littleton, A.C., "Structure of Accounting Theory", *Monograph No. 5* (Evanston, IL: American Accounting Association, 1953); Paton, W.A., and Littleton, A.C., "An Introduction to Corporate Accounting Standards", *Monograph No. 3* (Evanston IL: American Accounting Association, 1940); Ijiri, Yuji, "Theory of Accounting Measurement", *Studies in Accounting Research No. 10* (Evanston, IL: American Accounting Association, 1975).

63. Ijiri, Yuji, "Theory of Accounting Measurement", op. cit., p. 28.

64. Yu, S.C., *The Structure of Accounting Theory* (Gainesville: The University Presses of Florida, 1976), p. 20.

65. Scott, D.R., "The Basis for Accounting Principles", *The Accounting Review* (December, 1941), pp. 341–9.

66. Yu, S.C., *The Structure of Accounting Theory*, op. cit.

67. Patillo, James W., *The Foundations of Financial Accounting* (Baton Rouge: Louisiana State University Press, 1965), p. 11.

68. "Comments of Leonard Spacek", in R.T Sprouse and Maurice Moonitz, *Accounting Research Study* No. 3, "A Tentative Set of Broad Basic Accounting Principles for Business Enterprises" (New York: American Institute of Certified Public Accountants, 1962), p. 78.

69. Statement on Auditing Procedure No. 33, *Auditing Standards and Procedures* (New York: American Institute of Certified Public Accountants, 1963), pp. 69–74.

70. Rappaport, A., "Establishing Objectives for Published Corporate Accounting Reports", *The Accounting Review* (October, 1964), pp. 954–61.

71. Belkaoui, A., "The Whys and Wherefores of Measuring Externalities", *The Certified General Accountant* (January–February, 1975), pp. 29–32; Beams, Floyd A., and Fertig, Paul E., "Pollution Control Through Social Cost Conversion", *Journal of Accountancy* (November, 1971), pp. 37–42.

72. Ladd, D.R., *Contemporary Corporate Accounting and the Public* (Homewood, IL: Richard D. Irwin, 1963), p. ix; Littleton, A.C., and Zimmerman, V.K., *Accounting Theory: Continuity and Change* (New York: Prentice-Hall, 1962), pp. 261–2.

73. Brooks, L.L., Jr., "Accounting Policies Should Reflect Economic Reality", *The Canadian Chartered Accountant Magazine* (November, 1976), pp. 39–43.

74. Mueller, Gerhard G., *International Accounting*, op. cit., pp. 27–30.

75. Brooks, L.L., Jr., "Accounting Policies Should Reflect Economic Reality", *The Canadian Chartered Accountant Magazine* (November, 1976), pp. 39–43.

76. Zeff, A.S., "The Rise of 'Economic Consequences'", *Journal of Accountancy* (December, 1978), pp. 56–63.

77. Moonitz, Maurice, "Some Reflections on the Investment Credit Experience", *Journal of Accounting Research* (Spring, 1966), pp. 47–61.

78. Conference on the Economic Consequences of Financial Accounting Standards (Stamford, CT: Financial Accounting Standards Board, 1978).

79. Beaver, William H., *Financial Reporting – An Accounting Revolution* (Englewood Cliffs, NJ: Prentice-Hall, 1989), pp. 13–14.

References

Images of accounting

Belkaoui, A., "Linguistic Relativity in Accounting", *Accounting, Organizations and Society* (October, 1978), pp. 97–104.

Birnberg, J.G., "The Role of Accounting in Financial Disclosure", *Accounting, Organizations and Society* (June, 1980), pp. 71–80.

Buckley, J.W., "Policy Models in Accounting: A Critical Commentary", *Accounting, Organizations and Society* (June, 1980), pp. 49–64.

Burchell, S., Clubb, C., Hopwood, A., Hughes, J., and Napier, J., "The Roles of Accounting in Organizations and Society", *Accounting, Organizations and Society* (June, 1980), pp. 5–28.

Chambers, R.J., "The Myths and the Science of Accounting", *Accounting, Organizations and Society* (June, 1980), pp. 167–80.

Davis, S.W., Menon, K., and Morgan, G., "The Images That Have Shaped Accounting Theory", *Accounting, Organizations and Society* (December, 1982), pp. 307–18.

Jain, Tribhowan N., "Alternative Methods of Accounting and Decision Making: A Psycholinguistic Analysis", *The Accounting Review* (January, 1973), pp. 95–104.

Morgan, G., "Paradigms, Metaphors and Puzzle Solving in Organization Theory", *Administrative Science Quarterly* (Issue 3, 1980), pp. 605–22.

Theory construction and verification

American Accounting Association, "Report of the Committee on Foundations of Accounting Measurement", *The Accounting Review*, supplement to Vol. 46 (1971), pp. 37–45.

American Accounting Association, "Report of the Committee on Accounting Theory Construction and Verification", *The Accounting Review*, supplement to Vol. 46 (1971), pp. 53–79.

Buckley, J.W., Kircher, Paul, and Mathews, Russell L., "Methodology in Accounting Theory", *The Accounting Review* (April, 1968), pp. 274–83.

Gonedes, N.J., "Perception, Estimation, and Verifiability", *International Journal of Accounting Education and Research* (Spring, 1969), pp. 63–73.

McDonald, Daniel L., *Comparative Accounting Theory* (Reading, MA: Addison-Wesley, 1972).

Schrader, William J., and Malcolm, Robert E., "Note on Accounting Theory Construction and Verification", *Abacus* (June, 1973), pp. 93–8.

Sterling, Robert R., "An Explication and Analysis of the Structure of Accounting", Part 1, *Abacus* (December, 1971), pp. 137–52; Part 2. *Abacus* (December, 1972), pp. 145–62.

Sterling, Robert R., "On Theory Construction and Verification", *The Accounting Review* (July, 1970), pp. 444–57.

Nontheoretical approach

Beams, Floyd A., "Indications of Pragmation and Empiricism in Accounting Thought", *The Accounting Review* (April, 1968), pp. 382–97.

Cowan, T.K., "A Pragmatic Approach to Accounting Theory", *The Accounting Review* (January, 1968), pp. 94–100.

Fremgen, James M., "Utility and Accounting Principles", *The Accounting Review* (July, 1967), pp. 457–67.

Geijsbeek, J.B., *Ancient Double-Entry Bookkeeping: Luca Pacioli's Treatise* (Denver: University, Colorado, 1914).

Mueller, Gerhard G., "Accounting and Conventional Business Practices", *International Accounting* (New York: Macmillan, 1967), pp. 718–23.

Prince, R.T., *Extensions of the Boundaries of Accounting Theory* (Cincinnati, OH: South-Western 1963).

Deductive, inductive, and axiomatic approaches

Bedford, N.M., and Dopuch, N., "Research Methodology and Accounting Theory: Another Perspective", *The Accounting Review* (July, 1972), pp. 351–61.

Demski, Joel S., "The General Impossibility of Normative Accounting Standards", *The Accounting Review* (October, 1973), pp. 718–23.

Devine, C.T., "Research Methodology and Accounting Theory Formation", *The Accounting Review* (July, 1960), pp. 387–99.

Hakansson, Nils H., "Normative Accounting Theory and the Theory of Decision", *International Journal of Accounting Education and Research* (Spring, 1969), pp. 33–47.

Langenderfer, H.Q., "A Conceptual Framework for Financial Reporting", *Journal of Accountancy* (July, 1973), pp. 45–55.

Mattessich, R., *Accounting and Analytical Methods* (Homewood, IL: Richard D. Irwin, 1964).

Mattessich, R., "Methodological Preconditions and Problems of a General Theory of Accounting", *The Accounting Review* (July, 1972), pp. 469–87.

Moonitz, Maurice, "Why Do We Need 'Postulates' and 'Principles'?" *Journal of Accountancy* (December, 1963), pp. 42–6.

Pellicelli, Georgio, "The Axiomatic Method in Business Economics: A First Approach", *Abacus* (December, 1969), pp. 119–31.

Vernon, Kam, "Judgment and Scientific Trend in Accounting", *Journal of Accountancy* (February, 1973), pp. 57–67.

Ethical approach

Annett, Harold E., "The Concept of Fairness", *The Accounting Review* (April, 1967), pp. 291–7.

Burton, John C. (ed.), *Corporate Financial Reporting: Ethical and Other Problems* (New York: American Institute of Certified Public Accountants, 1972), pp. 17–27.

Patillo, James W., *The Foundation of Financial Accounting* (Baton Rouge: Louisiana State University Press, 1965).

Scott, D.R., "The Basis for Accounting Principles", *The Accounting Review* (December, 1941), pp. 341–9.

Spacek, Leonard, *A Search for Fairness in Financial Reporting to the Public* (Chicago, IL: Arthur Andersen & Co., 1965), pp. 38–77 and 349–56.

Sociological approach

Alexander, Michael O., "Social Accounting, If You Please!" *The Canadian Chartered Accountant Magazine* (January, 1973), pp. 23–7.

American Accounting Association, "Report of the Committee on Measures of Effectiveness for Social Programs", *The Accounting Review*, supplement to Vol. 47 (1972), pp. 337–98.

American Institute of Certified Public Accountants, *Social Measurement* (New York: American Institute of Certified Public Accountants, 1972).

Beams, Floyd, A., and Fertig, Paul E., "Pollution Control Through Social Cost Conversion", *Journal of Accountancy* (November, 19 71), pp. 37–42.

Belkaoui, A., "The Whys and Wherefores of Measuring Externalities", *The Certified General Accountant* (January–February, 1975), pp. 29–32.

Estes, Ralph W., "Socioeconomic Accounting and External Diseconomies", *The Accounting Review* (April, 1972), pp. 284–90.

Gambling, Trevor, *Societal Accounting* (London: George Allen & Unwin, 1974).

Ladd, D.R., *Contemporary Corporate Accounting and the Public* (Homewood, IL: Richard D. Irwin, 1963).

Mobley, Sybil C., "The Challenges of Socioeconomic Accounting", *The Accounting Review* (October, 1970), pp. 762–8.

Economic approach

Brooks, L.L., Jr., "Accounting Policies Should Reflect Economic Reality", *The Canadian Chartered Accountant Magazine* (November, 1976), pp. 39–43.

Enthoven, Adolf J.H., *Accountancy and Economic Development Policy* (New York: American Elsevier, 1973).

FASB Conference on the Economic Consequences of Financial Accounting Standards (Stamford, CT: Financial Accounting Standards Board, 1978).

Moonitz, Maurice, "Some Reflections on the Investment Credit Experience", *Journal of Accounting Research* (Spring, 1966), pp. 47–61.

Mueller, Gerhard G., "Accounting Within a Macroeconomic Framework", *International Accounting* (New York: Macmillan, 1967), pp. 27–30.

Zeff, A.S., "The Rise of 'Economic Consequences'", *Journal of Accountancy* (December, 1978), pp. 56–63.

The regulatory approach to the formulation of an accounting theory

5

Accounting has been generally slighted in literature. As stated by Henry Rand Hatfield:

> The public eye has generally, both in history and in fiction, been turned on the man on horseback, but nevertheless at times there comes upon the stage a more prosaic figure. Great masterpieces have grouped themselves about a scholar as Faust, about a carpenter as Adam Bede, about a manufacturer as in *Les Miserables*, about a sailor as Robinson Crusoe, about courtesans, thieves and beggars beyond recital. Even a horse and a dog have been made the heroes in *Black Beauty* and in *Rab and his Friends*. But never, so far as I recollect, has a bookkeeper been made the hero of novel, play or poem. The bookkeeper is not even honored by being made a noteworthy villain.[1]

This may be due to the ignorance of the role of accounting standards in creating an accounting order and thereby a social and economic order.

The establishment and enforcement of standards is an important problem to the accounting profession and to interested users. Determining the best mechanism to employ in establishing uniform accounting standards may be essential to the acceptability and usefulness of accounting standards. Should the free-market approach, the private-sector approach, or the public-sector approach be employed? First, however, the chapter explicates the nature of accounting standards, determines the entities concerned with accounting standards, and traces the development of accounting principles. In conclusion, the chapter elaborates on the legitimacy of the standard-setting process as well as the standards-overload problem.

5.1 The nature of accounting standards

Accounting standards dominate the accountant's work. These standards are being constantly changed, deleted, and/or added to, both in the United States and abroad. They provide practical and handy rules for the conduct of the accountant's work. They are generally accepted as firm rules, backed by sanctions for nonconformity. Accounting standards usually consist of three parts:

1. a description of the problem to be tackled;
2. a reasoned discussion (possibly exploring fundamental theory) or ways of solving the problem;
3. then, in line with decision or theory, the prescribed solution.[2]

In general, standards, especially auditing standards, have been restricted to point 3, which has generated a lot of controversy about the absence of supporting theories and the use of an ad hoc formulating approach. The general trend, however, is to include points 1 and 2, thereby providing a concise, theoretically supported rule of action. In considering the subject matter of standards, Edey divides requirements under standards into four main types:[3]

1. *Type 1* states that accountants must tell people what they are doing by disclosing the methods and assumptions (accounting policies) they have adopted.
2. *Type 2* aims at achieving some uniformity of presentation of accounting statements.
3. *Type 3* calls for the disclosure of specific matters in which the user may be called to exercise his or her own judgment.
4. *Type 4* requires implicit or explicit decisions to be made about approved asset valuation and income determination.[4]

Are standards of Type 4 – first, based on broad, debated principles and on a comparison of the pros and cons of rival theories, and second, selected on that basis by an authority (a standard-setting body) – possible? A lot of people will express serious doubt. In any case, all these types of standards continue to be promulgated. Some good reasons to establish standards are as follows:

1. They provide users of accounting information with information about the financial position, performance, and conduct of a firm. This information is assumed to be clear, consistent, reliable, and comparable.

2. They provide public accountants with guidelines and rules of action to enable them to exercise due care and independence in selling their expertise and integrity in auditing firms' reports and in attesting the validity of these reports.

3. They provide the government with databases on various variables that are deemed essential to the conduct of taxation, regulation of enterprises, planning and regulation of the economy and enhancement of economic efficiency and other social goals.

4. They generate interest in principles and theories among all those interested in the accounting disciplines. The mere promulgation of a standard generates a lot of controversy and debate both in practice and in academic circles, which is better than apathy.[5]

5.2 Goals of standard-setting

The enactment of a standard may benefit some and hurt others. It is a social choice. It forces the standard-setters to adopt a political process in order to find some accommodations. If any social welfare criteria are used to justify the enactment of a standard, then a serious question is raised about the legitimacy of any non-elected standard-setting body. The question then becomes to determine the right approach to accounting policy questions. Two approaches exist:

1. a representational faithfulness approach;
2. an economic consequences approach.

The first approach favors neutral reporting and the pursuit of faithful representations through the standard-setting process. Under such an approach, accounting is compared to financial map-making, where maps have to be accurate and faithful. The second approach favors the adoption of standards with good rather than bad economic consequences. Under such an approach, standards are enacted that have a positive, or at least nonnegative, impact on social welfare. The differences between the two approaches are best expressed as follows:

> If economic consequences are to be pursued, then accounting policy makers must provide information signals that will direct the decisions of information users. Pragmatically, this results in the policy makers acting as decision makers. If a user-oriented measurement objective is to be pursued, then accounting policy makers must provide information to facilitate users' decision making. Pragmatically, if the information provided is faithful and chosen based on user needs, it is the user that is acting as the decision maker.[6]

Another approach argues for the recognition of an explicit political economy of accounting. As stated by Cooper and Sherer:

Our position, that the objectives of and for accounting are fundamentally contested, arises out of the recognition that any accounting contains a representation of a specific social and political context. Not only is accounting policy essentially political in that it derives from the political struggle in society as a whole, but also the outcomes of accounting policy are essentially political in that they operate for the benefit of some groups in society and to the detriment of others. ... Social welfare is likely to be improved if accounting practices are recognized as being consistently partial; that the strategic outcomes of accounting practices consistently (if not invariably) favor specific interests in society and disadvantage others.[7]

This last approach, also known as the critical-interpretative approach, holds that financial reporting should be used as an instrument of social change, and even radical social change.

The difference between the three approaches, the representational faithfulness approach, the economic consequences approach and the critical-interpretative approach, arise from opposing normative commitments to financial reporting objectives. It may be argued that a consensus interpretation of epistemological objectivity and related principles of rationality make it possible to conduct a rational and objective debate about the merits of alternative financial reporting practices.[8] This consensus is represented in the form of five philosophical presuppositions of external financial reporting. They are shown in Exhibit 5.1. The first three presuppositions refer to the degree of correspondence between financial reporting schemes

---

P1. External realism (ontological objectivity and ontological subjectivity): External reality exists independently of the financial statements that attempt to represent it. Social phenomena are ontologically subjective but just as real as ontologically objective physical phenomena.

P2. Correspondence theory of truth (representational faithfulness): A financial representation is true if it corresponds (at least approximately) to the underlying economic reality that it purports to represent.

P3. Conceptual relativism of financial reporting schemes: All systems of representation, such as conceptual frameworks, are human creations and thus socially constructed. Different systems of representations can be used to represent the same reality, and one system may or may not be better than another. The objectives of financial reporting are based on nonnative values that cannot be verified or empirically validated.

P4. Subjective judgment (epistemological subjectivity): Accountants' judgments about what constitute valid descriptions of economic reality are influenced by many factors – cultural, economic, political, psychological, and so on. Absolute epistemological objectivity is not possible because all accounting judgments are made from a point of view, subject to various measurer and measurement biases, motivated by personal factors, and within a certain historical context.

P5. Commitment to rationalism (epistemological objectivity): Knowledge is epistemologically objective to the extent that a community can agree on the criteria for evaluating the justification or evidence for assertions. The idea that knowledge consists in having true representations for which we can give certain sorts of justification or evidence is the basis of Western rational science, the notion of due process in standard-setting, and the demand for attestation services. Absolute epistemological objectivity is rejected in favor of a pragmatic, intersubjective, and consensus view.

Source: Brian P. Shapiro, "Objectivity, Relativism, and Truth in External Financial Reporting: What's Really at Stake?", *Accounting, Organizations and Society* (22, 2, 1997), p. 167. Reprinted with permission.

Exhibit 5.1 Five presuppositions of external financial reporting

and the external reality that the schemes purport to represent, while the last two refer to the epistemological subjectivity and objectivity of accounting judgments, repectively.[9]

5.3 Entities concerned with accounting standards

5.3.1 Individual and public accounting firms

Individual and public accounting firms are responsible through their auditors for independently certifying that corporate financial statements present fairly and accurately the results of business activities.

Independent auditors are expected to be truly independent of the interests of their corporate clients. The work of public accounting firms consists principally of the performance of auditing, accounting, tax and management advisory services. The accounting and auditing services assist in the design of reliable record-keeping systems, check the systems periodically to ensure their effectiveness, prepare financial statements that convey accurate information and certify financial statements for accuracy.

5.3.2 The American Institute of Certified Public Accountants (AICPA)

The American Institute of Certified Public Accountants (AICPA) is the professional coordinating organization of practicing Certified Public Accountants in the United States. Its two important senior technical committees – the Accounting Standards Executive Committee (AcSEC) and the Auditing Standards Executive Committee (AudSEC) – are empowered to speak for the AICPA in the areas of financial and cost accounting, and auditing, respectively. These committees issue Statements of Position (SOPs) on accounting issues. These SOPs clarify and elaborate on controversial accounting issues and should be followed as guidelines if they do not contradict existing FASB pronouncements. Through its monthly publication, the *Journal of Accountancy*, the AICPA communicates with its members on controversial accounting problems and solutions. In fact, since its inception in 1937, its Committee on Accounting Procedures (CAP) has striven to "narrow the areas of difference in corporate reporting" by eliminating undesirable practices. Rather than developing a set of generally accepted accounting principles, the CAP adopted an ad hoc and pragmatic approach to controversial problems. Over a period of twenty years, through 1958, the CAP issued 51 Accounting Research Bulletins (ARBs) suggesting accounting treatments for various items and transactions. At the time, these Accounting Research Bulletins were supported by the Securities and Exchange Commission (SEC) and the stock exchanges, and consequently represented the only source of generally accepted accounting principles in the United States.

After the Second World War, the coexistence of many alternative accounting treatments, the new tax laws and financing techniques and complex capital structures, such as business combinations, leasing, convertible debts and investment tax credit, created the need for a new approach to the development of accounting principles. In 1959, the AICPA created a new body, the Accounting Principles Board (APB), "to advance the written expression of what constitutes generally accepted accounting principles". In addition, the AICPA appointed a director of accounting research and a permanent staff. Between 1959 and 1973, the APB issued opinions, intended to be used as guidelines for accounting practices unless superseded by FASB Statements. In addition to the opinions, the APB published four statements and a series of Accounting Interpretations intended to expand on the opinions or to communicate recommendations related to accounting problems. The statements are:

1. APB Statement No. 1, a report on the receipt of Accounting Research Studies No. 1 and No. 3.

2. APB Statement No. 2, *Disclosure of Supplementary Financial Information by Diversified Companies,* issued in September 1967.

3. APB Statement No. 3, *Financial Statements Restated for General Price-Level Changes*, issued in June 1969.

4. APB Statement No. 4, *Basic Concepts and Accounting Principles Underlying Financial Statements of Business Enterprises*, issued in October 1970.

To stimulate discussion of controversial topics before the APB acted on them, the Research Division of the AICPA commissioned research studies by independent investigators or by members of the research staff under the guidance of the director of research and an advisory committee. Accounting Research Study No. 1, entitled *The Basic Postulates of Accounting,* and Accounting Research Study No. 3, entitled *A Tentative Set of Broad Accounting Principles for Business Enterprises*, were published in 1961 and 1962, respectively. Maurice Moonitz and R.T. Sprouse[10] used a deductive approach in both studies. In the first study, the authors supported exit-value accounting; in the second study, they suggested that it might be necessary to account for both general and specific price-level changes. As might have been expected at the time, the AICPA rejected both studies, claiming that they were radically different from generally accepted accounting practices and therefore unacceptable. A new study was commissioned to review existing accounting principles. Thus, Accounting Research Study No. 7 by Paul Grady, entitled *Inventory of Generally Accepted Accounting Principles for Business Enterprises*, was nothing more than an inventory of existing accounting principles, practices and methods of the APB and the CAP (that is, APB and ARB's opinions). After the AICPA's rejection of Accounting Research Studies No. 1 and No. 3, the remaining studies reflected the assumptions and findings of the particular researcher who conducted the study. The APB opinions did not, in general, follow the recommendations of Accounting Research Studies No. 2 and No. 3. The other twelve Accounting Research Studies (ARS) are:

1. ARS No. 2, *Cash Flow Analysis and the Funds Statement*, by Perry Mason (1961).

2. ARS No. 4, *Reporting of Leases in Financial Statements*, by John H. Myers (1962).

3. ARS No. 5, *A Critical Study of Accounting for Business Combinations*, by Arthur B. Watt (1963).

4. ARS No. 6, *Reporting the Financial Effects of Price-Level Changes*, by the staff of the Research Division (1963).

5. ARS No. 8, *Accounting for the Cost of Pension Plans*, by Ernest L. Hicks (1966).

6. ARS No. 9, *Interperiod Allocation of Corporate Income Taxes*, by Howard A. Black (1966).

7. ARS No. 10, *Accounting for Goodwill*, by George R. Catlett and Norman O. Olson (1968).

8. ARS No. 11, *Financial Reporting in the Extractive Industries*, by Robert R. Field (1968).

9. ARS No. 12, *Reporting Foreign Operations of US Companies in US Dollars*, by Leonard Lorenson (1972).

10. ARS No. 13, *The Accounting Basis of Inventories*, by Horace G. Barden (1973).

11. ARS No. 14, *Accounting for R & D Expenditures*, by Oscar S. Gellein and Maurice S. Newman (1973).

12. ARS No. 15, *Stockholders' Equity*, by Beatrice Melcher (1973).

5.3.3 The American Accounting Association (AAA)

The American Accounting Association (AAA) is an organization of accounting academics and any individuals interested in the betterment of accounting practice and theory. Its quarterly journal, the *Accounting Review*, is devoted to the exchange of ideas and results among accounting researchers. The AAA serves as a forum within which academics express their views on various accounting topics and issues, either individually or through the organization's special appointed committees. In fact, the AAA has attempted through such special committees to provide a framework for corporate financial statements. These efforts, which have met with varying degrees of success, comprise the following studies:

1. *A Tentative Statement of Accounting Principles Underlying Corporate Financial Statements* published in 1936 and revised successively in 1941 and 1948, with eight supplementary statements prepared between 1950 and 1954 that clarify or expand on the 1948 statement: revised again in 1957, with five supplementary statements appearing between 1957 and 1964.

2. *An Introduction to Corporate Accounting Standards*, by W.A. Paton and A.C. Littleton, published in 1940.

3. *An Inquiry into the Nature of Accounting*, by Louis Golberg, published in 1964.

4. *A Statement of Basic Accounting Theory*, published in 1966.

5. *A Statement on Accounting Theory and Theory Acceptance*, published in 1977.

Initially based on an inductive approach, these attempts by the AAA to develop an accounting framework gradually shifted to a deductive approach with the 1957 revision, entitled *Accounting and Reporting Standards for Corporate Financial Statements – 1957 Revision*. The members of the AAA, primarily college and university professors, play one of the greatest roles in the formulation of accounting theory, through continuous innovative research and active participation in the principal standard-setting bodies. The enthusiasm of AAA members is indicated by their research output in the various accounting journals.

Academics rely on the results of their research to provide assistance to FASB and other policy makers. Ijiri has constructed a hypothetical conversation in which a standard-setter responds as follows to the question of what is needed from a researcher:

> Number one. Facts, concepts and theories which provide a basis for our discussion of standard setting. These are needed as general background. It is certainly our responsibility to keep up with research literature but researchers can only help us by calling interesting findings to our attention. Number two. For a specific decision on hand, we have to nail down all feasible alternatives and evaluate them in terms of objectives and guidelines for financial reporting, their consistency with other standards, and their possible consequences if adopted. Any research results that have a bearing on these matters will be useful, whether they are generated as part of a general research study or through a specific study tailored for a specific decision on hand. Finally, number three. Once a decision is made we need research results to persuade those who preferred alternative routes to go along with the selected one. Enormous effort has been expended in explaining why one alternative was chosen over the other as you can see from any pronouncement in recent years.[11]

5.3.4 The Financial Accounting Standards Board (FASB)

The Financial Accounting Standards Board (FASB) replaced the APB in 1973 as the body responsible for establishing accounting standards. The demise of the APB was due mainly to the following factors:

1. the continuing existence of alternative accounting treatments that allowed companies to show higher earnings per share, specially as a result of corporate mergers and acquisitions;

2. the lack of adequate accounting treatments for such new accounting problems as the investment-tax credit, accounting for the franchising industries, the land development business and long-term leases;

3. a number of cases of fraud and lawsuits implicating the accounting methods, which failed to disclose relevant information in many cases;

4. the failure of the APB to develop a conceptual framework.

After investigating the situation, a committee appointed by the AICPA, known as the Wheat Committee, proposed a new structure for establishing accounting standards. The proposed new structure consisted of a nonprofit organization, the Financial Accounting Foundation (FAF), that would operate the FASB and would be cosponsored by five interest groups:

1. The Financial Executive Institute;

2. The National Association of Accountants;

3. The American Accounting Association;

4. The Financial Analysts Federation;

5. The Security Industry Association.

The structure of FASB is depicted in Exhibit 5.2.

The FASB is the authoritative, independent body charged with establishing and improving financial accounting and reporting standards, that is, those standards concerned with recording meaningful information about economic events and transactions in a useful manner in financial statements. The members of the FASB are assumed to represent most

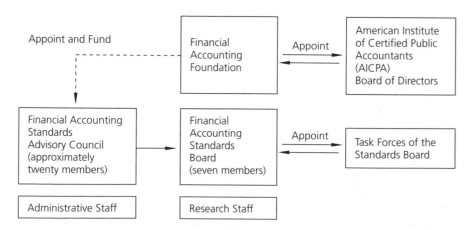

Source: American Institute of Certified Public Accountants, *Report of the Study on Establishment of Accounting Principles* (New York: AICPA, 1972). Reprinted with permission.

Exhibit 5.2   Structure of the Financial Accounting Standards Board (FASB)

parties interested in financial accounting. More specifically, four members are CPAs in public practice, and three members are from areas related to accounting (government, industry, and education). Although APB members had been permitted to retain their positions with firms, companies and institutions, FASB members must sever all such ties. Finally, FASB members are well-paid, full-time members, appointed for renewable five-year terms. This broader representation, increased independence and smaller full-time remunerated membership should make the FASB more successful than the APB.

The relationship of the accounting profession to the FASB was clarified by Rule 203 of the AICPA's Code of Professional Ethics which holds that a member of AICPA may not express an opinion that financial statements are presented fairly in conformity with generally accepted accounting principles if these statements depart from an FASB Statement or Interpretation or an APB Opinion or Accounting Research Bulletin, unless the member can demonstrate that, due to unusual circumstances, the financial statements would otherwise be misleading. Rule 203 constitutes an endorsement of the FASB, with the reservation that recognizes that, in unusual circumstances, literal compliance with presumptively binding, generally accepted accounting principles issued by a recognized standard-setting body may not invariably ensure that financial statements are presented fairly.

Since its inception, the FASB has adopted the following due-process procedure:

1. A reporting problem is identified and placed on the Board's agenda.
2. A task force composed of a group of knowledgeable individuals in the accounting and business community is appointed. The technical staff of the FASB, in consultation with the task force, prepares a Discussion Memorandum (DM) on the reporting problem. The DM exposes the principal questions and alternatives to be considered by the Board.
3. The DM is made available to the public for examination for a period of at least sixty days.
4. A public hearing is staged, during which viewpoints regarding the merits and limitations of various possible positions are presented to the Board.
5. Based on the oral and written comments received, the Board issues an Exposure Draft (ED) of a Proposed Statement of Financial Accounting Standards. Unlike the DM, the ED sets forth the definite position of the Board on the reporting problem.
6. The ED is made available to the public for examination for a period of at least thirty days.
7. Another public hearing is staged, during which viewpoints regarding the merits and limitations of the positions set forth in the ED are presented to the Board.
8. Based again on the oral and written comments received following the issuance of the ED, the Board may take any of the following actions:
   (a) Adopt the Proposed Standard as an Official Statement of Financial Accounting Standards (SFAS).
   (b) Propose a revision of the proposed standard, again following the due-process procedure.
   (c) Postpone the issuance of a standard and keep the problem on the agenda.
   (d) Not issue a standard and eliminate the issue from the agenda.

Public participation does not alter the fact that the actual decisions regarding accounting standards are made by the members of the FASB.

There are several important features that allow people with different interests to influence the FASB and policy making.

1. One feature is *partial inclusion* where people participate in FASB activities only on a segmental or partial basis and belong to many organizations.
2. A second feature is *fluid participation* where participants in FASB activities vary in how much time and effort they devote to FASB activities.
3. A third feature is *information asymmetry* where participants in FASB activities have deeper knowledge about financial accounting and reporting matters than others.
4. A fourth feature is *boundary conditions* where participants in FASB activities cross boundaries between FASB and other organizations and social *groupings*.
5. A fifth feature is *opportunities for influence and opportunism* where people who participate in FASB activities on a partial and fluid basis have different information, and operate at the boundaries of organizations which are likely to have opportunities for influence and opportunism.[13]

5.3.5 The Securities and Exchange Commission (SEC)

Created by an Act of Congress in 1934, the Securities and Exchange Commission (SEC) is primarily responsible for the administration of various laws intended to regulate securities and to ensure proper financial reporting and disclosure by American firms. Briefly, the various acts and their respective general registration requirements are:

1. *Securities Act of 1933*: Requires registration of new securities offered for public sale.
2. *Securities Exchange Act of 1934*: Requires continuous reporting of publicly-owned companies and registration of securities, security exchanges and certain brokers and dealers.
3. *Public Unity Holding Act of 1935*: Requires registration of trust indenture documents and supporting data.
4. *Trust Indenture Act of 1939*: Requires registration of trust indenture documents and supporting data.
5. *Investment Company Act of 1940*: Requires registration of investment companies.
6. *Investment Advisers Act of 1940*: Requires registration of investment advisers.

The Securities Acts of 1933 and 1934 gave the SEC the power to determine accounting standards. As Horngren explains, the SEC was the top management and the APB was the lower management.[14] Although the SEC has the power to regulate accounting practices and disclosure, in general, the SEC has relied on the accounting profession and used its power to set constraints and exert veto power. John C. Burton better expressed this position while he was chief accountant of the SEC:

> We are in partnership and our best interests are served in an atmosphere of mutual nonsurprise. The SEC does not view itself as being in a position of absolute authority and the FASB working for it.[15]

Thus, the SEC has generally concurred with the profession's pronouncements, APB opinions and FASB statements. Nevertheless, the SEC has retained its right to express its views in the following five ways:

1. Regulation S-X, which prescribes the form and content of the reports filed with the SEC. (The most important of these SEC corporate reports are the 10-K annual report, the 10-Q quarterly report, and the 8-K report of unscheduled material events or corporate exchanges of interest to shareholders or the SEC.)

2. Accounting Series Releases, which are pronouncements on accounting matters.
3. SEC Decisions and Reports.
4. The SEC Annual Report.
5. Speeches and articles by members of the Committee and its staff.

The SEC has not always concurred with the accounting profession's pronouncements. Some of its Accounting Series Releases (ASRs) on accounting, auditing and financial matters have been in conflict with, or have in fact amended or superseded, standards set by the standard-setting bodies. Three notorious examples are:

1. ASR No. 96, in which the SEC rejected APB Opinion No. 2 and granted acceptance to several methods of handling the investment credit;
2. ASR No. 147, in which the SEC characterized lessee disclosures required by APB No. 31 as inadequate and imposed additional disclosure requirements of its own;
3. ASR No. 146, in which the SEC provided an interpretation of APB Opinion No. 16 which prompted a CPA firm to sue the SEC.

After the failure of the APB and the creation of the FASB, the SEC issued a policy statement, Accounting Series Release No. 150, which specifically endorsed the FASB as the only standard-setting body whose standards would be accepted by the SEC as satisfying the requirements of the federal securities laws. The release states that "principles, standards, and practices promulgated by the FASB will be considered to have such support". It also states, however, that "the Commission will continue to identify areas where investor information needs exist and will determine the appropriate methods of disclosure to meet the needs". The SEC continues to permit the establishment of accounting standards by the private sector, and the Commission's intervention as the federal government's major participant in the accounting standard-setting process is in the form of cooperation, advice and occasional pressure, rather than in the form of rigid controls. In other words, the SEC endorses the FASB with some reservations, in that it has not delegated any of its authority or given up any right to reject, modify, or supersede FASB pronouncements through its own rule-making procedures.

5.3.6 Other professional organizations

Although the previously cited organizations traditionally have been involved with the development of accounting theory, other organizations in the United States and abroad have recently become active participants. A list of some of these organizations is shown in Appendix 5.A to this chapter.

Each of these organizations is actively involved in setting accounting standards in its respective country and in furthering the basic foundations of accounting.

5.3.7 Users of financial statements

The different groups interested in the results of the activities of a profit-oriented organization have been classified as direct users and indirect users.

Direct users include:

1. the owners of the corporation and its shareholders;
2. the creditors and suppliers;
3. the management of the firm;

4. the taxing authorities;

5. the laborers in an organization;

6. the customers.

Indirect users include:

1. financial analysts and advisers;

2. the stock exchanges;

3. lawyers;

4. regulatory or registration authorities;

5. the financial press and reporting agencies;

6. trade associations;

7. labor unions;

8. competitors;

9. the general public;

10. other governmental departments.

A useful list of constituencies in the financial reporting environment follows:

I. Investors
   A. Diversified vs. Undiversified
   B. Active vs. Passive
   C. Professional vs. Nonprofessional
II. Information Intermediaries
   A. Financial Analyst
   B. Bond Rating Agencies
   C. Stock Rating Agencies
   D. Investment Advisory Services
   E. Brokerage Firms
III. Regulators
   A. FASB
   B. SEC
   C. Congress
IV. Management
   A. Large vs. Small Firms
   B. Publicly vs. Closely Held Firms
V. Auditors
   A. National vs. Local
   B. SEC Practice vs. Non-SEC Practice.[16]

Direct and indirect users have diverse and conflicting sets of objectives. Basically, these two types of users have different information needs. Three kinds of financial statements may be prepared:

1. General-purpose financial statements meet the common needs of the users. In the designing of the financial statements presented in most annual reports, accountants assume that the reports will meet the common needs of users.

2. Specific-purpose financial statements meet the needs of specific user groups.

3. Differential disclosures present different figures for the user to select. Whatever kind of financial statement is used, most of the users act as pressure groups to

influence the development of accounting principles in such a way that their objectives are met.

The most important indirect users are generally the financial analysts and advisers. Analysts have been assumed to serve two functions: information intermediary and analysis. The intermediary function assumes that the analysts convey to clients information gathered from the companies, such as earnings forecasts and other relevant information. The analysis function assumes that the analyst uses his/her skills and talents to analyze the information. To accentuate the analysis role and to provide the general public with similar access to information, the Securities and Exchange Commission (SEC) adopted Regulation Fair Disclosure (FD) in August 2000, which prohibits firms from disclosing material nonpublic information to security analysts and other market professionals unless the information is disclosed broadly simultaneously. This reduced the role of the analyst to information analysis, still capable of providing value for investors by using their expertise in analyzing information. One may also argue that technological breakthroughs, such as conference calls over the Web and the SEC's Electronics Data Gathering and Retrieval (EDGAR), had already diminished the importance of the analyst's intermediary role.

Given these constituencies, management faces an information production and dissemination task. The information production includes (a) *proprietary information*, i.e., information that, if disseminated to outside users, would adversely affect future cash flows of the firm, and (b) *nonproprietary information*, i.e., information that does not directly affect firm cash flows and consisting of conventional financial statement information, including audits. Both types of information can be viewed as commodities to be produced and may be disseminated. Nonproprietary information is both produced and disseminated. Proprietary information is produced but rarely disseminated by management as the costs to the manager and firm of releasing proprietary information can be material. The quantity of either proprietary or nonproprietary information to be produced differs in terms of fineness, where finer information adds more value to conventional information, and permits better discrimination between realizations of states of nature.

5.4 Who should set accounting standards?

5.4.1 Theories of regulation

Regulation is generally assumed to be acquired by a given industry and is designed and operated primarily for its benefit. There are two major categories of regulation of a given industry:

1. public-interest theories;
2. interest-group or capture theories.

The *public-interest theories* of regulation maintain that regulation is supplied in response to the demand of the public for the correction of inefficient or inequitable market prices. They are instituted primarily for the protection and benefit of the general public.

The *interest-group or capture* theories of regulation maintain that regulation is supplied in response to the demands of special-interest groups, in order to maximize the income of their members. The main versions of this theory are:

1. the political ruling-elite theory of regulation;
2. the economic theory of regulation.[17]

The political ruling-elite theory concerns the use of political power to gain regulatory control; the economic theory concerns economic power.

Which of these theories better describes accounting standard-setting? Unfortunately, the theory of what constitutes maximizing behavior in an accounting regulatory agency is in its infancy. Benston attempted to explain the behavior of the SEC according to the economic theory's predictions of agency conservatism:

> An active regulatory agency has an incentive for insisting on conservative, explicit, even rigid accounting standards. Such standards reduce the risk to the agency that it will be criticized for "accepting" statements that, when viewed with the benefit of hindsight, appear misleading or fraudulent.
>
> It is not surprising that the SEC tends to want uniform, conservative reporting by corporations.[18]

Needless to say, this statement by Benston is inconsistent with the behavior of the SEC since the early 1970s.

Similarly, Hussein and Ketz examined and rejected the plausibility of the political ruling-elite version of the theory of regulation.[19] More empirical evidence is needed to develop a theory of regulation of accounting standards.

5.4.2 Should we regulate accounting?

A debate exists as to whether accounting should or should not be regulated.

Those arguing for an unregulated market use agency theory to question why incentives should exist for reliable and voluntary reporting to owners. To solve the conflict between owners and managers financial reporting is used to monitor employment contracts, to judge and reward managers. In addition, firms have an incentive to report voluntarily to the capital market and failure to report might be interpreted as bad news. Even if firms do not report voluntarily, those seeking the information may resort to private contractors for the information.

Those arguing for a regulated market use a public-interest argument. Basically, either market failures or the need to achieve social goals dictate a regulation of accounting. Market failures, as suboptimal allocation of issuances, may be the result of

1. a firm's reluctance to disclose information about itself, as it is a monopoly supplier of information about itself;
2. the occurrence of fraud;
3. the underproduction of accounting information as a public good.

The need to achieve desired social goals also argues for a regulation of accounting. These goals include fairness of reporting, information symmetry and the protection of investors, to name only a few.

While the debate on the benefits and limitations of regulation continue, standard-setting is a reality of the accounting environment. The advantages and limitations of various forms of standard-setting – regulatory or nonregulatory – may be assessed as a way of improving the process. In the following section, each of the approaches to standard-setting will be examined.

5.4.3 The free-market approach

The free-market approach to the production of accounting standards starts from the basic assumption that accounting information is an economic good, much the same as other goods or services. As such it is subject to the forces of demand by interested users and of supply by interested preparers. What results is an optimal amount of information disclosed at an optimal price. Whenever a given piece of information is needed and the right price is offered for it, the market will generate the information if the price exceeds the cost of the information. The market is thus presented as the ideal mechanism for determining the types of information to be disclosed, the recipients of the information and the accounting standards to govern the production of such information.

Advocates of a regulatory approach (whether private or public) maintain that there are both *explicit and implicit* market failures in the private market for the information:

1. In general, explicit market failure is assumed to happen when either the quantity or the quality of a good produced in an unregulated market differs from the private costs of, and benefits derived from, that good, and the market solution results in a non-Pareto resource allocation. The same explicit market failure is also applied to the private market for the accounting information, with the assumption that the quantity and the quality of the accounting information differ from the social optimum. More explicitly, accounting information is viewed as a public good and due to the inability to exclude nonpurchasers (free riders), there is a non-Pareto optimal production of the information of firms.[20]

2. Implicit market failure theories focus on one or more of the following claims that there are defects in the private markets for accounting information:

   (a) Monopoly control over information by management.
   (b) Naive investors.
   (c) Functional fixation.
   (d) Misleading numbers.
   (e) Diversity of procedures.
   (f) Lack of objectivity.[21]

   Each of these alleged defects is briefly examined next.

   (a) *Monopoly control over information by management*: The hypothesis claims that accountants possess a monopolistic influence over the data provided and used by the market. As a result, the market cannot really distinguish between real and accounting effects, and may be misled by the accounting changes.[22]

   (b) *Naive investors*: The hypothesis claims that those investors who are not well versed in some of the complex accounting techniques and transformations may be "fooled" by the use of different techniques by comparable firms and may not be able to adjust their decision-making process to take the diversity of accounting procedures into account.

   (c) *Functional fixation*: It is argued that under certain conditions investors may be unable to change their decision-making processes in response to a change in the underlying accounting process that provided them with the data. The failure of these investors to change their decision-making processes to conform to a change in accounting methods is attributed to the phenomenon of functional fixation.

   (d) *Misleading numbers*: Because accounting relies heavily on various asset-valuation bases and various allocation procedures deemed arbitrary and incorrigible, the accounting output is at best meaningless or misleading for the purpose of decision-making.

   (e) *Diversity of procedures*: Given the flexibility in the choice of accounting techniques used to report particular events and the inclination of management to present a "desired" picture, the accounting output from one firm to another firm is less than comparable and useful.

(f) *Lack of objectivity*: No objective criteria are available on which management can base its choice of accounting techniques: incomparable output is the obvious result.

Greater information asymmetry among market participants leads to higher transaction costs and lower liquidity for trading shares of the firm, causing a raise in the required rate of return and lowering in current stock prices.[23] Diamond and Verrecchia[24] suggest that if managers present a credible commitment to improve disclosures and hence increase the precision of public information about firm value, current stock prices will increase as a result of reduced information asymmetry and increased liquidity. This is the essence of the information asymmetry perspective in the sense that value-maximizing managers will choose from the set of available accounting techniques with the objective of reducing information symmetry to the level where the expected benefit of new disclosure is offset by the expected costs, such as the preparation and proprietary costs, of making the disclosure.

Based on these alleged defects, those who favor some form of regulation of accounting criticize the market approach as ineffective and claim that regulation is superior in improving accounting output. These allegations have not gone uncontested. The best challenge to the market failure theories as they affect accounting information is summarized by Leftwich:

> Market failure theories contain a fundamental flaw. The output identified by those theories as optimal is optimal in name only – it is defined independently of any institutional arrangements that can produce the output. None of these theories identifies a level of output which is optimal, given the existing technology of markets, regulations or any other regimes. Thus, unless market failure theories incorporate attainable institutional arrangements, they can yield no policy implications. It is illogical to condemn the actual output of an existing market (or government agency) merely because the quantity or quality of that output differs from an unattainable norm that is falsely described as optimal.[25]

The question of what would happen to financial accounting in the absence of regulation remains. Kripke proposes the following two possible consequences:

> First, there would continue to be adequate accounting disclosure, as issuers negotiated with lenders, investors and underwriters in the new issue market and felt the pressure of analysts in the trading market. Second, the accounting would be less uniform than it is now, because vast differences in views as to the appropriate interpretation and abstraction of events are concealed by the mandated system. But the pressures would be such that the disclosure would be adequate to enable the reader to make his own judgment.[26]

5.4.4 Private-sector regulation of accounting standards

The private-sector approach to the regulation of accounting standards rests on the fundamental assumption that the public interest in accounting is best served if standard-setting is left to the private sector. Private standard-setting in the United States has included the Committee on Accounting Procedures (1939–59) and the Financial Accounting Standards Board (1973–present). Given the FASB is the ongoing standard-setting body in the private sector, it will be used to illustrate the advantages and the limitations of private-sector regulation of accounting standards.

Advocates of the private-sector approach cite the following arguments in support of their position:

1. The FASB seems to be responsive to various constituents. First, it is composed of members of various interested groups in addition to the public accounting profession. Second, its financial support is derived from the contributions of a diverse group of individuals, companies, and associations. Third, it has adopted a complex due-process procedure that relies heavily on the responses of all interested constituents. Fourth, the due-process procedure generates an active concern about the consequences of its actions on the constituents.

2. The FASB seems to be able to attract, as members or as staff, people who possess the necessary technical knowledge to develop and implement alternative measurement and disclosure systems. As a unit, the standards are more likely to be acceptable to CPA firms, business firms, and external users.

3. The FASB seems to be successful in generating responses from its constituency base and in responding to such input. The volume of responses to controversial topics shows that the constituents have been expressing interest by participating and voicing their concern through at least three different mediums:

   (i) written responses to a discussion memorandum;
   (ii) oral responses to an exposure draft; and
   (iii) written responses to an exposure draft.

Such participation is deemed essential to the accounting standard-setting process. A former staff member of the FASB describes the importance of the constituent's input:

> The FASB represents a legislative body in the private sector that must pay careful attention to the views of all the elements of its constituency. Each constituent potentially affects formulation of the FASB decisions by providing thoughtful and theoretically sound input for the Board members to comprehend and evaluate, weigh against other constituent input, and synthesize with their own educated views on the particular issue of concern. The decision-making process, however, does not merely involve tallying these constituent preferences and resolving the issue by majority consensus. The FASB's responsibility in reaching its decision entails careful consideration of all constituent interests; it does not entail numerical-count comparisons or attempts to serve specific constituents over others.[27]

Opponents of the private-sector approach cite the following arguments in support of their position:

1. The FASB lacks statutory authority and enforcement power and faces the challenges of an override by either Congress or a governmental agency. Kaplan states the case as follows:

   > Acceptance of FASB standards requires voluntary agreement from the AICPA and the benevolent delegation of authority from the SEC. Lacking true statutory authority, the private standard-setting agency is always susceptible to end runs by aggrieved constituents when they feel their particular ox is about to be gored.[28]

   This situation is a result of the positions taken by Congress and the SEC on accounting standard-setting. Following the Securities Act of 1933 and the Securities Act of 1934, Congress became the legal authority for standard-setting. It then delegated its authority to the accounting profession. Finally, in Accounting Series Release No. 150, the SEC recognized the authoritative nature of the pronouncements of the FASB and at the same time retained its role as adviser and supervisor as a constant threat of override.

2. The FASB is often accused of lacking independence from its large constituents, public accounting firms and corporations. This lack of independence translates into a lack of responsiveness to the public interest. This theme gained popularity as a result of assertions made in the Metcalf Report that the accounting and financial reporting standard-setting process is dominated by the "Big Eight" accounting firms.[29] One way in which this domination may manifest itself is through pressure in the FASB to avoid standards that would involve subjective estimates, especially standards that would require the use of current-market prices. Kaplan states the case as follows:

> Because practitioners from CPA firms are primarily auditors, the auditing implications of any standard will receive a great deal of attention from a private standard-setting agency. There will be strong pressure for rules that can be implemented without requiring subjective estimates that are difficult to audit and even more difficult to defend should the financial statements be subject to question in a judicial proceeding. Given the present litigious climate, auditors wish to avoid having to certify figures for which objective verifiable evidence is unavailable. These feelings are reinforced by corporate executives, another principal constituency of the private standard-setting agency, who may also fear the repercussions from issuing "soft" data. In addition, the production of subjective data is expensive and introduces a degree of uncontrolled volatility to a company's financial statements.[30]

3. The FASB is often accused of responding slowly to major issues that are of crucial importance to some of its constituents. This situation is generally attributed to the length of time required for due process and extensive deliberations of the Board.

The defenders of the Board maintain, however, that these extensive deliberations may allow the Board to correct the unintended side-effects of some of its pronouncements. This brings to mind the additional problem that the proposed standards have a slim chance of being implemented without general support. Horngren provides the following details on problems associated with the Accounting Principles Board's issuance in October 1971 of an exposure draft supporting the deferral method:

> Without public support, which usually means without the widespread support of industry, significant changes are seldom possible. Perhaps the situations would be better expressed negatively. If there is widespread hostility to a suggested accounting principle, there is a small chance of implementing it – regardless of how impeccable or how heavy the support within the Board.

> The investment tax credit is a clear example of the impotency of both the SEC and the APB when hostility is rampant. Let me describe the events without getting tangled in the pros and cons of the conceptual issues:

> The APB did not issue its exposure draft of October 22, 1971, until receiving two written commitments. The SEC said it would support the APB position, and the Department of the Treasury indicated that it "will remain neutral in the matter." The Senate Finance Committee issued its version of the 1971 Revenue Act on November 9. In response to lobbying, the Committee clearly indicated that companies should have a free choice in selecting the accounting treatment of the new credit.

> On November 12, the Treasury sent a letter to the chairman of the Senate Finance Committee that stated:

> "Since any change in the preexisting, well-established financial accounting practice might operate to diminish the job-creating effect of the credit, the Treasury Department strongly supports a continuation of the optimal

treatment." Congress then cut the ground out from under the APB and the SEC by passing legislation that stated:

"No taxpayer shall be required, without his consent, to use … any particular method of accounting for the credit."

The APB's unanimous denunciation of congressional involvement was issued on December 9, 1971.[31]

5.4.5 Public-sector regulation of accounting standards

Public-sector regulation of any activity is always the subject of heated debate between advocates and opponents. Without a doubt, public-sector regulation has gained a high degree of legitimacy and become part of American and international traditions and legal frameworks. To be effective, however, regulation must ascribe to certain general principles. Elliot and Schuetze present the following:

> First, regulation must not violate constitutional rights or statutes. Second, it should be designed to prevent real or probable social change. Third, regulation must be in the public interest. A corollary to this principle is that costs must not exceed benefits and the regulation itself ought not to be superfluous. If the forces of the marketplace can resolve a question adequately, regulation is superfluous. Fourth, regulation should not be adopted by the public sector if its purpose can be achieved by private-sector institutions. Fifth, the potential regulatee should not bear the burden of proving regulation is warranted; rather, advocates of regulation must demonstrate that regulation is warranted. Sixth, regulatory action should not be used to correct occasional lawbreaking, which is the task of law enforcement; nor should regulatory responsibilities be established to combat occasional antisocial behavior that can be proscribed by statute.[32]

Even if all of these principles were met, regulation is still perceived to be suffering from various failures. Buckley and O'Sullivan identify the *zero-cost phenomenon*, *the regulatory lag* or *nonfeasance, the regulatory trap,* and *the tar-baby effect* as some of the observed regulatory failures.[33] The zero-cost phenomenon results from the fact that regulators do not bear the costs of their failures. The regulatory lag or nonfeasance results from delays in regulation. The regulatory trap refers to the difficulties of reversing a given regulation. Finally, the tar-baby effect results from the tendency of regulation to expand continually.

Given these strong arguments about regulation in general, what about public-sector regulation of accounting specifically? As we might expect, arguments for and against public-sector regulation of accounting standards abound in the literature. These arguments center generally around the role of the SEC.

Advocates of public-sector regulation of accounting standards cite the following arguments in favor of their position:

1. It is generally maintained that the process of innovation in accounting rests on the role of a governmental agency such as the SEC as a "creative irritant". Burton, a former chief accountant of the SEC, makes this point:

   > Since its inception in 1934, the Securities and Exchange Commission has been a principal source of creative irritation in accounting, and the practicing public accounting profession has generally served as the host that builds upon it. It is the hypothesis of this paper that this combination of SEC stimulation and professional reaction is one which emerges logically from the historical and economic forces at work that is likely to continue, and that the result is likely to

be a satisfactory balancing of diverse interests and objectives. In the financial reporting environment as it exists today, substantial change will not occur in the absence of SEC stimulation.[34]

The implication here is that the SEC is the most important catalyst for change, and that the private sector and market forces do not provide the leadership necessary to effect such change. The SEC has been instrumental in guiding the field from "safe" or "conservative" methods of accounting toward more innovative and realistic methods of accounting.

2. It is argued that the structure of securities regulation established by the Securities Acts of 1933 and 1934 serves to protect investors against perceived abuses. Thus public-sector regulation of accounting standards is motivated by the need to protect the public interest. It provides mechanisms to offset the preparer bias that institutionally exists in the standard-setting process, as well as to offset the economic limitations of investors seeking adequate information.[35] The mechanisms include suggestions through speeches, the exercise of rule-making powers granted by Congress under the Securities Act of 1933 and 1934, the use of a review and comment process, and the power not to accelerate the effectiveness of a registration statement and to discourage accounting applications in cases judged to be inappropriate, given the circumstances.[36]

3. The SEC is motivated by the desire to create a level of public disclosure deemed necessary and adequate for decision making. Burton suggests:

> The SEC has as its objective achieving a level of public disclosure at least equivalent to the disclosure that would likely be sought by a provider or capital user. If it errs in this objective, it seeks to do so on the side of providing more information rather than less, since an underlying premise of its regulatory purpose is to assure the existence of adequate information so that the capital-allocating mechanism of the marketplace will work effectively.[37]

To do so the SEC assumes the role of advocate for investors and attempts to determine their needs by continuously surveying analysts and other interested users.

4. Unlike the FASB, the SEC is secured greater legitimacy through its explicit statutory authority. Added to that is a greater enforcement power than a private agency and the absence of an explicit constituency that may "feel their particular ox is about to be gored". Kaplan provides the following illustration:

> For example, the replacement cost disclosure of Accounting Series Release No. 190 and the recently announced Reserve Recognition Accounting for oil and gas companies were accomplished by the SEC with little prior discussion and with considerable speed. Neither of these initiatives, which represented major departures from the conventional, historical, cost-based system, could have been accomplished by the FASB nearly so quickly or with so little public debate.[38]

In short, the SEC is better able to conduct experiments in disclosure policy when they are enforceable and can go uncontested by all participants in the standard-setting process.

5. Some claim that the private sector has to be watched and controlled, given that its objectives may sometimes contradict the public interest. A minimum of governmental intervention is deemed necessary to avoid the extreme and negative behaviors. Chetkovich emphasizes the same point:

> The private sector does not have all the answers; it is not immune to excesses, to shortsightedness, to deficiencies, and to failures. We need surveillance and

prodding and, at times, intervention by government. Left totally to our own devices, I am afraid we might destroy ourselves. On the other hand, government must exercise great restraint and not just because increasing governmental involvement is inconsistent with the concept of a free society, although that should be reason enough.[39]

6. Representative Richard H. Baker, Chairman of the House Banking Committee's subcommittee on capital markets, introduced in 1988 the *Financial Accounting Fairness Act*, which called for the SEC to vote on the pronouncements of the FASB before companies are required to comply with them. Under the bill, the SEC, in deciding whether to make FASB principles applicable to public companies, would have to consider the same set of questions as it does when it makes rules or approves the rules of self-regulatory organizations like the National Association of Securities Dealers.

There are, however, strong arguments against public-sector regulation of accounting standards:

1. It is generally maintained that there is a high corporate cost for compliance with government regulation of information. The problem is a matter of concern to opponents of public-sector regulation of accounting standards. The financial reports required by the federal government keep increasing to comply with such legislation as the Sherman Act, the Robinson–Patman Act, DOE pricing rules, OSHA, EPA, EEOC, NHTAS, NRC, NLRB, FDA, ICC, CPSC, FHLBB, MSHA, and NTSB. All of these reports have an impact on business organization in terms of paper costs and in terms of constant changes in organizational structure that cause the formation of new positions or departments. Added to these complaints are the following as yet unanswered questions:

   (a) What happens to the reports once they are sent to the federal government?
   (b) Do they end up in some agency's files never to be looked at again? or
   (c) Is the information from this one company's reports actually used, along with that from thousands of other corporations, to make important policy decisions?

   A study attempting to follow up on some of this information and see what happens to it would be interesting. Perhaps such a study would also give some indication of the possible benefits to society from such information-gathering.[40]

2. Some have argued that bureaucrats have a tendency to maximize the total budget of their bureau.[41] Applied to the SEC, this argument assumes that the SEC is staffed with people who tend to maximize their own welfare with no consideration for the costs and benefits of additional disclosures. Watts makes the same point:

   > If the SEC's budget is determined by politicians more concerned with appearance than substance, I would expect the SEC's actions to be more concerned with appearance rather than fact. The SEC's function is to issue regulations, to prosecute and to appear to be acting to remedy "perceived" abuses. Allowing serious calculations of costs to affect those regulations would be dysfunctional. That is why the SEC spends a small fraction of its budget on estimating costs and benefits and a large fraction on the lawyers who produce and enforce regulation.[42]

3. There is the danger that standard-setting may become increasingly politicized. Special-interest groups may possess the added initiative to lobby the governmental agency for special treatment. Moreover, political appointees may feel that "witch hunts" are necessary to protect the public interest. Another fear is that "uninformed

populists" may want some of the action at the expense of accounting standards and the accounting profession.[43]

4. Some have questioned the need for a governance system backed by a police power. It is claimed that such a situation may hinder the conduct of research and experimentation of accounting policy and is not essential to achieve standardization of measurement. For example, David Moss, then a member of the FASB, claimed that:

> ... the police power is not necessarily required for balancing the conflicting interests of the various parties in the capital-allocation process, including the interests of the state itself. The vast majority of interest conflicts in our society are resolved through systems of self-restraint.[44]

5.5 Legitimacy of the standard-setting process

5.5.1 The pessimistic prognosis

The legitimacy of the standard-setting process was sometimes linked to its ability to produce an optimal accounting system, that is "one for which the expected payoff to a user employing an optimal decision strategy is greater than or equal to the corresponding payoff for any other alternative system".[45] The implication is that no alternative financial statement presentations based on any other set of accounting rules can lead to better user-utility. Improved debate in the accounting literature concerns the attainability of such an optimal accounting system. The debate was sparked by Demski's use of the impossibility theorem to argue that:

1. an accounting standard-setting process must satisfy Arrow's condition[46] to be legitimate; and
2. no set of standards exists that will always seek alternatives in accordance with preferences and beliefs.[47]

He concludes as follows:

> We have interpreted accounting theory as providing a complete and transitive ranking of accounting alternatives at the individual level. It was then proven that no set of standards (applied to the accounting alternative *per se*) exist that will rank accounting alternatives in relation to consistent individual preferences and beliefs.[48]

This pessimistic prognosis was expanded to show:

1. that the selection of financial reporting alternatives "ultimately must entail trading off one person's gain for another",[49] and
2. that the resolution of financial reporting alternatives will require "value or ethical judgments as to whose well-being will be traded off and in what dimensions for whose".[50] What appears from these efforts is that rational choice theory offers no hope for solutions to the issues of choice among financial reporting alternatives. As stated by Cushing:

> Consider now an accounting policy-maker who implores this literature in searching for help in the discovery of optimal accounting principles. Under certain assumptions and conditions which seem logical and desirable, the policy-maker finds that attempts to use standards apparently will be fruitless, that optimal accounting principles apparently do not exist and that she/he must

reconcile herself or himself to a political role of trading off conflicting objectives of financial statement user groups.[51]

5.5.2 The optimistic prognosis

In fact, Cushing gave an optimistic prognosis about the sheer responsibility of optimal accounting principle, provided that the assumption of heterogeneous users is dropped and that the assumptions underlying the Arrow Paradox are challenged, namely the assumptions:

1. that Arrow's definition of a social welfare function requires that social choices be transitive, and

2. that Arrow's condition of "independence or irrelevant alternatives" is of questionable merit.[52]

Another optimistic prognosis is offered by Bromwich on the possibility of partial accounting standards; standards for one or more accounting problems, enacted in isolation from standards or other accounting problems.[53]

Chambers chose to counteract Demski's economic school and impossibility thesis by proposing a necessity school that assumes the existence of an ideal norm or standard that cuts across specific situations.[54] The norm is the information that represents the current money and money's worth of assets and the amount currently owing to others at any time.[55] Even if that norm is not available, Chambers suggests that the feasible alternative that most closely produces the necessary measure is the preferred alternative.

Cushing, Chambers and Bromwich, in demonstrating that under certain restrictive conditions it was possible to select accounting standards without isolating Arrow's conditions (or by violating only some minor aspects of one or more conditions), could have argued the legitimacy of the FASB by focusing on its feasibility and the irrelevancy of Arrow's Impossibility Theorem to the assessment of the legitimacy of the FASB standard-setting process. They would have used Tullock's argument when he examined the relevance of Arrow's Impossibility Theorem for purposes of assessing the legitimacy of certain voting processes, and concluded in these terms:

> One of the real problems raised by Arrow's book was why the real world democracies seemed to function fairly well in spite of the logical impossibility of rationally aggregating preferences. [Although] no decision process will meet Arrow's criteria perfectly, many [processes] meet them to a very high degree of approximation [and, therefore, the ability of a process to meet the strictly mathematical requirements imposed by Arrow is largely irrelevant in the real world].[56]

The problem remaining, however, is to assert the legitimacy of the FASB. To achieve that task, Johnson and Solomons relied on the "individualistic constitutional calculus".[57] This process involved mainly the economics/political science literature.[58]

It is defined as follows:

> Individualistic constitutional calculus is based on the premise that a process or institution is legitimate if it continues to be acceptable to its constituency in spite of the challenges posed to its credibility by the inevitable crisis that surrounds the exercise of such authority. In short, legitimacy implies acceptability in the face of uncertainty, and that, in turn, implies institutional durability.[59]

Basically, institutional constitutional calculus established the legitimacy of the FASB based on:

1. its ability to provide adequate procedural safeguards;
2. its ability to impose constraints on the choice set that are adequate to ensure an acceptable outcome;
3. the balance of procedural and outcome controls possessed by the standard-setting process of the FASB. The ability of the FASB to meet these conditions was assessed by showing that the FASB possess sufficient authority to ensure substantive due-process and ensure procedural due-process.[60]

5.6 Accounting standards overload

David Moss describes best the gravity of the standards-overload issue by the following statement:

> When I first encountered the subject, "standards overload" looked like the legendary Gordian knot, so intricate it couldn't be untied by any ordinary mortal. After five years of wrestling with the problem, however, I think maybe it isn't a Gordian knot after all – it looks like a hangman's noose.[61]

The accounting standards overload is generally associated with the proliferation of accounting standards. The following situations have also been identified with accounting standards overload:

1. too many standards;
2. too detailed standards;
3. no rigid standards, making selectivity of application difficult;
4. general-purpose standards failing to provide for differences in the needs of preparers, users and CPAs;
5. general-purpose standards failing to provide for differences between:
   (a) public and nonpublic entities;
   (b) annual and interim financial statements;
   (c) large and small enterprises; and
   (d) audited and nonaudited financial statements;
6. excessive disclosures, complex measurements, or both.

The situation took years to develop to the stage of becoming a serious problem. Various factors contributed to the standards-overload problem. First, with the numerous questions raised about what to disclose and what not to disclose, accountants began to issue a greater number of standards, which tended to leave less to judgment and to reduce the amount of litigation involving accounting principles. Second, the need to protect the public interest and to assist the individual investor generated various and numerous governmental and professional regulations and disclosures. Finally, the desire to satisfy the needs of many users required more detailed standards and disclosures.

What resulted is a complex and cumbersome situation. Mandated GAAP increased in number, complexity and specificity, affecting the costs of preparing financial statements for both small and large firms. Some believe the GAAP are becoming intolerable to some firms, their auditors and the users of information. Others think that the new and detailed GAAP requirements are more designed to serve the informational needs of investors and creditors at the expense of the particular users of financial statements of small or closely held businesses. This is in direct conflict with the accepted argument that serving the needs of users of financial statements is, or should be, the primary objective of financial reporting. In effect, that is exactly the main emphasis of FASB's Statement of Financial Accounting Concepts No. 1, *Objectives of Financial Reporting by Business Enterprises:*

> Financial reporting should provide information that is useful to present and potential investors and creditors and other users in making rational investment, credit, and similar decisions. The information should be comprehensible to those who have a reasonable understanding of business and economic activities and are willing to study the information with reasonable diligence.

The problem of overload is aggravated by the proliferation of standard-setting bodies. In addition to the FASB, the development of the GAAP and related disclosures are influenced by other bodies such as the SEC; the AICPA, including the Accounting Standards Executive Committee (AcSEC) and the Auditing Standards Board (ASB); and to some extent Congress. Examples of congressional actions having accounting consequences are the investment-tax credit and the enactment of the Foreign Corrupt Practices Act. In addition, the standards themselves are not only excessive in number, but too narrow in their application to cover all possible situations, and requiring too much detailed guidance.

5.6.1 Effects of accounting standards overload

The large number, narrowness and rigidity of accounting standards can have serious effects on the work performed by accountants, the value of financial information to users and business decisions made by management. The accountants may lose sight of their real jobs because of the excessive data required when complying with existing standards. Audit failures may result, because the accountant may lose the focus of the audit and may forget to perform basic audit procedures. The proliferation of complex accounting regulations may lead to noncompliance with those regulations by business, with the tacit agreement of CPAs. The embattled practitioner is in fact caught in the middle between the demands of professional standards and the discontent of small business clients with the burden these standards impose on them. This situation will undoubtedly have serious implications for legal liability, erosion of professional ethics, loss of public support and dissonance within the accounting profession.

One way out for practitioners faced with the GAAP departures is to give a modified opinion. Most CPAs, however, resist a modified opinion for the GAAP omissions in audited financial statements, because they think the negative connotation is not acceptable. What may be needed is an education of the public to greater acceptance of CPA reports that take note of omitted GAAP requirements.

The users may also be confused by the number and complexity of the notes used to explain the requirements under the existing standards. Users of financial reports of small businesses generally are concerned with the complexity introduced by the Financial Accounting Standards Board pronouncements. The jargon used in the notes can be understood only by accountants and other financial persons. Consider, for example, the following note from the 1981 United Leasing Corporation's Form 10-K, describing the company's method of recognizing revenue from a lease used to finance an asset:

> *Direct financial leases* – At the time of closing a direct financing lease, the company records on its balance sheet the gross sale receivable, estimated residual valuation of the leased equipment, and unearned lease income. The unearned lease income represents the excess of the gross lease receivable plus the estimated residual valuation over the cost of the equipment leased. A portion of the unearned income equal to the

initial direct costs incurred in consummating the lease plus an amount equal to the provision for losses is recognized as revenue at the time the lease is closed. Commencing with the second month of the lease, the remainder of the unearned lease income is recorded as revenue over the lease term so as to approximate a constant rate of return on the net investment in the lease.

The note can be understood only by a seasoned veteran familiar with the accounting jargon and body of knowledge.

The managers may also be overwhelmed by the number and complexity of the standards. In fact, they may be tempted to rewrite contracts and change business practices so as not to have to comply with some of the accounting standards. It is possible to restructure the terms of leases to avoid capitalization and the intricate requirements of Statement of Financial Accounting Standards No. 13 on leases. The major motivation for the restructuring of transactions by managers of small businesses is to avoid not only the detailed requirements of some accounting standards, but the excessive costs of preparing and verifying the information. Besides, the costs of complying with the standards may outweigh the benefits, given that users of financial reports of small businesses may be more interested in cash-flow projections than in the other financial statement information. In fact, because users of financial reports of small businesses have more immediate contact with management, they do not need to rely on financial reports as much as users of reports of large businesses.

5.6.2 Solutions to the standards-overload problem

The gravity of the standards-overload problem led various interest groups to address the problem and suggest solutions. The AICPA Special Committee on Accounting Standards evaluated the following possible approaches to dealing with accounting standards overload:

1. No change; retain status quo.
2. A change from the present concept of a set of unitary GAAP for all business enterprises to two sets of GAAP, thus creating a separate set of GAAP for certain entities, such as small nonpublic businesses.
3. Changes in GAAP to simplify application to all business enterprises.
4. Establishing differential disclosure and measurement alternatives.
5. A change in CPA's standards for reporting on financial statements.
6. An alternative to the GAAP as an optional basis for presenting financial statements.

Of all of these approaches, the committee recommended either establishing disclosure and measurement alternatives or adopting an alternative to the GAAP.

The approach based on differential disclosure and measurement alternatives for small nonpublic enterprises is a good solution to the standards-overload problem, in that it considers relevance to users and cost–benefit considerations with respect to small nonpublic entities. This is in line with the FASB's Statement of Financial Accounting Concepts No. 2, which states:

> The optimal information for one user will not be optimal for another. Consequently, the Board which must try to cater to many different users while considering the burdens placed on those who have to provide information, constantly treads a fine line between requiring disclosure of too much information and requiring too little.

The approach calls for a flexible concept of the GAAP with differential measurement alternatives to serve the specialized needs of small nonpublic companies. One way of implementing this approach would be for the standard-setting body to adopt a basis for exemption from the detailed requirements of each standard. The basis might be public versus private, or a size test based on asset values.

The approach that relies on an alternative to the GAAP rests on three possibilities:

1. a new basis accounting method (BAM);
2. the cash or modified cash basis;
3. the income tax basis.

A BAM is out of the question, because it would create more costs than benefits. Some of the conclusions of the committee include the following:

1. BAM will contain the essentials of the GAAP and allow significant departures from the measurement principles of the GAAP. As such, it would confuse everybody and undermine the GAAP in the process.
2. BAM will add rather than reduce the overload problem, given that it will create new requirements in addition to the GAAP.
3. BAM will require a position on each of the GAAP issues, which will be costly and time consuming.
4. BAM will need to be prepared by a new standard-setting body.
5. BAM will be perceived not as a subset of the GAAP but as a subset of the GAAP for special entities.

Given these constraints, the committee suggested that the issuance, in accordance with existing reporting standards, of compiled, reviewed or audited other comprehensive bases of accounting (OCBOA) financial statements, including income tax-basis financial statements, can help alleviate the burden of accounting standards overload for small nonpublic entities.

5.7 Accounting choice

In a situation of imperfect and incomplete markets, the demand for accounting and accounting regulation suggests that accounting disclosures and accounting-based contracts are efficient ways of addressing market imperfections. These accounting disclosures and accounting-based contracts are the results of an accounting choice, a choice that is meant to influence the output of the accounting system in a particular way. Three categories of goals or motivation for accounting choice may be determined, namely *contracting*, *asset pricing*, and *influencing external parties*.[62]

First, because of the presence of agency costs and the absence of complete markets, state-contingent contracts are used, often influenced by accounting choice. This category is termed the *efficient contracting perspective*.[63, 64] For example, while contractual arrangements such as executive compensation agreements and debt covenants can be used to alleviate agency costs, *ex-post* accounting choice may be used to increase compensation or to avoid covenant violation.

Second, because of information asymmetries, accounting choice may be used to influence asset prices, either by informed insiders imparting information to less well-informed parties about the turning, magnitude and risks of future cash flows, or by self-interested managers believing that higher earnings will lead to higher stock prices.

Third, accounting choice may be used to influence external parties other than actual and potential owners of the firm such as the Internal Revenue Service, government regulators, suppliers, competitors, and union negotiators.

5.8 Standard-setting strategies for the developing countries

The developing countries are characterized by relatively inadequate and unreliable accounting systems and generally new and untested standard-setting institutions. Theory development and academic and professional accounting research add to the economic, social, political and institutional problems that may be acting as deterrents to effective standard-setting. In spite of these limitations, the development of basic accounting systems and procedures and the process of standard-setting have accelerated, as evidenced by the increasing number of professional organizations, standard-setting books, and academic accounting associations, as well as by the increasing membership of these groups in international standard-setting bodies.

The standard-setting process in the developing countries has not followed a unique strategy proper to these countries and their context. In fact, four strategies may be identified:

1. the evolutionary approach;
2. development through transfer of accounting technology;
3. the adoption of international accounting standards;
4. the development of accounting standards based on analysis of accounting principles and practices in the advanced nations against the backdrop of their underlying investment.[65]

5.8.1 The evolutionary approach

The evolutionary approach consists of an isolationist approach to standard-setting whereby the developing country develops its own standard without any outside interference or influences. The particular developing country defines its own specific accounting objectives and needs and proceeds to meet them by developing its own techniques, concepts, institutions, profession and education in isolation. The particular country may feel its context to be unique enough to justify this drastic approach to standard-setting. The learning process in this approach has to come from local experiences rather than international experiences. It assumes the foreign partners will adapt to its own idiosyncratic rules and may have to if they want to continue to trade with the country and/or maintain operations. Naturally, it may create an additional cost to the foreign partners, who may feel the conditions onerous enough to justify complete cooperation. In addition, the absence of an adequate local accounting technology may hamper not only local firms, but also foreign firms operating in the country.

5.8.2 The transfer of technology approach

Development through transfer of accounting technology may result from either the operations and activities of international accounting firms, multinationals, and academicians practicing in the developing countries, or the various international treaties and cooperative arrangements calling for exchanges of information and technology. Adolf Enthoven, for example, describes the benefits of US accounting assistance to the developing world as follows:

US accounting and accountants have already had a positive effect on accounting systems, procedures and training in many developing economies. For example, the affiliates of US MNEs have developed sound financial management systems. Other US companies have entered into joint ventures with foreign companies or have set up their own organizations in these countries for the production and sale of goods and services. Good financial and managerial accounting methods have accompanied these investments. Many US CPA firms have either established corresponding relationships with foreign firms or set up branch offices abroad. Although much of value has been accomplished by US accountants in CPA firms and in industry-developing economies, such activities have generally been directed toward certain companies or to serve CPA firm clients. More might be done; however, I recognize that this task isn't the first priority of accountants in public practice and industry.[66]

Because most developing countries may not have given formal attention to the formulation and implementation of a strategy which facilitates the transfer of accounting technology, or the development of an indigenous accounting profession, Belverd Needles, Jr., proposed a conceptual framework by which a country may formulate a strategy for the international transfer of accounting technology as part of its overall economic plan.[67] Basically, national goals combine with the social, political and economic environment and general resources and constraints to influence the overall economic plan. The economic plan itself contains as a subplan a strategy for the transfer of accounting technology, composed of:

1. objectives for the accounting technology transfer;
2. strategy;
3. channels of transfer;
4. levels of accounting technology.

The three types of technology, individual, organizational, and independent professional, are defined as follows:

T_1: level of technical accounting knowledge possessed by individuals;

T_2: level of sophistication of accounting techniques used by government and business organizations;

T_3: level of advancement of an independent accounting profession.[68]

While the mere transfer of accounting technology may appear to be a direct benefit to the developing countries, there is the cost associated with (a) the transfer of the wrong or inapplicable technology, (b) the lack of appropriate infrastructure for the correct application of the technology, (c) the increased dependence on outside experts, (d) the lack of incentives for developing local standards, and (e) the horrible loss of pride by some culture groups. These costs ought to be compared with the benefits of technology transfer by each of the developing countries. It is a strategic decision which is an integral part of the overall economic plan, as suggested earlier. The whole process of development ought to include not only economic growth strategies but accounting growth strategies, and therein lies the question of the desirability of accounting technology transfer by the developing countries.

5.8.3 The adoption of international accounting standards

The strategy available to the developing countries consists of joining the International Accounting Standards Committee (IASC) or some of the other international standards bodies identified earlier and adopting "wholesale" their pronouncements. The rationale behind such strategy may be to:

(a) reduce the setup and production costs of accounting standards;

(b) join the international harmonization drive;

(c) facilitate the growth of foreign investment which may be needed;

(d) enable its profession to emulate well-established professional standards of behavior and conduct; and

(e) legitimize its status as a full-fledged member of the international community.

In fact, some of the developing countries give more credence to the IASC and other standards than do some of the developed countries that have a dominant influence in the preparation of such standards.

The question is whether the benefits described as accruing to the developing countries from the mere adoption of the international accounting standards may be outweighed by the misspecifying of costs. Indeed, the international standards for accounting for various transactions occurring in the advanced countries may be totally irrelevant to some of the developing countries, as these transactions have little chance of occurring or may be occurring in a fashion more specific to the context of the developing countries. The particular situations occurring in the developing countries call for specific and local standard-setting. In addition, the institutional and market factors of these countries are different enough in some contexts to justify a more "situationist" approach to standard-setting. Amenkhienan makes the same point as follows:

> The case against the adoption of international standards by developing nations as an alternative to developing their own local standards is a conclusive one. Accounting in each country should develop in a manner relevant to the needs and objectives of that country. The situational variables should determine the patterns of development.[69]

George Scott refers to the transfer of technology as a "fresh start", because its use established international standards as a basis toward a better fitting with the particular economic development context of the developing country. Scott elaborates as follows:

> The major alternative is to effect a relatively clean break with accounting tradition in developing nations and to attempt to develop accounting with a "fresh start" on the basis of the standards of accounting education, practices and professionalism that are embodied in economic evaluation accounting.[70]

5.8.4 The situationist strategy

The situationist strategy was also labeled as "the development of accounting standards based on an analysis of accounting principles and practices in the advanced nations against the backdrop of their underlying environments".[71] Basically, it calls for a consideration of the diagnostic factors which determine the development of accounting in the developing countries. A standard meeting the constraints imposed by these factors can be deemed relevant and useful to the developing countries. The total of these standards constitutes the system of reporting and disclosure of the developing country. The factors influencing it may be represented as being influenced by cultural linguistics, political and civil rights, economic and demographic characteristics, and the legal and tax environment of the country in question. In other words, based on cultural relativism, linguistic relativism, and legal and tax relativism, the accounting concepts and the reporting and disclosure systems in any given country rest on the varying aspects of that country.

5.9 Conclusions

The establishment and enforcement of accounting standards are emerging as complex problems. First, it does not appear that standards are based on broad, debated principles and a comparison of the pros and cons of relevant theories, and then chosen on that basis by the standard-setting body. Second, there are definite conflicts of interests and needs among the entities concerned with accounting principles. Third, the development of accounting principles has been a chaotic one – first dominated by management, then regulated by the profession, and finally becoming a truly political exercise. Fourth, every form of standard-setting in the free market, the private sector, or the public sector has its advantages and limitations; there is no clear-cut conceptual or practical winner. Fifth, the accounting standards-overload problem needs corrective solutions.

Appendix 5.A – Members of the International Accounting Standards Committee

Australia	Australian Society of Accountants
	The Institute of Chartered Accountants in Australia
Austria	Institut Osterreichischer Wirtschaftsprufer
Bahamas	The Bahamas Institute Of Chartered Accountants
Bahrain	The Bahrain Society of Accountants and Auditors
Bangladesh	The Institute of Chartered Accountants of Bangladesh
	The Institute of Cost and Management Accountants of Bangladesh
Barbados	The Institute of Chartered Accountants of Barbados
Belgium	L'Institut des Experts Comptables
	Institut des Reviseurs d'Entreprises
Botswana	The Association of Accountants in Botswana
Brazil	Instituto Brasileiro de Contadores
Canada	The Canadian Institute of Chartered Accountants
	Certified General Accountants' Association of Canada
	The Society of Management Accountants of Canada
Chile	Colegio de Contadores de Chile A.G.
Colombia	Instituto Nacional de Contadores Publicos de Colombia
Cyprus	The Institute of Certified Public Accountants of Cyprus
Denmark	Foreningen of Statsautoriserede Revisorer (FSR)
	Foreningen of Registrerede Revisor (FRR)
Dominican Republic	Instituto de Contadores Publicos Autorizados de la Republica Dominicana
Ecuador	Federacion Nacional de Contadores del Ecuador
Egypt	The Egyptian Society of Accountants and Auditors
Federal Republic of Germany	Institut der Wirtschaftsprufer in Deutschland e.V.
	Wirtschaftspruferkammer
Fiji	The Institute of Accountants
Finland	KHT – Yhidstys Foreningen CGR

France	Compagnie Nationale des Commissaires Aux Comptes
	Ordre des Experts Comptables et des Comptables Agrees
Ghana	The Institute of Chartered Accountants (Ghana)
Greece	Association of Certified Accountants and Auditors of Greece
	Institute of Certified Public Accountants of Greece
Hong Kong	Hong Kong Society of Accountants
Iceland	Felag Loggiltra Endurskooenda
India	The Institute of Chartered Accountants of India
	The Institute of Cost and Works Accountants of India
Indonesia	Indonesian Institute of Accountants
Iraq	The Association of Public Accountants and Auditors
Ireland	The Institute of Certified Public Accountants of Ireland
	The Institute of Chartered Accountants in Ireland
Israel	The Institute of Certified Public Accountants in Israel
Italy	Consiglio Nazionale dei Dottori Commercialisti
Jamaica	The Institute of Chartered Accountants of Jamaica
Japan	The Japanese Institute of Certified Public Accountants
Jordan	Arab Society of Certified Accountants
Kenya	Institute of Certified Public Accountants of Kenya
Korea	Korean Institute of Certified Public Accountants
Lebanon	The Lebanese Association of Certified Public Accountants
	The Middle East Society of Associated Accountants
Lesotho	Lesotho Institute of Accountants
Liberia	The Liberian Institute of Certified Public Accountants
Luxembourg	Ordre des Experts Comptables Luxembourgeois
Malawi	The Society of Accountants in Malawi
Malaysia	The Malaysian Association of Certified Public Accountants
	Institut Akauntan Malaysia
Malta	The Institute of Accountants
Mexico	Instituto Mexicano de Contadores Publicos A. C.
Morocco	Compagnie des Experts Comptables du Maroc
Netherlands	Netherlands Institute van Register accountants
New Zealand	New Zealand Society of Accountants
Nigeria	The Institute of Chartered Accountants of Nigeria
Norway	Norges Statsautoriscrte Revisorers Forening
	Norges Registrerte Revisorers Forening
Pakistan	Institute of Chartered Accountants of Pakistan
	Institute of Cost and Management Accountants of Pakistan
Paraguay	Colegio de Contadores del Paraguay
Philippines	Philippine Institute of Certified Public Accountants
Portugal	Camara dos Revisores Oficiais de Contas
Republic of Panama	Colegio de Contadores Publicos Autorizados de Panama
Singapore	Singapore Society of Accountants
South Africa	The South African Institute of Chartered Accountants
Spain	Instituto de Censores jurados de Cuentas de Espana
Sri Lanka	Institute of Chartered Accountants of Sri Lanka
Swaziland	The Swaziland Institute of Accountants
Sweden	Foreningen Auktoriserade Revisorer FAR
Switzerland	Schweizerische Treuhand-und Revisionskammer
Syria	Association des Experts Comptables Syrienne
Taiwan	National Federation of Certified Public Accountants
	Associations of the Republic of China

Tanzania	Tanzania Association of Accountants
	The National Board of Accountants and Auditors, Tanzania
Thailand	The Institute of Certified Public Accountants and Auditors of Thailand
Trinidad and Tobago	The Institute of Chartered Accountants of Trinidad and Tobago
Tunisia	Ordre des Experts Comptables et des Commissaires aux Comptes de Societes de Tunisie
Turkey	Experts Accountants' Association of Turkey
United Kingdom	The Chartered Association of Certified Accountants
	The Chartered Institute of Management Accountants
	The Chartered Institute of Public Finance and Accountancy
	The Institute of Chartered Accountants in England and Wales
	The Institute of Chartered Accountants in Ireland
	The Institute of Chartered Accountants in Scotland
United States of America	American Institute of Certified Public Accountants
	National Association of State Boards of Accountancy
	National Association of Accountants
	Institute of Internal Auditors
Uruguay	Colegio de Doctores en Ciencias Economicas y Contadores del Uruguay
Yugoslavia	The Social Accountancy Service of Yugoslavia
Zambia	The Zambia Institute of Certified Public Accountants
Zimbabwe	The Institute of Chartered Accountants of Zimbabwe

Notes

1. Rand Hatfield, Henry, "A Historical Defense of Bookkeeping", in W.T., Baxter and S. Davidson (eds.), *Studies in Accounting* (London: The Institute of Chartered Accountants in England and Wales, 1977), p. 2.
2. Baxter, W.T., "Accounting Standards – Boon or Curse?" in *The Emmanuel Saxe Distinguished Lectures in Accounting 1978–1979* (New York: The Bernard M. Baruch College, 1979), p. 30.
3. Edey, H.C., "Accounting Standards in the British Isles", in W.T., Baxter and Sydney Davidson (eds.), *Studies in Accounting*, 3rd edn (London: Institute of Chartered Accountants of England and Wales, 1977), pp. 295–8.
4. George J. Benston refers to the types of standards, respectively, as *disclosure-content*, *specific-instruction-content*, and *conceptually-based-content* standards. See Benston, George J., "Methods, Benefits, and Costs", *Accounting and Business Research* (Winter, 1980), p. 53.
5. Edey, H.C., "Accounting Standards in the British Isles", op. cit., p. 57.
6. Roland, Robert G., "Duty, Obligation, and Responsibility in Accounting Policy Making", *Journal of Accounting and Public Policy* (Fall, 1984), p. 225.
7. Cooper, David J., and Sherer, Michael J., "The Value of Corporate Accounting Reports: Arguments for a Political Economy of Accounting", *Accounting, Organizations and Society* (September, 1984), p. 184.
8. Shapiro, Brian P., "Objectivity, Relativism, and Truth in External Financial Reporting: What's Really at Stake in the Disputes?", *Accounting, Organizations and Society* (22, 2, 1997), pp. 165–85.
9. Ibid., p. 167.
10. Moonitz, Maurice, *The Basic Postulates of Accounting*, Accounting Research Study No. 1 (New York: American Institute of Certified Public Accountants, 1961); Sprouse, R.T., and

Moonitz, Maurice, *A Tentative Set of Broad Accounting Principles for Business Enterprises*, Accounting Research Study No. 3 (New York: American Institute of Certified Public Accountants, 1962).

11. Ijiri, Y., "A Dialogue on Research and Standard Setting in Accounting", in R.D. Nair and T.H. Williams (eds.), *Perspective in Research: Proceedings of the 1980 Beyer Consortium* (School of Business, University of Wisconsin, Radison, NY, 1980), p. 33.

12. Sevieringa, Robert J., "Accounting Research and Policy Making", *Accounting and Finance* (38, 1998), pp. 29–49.

13. Ibid., pp. 32–3.

14. Horngren, Charles, T., "Accounting Principles: Private or Public Sector?" *Journal of Accountancy* (May, 1972), p. 38.

15. The statement is from an interview with John C. Burton, "Paper Shuffling and Economic Reality", *Journal of Accountancy* (January, 1973), p. 26.

16. Beaver, William H., *Financial Reporting An Accounting Revolution* (Englewood Cliffs, NJ: Prentice-Hall, 1989), p. 13.

17. Peltzman, S., "Toward a More General Theory of Regulation", *The Journal of Law and Economics* (August, 1976), pp. 211–40.

18. Benston, George J., "Accounting Standards in the US and the UK: Their Nature, Causes, and Consequences", *Vanderbilt Law Review* (January, 1975), p. 255.

19. Hussein, M.E., and Ketz, J.E., "Ruling Elites of the FASB: A Study of the Big Eight", *Journal of Accounting, Auditing, and Finance* (Summer, 1980), pp. 354–67.

20. Gonedes, N.J., and Dopuch, N., "Capital–Market Equilibrium, Information Production, and Selecting Accounting Techniques: Theoretical Framework and Review of Empirical Work", *Studies on Financial Accounting Objectives*, supplement to *Journal of Accounting Research* (1974), pp. 48–129.

21. Leftwich, R.W., "Market Failure Fallacies and Accounting Information", *Journal of Accounting and Economics* (December, 1980), p. 200.

22. Ball, R., "Changes in Accounting Techniques and Stock Prices", *Empirical Studies in Accounting: Selected Studies, 1972*, supplement to *Journal of Accounting Research* (1972), p. 4.

23. Barta, Eli, and Bodnar, Gordon M., "Alternative Accounting Methods, Information Asymmetry and Liquidity: Theory and Evidence", *The Accounting Review* (July, 1996), pp. 357–418.

24. Diamond, D.W., and Verrecchia, R.E., "Disclosure, Liquidity and the Cost of Capital", *The Journal of Finance* (46, 1991), pp. 1325–6.

25. Leftwich, R.W., "Market Failure Fallacies and Accounting Information", op. cit., p. 208.

26. Kripke, Homer, "World Market Forces Cause Adequate Disclosure Without SEC Mandate", in A.R. Abdel-Khalik (ed.), *Government Regulation of Accounting and Information* (Gainesville: University Presses of Florida, 1980), p. 210.

27. Brown, P.R., "FASB Responsiveness to Corporate Input", *Journal of Accounting, Auditing, and Finance* (Summer, 1982), p. 283.

28. Kaplan, Robert S., "Should Accounting Standards Be Set in the Public or Private Sector?" in J.W. Buckley and J.F. Weston (eds.), *Regulation and the Accounting Profession* (Belmont, CA: Lifetime Learning Publications, 1980), p. 185.

29. US Senate Committee on Government Operations, Subcommittee on Reports, Accounting, and Management, *Summary of the Accounting Establishment. A Staff Study* (New York: National Association of Accountants, December, 1976).

30. Kaplan, Robert S., "Should Accounting Standards Be Set in the Public or Private Sector?" op. cit., p. 183.

31. Horngren, Charles T., "Accounting Principles: Private or Public Sector?" op. cit., p. 10.

32. Elliot, R.K., and Schuetze, W., "Regulation of Accounting: A Practitioner's Viewpoint", in A.R. Abdel-Khalik (ed.), *Government Regulation of Accounting Information* (Gainesville, FL: University Presses of Florida, 1980), pp. 109–10.

33. Buckley, J.W., and O'Sullivan, P., "Regulation and the Accounting Profession: What Are The Issues?" in J.W. Buckley and J.F. Weston (eds.), *Regulation and the Accounting Profession* (Belmont, CA: Lifetime Learning Publications, 1980), pp. 46–8.

34. Burton, John C., "The SEC and Financial Reporting: The Sand in the Oyster", in A.R. Abdel-Khalik (ed.), *Government Regulation of Accounting Information* (Gainesville, FL: University Presses of Florida, 1980), p. 74.

35. Ibid., pp. 79–80.

36. Ibid., p. 85.

37. Ibid., p. 80.

38. Kaplan, Robert S., "Should Accounting Standards Be Set in the Public or Private Sector?" op. cit., p. 187.

39. Chetkovich, M.N., "The Accounting Profession Responds to the Challenge of Regulation", in J.W. Buckley and J.F. Weston (eds.), *Regulation and the Accounting Profession* (Belmont, CA: Lifetime Learning Publications, 1980), p. 148.

40. Buchholz, R.A., "Corporate Cost for Compliance with Government Regulation of Information", in A.R. Abdel-Khalik (ed.), *Government Regulation of Accounting and Information* (Gainesville, FL: University Presses of Florida, 1980), p. 26.

41. Niskaven, W., *Bureaucracy and Representative Government* (Chicago, IL: Aldine Atherton Press, 1971).

42. Watts, R.L., "Beauty Is in the Eye of the Beholder: A Comment on John C. Burton's 'The SEC and Financial Reporting: The Sand in the Oyster'", in A.R. Abdel-Khalik (ed.), *Government Regulation of Accounting information* (Gainesville, FL: University Presses of Florida, 1980), pp. 99–100.

43. This point was suggested to me by Professor Ronald Picur, University of Illinois at Chicago.

44. Moss, David, "Regulation and the Accounting Profession: An FASB Member's View", in J.W. Buckley and J.F. Weston (eds.), *Regulation and the Accounting Profession* (Belmont, CA: Lifetime Learning Publications, 1980), p. 137.

45. Marshall, Ronald, "Determining an Optimal Accounting Information System for an Undefined User", *Journal of Accounting Research* (Fall, 1972), pp. 286–307.

46. Arrow, K., *Social Choice and Individual Values* (New York: Wiley, 1963).

47. Demski, Joel S., "The General Impossibility of Normative Accounting Standards", *The Accounting Review* (October, 1973), pp. 718–23.

48. Ibid., pp. 721–2.

49. Demski, Joel S., "Choice Among Financial Reporting Alternatives", *The Accounting Review* (April, 1974), pp. 221–32.

50. Beaver, William H., and Deusli, Joel S., "The Nature of Financial Accounting Objectives: A Summary and Synthesis", *Studies on Financial Accounting Objectives: 1974*, Supplement to *Journal of Accounting Research* (1974), pp. 170–87.

51. Cushing, Barry E., "On the Possibility of Optimal Accounting Principles", *The Accounting Review* (April, 1977), p. 310.

52. Ibid., p. 313.

53. Bromwich, Michael, "The Possibility of Partial Accounting Standards", *The Accounting Review* (April, 1980), pp. 288–300.

54. Chambers, R.J., "The Possibility of a Normative Accounting Standards", *The Accounting Review* (July, 1976), pp. 646–56.

55. Ibid., p. 651.

56. Tullock, G., "The General Irrelevance of the General Impossibility Theorem", *Quarterly Journal of Economics* (August, 1967), pp. 256–70.

57. Johnson, S.B., and Solomons, D., "Institutional Legitimacy and the FASB", *Journal of Accounting and Public Policy* (Fall, 1984), pp. 165–83.

58. Buchanan, J., and Tullock, G., *The Calculus of Consent: Logical Foundations of Constitutional Democracy* (Ann Arbor, MI: University of Michigan Press, 1962).

59. Johnson, S.B., and Solomons, D., "Institutional Legitimacy and the FASB", op. cit., p. 167.

60. Ibid., pp. 175–9.

61. Moss, David, "Standards Overload – No Simple Solution", *Journal of Accountancy* (November, 1983), p. 120.

62. Fields T., Lys, T., and Vincent, L., "Empirical Research in Accounting Choice", *Journal of Accounting and Economics* (31, 1–3, 2001), pp. 255–307.

63. Watts, Ross L., and Zimmerman, Jerold L., *Positive Accounting Theory* (Englewood Cliffs, NJ: Prentice-Hall, 1986).

64. Holthausen, R., and Leftwich, R., "The Economic Consequences of Accounting Choice: Implications of Costly Contracting and Monitoring", *Journal of Accounting and Economics* (5, 1983), pp. 77–117.

65. Amenkhienan, F.E., *Accounting in the Developing Countries: A Framework for Standard Setting*, op. cit., pp. 22–6.

66. Enthoven, Adolf J., "US Accounting and the Third World", *Journal of Accountancy* (June, 1983), p. 112.

67. Needles, Jr., B.E., "Implementing a Framework for the International Transfer of Accounting Technology", *International Journal of Accounting Education and research* (Fall, 1976), p. 51.

68. Ibid., p. 51.

69. Amenkhienan, F.E., *Accounting in the Developing Countries*, op. cit., p. 74.

70. Scott, G.M., *Accounting and the Developing Nations* (Seattle: University of Washington, 1970), p. 12.

71. Ibid., p. 25.

References

Goals of standard-setting

Buckley, John W., "The FASB and Impact Analysis", *Management Accounting* (April, 1976), pp. 13–17.

Cooper, David J., and Sherer, Michael J., "The Value of Corporate Accounting Reports: Arguments for a Political Economy of Accounting", *Accounting, Organizations and Society* (September, 1984), pp. 207–32.

Gellein, Oscar S., "Neutrality has Consequences", *FASB Viewpoints* (Stamford, CT: FASB, 1978).

Kirk, Donald J., "Concepts, Consensus, Compromise and Consequences: Their Setting", *Journal of Accountancy* (April, 1981), pp. 83–6.

May, Robert G., and Sundem, Gary L., "Research in Accounting Policy: An Overview", *The Accounting Review* (October, 1976), pp. 747–63.

Ruland, Robert G., "Duty Obligations and Responsibility in Accounting Policy Making", *Journal of Accounting and Public Policy* (Fall, 1984), pp. 223–38.

Solomons, David, "The Politicization of Accounting", *Journal of Accountancy* (November, 1978), pp. 65–72.

Tinker, Anthony, "Theories of The State and State Accounting: Economic Reduction and Polity Voluntarism in Accounting Regulation Theory", *Journal of Accounting and Public Policy* (Spring, 1984), pp. 55–74.

Tinker, Anthony, "Towards a Political Economy of Accounting", *Accounting, Organizations and Society* (May, 1980), pp. 147–60.

Who should set accounting standards?

Armstrong, Marshall S., "The Politics of Establishing Accounting Standards", *Journal of Accountancy* (February, 1971), pp. 76–9.

Benston, George, "The Market for Public Accounting Services: Demand, Supply, and Regulation", *Journal of Accounting and Public Policy* (Spring, 1985), pp. 33–80.

Bromwich, Michael, *The Economics of Accounting Standard Setting* (Prentice Hall/Institute of Chartered Accountants in England and Wales, 1985).

Brown, P.R., "FASB Responsiveness to Corporate Input", *Journal of Accounting, Auditing, and Finance* (Summer, 1982), pp. 282–90.

Chatov, Robert, *Corporate Financial Reporting: Public or Private Control* (New York: The Free Press, 1975).

Committee, Bruce Edward, "The Delegation and Privatization of Financial Accounting Rulemaking Authority in the United States of America", *Critical Perspectives on Accounting* (June, 1990), pp. 145–66.

Chow, Chee W., "Empirical Studies of the Effects of Accounting Regulations on Security Prices: Findings, Problems, and Prospects", *Journal of Accounting Literature* (Spring, 1983), pp. 73–109.

Ellyson, R.C., and Van Reusselaer, W.H., "Sunset – Is the Profession Ready for It?" *Journal of Accountancy* (June, 1980), pp. 52–61.

Foster, George, "Externalities and Financial Reporting", *Journal of Finance* (May, 1980), pp. 521–33.

Foster, George, "Accounting Policy Decisions and Capital Market Research", *Journal of Accounting and Economics* (June, 1980), pp. 29–62.

Haring, J.R., Jr., "Accounting Rules and 'The Accounting Establishment'", *Journal of Business* (October, 1979), pp. 507–19.

Holthausen, Robert W., and Leftwich, Richard W., "The Economic Consequences of Accounting Choice: Implications of Costly Contracting and Monitoring", *Journal of Accounting and Economics* (August, 1983), pp. 77–117.

Horngren, Charles T., "Accounting Principles: Private or Public Sector?", *Journal of Accountancy* (May, 1972), pp. 37–41.

Horngren, Charles T., "Accounting Principles: Private or Public Sector?", *Journal of Accountancy* (May, 1972), pp. 38–42.

Hussein, M.E., and Ketz, J.E., "Ruling Elites of the FASB: A Study of the Big Eight", *Journal of Accounting, Auditing, and Finance* (Summer, 1980), pp. 357–67.

Ingram, Robert W., and Chewning, Eugene G., "The Effect of Financial Disclosure Regulation on Security Market Behavior", *The Accounting Review* (July, 1983), pp. 562–80.

Johnson, S.B., and Messier, W.F., Jr., "The Nature of Accounting Standards Setting: An Alternative Explanation", *Journal of Accounting, Auditing, and Finance* (Spring, 1982), pp. 195–213.

Kelly-Newton, L., *Accounting, Policy Formulation: The Role of Corporate Management* (Reading, MA: Addison-Wesley, 1980).

Kirk, Donald J., "How to Keep Politics Out of Standard Setting: Making Private Sector Rule Making Work", *Journal of Accountancy* (September, 1978), pp. 92–4.

Leftwich, Richard W., "Market Failure Fallacies and Accounting Information", *Journal of Accounting Economics* (December, 1980), pp. 193–211.

Lindahl, Frederick W., "Accounting Standards and Olson's Theory of Collective Action", *Journal of Accounting and Public Policy* (Spring, 1987), pp. 59–72.

Merino, Barbara Dubois, and Neimark, Marilyn Dale, "Disclosure Regulation and Public Policy: A Sociohistorical Reappraisal", *Journal of Accounting and Public Policy* (Fall, 1982), pp. 33–57.

Miller, Paul B.W., and Redding, Rodney, *The FASB: The People, the Process and the Politics* (Homewood, IL: Richard D. Irwin, 1986).

Moonitz, Maurice, "Obtaining Agreement on Standards in the Accounting Profession", *Studies in Accounting Research No. 8* (American Accounting Association, 1974).

O'Leary, Ted, "Observations on Corporate Financial Reporting in the Name of Politics", *Accounting, Organizations and Society 10* (1985, no. 1), pp. 87–102.

Olson, W.E., "Self-Regulation: What's Ahead?", *Journal of Accountancy* (March, 1980), pp. 46–9.

Peltzman, S., "Toward a More General Theory of Regulation", *The Journal of Law and Economics* (August, 1976), pp. 211–40.

Phillips, Susan M., and Zecher, J., Richard, *The SEC and the Public Interest* (Boston, MA: Cambridge: MIT Press, 1981).

Posner, R.A., "Theories of Economic Regulation", *Bell Journal of Economics* (Autumn, 1974), pp. 335–58.

Puro, Marsha, "Audit Firm Lobbying Before the Financial Accounting Standards Board: An Empirical Study", *Journal of Accounting Research* (Autumn, 1984), pp. 624–46.

Puxty, A.G., Wilmott, Hugh C., Cooper, David J., and Lowe, Tony, "Modes of Regulation in Advanced Capitalism: Locating Accountancy in Four Countries", *Accounting, Organizations and Society* (12, 3, 1987), pp. 273–91.

Sterling, Robert R. (ed.), *Institutional Issues in Public Accounting* (Houston: Lawrence, KS: Scholars Book Company, 1974).

Stigler, G.J., "Theory of Economic Regulation", *Bell Journal of Economics* (Spring, 1971), pp. 3–21.

Solomons, David, *Making Accounting Policy: The Quest for Credibility in Financial Reporting* (New York: Oxford: Oxford University Press, 1986).

US Senate Committee on Government Operations, Subcommittee on Reports, Accounting, and Management, *Summary of The Accounting Establishment, A Staff Study* (New York: National Association of Accountants, December 1976).

Watts, Ross L., "Corporate Financial Statements; Product of the Market and Political Processes", *Australian Journal of Management* (April, 1977), pp. 53–75.

Watts, Ross L., "Can Optimal Information Be Determined by Regulation?" in John W. Buckley and J. Fred Weston (eds.), *Regulation and the Accounting Profession* (Belmont, CA: Lifetime Learning Publication, 1980), pp. 153–62.

Legitimacy of the standard-setting process

Beaver, W.H., and Demski, Joel S., "The Nature of Financial Accounting Objectives: A Summary and Synthesis", *Studies in Financial Accounting Objectives*, 1974, supplement to *Journal of Accounting Research* (1974), pp. 170–87.

Bromwich, Michael, "The Possibility of Partial Accounting Standards", *The Accounting Review* (April, 1980), pp. 288–300.

Chambers, R.J., "The Possibility of a Normative Accounting Standard", *The Accounting Review* (July, 1976), pp. 646–56.

Cushing, Barry E., "On the Possibility of Optimal Accounting Principles", *The Accounting Review* (April, 1977).

Demski, Joel S., "The General Impossibility of Normative Accounting Standards", *The Accounting Review* (October, 1973), pp. 718–23.

Demski, Joel S., "Choice Among Financial Reporting Alternatives", *The Accounting Review* (April, 1974), pp. 221–32.

Johnson, S.B., and Solomons, D., "Institutional Legitimacy and the FASB", *Journal of Accounting and Public Policy* (Fall, 1984), pp. 165–83.

Marshall, Ronald, "Determining an Optimal Accounting Information System for an Unidentified User", *Journal of Accounting Research* (Fall, 1978), 286–307.

Accounting standards overload

Alderman, C.W., Gary, D.M., and Meals, D.R., "Other Comprehensive Bases of Accounting: Alternative to GAAP?" *Journal of Accountancy* (August, 1982), pp. 52–62.

Chazen, C., and Benson, B., "Fitting GAAP to Smaller Businesses", *Journal of Accountancy* (February, 1978), pp. 46–51.

Hepp, G.W., and McRae, T.W., "Accounting Standards Overload: Relief is Needed", *Journal of Accountancy* (May, 1988), pp. 52–62.

Larson, R.E., and Kelly, T.P., "Differential Measurement in Accounting Standards: The Concept Makes Sense", *Journal of Accountancy* (November, 1984), pp. 78–90.

Lee, B.Z., Larson, R.E., and Chenok, P.B., "Issues Confronting the Accounting Profession", *Journal of Accountancy* (November, 1983), pp. 78–85.

A conceptual framework for financial accounting and reporting

6

Accounting theory constitutes the frame of reference on which the development of accounting techniques is based. This frame of reference, in turn, is based primarily on the establishment of accounting concepts and principles. Of vital importance to the accounting disciplines is that the accounting profession and other interest groups accept these concepts and principles. To guarantee such a consensus, a statement of the reasons or objectives that motivate the establishment of the concepts and principles must be the first step in the formulation of an accounting theory.

A statement of the objectives of financial statements has always been recognized as urgent and essential if the debate over alternative standards and reporting techniques is to be resolved by reason and logic. For example, in 1960, Devine argued that:

> ... the first order of business in constructing a theoretical system for a service function is to establish the purpose and the objectives of the function. The objectives and purposes may shift through time, but for any period, they must be specified or specifiable.[1]

Watts and Zimmerman note that financial accounting theory has had little substantive, direct impact on accounting theory and practice and offer the following explanation:

> Often the lack of impact is attributed to basic methodological weakness in the research. Or, the prescriptions offered are based on explicit or implicit objectives that frequently differ from writers. Not only are the researchers unable to agree on the objectives of financial statements, but they also disagree over the methods of deriving the prescriptions from the objectives.[2]

Aware of the importance of objectives, the accounting professions in the United States, the United Kingdom and Canada have made various attempts to formulate the objectives of financial statements. In the United States, the importance of the development of financial statements objectives was first expressed by the report of the Study Group on the Objectives of Financial Statements[3] and emphasized the FASB attempts to develop a conceptual framework or constitution.[4] In the United Kingdom, the importance of these objectives was highlighted by the publication of *The Corporate Report*[5] by the Institute of Chartered Accountants in England and Wales. In Canada, interest in the subject resulted in the publication of *Corporate Reporting*.[6] Although relatively recent, all of these efforts are directly influenced to a great extent by Chapter 4 of APB Statement No. 4.[7]

In this chapter, we will elaborate on the various attempts to formulate the objectives of financial statements and a conceptual framework for financial accounting and reporting in the United States, the United Kingdom and Canada.

6.1 Classification and conflicts of interests

Formulating the objectives of accounting depends on resolving the conflicts of interests that exist in the information market. More specifically, financial statements result from the interaction of three groups: firms, users and the accounting profession.[8]

Firms comprise the main party engaged in the accounting process. By their operational, financial and extraordinary (that is, nonoperational) activities, they justify the production of financial statements. Their existence and behavior produce financial results that are partly measurable by the accounting process. Firms are also the preparers of accounting information.

Users comprise the second group. The production of accounting information is influenced by their interests and needs. Although it is not possible to compile a complete list of users, the list would include shareholders, financial analysts, creditors and government agencies.

The accounting profession constitutes the third group that may affect the information to be included in financial statements. Accountants act principally as "auditors" in charge of verifying that financial statements conform to generally accepted accounting principles.

The interaction between these three groups may be represented by a Venn diagram, as shown in Exhibit 6.1, where circle U represents the interests of the users in the information deemed useful for their economic decision-making, circle C represents the set of information that the corporation publishes and discloses (whether or not it is within the boundaries of generally accepted accounting principles) and circle P represents the set of information that the accounting profession is capable of producing and verifying. The area labeled I represents the set of information that is acceptable to all three groups. In other words, these data are disclosed by the firm, accountants are capable of producing and verifying them, and they are perceived as relevant by users. Areas II–VII represent areas of conflicts of interest.

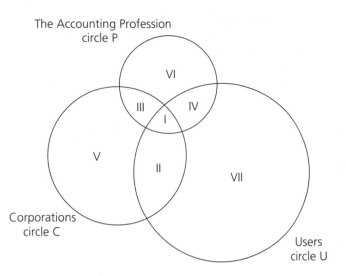

The Accounting Profession
circle P

Corporations
circle C

Users
circle U

Source: Richard M. Cyert, and Yuji Ijiri, "Problems of Implementing the Trueblood Objectives Report",
Journal of Accounting Research, Studies on Financial Accounting Objectives, supplement to vol. 12
(1974), diagram 1, p. 30. Reprinted with permission.

Exhibit 6.1

Given these conflicts, there are three possible approaches to the formulation of accounting objectives. The first approach considers the set of information that the firm is ready to disclose and attempts to find the best means of measuring and verifying it (in other words, area C is kept fixed and areas P and U are moved toward it). The second approach considers the information that the profession is capable of measuring and verifying and attempts to accommodate users and firms through various accounting options (in other words, area P is kept fixed and areas C and U are moved toward it). The third approach views the set of information deemed relevant by users as central and encourages the profession and the firms to produce and verify that information (in other words, area U is kept fixed and areas P and C are moved toward it).

Stated simply, the first approach is *firm-oriented*, the second approach is *profession-oriented* and the third approach is *user-oriented*. Needless to say, given the dominance of the political and legislative approaches to the formulation of an accounting theory, as we saw in Chapter 4, the user-oriented approach will prevail when future objectives of financial statements are formulated. In fact, the user-oriented approach is employed both by the group on the objectives of financial statements in the United States and by *The Corporate Report* in the United Kingdom; other approaches have been utilized for APB Statement No. 4.

6.2 Toward a formulation of the objectives of financial statements

6.2.1 The objectives of financial statements as stated in APB Statement No. 4

The Accounting Research Division of the Accounting Principles Board was created to motivate research on the basic postulates and principles of accounting. Accounting Research Statements (ARS) Nos 1 and 3 were rejected, however, and although ARS No. 7

was accepted, it did not lead to a statement of broad principles of accounting. Subsequently, the Accounting Principles Board recommended that the objectives of accounting be defined and that the basic concepts, principles and terminology known as "generally accepted accounting principles" be enumerated and described. This recommendation resulted in the publication of APB Statement No. 4, *Basic Concepts and Accounting Principles Underlying Financial Statements of Business Enterprises*. Although it was basically descriptive, which diminished its chances of providing the first accounting conceptual framework, the statement did influence most subsequent attempts to formulate the objectives of financial statements and to develop a basic conceptual framework for the field of accounting. Chapter 4 of APB Statement No. 4 classifies objectives as particular, general and qualitative, and places them under a set of constraints. These objectives may be summarized as follows:

1. The *particular* objectives of financial statements are to present fairly and in conformity with generally accepted accounting principles, financial position, results of operations, and other changes in financial position.

2. The *general* objectives of financial statements are as follows:

   (a) To provide reliable information about the economic resources and obligations of a business enterprise in order to:
      (i)   evaluate its strengths and weaknesses;
      (ii)   show its financing and investments;
      (iii) evaluate its ability to meet its commitments;
      (iv)   show its resource base for growth.

   (b) To provide reliable information about changes in net resources resulting from a business enterprise's profit-directed activities in order to:
      (i)   show expected dividend return to investors;
      (ii)   demonstrate the operations ability to pay creditors and suppliers, provide jobs for employees, pay taxes and generate funds for expansion;
      (iii) provide management with information for planning and control;
      (iv)   show its long-term profitability.

   (c) To provide financial information that can be used to estimate the earnings potential of the firm.

   (d) To provide other needed information about changes in economic resources and obligations.

   (e) To disclose other information relevant to statement users' needs.

3. The *qualitative* objectives of financial accounting are the following:

   (a) *Relevance*, which means selecting the information most likely to aid users in their economic decisions.

   (b) *Understandability*, which implies not only that selected information must be intelligible, but also that the users can understand it.

   (c) *Verifiability*, which implies that the accounting results may be corroborated by independent measures, using the same measurement methods.

   (d) *Neutrality*, which implies that the accounting information is directed toward the common needs of users, rather than the particular needs of specific users.

   (e) *Timeliness*, which implies an early communication of information, to avoid delays in economic decision-making.

   (f) *Comparability*, which implies that differences should not be the result of different financial accounting treatments.

   (g) *Completeness*, which implies that all the information that "reasonably" fulfills the requirements of the other qualitative objectives should be reported.

The objectives expressed by APB Statement No. 4 appear to provide a rationale for the form and the content of conventional financial reports. The statement even admits that the particular objectives are stated in terms of accounting principles that are generally accepted at the time the financial statements are prepared. The general objectives fail to identify the informational needs of users. The statement implicitly recognizes these limitations when it admits that "the objectives of financial accounting and financial statements are at least partially achieved at present". Despite these limitations, APB Statement No. 4 has been a necessary step toward the development of a more consistent and comprehensive structure of financial accounting and of more useful financial information. As we will see, it has directly influenced both the "Trueblood Report" (discussed in the following sections) and *The Corporate Report* in their search for the objectives of financial statements as well as the FASB's attempts to develop a conceptual framework for financial accounting and reporting.

6.2.2 Report of the study group on the objectives of financial statements

Methodology used

In response to the criticism of corporate financial reporting and the realization that a conceptual framework of accounting is urgently needed, the Board of Directors of the American Institute of Certified Public Accountants announced the formation of two study groups in April 1971. The study group on the establishment of accounting principles, known as the "Wheat Committee", was charged with the task of improving the standard-setting process. Its report resulted in the formation of the Financial Accounting Standards Board (FASB). A second study group, known as the "Trueblood Committee", was charged with the development of the objectives of financial statements; that is, with determining:

1. who needs financial statements;
2. what information they need;
3. how much of the needed information can be provided through accounting; and
4. what framework is required to provide the needed information.

The Trueblood Committee was composed of nine members, representing the accounting profession, the academic world, industry and the Financial Analysts Federation. A team of academics, practitioners and consultants served as advisers. The Committee conducted meetings and interviews to assess the informational needs of various interested groups from all sectors of government and the business and professional communities. Relevant literature in accounting, economics and finance provided the basic conceptual foundations. On the basis of the empirical and conceptual data gathered, the study group issued two reports. The first and more important *Report of the Study Group on the Objectives of Financial Statements* contains the principal conclusions and the stated objectives of financial statements. The second report contains a selection of articles by the team of advisers that the study group considered when forming the conclusions and objectives in the first report.[9]

The objectives of financial statement as expressed in the "Trueblood Report"

Although the twelve objectives in the study group's report were intended to be equal, there is a justifiable tendency to distinguish a definite hierarchical structure to the objectives.[10] Differences in emphasis and the relative dependency among the objectives justify such a hierarchy. Accordingly, Exhibit 6.2 illustrates a hierarchical structure of the objectives of accounting; the basic objective appears at the top, and specific recommendations are arranged below it. The following six objective levels may be derived from the "Trueblood Report":

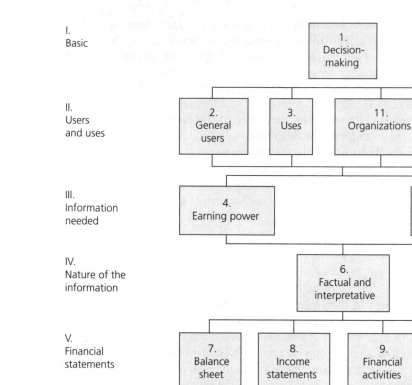

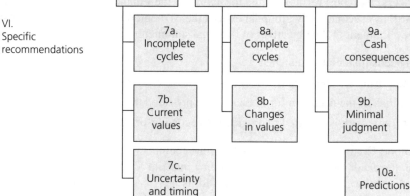

Exhibit 6.2 Trueblood's objectives

1. The basic objective (No. 1).

2. Four objectives (Nos 2, 3, 11 and 12) that specify the diverse users and uses of accounting information.

3. Two objectives (Nos 4 and 5) that specify enterprise earning power and management ability (accountability) as the type of information needed.

4. One objective (No. 6) that specifies the nature of the needed information as factual and interpretive.

5. Four objectives (Nos 7, 8, 9 and 10) that describe the financial statements required to meet objective No. 6.

6. A number of specific recommendations for the financial statements are made in order to meet each of the preceding objectives (Nos 7, 8, 9 and 10).

We will analyze each of the objectives:

> No. 1: *The basic objective of financial statements is to provide information on which to base economic decisions.*

The first objective clearly and directly links accounting to decision-making. The emphasis again is directed to the usefulness of accounting information. Decisions are characterized as "economic" in the sense that they refer to resource allocation. In other words, there is a direct link between the relevance of accounting information and the efficient allocation of resources.

> No. 2: *An objective of financial statements is to serve primarily those users who have limited authority, ability, or resources to obtain information and who rely on financial statements as their principal source of information about an enterprise's activity.*

Objective No. 2 seems to designate a "primary audience" for financial statements. This audience consists of those who have limited access to the information and therefore must rely on accounting reports. If we interpret the objective literally, the primary users of accounting information are shareholders who depend on financial statements for information about a firm's financial position, performance and changes in financial position. It may appear, therefore, that accountants should present a set of financial statements that, standing alone, contain relevant information for shareholders.

> No. 3: *An objective of financial statements is to provide information useful to investors and creditors for predicting, comparing, and evaluating potential cash flows to them in terms of amount, timing and related uncertainty.*

Objective No. 3 identifies two important users: investors and creditors. The basis of their interest in financial statements is the cash flow from the enterprise: no mention is made of net income. The decision models of both investors and creditors involve the tasks of prediction, comparison and evaluation of cash flows. The characteristics of cash flows of interest to investors and creditors pertain to amount, timing and degree of uncertainty. We may perceive an emphasis on the stochastic nature of accounting information in general and cash flow in particular.

> No. 4: *An objective of financial statements is to provide users with information for predicting, comparing and evaluating enterprise earning power.*

Although the third objective specifies the information and the decision model of investors and creditors, the fourth objective accomplishes the same task for all users. The decision model is still expressed in terms of the activities of prediction, comparison and evaluation, but the information needed is specified in terms of "earning power". This objective is important because it designates earning power rather than accounting income as the information primarily needed by users. Earning power is perceived as the ability to bring in cash, rather than as the ability to produce earnings. The emphasis on earning power and consequently on *cash flow* is a shift in emphasis from traditional accounting objectives.

> No. 5: *An objective of financial statements is to supply information useful in judging management's ability to utilize enterprise resources effectively in achieving the primary enterprise goal.*

To cash flows and earning power, specified by the third and fourth as the information needed, the fifth objective adds *management ability*. This implies that accounting data may be used to evaluate the economic behavior of management. This economic behavior includes the fiduciary stewardship function, or safekeeping of assets to prevent their loss. It goes beyond the stewardship function, however, to include all of management's decisions regarding the use of assets. Objective No. 5 assumes that accounting data can measure management's ability to use resources effectively to achieve the primary enterprise goal.

> No. 6: *An objective of financial statements is to provide factual and interpretive information about transactions and other events that is useful for predicting, comparing and evaluating enterprise earning power. Basic underlying assumptions with respect to matters subject to interpretation, evaluation, prediction or estimation should be disclosed.*

Objective No. 6 expands the scope of accounting measurement to include not only factual or objective information but also interpretive or subjective information. The prediction, comparison and evaluation of enterprise earning power rest not only on objective and verifiable information, but also subjective information, which may be subject to interpretation. Such factual and interpretive information is the result of both transactions and events. We may interpret the sixth objective as an application of the events approach. Because information may be interpretive rather than factual and because it may result from events rather than transactions, the sixth objective specifically recommends that the accountant discloses the assumptions from which the information was derived. Such disclosure facilitates the interpretation, evaluation, prediction or estimation on the basis of factual and interpretive information about transactions and events.

> No. 7: *An objective is to provide a statement of financial position that is useful for predicting, comparing and evaluating enterprise earning power. This statement should provide information concerning enterprise transactions and other events that are part of incomplete earnings cycles. Current values should also be reported when they differ significantly from historical cost. Assets and liabilities should be grouped or segregated by the relative uncertainty of the amount and timing of prospective realization or liquidation.*

Objective No. 7 refers to a concept of a balance sheet or a statement of financial position. The objective specifically recommends that the *balance sheet* or *statement of financial position* includes transactions and events of incomplete earnings cycles, the possible reporting of current values and the criteria for grouping or segregating assets and liabilities. The seventh objective distinguishes between a *complete* earnings cycle (a chain of events with an impact on earning power that lies in the past), an *incomplete* cycle (a chain of events that has commenced but is not yet complete) and a *prospective* cycle (a chain of events that lies wholly in the future). Thus, a statement of financial position reports on the transactions and events that are not yet complete. More specifically,

> [an] earnings cycle is defined as incomplete when:
> (i) a realized sacrifice or a benefit has occurred, but the related benefit or sacrifice has not been realized;
> (ii) both sacrifice and benefit are not realized; or
> (iii) the effort has not taken place.[11]

Given this objective, a timid step is made toward the disclosure of current values. The uncertainty of the amount and timing of prospective realization or liquidation seems to call for probabilistic values.

> No. 8: *An objective is to provide statement of periodic earnings useful for predicting, comparing and evaluating enterprise earning power. The net result of completed earnings cycles and enterprise activities resulting in recognizable progress toward completion of incomplete cycles should be reported. Changes in the values reflected in successive statements of financial position should also be reported, but separately, since they differ in terms of their certainty of realization.*

Objective No. 8 refers to a concept of a profit-and-loss statement or a statement of periodic earnings. The objective recommends that the profit-and-loss statements or the statement of periodic earnings include transactions and events of completed earnings cycles, results of the progress of incomplete cycles and changes in values. Specifically, the reporting of transactions and events that are complete and the progress of incomplete cycles is recommended:

> For an earnings cycle to be defined as completed, three conditions should be fulfilled:
>
> (1) a realized sacrifice (an actual or high disbursement of cash);
> (2) a related realized benefit (an actual or high probable receipt of cash);
> (3) no further related substantive effort.[12]

The eighth objective states that the inclusion of unrealized value changes in earnings is both desirable and practical as long as they are disclosed separately to emphasize the uncertainty of their realization.

> No. 9: *An objective is to provide a statement of financial activities useful for predicting, comparing and evaluating enterprise earning power. This statement should report mainly on factual aspects of enterprise transactions having or expected to have significant cash consequences. This statement should report data that require minimal judgment and interpretation by the preparer.*

The statement refers to a *concept of funds statement*, or a *statement of financial activities*. Objective No. 9 specifically recommends reporting transactions that establish highly probable receipts and disbursements of cash and factual information with minimal intervention by the preparer. The statement of earnings shows *progress* and *results* and the statement of financial position shows *structure*, but the statement of financial activities shows *conduct*. The statement of earnings reports the relationship between sacrifice and benefits during different periods through matching and allocation procedures. The statement of financial activities reports only the enterprise's financial transactions (the benefits and sacrifices) made during the period that are presumed to have cash consequences.

> No. 10: *An objective of financial statements is to provide information useful for the predictive process. Financial forecasts should be provided when they will enhance the reliability of users' predictions.*

Again, the objective emphasizes the importance of predicting and forecasting in the economic decision-making process. Publication of explicit forecasts of enterprise activities is deemed an important objective of financial statements. Specifically, Objective No. 10

recommends that, in order to be published, these forecasts must enhance the relative accuracy of users' predictions.

> No. 11: *An objective of a financial statement for governmental and not-for-profit organizations is to provide information useful for evaluating the effectiveness of the management of resources in achieving the organization's goals that are primarily nonmonetary. Performance measures should be expressed in terms of the not-for-profit organization's goals.*

Objective No. 11's expansion of the scope of financial accounting to the measurement of the performance and goal attainment of governmental and not-for-profit organizations is rather difficult, and because the goals of such organizations are primarily nonmonetary, performance measures should be expressed in terms of the not-for-profit organization's goals.

> No. 12: *An objective of financial statements is to report on those activities of the enterprise affecting society which can be determined and described or measured and which are important to the enterprise in its social environment.*

Objective No. 12 adds a socioeconomic dimension to the scope of financial accounting. It recognizes the possible interactions between the private goals of the enterprise and its social goals. There may be *reciprocal* or *direct* interactions when the enterprise derives social benefits, such as fire and police protection, in exchange for tax payments or private costs. In the case of direct and reciprocal interactions, therefore, the firm enjoys benefits and incurs costs. Interactions may also be *nonreciprocal* or *indirect*. Examples are situations in which a firm contributes to the social welfare, which is a social benefit, or when the firms impose a burden on society, which is a social cost. Objective No. 12 seems to call for reporting both the sacrifices and the benefits accruing to a firm that result from direct and reciprocal interactions and indirect and nonreciprocal interactions. The stewardship function may be perceived not only as the safeguarding of assets of the firm but also the safeguarding of the social welfare.

Qualitative characteristics of reporting

To satisfy users' needs, information contained in financial statements must possess certain characteristics. The "Trueblood Report" mentions seven qualitative characteristics of reporting:

1. relevance and materiality;
2. form and substance;
3. reliability;
4. freedom from bias;
5. comparability;
6. consistency; and
7. understandability.

In the Report's words:

> The qualitative characteristics of financial statements should be based largely on the needs of users of the statements. Information should be as free as possible from any bias of the preparer. In making decisions, users should not only understand the information

presented, but also should be able to assess its reliability and compare it with information about alternative opportunities and previous experience. In all cases, information is more useful if it stresses economic substance rather than technical form.[13]

6.3 Toward a conceptual framework

6.3.1 The nature of a conceptual framework

The "Trueblood Report" specified twelve objectives and seven qualitative characteristics of financial reporting. Since its inception, the FASB has recognized the importance of the objectives of financial statements in the adoption of financial standards. The FASB has also realized that the whole problem of standard-setting rests not only on the objectives, but also on an established body of concepts and objectives. In fact, the Board has acknowledged the erosion of the credibility of financial reporting in recent years, and has criticized the following situations:

- Two or more methods of accounting are accepted for the same facts.
- Less conservative accounting methods are being used rather than the earlier, more conservative methods.
- Reserves are used to artificially smooth earning fluctuations.
- Financial statements fail to warn of impending liquidity crunches. Deferrals are followed by "big bath" write-offs.
- Unadjusted optimism exists in estimates of recoverability.
- Off-balance-sheet financing (that is, disclosure in the notes to the financial statements) is common.
- An unwarranted assertion of immateriality has been used to justify nondisclosure of unfavorable information or departures from standards.
- Form is relevant over substance.[14]

To correct some of these situations and to provide a more rigorous way of setting standards and increasing financial statement users' understanding and confidence in financial reporting, the FASB instituted a conceptual-framework project. The Board described this project as follows:

> A conceptual framework is a constitution, a coherent system of interrelated objectives and fundamentals that can lead to consistent standards and that prescribes the nature, function, and limits of financial accounting and financial statements. The objectives identify the goals and the purposes of accounting. The fundamentals are the underlying concepts of accounting concepts that guide the selection of events to be accounted for, the measurement of those events and the means of summarizing and communicating to interested parties. Concepts of that type are fundamental in the sense that other concepts flow from them and repeated references to them will be necessary in establishing, interpreting and applying accounting and reporting standards.[15]

The conceptual framework, therefore, is intended to act as a constitution for the standard-setting process. Its purpose is to guide in resolving disputes that arise during the standard-setting process by narrowing the question to whether or not specific standards conform to the conceptual framework. In fact, the FASB has identified four specific benefits that would result from a conceptual framework. A conceptual framework, when completed, would:

- guide the FASB in establishing accounting standards;
- provide a frame of reference for resolving accounting questions in the absence of specific promulgated standards;
- determine the bounds of judgment in preparing financial statements;
- enhance comparability by decreasing the number of alternative accounting methods.[16]

6.3.2 Conceptual framework issues

Before starting effective work on the conceptual framework, the FASB attempted to identify the most important conceptual issues of concern to standard-setting. Nine issues were presented for discussion and resolution.

Issue 1: Which view of earnings should be adopted?

Three distinct views about measuring earnings are identified:

- the asset/liability view;
- the revenue/expense view;
- the nonarticulated view.

For both the asset/liability view and the revenue/expense view, the statement of earnings "articulates" with the statement of financial position, in the sense that they are both part of the same measurement process. The difference between revenues and expenses is also equivalent to the increase in net capital.

The asset/liability view, also called the balance sheet or capital-maintenance view, holds that revenues and expenses result only from changes in assets and liabilities. Revenues are increases in assets and decreases in liabilities; expenses are decreases in assets and increases in liabilities. Some increases and decreases in net assets are excluded from the definition of earnings – namely, capital contributions, capital withdrawals, corrections of earnings of prior periods and holding gains and losses. The asset/liability view should not be interpreted as an abandonment of the matching principle. In fact, matching revenues and expenses result from clear definitions of assets and liabilities.

The revenue/expense view, also called the income statement or matching view, holds that revenues and expenses result from the need for a proper matching. Earnings are merely the differences between revenues in a period and the expenses incurred earning those revenues. Matching, the fundamental measurement process in accounting, is comprised of two steps:

1. Revenue recognition or timing through the realization principle.
2. Expense recognition in three possible ways:
    (a) Associating cause and effect, such as for cost of good sold.
    (b) Systematic and rational allocation, such as for depreciation.
    (c) Immediate recognition, such as for selling and administrative costs.

Thus, contrary to the asset/liability view, the revenue/expense view primarily emphasizes measuring the earnings of the firm, and not the increase or decrease in net capital. Assets and liabilities, including deferred charges and credits, are considered residuals that must be carried to future periods in order to ensure proper matching and avoid distortion of earnings.

The nonarticulated view is based on the belief that articulation leads to redundancy, "since all events reported in the income statement are also reported in the balance sheet, although from a different perspective".[17] According to this view, the definitions of assets and liabilities may be critical in the presentation of financial position and the definitions of revenues and expenses may dominate the measurement of earnings. The two financial statements have independent existence and meanings; therefore, different measurement schemes may be used for them. An example of the nonarticulted view would be the use of LIFO in the income statement and of FIFO in the balance sheet. The nonarticulated view gained some ground in 1966. In fact, the American Accounting Association's *Statement of Basic Accounting Theory* criticizes articulation:

> We find no logical reason why external financial reports should be expected to "balance" or articulate with each other. In fact, we find that forced balancing and articulation have frequently restricted the presentation of relevant information. The important guide should be the disclosure of all relevant information with measurement procedures that meet the other standards suggested in ASOBAT [A Statement of Basic Accounting Theory].[18]

In a world of uncertainty, it is not possible to create an accounting system where book equity (a balance sheet approach) and earnings (an income statement approach) both give estimates of equity value. The choice, as articulated by Black,[19] is to choose among the following paths.

1. We can refine our accounting rules (continuing to emphasize objectivity) to improve the relation between book equity and equity value. Then net income will be highly erratic and will give little information on value.

2. We can refine our accounting rules (continuing to emphasize objectivity) to improve the relation between earnings and equity value. Then book equity will be very sluggish and will give little information on anything.

3. We can continue the current practice of making some choices that improve the relation between book equity and equity value, and other choices that improve the relation between earnings and equity value. This compromises both sources of information and leaves us unclear how to combine them (with other information) into a single best estimate of value.

4. We can abandon conventional articulation. This will let us make choices that improve both the relation between book equity and equity value and the relation between earnings and equity value. For example, we can make greater use of entries that change assets and liabilities with only minor effects on earnings.[20]

Which view of earnings should be adopted as the basis of a conceptual framework for financial accounting and reporting? If articulation can be proved not only to be necessary but also to be advantageous, then the choice is between the asset/liability view and the revenue/expense view. The choice between these two views rests on which view constitutes the fundamental measurement process:

1. measurement of the attributes of assets and liabilities and changes in them; or
2. the matching process.

If the measurement of attributes of assets and liabilities and changes in them is deemed the fundamental measurement process (as in the asset/liability view), then earnings are only the consequences and the result of certain changes in assets and liabilities. On the other hand, if the matching process is deemed the fundamental measurement process (as in the revenue/expense view), then changes in assets and liabilities are merely the consequences and results of revenues and expenses. This latter view has led to the recognition in the statement of financial position of such items as "deferred charges", "deferred credits" and "reserves", which do not represent economic resources and obligations but which are necessary to ensure a proper matching and income determination. The asset/liability view would reject the deferral method of intraperiod tax allocation in favor of either the liability method or the net-of-tax method. By rejecting these new items in the balance sheet, the asset/liability view faces a major criticism, which concerns its unwillingness to recognize as revenues and expenses anything except current changes in economic resources and obligations to transfer resources, making it incapable of dealing with the complexities of the modern business world.

A choice between these views would provide not only an underlying basis for a conceptual framework for financial accounting and reporting but also definitions of the elements of financial statements.

Issues 2–7: Definitions

Definitions of each element of financial statements may be provided by both the asset/liability view and the revenue/expense view.

According to the asset/liability view, assets are the economic resources of a firm; they represent future benefits that are expected to result directly or indirectly in a net cash inflow. Alternatively, we may exclude from the definition of "assets" economic resources that do not have the characteristics of exchangeability or severability. In either case, based on the asset/liability view, assets are restricted to representations of economic resources of the firm. The economic resources of the firm are:

1. productive resources of the enterprise;
2. contractual rights to productive resources;
3. products;
4. money;
5. claims to receive money;
6. ownership interests in other enterprises.

According to the revenue/expense view, assets include not only the assets defined from the asset/liability viewpoint, but also all items that do not represent economic resources but are required for proper matching and income determination.

A third view of assets arises from the perception of the balance sheet not as a statement of financial position, but as "a statement of the sources and composition of company capital". According to this view, assets constitute the "present composition of invested capital".

If we exclude the problem of the element of "deferred charges" on the statement of financial position, the definitions of assets presented in these three different views have the following characteristics in common:

1. An asset represents potential cash flow to a firm.
2. Potential benefits are obtained by the firm.
3. The legal concept of property may affect the accounting definition of assets.
4. The way an asset is acquired may be part of the definitions. It may have been acquired in a past or current transaction or event; the event includes either an exchange transaction, a nonreciprocal transfer from owners or nonowners, or a windfall, and may exclude executory contracts.
5. Exchangeability may be an essential characteristic of assets.

Which of these definitions or modifications of these definitions should comprise the substance of a definition of "assets" for a conceptual framework for financial accounting and reporting? What is needed is a definition that lends itself to the generality of application required for a conceptual framework. Such a definition should take into account the following characteristics:

1. An asset represents only economic resources and does not include "deferred charges".
2. An asset represents potential cash flows to a firm.
3. Potential benefits are obtainable by the firm.
4. An asset represents the legal binding right to a particular benefit, results from a past or current transaction and includes all commitments, as in wholly executory contracts.
5. Exchangeability is not an essential characteristic of assets except for "deferred charges", in order to keep most intangibles as assets and exclude "deferred charges".

The second element to be defined is liabilities. According to the asset/liability view, liabilities are the obligations of the firm to transfer economic resources to other entities in the future. We may expand this definition to exclude items that do not represent binding obligations to transfer economic resources to other entities in the future.

According to the revenue/expense view, liabilities comprise not only the liabilities defined from the asset/liability viewpoint but also certain deferred credits and reserves that do not represent obligations to transfer economic resources but that are required for proper matching and income determination.

A third view of liabilities arises from the perception of the balance sheet as "a statement of the sources and composition of company capital". According to this view, liabilities constitute sources of capital and include certain deferred credits and reserves that do not represent obligations to transfer economic resources.

If we disregard the element of "deferred credits", the definitions of liabilities presented in these three different views have the following characteristics in common:

1. A liability is a future sacrifice of economic resources.
2. A liability represents an obligation of a particular enterprise.
3. A liability may be restricted to legal debt.
4. A liability results from past or current transactions or events.

APB Statement No. 4 summarizes these characteristics of liabilities in paragraph 58:

> The economic obligations of an enterprise at any time are its present responsibilities to transfer economic resources or provide services to other entities in the future. Obligations usually arise because the enterprise has received resources from other entities through purchases or borrowing. Some obligations, however, arise by other means (for example, through the imposition of taxes or through legal action). Obligations are general claims against the enterprise, rather than claims to specific resources of the enterprise, unless the terms of the obligation or applicable legal rules provide otherwise.

Which of these definitions or modifications of these definitions should comprise the substance of a definition of "liabilities" for a conceptual framework for financial accounting and reporting? As in the case of assets, what is needed is a definition of liabilities that lends itself to the generality of application required for a conceptual framework.

The third element to be defined is earnings. According to the asset/liability view, earnings are the increase in the net assets of the firm except for "capital" charges.

According to the revenue/expense view, earnings result from the matching of revenues and expenses and, perhaps, from the gains and losses. Gains and losses, therefore, may be distinguished from the revenues and expenses, or they may be considered part of them. Each possible component of earnings (revenues, expenses, gains and losses) may be defined as follows:

1. *Revenues and expenses*: According to the asset/liability view, revenues, which encompass gains and losses, are defined as increases in the assets or decreases in the liabilities that do not affect capital. Similarly, expenses, which encompass gains and losses, are defined as decreases in the assets or increases in the liabilities arising from the use of economic resources and services during a given period.

   According to the revenue/expense view, revenues, which encompass gains and losses, result from the sale of goods and services and include gains from the sale and exchange of assets other than inventories, interest and dividends earned on investments, and other increases in owners' equity during a period other than capital contributions and adjustments. Similarly, expenses comprise all of the expired costs that correspond to the revenues of the period. If gains and losses are defined as a separate element of earnings, however, revenues are defined as measures of enterprise outputs that result from the production or delivery of goods and the rendering of services during a period. Similarly, expenses are the expired costs corresponding to the revenues of the period.

   Which of these definitions of earnings should comprise the substance of "revenues" and "expenses" for a conceptual framework for financial accounting and reporting? In other words, which definition lends itself to the generality of application needed for a conceptual framework? The definitions generated by the revenue/expense viewpoint rely on a listing of all items that may be perceived as revenues or expenses. First, such a list is not necessarily exhaustive and second, the items in the list may change. As a result, the revenue/expense view of earnings and the ensuing definitions of revenues and expenses lack the generality of application needed for a conceptual framework.

2. *Gains and losses*: According to the asset/liability view, gains are defined as increases in net assets other than increases from revenues or from changes in capital. Similarly, losses are defined as decreases in net assets other than decreases from expenses or from changes in capital. Thus, gains and losses constitute that part of earnings not explained by revenues and expenses.

   According to the revenue/expense view, gains are defined as the excess of proceeds over the cost of assets sold, or as windfalls and other benefits obtained at no cost or sacrifice. Similarly, losses are defined as the excess over the related proceeds, if any, of all or an appropriate portion of the costs of assets sold, abandoned, or wholly or partially destroyed by casualty (or otherwise written off), or as costs that expire without producing revenues. Thus, according to the revenue/expense view, gains and losses are independent from the definitions of other elements of financial statements.

   Which of these definitions of gains and losses contains the generality of application required for a conceptual framework? According to the revenue/expense view, the definitions are independent of the definitions of the other elements and may, for that reason, be viewed as lacking generality of application. According to the asset/liability view, the definitions are derived from the other definitions and emphasize the incidental nature of gains and losses; they appear to contain the generality of application required for a conceptual framework.

In any case, gains and losses may be either gains and losses from exchanges, "holding" gains and losses resulting from a change in the value of assets and liabilities held by the firm, or gains and losses from nonreciprocal transfers.

3. *Relationships between earnings and the component of earnings*: Three major relationships exist between earnings and the component of earnings:

(a) Earnings = Revenues – Expenses + Gains – Losses
(b) Earnings = Revenues – Expenses
(c) Earnings = Revenues (including gains) – Expenses (including losses)

In the first relationship, each component is separate and essential to a definition of earnings. The different sources of earnings are distinguished, thereby providing greater flexibility in the classification and analysis of a firm's performance.

In the second relationship, gains and losses are not separate and are not essential to the definition of earnings. All increases and decreases are treated similarly as either revenues or expenses. Such a definition does not fit all the gains and losses from nonreciprocal transfers, windfalls, casualties, and holding gains and losses.

In the third relationship, although gains and losses are separate concepts, they are part of revenues and expenses. Such a definition has the same advantages as the first relationship and avoids the disadvantages of the second relationship. The definitions of revenues and expenses, however, must mix different items and may require a complete identification and listing of the items that comprise revenues, expenses, gains and losses.

The first relationship appears to present the least disadvantage according to both the asset/liability view and the revenue/expense view. It allows identification and disclosure of the three kinds of gains and losses: gains and losses from exchanges, holding gains and losses, and gains and losses from nonreciprocal transfers, windfalls and casualties.

4. *Accrual accounting*: The elements of financial statements are accounted for and included in financial statements through the use of accrual accounting procedures. Accrual accounting rests on the concepts of accrual, deferral, allocation, amortization, realization and recognition. The FASB opted for the following definitions of these concepts:

> Accrual is the accounting process of recognizing noncash events and circumstances as they occur, specifically, accrual entails recognizing revenues and related increases in assets and expenses and related increases in liabilities for amounts expected to be received or paid, usually in cash, in the future …
>
> Deferral is the accounting process of recognizing a liability for a current cash receipt or an asset for a current cash payment (or current incurrence of a liability) with an expected future impact on revenues and expenses …
>
> Allocation is the accounting process of assigning or distributing an amount according to a plan or a formula. It is a broader term than "amortization", that is, amortization is an allocation process …
>
> Amortization is the accounting process of systematically reducing an amount by periodic payments, or write-downs …
>
> Realization is the process of converting noncash resources and rights into money; it is most precisely used in accounting and financial reporting to refer to sales of assets for cash or claims of cash. The related terms, "realized" and "unrealized", therefore identify revenues or gains and losses on assets sold and unsold, respectively …
>
> Recognition is the process of formally recording or incorporating an item in the accounts and financial statements of an enterprise. Thus, an element may be

recognized (recorded) or unrecognized (unrecorded). "Realization" and "recognition" are not used synonymously, as they sometimes are in the accounting and financial literature.[21]

Issue 8: Which capital maintenance or cost recovery concepts should be adopted?

The concept of capital maintenance allows us to make a distinction between the return on capital or earnings and the return of capital or cost recovery. Earnings follow from recovery or maintenance of capital. Two concepts of capital maintenance exist: the financial capital concept, and the physical capital concept. Both concepts use measurements in terms of units of money or units of the same general purchasing power, resulting in four possible concepts of capital maintenance:

1. financial capital measured in units of money;
2. financial capital measured in units of the same general purchasing power;
3. physical capital measured in units of money;
4. physical capital measured in units of the same general purchasing power.

Note that the comprehensive income is a return on financial capital, as distinguished from a return on physical capital. The essential difference between the two concepts is that "holding gains and losses" are included in income under the financial capital concept, but are treated as "capital maintenance adjustments" under the physical capital concept.

Issue 9: Which measurement method should be adopted?

The issue of measurement method concerns the determination of both the unit of measure and the attribute to be measured. As far as the unit of measure is concerned, the choice is between actual dollars and general purchasing power adjusted dollars. As far as the particular attribute to be measured is concerned, we have five options:

1. historical cost method;
2. current cost;
3. current exit value;
4. expected exit value; and
5. present value of expected cash flows.

6.3.3 Development of a conceptual framework

Exhibit 6.3 illustrates the overall scope of the conceptual framework and lists the related documents issued to 1982 by the FASB.[22]

At the first level, the objectives identify the goals and the purposes of accounting. Statement of Financial Accounting Concepts No. 1 (*Objectives of Financial Reporting by Business Enterprises*) presents the goals and purposes of accounting for business enterprises. Statement of Financial Accounting Concepts No. 4 (*Objectives of Financial Reporting by Nonbusiness Organizations*) presents the goals and purposes of accounting for nonbusiness organizations.

At the second level, the fundamentals include the qualitative characteristics of accounting information (*Statement of Financial Accounting Concepts No. 2*) and the definitions of the elements of financial statements (*Statement of Financial Accounting Concepts No. 3*). In summary the five Statements of Financial Accounting Concepts issued relating to financial reporting for business enterprises are:

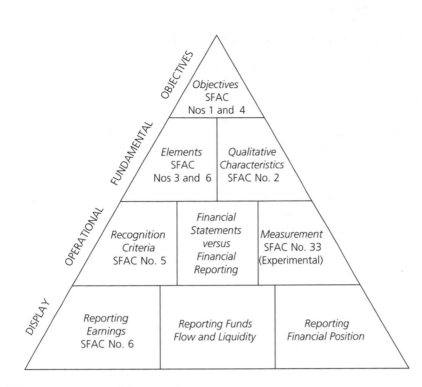

Exhibit 6.3 Conceptual framework

1. SFAC No. 1, "Objectives of Financial Reporting by Business Enterprises", which presents the goals and purposes of accounting.
2. SFAC No. 2, "Qualitative Characteristics of Accounting Information", which examines the characteristics that make accounting information useful.
3. SFAC No. 3, "Elements of Financial Statements of Business Enterprises", which provides definitions of items in financial statements, such as assets, liabilities, revenues and expenses.
4. SFAC No. 5, "Recognition and Measurement in Financial Statements of Business Enterprises", which sets forth fundamental recognition and measurement criteria and guidance on what information should be formally included in financial statements.
5. SFAC No. 6, "Elements of Financial Statements", which replaces SFAC No. 3 and expands its scope to include not-for-profit organizations.
6. SFAC No. 7, "Using Cash Flow Information and Present Value in Accounting Measurements", provides a framework for using cash flows and present values a basis for measurement.

At the third level, the operational guidelines that the accountant uses in establishing and applying accounting standards include the recognition criteria, financial statements versus financial reporting and measurement (Statement of Financial Accounting Standards No. 33).

At the fourth level, the display mechanisms that accounting uses to convey accounting information include reporting earnings, reporting funds flow and liquidity, and reporting financial position.

Each of these levels and components will be examined in the next section.

6.3.4 The objectives of financial reporting

The objectives of financial reporting by business enterprises

The FASB began its efforts to develop a constitution for financial accounting and reporting in November 1978 when it issued authoritative, broadly based guidelines spelling out the objectives of financial reporting in Statement of Financial Accounting Concepts No. 1, *Objectives of Financial Reporting by Business Enterprises*. The statement was not limited to the contents of financial statements:

> Financial reporting includes not only financial statements but also other means of communicating information that relates, directly or indirectly, to the information provided by the accounting system – that is, information about an enterprise's resources, obligations, earnings, etc.[23]

The objectives of financial reporting are summarized in the following excerpts from the statements:

> Financial reporting should provide information that is useful to present and potential investors and creditors and other users in making rational investment, credit, and similar decisions. The information should be comprehensible to those who have a reasonable understanding of business and economic activities and are willing to study the information with reasonable diligence. [Paragraph 34]
>
> Financial reporting should provide information to help present and potential investors and creditors and other users in assessing the amounts, timing, and uncertainty of prospective cash receipts from dividends or interests and proceeds from the sale, redemption, or maturity of securities or loan. The prospects for those cash receipts are affected by an enterprise's ability to generate enough cash to meet its obligations when due and its other cash operating needs, to reinvest in operations, and to pay cash dividends, and may also be affected by perceptions of investors and creditors generally about that ability, which affect market prices of the enterprise's securities. Thus, financial reporting should provide information to help investors, creditors, and others assess the amount, timing, and uncertainty of prospective net cash inflows to the related enterprise. [Paragraph 37]
>
> Financial reporting should provide information about the economic resources of an enterprise, the claims to those resources (obligations of the enterprise to transfer resources to other entities and owners' equity), and the effects of transactions, events, and circumstances that change resources and claims to those resources. [Paragraph 40]
>
> Financial reporting should provide information about an enterprise's financial performance during a period. Investors and creditors often use information about the past to help in assessing the prospects of an enterprise. Thus, although investment and credit decisions reflect investors' and creditors' expectations about the future enterprise performance, those expectations are commonly based at least partly on evaluations of past enterprise performance. [Paragraph 42]
>
> The primary focus of financial reporting is information about an enterprise's performance provided by measures of earnings and its components. [Paragraph 43]
>
> Financial reporting should provide information about how an enterprise obtains and spends cash, about its borrowing and repayment of borrowing, about its capital transactions, including cash dividends and other distributions of enterprise resource to owners, and about other factors that may affect an enterprise's liquidity or solvency. [Paragraph 49]

Financial reporting should provide information about how management of an enterprise has discharged its stewardship responsibility to owners (stockholders) for the use of enterprise resources entrusted to it. [Paragraph 50]

Financial reporting should provide information that is useful to managers and directors in making decisions in the interests of owners. [Paragraph 52]

The Statement also points out that:

Financial reporting is not an end in itself, but is intended to provide information that is useful in making business and economic decisions.

The objectives of financial reporting are not immutable – they are affected by the economic, legal, political, and social environment in which financial reporting takes place.

The objectives are also affected by the characteristics and limitations of the kind of information that financial reporting can provide.

The objectives in this statement are those of general-purpose external financial reporting by business enterprises.

The terms "investor" and "creditor" are used broadly, and apply not only to those who have or contemplate having a claim to enterprise resources, but also those who advise or represent them.

Although investment and credit decisions reflect investors' and creditors' expectations about future enterprise performance, such expectations are commonly based, at least partly, on evaluations of past enterprise performance.

The primary focus of financial reporting is information about earnings and its components. Information about enterprise earnings based on actual accounting generally provides a better indication of an enterprise's present and continuing ability to generate favorable cash flows than information limited to the financial effects of cash receipts and payments.

Financial reporting is expected to provide information about an enterprise's financial performance during a period and about how management of an enterprise has discharged its stewardship responsibility to owners.

Financial accounting is not designed to measure directly the value of a business enterprise, but the information it provides may be helpful to those who wish to estimate its value.

Investors, creditors, and others may use reported earnings and information about the elements of financial statements in various ways to assess the prospects for cash flows. They may wish, for example, to evaluate management's performance, estimate "earning power", predict future earnings, assess risk, or to confirm, change, or reject earlier predictions or assessments. Although financial reporting should provide basic information to aid them, users do their own evaluating, estimating, predicting, assessing, conforming, changing, and rejecting.

Management knows more about the enterprise and its affairs than investors, creditors, or other "outsiders" and, accordingly, may often increase the usefulness of financial information by identifying certain events and circumstances and explaining their financial effects on the enterprise.

After issuing this statement on the objectives of financial reporting, the FASB is in a better position to evaluate existing standards that are inconsistent with the stated objectives and to complete the remaining phases of the conceptual framework project.

The objectives of financial reporting by nonbusiness organizations

Nonbusiness organizations differ from business organizations in at least two respects. Nonbusiness organizations:

1. have no indicator of performance comparable to a business enterprise's profit;
2. generally are not subject to the test of competition in markets.

Three major distinguishing characteristics of nonbusiness organizations are:

1. Significant amounts of resources are received from resource providers, who do not expect to receive either repayment or economic benefits proportionate to the resources they provide.
2. The business operates primarily for purposes other than the provision of goods or services at a profit or a profit equivalent.
3. There are no defined ownership interests that can be sold, transferred, or redeemed, or that would convey entitlement to a share of residual distribution of the resources in the event of liquidation of the organization.

On the basis of this definition, the FASB exposure draft on the "Objectives of Financial Reporting by Nonbusiness Organizations," issued September 15, 1980, cites examples of nonbusiness organizations, which include private, nonprofit and philanthropic organizations such as colleges and universities; hospitals; health and welfare agencies; churches; foundations; state and local governmental units; and such membership organizations as trade and professional associations. Examples of organizations that do not possess all of the distinguishing characteristics of nonbusiness organizations are membership clubs in transferable entity interests; investor-owned hospitals and educational institutions; mutual insurance companies; and types of mutual and cooperative organizations that provide dividends, lower costs, or economic benefits directly to their owners, members, or participants.

Four particular groups are especially interested in the information provided by the financial reporting of nonbusiness organizations:

1. The resource providers: lenders, suppliers, employees, taxpayers, members and contributors.
2. The constituents who use and benefit from the services rendered by the organization.
3. The governing and overseeing bodies responsible for setting policies and overseeing and appraising the managers of nonbusiness organizations.
4. The managers of nonbusiness organizations.

To meet the needs of these particular users of information provided by nonbusiness organizations, the FASB exposure draft presents the following objectives:

> Information useful in making resource allocation decisions: financial reporting by nonbusiness organizations should provide information that is useful to resource providers in making rational decisions about the allocation of resources in those organizations.
>
> Information useful in assessing services and the ability to provide services: financial reporting by nonbusiness organizations should provide information that is useful to present and potential resource providers in assessing the services that a nonbusiness organization provides and its ability to continue to provide those services.
>
> Information useful in assessing management stewardship and performance: financial reporting by nonbusiness organizations should provide information that is

useful to present and potential resource providers in assessing how managers of a nonbusiness organization have discharged their stewardship responsibilities and other aspects of their performance. Information about an organization's performance should be the focus for assessing the stewardship, or accountability, of managers. Information about departures from such spending mandates as formal budgets and donor restrictions on the use of resources that may impinge on an organization's financial performance or on its ability to provide a satisfactory level of services is also important in assessing how well managers have discharged their stewardship responsibilities.

Information about economic resources, obligations, net resources, and charges on them: financial reporting by nonbusiness organizations about interest in those resources.

Organizational performance: financial reporting by nonbusiness organizations should provide information about the performance of an organization during a given period. Periodic measurement of the changes in the amount and nature of the net resources of a nonbusiness organization and information about the service's efforts and accomplishments of an organization, taken together, represent the information most useful in assessing organizational performance.

Liquidity: financial reporting by nonbusiness organizations should provide information about how a nonbusiness organization obtains and spends cash, about its borrowing and repayment of borrowing, and about other factors that may affect an organization's liquidity.

Managers' explanations and interpretations: financial reporting by nonbusiness organizations should include explanations and interpretations to help resource providers and other users understand the financial information they receive. Because managers usually know more about an organization and its affairs than resources providers or others outside the organization, managers can often increase the usefulness of financial reporting information by identifying certain transactions, events, and circumstances that affect the organization, and by explaining their financial impact.

6.3.5 Fundamental concepts

The fundamental concepts include both qualitative characteristics of accounting information and the definitions of the elements of financial statements.

The qualitative characteristics of accounting information

The FASB issued Statement of Financial Accounting Concepts No. 2, "Qualitative Characteristics of Accounting Information", to provide criteria for choosing between:

1. alternative accounting and reporting methods; and
2. disclosure requirements.[24]

Basically, these criteria indicate which information is better (more useful) for decision-making purposes. The characteristics may be viewed as a hierarchy – see Exhibit 6.4. Usefulness of decision-making is presented as the most important informational quality. Relevance and reliability are the two primary qualities, with related ingredients. Comparability and consistency are presented as secondary and interactive qualities.

Finally, the concepts of cost–benefit considerations and materiality are recognized, respectively, as a pervasive constraint and a threshold for recognition. Each of these qualitative characteristics of accounting information will now examined.

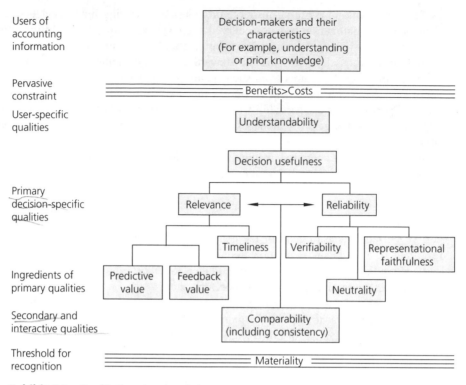

Exhibit 6.4 Qualitative characteristics

Relevance has been loosely defined as follows:

> For information to meet the standard of relevance, it must bear on or be usefully asso-
> ciated with the action it is designed to facilitate or the result it is desired to produce.
> This requires that either the information or the act of the communicating exert
> influence … on the designated actions.[25]

Relevance therefore refers to the ability of the information to influence the managers' decisions by changing or confirming their expectations about the results or consequences of
actions or events.

There can be degrees of relevance. The relevance of particular information will vary
among users and will depend on their needs and on the particular context in which the decisions are made. In the concept of the conceptual framework, the relevant information helps
investors, creditors and other users to evaluate the past, present and future events (predictive
value) or to confirm or correct prior expectations (feedback value). To be relevant, the information must also be available to a decision maker before it loses its capacity to influence
decisions (timeliness).

In short, to be relevant, information must have predictive value and feedback value and
at the same time must be conveyed on a timely basis.

Reliability refers to the "quality which permits users of data to depend on it with confidence as representative of what it proposes to present".[26] Thus, the reliability of information
depends on its degree of faithfulness in the representation of an event. Reliability will differ
between users, depending on the extent of their knowledge of the rules used to prepare
information. Similarly, different users may seek information with different degrees of reliability. In the context of the conceptual framework, to be reliable, information must be verifiable, neutral and faithfully presented.

Verifiability is the "attribute ... which allows qualified individuals working independently of one another to develop essentially similar measures or conclusion from an examination of the same evidence, data, or records".[27] It implies consensus and absence of measurer bias. Verifiable information can be substantially reproduced by independent measurers using the same measurement methods. Notice that verifiability refers only to the correctness of the resulting information, not to the appropriateness of the measurement methods used.

Representation faithfulness and completeness refer to the correspondence between accounting data and the events those data are supposed to represent. If the measure portrays what it is supposed to represent, it is considered to be free of measurement and measurer bias.

Neutrality refers to the absence of bias in the presentation of accounting reports or information. Thus, neutral information is free from bias toward attaining some desired result or inducing a particular mode of behavior. This is not to imply that the preparers of information do not have a purpose in mind when preparing the reports; it only means that the purpose should not influence a predetermined result.

Secondary qualities Comparability and consistency are the second qualities suggested by the FASB Statement of Financial Accounting Concepts No. 2.

Comparability describes the use of the same method over time by a given firm. The consistency principle does not, however, mean that a particular method of accounting cannot be changed once it is adopted. Environmental circumstances may dictate a more desirable change in accounting policy or technique if properly justified. APB Opinion No. 2 *Accounting Changes*, states that:

> The presumption that an entity should not change an accounting principle may be overcome only if the enterprise justifies the use of an alternative acceptable accounting principle on the basis that it is preferable. ... The nature and justification for a change in accounting principle and its effect on income should be disclosed. ... The justification for the change should explain why the newly adopted accounting principle is preferable.[28]

Cost–benefit considerations are recognized as one pervasive constraint. Financial accounting information will be sought if the benefit to be derived from the information exceeds its cost. Thus, before preparing and disseminating financial information, the benefits and costs of providing the information must be compared. The FASB emphasizes the importance of cost–benefit considerations:

> Before a decision is made to develop a standard, the Board needs to satisfy itself that the matter to be ruled on represents a significant problem, and that a standard that is promulgated will not impose costs on the many for the benefit of the few. If the proposal passes that first test, a second test may subsequently be useful. There are usually alternative ways of handling an issue. Is one of them less costly and only slightly less effective? Even if absolute magnitudes cannot be attached to costs and benefits, a comparison between alternatives may yet be possible and useful.[29]

Materiality is regarded as a threshold for recognition. Materiality is a state of relative importance. Basically, consideration must be given to whether or not the information is likely to have a significant or material impact on decisions. The question of crucial importance is who should determine the materiality rules, and how? (This question will be fully examined in Chapter 7.) The FASB's position on the subject is best illustrated by the following statement:

The Board's present position is that no general standards of materiality could be formulated to take into account all the considerations that enter an experienced human judgment. However, that position is not intended to imply either that the Board may not in the future review that conclusion or that quantitative guidance on materiality of specific items may not approximately be written into the Board's standards from time to time. That has been done on occasion already (for example, in the statement on financial reporting by segments of a business enterprise), and the Board recognizes that quantitative materiality guidance is sometimes needed. ... However, whenever the Board or any other authoritative body imposes materiality rules, it is substituting generalized collective judgment for specific individual judgments, and there is no reason to suppose that the collective judgments are always superior.[30]

The basic elements of financial statements of business enterprises

Statement of Financial Accounting Concepts No. 3, *Elements of Financial Statements of Business Enterprises*, defines ten interrelated elements that are directly related to measuring the performance and status of an enterprise: assets, liabilities, equity, investments by owners, distributions to owners, comprehensive income, revenue, expenses, gains, and losses.[31] These elements are defined as follows:

Assets: probable future economic benefits obtained or controlled by a particular entity as a result of past transactions or events.

Liabilities: probable future sacrifices of economic benefits arising from the present obligations of a particular entity to transfer assets or provide services to other entities in the future as a result of past transactions or events.

Equity: residual interests in the assets of an entity that remains after deducting its liabilities. In a business enterprise, the equity is the ownership interest.

Investments by owners: increases in the net assets of a particular enterprise that result from transfers to it from other entities of something of value to obtain or increase ownership interests (or equity) in the enterprise. Assets are most commonly received as investments by owners, but may also include services or satisfaction or conversion of liabilities of the enterprise.

Distributions to owners: decreases in the net assets of a particular enterprise that result from transferring assets, rendering services, or incurring liabilities by enterprise to owners. Distributions to owners decrease ownership interests (or equity) in the enterprise.

Comprehensive income: the change in the equity (net assets) of an entity during a given period that results from transactions and other events and circumstances from nonowner sources. Comprehensive income includes all changes in equity during a period except those that result from investments by owners and distribution to owners.

Revenues: inflows or other enhancements of the assets of an entity or settlement of the liabilities of an entity (or a combination of both) during a given period that result from delivering or producing goods, rendering services, or carrying out other activities that constitute the entity's ongoing major or central operations.

Expenses: outflows or other using-up of the assets of an entity or incurrence of the liabilities of an entity (or a combination of both) during a given period that result from delivering or producing goods, rendering services, or carrying out other activities that constitute the entity's ongoing major or central operations.

Gains: increase in equity (net assets) from the peripheral or incidental transactions of an entity and from all other transactions and other events and circumstances affecting the entity during a given period except those resulting from revenues or investments by owners.

Losses: decreases in equity (net assets) from the peripheral or incidental transactions of an entity and from all other transactions and other events and circumstances affecting the entity during a given period except those resulting from expenses or distributions to owners.[32]

These definitions provide a significant first screening method for determining the content of financial statements. They describe the essential characteristics to be met before events and circumstances are considered to be any element of financial statements. Three points are worth noting:

First, the concept of comprehensive income is more inclusive than the traditional concept of accounting income. Comprehensive income can be included in a statement that covers the change in a firm's net assets for a period from all sources except transactions with owners. It is an all-inclusive term that can be helpful to the user searching for the elusive true income number by (a) providing details highlighting the complicated nature of the number and allowing the users to make their own assessments, and (b) by portraying the performance of a firm as a continuum "with transactions and events occurring both regularly and irregularly throughout the company's existence".[33]

Second, the definitions of assets, liabilities and equities relate to amounts of resources and claims to resources at a given point in time, whereas the definitions of revenues, expenses, gains and losses relate to the impact of transactions, events and circumstances over a period of time.

Third, the values of assets, liabilities and equities are assumed to change as a result of revenues, expenses, gains and losses, which imply "articulation". In other words, the financial statements are assumed to interact and to interrelate.

Statement of Financial Accounting Concepts No. 3 was later replaced by Statement of Financial Accounting Concepts No. 6. The definitions of the elements are virtually identical to those in Statement No. 3, except that they are now applicable to nonbusiness organizations also.

6.3.6 Recognition and measurement

Statement of Financial Accounting Concepts No. 5 was intended to tackle the problems of recognition and measurement.

With regard to recognition, the statement was a cop-out as it stated at the outset that recognition and guidance criteria are generally consistent with current accounting practice and do not imply radical change. In addition, it states that disclosure by other means than the financial statements is not recognition.

The statement made a useful distinction between income, earnings and comprehensive income. Basically, earnings differed from income by excluding certain accounting adjustments of earlier periods that are not recognized in the current period, like the cumulative effects of a change in accounting principle. An example of the difference between present net income and earnings is shown in Exhibit 6.5.

The difference between earnings and comprehensive income is shown in Exhibit 6.6 Basically, comprehensive income recognizes two classes of items that are excluded from earnings; these are the effects of certain accounting adjustments of earlier periods that are recognized in the current period, and certain other changes in net assets (principally certain holding gains and losses) that are recognized in the period but excluded from earnings, such as some changes in market value of investments in marketable securities classified as noncurrent assets, some changes in market values of investments in industries having specialized accounting practices for marketable securities and foreign currency translation adjustments.

	Present net income	Earnings
Revenues	200	200
Expenses	140	140
Gain from unusual source	(10)	(10)
Income from continuing operations	70	70
Losses on discontinued operations		
Income from operating discontinued segment		
Loss on disposal of discontinued segment	10	10
Income before extraordinary items and effect of a change in accounting principle	60	60
Extraordinary loss		10
Cumulative effect on year of a change in accounting principle	30	
Earnings		50
Net income	30	

Exhibit 6.5 Income versus earnings

+	Revenues	200	+	Earnings	50
−	Expenses	140	−	Cumulative accounting adjustments	20
+	Gains	10	+	Other non-owner changes in equity	10
−	Losses	20	=	Comprehensive income	40
=	Earnings	50			

Exhibit 6.6 Earnings and comprehensive income

The recognition criteria include:

- *Definition*: The item meets the definition of an element of financial statements.
- *Measurability*: It has a relevant attribute measurable with sufficient reliability.
- *Relevance*: The information about it is capable of making a difference in user decisions.
- *Reliability*: The information is representational, faithful, verifiable and neutral.

With regard to measurement, the statement recognizes the five different attributes of assets and liabilities presented in the discussion memorandum, namely:

1. historical cost;
2. current replacement cost;
3. current market value;
4. net realizable (settlement) value;
5. present (or discounted) value of future cash flows.

6.4 The other reports

6.4.1 The Corporate Report

In 1975, the Accounting Standards Steering Committee of the Institute of Chartered Accountants in England and Wales published *The Corporate Report*, a discussion paper intended as a first step toward a major review of users, purposes and methods of modern financial reporting in the United Kingdom. The report presented the efforts of an eleven-member party, working within the following frame of reference:

> The purpose of this study is to reexamine the scope and aims of published financial reports in the light of modern needs and conditions.
>
> It will be concerned with the public accountability of economic entities of all kinds, but especially of business enterprises.
>
> It will seek to establish a set of working concepts as a basis for financial reporting. Its aims will be to identify the persons or groups for whom published financial reports should be prepared, and the information appropriate to their interests.
>
> It will consider the most suitable means of measuring and reporting the economic position, performance, and prospects of undertakings for the purposes and persons identified above.[34]

How well the report lives up to its stated aims is evidenced by its major findings and recommendations.

First, the basic philosophy and starting point of *The Corporate Report* is that financial statements should be appropriate to their expected use by potential users. In other words, financial statements should attempt to satisfy the informational needs of their users.

Second, the report assigns responsibility for reporting to the "economic entity" having an impact on society through its activities. The economic entities are itemized as limited companies, listed and unlisted; pension schemes, charitable and other trusts; and not-for-profit organizations; noncommercially oriented central government departments and agencies; partnerships and other forms of unincorporated business enterprises; trade unions and trade and professional associations; local authorities; and nationalized industries and other commercially oriented public sector bodies.

Third, the report defined users as those having a reasonable right to information whose information needs should be recognized by corporate reports. The users are identified as the equity investor group, the loan creditor group, the employee group, the analyst adviser group, the business contract group, the government and the public.[35]

Fourth, to satisfy the fundamental objectives of annual reports established by the basic philosophy, seven desirable characteristics are cited – namely, that the corporate report be relevant, understandable, reliable, complete, objective, timely and comparable.

Fifth, after documenting the limitations of current reporting practices, the report suggests the need for the following additional statements:

1. A statement of value added, showing how the benefits of the efforts of an enterprise are shared among employees, providers of capital, the state and reinvestment. Exhibit 6.7 is an example of a statement of value added.

2. An employment report, showing the size and composition of the workforce relying on the enterprise for its livelihood, the work contribution of employees and the benefits earned.

3. A statement of money exchange with government, showing the financial relationship between the enterprise and the state.

4. A statement of transactions in foreign currency, showing the direct cash dealings between Great Britain and other countries.

5. A statement of future prospects, showing likely future profit, employment and investment levels.

6. A statement of corporate objectives, showing management policy and medium-term strategic targets.

	Year to December 31, 1999
Turnover	$
Brought-in material and services	100
Value added	_60_
	_40_
Applied the following way:	
To pay employees	
Wages, pensions, and fringe benefits	19
To pay providers of capital:	
Interests on loans 0.1	
Dividends to shareholders _0.9_	
	1
To pay government	
Corporation tax payable	5
To provide for maintenance and expansion of assets	
Depreciation 5	
Retained profits _10_	
	_15_
Value added	_40_

Exhibit 6.7 A manufacturing company statement of value

Finally, after assessing six measurement bases (historical cost, purchasing power, replacement cost, net realizable value, value to the firm and net present value) against three criteria (theoretical acceptability, utility and practicality), the report rejected the use of historical cost in favor of current values accompanied by the use of general index adjustment.

In conclusion, a comparison of the principal findings and recommendations of *The Corporate Report* and the "Trueblood Report" cannot be made without considering the different economic and political environments in Great Britain and the United States. In general, *The Corporate Report* expresses a more pronounced concern for statements that can be used to improve both the social and economic welfare of society.

Following *The Corporate Report*, the research for a British conceptual framework continued, despite the British tradition of pragmatism militating against Grand Designs, with various calls for reforms.[36,37]

6.4.2 The "Stamp Report"

The Canadian Institute of Chartered Accountants (CICA) published a research study in June 1980 entitled *Corporate Reporting: Its Future Evolution*, written by professor Edward Stamp and hereafter referred to as the "Stamp Report".[38] The main motivations behind this effort are that, first, the FASB conceptual framework is not suitable for Canada, given the environmental, historical, political and legal differences between the United States and Canada; and second, the framework will provide a Canadian solution to the problem of improving the quality of corporate financial accounting standards.

The approach advocated in the "Stamp Report" is evolutionary. It identifies problems and conceptual issues and provides solutions in terms of the identification of the objectives of corporate financial reporting, the users of corporate reports, the nature of the users' needs and the criteria for the assessment of the quality of standards and of corporate account-ability as the possible components of a Canadian conceptual framework. Each of these components will be examined later.

Problems faced by standard-setters

The "Stamp Report" begins with an examination of some of the problems accounting standard-setters have to face:

- How is economic reality to be measured in an unambiguous manner?
- What is the nature of accounting, since the question of how best to develop accounting standards rests on it?
- Are there permanent and universal concepts on which financial reporting and accounting standards rest?
- Who are the users, what kind of decisions are they apt to make as the result of reading an annual report and what kind of information will they be looking for in the report on which to base these decisions?
- What criteria do standard-setters, preparers and users need to judge the quality of accounting standards, to choose between the possible alternative standards on any given subject, and to assess the utility of published accounting reports?
- How can the costs and benefits be estimated when deciding what action to take in the area of standard-setting?
- Can standards resolve the conflicts of interests between preparers and users and between different users by achieving neutrality?
- How useful is a published accounting report in the light of the "efficient market" evidence? Is the report predictive? Is it too concise and does it include too much information?
- Should there be extensions to disclosure? Should these extensions include disclosure?
- Given that the process of accounting standardization is to narrow the areas of difference, is the resulting increase in uniformity possible? How can stifling the process of legitimate innovation in accounting measurement be avoided and the trend toward the "book of rules" be decelerated?
- Should information be made available regarding the size of the margins of error in preparing accounts, or should the illusion of precision be presented?
- Are general-purpose reports enough? If not, should additional information be published in the form of supplementary statements or by adding further columns to the present financial reports?
- How should standards be enforced? (It is, however, noted that since 1975 the Canada Business Corporate Act specified that the operational definition of generally accepted accounting principles is the set of accounting pronouncements in the Canadian Institute of Chartered Accountants Handbook.)

Conceptual issues in standard-setting

In addition to the problems just outlined, Stamp has identified some complex conceptual issues that accountants must face in formulating their standards:

- *Allocation problems*: Accountants must make periodic measurements of the financial position and performance of an enterprise and in the process, develop systematic and rational methods of allocation. Unfortunately, these allocations are generally arbitrary and incorrigible.
- *Income problems*: Should income be regarded and defined as the result of matching costs against revenues or as the change in the net assets of equity during a period?

- *Reporting focus:* Should the proprietary concept (which looks at the financial affairs of an enterprise through the eyes of its owners) or the entity concept (which looks at the financial affairs of the enterprise from within, as it were) be used?

- *Capital-maintenance concepts:* Which capital-maintenance concept is most suitable?

- *Assets-valuation base:* Which asset-valuation base is to be used – historical cost, replacement cost, net realizable value, or value to the firm?

- *Economic reality:* What is economic reality? Can the balance sheet measure the current worth of an enterprise? As an example, the goodwill problem is presented as insolvable, As Stamp states:

> The problem of how to account for goodwill, especially internally generated goodwill, is probably the most perplexing problem in accounting, and one that is almost certainly irresolvable. Human talent, technical and other know-how, and many other largely unquantifiable assets are involved, making the measurement task virtually insoluble … many of the perplexing problems of accounting are indeed irresolvable in the sense that a unique solution is neither possible nor necessary.[39]

The objectives of corporate financial reporting

Now that we have outlined the problems and conceptual issues of, and the need for, accounting standards, we will examine the objectives of financial reporting. These objectives are assumed to apply to all legitimate users of published corporate financial reports. The first major objective concerns accountability:

> One of the primary objectives of published corporate financial reports is to provide an accounting by management exercise of its stewardship function but also of its success (or otherwise) in achieving the goal of producing a satisfactory economic performance by the enterprise and maintaining it in a strong and healthy financial position.[40]

The objective is then extended to all types of users:

> In short, an important objective of financial reporting is the provision of useful information to all of the potential users of such information in a form and in a time frame that is relevant to their various needs.[41]

The second major objective concerns uncertainty and risk. Although it is impossible to eliminate uncertainty and risk,

> … it is an objective of good financial reporting to provide such information in such a form as to minimize uncertainty about validity of the information, and to enable the user to make his or her own assessment of the risks associated with the enterprise.[42]

The third major objective concerns change and innovation:

> it is therefore necessary that the standards governing financial reporting should have ample scope for innovation and evolution as improvements become feasible.[43]

The fourth major objective concerns complexity and the unsophisticated user. The objectives of financial reporting

... should be taken to be directed towards the needs of users who are capable of comprehending a complete (and necessarily sophisticated) set of financial statements or, alternatively, to the needs of experts who will be called on by unsophisticated users to advise them.[44]

Users of corporate reports

Attention now shifts to the users. Users demand accountability, but a major issue must be resolved to strike the right balance between accountability and the right to privacy. Because accountability is a broader concept in Canada than it is in the United States, the range of users is broader in Canada than the range of users considered by the FASB's conceptual-framework project. The range of Canadian users includes the following fifteen categories:

- shareholders (present and potential);
- long-term creditors (present and potential);
- short-term creditors (present and potential);
- analyst and advisers serving the above (present);
- employees (past, present and potential);
- nonexecutive directors (present and potential);
- customers (past, present and potential);
- suppliers (present and potential);
- industry groups (present);
- labor unions (present);
- governmental departments and ministers (present);
- the public (present);
- regulatory agencies (present);
- other companies, both domestic and foreign (present); and
- standard-setters and academic researchers (present).

Users' needs

After the types of users are determined, the next step is to determine their informational needs. This task is complicated by the difficulties of determining the users' decision models. The "Stamp Report" emphasized that one of the most difficult problems in developing accounting standards arises from our ignorance about the nature of users' decision-making processes and about the rational (and often irrational) mental processes that users go through in reaching their decisions. In any case, the following thirteen categories of user needs are proposed:

- assessing performance;
- assessing management quality;
- estimating future prospects;
- assessing financial strength and stability;
- assessing solvency;
- assessing liquidity;
- assessing risk and uncertainty;
- aiding resource allocation;

- making comparisons;
- making valuation decisions;
- assessing adaptability;
- determining compliance with the law or regulations; and
- assessing contributions to society.

Criteria for assessment of the quality of standards and of corporate accountability

The next step is to define the criteria for assessment that are "the yardsticks whereby standard setters, as well as preparers and users of published financial statements, can decide whether … published financial statements are indeed meeting the needs of users and objectives of financial reporting".[45] These criteria are to be used to decide which information can and ought to be excluded from financial statements. They included objectivity, comparability, full disclosure, freedom from bias, uniformity, materiality and cost–benefit effectiveness, flexibility, consistency, and conservatism.

Toward a Canadian conceptual framework

A conceptual framework project for Canada (and elsewhere), based on an evolutionary approach and resting on the concepts (objectives and criteria for assessment), is offered at the end of the "Stamp Report". Unlike the FASB's conceptual framework, which it deemed too normative (if not axiomatic) and too narrow in its scope (its primary concern is with the investors), the Canadian conceptual framework is based on an evolutionary (rather than revolutionary) approach and would be less narrow in its scope (its primary concern is with the reasonable needs of the legitimate users of published financial reports). Furthermore, a public justification and explanation of the standards is suggested, to win general acceptance of the Canadian conceptual framework.

The "Stamp Report" is successful in listing the major conceptual problems encountered in developing any framework and also provides a basis or background so that more and more research can be conducted.

Reactions to the "Stamp Report" have been mixed. It has been rightfully perceived as an opinion document:

> In the final analysis, Corporate Reporting is an opinion document. It is not, nor do I believe it attempts to be, a classic inquiry-type research study. Rather, it is based on the informed opinion of a group of experienced and capable accountants.[46]

The Report has also been characterized as confusing, before it finally opts for a socioeconomic-political world view:

> We might conclude that the "Stamp Report," though arriving at many blind alleys, going through several iterations, and making several detours, does arrive at a position on a world view that might prove to be very fruitful in the development of public accounting theory and standards – the socioeconomic-political world view.[47]

Finally, practitioners found the Report's recommendations either far from practical,[48] or too costly to implement.[49] Following the publication of the Report, the Canadian Institute of Chartered Accountants issued in 1991 in their CICA Handbook a section 1000 on "Financial Statement Concepts" to serve as the beginning of a Canadian conceptual framework.

6.5 Taxonomy of normative characteristics that accounting pronouncements should reflect

A good quote about the importance of the quality of pronouncements was made by Arthur Levitt, a former chairman of the SEC, as follows:

> I firmly believe that the success of capital markets is directly dependent on the quality of the accounting and disclosure system. Disclosures systems that are founded on high quality pronouncements give investors confidence in the credibility of financial reporting – and without investor confidence, markets cannot thrive.[50]

The question is to define what is meant by "high quality" pronouncement. Some commentaries on quality management were published in *Accounting Horizons*.[51, 52, 53, 54, 55] Based on these commentaries, Collins et al.[56] proposed an excellent general model of taxonomy of desirable normative characteristics composed of three categories:

(a) *Formational characteristics* that relate to the development of the pronouncement and to subsequent assessment of its usefulness.

(b) *Operational characteristics* that relate to implementing and fulfilling pronouncement requirements.

(c) *Informational characteristics* that relate to the ability to generate data useful in decision making.[57]

The taxonomy of accounting pronouncements characteristics that accounting pronouncements should reflect is shown in Exhibit 6.8.

6.6 Discussion and conclusions

Logically, the formulation of an accounting theory entails a sequential process that begins with the development of the objectives of financial statements and ends with the derivation of a conceptual framework or constitution to be used as a guide to accounting techniques. Such a process was initiated and is manifested by:

• APB Statement No. 4;

• the "Trueblood Report";

• *The Corporate Report*;

• the "Stamp Report";

• the FASB's conceptual-framework project.

The FASB's conceptual framework was by far the most advanced project in the creation of an accounting constitution. Its major benefit was to facilitate the resolution of conceptual disputes in the standard-setting process. To be effective, this constitution would have to gain general acceptance, represent collective behavior and protect the public interest in areas in which it is affected by financial reporting. Could this be achieved? Several issues would have to be resolved before this question could be adequately answered.

The conceptual framework may not be sufficient to resolve certain standard-setting problems. Some of these problems are related to the social choice aspect of accounting standard-setting. One prevailing idea is that it is impossible to develop a set of accounting standards that can be applied to accounting alternatives in a way that will satisfy

Short explanation	Keywords for evaluation of best	Keywords for evaluation of worst	Source*
Informational characteristics			
Economic reality	Recognizes a liability/ obligation/asset/benefit, economic reality	Lacks economic logic, fails to recognize a liability/ obligation/asset/benefit	K5, R2, S1, W1, W3
Provides better information	Decision-relevant, better information for users	Not decision-relevant, does not improve information/ reporting	K1, K2, L2, W2
Adheres to conceptual framework	Adheres to conceptual framework, uses accrual basis	Ignores conceptual framework, no conceptual basis, violates accrual basis	K4, L5, R1, S3, S4
Solves a problem	Satisfies deficiency or problem, corrects or improves current condition	Wrong answer, does not solve problem, does not correct or improve condition	L1, R4, R7, W4
Increases comparability	Increases comparability, provides standardization	Reduces comparability, does not provide standardization	S2
Favors current value	Favors current value over historical cost	Ignores current values, increases gap between book and fair market value	K6
Provides proper income recognition	Indicates performance, income recognition, prevents smoothing	Allows smoothing, ignores an expense	K7, K8
Conforms to international standards	Adheres to international guidelines or practices	No corresponding worst characteristic mentioned by participants	R6, W7
Operational characteristics			
Clear	Clear, concise, simple	Complex, not clear, too detailed	R1, R3, W9, W10
Provides implementation guidance	Improves guidance, provides rules, codification	Arbitrary, vague, lacks rules or guidance	S5
Benefits exceed cost	Benefits exceed cost, easy to implement	Costly, not operational, hard to maintain records	L3, R1, W6
Flexible	Allows flexibility or judgment, general	Does not allow flexibility, micro-manages	W8
Verifiable results	Easy to audit, verifiable	No corresponding worst characteristic mentioned by participants	K3
Formational characteristics			
Uses external input	Includes external input in formation, utilizes task force, utilizes research	No corresponding worst characteristic mentioned	L4, R5
Timely	Timely, issued quickly	No corresponding worst characteristic mentioned	R9, W5
Subject to sunset	Subject to sunset	No corresponding worst characteristic mentioned	R8, W11

* *Accounting Horizons* articles: Knutson and Napolitano (1998), Linsmeier *et al.* (1998), Rogero (1998), Smith (1998), and Wulff and Koski-Grafer (1998).

Source: Denton Collins, William R. Pasewark, and Jerry R. Strawser, "Characteristics Influencing Perceptions of Accounting Pronouncement Quality", *Accounting Horizons* (16, 2, June, 2002), p. 40. 2002 American Accounting Association. Reprinted with permission.

Exhibit 6.8 Taxonomy of accounting pronouncement characteristics

everybody.[58] In response to this pessimistic view, Cushing suggests that those who reject the possibility of finding an unobjectionable social-welfare function may be overstating the problem.[59] A partial, piecemeal approach is recommended by Cushing as a way of tackling accounting problems. Bromwich, however, feels that the conditions for successful use of the partial approach are fairly restrictive.[60] His analysis suggests that:

> Cushing's approach of seeking the best out of a set of mutually exclusive standards for a given accounting problem, while holding all other standards constant, will be successful only where interdependence of the utility, attached to the outcomes addressed by that standard, from all the outcomes affected by other standards can be assumed.[61]

The conceptual framework must be workable and acceptable to all interested parties. The workability of the conceptual framework may be hampered by the level of abstractness of some of the qualitative characteristics and other recommendations. The acceptability of the conceptual framework may be hampered by the difficulty of resolving the conflicts of interest of all users and by the fear that the framework may be calling for radical changes in business reporting. One way of determining acceptability is to reaffirm the soundness of the reasoning underlying the elements of the framework.

As Horngren states:

> A major role of the conceptual framework is ultimately to enhance the likelihood of acceptability of specific statements to be proposed or already in place. The more plausible the assumptions and the more compelling the analysis of the facts, the greater the chance of winning the support of diverse interests – and retaining and enhancing the Board's power.[62]

The ultimate test of the conceptual framework is its implementation and survival. In substance, the framework should exist in more than form. A view that the conceptual framework may be forgotten presents the following argument:

> Our initial guess is that the objectives selected by the board will be ignored in future rule-making activities, just as were those from previous authoritative attempts. Following the publication of these objectives, the Board will probably feel obligated to pay lip service to them in future pronouncements, but these pronouncements will not be affected in any substantive way by what is contained in the present documents.[63]

One way of dismissing this view is to ensure that the conceptual framework be used to resolve controversial accounting issues. But will the conceptual framework guide the FASB in correcting some of these accounting problems? Dopuch and Sunder make a strong argument that the framework is unlikely to help resolve major accounting issues or to set standards.[64] They illustrate their point by analyzing three much-debated accounting techniques:

> The FASB's definition of liabilities is so general that at this stage we cannot predict the Board's position on deferred taxes. However, those who favor the recognition of deferred taxes can adopt a somewhat broad interpretation of the FASB's definition of liabilities to justify the conclusion of deferred taxes as an element of financial statements, particularly at the individual asset level. In contrast, those who do not could take the FASB's statements literally and just as easily argue against the inclusion of deferred taxes.[65]

The conceptual framework is also shown to support either a full-cost or a successful-efforts method for oil and gas accounting. The only explicit statement bearing on this problem is that "information about enterprise earnings and its components measured by accrual accounting generally provides a better indication of enterprise performance than information about current cash receipt and payments". However, both full-cost and successful-efforts accounting are forms of accrual accounting, so that proponents of the former (for example, the Federal Trade Commission) have the same support for their position as do the proponents of the latter (for example, the FASB).[66]

Finally, with regard to the asset-valuation debate, Dopuch and Sunder conclude that:

> no conceptual framework, however logically conceived, can counter practical issues regarding the reliability of estimates of say, replacement costs. So the issue is not whether costs are useful in making economic decisions; rather, the issue is what criteria may be used to determine alternative estimates of unknown parameters.[67]

Three other issues concern the conceptual framework:

First, the conceptual framework has often been referred to as a kind of constitution. Yet there may be great differences that make the analogy an imperfect one, and at the same time a strong case for the conceptual framework. Solomons, for example, cites the following three differences:

1. A constitution has the force of law. A conceptual framework has no authority except that which flows from its intellectual pervasiveness.
2. Constitutions contain many arbitrary elements, for example, the number of senators each state is to have, the length of the interval between elections, and so forth. There is no room for arbitrariness in a conceptual framework.
3. There are significant differences among the nations of the world in their constitutional arrangements. There could be important national differences among conceptual frameworks – this is mere speculation because no country other than the United States has yet made any attempt to construct one.[68]

Second, Miller points to eight myths about conceptual frameworks:

> The myth that Accounting Principles Board failed because it did not have a conceptual framework.
> FASB cannot succeed unless it has a conceptual framework.
> A conceptual framework will lead to consistent standards.
> That a conceptual framework will eliminate the problem of standard overload.
> That the FASB's conceptual framework captures only the status quo of accounting practice.
> That the conceptual framework project has cost more than it should have.
> That the FASB will revise the existing standards to make them consistent with the conceptual framework.
> That the FASB has abandoned the conceptual framework project.[69]

The realities are that the framework is a political document that is not the ultimate authority for resolving issues; it is neither a complete description of existing practice nor a blueprint for the future. It is a point of departure for future debates.[70]

Third, the conceptual framework is not going to provide all the answers, but at least it will provide a direction for setting standards and reduce the influence of personal biases and political pressures in making accounting judgments.[71]

Various scenarios await the conceptual framework project. Sterling offers his views of the future as follows:

> The most pessimistic one is that the Board meets so much resistance that it fails to complete the task and reverts to "ad hocery". The most optimistic scenario, indeed widely optimistic, is that I can convince everyone that it is possible for accounting to become a scientific discipline and thereby rely more on the method of science – empirical and logical testing – and less on the method of authority. The most likely scenario is that the Board will complete this task, albeit faced with increasing resistance, and will therefore be forced to slow it down or water it down or both. Thus, the most likely scenario is that the Board will continue to make progress, continue to improve accounting, but that this will occur by inching along and not by quantum leap.[72]

It is very hard not to agree with the most likely scenario as described, as the Board continue to improve gradually through a "muddling through" process created by the political quagmire that characterizes the accounting environment and its interests groups. The Board, however, ought to consider the useful suggestions offered in the literature. The best suggestions for improvement, offered by Agrawal, are as follows:

> The need to make an explicit distinction between what the FASB considers to be the basic concepts and policy issues. Only the basic concepts should be the subject matter of the conceptual framework. Policy issues are those that depend upon the particular circumstance of each case and may need to be changed with changes in circumstances over time. These issues should be addressed by FASB's standard-setting function. The primary accounting model will be the connecting link between the two categories. This, in turn, would involve specification of:
>
> (a) the attribute to be measured;
> (b) the capital maintenance concept;
> (c) timing of recognition (particularly of revenues/gains and expenses/losses);
> (d) relative importance to be placed on the Income Statement and Balance Sheet; and
> (e) the unit of measurement.
>
> FASB should indicate the primary model it implies in its standards currently, with a proviso that exceptions may be made for dominant, but specific, reasons. The justification must be based upon the objectives of financial reporting, qualitative characteristics of information, definitions of elements and the recognition criteria. FASB should also state that it might experiment with other models under appropriate circumstances and that a different model might be adopted as the primary model when considered appropriate.
>
> There is a need to specify a temporal hierarchy of objectives and needs. The first tier should consist of those the fulfillment of which is sought currently (or in the near future). Subsequent tiers should be aimed for achievement in a more distant future when:
>
> (a) there is a better understanding of information needed, and
> (b) means are available to provide such information.
>
> The ideas of "freedom from error" and "precision" that have been used rather ambiguously should be integrated properly in the qualitative characteristics. This will require consideration of several related concepts that have been considered only briefly in the network, including:

(a) accuracy;

(b) truth or truthfulness; and

(c) evenhandedness or fairness.

The need to provide criteria for the disclosure of items that are not formally "recognized". These criteria may be the same as for formal recognition but might also provide for:

(a) disclosure of attributes in addition to those under the primary accounting model; and

(b) explanation of further details of items that are formally recognized.[73]

The benefits of a conceptual framework include:

(a) providing the foundation that can provide the guidance for standard-setting;

(b) allowing the standard-setting body to utilize economies in their efforts to develop standards;

(c) providing broad prescriptive concepts to allow other concepts to flow from them; and

(d) resulting in standards that are apolitical.[74]

The benefits are strong enough to overcome the antiquated thinking of opponents of the conceptual framework who claim that the conceptual framework is unnecessary and potentially rigid,[75,76] and to support the view of the conceptual framework as a process of constant reformation of the status quo followed by instances of counterreformation by those who acted to protect their power under the status quo.[77] The success of the conceptual framework is to continue on the momentum of reforms after dealing with the expected counterreformation it will encounter along the way. At the same time, it needs to take care of noted cases of incompleteness, internal inconsistencies, ambiguities, circular reasoning, and unsubstantiated assertions.[78]

An operational measure of the success of the conceptual framework concept is the proliferation of conceptual frameworks to include the following countries:

• United States;

• Australia;

• New Zealand;

• Canada;

• United Kingdom;

• Tunisia; and

• China.

Notes

1. Devine, C.T., "Research Methodology and Accounting Theory Formulation", *The Accounting Review* (July, 1960), p. 399.
2. Watts, R.L., and Zimmerman, J.L., "The Demand for and Supply of Accounting Theories: The Market for Excuses", *The Accounting Review* (April, 1979), pp. 273–305.
3. *Objectives of Financial Statements* (New York: American Institute of Certified Public Accountants, 1973).

4. FASB Discussion Memorandum, *Conceptual Framework for Financial Accounting and Reporting: Elements of Financial Statements and Their Measurement* (Stamford, CT: Financial Accounting Standards Board, 1976).

5. The Accounting Standards Steering Committee, *The Corporate Report* (London: The Institute of Chartered Accountants in England and Wales, 1975).

6. Stamp, Edward, *Corporate Reporting: Its Future Evolution* (Toronto: Canadian Institute of Chartered Accountants, 1980).

7. APB Statement No. 4, *Basic Concepts and Accounting Principles Underlying Financial Statements of Business Enterprises* (New York: American Institute of Certified Public Accountants, 1970).

8. Cyert, R.M., and Ijiri, Yuji, "Problems of Implementing the Trueblood Objectives Report", in *Studies on Financial Accounting Objectives*, supplement to Vol. 12, *Journal of Accounting Research* (1974), p. 29.

9. Cramer, J.J., Jr., and Sorter, G.H. (eds.), *Objectives of Financial Statements: Selected Papers*, Vol. 2 (New York: American Institute of Certified Public Accountants, 1973).

10. Sorter, G.H., and Gans, M.S., "Opportunities and Implications of the Report on Objectives of Financial Statements", in *Studies on Financial Accounting Objectives*, supplement to Vol. 12, *Journal of Accounting Research* (1974), pp. 1–12.

11. *Objectives of Financial Statements: Selected Papers*, op. cit., p. 29.

12. Ibid., p. 29.

13. Ibid., p. 60.

14. *The Conceptual Framework for Financial Accounting and Reporting: Elements of Financial Statements and Their Measurement* (Stamford, CT: Financial Accounting Standards Board, 1976), p. 4.

15. Ibid., p. 2.

16. *Scope and Implications of the Conceptual Framework Project* (Stamford, CT: Financial Accounting Standards Board, 1976), pp. 7–8.

17. Sorter, G.H., "The Partitioning Dilemma", in J.J. Cramer, Jr., and G.H. Sorter (eds.), *Objectives of Financial Statements: Selected Papers*, Vol. 2 (New York: American Institute of Certified Public Accountants, 1974), p. 117.

18. *A Statement of Basic Accounting Theory* (Evanston, IL: American Accounting Association, 1966), p. 118.

19. Black, Fisher, "Choosing Accounting Rules", *Accounting Horizons* (December, 1993), pp. 1–17.

20. Ibid., p. 6.

21. Ibid., pp. 35–7.

22. Norby, W.C., *The Financial Analysts Journal* (March/April, 1982), p. 22.

23. Statement of Financial Accounting Concepts No. 1, *Objectives of Financial Reporting by Business Enterprises* (Stamford, CT: Financial Accounting Standards Board, 1980).

24. Statement of Financial Accounting Concepts No. 2, *Qualitative Characteristics of Accounting Information* (Stamford, CT: Financial Accounting Standards Board, 1980).

25. *A Statement of Basic Accounting Theory* (Evanston, IL: American Accounting Association, 1966), p. 9.

26. *Statement of Accounting Theory and Theory Acceptance* (Sarasota, FL: American Accounting Association, 1977), p. 16.

27. *A Statement of Basic Accounting Theory*, op. cit., p. 10.

28. APB Opinion No. 21, *Accounting Changes* (New York: American Institute of Certified Public Accountants, 1971), p. 391.

29. Statement of Financial Accounting Concepts No. 2, op. cit., p. 58.

30. Ibid., p. 53.

31. Statement of Financial Accounting Concepts No. 3, *Elements of Financial Statements of Business Enterprises* (Stamford, CT: Financial Accounting Standards Board, 1980).

32. Ibid., pp. xi–xii.

33. Robinson, Londell Ellis, "The Time Has Come to Report Comprehensive Income", *Accounting Horizons* (June, 1991), p. 111.

34. *The Corporate Report*, op. cit., p. 10.

35. Ibid., p. 17.

36. McMonnies, P. (ed.), *Making Corporate Reports Valuable* (London: Institute of Chartered Accountants of Scotland and Kogan Page, 1988).

37. Solomons, D., *Guidelines for Financial Reporting* (London: Institute of Chartered Accountants in England and Wales, 1989).

38. Stamp, Edward, *Corporate Reporting: Its Future Evolution*, op. cit.

39. Ibid., p. 19.

40. Ibid., p. 33.

41. Ibid., p. 34.

42. Ibid., p. 35.

43. Ibid., p. 36.

44. Ibid., p. 38.

45. Ibid., p. 52.

46. Archibald, T. Ross, "A Research Perspective on *Corporate Reporting: Its Future Evolution*" in S. Basu and J. Alex Milburn (eds.), *Research to Support Standard Setting in Financial Accounting: A Canadian Perspective* (Toronto: The Clarkson Gordon Foundation, 1982), p. 229.

47. Dewhirst, John E., "An Evaluation of *Corporate Reporting: Its Future Evolution* Based on Different 'World Views'", in *Research to Support Standard Setting in Financial Accounting: A Canadian Perspective*, op. cit., p. 244.

48. Fowler, G.C., "A Public Practitioner's View of *Corporate Reporting: Its Future Evolution*", in *Research to Support Standard Setting in Financial Accounting: A Canadian Perspective*, op. cit., p. 253.

49. Park, R.W., "Is Corporate Reporting Asking too Much?" *The Canadian Chartered Accountant Magazine* (December, 1981), pp. 34–7.

50. Levitt, A., "The Importance of High Quality Accounting Standards", *Accounting Horizons* (12, June, 1998), pp. 78–83.

51. Linsmeier, T.J., Boatsman, J.R., Herz, R.H., Jennings, R.G., Jonas, G.J., Lang, R.H., Petioni, K.R., Shores, D., and Wahlen, J.N., "Criteria for Assessing the Quality of an Accounting Standard", *Accounting Horizons* (12, June, 1998), pp. 161–2.

52. Smith, J.T., "Responding to FASB Standard Setting Proposals", *Accounting Horizons* (12, June, 1998), pp. 163–9.

53. Knutson, P.H., and Napolitano, G.U., "Criteria Employed by AIMR Financial Accounting Policy Committee in Evaluating Financial Accounting Standards", *Accounting Horizons* (12, June, 1998), pp. 170–6.

54. Rogero, L.H., "Characteristics of High Quality Standards", *Accounting Horizons* (12, June, 1998), pp. 177–83.

55. Wulff, J.K., and Koski-Grafer, S., "Characteristics of High Quality Accounting Standards: Perspective of the Corporate Preparer", *Accounting Horizons* (12, June, 1998), pp. 188–91.

56. Collins, D.L., Pasewark, W.R., and Strawser, J.R., "Characteristics Influencing Perceptions of Accounting Pronouncement Quality", *Accounting Horizons* (12, June, 1998), pp. 137–51.

57. Ibid., pp. 139–41.

58. Demski, Joel S., "The Choice Among Financial Reporting Alternatives", *The Accounting Review* (April, 1974), pp. 718–83.

59. Cushing, B.E., "On the Possibility of Optimal Accounting Principles", *The Accounting Review* (April, 1977), pp. 380–421.

60. Bromwich, M., "The Possibility of Partial Accounting Standards", *The Accounting Review* (April, 1980), pp. 288–300.

61. Ibid., p. 299.

62. Horngren, Charles T., "Uses and Limitations of a Conceptual Framework", *Journal of Accountancy* (April, 1981), p. 90.

63. Ibid., p. 8.

64. Dopuch, N., and Sunder, S., "FASB's Statements on Objectives and Elements of Financial Accounting: A Review", *The Accounting Review* (January, 1980), p. 8.

65. Ibid., pp. 6–7.

66. Ibid., p. 7.

67. Ibid., pp. 7–8.

68. Solomons, David, "The FASB's Conceptual Framework: An Evaluation", *Journal of Accountancy* (June, 1986), p. 115.

69. Miller, Paul B., "The Conceptual Framework: Myths and Realities", *Journal of Accountancy* (March, 1985), pp. 62–71.

70. Ibid.

71. Pacter, Paul A., "The Conceptual Framework: Make No Mystique About It", *Journal of Accountancy* (July, 1983), p. 88.

72. Sterling, Robert R., "The Conceptual Framework: An Assessment", *The Journal of Accountancy* (November, 1982), p. 108.

73. Agrawal, Surendra P., "On the Conceptual Framework of Accounting", *Journal of Accounting Literature* (June, 1987), pp. 176–7.

74. Nussbaumer, Norma, "Does the FASB's Conceptual Framework Help Solve Real Accounting Issues?" *Journal of Accounting Education* (Spring, 1992), pp. 235–42.

75. Hichok, R.S., "The FASB's Conceptual Framework Project: A Critique", *CPA Journal* (52, 1982), pp. 75–7.

76. Beresford, D.R., "A Practitioner's View of The FASB Conceptual Framework", *The Ohio CPA Journal* (40, 1981), pp. 65–7.

77. Miller, Paul B.W., "The Conceptual Framework as Reformation and Counterreformation", *Accounting Horizons* (June, 1990), pp. 23–32.

78. Agrawal, Surendra, P., "On the Conceptual Framework of Accounting", *Journal of Accounting Literature* (6, 1987), pp. 165–78.

References

The "Trueblood Report"

Anton, H.R., "Objectives of Financial Accounting: Review and Analysis", *Journal of Accountancy* (January, 1976), pp. 40–51.

Beaver, W.H., "What Should Be the FASB's Objectives?" *Journal of Accountancy* (August, 1973), pp. 49–56.

Beaver, W.H., and Demski, Joel, "The Nature of Financial Objectives: A Summary and Synthesis", in *Studies in Financial Accounting Objectives: 1974*, supplement to Vol. 12, *Journal of Accounting Research* (1974), pp. 170–87.

Bird, P., "Objectives and Methods of Financial Reporting: A Generalized Search Procedure", *Accounting and Business Research* (Summer, 1974), pp. 23–32.

Carlsberg, B., Hope, A., and Scapens, R.W., "The Objectives of Published Accounting Reports", *Accounting and Business Research* (Summer, 1974), pp. 34–50.

Chastain, C.E., "Accounting Objectives and User Needs: A Behavioral View", *National Public Accountant* (May, 1974), pp. 24–7.

Chastain, C.E., "Accounting Objectives and User Needs: A Behavioral View", *National Public Accountant* (June, 1974), pp. 26–31.

Chen, R.S., "Social and Financial Stewardship", *The Accounting Review* (July, 1975), pp. 533–43.

Clinton, R.E., "Objectives of Financial Statements", *Journal of Accountancy* (November, 1972), pp. 56–68.

Cramer, J.J., Jr., and Sorter, G.H. (eds.), *Objectives of Financial Statements: Selected Papers*, Vol. 2 (New York: American Institute of Certified Public Accountants, 1973).

Cyert, R.M., and Ijiri, Yuji, "Problems of Implementing the Trueblood Objectives Report", in *Studies on Financial Accounting Objectives*, supplement to Vol. 12, *Journal of Accounting Research* (1974), pp. 29–42.

Mautz, R.K., "Accounting Objectives – The Conservative View", *CPA Journal* (September, 1973), pp. 771, 774–7.

Most, K.S., and Winters, A.L., "Focus on Standard Setting: From Trueblood to the FASB", *Journal of Accountancy* (February, 1977), pp. 67–75.

Scott, G., and Decelles, M., "United States: Objectives of Financial Reporting Revisited", *Accountant's Magazine* (February, 1980), pp. 16–23.

Sorter, G.H., and Gans, M.S., "Opportunities and Implications of the Report on Objectives of Financial Statements", in *Studies on Financial Accounting Objectives*, supplement to Vol. 12, *Journal of Accounting Research* (1974), pp. 1–12.

Williams, R.J., "Differing Opinions on Accounting Objectives", *CPA Journal* (August, 1973), pp. 651–6.

The conceptual framework

Agrawal, Surendra, E., "On the Conceptual Framework of Accounting", *Journal of Accounting Literature* (6, 1987), pp. 165–78.

Brown, W.W., "Industry and Conceptual Framework", *Journal of Accountancy* (August, 1980), pp. 20–5.

Depree, C.M., Jr., "Testing and Evaluating a Conceptual Framework of Accounting", *Abacus* (September, 1989), pp. 61–73.

Edwards, J.D., Wyatt, A.R., and Defliese, P.L., "Conceptual Framework for Accounting Standards", in D.D. Alhasim and J.W. Robertson (eds.), *Contemporary Issues in Accounting* (Indianapolis, IN: Bobbs-Merrill Educational Publishing, 1975), pp. 1–54.

Gerboth, Dale, "The Conceptual Framework: Not Definitions, But Professional Values", *Accounting Horizons* (September, 1987), pp. 1–9.

Heath, Lloyd C., "The Conceptual Framework as Literature", *Accounting Horizons* (June, 1988), pp. 100–4.

Holder, W.W., and Hanendy, K., "A Framework for Building an Accounting Constitution", *Journal of Accounting, Auditing, and Finance* (Winter, 1982), pp. 110–25.

Horngren, Charles T., "Uses and Limitations of a Conceptual Framework", *Journal of Accountancy* (April, 1981), p. 86–95.

Ijiri, Yuji, "Critique of the APB Fundamentals Statement", *Journal of Accountancy* (November, 1971), pp. 43–50.

Kirk, D.J., "Concepts, Consensus, Compromise, and Consequence: Their Roles in Standard Setting", *Journal of Accountancy* (April, 1981), pp. 85–6.

Koepper, David R., "Using the FASB's Conceptual Framework: Fitting the Pieces Together", *Business Horizons* (June, 1988), pp. 18–26.

Langenderfer, H.Q., "Conceptual Framework for Financial Reporting", *Journal of Accountancy* (July, 1973), pp. 46–55.

Miller, Paul B.W., "The Conceptual Framework as Reformation and Counterreformation", *Business Horizons* (June, 1990), pp. 23–32.

Murray, Dennis, and Johnson, Raymond, "Differential GAAP and the FASB's Conceptual Framework", *Journal of Accounting, Auditing and Finance* (Fall, 1983), pp. 4–16.

Peasnell, K.V., "The Function of a Conceptual Framework for Corporate Financial Reporting", *Accounting and Business Research* (Autumn, 1982), pp. 243–56.

Pacter, Paul A., "The Conceptual Framework: Make No Mystique About It", *Journal of Accountancy* (July, 1983), pp. 76–88.

Schattke, R.W., "An Analysis of APB Statement No. 4", *The Accounting Review* (April, 1972), pp. 233–44.

Shultis, R.L., "Opinion: FASB – The Only 'Game' in Town", *Management Accounting* (March, 1981), pp. 6, 47.

Sprouse, Robert T., "The Importance of Earnings in the Corporate Framework", *Journal of Accountancy* (January, 1978), pp. 64–71.

Solomons, David, "The FASB's Conceptual Framework: An Evaluation", *Journal of Accountancy* (June, 1986), pp. 114–25.

Statement of Financial Accounting Concepts No. 1, *The Objectives of Financial Reporting by Business Enterprises* (Stamford, CT: Financial Accounting Standard Board, 1978).

Statement of Financial Accounting Concepts No. 2, *Qualitative Characteristics of Accounting Information* (Stamford, CT: Financial Accounting Standards Board, 1980).

Statement of Financial Accounting Concepts No. 3, *Elements of Financial Statements of Business Enterprises* (Stamford, CT: Financial Accounting Standards Board, 1980).

Statement of Financial Accounting Concepts No. 4, *Objectives of Financial Reporting by Nonbusiness Organizations* (Stamford, CT: Financial Accounting Standard Board, 1975).

Statement of Financial Accounting Concepts No. 5, *Recognition and Measurement in Financial Statement of Business Enterprises* (Stamford, CT: Financial Accounting Standard Board, 1984).

Statement of Financial Accounting Concepts No. 6, *Elements of Financial Statements: A Replacement of FASB Concepts Statement No. 3* (Stamford, CT: Financial Accounting Standard Board, 1985).

Storey R.K., "Conditions Necessary for Developing a Conceptual Framework", *FASB Viewpoints* (March 3, 1981), pp. 1–6.

Storey, R.K., "Conditions Necessary for Developing a Conceptual Framework", *Journal of Accountancy* (June, 1981), pp. 84–96.

Walter, H.E., II, and Sale, J.T., "Financial Reporting: A Two-Perspective Issue", *Management Accounting* (June, 1981), pp. 33–7.

The Corporate Report

The Accounting Standards Steering Committee, *The Corporate Report* (London: The Institute of Chartered Accountants in England and Wales, 1975).

Climo, Tom, "What's Happening in Britain?" *Journal of Accountancy* (February, 1976), pp. 55–9.

Harrison, R.B., "Corporate Report: A Critique", *The Chartered Accountant Magazine* (December–January, 1976), pp. 27–33.

The "Stamp Report"

Archibald, T. Ross, "A Research Perspective on *Corporate Reporting: Its Future Evolution*", in S. Basu and J. Alex Milburn (eds.), *Research to Support Standard Setting in Financial*

Accounting: A Canadian Perspective (Toronto: The Clarkson Gordon Foundation, 1982), pp. 218–30.

Denman, J.H., "Corporate Reporting and the Conceptual Framework Issue", *The Chartered Accountant Magazine* (April, 1981), pp. 74, 76–8.

Dewhirst, John E., "An Evaluation in *Corporate Reporting: Its Future Evolution*", in *Research to Support Standard Setting in Financial Accounting: A Canadian Perspective*, op. cit., pp. 231–46.

Falk, H., "Do We Really Need Accounting and Auditing Standards?" *The Chartered Accountant Magazine* (October, 1980), pp. 40–5.

Fowler, G.C., "A Public Practitioner's View of Corporate Reporting; Its Future Evolution", in *Research to Support Standard Setting in Financial Accounting: A Canadian Perspective*, op. cit., pp. 247–53.

Park, R.W., "Is Corporate Reporting Asking Too Much?" *The Chartered Accountant Magazine* (December, 1981), pp. 34–7.

Stamp, Edward, "Accounting Standard Setting – A New Beginning", *The Chartered Accountant Magazine* (September, 1980), pp. 38–42.

Stamp, Edward, *Corporate Reporting: Its Future Evolution* (Toronto: Canadian Institute of Chartered Accountants, 1980).

Stephen, Elliot, "Accounting and Canada", *Arthur Andersen Chronicle* (July, 1974), pp. 78–82.

The structure of accounting theory

7

The general boundaries of accounting theory have previously been defined to be the measurement and communication of data revealing economic activity consisting of three elements:

1. data revealing economic activity;
2. the measurement of data revealing economic activity;
3. communication of data revealing economic activity.[1]

A full appreciation of the current and future scope of accounting depends, however, on an understanding not only of accounting techniques but also of the structure of accounting theory from which the techniques are derived. The development of a structure of accounting theory to better justify the existing rules and techniques began with Paton's examination of the basic foundations of accounting.[2] The effort was continued by a number of accounting theorists who used either a deductive approach[3] or an inductive approach.[4] Their primary objectives were to codify the postulates and principles of accounting and to formulate a coherent accounting theory to enable accountants to improve the quality of financial reporting.

Although the resulting theories differ in terms of who uses accounting information, what constitutes the "use" of accounting data and the nature of the environment assumed by users and preparers of the accounting data, all of these theories provide a frame of reference, or a structure of accounting theory, within which the adequacy of specific methods may be judged. Although the elements of the structure may differ, according to the methodologies used and the assumptions made, a consensus exists in the literature and in practice regarding the primacy of certain elements as essential foundations of accounting theory.

7.1 The nature of the structure of an accounting theory

Whatever approaches and methodologies are used in the formulation of an accounting theory (deductive or inductive, normative or descriptive), the resultant frame of reference is based on a set of elements and relationships that govern the development of accounting techniques. As shown in Exhibit 7.1, the structure of an accounting theory contains the following elements:

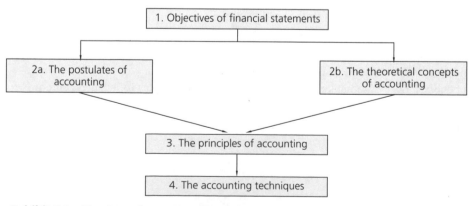

Exhibit 7.1 Structure of an accounting theory

1. A statement of the objectives of financial statements.
2. A statement of the postulates and the theoretical concepts of accounting concerned with the environment assumptions and the nature of the accounting unit. These postulates and theoretical concepts are derived from the stated objectives.
3. A statement of the basic accounting principles based on both the postulates and the theoretical concepts.
4. A body of accounting techniques derived from the accounting principles.

We discussed the first element – the formulation of the objectives of financial statements – in Chapter 6. Recall the importance of the objectives in the development of a structure theory. The fourth element – a body of knowledge or techniques for accountants – is the subject of other technique-oriented courses and will not be covered here. In this chapter, we will discuss the remaining three elements of an accounting theory, which are:

1. the postulates of accounting;
2. the theoretical concepts of accounting;
3. the principles of accounting.

7.2 The nature of accounting postulates, theoretical concepts and principles

The development of the postulates, theoretical concepts and principles of accounting has always been one of the most challenging and difficult tasks in accounting. The lack of a precise terminology, which has been recognized by most theorists, has compounded the problem. Littleton refers to this problem when he states that:

> Each book usually contains a mixture of axioms, conventions, generalizations, methods, rules, postulates, practices, procedures, principles, and standards. These terms cannot all be synonymous.[5]

Such confusion may be avoided by considering the formulation of the structure of accounting theory as a deductive, interactive process in which the objectives of accounting provide the basis for both the postulates and the theoretical concepts from which the techniques are derived. We begin with the following definitions:

1. The *accounting postulates* are self-evident statements or axioms, generally accepted by virtue of their conformity to the objectives of financial statements, that portray the economic, political, sociological and legal environments in which accounting must operate.
2. The *theoretical concepts* of accounting are also self-evident statements or axioms, also generally accepted by virtue of their conformity to the objectives of financial statements, that portray the nature of accounting entities operating in a free economy characterized by private ownership of property.
3. The *accounting principles* are general decision rules, derived from both the objectives and the theoretical concepts of accounting, that govern the development of accounting techniques.
4. The *accounting techniques* are specific rules derived from the accounting principles that account for specific transactions and events faced by the accounting entity.

7.3 The accounting postulates

7.3.1 The entity postulate

Accounting measures the results of the operations of specific entities, which are separate and distinct from owners of entities. The entity postulate holds that each enterprise is an accounting unit separate and distinct from its owners and other firms. The postulate defines the accountant's area of interest and limits the number of objects, events and events attributes that are to be included in financial statements. The postulate enables the accountant to distinguish between business and personal transactions: the accountant is to report the transactions of the enterprise, rather than the transactions of the enterprise's owners. The postulate also recognizes the fiduciary responsibility of management to stockholders. The entity concept applies to partnerships, sole proprietorships, corporations (incorporated and unincorporated), and small and large enterprises. It may also apply to a segment of a firm (such as a division) or to several firms (such as a consolidation of interrelated firms).

One way to define an *accounting entity* is to define the economic unit responsible for the economic activities and the administrative control of the unit. Postulate A.2 of Accounting Research Study No. 1 states that the "economic activity is carried on through specific units or entities".[6] This approach is better exemplified by the consolidated reporting of different entities as a single economic unit, regardless of their legal differences.

Another way to define an accounting entity is in terms of the economic interest of various users, instead of the economic activities and administrative control of the unit. This approach is user-oriented rather than firm-oriented. The interests of the users, not of the economic activities of the firm, define the boundaries of the accounting entity and the information to be included in the financial statements. The American Accounting Association's 1964 Concepts and Standards Research Study Committee on the Business Entity Concept supported this view, stating "the boundaries of such an economic entity are identifiable:

1. by determining the interested individual or group; and
2. by determining the nature of that individual's or that group's interest."[7]

This second approach justified the possible data expansion that may result from the new scope of accounting as it attempts to meet the potential informational needs of all users. For example, information generated by the possible adoption of human resource accounting, socioeconomic accounting, accounting for the cost of capital, and the reporting of financial forecasts may be more easily included in financial reports that are based on the user approach rather than on the firm approach to the definition of an accounting entity.

7.3.2 The going-concern postulate

The going-concern postulate, or continuity postulate, holds that the business entity will continue its operations long enough to realize its projects, commitments and ongoing activities. The postulate assumes either that the entity is not expected to be liquidated in the foreseeable future or that the entity will continue for an indefinite period of time. Such a hypothesis of stability reflects the expectations of all parties interested in the entity. Thus, the financial statements provide a tentative view of the financial situation of the firm and are only part of a series of continuous reports. Except for the case of liquidation, the user will interpret the information as computed on the basis of the assumption of the continuity of the firm. Accordingly, if an entity has a limited life, the corresponding reports will specify the terminal data and the nature of the liquidation.

The going-concern postulate justifies the valuation of assets on a nonliquidation basis and provides the basis for depreciation accounting. First, because neither current values nor liquidation values are appropriate for asset valuation, the going-concern postulate calls for the use of historical cost for many valuations. Second, the fixed assets and intangibles are amortized over their useful life, rather than over a shorter period in expectation of early liquidation.

The going-concern postulate may also be employed to support the *benefit theory*. Expectations of future benefits encourage managers to be forward looking and motivate investors to commit capital to an enterprise. The going concern (that is, an indefinite continuance of the accounting entity) is essential for the justification of the benefit theory.

Many accounting theorists consider the going-concern postulate to be a necessary and essential accounting convention. Paton and Littleton simply state that "the possibility of abrupt cessation of activity cannot afford a foundation for accounting".[8]

All accounting theorists do not share this interpretation of the going-concern postulate. Storey and Sterling separately argue that the going-concern postulate does not provide justification for valuing inventories at cost.[9] Storey argues that "it is the realization convention and not the going-concern convention which requires valuation of inventories at cost".[10] Sterling argues that assuming that an accounting entity has an indefinite life does not justify the use of liquidation value, but also that this assumption is not a sufficient reason for using historical cost when other relevant valuation alternatives exist. Furthermore, if the going-concern postulate is to be retained, it should be perceived as a *prediction*.

Some accounting theorists prefer not to include the going-concern postulate in the structure of accounting theory. Chambers views a going concern as an entity that is in a continuous state of orderly liquidation, rather than in forced liquidation.[11] This interpretation of a going concern conforms with the use of the "current cash equivalent" Chambers proposes as a valuation base. Other theorists do not include the going-concern postulate, because they assume it is irrelevant to a structure of accounting theory.[12]

All these objections point to the necessity of reinterpreting the going-concern postulate. The postulate may be viewed as a judgment on continuity based on actual evidence to that effect. Fremgen offers a definition consistent with the view that the going-concern postulate is a conclusion or a judgment, rather than an assumption, when he states that "the entity is viewed as remaining in operation indefinitely" *in recognition of evidence to that effect*, not "in the absence of evidence to the contrary".[13]

7.3.3 The unit-of-measure postulate

A unit of exchange and of measurement is necessary to account for the transactions of firms in a uniform manner. The common denominator chosen in accounting is the *monetary unit*. The exchangeability of goods, services and capital is measured in terms of money. The unit-of-measure postulate holds that accounting is a measurement and communication process of the activities of the firm that are measurable in monetary terms.

The unit-of measure postulate, or the monetary-unit postulate, implies two principal limitations of accounting. First, accounting is limited to the prediction of information expressed in terms of a monetary unit; it does not record and communicate other relevant but nonmonetary information. Accounting information is perceived as essentially monetary and quantified; nonaccounting information is perceived as nonmonetary and nonquantified. This view leads us to define accounting information as "quantitative, formal, structured, audited, numerical, and past-oriented" and to define nonaccounting information as "qualitative, informal, narrative, unaudited, and future-oriented".[14]

These definitions show, however, that although accounting is a discipline concerned with the measurement and communication of monetary activities, it has been expanding into areas previously viewed as qualitative in nature. In fact, a number of empirical studies refer to the relevance of nonaccounting information compared with accounting information.[15]

The limitation implied by the unit-of-measure postulate concerns the monetary unit itself as a unit of measure. The primary characteristic of the *monetary-unit purchasing power*, or the quantity of goods or services that money can acquire, is of concern. Unlike the meter, which is invariably 100 centimeters long, the purchasing power of the monetary unit, which is the dollar, is subject to change. Conventional accounting theory deals with this problem by stating that the unit-of-measure postulate is also a "stable monetary postulate" in the sense that the postulate assumes that the purchasing power of the dollar is either stable over time or changes insignificantly. Although it is still employed in current financial reporting, the *stable monetary postulate* is the object of continuous and persistent criticism. The accounting profession faces the challenge of choosing between units of money and units of general purchasing power as the unit of accounting measurement.

7.3.4 The accounting-period postulate

Although the going-concern postulate holds that the firm will exist for an indefinite period of time, users require a variety of information about the financial position and performance of a firm to make short-term decisions. In response to this constraint imposed by the user environment, the accounting-period postulate holds that financial reports depicting changes in the wealth of the firm should be disclosed periodically. The duration of the period may vary, but income tax laws, which require income determination on an annual basis, and traditional business practices, result in a normal period of a year. Although most companies use an accounting period that corresponds to the calendar year, some companies use a fiscal or a "natural" business year. When the business cycle does not correspond to the calendar year, it is more meaningful to end the accounting period when the business activity has reached its lowest point. Owing to the need for more timely, relevant and frequent information, most companies also issue interim reports that provide financial information on a quarterly or a monthly basis. Empirical studies on stock market reactions to the issuance of interim reports and their impact on users' investment decisions indicate the usefulness of interim reports. To ensure the credibility of interim reports, the Accounting Principles Board issued APB Opinion No. 28, which requires interim reports to be based on the same accounting principles and practices employed in the preparation of annual reports.

By requiring the entity to provide periodic, short-term financial reports, the accounting period postulate imposes *accruals and deferrals*, the application of which is the principal difference between *accrual* and *cash accounting*. Each period, the use of accruals and deferrals is required in the preparation of the financial position of the firm in terms of prepaid expenses, uncollected revenues, unpaid wages and depreciation expense. The accountant may have to rely on experience and judgment to reconcile the postulate of continuity with the necessity for accruals and deferrals. Although short-term financial reports may be arbitrary and imprecise, such drawbacks are overridden by their significance to users, thereby dictating that the accounting process continue to produce them.

7.4 The theoretical concepts of accounting

7.4.1 The proprietary theory

According to the proprietary theory, the entity is the "agent, representative or arrangement through which the individual entrepreneurs or shareholders operate".[16] The viewpoint of the proprietor group as the center of interest is reflected in the ways in which accounting records are kept and financial statements are prepared. The primary objective of the proprietary theory is the determination and analysis of the proprietor's *net worth*. Accordingly, the accounting equation is

$$\text{Assets} - \text{Liabilities} = \text{Proprietor's Equity}$$

In other words, the proprietor owns the assets and the liabilities. If the liabilities may be considered negative assets, the proprietary theory may be said to be asset "centered" and, consequently, balance sheet oriented. Assets are valued and balance sheets are prepared to measure the changes in the proprietary interest or wealth. Revenues and expenses are considered to be increases or decreases respectively in proprietorship that do not result from proprietary investments or capital withdrawals by the proprietor. Thus, net income on debt and corporate income taxes are expenses; dividends are withdrawals of capital.

Although the proprietary theory is generally viewed as primarily adaptable to such closely held corporations as proprietorships and partnerships, the influence of the proprietary theory may be found in some of the accounting techniques and terminology used by widely held corporations. For example, the corporate concept of income, which is arrived at after treating interest and income taxes as expenses, represents "net income to the stockholders" rather than to all providers of capital. Similarly, terms such as "earnings per share" and "dividend per share" connote a proprietary emphasis. The equity method of accounting for nonconsolidated investments in subsidiaries recommends that the firm's share of the unconsolidated subsidiary net income be included in the net income. Thus practice also implies a proprietary concept.

The proprietary theory can assume at least two forms, which differ on the basis of who is included in the proprietary group. In the first form, only the common stockholders are part of the proprietary group and preferred stockholders are excluded.[17] Thus, preferred dividends are deducted when calculating the earnings of the proprietor. This narrow form of the proprietary theory is identical to the *residual equity concept* set forth by Staubus.[18] Consistent with this form of the proprietary theory, the net income is extended to deduct preferred dividends to arrive at a net income to the residual equity on which the computation of earnings per share will be based. In the second form of the proprietary theory, both common stock and preferred stock are included in the proprietor's equity.[19] This wider view of the theory focuses attention on the shareholders' equity section of the balance sheet and the amount to be credited to all shareholders on the income statement.

7.4.2 The entity theory

The entity theory views the entity as something separate and distinct from those who provide capital to the entity. Simply stated, the business unit, rather than the proprietor, is the center of accounting interest. The business unit owns the resources of the enterprise and is liable to both the claims of the owners and the claims of the creditors. Accordingly, the accounting equation is:

$$\text{Assets} = \text{Equities}$$
$$\text{Assets} = \text{Liabilities} + \text{Stockholders' Equity}$$

Assets are rights accruing to the entity; equities represent sources of the assets and consist of liabilities and the stockholders' equity. Both the creditors and the stockholders are equity holders, although they have different rights with respect to income, risk control and liquidation. Thus, income earned is the property of the entity until it is distributed as dividends to the shareholders. Because the business unit is held responsible for meeting the claims of the equity holders, the entity theory is said to be "income centered" and consequently income statement oriented. Accountability to the equity holders is accomplished by measuring the operating and financial performances of the firm. Accordingly, income is an increase in the stockholders' equity after the claims of other equity holders (for example, interest on long-term debt and income taxes) are met. The increase in the stockholders' equity is considered income to the stockholders only if a dividend is declared. Similarly, undistributed profits remain the property of the entity because they represent the "corporation's proprietary equity in itself".[20] Note that strict adherence to the entity theory dictates that income taxes and interest on debt be considered distributions of income rather than expenses. The general belief and the interpretation of the entity theory, however, is that interest and income taxes are expenses.

The entity theory is most applicable to the corporate form of business enterprise, which is separate and distinct from its owners. The impact of the entity theory may be found in some of the accounting techniques and terminology used in practice. First, the entity theory favors the adoption of LIFO rather than FIFO inventory valuation, because LIFO valuation achieves a better income determination, due to its application under the proprietary theory. Second, the common definitions of revenues as products of an enterprise and expenses as goods and services consumed to obtain these revenues are consistent with the entity theory's preoccupation with an index of performance and accountability to equity holders. Third, the preparation of consolidated statements and the recognition of a class of minority interests as additional equity holders are also consistent with the entity theory. Finally, both the entity theory, with its emphasis on the proper determination of income to equity holders, and the proprietary theory, with its emphasis on proper asset valuation, may be perceived to favor the adoption of current values, or valuation bases other than historical costs.

7.4.3 The fund theory

Under the fund theory, the basis of accounting is neither the proprietor nor the entity, but a group of assets and related obligations and restrictions, called a *fund*, that governs the use of the assets.[21] Thus, the fund theory views the business unit as consisting of economic resources (funds) and related obligations and restrictions regarding the use of these resources. The accounting equation is:

$$\text{Assets} = \text{Restrictions of Assets}$$

The accounting unit is defined in terms of assets and the uses to which these assets are committed. Liabilities represent a series of legal and economic restrictions on the use of the assets. The fund theory is therefore "asset-centered" in the sense that its primary focus is on the administration and the appropriate use of assets. Instead of the balance sheet or the financial statement, the statement of sources and uses of funds is the primary objective of financial reporting. This statement reflects the conduct of the operations of the firm in terms of sources and dispositions of funds.

The fund theory is useful primarily to government and nonprofit organizations. Hospitals, universities, cities and governmental units, for example, are engaged in multifaceted operations that warrant separate funds. Each self-balanced fund produces separate reports through a separate accounting system and a proper set of accounts. A fund may be defined as:

… an independent fiscal and accounting entity with a self-balancing set of accounts recording cash and/or other resources together with all related liabilities, obligations, reserves, and equities which are segregated for the purpose of carrying on specific activities or attaining certain objectives in accordance with special regulations, restrictions, or limitations.[22]

The number of funds used by any nonprofit institution depends on the number and type of activities on which legal restrictions are imposed regarding the use of the assets entrusted to the organization. For instance, the following eight major funds are recommended for the sound financial administration of a governmental unit:

1. The General Fund to account for all financial transactions not properly accounted for in another fund.
2. Special Revenue Funds to account for the proceeds of specific revenue sources (other than special assessments) or to finance specified activities as required by law or administrative regulation.
3. Debt Service Funds to account for the payment of interest and principal on long-term debts other than special assessment and revenue bonds.
4. Capital Projects Funds to account for the receipt and disbursement of moneys used for the acquisition of capital facilities other than those financed by special assessment and enterprise funds.
5. Enterprise Funds to account for the financing of services to the general public, where all or most of the costs involved are paid in the form of charges by users of such services.
6. Trust and Agency Funds to account for assets held by a governmental unit as trustee or agent for individuals, private organizations, and other governmental units.
7. Intragovernmental Service Funds to account for the financing of special activities and services performed by a designated organization unit within a government jurisdiction.
8. Special Assessment Funds to account for special assessments levied to finance public improvements or services deemed to benefit the properties against which the assessments are levied.[23]

The fund theory is also relevant to profit-oriented organizations, which use funds for such diverse activities as sinking funds, accounting for bankruptcies and estates and trusts, branch or divisional accounting, segregation of assets into current or fixed assets, and consolidation.

7.5 The accounting principles

7.5.1 The cost principle

According to the cost principle, the *acquisition cost* or *historical cost* is the appropriate valuation basis for recognition of the acquisition of all goods and services, expenses, costs, and equities. In other words, an item is valued at the exchange price at the date of acquisition and is recorded in the financial statements at that value or an amortized portion of that value. Accordingly, APB Statement No. 4 defines cost as follows:

Cost is the amount, measured in money, of cash expended or other property transferred, capital stock issued, services performed, or a liability incurred, in consideration of goods or services received or to be received. Costs can be classified as unexpired or expired. Unexpired costs (assets) are those which are applicable to the production of future revenues. ... Expired costs are not applicable to the production of future revenues, and for that reason are treated as deductions from current revenues or are charged against retained earnings.[24]

Cost represents the exchange price of, or the monetary consideration given for the acquisition of, goods or services. If the consideration comprises nonmonetary assets, the exchange price is the cash equivalent of the assets or services given up. The cost principle is equally applicable to the measurement of liabilities and capital transactions.

The cost principle may be justified in terms of both its objectivity and the going-concern postulate. First, acquisition cost is objective, verifiable information. Second, the going-concern postulate assumes that the entity will continue its activities indefinitely, thereby eliminating the necessity of using current values or liquidation values for asset evaluation.

The precarious validity of the unit-of-measure postulate, which assumes that the purchasing power of the dollar is stable, is a major limitation to the application of the cost principle. Historical cost valuation may produce erroneous figures if changes in the values of assets over time are ignored. Similarly, the values of assets acquired at different times over a period during which the purchasing power of the dollar is changing cannot be added together in the balance sheet and provide meaningful results.

7.5.2 The revenue principle

The revenue principle specifies:

1. the nature of the components of revenue;
2. the measurement of revenue; and
3. the timing of revenue recognition.

Each fact of the revenue principle raises interesting and controversial issues in accounting theory.

The nature and components of revenue

Revenue has been interpreted as:

1. an inflow of *net* assets resulting from the sale of goods or services;[25]
2. an outflow of goods or services from the firm to its customers;[26] and
3. a product of the firm resulting from the mere creation of goods or services by an enterprise during a given period of time.[27]

Hendriksen considers that:

1. the product concept is superior to the outflow concept, which is superior to the inflow concept; and
2. the product concept is neutral with respect to both the measurement (amount) and timing (date of recognition) of revenue, but the inflow concept confuses both measurement and timing with the revenue process.[28]

The different interpretations of the nature of revenue are compounded by different views on what should be included in revenue. Basically, there are two views of the components of revenue. The broad or comprehensive view of revenue includes all of the proceeds from business and investment activities. This view identifies as revenue all changes in the net assets resulting from the revenue-producing activities and other gains or losses resulting from the sale of fixed assets and investments. Applying this view, Accounting Terminology Bulletin No. 2 defines revenue as follows:

> Revenue results from the sale of goods and the rendering of services and is measured by the charge made to customers, clients or tenants for goods and services furnished to them. It also includes gains from the sale or exchange of assets (other than stock in trade), interest and dividends earned on investments, and other increases in the owners' equity except those arising from the capital contributions and capital adjustments.[29]

The narrower view of revenue includes only the results of the revenue-producing activities and excludes investment income and gains and losses on the disposal of fixed assets. This view requires that a clear distinction be made between revenue and gains and losses. Adopting the narrower view of revenue, the American Accounting Association in a 1957 statement defined *net income* as:

> ... the excess of deficiency of revenue compared with related expired costs and other gains and losses to the enterprise from sales, exchanges, or other conversions of assets.[30]

The measurement of revenue

Revenue is measured in terms of the value of the products or services exchanged in an "arm's-length" transaction. This value represents either the net cash equivalent or the present discounted value of the money received or to be received in exchange for the products or services that the enterprise transfers to its customers. Two primary interpretations arise from this concept of revenue:

1. Cash discounts and any reductions in the fixed prices, such as bad debt losses, are adjustments necessary to compute the true net cash equivalent or the present discounted value of the money claims and consequently should be deducted when computing revenue. (This interpretation conflicts with the view that cash discounts and bad debt losses should be considered expenses.)
2. For noncash transactions, the exchange value is set equal to the fair market value of the consideration given or received, whichever is more easily and clearly computed.

The timing of revenue recognition

It is generally admitted that revenue and income are earned throughout all stages of the operating cycle (that is, during order reception, production, sale and collection). Given the difficulties of allocating revenue and income to the different stages of the operating cycle, accountants employ the realization principle to select a "critical event" in the cycle for the timing of revenue and recognition of income. The critical event is chosen to indicate when certain changes in assets and liabilities may be accounted for appropriately An early definition of the realization principle is:

> The essential meaning of realization is that a change in asset or liability has become sufficiently definite and objective to warrant recognition in the accounts. This recognition may rest on an exchange transaction between independent parties, or on established trade practices, or on the terms of a contract performance which is considered to be virtually certain.[31]

The broad nature of this statement has led accountants to search for specific rules or considerations necessary to the recognition of certain asset and liability changes. Naturally, the realization principle and the corresponding criteria for the recognition of asset and liability changes have been subject to different interpretations.[32] As reported by the 1973–1974 American Accounting Association Committee on Concepts and Standards External Reporting, the specific criteria for revenue and income recognition are:

1. earned, in some sense or another;
2. in distributable form;
3. the result of a conversion brought about in a transaction between the enterprise and someone external to it;
4. the result of a legal sale or similar process;
5. severed from capital;
6. in the form of liquid assets;
7. both its gross and net effects on shareholder equity must be estimable with a high degree of reliability.[33]

The committee tied the realization principle to a concept of a *reliable income measurement*. The realization principle is an expression of the level of certainty of the profit impact of an event reported as revenue. More explicitly, the Committee defined realization as follows:

> Income must always be in existence before the question of realization can arise. Realization is not a determinant in the concept of income; it only serves as a guide in deciding when events, otherwise resolved as being within the concept of income, can be entered in the accounting records in objective terms; that is, when the uncertainty has been reduced to an acceptable level.[34]

Given these different interpretations of the realization principle and of the criteria to be used for the recognition of asset and liability changes, reliance on the realization principle may be misleading.[35] In general, revenue is recognized on an accrual basis or on a critical event basis.

The *accrual basis* for revenue recognition may imply that revenue should be reported during production (in which case the profit may be computed proportionally to the work completed or the service performed), at the end of production, on sale of goods, or on collection of sale. Revenue is generally recognized during production in the following situations:

1. Rent, interest and commission revenue are recognized as earned, given the existence of a prior agreement or a contract specifying the gradual increase in the claim against the customer.
2. An individual or a group rendering professional or similar services might better use an accrual basis for the recognition of revenue, given that the nature of the claim against the customer is a function of the proportion of services rendered.
3. Revenues on long-term contracts are recognized on the basis of the progress of construction or the "percentage of completion". The percentage of completion is computed as either:
   (a) the engineering estimates of the work performed to date compared with the total work to be completed in terms of the contract; or
   (b) the total costs incurred to date compared with the total costs estimated for the total project in the contract.

4. Revenues on "cost plus fixed-fee contracts" are better recognized on the accrual basis.

5. Asset changes due to accretion give rise to revenue (for example, when liquor or wines age, timber grows, or livestock matures). Although a transaction must occur before revenue is recognized in these examples, accretion revenue is based on comparative inventory valuations.

The *critical event basis* for revenue recognition is triggered by a crucial event in the operating cycle. That may be:

- the time of sale;
- the completion of production; or
- the receipt of payment subsequent to sale.

The *sales basis* for the recognition of revenue is justified because:

1. the price of the product is then known with certainty;
2. the exchange has been finalized by delivery of goods, leading to an objective knowledge of the costs incurred; and
3. in terms of realization, a sale constitutes a crucial event.

The *completion-of-production basis* for the recognition of revenue is justified when a stable market and a stable price exist for a standard commodity. The production process rather than the sale therefore constitutes the crucial event for the recognition of revenue. This rule is primarily applicable to "precious metals that have a fixed selling price and insignificant market prices".[36] The completion-of-production treatment is appropriate for gold, silver, and other precious metals and may also be appropriate for agricultural and mineral products that meet the required criteria.

The *payment basis* for the recognition of revenue is justified when the sale will be made and when a reasonably accurate valuation cannot be placed on the product to be transferred. This method, which amounts to a mere deferral of revenue, is primarily identified with the "installment method" of recognizing revenue.

7.5.3 The matching principle

The matching principle holds that expenses should be recognized in the same period as the associated revenues; that is, revenues are recognized in a given period according to the revenue principle, and the related expenses are then recognized. The association is best accomplished when it reflects the cause-and-effect relationship between costs and revenues. Operationally, it consists of a two-stage process for accounting for expenses. First, costs are capitalized as assets representing bundles of service potentials or benefits. Second, each asset is written off as an expense to recognize the proportion of the assets' service potential that has expired in the generation of the revenue during this period. Thus, accrual accounting rather than cash accounting is implied by the matching principle in terms of capitalization and allocation.

The association between revenues and expenses depends on one of four criteria:

1. Direct matching of expired costs with a revenue (for example, cost of goods sold matched with related sale).
2. Direct matching of expired cost with the period (for example, president's salary for the period).

3. Allocation of costs over periods benefited (for example, depreciation).

4. Expensing all other costs in the period incurred, unless it can be shown that they have future benefit (for example, advertising expense).

Unexpired costs (that is, assets) not meeting one of these four criteria for expensing the current period are chargeable to future periods and may be classified under different categories according to their different uses in the firm. Such varying uses may justify differences in the application of the matching principle.

We will now examine the major asset and cost categories and the corresponding rules for the time of expenses.

Costs of producing finished goods for sale

The costs of producing finished goods for sale generally include raw materials, direct labor and factory overhead. A two-stage process is employed to account for these costs:

1. inventory valuation, or the determination of the product costs attached to the product; and

2. income determination, or the matching of product costs with revenues.

When determining the amount of inventory valuation, the problem is to decide which costs are product costs (because they benefit future periods and should be inventoried) and which costs are period costs (because they benefit only the current period and should be charged against current income). The absorption (or full) costing method and the direct (or variable) costing method produce different answers.

The *absorption costing* method treats all production costs as product costs that are attached to the product, carried forward, and only released as period costs at the time of sale. The *direct costing* method treats only the variable production costs as product costs and all of the fixed manufacturing overhead costs as period costs. The choice between these two methods has posed a major controversy in the accounting literature for many years. Neither method has emerged as the primary victor.[37] It is generally admitted, however, that direct costing is more relevant to internal decision-making. The separate reporting of fixed and variable costs is assumed to facilitate incremental profit analysis and to remove the impact of inventory changes from income.

Depreciable operating assets

Depreciable operating assets are also referred to as *wasting capital assets*. Because a depreciable operating asset is assumed to benefit more than one period, the asset is capitalized at its acquisition cost, which is then allocated on some logical basis over the asset's useful life. This allocation process is known as *depreciation* for such tangible assets as building, equipment, tools and furniture, as *depletion* for assets represented by a natural resource (such as mineral deposits and timber tracts), and *amortization* for such intangible assets as special rights or benefits (examples are patents, copyrights, franchises, trademarks, goodwill, deferred charges, research and development costs, organizational costs, and leaseholds). Depreciation accounting has been defined as follows:

> Depreciation accounting is a system of accounting which aims to distribute the cost or other basic value of tangible capital assets, less salvage (if any), over the estimated useful life of the unit (which may be a group of assets) in a systematic and rational manner. It is a process of allocation, not of valuation. Depreciation for the year is the portion of the total charge under such a system that is allocated during

the year. Although the allocation may properly take into account occurrences during the year, it is not intended to be a measurement of the effect of all such occurrences.[38]

A number of depreciation methods have been developed, each of which is based on a different pattern of depreciation charges over the life of the tangible asset. A depreciation method may be based on:

1. *time*, such as the straight-line method;
2. *output*, such as the service-hours and the unit-of-output method;
3. *reducing depreciation charge*, such as the sum of years' digit method, the fixed percentage on declining base amount method, the declining rate on cost method, and the double-declining balance method;
4. *investment and interest concepts*, such as the annuity method and the sinking-fund method.[39]

Nondepreciable operating assets

The third major asset and cost category consists of nondepreciable operating assets, which are also referred to as permanent capital assets, because it is assumed that they are not consumed while the operations of the business are being conducted. Their value is not affected by productive activities and they have no impact on income determination until they are sold or revalued. Accordingly, the matching principle is not applicable to nondepreciable operating assets.

Costs of selling and administration

The costs of selling and administration are all of the nonmanufacturing costs necessary to maintain a basic selling and administrative organization. They are treated as period costs in the period in which they are incurred, under either the direct or absorption costing method.

7.5.4 The objectivity principle

The usefulness of financial information depends heavily on the *reliability* of the measurement procedure used. Because ensuring maximum reliability is frequently difficult, accountants have employed the objectivity principle to justify the choice of a measurement procedure. The principle of objectivity, however, has been subject to different interpretations:

1. An objective measurement is an "impersonal" measure, in the sense that it is free from the personal bias of the measurers. "In other words, objectivity refers to the external reality that is independent of the persons who perceive it."[40]
2. An objective measurement is a variable measurement, in the sense that it is based on evidence.[41]
3. An objective measurement is the result of a "consensus among a given group of observers or measurers".[42] This view also implies that objectivity will depend on the given group of measurers.
4. The size of the dispersion of the measurement distribution may be used as an indicator of the degree of objectivity of a given measurement system.

Ijiri and Jaedicke employ the fourth interpretation of objectivity.[43] Specifically, they define objectivity V as:

$$V = \frac{1}{n} \sum_{i=1}^{n} (x_i - \bar{x})^2$$

where:

n = the number of measures in the reference group
x_i = the quantity that the ith measure reports
$\bar{x}$ = the average of x_is over all measures in the reference group

In other words, when choosing between accounting measurement techniques that result in two measurement distributions, the technique that results in the smaller variance is the more objective. This concept is illustrated in Exhibit 7.2 by two measurement techniques, which both yield the same average value.

Measurement technique A is more objective than measurement technique B, because A exhibits a narrower dispersion of values around the mean. However, as we learned earlier, objectivity does not reflect *reliability*, which is a more useful concept for accountants. Ijiri and Jaedicke suggest the use of the mean square error as a measure of reliability.[44] Specifically, they define reliability R as:

$$R = \frac{1}{n} \sum_{i=1}^{n} (x_i - \bar{x})^2$$

where x^* is the alleged value, or

$$R = \frac{1}{n} \sum_{i=1}^{n} (x_i - \bar{x})^2 + (\bar{x} - x^*)^2$$

From the second expression of reliability, Ijiri and Jaedicke state that the degree of reliability is equal to the degree of objectivity (first term) plus a reliance bias (second term). Note that the *reliance bias* is equal to the differences between the mean value and the alleged value of the measurement.

The application of this reliability measure is illustrated in Exhibit 7.3 in two measurement procedures, which yield different average values, although they have similar values.

From this analysis, we may conclude that the accounting profession should define a trade-off point between objectivity and bias that leads to acceptable levels of reliability. This is only when a consensus exists as to the alleged values that should be measured.

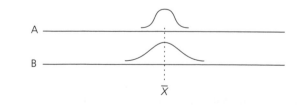

Exhibit 7.2 Results of two different measurement techniques

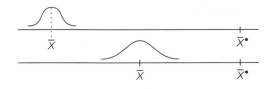

Exhibit 7.3 Application of the reliability measure

7.5.5 The consistency principle

The consistency principle holds that similar economic events should be recorded and reported in a consistent manner from period to period. The principle implies that the same accounting procedures will be applied to similar items over time. Application of the consistency principle makes financial statements more comparable and more useful. Trends in accounting data and relationships with external factors are more accurately revealed when comparable measurement procedures are used. Similarly, the distortion of income and balance sheet amounts and the possible manipulation of financial statements are avoided by the consistent application of accounting procedures over time. Consistency is therefore a user constraint intended to facilitate the user's decision by ensuring the comparable presentation of the financial statements of a given firm over time, thereby enhancing the utility of the statements. In the standard opinion, the certified public accountant recognizes the consistency principle by noting whether or not the financial statements have been prepared in conformity with generally accepted accounting principles applied on a basis "consistent with that of the preceding year".

The consistency principle does not preclude a firm changing accounting procedures when this is justified by changing circumstances, or if the alternative procedure is preferable (the rule of preferability). According to APB Opinion No. 20, changes that justify a change in procedure are:

1. a change in accounting principle;
2. a change in accounting estimate;
3. a change in reporting entity.

These changes are to be reflected in the accounts and reported in the financial statements *retroactively* for a change in accounting entity, *prospectively* for a change in accounting estimate, and *generally* and *currently* for a change in accounting principle.

7.5.6 The full disclosure principle

There is a general consensus in accounting that there should be "full", "fair" and "adequate" disclosure of accounting data. *Full disclosure* requires that financial statements be designed and prepared to portray accurately the economic events that have affected the firm for the period and to contain sufficient information to make them useful and not misleading to the average investor. More explicitly, the full disclosure principle implies that no information of substance or of interest to the average investor will be omitted or concealed.

The principle is further reinforced by the various disclosure requirements set forth by the APB Opinions, the FASB Statements and the SEC Accounting Releases and requirements. Full disclosure is, however, a broad, open-ended construct that leaves several questions unanswered or open to different interpretations. First, what is meant by "full", "fair" and adequate disclosure? "Adequate" connotes a minimum set of information to be disclosed;

"fair" implies an ethical constraint dictating an equitable treatment of users; and "full" refers to complete and comprehensive presentation of information. Another accepted position is to view "fairness" as the central objective and trade-off point between full and adequate disclosure. Hence, under the title *Fair Presentation in Conformity with Generally Accepted Accounting Principles*, APB Statement No. 4 states that "fair" presentation is met when:

> ... a proper balance has been achieved between the conflicting needs to disclose important aspects of financial positions and results of operations in accordance with conventional aspects and to summarize the voluminous underlying data into a limited number of financial statement captions and supporting notes.

Second, what should be disclosed so that a "prudent, average investor" will not be misled? Should the data be essentially accounting information? Should the data include novel information and such additions as human-asset accounting, socioeconomic accounting, inflation accounting and segment reporting?

The answers to these questions rest on proper determination of the users, their needs, their level of sophistication and, more importantly; their information-processing capabilities, given the risks of information overload caused by data expansion. Skinner draws attention to some matters that should be the subject of full disclosure:

1. details of accounting policies and methods, particularly when judgment is required in the application of an accounting method, when the method is peculiar to the reporting entity, or when alternative accounting methods can be used;

2. additional information to aid in investment analysis or to indicate the rights of various parties that have claims on the reporting entity;

3. changes from the preceding year in accounting policies or methods of applying them and the effects of such changes;

4. assets, liabilities, costs and revenues arising from transactions with parties that have controlling interests or with directors or officers that have special relationships with the reporting entity;

5. contingent assets, liabilities and commitments;

6. financial or other nonoperating transactions occurring after the balance sheet date that have a material effect on the entity's financial position as indicated in the Year-end statement.[45]

7.5.7 The conservatism principle

The conservatism principle is an exception or modifying principle in the sense that it acts as a constraint to the presentation of relevant and reliable accounting data. The conservatism principle holds that when choosing among two or more acceptable accounting techniques, some preference is shown for the option that has the least favorable impact on the stockholder's equity. More specifically, the principle implies that preferably the lowest values of assets and revenues and the highest values of liabilities and expenses should be reported. The conservatism principle therefore dictates that the accountant displays a generally pessimistic attitude when choosing accounting techniques for financial reporting. To accomplish the objectives of understanding current income and assets, the conservatism principle may lead to treatments that constitute a departure from acceptable or theoretical approaches. For example, the adoption of the "lower-of-cost-or-market" concept conflicts with the historical principle. Although the LIFO valuation and accelerated depreciation are generally perceived as counter inflationary measures, they may be viewed as resulting from the adoption of the conservatism principle. Thus Chatfield maintains that:

> Both [LIFO and accelerated depreciation] reinforced an older tradition of balance sheet conservatism, so much so that taxpayers are still allowed to use LIFO together with lower-of-cost-or-market inventory valuation. Both gave precedence to management's need for more precise valuation.[46]

In the past, conservatism has been employed when dealing with uncertainty in the environment and possible over-optimism of managers and owners and also when protecting creditors against an unwarranted distribution of the firm's assets as dividends. Conservatism was a more highly esteemed virtue in the past than it is today. It has led to arbitrary and inconsistent provisions or liabilities or both.

Sterling calls conservatism "the most ancient and probably the most pervasive principle of accounting valuation".[47] Today, the emphasis on objective and fair presentation and the primacy of the investor as user has lessened the reliance on conservatism. It is now perceived more as a guide to be followed in extraordinary situations, than as a general rule to be rigidly applied to all circumstances. Conservatism is still employed in some situations that require the accountant's judgment, such as choosing the estimated useful life and residual value of an asset for depreciation accounting and the corollary rule of applying the "lower-of-cost-market" concept in valuing inventories and marketable equity securities. Because it is essentially the manifestation of the accountant's intervention that may result in the introduction of bias, errors, possible distortions and misleading statements, the present view of conservatism as an accounting principle is bound to disappear.

7.5.8 The materiality principle

Like conservatism, the materiality principle is an exception or modifying principle. The principle holds that transactions and events having insignificant economic effects may be handled in the most expeditious manner, whether or not they conform to generally accepted principles, and need not be disclosed. Materiality serves as an implicit guide for the accountant in terms of what should be disclosed in the financial reports, enabling the accountant to decide what is not important or what does not matter on the basis of record-keeping costs, accuracy of financial statements, and relevance to the user.

In general, the accounting bodies have left the application of materiality to the accountant's judgment, at the same time stressing its importance. According to APB Statement No. 4, materiality implies that "financial reporting is only concerned with information that is significant enough to affect evaluations or decisions".[48] APB Opinion No. 30 relies on an undefined concept of materiality to describe extraordinary items. Similarly, APB Opinion No. 22 recommends the disclosure of all policies or principles that materially affect the financial position, results of operations and changes in the financial position of the entity. In 1975 the FASB issued a Discussion Memorandum on the materiality issue, stressing the importance of this principle.[49]

The materiality principle lacks an operational definition. Most definitions of materiality stress the accountant's role in interpreting what is and what is not material. For example, Frishkoff defines materiality as the "relative, quantitative importance of some piece of financial information to a user, in context of a decision to be made".[50]

A 1974 study by the Accountants' International Study Group characterizes materiality as follows:

Materiality is essentially a matter of professional judgment. An individual item should be judged material if the knowledge of that item could reasonably be deemed to have influence on the users of the financial statements.[51]

Guidelines or criteria to be used in determining materiality are urgently needed. Two basic criteria have been recommended. The first, referred to as the *size approach*, relates the size of the item to another relevant variable, such as net income. For example, Bernstein suggests a border zone of 10–15 percent of net income after taxes as the point of distinction between what is and what is not material.[52] Similarly, the FASB Discussion Memorandum on materiality suggests criteria based on the size approach:

If the amount of its current or potential effect equals or exceeds 10 percent of a pertinent financial statement amount, the matter should be presumed to be material.

If its amount or current potential effect is between 5 and 10 percent of a pertinent financial statement amount, the materiality of the manner depends on the surrounding circumstances.[53]

The second criterion, referred to as the *change criterion approach*, evaluates the impact of an item on trends or changes between accounting periods. This approach is advocated primarily by Rappaport, who contends that materiality criteria can be stated in terms of financial averages, trends, and ratios that express significant analytic relationships in terms of accounting information.[54] The change criterion approach has influenced the Accountants' International Study Group, as the following excerpt from *Materiality in Accounting* indicates:

An amount is not material solely by reason of its size; other factors including those set out below must be considered in making decisions as to materiality: The nature of the item, whether it is:

- a factor entering into the determination of net income;
- unusual or extraordinary;
- contingent on an event or condition;
- determinable based on existing facts and circumstances;
- required by statute or regulation.

The amount itself, in relationship to:

- the financial statements taken as a whole;
- the total of the accounts of which it forms, or should form, a part;
- related items;
- the corresponding amount in previous years or the expected amount in future years.[55]

7.5.9 The uniformity and comparability principles

The consistency principle refers to the use of the same procedures for related items by a given firm over time; the uniformity principle refers to the use of the same procedures by different firms. The desired objective is to achieve comparability of financial statements by reducing the diversity created by the use of different accounting procedures by different firms. In fact, a constant debate is taking place over whether flexibility or uniformity should prevail in accounting and financial reporting. The principal supports for *uniformity* are the claims that it would:

1. reduce the diverse use of accounting procedures and the inadequacies of accounting practices;
2. allow meaningful comparisons of the financial statements of different firms;
3. restore the confidence of users in the financial statements;
4. lead to governmental intervention and regulation of accounting practices.

The main supports for *flexibility* are the claims that:

1. the use of uniform accounting procedures to represent the same item occurring in many cases poses the risk of concealing important differences among cases;
2. comparability is a utopian goal; "it cannot be achieved by the adoption of firm rules that do not take adequate account of different factual situations";[56]
3. "differences in circumstances" or "circumstantial variables" call for different treatments, so that corporate reporting can respond to circumstances in which transactions and events occur. The circumstantial variables are defined as:

   "… environmental conditions which vary among companies and which influence:

   (a) the feasibility of accounting methods, and/or
   (b) the objectivity of the measures resulting from applying the accounting methods".[57]

The implicit objective of both uniformity and flexibility is to protect the user and to present the user with meaningful data. Both principles fail due to their extreme positions on the issue of financial reporting. Uniformity does not lead to comparability, an admittedly unfeasible goal. Flexibility evidently leads to confusion and mistrust. A trade-off solution may be provided by encouraging uniformity by narrowing the diversity of accounting practices and, at the same time, allowing a proper recognition of market and economic events peculiar to a given firm and a given industry by a proper association of certain economic circumstances with related accounting techniques. This middle position calls for an operational definition of "differences in circumstances" and for better guidelines for relating differences in circumstances to various procedures.[58]

7.5.10 Timeliness of accounting earnings and conservatism

Timeliness of accounting earnings has been defined as the extent to which current-period accounting income incorporates current-period economic income.[59] While economic income and accounting income summed over the lifetime of a firm are identical, they are different in the short term. Economic income immediately recognizes the changes in expectations of present values of future cash flows, while accounting income uses the accounting "recognition" principles to incorporate the same changes gradually over time, generally at points close to when the actual cash-flow realizations occur.[60] What results is a lag between accounting income and economic income that may extend over multiple periods. As preferably stated by Ball et al.[61]: "The recognition principle therefore causes economic income to be incorporated in accounting income in a lagged and 'smoothed' fashion over time." Accounting income's relation to economic income defines its timeliness as follows:

$$\text{EARN}_{it} = a_{0j} + a_{1j} \, \text{RET}_{it} + \epsilon_{it}$$

where:

EARN_{it} = Earnings before extraordinary items, discontinued operations, and special items, deflated by the beginning of year market value of equity of a given firm in year t.
RET_{it} = Annual stock return for year t.

Conservatism is defined by Basu[62] as the extent to which current-period accounting income asymmetrically incorporates economic losses, relative to economic gains. Therefore, while timeliness measures the degree of incorporation of economic income in contemporaneous accounting income, conservatism measures the heightened timeliness in incorporating value decreases, or negative economic income. Therefore conservative asymmetry in accounting income timeliness is introduced by modifying the previous equation for asymmetric incorporation of economic income as follows:

$$EARN_{it} = a_{0j} + a_{1j} NEG_{it} + a_{2j} RET_{it} + a_{3j} RET_{it} NEG_{it} + \epsilon_{it}$$

where:

NEG_{it} = Dummy variable equal to 1 if RET is negative and 0 otherwise. Therefore a_{2j} and $a_{2j} + a_{3j}$ capture the incorporation in current year income respectively for good news and bad news.

7.6 Truth in accounting

The lack of concern with truth in accounting has always been a major issue in the accounting literature. Witness the following concern expressed by K. MacNeal in 1939:

> For more than four hundred years since the publication of Pacioli's book on double entry bookkeeping in 1454, accounting methods, and hence accounting reports, have been based on expediency rather than on truth. Financial statements today are composed of a bewildering mixture of accounting conventions, historical data, and present facts, wherein even accountants are often unable to distinguish between truth and fiction.[63]

MacNeal may have been a little bit too hard on accountants, given the possibilities and impossibilities of truth in accounting. They are examined next, showing that the idea of truth in accounting is at best a normative idea that has few chances of being applied in accounting.

7.6.1 Notions of truth in philosophy

Knowledge of a proposition arises from its truthfulness. If we know of a proposition, we know it to be true. The question becomes: What makes a proposition a true one? In everyday life we encounter states of affairs occurring or existing in the world that we report using language. A true proposition relates to a state of affairs that occurs. The truth relates to the reporting of the occurrence or the existence of a state of affairs. The truth may be framed differently.[64]

- It can be *truth as correspondence* when the proposition is true if it corresponds to a fact. The notion of correspondence is best explicated as follows:

> The word "correspondence" suggests that, when we make a true judgment, we have a sort of picture of the real in our minds and that our judgment is true because this picture is like the reality it represents. But our judgments are not like the physical things to which they refer. The images we use in judging may indeed in certain respects copy or resemble physical things, but we can make a judgment without using any imagery except words, and words are not in the least similar to the things which they represent. We must not understand "correspondence" as meaning copying or even resemblance.[65]

- It can be *truth as coherence* when the proposition is true because it is coherent with other propositions. The propositions must be mutually supporting.
- It can be *truth as what "works"*, implying that a true proposition is what works.

A distinction should be made between truth or falsity of propositions and the belief of people about them. Beliefs do not necessarily correspond to the state of affairs. A statement believed to be true or false still needs to be proven true or false. The proof will show that the truth of a proposition is not relative to time, space, or speaker, although it might be about time, space, or speaker. As J. Hospers states, "Caesar's assassination occurred at only one point in space and time; and the burning of people as witches, though it occurred at different spaces and times, did not on that account occur at *all* spaces and times. States-of-affairs come and go, but truths are eternal."[66]

The truthfulness of propositions can be ascertained with different degrees of complexity. An analytical proposition, such as "all American accountants are American", is obviously true without further proof, since negation of it is self-contradictory. Synthetic propositions (propositions that are not analytic) need to be proven as true or false. The synthetic proposition, "Tunis is the capital of Tunisia", is a true synthetic proposition.

7.6.2 The possibilities of truth in accounting

a. Truth as neutrality

To be able to report the truth, accounting needs to avoid injecting any bias. It may be difficult. Witness the following comment:

> First, the difficulty is of knowing the facts. Secondly, the difficulty of describing them. It is well understood nowadays that the record of events cannot be dissociated from the recorder. There is no history without bias.[67]

… The other half of the problem is the right use of words. This is not a talent that everyone has, and these days one may justifiably conclude that fewer people have it than before. Many of the matters to be communicated in a set of accounts are of their nature difficult or obscure (e.g., most things to do with tax); some are highly delicate (e.g., liabilities under guarantee or contingencies); some are, as explained above, simply uncertain; and to convey an exact shade of uncertainty is a searching test of verbal skill.[68]

To avoid injecting bias in the knowledge, description, and communication of facts, accountants are expected to be neutral. The important characteristic of the information provided is to be "free from bias" or neutral. Neutrality is considered an important qualitative characteristic of accounting information.[69] Neutrality, in this context, refers to the absence of bias in the presentation of accounting information or reports. Thus, neutral information is free from bias toward attaining some desired result or inducing a particular mode of behavior. This is not to imply that the preparers of information do not have a purpose in mind when preparing the reports; it means only that the purpose should not influence a predetermined result. The accountant is expected to "tell it like it is" rather than the way any interest group might or would like to see it. This is generally stated as the criteria of "representational faithfulness and completeness". They refer to the correspondence between accounting data and the events those data are supposed to represent. If the measure portrays what it is supposed to represent, it is considered to be free of measurement and measurer bias. Therefore neutrality, representational faithfulness, and completeness establish truth in accounting as a correspondence. The accounting information is true because it corresponds to a fact.

b. Truth as objectivity

To establish the accuracy of the attributes measured, accountants have relied on the principle of objectivity as a way of justifying their choice of procedures. Objectivity, however, has been given at least four possible meanings:

> (1) measurements that are impersonal or existing outside the mind of the person making the measurement, (2) measurements based on verifiable evidence, (3) measurements based on a consensus of qualified experts, and (4) the narrowness of the statistical dispersions of the measurements of an attribute when made by different measurers.[70]

The first meaning of objectivity refers to the truth as neutrality examined earlier in the chapter. The second meaning refers to the need for evidence as a test of the accuracy of the information.[71] The third meaning refers to the need for consensus evidence as a test of the accuracy of the information. The fourth meaning refers to the narrowness of the dispersion of the measurement values around a mean or average figure. This fourth meaning is the most interesting criterion of objectivity. It arises from the tendency of accounting theorists to give accounting information the characteristic of an average or expected value of a probability distribution. The average or mean is not considered as precise as other statistics. As Norton Bedford pointed out,

> the main theoretical objection to the use of expected value as the accounting disclosure is the sin of omitting a measure of the dispersion around the expected value disclosed. In a sense, the theoretical objection is that accounting disclosures have been determined according to precise laws, when statistical laws are the relevant ones.[72]

As a result, variance and standard deviation are generally offered as a measure of objectivity and verifiability. The narrower the dispersion, the more objective is the measure. The variance is considered to be a function of the attribute measured (A), the object whose attribute is measured (O), the individual measurers making the measurement (M), the measurement rules they followed (R), and the constraints imposed on them (C), as follows:

$$\text{Variance } X_i = f(A, O, M, R, C)^{73}$$

Its benefits are as follows:

> An advantage of dispersion as an objectivity criterion is its applicability to predictions before they can be validated by correlation analysis. Second, dispersion can be expressed as a continuum. Another advantage of dispersion is its ability to test hypothesized relationships of changes resulting from modifying one of the measurement parameters such as the attribute, object, measurer, etc.[74]

c. Truth, objectivity, and reliability

An item of information could be considered verifiable based on the narrowness of the dispersion measurement values around a mean and yet be less reliable because of a bias factor.

Reliability refers to the "quality which permits users of data to depend on it with confidence as representative of what it proposes to represent".[75] Thus, the reliability of information depends on its degree of faithfulness in the representation of an event. Reliability will differ between users, depending on the extent of their knowledge of the rules used to prepare the information. Similarly, different users may seek information with different degrees of reliability. In the context of the conceptual framework, to be reliable, information must be verifiable, neutral, and faithfully represented.

The term "bias" or "displacement" is the systematic difference between the mean of the sample estimates of a parameter and the true value of the parameter.

Y. Ijiri and R.K. Jaedicke define reliability as the degree of objectivity or verifiability plus the bias or displacement factor.[76] If the mean square error is used as the measure of reliability, then the relationship can be expressed as follows:

$$\text{Reliability} = \text{Objectivity} + \text{Bias}^{[77]}$$

or

$$\text{Mean square error} = \text{Variance} + \text{Displacement}$$

or

Variance of observations about the true value of parameter $= $ Variance of observations about the mean of the observations $+ (\text{true} - \text{mean})^2$

$$\sum_{i=1}^{N} \frac{(X_i - X^*)^2}{N} = \sum_{i=1}^{N} \frac{(X_i - \bar{X})^2}{N} + (X^* - \bar{X})^2$$

where

$X_i = i$th observation used as an estimate of the true parameter X^*

$\bar{X} = $ mean of the X_i

$X^* = $ the true value of the parameter being estimated.

An evaluation of the relationship is stated as follows:

> The greater dispersion of measures the more likely are incorrect decisions based on them because of the sampling errors they contain. The greater the displacement the more likely are incorrect decisions because the expected value of the measure is not equal to a more true measure of the attribute. Dispersion and displacement are undesirable to the extent wrong decisions have a high cost. To the extent resources must be consumed in reducing dispersion and displacement, poor measures can be accepted as long as the costs of improving them are greater than the cost of wrong decisions arising further.[78]

Another problem arises from the fact that the dispersion criterion is applicable to both assessments and predictors while the displacement criterion applies only to assessment measures, not to predictor measures.

d. Truth, objectivity, and hardness

The previous section on truth, objectivity, and reliability focused on a comparison between what accountants do and what users of accounting measures expect them to do.[79] This section is a comparison among different groups of accountants. The relationship is between objectivity and hardness. Objectivity in this case is a high degree of consensus among diverse groups of accountants, in the sense that different groups of accountants produce a set of measures with the same mean u and the same variance 6^2, given their neutrality in terms of their interest in the outcome of the measurement.[80] Hardness, however, assumes a competitive environment such that different incentives may push the different groups of accountants to produce a different set of measures. The resulting distribution from all groups will have a wider distribution than in the original distribution. Ijiri shows that the degree of dispersion in the combined distribution by biased measurers is greater than the degree of dispersion by neutral measurers by an amount directly proportional to the size of the bias introduced by the incentive.[81]

More explicitly, assume the groups of accountants, one including m subjects and the other n subjects, produce a set of measures with the same mean u and the same variance 6^2.[82] Both groups are now induced to produce different numbers, one group induced to increase the measure by a constant c and the other induced to decrease the measure by a constant d. The distribution resulting from putting the two "biased" groups together produces a mean $\bar{z}$ and a variance h^2 as follows:

$$\bar{Z} = u + z\frac{mc - nd}{m + n}$$

and

$$h^2 = 6^2 + pqs^2$$

where

$s = c + d$ ("measurement slack")

$p = m / (m + n)$

$q = n / (m + n)$

The new relationship is that hardness (h^2) is equal to objectivity (6^2) plus the pqs^2 factor. Therefore, comparing two measures may lead to the result that one is more objective than the other but less hard. The hard measure is the one constructed in such a way as to make disagreement arising among measurers difficult.

The measurement of truth in accounting is therefore best set in a competitive environment to allow the distinction between objectivity and hardness of the measure. As stated by Ijiri:

> The outcome of the measurement under competitive circumstances is often far more revealing than the result in a neutral situation. This is because people may overlook many things when they are neutral and indifferent to the outcome of the measurement. They tend to tolerate ambiguities so long as their choice is not considered to be "out-of-line." In a competitive environment, not being "out-of-line" is not enough. One must justify his particular choice by stronger reasoning. Thus, the extent of ambiguity is highlighted by the difference in the measures produced by two parties with conflicting interests.[83]

e. Truth and roles of accounting

The kind of truth conveyed in accounting practices and discourses may be contingent on the roles accounting actually plays in organizations. There is naturally the traditional role of a useful aid to rational decision-making with a view of measuring organizational efficiency and effectiveness. The truth in accounting in this traditional context is to provide useful and known accounting numbers along technically based rules. But notwithstanding the evidence that accounting numbers may not be used as extensively as the traditional roles suggest, the literature presents a distinction between the traditional "real/actual" and nontraditional "espoused/articulated/intended" roles of accounting information that suggests different kinds of truths conveyed by accounting information.[84] In effect, examination of each of the roles of accounting will show a gradual move from accounting as a neutral portrayer of economic reality to accounting as an interpreter of the interplay of various sources of powers. For example, Lars Samuelson describes the coexistence of different expressions of the role of the budget at the same point in time as follows:

> According to his view, senior management often articulate one role for the budget but budgeters then perceive that another very different role may be intended, with senior management actions following the course of the latter rather than the former role. Such conflicting expressions of the roles of the budgeting are here seen to be a major factor underlying both attitudes and behaviors orientated towards budgetary control systems.[85]

Similarly, Shahid Ansari and K.J. Euske classify different roles of accounting by emphasizing two dimensions: a traditional internal-external dichotomy of the use of accounting information, and a focus of organizational process congruent with either a rational or technical perspective.[86]

d. The impossibility of truth in accounting

Truth in accounting implies the need to avoid secrecy. Secrecy is the act of concealing a fact or blocking information about it or evidence of it from reaching interested publics that can benefit from knowing it. Moral considerations argue against secrecy. As stated by Sissela Bok,

> given both the legitimacy of some control over secrecy and openness, and the damages this control carries for all involved, there can be no presumption either for or against secrecy in general. Secrecy differs in this respect from lying, promise-breaking, violence and other practices for which the burden of proof rests on those who would depend on them. Conversely, secrecy differs from truthfulness, friendship, and other practices carrying a favorable presumption.[87]

Because accountants are not at liberty to disclose secrets that may benefit users, it raises questions about the limitations of narrative truth in accounting as compared to historical truth.

It has been clearly posited that truth in accounting is an elusive goal; it is not attainable. It is best stated by William Vatter as follows:

> It is perhaps inevitable that the human mind should tend to view truth as an absolute or an ideal; such a view has merit in the attempt to make really precise explanations of scientific phenomena. But there are places where this ideal cannot be applied. The real world of business is nearly always too complicated for simple answers to questions, and accounting is no exception. Yet the search for single-valued truth persists in the notion that there should be some "right" or "best" way to present facts. This appears to some extent to underlie the general-purpose report, but it may be seen elsewhere. The search for "uniformity" or comparability in the presentation of financial

data (even the idea that like things ought to be reported by the same methods, while unlike ones should not), the emphasis upon consistency, the pressure for conforming to specified forms of analysis and presentation, are all expressions of the single-valued truth idea. This conception affects the specification of accounting principles, supporting the view that there must be some basic formula or set of rules which, if established, could be depended upon to produce correct or proper results that some set of principles can be established as "the" basic way to report financial "facts." The trouble is that truth is not simple and unitary; facts arise only in context, and they must be abstracted and interpreted for communication.[88]

Accounting is reduced to scenarios where possibilities of truths are present if approximated by such criteria as neutrality, objectivity, reliability, and/or hardness and adapted to different roles of accounting and scenarios where impossibilities of truth are prevalent in cases involving measurement, income smoothing, choice of accounting techniques, asset valuation, cost allocation, relying on a standard of evidence, and using narrative truth.

The failure to capture the truth argues for the unscientific nature of accounting. The argument against the notion of accounting as a science capable of delivering the truth was made very early by A.C. Littleton as follows:

> It is clear that accounting theory cannot justifiably be said to consist of scientific explanation. There are no immutable laws of accountancy comparable to the immutable laws of nature; there are no laboratory tests and controlled experiments to yield data which may be set up as mathematical formulas to express existing relationships.[89]

The accounting discipline is indeed socially constructed, and has no immutable laws or truths.[90] The man-made rules in accounting rely on a judgment process for both the preparation and use of accounting information.

7.7 Conclusions

Existing accounting rules and techniques are based on foundations of accounting theory. These foundations are composed of hierarchical elements that function as a frame of reference or a theoretical structure. In this chapter, we have viewed the formulation of such a theoretical structure as a deductive, interactive process consisting of the successive formulation of the objectives, the postulates, the concepts, the principles and the techniques of accounting. An understanding of these elements and relationships of accounting theory guarantees an understanding of the rationale behind actual and future practices. The financial statements presented in the formal accounting reports are merely reflections of the application of the theoretical structure of accounting. Improving the content and the format of financial statements is definitely linked to improving the theoretical structure of accounting. Foremost on the agenda of accounting bodies should be the formulation of the elements of accounting theory – namely, the objectives of accounting, the environmental postulates, the theoretical concepts and the principles of accounting.

Appendix 7.A – The basic postulates of accounting (ARS 1)

Postulates stemming from the economic and political environment

Postulate A.1: Quantification Quantitative data are helpful in making rational economic decisions, i.e. in making choices among alternatives so that actions are correctly related to consequences.

Postulate A.2: Exchange Most of the goods and services that are produced are distributed through exchange and are not directly consumed by the producers.

Postulate A.3: Entities (including identification of the entity) Economic activity is carried on through specific units or entities. Any report on the activity must identify clearly the particular unit or entity involved.

Postulate A.4: Time period (including specification of the time period) Economic activity is carried on during specifiable periods of time. Any report on that activity must identify clearly the period of time involved.

Postulate A.5: Units of measure (including identification of the monetary unit) Money is the common denominator in terms of which goods and services, including labor, natural resources and capital are measured. Any report must clearly indicate which money (e.g. dollars, euros, pounds) is being used.

Postulates stemming from the field of accounting itself

Postulate B.1: Financial statements (related to A.1) The results of the accounting process are expressed in a set of fundamentally related financial statements which articulate with each other and rest upon the same underlying data.

Postulate B.2: Market price (related to A.2) Accounting data are based on prices generated by past, present or future exchanges which have actually taken place or are expected to.

Postulate B.3: Entities (related to A.3) The results of the accounting process are expressed in terms of specific units or entities.

Postulate B.4: Tentativeness (related to A.4) The results of operations for relatively short periods of time are tentative whenever allocations between past, present and future periods are required.

The imperatives

Postulate C.1: Continuity (including the correlative concept of limited life) In the absence of evidence to the contrary; the entity should be viewed as remaining in operation indefinitely. In the presence of evidence that the entity has a limited life, it should not be viewed as remaining in operation indefinitely.

Postulate C.2: Objectivity Changes in assets and liabilities, and the related effects (if any) on revenues, expenses, retained earnings and the like, should not be given formal recognition in the accounts earlier than the point of time at which they can be measured in objective terms.

Postulate C.3: Consistency The procedures used in accounting for a given entity should be appropriate for the measurement of its position and its activities and should be followed consistently from period to period.

Postulate C.4: Stable unit Accounting reports should be based on a stable measuring unit.
Postulate C.5: Disclosure Accounting reports should disclose that which is necessary to make them not misleading.

Appendices 7.A and 7.B are reprinted by permission of the American Institute of Certified Public Accountants.

Appendix 7.B – A tentative set of broad accounting principles for business enterprises (ARS 3)

The principles summarized below are relevant primarily to formal financial statements made available to third parties as representations by the management of the business enterprise. The "basic postulates of accounting" developed in Accounting Research Study No. I are integral parts of this statement of principles.

Broad principles of accounting should not be formulated mainly for the purpose of validating policies (e.g. financial management, taxation, employee compensation) established in other fields, no matter how sound or desirable those policies may be in and of themselves. Accounting draws its real strength from its neutrality as among the demands of competing special interests. Its proper functions derive from the measurement of the resources of specific entities and of changes in these resources. Its principles should be aimed at the achievement of these functions.

The principles developed in this study are as follows:

A. Profit is attributable to the whole process of business activity. Any rule or procedure, therefore, which assigns profit to a portion of the whole process should be continuously re-examined to determine the extent to which it introduces bias into the reporting of the amount of profit assigned to specific periods of time.

B. Changes in resources should be classified among the amounts attributable to the following:

1. Changes in the dollar (price-level changes) which lead to restatements of capital but not to revenues or expenses.

2. Changes in replacement costs (above or below the effect of price-level changes) which lead to elements of gain or loss.

3. Sale or other transfer, or recognition of net realizable value, or which lead to revenue or gain.

4. Other causes, such as accretion or the discovery of previously unknown natural resources.

C. All assets of the enterprise, whether obtained by investments of owners or of creditors, or by other means, should be recorded in the accounts and reported in the financial statements. The existence of an asset is independent of the means by which it was acquired.

D. The problem of measuring (pricing, valuing) an asset is the problem of measuring the future services, and involves at least three steps:

1. A determination if future services do in fact exist. For example, a building is capable of providing space for manufacturing activity.

2. An estimate of the quantity of services. For example, a building is estimated to be usable for twenty more years, or for half of its estimated total life.

3. The choice of a method or basis or formula for pricing (valuing) the quantity of services arrived at under (2) above. In general, the choice of a pricing basis is made from the following three exchange prices:

    (a) A past exchange price, e.g., acquisition cost or other initial basis. When this basis is used, profit or loss, if any, on the asset being priced will not be recognized until the sale or other transfer out of the business entity.

    (b) A current exchange price, e.g., replacement cost. When this basis is used profit or loss on the asset being priced will be recognized in two stages. The first stage will recognize part of the gain or loss in the period or periods from time of acquisition to time of usage or other disposition; the second stage will recognize the remainder of the gain or loss at the time of the sale or other transfer out of the entity, measured by the difference between sale (transfer) price and replacement cost. This method is still a cost method; an asset priced on this basis is being treated as a cost factor awaiting disposition.

    (c) A future exchange price, e.g., anticipated selling price. When this basis is used, profit or loss, if any, has already been recognized in the accounts. Any asset priced on this basis is therefore being treated as though it were a receivable, in that sale or other transfer out of the business (including conversion into cash) will result in no gain or loss, except for any interest (discount) arising from the passage of time.

    The proper pricing (valuation) of assets and the allocation of profit to accounting periods are dependent in large part upon estimates of the existence of future benefits, regardless of the bases used to price the assets. The need for estimates is unavoidable and cannot be eliminated by the adoption of any formula as to pricing.

4. All assets in the form of money or claims to money should be shown at their discounted present value or the equivalent. The interest rate to be employed in the accounting process is the market (effective) rate at the date the asset was acquired.

    The discounting process is not necessary in the case of short-term receivables where the force of interest is small. The carrying value of receivables should be reduced by allowance for uncollectable elements; estimated collection costs should be recorded in the accounts.

    If the claims to money are uncertain as to time or amount of receipt, they should be recorded at their current market value. If the current market value is so uncertain as to be unreliable, these assets should be shown at cost.

5. Inventories which are readily saleable at known prices with readily predictable costs of disposal should be recorded at net realizable value, and the related revenue taken up at the same time. Other inventory items should be recorded at their current (replacement) cost, and the related gain or loss separately reported. Accounting for inventories on either basis will result in recording revenues, gains, or losses before they are validated by sale but they are nevertheless components of the net profit (loss) of the period in which they occur.

    Acquisition costs may be used whenever they approximate current (replacement) costs, as would probably be the case when the unit prices of inventory components are reasonably stable and turnover is rapid. In all cases the basis of measurement actually employed should be "subject to verification by another competent investigator".

6. All items of plant and equipment in service, or held in stand-by status, should be recorded at cost of acquisition or construction, with appropriate modification for the effect of the changing dollar either in the primary statements or in supplementary statements. In the external reports, plant and equipment should be restated in terms of

current replacement costs whenever some significant event occurs, such as reorganization of the business entity or its merger with another entity or when it becomes a subsidiary of a parent company. Even in the absence of a significant event, the accounts could be restated at periodic intervals, perhaps every five years. The development of satisfactory indexes of construction costs and of machinery and equipment prices would assist materially in making the calculation of replacement costs feasible, practical and objective.

7. The investment (cost or other basis) in plant and equipment should be amortized over the estimated service life. The basis for adopting a particular method of amortization for a given asset should be its ability to produce an allocation reasonably consistent with the anticipated flow of benefits from the asset.

8. All "intangibles" such as patents, copyrights, research and development, and goodwill should be recorded at cost, with appropriate modification for the effect of the changing dollar either in the primary statements or in supplementary statements. Limited-term items should be amortized as expenses over their estimated lives. Unlimited-term items should continue to be carried as assets, without amortization.

   If the amount of the investment (cost or other basis) in plant and equipment or in the "intangibles" has been increased or decreased as the result of appraisal or the use of index-numbers, depreciation or other amortization should be based on the changed amount.

E. All liabilities of the enterprise should be recorded in the accounts and reported in the financial statements. Those liabilities which call for settlement in cash should be measured by the present (discounted) value of the future payments or the equivalent. The yield (market, effective) rate of interest at date of incurrence of the liability is the pertinent rate to use in the discounting process and in the amortization of "discount" and "premium". "Discount" and "premium" are technical devices for relating the issue price to the principal amount and should therefore be closely associated with principal amount in financial statements.

F. Those liabilities which call for settlement in goods or services (other than cash) should be measured by their agreed selling price. Profit accrues in these cases as the stipulated services are performed or the goods produced or delivered.

G. In a corporation, stockholders' equity should be classified into invested capital and retained earnings (earned surplus). Invested capital should, in turn, be classified according to source, that is, according to the underlying nature of the transactions giving rise to invested capital.

   Retained earnings should include the cumulative amount of net profits and net losses, less dividend declarations and less amount transferred to invested capital.

   In an unincorporated business, the same plan may be followed, but the acceptable alternative is more widely followed of reporting the total interest of each owner or group of owners at the balance sheet date.

H. A statement of the results of the operations should reveal the components of profit in sufficient detail to permit comparisons and interpretations to be made. To this end, the data should be classified at least into revenues, expenses, gains and losses.

   1. In general, the revenue of an enterprise during an accounting period represents a measurement of the exchange value of the products (goods and services) of that enterprise during that period. The preceding discussion, under D.3(b) is also pertinent here.

2. Broadly speaking, expenses measure the costs of the amount of revenue recognized. They may be directly associated with revenue-producing transactions themselves (e.g., so-called "product costs") or with the accounting period in which the revenues appear (e.g., so called "period costs").

3. Gains include such items as the results of holding inventories through a price rise, the sale of assets (other than stock-in-trade) at more than book value, and the settlement of liabilities at less than book values. Losses include such items as the result of holding inventories through a price decline, the sale of assets (other than stock-in-trade) at less than book value or their retirement, the settlement of liabilities at more than book value, and the imposition of liabilities through a lawsuit.

Notes

1. Prince, Thomas R., *Extensions of the Boundaries of Accounting Theory* (Cincinatti, OH: South Western Publishing Co., 1963), p. 4.
2. Paton, W.A., *Accounting Theory* (New York: The Ronald Press, 1922).
3. Canning, John B., *The Economics of Accountancy* (New York: The Ronald Press, 1929); Sweeney, Henry W., *Stabilized Accounting* (New York: Harper & Row, 1936); MacNeal, Kenneth, *Truth in Accounting* (Philadelphia: University of Pennsylvania Press, 1939); Alexander, Sidney S., "Income Measurement in a Dynamic Economy", *Five Monographs On Business Income* (New York: American Institute of Certified Public Accountants, 1950); Edwards, E.O., and Bell, P.W., *The Theory and Measurement of Business Income* (Berkeley: University of California Press, 1961); Moonitz, Maurice, Accounting Research Study No. 1, *The Basic Postulates of Accounting* (New York: American Institute of Certified Public Accountants, 1961); Sprouse, R.T., and Moonitz, Maurice, Accounting Research Study No. 3, *A Tentative Set of Broad Accounting Principles for Business Enterprises* (New York: American Institute of Certified Public Accountants, 1962).
4. Hatfield, H.R., *Accounting: Its Principles and Problems* (New York: D. Appleton & Company, 1927); Gilman, Stephen, *Accounting Concepts of Profits* (New York: The Ronald Press, 1939); Paton, W.A., and Littleton, A.C., Monograph No. 3, *An Introduction to Corporate Accounting Standards* (Columbus, OH: American Accounting Association, 1940); Littleton, A.C., AAA Monograph No. 5, *Structure of Accounting Theory* (Iowa City: American Accounting Association, 1953); Ijiri, Yuji, Studies in Accounting Research No. 10, *Theory of Accounting Measurement* (Sarasota, FL: American Accounting Association, 1975); Skinner, R.M., *Accounting Principles* (Toronto: Canadian Institute of Chartered Accountants, 1973).
5. Littleton, A.C., "Tests for Principles", *The Accounting Review* (March, 1938), p. 16.
6. Moonitz, Maurice, Accounting Research Study No. 1, op. cit., p. 22.
7. Concepts and Standards Research Study Committee on the Business Entity Concept, "The Entity Concept", *The Accounting Review* (April, 1965), pp. 358–67.
8. Paton, W.A., and Littleton, A.C., *An Introduction to Corporate Accounting Standards*, op. cit., p. 9.
9. Storey, R.K., "Revenue Realization, Going Concern, and Measurement of Income", *The Accounting Review* (April, 1959), pp. 232–8; Sterling, Robert R., "The Going Concern: An Examination", *The Accounting Review* (July, 1968), pp. 481–502.
10. Storey, R.K., "Revenue Realization, Going Concern, and Measurement of Income", op. cit., p. 238.
11. Chambers, R.J., *Accounting Evaluation, and Economic Behavior* (Englewood Cliffs, NJ: Prentice-Hall, 1966), p. 218.

12. Ijiri, Yuji, "Axioms and Structures of Conventional Accounting Measurement", *The Accounting Review* (January, 1965), pp. 36–53; Sterling, Robert R., "Elements of Pure Accounting Theory", *The Accounting Review* (January, 1967), pp. 62–73.

13. Fremgen, James M., "The Going-Concern Assumption: A Critical Appraisal", *The Accounting Review* (October, 1968), pp. 649–56.

14. Hofstedt, T.R., "Some Behavioral Parameters of Financial Analysis", *The Accounting Review* (October, 1972), pp. 680, 681.

15. Ibid., pp. 679–92; Belkaoui, A., and Cousineau, A., "Accounting Information, Nonaccounting Information, and Common Stock Perception", *Journal of Business* (July, 1977), pp. 334–42.

16. Coughlan, J.W., *Guide to Contemporary Theory of Accounts* (Englewood Cliffs, NJ: Prentice-Hall, 1965), p. 155.

17. Husband, G.R., "The Entity Concept in Accounting", *The Accounting Review* (October, 1954), p. 561.

18. Staubus, G.J., "The Residual Equity Point of View in Accounting", *The Accounting Review* (January, 1959), p. 12.

19. Lorig, A.N., "Some Basic Concepts of Accounting and Their Implications", *Accounting Review* (July, 1964), p. 565.

20. Husband, G.R., "The Entity Concept in Accounting", op. cit., p. 554.

21. Vatter, W.J., *The Fund Theory of Accounting and Its Implications for Financial Reports* (Chicago: University of Chicago Press, 1947), p. 20.

22. National Committee on Governmental Accounting, *Governmental Accounting, Auditing, and Financial Reporting* (Chicago: Municipal Finance Officers Association of the United States and Canada, 1968), pp. 6–7.

23. Ibid., pp. 7–8.

24. APB Statement No. 4 (New York: American Institute of Certified Public Accountants, 1970), p. 57.

25. American Institute of Certified Public Accountants. *Professional Standards* (Chicago, IL: Commerce Clearing House, 1975), p. 7248.

26. Staubus, G.J., "Revenue and Revenue Accounts", *The Accounting Review* (July, 1956), pp. 284–94.

27. Paton, W.A., and Littleton, A.C., "An Introduction to Corporate Accounting Standards", op. cit., p. 46.

28. Hendriksen, E.S., *Accounting Theory* Third Edition (Homewood, IL: Richard D. Irwin, 1977), pp. 177–8.

29. Accounting Terminology Bulletin No. 2, *Proceeds, Revenue, Income, Profit and Earnings* (New York: American Institute of Certified Public Accountants, 1955), p. 2.

30. AAA Committee on Accounting Concepts and Standards, *Accounting and Reporting Standards for Corporate Financial Statements and Preceding Statements and Supplements* (Columbus, OH: American Accounting Association, 1957), p. 5.

31. Ibid., p. 3.

32. Meyers, J.H., "The Critical Event and Recognition of New Profit", *The Accounting Review* (October, 1959), pp. 528–32; Windal, F.W., Occasional Paper No. 5. *The Accounting Concept of Realization* (East Lansing: Bureau of Business and Economic Research, Michigan State University, 1961); AAA Committee on Concepts and Standards Research, "The Realization Concept", *The Accounting Review* (April, 1965), pp. 312–22.

33. Report of the 1973–1974 Committee on Concepts and Standards – External Reporting, supplement to Vol. 40, *The Accounting Review* (1974), pp. 207–8.

34. Ibid., p. 209.

35. Arnett, H.E., "Recognition as a Function of Measurement in the Realization Concept", *The Accounting Review* (October, 1963), pp. 733–41.

36. American Institute of Certified Public Accountants, *Professional Standards*, op. cit. p. 7301.

37. Green, David G., Jr., "A Moral to Direct-Costing Controversy?" *Journal of Business* (July, 1960), pp. 218–26; Staubus, G.J., "Direct, Relevant, or Absorption Costing?" *The Accounting Review* (January, 1963), pp. 64–75; Fremgen, James M., "The Direct-Costing Controversy: An Identification of Issues", *The Accounting Review* (January, 1964) pp. 43–71; Horngren, Charles T. and Sorter, G.H., "The Effects of Inventory Costing Methods on Full and Direct Costing", *Journal of Accounting Research* (Spring, 1965) pp. 63–74; Fekrat, A.M., "The Conceptual Foundation of Absorption Costing", *The Accounting Review* (April, 1972), pp. 351–5.

38. Accounting Terminology Bulletin No. 1 (New York: American Institute of Certified Public Accountants, 1955), p. 100.

39. Welsh, G.A., Zlatkovitch, C.T., and White, J.A., *Intermediate Accounting* (Homewood, IL: Richard D. Irwin, 1976), pp. 547–8.

40. Ijiri, Yuji, and Jaedicke, R.K., "Reliability and Objectivity of Accounting Measurement", *The Accounting Review* (July, 1966), p. 476.

41. Paton, W.A., and Littleton, A.C., "An Introduction to Corporate Accounting Standards", op. cit., p. 18.

42. Ijiri, Yuji, and Jaedicke, R.K., "Reliability and Objectivity of Accounting Measurements", op. cit., p. 476.

43. Ibid., p. 477.

44. Ibid., p. 481.

45. Skinner, R.M., *Accounting Principles*, op. cit., p. 234.

46. Chatfield, M., *A History of Accounting Thought* (New York: Dryden Press, 1974), p. 244.

47. Sterling, Robert R., "Conservatism: The Fundamental Principle of Valuation in Traditional Accounting", *Abacus* (December, 1967), p. 110.

48. APB Statement No. 4, op. cit., p. 18.

49. APR Opinion No. 22, *Disclosure of Accounting Policies* (New York: American Institute of Certified Public Accountants, 1972), paragraph 12; APB Opinion No. 30, *Reporting the Results of Operations* (New York: American Institute of Certified Public Accountants, 1973), paragraph 24; FASB Discussion Memorandum, *An Analysis of Issues Related to Criteria for Determining Materiality* (Stamford, CT: Financial Accounting Standards Board, March 21, 1975).

50. Frishkoff, P., "An Empirical Investigation of the Concept of Materiality in Accounting", *Empirical Research in Accounting: Selected Studies*, supplement to Vol. 8, *Journal of Accounting Research* (1970), p. 116.

51. Accountants' International Study Group, *Materiality in Accounting* (London: AISG, 1974), p. 30.

52. Bernstein, L.A., "The Concept of Materiality", *The Accounting Review* (January, 1967), p. 93.

53. FASB Discussion Memorandum, op. cit., p. 50.

54. Rappaport, A., "Materiality", *The Journal of Accountancy* (April, 1964), p. 48.

55. Accountants' International Study Group, *Materiality in Accounting*, op. cit., p. 30.

56. Keller, T.F., "Uniformity Versus Flexibility: A Review of the Rhetoric", *Law and Contemporary Problems* (Autumn, 1965), p. 637.

57. Cadenhead, G.M., "Difference in Circumstances: Fact or Fantasy?" *Abacus* (September, 1970), p. 72.

58. Dewhirst, John F., "Is Accounting Too Principal?", *The Canadian Chartered Accountant Magazine* (July, 1976), pp. 44–9.

59. Ball, Ray, Kothari, S.P., and Ashok, Robin, "The Effect of International Institutional Factors on Properties of Accounting Earnings", *Journal of Accounting and Economics* (29, 2000), pp. 1–151.

60. Ibid.

61. Ibid., p. 6.

62. Basu, S., "The Conservatism Principle and the Asymmetric Timeliness of Earnings", *Journal of Accounting and Economics* (24, 1997), pp. 3–37.

63. MacNeal, Kenneth, *Truth in Accounting* (Houston: Scholars Book Co., 1939), p. vii.

64. Hospers, John, *An Introduction to Philosophical Analysis*, 2nd edn (Englewood Cliffs, NJ: Prentice-Hall, 1967), pp. 115–22.

65. Ewing, A.C., *The Fundamental Questions of Philosophy* (New York: Macmillan, 1951), pp. 54–5.

66. Hospers, *An Introduction to Philosophical Analysis*, p. 121.

67. Morison, A.M.C., "The Role of the Reporting Accountant Today", in W.T. Baxter and S. Davidson (eds.), *Studies in Accounting* (London: Institute of Chartered Accountants in England and Wales, 1977), p. 271.

68. Ibid., p. 272.

69. Financial Accounting Standards Board, Statement of Financial Accounting Concepts.

70. Hendriksen, Eldon S., *Accounting Theory*, 3rd edn (Homewood, IL: Richard D. Irwin, 1977), p. 128.

71. Paton, W.A., and Littleton, A.C., *An Introduction to Corporate Accounting Standards* (Sarasota, FL: American Accounting Association, 1955), pp. 18–21.

72. Bedford, Norton M., *Extensions in Accounting Disclosures* (Englewood Cliffs, NJ: Prentice-Hall, 1973), p. 158.

73. Committee on Accounting Valuation Bases, "Report of the Committee on Valuation Bases", *The Accounting Review*, supplement to Vol. 47 (1972), p. 562.

74. Ibid., p. 563.

75. *Statement of Accounting Theory and Theory Acceptance* (Sarasota, FL: American Accounting Association, 1977), p. 16.

76. Ijiri, Y., and Jaedicke, R.K., "Reliability and Objectivity of Accounting Measurements", *The Accounting Review* (July, 1966), pp. 480–3.

77. Committee on Accounting Valuation Bases, "Report of the Committee On Valuation Bases", p. 563.

78. Ibid., p. 567.

79. Ijiri, Yuji, "Theory of Accounting Measurement", *Studies in Accounting Research No. 1* (Sarasota, FL: American Accounting Association, 1975), p. 39.

80. Ibid., p. 37.

81. Ibid.

82. Ibid., pp. 38–9.

83. Ibid., p. 40.

84. Chua, Wai-Fong, "Accounting as Social Practice in Organizations: Critical Review," paper presented at the Inaugural Management Accounting Research Conference, University of New South Wales, Australia, September 9–10, 1988.

85. Samuelson, Lars A., "Discrepancies Between the Roles of Budgeting", *Accounting, Organizations, and Society* (11, 1, 1986), p. 35.

86. Ansari, Shahid, and Euske, K.J., "Rational, Rationalizing and Reifying Uses of Accounting Data in Organizations," *Accounting, Organizations and Society* (12, 1987), pp. 549–70.

87. Bok, Sissela, *Secrets: On the Ethics of Concealment and Revelation* (New York: Pantheon Books, 1982), pp. 26–7.

88. Vatter, William J. "Obstacles to the Specification of Accounting Principles," in R.K. Jaedicke, Y. Ijiri, and O. Nielsen (eds.), *Research in Accounting Measurement* (Sarasota, FL: American Accounting Association, 1966), p. 81.

89. Littleton, A.C., *Structure of Accounting Theory* (Columbus, OH: American Accounting Association, 1953), p. 153.

90. Tilley, Ian, "Accounting as a Specific Endeavor: Some Questions the American Theorists Tend to Leave Unanswered", *Accounting and Business Research* (Autumn, 1972), pp. 287–97.

References

Equity theories

Bird, Francis A., Davidson, Lewis F., and Smith, Charles H., "Perceptions of External Accounting Transfers Under Entity, and Proprietary Theory", *The Accounting Review* (April, 1974), pp. 233–44.

Goldberg, Louis, *An Inquiry Into the Nature of Accounting* (Evanston, IL: American Economic Association, 1965).

Gynther, Reginald S., "Accounting-Concepts and Behavioral Hypotheses", *The Accounting Review* (April, 1967), pp. 274–90.

Husband, G.R., "The Entity Concept in Accounting", *The Accounting Review* (October, 1954), p. 561.

Lorig, A.N., "Some Basic Concepts of Accounting and Their Implications", *The Accounting Review* (July, 1964).

Moore, K., and Steadman, G., "The Comparative Viewpoints of Groups of Accountants: More on the Entity-Proprietary Debate", *Accounting, Organizations and Society* (February, 1986).

Ricchiute, David N., "Standard Setting and the Entity-Proprietary Debate", *Accounting, Organizations and Society* (January, 1980), pp. 67–76.

Staubus, G.J., "The Residual Equity Point of View in Accounting", *The Accounting Review* (January, 1959).

Vatter, W.J., *The Fund Theory of Accounting and Its Implications for Financial Reporting* (Chicago: University of Chicago Press, 1947).

Postulates, concepts, and principles

American Accounting Association, *A Statement of Basic Accounting Theory* (New York: American Accounting Association, 1966).

Burton, John C., "Some General and Specific Thoughts on the Accounting Environment", *Journal of Accountancy* (October, 1973), pp. 40–6.

Byrne, Gilbert R., "To What Extent Can the Practice of Accounting Be Reduced to Rules and Standards?" *Journal of Accountancy* (November, 1937), pp. 364–79.

Carlson, Marvin L., and Lamb, James W., "Constructing a Theory of Accounting – An Axiomatic Approach", *The Accounting Review* (July, 1981), pp. 544–73.

Chambers, R.J., "The Anguish of Accountants", *Journal of Accountancy* (March, 1972), pp. 68–74.

Deinzer, Harvey T., *Development of Accounting Thought* (New York: Holt, Rinehart, & Winston, 1965), Chapters 8 and 9.

Grady, Paul, "Inventory, of Generally Accepted Accounting Principles in the United States of America", *The Accounting Review* (January, 1965), pp. 21–30.

Hicks, E.L., "APB: The First 360 Days", *Journal of Accountancy* (September, 1969), pp. 56–60.

Higgins, T.S., and Bevis, Herman, "Generally Accepted Accounting Principles Their Definition and Authority", *The New York Certified Public Accountant* (February, 1964), pp. 93–4.

Horngren, Charles T., "Accounting Principles: Private or Public Sector?" *Journal of Accountancy* (May, 1972), pp. 37–41.

Husband, G.R., "The Entity Concept in Accounting", *The Accounting Review* (October, 1954), pp. 560–2.

Lambert, Samuel Joseph, III, "Basic Assumptions in Accounting Theory Construction", *Journal of Accountancy* (February, 1974), pp. 41–8.

Lorig, A.N., "Some Basic Concepts on Accounting and Their Implications", *The Accounting Review* (July, 1964), pp. 563–73.

Mautz, Robert K., "The Place of Postulates in Accounting", *Journal of Accountancy* (January, 1965), pp. 46–9.

May, George O., "Generally Accepted Principles of Accounting", *Journal of Accountancy* (January, 1958), p. 26.

Metcalf, Richard W., "The Basic Postulates in Perspective", *The Accounting Review* (January, 1964), pp. 16–21.

Murphy, George, "A Numerical Representation of Some Accounting Conventions", *The Accounting Review* (April, 1974), pp. 233–44.

Popoff, Boris, "Postulates, Principles and Rules", *Accounting and Business Research* (Summer, 1972), pp. 182–93.

Staubus, G.J., "The Residual Equity Point of View in Accounting", *The Accounting Review* (January, 1959), pp. 11–15.

Storey, R.K., *The Search for Accounting Principles – Today's Problems in Perspective* (New York: American Institute of Certified Public Accountants, 1964).

Vatter, W.J., *The Fund Theory of Accounting and Its Implications for Financial Reports* (Chicago: University of Chicago Press, 1947).

Zeff, Stephen A., *Forging Accounting Principles in Five Countries: A History and an Analysis of Trends* (Champaign, IL: Stipes Publishing, 1971).

The going-concern postulate

Devine, C.T., "Entity, Continuity, Discount, and Exit Values", *Essays in Accounting Theory* (3, 1971), pp. 111–35.

Fremgen, James M., "The Going-Concern Assumption: A Critical Appraisal", *The Accounting Review* (October, 1968), pp. 649–56.

Sterling, Robert R., "The Going Concern: An Examination", *The Accounting Review* (July, 1968), pp. 481–502.

Storey, R.K., "Revenue Realization, Going Concern, and Measurement of Income", *The Accounting Review* (April, 1959), pp. 232–8.

Van Seventer, A., "The Continuity Postulate in the Dutch Theory of Business Income", *International Journal of Accounting, Education, and Research* (Spring, 1969), pp. 1–9.

Yu, S.C., "A Reexamination of the Going-Concern Postulate", *International Journal of Accounting, Education, and Research* (Spring, 1971), pp. 37–58.

The revenue principle

AAA Committee on Concepts and Standards Research, "The Realization Concept", *The Accounting Review* (April, 1965), pp. 312–22.

Arnett, H.E "Recognition as a Function of Measurement in the Realization Concept", *The Accounting Review* (October, 1963), pp. 733–41.

Horngren, Charles T., "How Should We Interpret the Realization Concept?" *The Accounting Review* (April, 1965), pp. 323–33.

Myers, I.H., "The Critical Event and the Recognition of Net Profit", *The Accounting Review* (October, 1959), pp. 528–32.

Staubus, G.I., "Revenue and Revenue Accounts", *The Accounting Review* (July, 1956), pp. 284–94.

The matching principle

Fekrat, A.M., "The Conceptual Foundations of Absorption Costing", *The Accounting Review* (April, 1972), pp. 351–5.

Fremgen, James M., "The Direct Costing Controversy: An Identification of Issues", *The Accounting Review* (January, 1964), pp. 43–51.

Green, David G., Jr., "A Moral to Direct-Costing Controversy?" *Journal of Business* (July, 1960), pp. 218–26.

Horngren, Charles T., and Sorter, G.H., "The Effects of Inventory Costing Methods on Full and Direct Costing", *Journal of Accounting Research* (Spring, 1965), pp. 63–74.

Staubus, G.J., "Direct Relevant or Absorption Costing?" *The Accounting Review* (January, 1963), pp. 64–75.

Materiality

Barley, B., "On the Measurement of Materiality", *Accounting and Business Research* (Summer, 1972), pp. 194–7.

Barries, D.E, "Materiality – An Illusive Concept", *Management Accounting* (October, 1976), pp. 19–20.

Bernstein, L.A., "The Concept of Materiality", *The Accounting Review* (January, 1967), pp. 86–95.

FASB Discussion Memorandum, *An Analysis of Issues Related to Criteria for Determining Materiality* (Stamford, CT: Financial Accounting Standards Board, March 22, 1975).

Financial Accounting Standards Board, *An Analysis of Issues Related to Criteria for Determining Materiality* (Stamford, CT: Financial Accounting Standards Board, March 22, 1975).

Frishkoff, P., "An Empirical Investigation of the Concept of Materiality in Accounting", *Journal of Accounting Research, supplement, Empirical Research in Accounting: Selected Studies* (1970), pp. 138–53.

Hicks, E.L., "Some Comments on Materiality", *The Arthur Young Journal* (April, 1958), p. 15.

Holmes, W., "Materiality – Through the Looking Glass", *Journal of Accountancy* (February, 1972), pp. 44–9.

Leitch. R.A., and Williams, I.R., "Materiality in Financial Statement Disclosure", *The Canadian Chartered Accountant Magazine* (December, 1975/January, 1976), pp. 53–8.

O'Connor, Melvin, and Collins, Daniel W., "Toward Establishing User-Oriented Materiality Standards", *Journal of Accountancy* (December, 1974), pp. 171–9.

Rappaport, A., "Materiality", *Journal of Accountancy* (April, 1964), pp. 45–52.

Rose, J.W., and Sorter, G.H., "Toward an Empirical Measure of Materiality", *Journal of Accounting Research, supplement, Empirical Research in Accounting: Selected Studies* (1970), pp. 138–53.

Woolsey, S., "Approach to Solving the Materiality Problem", *Journal of Accountancy* (March, 1973), pp. 47–50.

Woolsey, S., "Materiality Survey", *Journal of Accountancy* (September, 1973), pp. 91–2.

Conservatism

Devine, C.T., "The Rule of Conservatism Reexamined", *Journal of Accounting Research* (Autumn, 1963), pp. 137–8.

Landry, M., "Le Conservatism en Compatibilite – Essai d'Explication", *The Canadian Chartered Accountant Magazine* (November, 1970), pp. 321–4; (January, 1970), pp. 44–9.

Sterling, Robert R., "Conservatism: The Fundamental Principle of Valuation in Traditional Accounting", *Abacus* (December, 1967), p. 110.

Reliability, objectivity, and freedom from bias

Arnett, H.E., "What Does Objectivity Mean to Accountants?" *Journal of Accountancy* (May, 1961), pp. 65–70.

Ijiri, Yuji, and Jaedicke, R.K., "Reliability and Objectivity of Accounting Measurements", *The Accounting Review* (July, 1966), pp. 474–83.

McFarland, W.B., "Concept of Objectivity", *Journal of Accountancy* (September, 1961), pp. 25–32.

Murphy, G.J., "A Numerical Representation of Some Accounting Conventions", *The Accounting Review* (April, 1976), pp. 277–86.

Consistency, uniformity, and comparability principles

Bedford, Norton, and Toshio, Iino, "Consistency Reexamined", *The Accounting Review* (July, 1968), pp. 453–8.

Cadenhead, G.M., "Differences in Circumstances: Fact or Fantasy?" *Abacus* (September, 1970), pp. 71–80.

Chasteen, L.G., "An Empirical Study of Differences in Economic Circumstances as a Justification for Alternative Inventory Pricing Methods", *The Accounting Review* (July, 1971), pp. 504–8.

Frishkoff, P., "Consistency in Auditing and APB Opinion No. 20", *Journal of Accountancy* (August, 1972), pp. 64–70.

Hendriksen E.S., "Toward Greater Comparability Through Uniformity of Accounting Principles", *CPA Journal* (February, 1967), pp. 105–15.

Keller, T.F., "Uniformity Versus Flexibility: A Review of the Rhetoric", *Law and Contemporary Problems* (Autumn, 1965), pp. 637–51.

Mautz, R.K., "An Approach to the Uniformity-Flexibility Issues in Accounting", *Financial Executive* (February, 1971), pp. 14–19.

Revsine, Lawrence, "Toward Greater Comparability in Accounting Reports", *Financial Analysts Journal* (January/February 1975), pp. 45–51.

Simmons, John K., "A Concept of Comparability in Financial Reporting", *The Accounting Review* (October, 1967), pp. 680–92.

Sterling, Robert, R., "A Test of the Uniformity Hypotheses", *Abacus* (September, 1969), pp. 37–47.

Fairness, disclosure and future trends in accounting

8

8.1 Introduction

Fairness occupies an important role in accounting as it presents to the users and the market the guarantee that the accountant (as preparer) and the auditor (as attestor) have striven to be fair. The conventional nature of the concept of fairness is fairness in presentation, a guarantee that the diligence and care in the preparation and attestation of the financial statements are to ensure an adequate presentation of the financial affairs of the firm. Because the central meaning of fairness is fairness in presentation, this chapter explicates the concept understood in the United States as the fairness doctrine and in Europe as the "True and Fair" doctrine. The chapter extends the concept of fairness to the more progressive notions of fairness in distribution and in disclosure to motivate calls for expanded disclosure and accounting innovations.

8.2 Fairness in accounting

8.2.1 Fairness as neutrality in presentation

Fairness is best understood in the professional accounting literature and pronouncements as an expression of neutrality of the accountant in the preparation of financial reports. The first suggestion of the use of fairness in accounting was made by Scott in 1941 when he listed it as a principle of accounting and stated: "Accounting rules, procedures and techniques should be fair, unbiased and impartial. They should not serve a special interest."[1] Since then fairness has become a value statement that is variously applied to accounting. Arthur Andersen & Co., in 1960, published a monograph on the subject that states the following:

> Thus, the one basic accounting postulate underlying accounting principles may be stated as that of fairness – fairness to all segments of the business community (management, labor, stockholders, creditors, customers, and the public), determined and measured in the light of the economic and political environment and the modes of thought and customs of all such segments to the end that the accounting principles based upon this postulate shall produce financial accounting for the lawfully established economic rights and interests that is fair to all segments.[2]

Patillo followed by making fairness the subject of a book and ranking it as a basic standard to be used in the evaluation of other standards because it is the only standard that implies "ethical considerations".[3] He states:

> From these observations on the relation between accounting and the current social concepts and attitudes, it is concluded that accounting is essentially social in nature and has significant responsibilities to society. Furthermore, relating these ideas to the objective of financial accounting results in an emphasis on the communication of economic interests of the economy segments. Finally, from contrasting the connotations of justice, truth, and fairness, the current social concept of fairness is selected as the basic standard by which to measure the propriety of accounting principles and rules which purport to be means of attaining the objective. Fairness to all parties, therefore, is formulated to be the single basic standard of accounting, that criterion or test which all accounting propositions must reflect before being included into the accounting structure.[4]

The importance of fairness was also in evidence when Devine gave preserving equity among conflicting groups a central place among accounting concerns.[5]

Historically, fairness or the "fairness doctrine" evolved from the application of the concept of conservatism. The evolution went from a concern with liquidity and credit granting, generally associated with conservatism, to the idea that financial statement presentations should be fair to all users.[6] Fairness is then basically an extension of the user set from creditors to stockholders. This attempt was doomed to fail. As stated by Chatfield: "But what was fair (or conservative) for credit granters might not be for stockholders. The concept of conservatism in its corporate context required specifying the financial statement audience, which the doctrine itself was not helpful in doing."[7]

Having failed at producing useful information, some accounting writers put more emphasis on fairness in presentation. As explained by Skinner:

> This test extends the concept of usefulness, since it is conceivable that a distorted presentation would be more useful to some parties (using the word "useful" in a narrow, selfish sense) than would be an unbiased presentation.[8]

Fairness is generally associated with the measurement and reporting of information in an objective and neutral way. Information is fair if it is objective and neutral. As stated by Lee:

> It must be based on firm, verifiable evidence (whenever possible), and it must not be such as to tend to benefit a particular user (or group of users) to the relative detriment of others.[9]

Fairness is much more achievable in managerial and cost accounting where any hint of impartiality or bias may distort the decision-making processes that rely heavily on managerial accounting data. Fairness becomes a necessary criterion of information in managerial accounting to ensure the integrity and accuracy of decision-making. As stated by Flegm:

> In practice, managerial accountants continually strive to "call them as they see them" since it is essential that top management have faith that the comparative analyses of actual results with budget and forecast data are as impartial and free from bias as is humanly possible. The reason for this objectivity seems obvious since any other course would have the effect of influencing and perhaps misleading the decisions of management. Of course, public accountants too are striving for this same objectivity.[10]

In spite of contentions that fairness is subjective, ambiguous and therefore cannot serve as a basis for developing accounting theory, it has become one of the basic objectives of accounting. A first evidence of this importance is the reference by the American Institute of Certified Public Accountants' (AICPA) Committee on Auditing Procedures to the criteria of "fairness of presentation" as conformity with generally accepted accounting principles, disclosure, consistency and comparability. In an unqualified report, "present fairly" connotes compliance with generally accepted accounting principles and generally accepted auditing standards.

Since then, the fairness concept has become an implicit ethical norm. In general, the fairness concept implies that accounting statements have not been subject to undue influence or bias. Fairness implies that the preparers of accounting information have acted in good faith and employed ethical business practices and some accounting judgment in the presentation, production and auditing of accounting results. The professional interpretation is now restricted to fairness in presentation.

The perception and application of fairness in presentation as the production and presentation of financial statements in conformity with generally accepted accounting principles result sometimes in some unfortunate consequences:

1. A first consequence of fairness in presentation is the failure to rely on concepts of justice that dedicate instead a fairness in distribution.

2. A second consequence of fairness in presentation is the failure to expand the scope of the disclosure in financial statements beyond conventional financial accounting information toward a fairness in disclosure.

3. A third consequence of fairness in presentation is the flexibility it creates in the management of earnings and income smoothing.

4. A fourth consequence of fairness in presentation is the climate it creates for fraudulent practices.

8.2.2 "True and fair" doctrine

Financial statements of British companies are required by law to present a true and fair view of the state of affairs, making it the ultimate foundation of financial reporting in Great

Britain.[11] A history of the concept is provided by Chastney.[12] It has been, however, a concept in continuous search for comprehensive definition, along with a reasonable consensus that more than a single presentation may satisfy the true and fair doctrine.[13,14] The lack of clear explication is best illustrated in the following quotation:

> On the surface the true and fair view towers over British accounting but with the curious characteristic that no-one knows what it means, and very little academic analysis has been done on its role in accounting. As regards its meaning it is a legal term in origin and yet the Companies Acts have never defined it (nor has the Fourth Directive, of course) and there is little jurisprudence which bears upon it. There is no definition of it in accounting standards, auditing standards or other professional pronouncements. Most tellingly, a television broadcast in 1992 included interviews with senior British accountants: when asked to define the true and fair view, one (partner in Ernst and Young) laughed, another (senior partner of a major non big 6 firm) would say nothing and a third, the finance director of an Anglo-American multinational, asked for time to think about the question.[15]

Academic accountants were not successful either. Witness the following two attempts at defining true and fair:

> It is generally understood to mean a presentation of accounts, drawn up according to accepted accounting principles, using accurate figures as far as possible, and reasonable estimates otherwise; and arranging them to show, within the limits of current accounting practice, as objective a picture as possible, free from willful bias, distortion, manipulation, or concealment of material facts.[16]

> True means that the accounting information contained in the financial statements has been quantified and communicated in such a way as to correspond to the economic events, activities and transactions it is intended to describe. ... Fair means that the accounting information has been measured and disclosed in a manner which is objective and without prejudice to any particular sectional interests in the company.[17]

The two definitions link "true and fair" basically to accurate and free from bias. This noble attempt does not, however, detract from the professional and legal implied definitions of "true and fair" as a technical term implying a compliance with sound accounting principles. The problem was not solved even with the Fourth Directive, which required that all financial statements of limited liability companies subject to European Economic Community company law should present a "true and fair" view as follows:

1. The annual accounts shall comprise the balance sheet, the profit and loss account and the notes on the accounts. These documents shall constitute a composite whole.
2. They shall be drawn up clearly and in accordance with the provisions of this Directive.
3. The annual accounts shall give a true and fair view of the company's assets, liabilities, financial position and profit or loss.
4. Where the application of the provisions of the Directive would not be sufficient to give a true and fair view within the meaning of paragraph 3, additional information must be given.
5. Where in exceptional cases the application of a provision of this Directive is incompatible with the obligation laid down in paragraph 5, that provision must be

departed from in order to give a true and fair view within the meaning of paragraph 5. Any such departure must be disclosed in the notes on the accounts together with an explanation of the reasons for it and a statement of its effects on the assets, liabilities, financial position and profit or loss. The Member States may define the exceptional cases in question and lay down the relevant special rules.[18]

No clear definition of the "true and fair" doctrine was provided, leading to different interpretations by the members of the European Community and a tendency to interpret it in the context of national culture, national accounting tradition and national generally accepted accounting principles.[19]

In addition to the lack of a comprehensive definition, there is definitely much confusion among producers and users of accounting information on the exact meaning of "true and fair".[20,21,22,23] The interpretation of the word "true" and the word "fair" by the technical partners of the top twenty UK audit firms provided for "true": based on fact, undistorted facts, correct, complies with rules, not in conflict with facts, objective, correct within material, adherence to events, and factual accuracy; and for "fair": not misleading, substance over form, proper reflection, putting in right context, consistent with underlying reality, ability to understand what has really gone on, in accordance with rules in context, reasonable, give right impression, and whether reader receives the right message.[24]

8.3 Fairness in distribution

Fairness judgments are taken for granted in accounting, although their clear meaning is not well specified. Two generally accepted meanings concern the idea of neutrality in preparation and presentation of financial reports and the idea of justice in outcome. While both notions play a useful role in accounting, the expansion of the notion of fairness to deal with distribution considerations links it to alternative philosophical concepts more compatible with moral concepts of justice. Basically, fairness may be viewed as a moral concept of justice subject to three different interpretations of the notions of distributive justice. Accordingly, this section expands the accounting discussion of fairness by introducing the main philosophical concepts of distributive justice in the accounting context. The end result is the possibility of viewing and comparing the concept of fairness through different distributive justice frameworks.

8.3.1 Concerns with distribution questions

The problems of distribution have almost been ignored in the conventional view of fairness as neutrality, in presentation. The concern here was merely the final production and disclosure of accounting results rather than their distribution. The view of fairness as neutrality in presentation is not without its critics. Williams characterized it as an evaluation process with the following two attributes:

1. that the evaluator is aware of the conditions that any consequences of his or her actions be judged as fair or unfair; and
2. that the evaluation attempts to adopt a perspective of impartiality.[25]

Williams presented two interesting arguments. The first argument is that decision usefulness, the principle of organizing accounting research and practice, is incomplete, while accountability, at least, possesses fairness as an inherent property. The second argument is that the concern of accounting with efficiency makes accounting's fairness judgment implicit, not absent. Explicit concern with fairness is warranted:

If more explicit consideration of fairness is granted, certain implications emerge for the study and practice of accounting. One of the most obvious is that accounting has a moral dimension. Consequences of accounting activity have moral implications as well as "efficiency" ones. For a profession, becoming more scientific does not necessarily require abandoning moral decision-making and the cultivation of modes for doing so. The two most notable professions, law and medicine, accommodate schools concerned only with legal or medical ethics. For unknown reasons, the ethics of accounting has virtually vanished as a subject worthy of scholarly concern.[26]

Williams' arguments were supported by Pallot.[27] She agreed with the suggestion that fairness in accountability and fairness in distribution stem from different ethical frameworks and different, though complementary, assumptions about society. In addition, she made some preliminary suggestions as to how a community perspective might be added to the predominantly individualistic one in accounting as a step toward developing new approaches to the issues of accountability and distributive practice. The concept of "community assets"[28] fits well within Chen's model of social and financial stewardship, where management's performance is evaluated in terms of both profit and social objectives.[29] Pallot explains:

> This sort of accountability framework is fundamentally different from those where the starting assumption is one of private property and social responsibility accounting is seen as a matter of accounting for social costs and benefits viewed as externalities. In a world where a commitment to shared values, rather than the pursuit of self interest, was the norm, accountability might be seen as a voluntary obligation in the public interest rather than a mechanism for constraining self seeking behavior and protecting rights.[30]

There are three other notable exceptions in the accounting literature that have shown concern with distributive questions. The first exception emanates from the social accounting concern with accounting for externalities and reporting some forms of a social report. A first example includes Scott's view of the social role of accounting in the revolution of conflicting social interest:

> The compromise of conflicting interests is a process of valuation. It accomplishes social organization and results in a distribution of economic incomes. Value and distribution constitute a simple problem and accounting theory is especially and peculiarly a treatment of that problem.[31]

A second example includes the various calls for the role of social accounting in some form of the rectification of society's ills.[32] It is best stated by Schreuder and Ramanathan:

> In the context of traditional economic analysis, the issue boils down to a distribution problem, namely the apportionment in a society of the costs and benefits of economic activity. Economists have long recognized that such distributional issues cannot be addressed without taking a normative position.[33]

Fairness in the social accounting literature becomes a matter of distribution of social responsibility in general, and social responsiveness as the capacity of corporations to respond to social pressures. Thus corporate social responsiveness, as an expression of fairness, goes beyond the moral and ethical connotation of social responsibility to the managerial process of response. The response to be fair involves the identification, measurement and disclosure, where necessary, of the social costs and benefits created by the economic activities of the firm, as well as the adequate responses to these problems.

The second exception emanates from advocates of the political economy of accounting and the critical and Marxist approach to accounting.[34] They advocate a political economy approach that recognizes power and conflict in society and the effects of accounting reports on the distribution of income, wealth and power in society.

The third exception emanates from the positive theory of accounting view that accounting can be used to optimally resolve conflicts over resource allocation to a limited set of participants.[35] Fairness in this context is ultimately in the shareholder's interest.[36]

8.3.2 Fairness as a moral concept of justice

For fairness to be perceived as a moral concept of justice, parallels must be made to the main theories of distributive justice, those of J.A. Rawls, R. Nozick, and A. Gerwith.

A. Rawls' contribution

1. Rawls' theory of justice

The goal of Rawls' theory of justice is to develop a theory about justice in the form of principles to apply to the development of the basic structure of society and that presents a direct challenge to utilitarianism.[37] As an egalitarian theory, its main contention is the distribution of all economic goods and services equally except where an unequal distribution would actually work to everyone's advantage, or at least would benefit the worst-off in society. Using what he calls the "Kantian concept of equality", Rawls starts by comparing life to a game of chance where nature bestows on each individual a generation, culture, a social system, a family and a set of personal attributes that determines his or her happiness. Accepting this random allocation is viewed as unjust and a set of just institutions is required. To establish just institutions, Rawls suggests that individuals step behind a "veil of ignorance" that eliminates any knowledge about potential positions and benefits under a given set of principles. Then, to reach a social contract, they must choose from this original position principles of justice leading to the just society. From this original position and under the veil of ignorance, individuals will choose two principles of justice:

> First: Each person is to have an equal right to the most extensive basic liberty compatible with a similar liberty for others. Second: social and economic inequalities are to be arranged so that they are both (a) reasonably expected to be to everyone's advantage, and (b) attached to positions and offices open to all.[38]

Rawls maintains that the two principles are lexicographically ordered, the first one over the second:

> Now it is possible, at least theoretically, that by giving up some of their fundamental liberties men are sufficiently compensated by the resulting social and economic gains. The general conception of justice implies no restrictions on what sort of inequalities; it only requires that everyone's position be improved ... Imagine ... that men forgo certain political rights when the economic returns are significant and their capacity to influence the course of policy by the exercise of these rights would be marginal in any case. It is this kind of exchange which the two principles as stated rule out; being arranged in serial order they do not permit exchanges between basic liberties and economic and social gains.[39]

The first principle shows the emphasis placed by Rawls on liberty and the precedence of liberty over the second principle of justice. Liberty can be restricted only when it is formulated as follows:

> The principles of justice are to be ranked in lexical order and therefore, liberty can be restricted only for the sake of liberty. There are two cases: (a) a less restrictive liberty shared by all, and (b) a less than equal liberty must be acceptable to those citizens with the lesser liberty.[40]

The second principle of justice, which Rawls labeled the difference principle, contains a second lexicographic ordering of the welfare of the individuals from the lowest to the highest, where the welfare of the worst-off individual is to be maximized first before proceeding to higher levels. In its most general form, the difference principle states that:

> In a basic structure with no relevant representatives, first maximize the welfare of the worst-off representative, maximize the welfare of the second, worst-off man, and so on until the last case, which is for equal welfare of all the preceding n–1 representatives, maximize the welfare of the best-off representative man. We think of this as the lexical difference principle.[41]

These two principles show a democratic conception that eliminates those aspects of the social world that seem arbitrary from a moral point of view. This does not necessarily eliminate economic inequality. Rawls justifies some difference in income first: as incentives to attract people into certain positions and motivate them to perform; and as a guarantee that certain public-interest positions will be filled. To implement Rawls' theory, the idea of "basic structure" may be "a constitutional democracy", which preserves equal basic liberties, with a government that promotes equality of opportunity and guarantees a social minimum and a market-based economic system. Rawls suggests that this social minimum be established before allowing the rest of the total income to be settled by the price system. It is to be settled by special payments for sickness and unemployment and monetary transfer systems such as negative income tax. Rawls, however, gives little attention to the identification of the worst-off representative. He offers only two alternatives:

1. to choose a particular social position, say that of the unskilled worker, and then to count as the least advantaged all those with the average income of this group, or less; or

2. to focus on the relative income and wealth with no reference to social position, that is, all persons with less than half of the median income and wealth may be taken as the least advantaged segment.[42]

With regard to redistribution, Rawls finds large inequalities to be permissible if lowering them would make the working class even worse off. Basically, with the raising of expectations of the more advantaged, the situation of the worst-off is continuously improved. Inequalities will tend to be leveled down by the increasing availability of education and ever-widening expectations. However, Rawls calls for the establishment of social minimums through various transfers and redistributive mechanisms. But would Rawls' difference principle assure an adequate level of the necessary goods and services? There are a host of disagreements on this issue.[43]

Derek Phillips joins the opposite chorus:

> The major reason for this concerns Rawls' emphasis on incentives. With the difference principle … an unequal distribution of wealth and income is justified if and

only if it will maximize benefits to the least advantaged segments within a society. But if, as Rawls assumes, these inequalities must be rather large, then it seems likely that the actual benefits even if maximized will not be sufficient to provide an adequate level for the least advantaged segment, they will fail to do so for those persons who require extra medical care, protection and other basic goods. This is a consequence of the fact ... that the difference principle makes no allowances for the particular needs of especially disadvantaged individuals.[44]

While better criteria still need to be developed to resolve these issues, Gerwith asserts that what is needed is a drastic redistribution of wealth and an effective exercise of the fundamental rights to freedom and well-being.[45] Basically, Rawls and Gerwith disagree on how the needs of the disadvantaged are to be met. While Rawls is willing to accept an unequal distribution of economic rewards, if it benefits the least advantaged, Gerwith maintains that the wealthy have an obligation to assist the disadvantaged.

2. Fairness in accounting according to Rawls

Rawls' contract theory – a theory of just social institutions – may be offered as a concept of fairness in accounting. Applied to accounting, it suggests first the potential reliance on the veil of ignorance in all the situations calling for an accounting choice eventually to yield solutions that are neutral, fair and socially just. Second, it also suggests the expanded role of accounting in the creation of just institutions and the definition of the social minimum advocated by Rawls. This role, as also espoused by advocates of social accounting, will lead to the elimination of those aspects of the social world in general and the accounting world in particular, that seem arbitrary from a moral point of view. This view of fairness would be most welcome to advocates of social accounting. As stated by Williams:

> Rawlsian principles also may prove to be a useful set of premises for speculation about alternative accounting systems. For example, one plausible reason for the slow theoretical development of social accounting, at least in the United States, could be the constraining effect of conventional accounting premises about character and legitimacy of institutions, both public and private. Accounting scholars with interests in social accounting are certainly free to generate and test hypotheses about measuring and reporting, in Rawlsian, or any other institutional setting.[46]

B. Nozick's contribution

1. Nozick's theory of justice

While Rawls is interested in the justice of one or another pattern of distribution, Nozick is interested in the process through which distribution comes about.[47] He first argued that Rawls' theory of justice violates people's rights, and consequently cannot be morally justified; that it ignores people's entitlement and is, like most other theories of justice, patterned. Patterned theories of justice imply that a distribution is to vary along some natural dimension, weighted sum of natural dimensions, or lexicographic ordering of natural dimensions.[48] Examples of such distributions include those based on need, merit, or work. Nozick maintains: "To think that the task of a theory of justice is to fill in the blank in each according to his _____ is to be predisposed to search for a pattern; and separate treatment from each according to his _____ treats production and distribution as two separate and independent issues".[49]

Nozick argues that such theories of justice, based on the patterned and end-state principles, violate people's rights and exclude recognition of an entitlement principle of distributive justice, whereby individuals are entitled to their possessions as long as they acquired them by legitimate means, including voluntary transfers, exchanges and cooperative productive activity. Nozick's theory focuses on the importance of historical principles, in the sense that a distribution is just or not depending on how it came about. He justifies his theory as follows:

1. A person who acquires a holding in accordance with the principle of justice in acquisition is entitled to that holding.
2. A person who acquires a holding in accordance with the principle of justice in transfer, from someone else entitled to that holding, is entitled to the holding.
3. No one is entitled to a holding except by (repeated) applications of 1 and 2.[50]

The principles involve, respectively, the question of original acquisition of holdings and the rectification of injustices in holdings. Nozick introduced a proviso, however, to ensure that an individual's entitlement does not result in a net loss in what remains for other persons to use. Nozick's theory is, then, a theory of justice in holdings. It is a very special kind of theory of distributive justice, as Nozick emphasizes:

> The term "distributive justice" is not a neutral one. Hearing the term "distribution", most people presume that some thing or mechanism uses some principle or criterion to give out a supply of things … However, we are not in the position of children who have been given portions of pie by someone who now makes last-minute adjustments to rectify careless cutting. There is no central distribution, no person or group entitled to control all the resources, jointly deciding how they are to be doled out. What each person gets, he gets from others who give it to him in exchange for something, or as a gift. In a free society diverse persons control different resources, and new holdings arise out of the voluntary exchanges and action of persons. There is no more a distribution of shares than there is a distribution of mates in a society in which persons choose whom they shall marry. The total result is the product of many individuals' decisions which the different individuals involved are entitled to make.[51]

Although some criteria remain to be used, Nozick's theory has been criticized for its failure to recognize the right to well-being. The question generally asked is: Is it just to tie the socioeconomic standing of other family members entirely to the moral acceptability of the historical process through which the breadwinner has acquired his or her holdings? Those answering "no" argue that it may appear to anyone involved with a sense of justice and concerned about some family members reducing their standard of living radically, when, in other cases, correction is required because of someone else's unjust acquisition; and feeling something morally unsatisfactory about some people being very well compared to others.[52]

2. Fairness in accounting according to Nozick

The use of economic man theory in accounting and the decision usefulness criterion used in empirical accounting research link fairness and distributive justice to a free market mechanism. Accounting is viewed as essential to the efficient running of an organization, and the mere reaching of efficiency is presumed to make everybody better off in possession of their just share.[53] Fairness to the positivists and the rationality theorists is linked to an efficient market that allows a just transfer to shareholders.

It is essentially a libertarian theory of distribution according to Nozick, based on a principle of justice in acquisition and in transfer. This concept of distributive justice, with its reliance on a free market mechanism, does not allow for dealing adequately with fairness as a distributive function, because it is assumed to fail in the discussion of the social obligations of humans to each other, to perpetuate past violations of principles of acquisition and transition, and to distort the meaning of well-offness in a world of scarcity. The reliance on the market mechanism, the absence of a moral language to discuss social obligations, as well as the absence of a concept of redistributive justice are some of the cited failures of the libertarian theory of justice. In addition, the growing importance of meritocracy in the context of a basically market system has created problems for a Nozickean theory of justice. The conflicting rules of distribution are not well accepted in contemporary culture. Most often, members of the organization demand to receive what they justly deserve.

Under the tutoring of the school system, and reinforced by other meritocratic organizations, a person has been socialized to feel that he or she ought to get what has been earned and to be protected from the vagaries and irrationalities of the market. Basically, stakeholders and other shareholders may not be satisfied by the conventional reporting emphasis on returns to shareholders. For example, labor may feel that the profit generated dictates a different distribution than the one dictated by justice in holding and transfer, and a reporting system emphasizing the "mere" just distribution is warranted.

A good evaluation of the Nozickean libertarian view of accounting follows:

> In summary, a Libertarian interpretation of accounting's deference to a market mechanism for making its fairness judgments leaves accounting inadequately equipped to deal with the distributive aspects of the accounting process. Without a moral language to discuss the social obligations of humans to each other, the principles of justice in acquisition and transition have no substance. Without a concept of redistributive justice, past violations of principles of acquisition and transition are perpetuated. And in a world of scarcity well-offness acquires a meaning beyond the capabilities of the language of property rights to define. Markets do distribute society's prizes, but a Libertarian interpretation of that mechanism certainly provides no assurance that it is fair or even that fairness is a mediating process.[54]

C. Gerwith's contribution

1. Gerwith's theory of justice

The goal of Gerwith's theory of justice was to provide a rational justification for moral principles to objectively distinguish morally right actions and institutions from morally wrong ones.[55] The necessary content of morality is in actions and their generic features. The actions are distinguished in terms of two categorical features: voluntariness and purposiveness. Given the importance of action as the necessary and universal matter of all moral and other practical precepts, Gerwith presents his doctrine of the structure of actions in three main steps:

> First, every agent implicitly makes evaluative judgments about the goodness of his purposes and hence about the necessary goodness of the freedom and well-being that are necessary conditions of his acting to achieve his purposes. Second, because of this necessary goodness, every agent implicitly makes a deontic judgment in which he claims that he has no freedom and well-being. Third, every agent must claim these rights for the sufficient reason that he is a prospective agent who has purposes he wants to fulfill, so that he logically must accept the generalization that all prospective agents have rights to freedom and well-being.[56]

The rights to freedom and well-being are seen as generic, fundamental and universal. As a result, Gerwith asserts that every agent logically must acknowledge certain generic obligations:

> Negatively, he ought to refrain from coercing and from banning his recipients; positively, he ought to assist them to have freedom and well-being whenever they cannot

otherwise have the necessary goods and he can help them at no comparable loss to himself. The general principle of these obligations and rights may be expressed as the following precepts addressed to every agent; act in accord with the generic rights of your recipients as well as yourself. I call this the Principle of Generic Consistency (PGC) since it combines the formal consideration of rights to generic features or goods of action.[57]

Gerwith calls the PGC the supreme moral principle, as it requires the agents not to interfere with the freedom and well-being of others. It remains that the PGC has both direct and indirect application. The direct application concerns the requirement for agents to act in accord with the right to freedom and well-being of all other persons. The indirect application concerns the requirement that institutional arrangements must express or serve the freedom and well-being of all other persons.

The indirect application involves specifically social rules and arrangements to be implemented in a static and dynamic phase. The static phase generates rules to protect an existing equality of generic rights, while the dynamic phase calls for redistributive justice to eliminate inequalities through a "supportive state". The social rules between the two extremes are as follows:

1. a certain libertarian extreme that would defend the existing distribution of wealth, arising presumably from just acquisition, and
2. an egalitarian extreme that calls for a drastic redistribution to be guided solely by the aim of maximally benefiting those who are the least advantaged.

Both extremes appear deficient.[58]

2. Fairness in accounting according to Gerwith

Gerwith's theory of justice may be offered as a concept of fairness in accounting. Applied to accounting, it suggests the primacy of the concerns for the rights of freedom and well-being of all persons affected by the activities of the firm and for the creation of institutional and accounting arrangements to guarantee these rights. These arrangements call for some form of rectification through the creation of a "supportive system" and specific social rules to be followed by organizations and members within the organization. Accounting may be called on to facilitate a drastic redistribution of wealth and an effective exercise of the fundamental rights to freedom and well-being of the stakeholders in organizations. Gerwithian principles may prove to be a useful set of premises for speculation about the merit of value-added reporting. This supports the emphasis in value-added reporting to report the total return of all members of the "production team": shareholders, bondholders, suppliers, labor, government and society. Not one of these members is relegated to the position of "disadvantaged" as in other concepts of distributive justice, as they are all given a place of importance in the measurement, reporting and allocation of the total return of the firm. Basically, the Gerwithian principles applied to fairness in accounting include a recognition of the rights of all those affected by the activities of the organization,[59] and as stated by Gerwith himself.

> It calls for action that is voluntary and purposive to affirm an egalitarian universalist moral principle. As Marx's "man makes its own history", the role of action toward making moral judgments applies to accounting making efficiency and distribution judgments that protect the generic rights of all the recipients of accounting information. Accounting will create its own history of a moral agent in the marketplace, an agent concerned with the rights of the recipients of accounting information. The

merits of applying the principle of generic consistency to the concept of fairness in accounting derives from its capacity of presenting the accountant with rationally grounded answers to each of the three questions of moral philosophy:

1. The distributive question of which persons' interests ought to be favorably considered is answered by calling for the respect of the generic rights of all recipients and for the equality of the rights of all prospective agents.

2. The substantive question of which interests ought to be favorably considered is answered by focusing on the primacy of freedom and well-being.

3. The authoritative question of why should anyone be moral in the sense of taking favorable account of other people's interests is justified by the reason of avoiding self-contradiction. Basically, an action that violates the PGC principle cannot be rationally justified.[60]

8.4 Fairness in disclosure

The previous two sections examined the principle of fairness in presentation and the principle of fairness in distribution. This section extends the discussion of improving the concept of fairness by examining the principle of fairness in disclosure. Basically, as a result of the more equitable concept of fairness in distribution, the principle of fairness in disclosure calls for an expansion of the conventional accounting disclosures to accommodate all the other interest groups, in addition to investors and creditors that have a vested interest in the affairs of the firm. For example, the SEC had historically recognized three levels of disclosure: protective, informative and differential.

8.4.1 Calls for expanded disclosures

The reliance on conventional fairness in presentation in conformity with generally accepted accounting principles has created some limitations and unfairness in reporting and disclosure. Three proposals for reducing and/or eliminating this unfairness in reporting and disclosure are examined next.

A. Bedford's disclosure proposals

Bedford proposed extensions in accounting disclosure to alleviate the problems created by the fairness doctrine in accounting.[61] Rather than merely relying on generally accepted accounting principles as the only measurement method, Bedford called for the development of new tools to provide management and decision-makers with useful information. These tools are described as follows:

> These new tools have been gathered together under diverse new disciplines, such as Administrative Science, Management Science, Operations Research, and Organizational Theory, *competitors* of traditional accounting in the sense that the information they provide may be more useful to management than traditional accounting information which are typically interdisciplinary arrangements of traditional disciplines. They are made up of parts of such basic disciplines as Economics, Sociology, Psychology Mathematics, Statistics, Political Science, Neurology, Servomechanism Engineering, Anthropology and Advanced Computer Design.[62]

With the expansion of accounting measurements comes the expansion of accounting disclosures for covering wealth-structures to socioeconomic structures, and from being limited to the measurement and communication of economic data to the measurement and communication of data revealing socioeconomic activities that use economic resources.[63] The expansion of accounting disclosures dictates the expansion of the following characteristics of disclosure:

1. an expansion of the scope of users from shareholders, creditors, managers and the general public to public groups;

2. an expansion of the scope of users from evaluating economic progress, enabling base assessments and aiding investment decisions to providing for intercompany coordination, meeting specific user information needs and developing public confidence in firm activities;

3. an expansion of the type of information from transaction-based monetary valuations of internal activities of the firm to internal and external data to reveal both internal activities and the environmental setting of the internal activities of a socioeconomic nature;

4. an expansion of measurement techniques from arithmetic and the bookkeeping system to the total management science area;

5. an expansion of the quality of disclosure from excellent in terms of past needs to improved relevance for specific decisions;

6. an expansion of disclosure devices from conventional financial statements to multimedia disclosures based on the psychology of human communications.[64]

These expansions are influenced and motivated by a series of attitudes of "theorists" influencing accounting. The following theories are representative:

1. The theory of the "right to know" identifies both the general public and the owners as having a "right" to information which should concern accountants in the performance of the disclosure function.

2. The theory of "information overload" suggests limitations in human information processing of expanded accounting disclosures and considerations for contracting the amount of information disclosed and compressing the disclosed information itself.

3. The theory of "retrieved systems" leaves to the accountant the function of production and storage of data and presenting the user with either an information self-retrieval system or an information project retrieval system.

4. The theory of "relevance" is used to determine the relevant disclosure requirements and supports the disclosure of additional information having a high relevance evaluation, such as human asset, market value and nonfinancial measures.

5. The theory of "preciseness" dictates a rigor of analysis and unambiguous concepts.[65]

The clear implication of Bedford's proposals is an expanded disclosure-based notion of fairness.

B. Lev's theory of equitable and efficient accounting policy

Lev proposed a theory of equitable and efficient accounting policy.[66] Lev argued that progress in addressing the fundamental accounting policy issue can be achieved by including the explicit concern of policy makers – equity of the capital markets. This equity is defined as equality of opportunity or symmetric information when all investors would be equally endowed with information and risk-adjusted expected returns would be identical across investors. This is important since both theoretical analysis and empirical evidence show that the existing increased information asymmetry, or inequity, is associated with a lower number of investors, higher transaction costs, lower liquidity of securities, thinner volumes of trade and, in general, decreased social gains from trade. The equity concept will eliminate the major source of inequity, which is the informational advantage held by informed investors, lessen the generally harmful effects of the defensive measures that are naturally taken by the uninformed, and as a result improve overall welfare. The standard for the equity concept is stated as follows. *"The interests of the less informed investors should, in general, be favored in favor of the more informed investors."*[67] This standard entails the systematic decrease of information asymmetries and offers accounting policy makers operational and rather simple "public interest" criterion for disclosure choices. It is in fact based on a well-known principle in public policy:

> It is possible in our society to argue for a government program to the poor. But, the argument is not that the poor, being part of the winning coalition, should benefit at the expense of others. The argument is that by helping the poor we can make everyone better off: that helping the poor is not merely a means to make the poor happier but a means to reduce crime, make us all feel less guilty, make the cities livable, etc. What may, from the standpoint of wealth, be (small) redistribution is defended as, from the standpoint of utility, a Pareto improvement.[68]

C. Gaa's user primacy

Corporate financial reporting policy faces collective device problems that affect the allocation of resources to the production and consumption of information.[69] The following dilemma faces any standard-setting body set to resolve the allocation problems:

> Every policy choice represents a trade-off among different individual preferences, and possibly among alternative consequences, regardless of whether the policy makers see it that way or not. In this sense, accounting policy choice can never be neutral. There is someone who is granted his preference, and someone who is not. The ethical question is what morality should guide the policy-making process.[70]

Two alternatives are available. A first alternative is that the interests of all individuals will be connected equally by the standard-setter. It is a principle of neutrality that dictates the selection of standards that maximize social welfare. A second alternative is that the interests of one group of users would be given preferential treatment. One such group is the user group. This second alternative is therefore the user primacy guide to accounting reporting policy. Two versions of the user primacy principle have been advocated in the literature. The version known as the basic user primacy principle focuses on needs of users with limited abilities. As stated in *Objectives of Financial Statements*, published by the American Institute of Certified Public Accountants: "an objective of financial statements is to serve primarily those who have limited authority, ability, or resources to obtain information and who rely on financial statements as their principal source of information about an enterprise's economic activities".[71] Another version, known as extended user primacy, focuses on the information needs of sophisticated users. As stated in the Conceptual Framework of the Financial Accounting Standards Board:

> Financial Reporting should provide information that is useful to present and potential investors and creditors and other users in making rational investment, credit, and similar decisions. The information should be comprehensible to those who have a reasonable understanding of business and economic activities and are willing to study the information with reasonable diligence.[72]

Gaa investigated the logical formulations of the user primacy principle, based on contemporary work in ethics and social and political philosophy, in which humans are regarded as decision-makers, and in which principles governing individual and group behavior are the result of rational decisions. Basically:

> A standard setter would be established to enforce user primacy, thereby redressing an imbalance between investors (users) and managers. By acting in accordance with this principle, the standard setter aids all securities market agents in exploiting the potential trading gains provided by such a market. At the same time, investors are protected from possible losses arising from the basic relationship between them and managers of widely held corporations.[73]

D. The Jenkins Committee findings

In order to improve external reporting, the AICPA established in 1991 the Special Committee on Financial Reporting, or Jenkins Committee (Edmond L. Jenkins was the chairman). The committee was charged with the determination of (a) the nature and extent of information that should be made available to others by management, and (b) the extent to which the auditors should report on the various elements of that information. After two years of research into the needs of external reporting users (investors, creditors, and their advisers), the committee issued in November 1995 its report titled *The Information Needs of Investors and Creditors*. The report identified the following areas in financial statements that should be enhanced to meet users' need for information.

1. Improve disclosure of business segment information.
2. Address the disclosures and accounting for innovative financial instruments.
3. Improve disclosures about the identity, opportunities and risks of off-balance-sheet financing arrangements and reconsider the accounting for those arrangements.
4. Report separately the effects of core and noncore activities and events, and measure at fair value noncore assets and liabilities.
5. Improve disclosures about the uncertainty of measurements of certain assets and liabilities.
6. Improve quarterly reporting by reporting in the fourth quarter separately and including business segment data.

The report also proposed a comprehensive model including ten elements within five broad categories of information that are designed to fit the decision process users employ to make projections, value companies, or assess the prospect of loan repayment.

These elements are as follows:

1. *Financial and nonfinancial data:*
   - Financial statements and related disclosures.
   - High-level operating data and performance measurements that management uses to manage the business.
2. *Management's analysis of the financial and nonfinancial data:*
   - Reasons for changes in the financial, operating and performance related data, and the identity and past effect of key trends.
3. *Forward-looking information:*
   - Opportunities and risks, including those resulting from key trends.
   - Management's plans, including critical success factors.

- Comparison of actual business performance to previously disclosed opportunities, risks and management's plans.

4. *Information about management and shareholders*
   - Directors, management, compensation, major shareholders, and transactions and relationships among related parties.

5. *Background about the company*
   - Broad objectives and strategies.
   - Scope and description of business and properties.
   - Impact of industry structure on the company.[74]

E. Multilayered reporting model

Steven Wallman, who was an SEC commissioner at the time, suggested the following four broad accounting and disclosure issues that may be critically important to the future of financial reporting:

1. recognition and measurement of the benefits and obligations of a business – in other words, *what* is it that we should report in the financial statements of an enterprise;
2. the timeliness of financial reporting – in other words, *when* should recognized items be reported;
3. the concept of the firm – in other words, *who* are we measuring; and
4. the distribution channel and medium – in other words, *where* and *how* are we distributing this information.[75]

The first issue raises (a) the inadequacy of historical cost in the recognition and measurement of most assets, and (b) the inability to recognize at all as assets some of the new and most significant building blocks of business such as the value of trademarks, intellectual property, and human assets.

The second issue posits the needs for more timely information that increases the flow of relevant financial information to the market and lowers the cost of capital by decreasing risks and demanded returns.

The third issue raises (a) the problem of defining the outer edges of a firm, like in the case of public companies with multiple public subsidiaries, each with joint ventures, licensing arrangements and other affiliations, and (b) the need to recognize "virtual firms" with people networked together in combinations that form and dissolve as tasks are required to be performed.

The fourth issue raises (a) the need to offer more disaggregated information, and (b) the possibility of offering the users online access to selected portions of a firm's management information system.

A multilayered reporting model is offered as follows: [76]

1. The first layer is devoted to items that satisfy recognition criteria and would resemble the current core financial statements.
2. The second layer is devoted to items that satisfy recognition criteria but are not included in the core section because of reliability concerns, such as research and development, advertising, value of brands and deposit intangibles.
3. The third layer is devoted to items that have both reliability and definition concerns, such as measures of customer satisfaction.
4. The fourth layer is devoted to items that satisfy measurement, reliability and relevance criteria but do not meet the definitions of financial statement elements, such as risk sensitivity metrics.

5. The fifth layer is devoted to relevant items that do not meet the definition of elements and cannot be reliably measured, such as the intellectual capital of employees.

F. Expanded accounting disclosures

The principle of fairness in presentation restricts recognition and disclosures to the situations governed by existing generally accepted accounting principles. The distinction between recognition and disclosure is emphasized by the Financial Accounting Standards Board (FASB). According to the FASB Concepts Statement No. 5, *Recognition and Measurement in Financial Statements of Business Enterprises:*

> Recognition is the process of formally recording or incorporating an item into the financial statements of an entity as an asset, liability, revenue, expense, or the like. Recognition includes depiction of an item in both words and numbers, with the amount included in the totals of the financial statements.[77]

The same statement states that:

> since recognition means depiction of an item in both words and numbers, with the amount included in the totals of the financial statements, disclosure by other means is not recognition. Disclosure of information about the items in financial statements and their measures that may be provided by notes or parenthetically on the face of financial statements, by supplementary information, or by other means of financial reporting is not a substitute for recognition in financial statements for items that meet recognition criteria.[78]

The purposes of disclosure were stated as follows:

1. To describe recognized items and to provide relevant measures of those items other than the measures in the financial statements.
2. To describe unrecognized items and to provide a useful measure of those items.
3. To provide information to help investors and creditors assess risks and potentials of both recognized and unrecognized items.
4. To provide important information that allows financial statement users to compare within and between years.
5. To provide information in future cash inflows or outflows.
6. To help investors assess return on their investment.[79,80]

Examples are provided in Exhibit 8.1. An analysis of required financial statement disclosures led to the following five conclusions:

1. The most frequently required disclosures relate to amounts recognized in the financial statements, particularly to disaggregating them and providing relevant measures other than the measure in the financial statements – disaggregation of recognized amounts represents 26 percent of all required disclosures.
2. Six subjects – stockholders' equity, leases, pensions, income taxes, other postretirement employee benefits, and commitments and contingencies – account for 45 percent of all required disclosures; five standards – SFAS nos 15, 87, 88, 106 and 109 – account for 28 percent.
3. Few disclosures explicitly provide information on future cash inflows or outflows.
4. Few provide measures of unrecognized items.
5. Disclosure requirements have increased over time; few have been eliminated.[81]

Purpose	Example
1. Describe recognized items and provide relevant measures of those items other than the measure in the financial statements.	
1(a) Describe item.	General character, including interest rate, of recorded obligation.
1(b) Disaggregate item.	Components of net periodic pension cost.
1(c) Provide alternative measure.	Estimated fair value of on balance sheet financial instruments.
1(d) Disclose critical assumption used in determining amounts.	Weighted-average expected long-term rates of return on pension plan assets.
2. Describe unrecognized items and provide a useful measure of those items.	
2(a) Describe item.	Description of direct and indirect guarantees of indebtedness of others.
2(b) Disaggregate item.	Amount of unrecognized deferred tax liability for temporary differences related to essentially permanent investments in foreign subsidiaries.
2(c) Provide alternative measure.	Estimates of fair values of off balance sheet financial instruments.
2(d) Disclose critical assumption used in determining amounts.	Significant assumptions used to estimate fair values of off balance sheet financial instruments.
3. Provide information to help investors and creditors assess risks and potentials of both recognized and unrecognized items.	
3(a) Provide description of underlying economic situations.	Description of substantive defined benefit postretirement plan(s).[1]
3(b) Provide description to assess risks and potentials.	Company's collateral policy for each significant concentration of credit risk.
3(c) Provide maximum amount involved.	Number and option price for shares under options.
3(d) Provide information necessary for user to make independent calculation of an amount.	Number of shares exercisable under stock options.
4. Provide information that allows financial statement users to compare numbers to other companies and between years.	
4(a) Describe company's accounting policies and practices.	Method of inventory cost determination.
4(b) Describe effects of unusual transactions.	Portion of income tax expense relating to extraordinary items, cumulative effect of an accounting change, and prior period adjustments.[2]
4(c) Describe effect of unusual transaction on a prior year, or portion of a period.	In purchase business combinations, results of operations for immediately preceding period as though the companies had combined at the beginning of that period.
5. Provide information on future cash inflows or outflows.	Combined aggregate amount of maturities and Sinking fund requirements for all long-term borrowings for each of the next five years.
6. Help investors assess return on their investment.	Preferred stock dividend rate.

[1] (3a) is similar to describing a recognized or unrecognized item (1a or 2a) except that (3a) descriptions typically provide general background information whereas items (1a) or (2a) provide specific information directly relating to the recognized or unrecognized item. To avoid unnecessary duplication we classify a disclosure as (3a) if it could be classified as either (3a) or (1a) or (2a).

[2] (4b) is similar to disaggregating a recognized amount (1b). However, (4b) disclosures go beyond disaggregation to enable financial statement users to adjust for unusual items, permitting comparability between years. We classify disclosures as (4b) that could be classified as (1b).

Source: Mary E. Barth, and Christine M. Murphy, "Required Financial Statement Disclosures: Purposes, Subject, Number, and Trend", *Accounting Horizons* (December, 1994), p. 5. Reprinted with permission.

Exhibit 8.1 Purposes of required financial statement disclosures

All the previous calls for expanded disclosures are motivated by the principle of fairness in disclosure. The principle would advocate expanding the scope of accounting information beyond conventional accounting information. Examples of new accounting disclosures under this principle of fairness in disclosure include:

1. value added reporting;
2. employee reporting;
3. human resource accounting;
4. social accounting and reporting;
5. budgetary information disclosures;
6. cash-flow accounting and reporting.

These are examined next.

8.4.2 Value added reporting

Conventional reporting in most countries does not include value added reporting. Instead, it measures and discloses the financial position (through the balance sheet), the financial performance of the firm (through the income statement), and the financial conduct of the firm (through the statement of changes in the financial position). Although the usefulness of these statements has been established by their sheer use over time, they fail to give important information on the total productivity of the firm and the share of each team of members involved in the management of resources, shareholders, bondholders, employees and the government. The value added statement can fill that crucial role. Value added is the increase in wealth generated by the productive use of the firm's resources before its allocation among shareholders, bondholders, workers and the government. It can be easily computed by a modification of the income statement as follows:

Step 1: The income statement computes retained earnings as a difference between sales revenue, on one hand, and costs, taxes and dividends, on the other:

$$R = S - B - DP - W - I - DD - T \tag{1}$$

where:

R   = retained earnings
S   = sales revenue
B   = bought-in materials and services
DP   = depreciation
W   = wages
I   = interest
DD   = dividends
T   = taxes.

Step 2: The value added equation can be obtained by rearranging the profit equation as:

$$S - B = R + DP + W + I + DD + T \tag{2}$$

or

$$S - B - DP = R + W - t - I + DD + T \tag{3}$$

Equation 2 expresses the gross value added method. Equation 3 expresses the net value added method. In both cases, the left part of the equation shows the value added among the groups involved in the managerial production team (the workers, the shareholders, the bondholders, and the government). The right-hand side is also known as the additive method and the left-hand side as the subtractive method.

Exhibit 8.2 shows the value added statement can be derived from a regular income statement. The company in this example deducted bought-in materials, services and depreciation from sales, to arrive at a value added of $2,240,000. The $2,240,000 was divided among the team of workers ($800,000), shareholders ($200,000), bondholders and creditors ($240,000) and the government ($600,000), leaving $400,000 for retained earnings.

The value added statement can be presented in either the gross or net format. The value added statement has some very good benefits:

1. With the disclosure of value added, employees get the satisfaction of knowing the value of their contribution to the total wealth of the firm.

2. Value added represents a better base for the computation of worker bonuses.

3. Value added information has been proven to be a good predictor of economic events and market reaction.[82]

4. Value added is a better measurement of size than sales.

5. Value added may be useful to employee groups because it can affect the aspirations and thoughts of its negotiating representatives.

6. Value added may be extremely useful in financial analysis by relating various crucial events to value added variables. A summary of the empirical research is shown in three tables in Exhibit 8.3.

A. The conventional income statement of a company for 19X8 was:

	$	$
Sales		4,000,000
Less: Materials used	400,000	
Wages	800,000	
Services purchased	1,200,000	
Interest paid	240,000	
Depreciation	160,000	
Profit before tax		1,200,000
Income tax (assume 50% tax rate)		600,000
Profit after tax		600,000
Less: Dividend payable		200,000
Retained earnings for the year		400,000

B. A value added statement for the same year would be:

Sales		4,000,000
Less: Bought-in materials and services and depreciation		1,760,000
Value added available for distribution or retention		2,240,000
Applied as follows:		
To employees		800,000
To providers of capital		
Interest	240,000	
Dividends	200,000	440,000
To government		600,000
Retained earnings		400,000
Value added		2,240,000

Exhibit 8.2   Deriving the value added statement

8.4.3 Employee reporting

With the emergence of employees and unions as potential users of accounting information, it also appears, and for a good many reasons, that the annual report to shareholders is not the all-inclusive document suitable for all unions. The solution lies in the production of a special report to employees and unions. This solution has been accepted in many country members of the Organization of Economic Cooperation and Development, including the United States, West Germany, Canada, France, Denmark, Norway, Sweden and the United Kingdom. The idea has been accepted not only operationally but conceptually. For example, in the United Kingdom, *The Corporate Report* identifies employees as a user group of published company annual reports.[83]

Because different factors apply for employees and unions, each will be reviewed separately. In fact, a sample employment report, included as an appendix to *The Corporate Report*, showed quantitative data under the following headings:[84]

1. Number employed (analyzed in various ways)
2. Location of employment
3. Age distribution of permanent workforce
4. Hours worked during the year (analyzed)
5. Employee costs

Table 1 Value added performance of firms

Study	Context	Results
1. Riahi-Belkaoui (1997c)	Multidivisional structure and diversification strategy.	Following the M-form implementation, productive efficiency decreases for vertically integrated firms and increases for related diversified firms. The moderate increase in productivity is not significant for unrelated diversifiers.
2. Riahi-Belkaoui and Pavlik (1994)	Effects of ownership structure.	There is a significant nonmonotonic relationship between value added performance and ownership structure.
3. Askren *et al.* (1994)	Performance plan adoption.	Firms adopting accounting-based performance plans do not experience any greater gains in accounting return or productivity measure than do a set of control firms.
4. Riahi-Belkaoui (1997a)	Performance plan adoption and ownership structure.	Following performance plan adoption, profitability will increase in owner-controlled firms, but not manager controlled firms.

Exhibit 8.3

Table 2 Market valuation and value added versus conventional data

Study	Research question	Model used	Results
1. Bao and Bao (1989)	Association between productivity and firm value.	Litzenberger and Rao (1971) valuation model.	The association between firm value and productivity in the oil-refining and apparel industries is stronger than between firm value and earnings measures.
2. Riahi-Belkaoui (1993)	Relative and incremental content of value added, earnings and cash flow.	Earnings valuation model.	Value added information can supply some explanatory power beyond that provided by earnings or cash-flow measures.
3. Riahi-Belkaoui and Fekrat (1994)	Merits of derived accounting indicator numbers.	Accounting indicator numbers (Barlev and Levy, 1979).	The derived indicator numbers based on net value added had lower variability and higher persistency than~ corresponding numbers based on either earnings or cash flows.
4. Riahi-Belkaoui and Picur (1994)	Relative and incremental information content of value added and earnings	Combined earnings value added valuation model.	The study confirms association between both relative changes in earnings and net value added and the relative changes in security prices.
5. Riahi-Belkaoui and Picur (1994)	Information content of level versus change in net value added.	Book value and wealth models.	Both the levels of net value added and the changes in net value added play a role in security valuation.
6. Riahi-Belkaoui (1996)	Functional specification relating unexpected earnings or net value added to market-adjusted returns.	Linear and nonlinear valuation models.	Models relating accounting and market returns have more explanatory power when: (a) the accounting returns are expressed by the relative changes in net value added, and (b) the relation is a nonlinear convex-concave function.

Exhibit 8.3 *continued*

Study	Research question	Model used	Results
7. Riahi-Belkaoui (1997b)	Informational content of net value added components disclosed concurrently with earnings.	Earnings valuation model.	Earnings component of value added is viewed favorably by the market while the nonearnings components (interest, tax and wages) are negatively related to market return.

Table 3 Predictive ability of value added data

Study	Nature of prediction	Model used	Results
1. Karpik and Belkaoui (1989)	Explaining market risk.	Market model.	Value added variables process incremental information beyond accrual earnings and cash flows in the context of explaining market risk.
2. Bannister and Riahi-Belkaoui (1991)	Explaining target firm's abnormal returns during the takeover period.	Market model.	Takeover targets have lower value added to total ratios rather than other firms in their industries in the year preceding the completion of the takeover, and target firm abnormal returns observed during the takeover period are related to the difference between target firm and average industry value added.
3. Bao and Bao (1996)	Examining the structure and the forecasting accuracy of firm value added measure.	Four time-series models.	The four value added measures can be diversified as a random walk model. The process/model has the lowest forecast errors in terms of two error metrics.

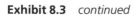

Exhibit 8.3 *continued*

6. Pension information

7. Education and Training (including costs)

8. Recognized trade unions

9. Additional information (race relations, health and safety statistics, etc.)

10. Employment ratios.[85]

Similarly, in Canada, the Canadian Institute of Chartered Accountants published a research study in June 1980 entitled *Corporate Reporting: Its Future Evolution*.[86] The report explicitly identified employees (past, present and future) as users of corporate reports.

Firms do have a continuous communications process with employees through various media, including plant-level discussions, quality circles, audiovisual presentations, and in-house journals and notices. The purpose of the formal employees' annual report is to provide an integrative and exhaustive report rather than a piecemeal approach. The same point is argued as follows:

> It must be a report, capable of satisfying additional information needs of employees, rather than simply supply information already provided through alternative internal channels, or providing unwanted information. Unless the preparers of an annual report to employees can identify a genuine information void left by other internal communication media, and can justifiably believe that such a report can fill this void, then the report has no real justification.[87]

The literature has identified various aims and reasons for reporting to employees. A survey of the literature on financial reporting to employees between 1919 and 1979 identified the following reasons: (a) heralding changes, (b) presenting management propaganda, (c) promoting interest in understanding of company affairs and performance, (d) explaining management decisions, (e) explaining the relationship between employees, management and shareholders, (f) explaining the objectives of the company, (g) facilitating greater employee participation, (h) responding to legislative or union pressure, (i) building company image, (j) meeting information requirements peculiar to employees, (k) responding to management fear of wage demands, strikes, and competitive disadvantages, and (l) promoting a higher degree of employee interest.[88] The same survey shows that the level of interest in reporting to employees reached a higher level when the following four socioeconomic factors were also present: (a) the use of new technology in the workplace, (b) increased mergers in the corporate sector, (c) the emergence of antiunion sentiment, and (d) fears of economic recessions.[89] It seems that management may have increased the level of employee reporting in reaction to the potential consequence of each of these factors or a combination of these factors. Lewis *et al.*, the authors of the survey, speculated that management may have hoped to:

1. allay fear of lost rank, skill, or employment through technological advances;

2. counter fears of "bigness", monopoly power, employee relocation, and loss of identity through corporate mergers;

3. take advantage of community antiunion sentiments by bypassing union communication channels (reporting directly to employees), emphasizing management prerogatives and the need to control wages and associated costs, and generally weakening the unions' potential to disrupt operations;

4. prepare employees for hard times, confirm or dispel rumors of imminent company failure, allay fears of unemployment, and urge employees to greater efforts in difficult economic times.[90]

Taylor, Webb and McGinley identified the following personal benefits which management might attempt to seek for itself by providing an annual report to employees in addition to using the conventional management–employee communication media:

(a) building a favorable employee impression of the management group;

(b) reducing the resistance of employees to changes initiated by management; and

(c) providing a useful response to union pressure for more corporate financial information from management.[91]

They also identified the following personal benefits which might accrue to employees with employee reporting:

(a) having the basis for deciding whether to continue employment with the company or an organization section of the company;

(b) having the basis for assisting the relative position of the employees within the corporate structure, particularly in terms of getting a "fair go"; and

(c) understanding the image of the company, as a basis for deciding at a personal level whether to identify with this image.[92]

Finally, Foley and Maunders identified arguments supporting disclosure direct to employees:

(a) feedback of information to employees will improve job performance via learning effects and also serve to increase motivation;

(b) the role of employee reporting is crucial to effective worker participation which will contribute to the efficiency of the company;

(c) the fundamental change in the nature of the firm and its "social responsibility" legitimizes employee reporting;

(d) employee reporting may be seen by some employers as a possible way of resurrecting the concept of joint consultation as a means of avoiding unionization;

(e) finally, the socialist tradition, with its ultimate objective of changing the basis of ownership and the control of resources, sees employee reporting as a step to increase "workers' control" and develop "workers' self confidence".[93]

The case for employee reporting using the socialist argument rests on two fundamental principles:

1. that it is a technique which helps employees establish greater democratization of decision-making in industry;

2. that it may usefully act as a check on those aspects of the market system which result in adverse external effects in the form of pollution and environmental degradation.

8.4.4 Social accounting and reporting

The measurement of social performance falls in the general area of social accounting.[94] Under this area there are four various activities that may be delineated: social responsibility accounting (SRA), total impact accounting (TIA), socioeconomic accounting (SEA), and social indicators accounting (SIA).[95] Exhibit 8.4 shows the characteristics of the various component parts of social accounting. One can see that the general concepts and disclosure of social performance are products of SEA and TIA, and social accounting is appropriately defined as "the process of selecting firm-level social performance variables, measures and measurements procedures; systematically developing information useful for evaluating the firm's social performance, and communication of such information to concerned social groups, both within and outside the firm".[96] This is a good conceptual framework for social accounting, proposed by Ramanathan, and comprises three objectives and six concepts. This framework applies equally to SRA and TIA.

A question arises about who is "pushing" for corporate social reporting. Are they to the right or to the left of the political spectrum? Gray *et al.* presented corporate social reporting (CSR) as a dialectic between four positions: "(1) The extreme left-ring of politics ('left-wing radicals'); (2) the acceptance of the *status quo*; (3) the pursuit of subject/intellectual property rights; (4) the extreme right-wing of politics (the 'pristine capitalists' or 'right-wing radicals'".[97] The second group appears to represent those true advocates of corporate social reporting. They are represented by people:

1. who assume that the purpose of CSR is to enhance the corporate image and hold the, usually implicit, assumption that corporate behavior is fundamentally benign;

Division	Purpose	Area of main use	Time scale	Measurements used	Associated areas
1. Social responsibility accounting (SRA)	Disclosure of individual items having a social impact	Private sector	Short term*	Levels I, II, mainly non-financial and qualitative	Employee reports, human resource accounting, industrial democracy
2. Total impact accounting (TIA)	Measures the total cost (both public and private) of running an organization	Private sector	Medium and long term	Financial AAA Level III	Strategic planning, cost–benefit analysis
3. Socio-economic accounting (SEA)	Evaluation of publicly funded projects both financial and nonfinancial	Public sector	Short and medium term	Financial, nonfinancial, Levels II and and III	Cost-benefit analysis, planned programmed budgeting systems, zero-based budgeting, institutional performance indicators
4. Social indicators accounting (SIA)	Long-term nonfinancial quantification of societal statistics	Public sector	Long term	Nonfinancial quantitative AAA Level II	National income accounts, census statistics

*Normally short term to fit annual reporting patterns.

Source: Reprinted from M.R. Mathews, "A Suggested Classification for Social Accounting Research", *Journal of Accounting and Public Policy* (3, 3, 1984), p. 202. ©1984 Elsevier Science Inc. Reprinted with permission.

Exhibit 8.4   The characteristics of the various component parts of social accounting

2. who assume that the purpose of CSR is to discharge an organization's accountability under the assumption that a social contract exists between the organization and society. The existence of this social contract demands the discharge of social accountability;

3. who *appear* to assume that CSR is effectively an extension of traditional financial reporting and its purpose is to inform investors.[98]

Various arguments are used for the measurement and disclosure of social performance:

1. The first argument is that of *social contract*. Implicitly, it is assumed that organizations ought to act in a manner that maximizes social welfare, as if a social contract existed between the organization and society. By doing so, organizations gain a kind of organizational legitimacy vis-à-vis society. While the social contract may be assumed to be implicit, various societal laws may render certain covenants of the contract more explicit. These laws that constitute the rules of the game in which organizations choose to play become the terms of the social contract.[99] Through these implicit and explicit laws, society defines the rules of accountability for organizations.

   The state, however, plays a primary role in the formulation of these laws and the specification of the rules of the game. In the US context, these laws and the general concern with social performance created a need for tracking environmental risk. With the 1989 SEC requirement that companies disclose any potential environmental cleanup liabilities they may face under the federal Superfund law, the 1990 annual reports of companies started the disclosure process. The 10k disclosures, added to the host of required filings with state and federal environment agencies, led to the creation of data banks that provided information on companies specializing in the tracking of environmental risk. Examples of these companies include Ersite, based in Denver; Environmental Audits, in Lyonville, Pennsylvania; the Environmental Risk Information Center in Alexandria, Virginia; the Petroleum Information Corporation, Littleton, Colorado; Toxicheck, in Birmingham, Michigan; Vista Environmental Information in San Diego; Environmental Data Resources in Southport, Connecticut.[100] This new industry gives a glimpse of a future characterized by concerned shareholders regarding the social performance of firms and more accurate and reliable information on the environmental risks of US corporations.

2. Rawls' theory of justice, as presented in his book *A Theory of Justice*,[101] Nozick's "entitlement theory" as presented in his book *Anarchy, State, and Utopia*,[102] and Gerwith's theory of justice as presented in *Reason and Morality*[103] contain principles for evaluating laws and institutions from a moral standpoint. Both Rawls' and Gerwith's models argue for a concept of fairness favorable to social accounting.

3. The third argument is that of users' needs. Basically, users of financial statements need social information for their revenue allocation decisions. An argument may be made by some that shareholders are conservative and care only about dividends. In fact, according to a recent survey of shareholders, they want corporations to direct resources toward cleaning up plants, stopping environmental pollution and making safer products.[104] As a result, Marc Epstein advises corporations to do the following in order to manage expenditures on social concerns:

   ● Integrate corporate awareness of social, ethical and environmental issues into corporate decisions at all levels, and make sure such concerns have representation on the board of directors;

   ● Develop methods to evaluate and report on the social and environmental impacts of corporate activities;

- Modify the corporate structure to set up a mechanism to deal with social, environmental and ethical crisis. Then a company can be a crisis-prepared organization rather than a crisis-prone organization. Companies that do not prepare themselves for crises simply flounder;

- Create incentives for ethical, environmental and socially responsible behavior on the part of employees and integrate those incentives into the performance evaluation system and corporate culture. Unless this is institutionalized it never enters the corporate culture and significant, permanent change cannot occur;

- Recognize that if the environment is to be cleaned up, business must take a leadership role in the reduction of pollutants and the wise use of natural resources.[105]

There is, however, a lack of normative and/or descriptive models on the users' needs in terms of social information.

4. The fourth argument is that of *social investment*. Basically, it is assumed that an *ethical investor* group is now relying on social information provided in annual reports for making investment decisions. The disclosure of social information becomes, therefore, essential if investors are going to consider properly the negative effects of social awareness expenditures on earnings per share, along with any compensating positive effects that reduce risk or create greater interest from a particular investment clientele. Some argue that the risk-reducing effects will more than compensate for social awareness expenditures:

> Between firms competing in the capital markets those perceived to have the highest expected future earnings in combination with the lowest expected risk from environmental and other factors will be most successful at attracting long term funds.[106]

Others believe that "ethical investors" form a clientele that responds to demonstrations of corporate social concern.[107] Investors of this type would like to avoid particular investments entirely for ethical reasons and would prefer to favor socially responsible corporations in their portfolios.[108] A survey by Rockness and Williams identifies an emerging consensus on the primary characteristics of social performance among fund managers.[109] The performance factors include environmental protection, treatment of employees, business relations with repressive regimes, product quality and innovation, and defense criteria considered investment criteria by most of the managers.

An emerging theory of social investment is provided by Bruyn who suggests that social and economic values can be maximized together, and this creative synergism is the practical direction taken by the social investor today.[110] Bruyn's investor is assumed to contribute to the development of social economy design to promote human values and institutions, as well as self-interests. The social investor bases investment decisions not only on economic and financial considerations, but also on sociologically grounded considerations. Both "social inventions" and technological inventions hold an expectation of profit and economic development. With regard to accountability, social investors, while concerned with the management of profits and scarce resources, are also interested in the corporations' accountability to other stakeholders in the environment besides stockholders.

8.4.5 Budgetary information disclosures

Faced with the challenge from diverse users to develop more relevant financial reporting techniques, accountants and nonaccountants alike have recommended that forecasted information can be incorporated into financial statements. Proposals vary from the suggestion that budgetary data be disclosed to the suggestion that public companies provide earnings forecasts in their annual or interim reports and prospectuses. One objective of financial reporting set forth in the "Trueblood Report" supports this type of disclosure: "An objective of financial statements is to provide information useful for the predictive process. Financial forecasts should be provided when they will enhance the reliability of users' prediction."[111]

Although the objective does not constitute a strong recommendation for corporate financial forecasts, steps have been taken to ensure that forecasts are included in accounting reports. In Great Britain, the revised version of the *City Code on Takeovers and Mergers* requires profit forecasts to be included in takeover-bid circulars and prospectuses.[112] In the British case, the interest of the accounting profession was created by the requirement that not only must "the assumptions, including the commercial assumptions", be stated but the "accounting bases and calculations must be examined and reported on by the auditors or consultant accountants".[113] In the United States, in February 1975, the SEC first announced its intention to require companies disclosing the forecasts to conform with certain rules to be laid down by the Commission. In April 1976, in reaction to public criticism, the SEC called for voluntary filings of forecasts. The SEC's amended position presents some problems in terms of:

1. the definition of earnings forecasts,
2. whether disclosure should be mandatory or optional, and
3. the possible advantages of such disclosures.

The first problem concerns determining which forecasted items are to be disclosed. The two possible solutions are disclosing budgets or disclosing probable results (forecasts). This distinction may be made because budgets are prepared for internal use and, for motivational reasons, may be stated in a way that differs from expected results. Ijiri makes the distinction as follows: "Forecasts are estimates of what the corporation considers to be the most likely to occur, whereas budgets may be inflated from what the corporation considers to be most likely to occur in order to take advantage of the motivational function of the budget."[114] From the point of view of the user, therefore, the disclosure of forecasts, rather than budgets, may be more relevant to his or her decision-making needs. In fact, the trend seems to be in favor of the disclosure of forecasts of specific accounts in general and earnings in particular.

The second problem is whether the disclosure of earnings forecasts should be mandatory or optional. Each position may be easily justified. The principal argument in favor of mandatory disclosure is that it creates a similar and uniform situation for all companies. However, mandatory disclosure could create an unnecessary burden in terms of competitive advantage and certain firms would have to be viewed as exceptions (for example, private companies, companies in volatile industries, companies in the process of major changes and companies in developmental stages).[115] Another argument against mandatory disclosure is that some firms lack adequate technology, experience, and competence to disclose forecasts adequately and that the outlays to correct this situation may create an unnecessary burden on these firms. Such a firm may doubt the benefits of a forecast-disclosure procedure that justifies the cost of installing a new reporting system.

The third problem concerns the desirability of forecast publication. Several arguments have been advanced against the reporting of corporate financial forecasts. One argument is that both companies and analysts have been unsuccessful in accurately forecasting earnings. Daily points out that budgeted "information must be reasonably accurate to be relevant; otherwise the investors will have no confidence in the information and consequently not utilize it".[116] Both his study and McDonald's study[117] support the contention that, on average, management earnings forecasts are likely to be materially inaccurate. A number of factors may affect the accuracy of forecasts, for example the length of time covered by the forecasts, the nature of the industry in which the company operates, the external environment and the degree of sophistication and experience of the company making the forecast. Ijiri classifies the primary issues involved in corporate financial forecasts as:

1. reliability,
2. responsibility; and
3. reticency.[118]

Reliability is related to the relative accuracy of the forecasts; *responsibility*, to the possible large liabilities of firms making forecasts and accountants auditing these forecasts; and *reticency*, to the degree of silence and inaction of firms that are at a competitive disadvantage due to forecast disclosure. Similarly, Mautz suggests that three kinds of differences must be considered in evaluating the overall usefulness of published forecasts:

● differences in the forecasting abilities of publicly owned firms;
● differences in the attitudes with which managements in publicly owned companies might be expected to approach the forecasting task;
● differences in the capacities of investors to use forecasts.[119]

Finally, given the difficulties associated with identifying and estimating forecasts, to what is an accountant expected to attest? Mautz suggests the following range of possibilities:

1. arithmetic accuracy,
2. internal integrity of the forecast data,
3. consistency in the application of accounting principles,
4. adequacy of disclosure,
5. reasonableness of assumptions, and
6. reasonableness of projections.[120]

8.4.6 Cash-flow accounting and reporting

A dominant characteristic in early views of the purpose of financial statements is the stewardship function. According to this view, management is entrusted with control of the financial resources provided by capital suppliers. Accordingly, the purpose of financial statements is to report to concerned parties to facilitate the evaluation of management's stewardship. To accomplish this objective, the reporting system favored and deemed essential and superior to others is the *accrual system*. Simply stated, the *accrual basis of accounting* refers to a form of keeping those records not only of transactions that result from the receipt and disbursement of cash but also of the amounts that the entity owes others and that others owe the entity.[121] At the core of this system is the matching of revenues and expenses. Interest in the accrual method has generated a search for the "best" accrual method in general and the "ideal income" in particular. For a long time, this accounting paradigm governed the evaluation of accounting alternatives and the asset valuation and income-determination proposals. However, this approach was constantly challenged by proponents of *cash-flow accounting*. *The cash-flow basis of accounting* has been correctly defined as the recording not only of cash receipts and disbursements of the period (the cash basis of accounting) but also of the *future cash flows* owed to or by the firm as a result of selling and transferring the title to certain goods (the *accrual basis* of accounting).[122] The advocacy of cash-flow accounting is more evident in a questioning of the importance and efficacy of accrual accounting and a shift toward the cash-flow approach in security analysis.[123]

The question of the superiority of accrual accounting over cash-flow accounting is central to the determination of the objectives and the nature of financial reporting. Accrual accounting facilitates the evaluation of management's stewardship and is essential to the matching of revenues and expenses, which is required to properly align efforts and accomplishments. The efficiency of the accrual system has been questioned, however. Thomas states that all allocations are arbitrary and incorrigible and recommends the minimization of such allocations.[124] Hawkins and Campbell report a shift in security analysis from earnings-oriented valuation approaches to cash-flow-oriented valuation approaches.[125] Many decision-usefulness theorists advocate a cash-flow accounting system based on the investor's desires to predict cash flows.[126,127] Most advocates of cash-flow accounting feel that the problems of asset valuation and income determination are so formidable that they warrant the derivation of a separate accounting system and propose the inclusion of a comprehensive cash-flow statement in company reports. For instance, Lee describes how cash-flow accounting and net-realizable-value accounting can be combined in a series of articulating statements that provide more relevant information about cash and cash management than either system can provide individually.[128]

Cash-flow accounting is viewed by supporters as superior to conventional accrual accounting because:

1. A system of cash-flow accounting might provide an analytic framework for linking past, present and future financial performance.[129]

2. From the perspective of investors, the projected cash flow would reflect both the company's ability to pay its way in the future and its planned financial policy.[130]

3. A price-discounted flow ratio would be a more reliable investment indicator than the present price-earnings ratio, due to the numerous arbitrary allocations used to compute earnings per share.[131]

4. Cash-flow accounting may be used to correct the gap in practice between the way in which an investment is made (generally based on cash flows) and the way in which the results are evaluated (generally based on earnings).[132]

The important question remaining is whether or not cash-flow accounting will be restored to its predominant position as an important and relevant source of financial information. All trends seem to indicate that the answer is in the affirmative. Witness the following eloquent and optimistic statement:

> Of all the available systems of financial reporting, cash flow accounting is one of the most objective and understandable. It attempts to state facts in financial-accounting terms, without the accountant having to become involved in making subjective judgments as to which period the data relate. And it is expressed in terms that should be familiar to all nonaccountants. Cash resources and flows are things that anyone in a developed economy has to administer from day to day. Thus, cash flow reports are potentially comprehensible, a matter that is of increasing concern to accountants as the number of report users and groups increases year by year.[133]

How would users react to cash-flow information? Evidence to date seems to indicate that security analysts use earnings information more often than they use cash-flow information in their professional reports.

8.4.7 Human-resource accounting

A. The usefulness of human resources

The objective of financial accounting is to provide information that is relevant to the decisions that users (investors) must make, including adequate information about one "neglected" asset of a firm – the human asset. More specifically, investors may greatly benefit from knowledge of the extent to which the human assets of an organization have increased or decreased during a given period. The conventional accounting treatment of human-resource outlays consists of *expensing* all human-capital formation expenditures and *capitalizing* similar outlays on physical capital. A more valid treatment would be to capitalize human-resource expenditures to yield future benefits and to reveal when such benefits can be measured. In fact, this treatment has created a new concern with the measurement of the cost or value of human resources to an organization and has led to the development of a new field of inquiry in accounting, known as *human-resource accounting*. A broad definition of human-resource accounting is:

> the process of identifying and measuring data about human resources and communicating this information to interested parties.[134]

This definition implies that there are three major objectives of human-resource accounting:

1. identification of "human-resource value",
2. measurement of the cost and value of people to organizations, and
3. investigation of the cognitive and behavioral impact of such information.

Human-resource accounting has led to a few applications, including those of the R.G. Barry Corporation, Touche Ross & Company, and a midwest branch of a mutual insurance company.[135] Despite the lack of enthusiasm of many firms to disclose the value of their human assets, most empirical studies investigating the cognitive and behavioral impact show a favorable predisposition of users to human-resource accounting information.[136] We may wonder, in fact, why the R.G. Barry Corporation, a small shoe-manufacturing company listed on the American Stock Exchange, would develop a human-resource accounting system. As one of its officers rhetorically observed:

> Why in the world is a little company with good – but unspectacular – growth, good but unromantic products, good but unsophisticated technology, good but undramatic profitability interested in the development of a system of accounting for the human resources of the business? This is a fair question and deserves an answer.[137]

To answer this question – and any similar questions asked by other corporations – we may cite three facts:

1. Capitalizing human-resource costs is conceptually more valid than the expensing approach.
2. The information concerning "human assets" is likely to be relevant to a great variety of decisions made by external or internal users, or both.
3. Accounting for human assets constitutes an explicit recognition of the premise that people are valuable organizational resources and an integral part of a mix of resources.

B. Human-resource value theory

The concept of *human value* may be derived from the general economic value theory. Values may be attributed to individuals or groups like physical assets, based on their ability to render future economic services. In line with the economic thinking that associates the value of an object with its ability to render benefits, the individual or group value is usually defined as the present worth of the services rendered to the organization throughout the individual's or the group's expected service life.

How do we determine the value of a human asset? To measure and disclose *human-resource value*, we must devise a theoretical framework, or *human-resource value theory*, to explicate the nature and determinants of the value of people to an organization. Basically, two models of the nature and determinants of human-resource value exist – one advanced by Flamholtz and one advanced by Likert and Bowers.[138] We will discuss each of these models here.

1. Determinants of individual value

In Flamholtz's model, the measure of a person's worth is his or her expected realizable value. Flamholtz's model suggests that such a measure of *individual value* results from the interaction of two variables: (1) the individual's expected conditional value, and (2) the probability that the individual will maintain membership in the organization.

The individual's *conditional value* is the amount the organization would potentially realize from that person's services. Conditional value is a multi-dimensional variable comprised of three factors: *productivity, transferability* and *promotability*. The elements of conditional value are perceived to be the products of certain attributes of the person and certain dimensions of the organization. Two important individual determinants are identified as the person's *skills* and *activation level*. Similarly, the organizational determinants that interact with the individual values are identified as the *organizational role* of the individual and the *rewards* that people expect from the different aspects of their membership in a firm.

The probability of maintaining the organizational membership is considered to be related to a person's degree of job satisfaction.

2. Determinants of group value

Flamholtz's model examines the determinants of an individual's value to an organization; the Likert-Bowers model examines the determinants of *group value*. Intended to represent the "productive capability of the human organization of any enterprise or unit within it",[139] the model identifies three variables that influence the effectiveness of a firm's "human organization":

1. The *causal variables* are independent variables that can be directly or purposely altered or changed by the organization and its management and that in turn determine the course of developments within an organization. These causal variables include only those that are controllable by the organization and its management. General business conditions, for example, although an independent variable, are not viewed as causal because they are not controllable by the management of a particular enterprise. Causal variables include the structure of the organization and management's policies, decisions, business and leadership strategies, skills, and behavior.

2. The *intervening variables* reflect the internal state, health and performance capabilities of the organization; that is, the loyalties, attitudes, motivations, performance goals and perceptions of all members and their collective capability for effective action.

3. The *end-result variables* are the dependent variables that reflect the results achieved by that organization, such as its productivity, costs, scrap loss, growth, share of the market and earnings.[140]

The Likert-Bowers model states that certain causal variables induce certain levels of intervening variables, which yield certain levels of end-result variables. The *causal variables* are managerial behavior, organizational structure and subordinate peer behavior. The *intervening variables* are such organizational processes as perception communication, motivation, decision-making, control and coordination. The *end-result variables* are health, satisfaction, productivity and financial performance.

C. Measures of human assets

Monetary measures of human assets are historical cost (acquisition cost), replacement cost, opportunity cost, the compensation model and adjusted discounted future wages. The principal nonmonetary measure is the "survey of organizations" model.

1. The historical-cost (acquisition-cost) method

The historical-cost, or acquisition-cost, method consists of capitalizing all of the costs associated with recruiting, selecting, hiring, training, placing and developing an employee (a human asset), and then amortizing these costs over the expected useful life of the asset, recognizing losses in case of liquidation of the asset or increasing the value of the asset to offset any additional cost that is expected to increase the benefit potential of the asset. Similar to the conventional accounting treatments for other assets, this treatment is practical and objective in the sense that the data are verifiable.[141]

However, the use of these measurements is limited in several ways. First, the economic value of a human asset does not necessarily correspond to its historical cost. Second, any appreciation or amortization may be subjective and have no relationship to any increase or decrease in the productivity of the human assets. Third, because the costs associated with recruiting, selecting, hiring, training, placing and developing an employee may differ from one individual to another within a firm, the historical-cost method does not result in comparable human-resource values.

2. The replacement-cost method

The replacement-cost method consists of estimating the costs of replacing a firm's existing human resources. Such costs include all of the costs of recruiting, selecting, hiring, training, placing and developing new employees until they reach the level of competence of existing employees. The principal advantage of the replacement-cost method is that it is a good surrogate for the economic value of the asset in the sense that market considerations are essential in reaching a final figure. Such a final figure is also generally intended to be conceptually equivalent to a concept of an individual's economic value.[142]

However, the use of the replacement-cost method is also limited in several ways. First, the value of a particular employee may be perceived by the firm to be greater than the relevant replacement cost. Second, there may be no equivalent replacement for a given human asset.[143] Third, as noted by Likert and Bowers, managers may have difficulty estimating the cost of completely replacing their human organization, and different managers may arrive at quite different estimates.[144]

3. The opportunity-cost method

Hekimian and Jones propose the opportunity-cost method to overcome the limitations of the replacement-cost method.[145] They suggest that human-resource values be established through a competitive bidding process within the firm, based on the concept of "opportunity" cost. More specifically, investment-center managers are to bid for the scarce employees they need to recruit. These "scarce" employees include only those employees within the firm who are the subject of a recruitment request by an investment center manager. In other words, employees who are not considered "scarce" are not included in the human-asset base of the organization.

Obviously, the opportunity-cost method has several limitations. First, the inclusion of only "scarce" employees in the asset base may be interpreted as "discriminatory" by other employees. Second, less profitable divisions may be penalized by their inability to outbid more profitable divisions to acquire better employees. Third, the method may be perceived as artificial and even immoral.[146]

4. The compensation model

Given the uncertainty and the difficulty associated with determining the value of human capital, Lev and Schwartz suggest the use of an individual employee's future compensation as a surrogate of his or her value. Accordingly, the "value of human capital embodied in a person of age T is the present value of his or her remaining future earnings from employment".[147] This valuation model is expressed:

$$V\tau = \sum_{t=\tau}^{T} \frac{I(t)}{(1+r)^{t-r}}$$

where

$V\tau$ = the human-capital value of an individual t years.
$I(t)$ = the individual's annual earnings up to retirement.
τ = a discount rate specific to the individual.
T = retirement age.

Because $V\tau$ is an ex-post value, given that $I(t)$ is obtained only after retirement and $V\tau$ ignores the possibility of death before retirement age, Lev and Schwartz have refined the valuation model as follows:

$$E(V^*_T) = \sum_{t=\tau}^{T} P\tau(t+1) \sum_{t=\tau}^{T} \frac{I^*_1}{(1+r)^{t-\tau}}$$

where

I^* = future annual earnings.
$E(V^*_T)$ = the expected value of an individual's human capital.
$P\tau(t)$ = the probability of an individual dying at age t.

The principal limitation of the compensation model is the subjectivity associated with the determination of the level of future salary, the length of expected employment within the firm and the discount rate.

5. The adjusted discounted-future-wages method

Hermanson proposes using an adjusted compensation value to approximate the value of an individual to a firm.[148] Discounted future wages are adjusted by an *efficiency factor* intended to measure the relative effectiveness of the human capital of a given firm. This efficiency factor, which is a ratio of the return on investment of the given firm to all other firms in the economy for a given period, is computed

$$\text{Efficiency Ratio} = \frac{\dfrac{5RF_0 + 4RF_1 + 3RF_2 + 2RF_3 + RF_4}{RE_0 + RE_1 + RE_2 + RE_3 + RE_4}}{15}$$

where

RF_i = the rate of accounting income on owned assets for the firm for the year i.
RE_i = the rate of accounting income on owned assets for all firms in the economy for the year i.
i = years (0 to 4).

The justification of this ratio rests on the thesis that differences in profitability are primarily due to differences in human-asset performance. Thus, it is necessary to adjust the compensation value by the efficiency factor.

6. Nonmonetary measures

Many nonmonetary measures of human assets may be used, such as a simple inventory of the skills and capabilities of individuals, the assignment of ratings or rankings to individual performances and the measurement of attitudes. The most frequently used nonmonetary measure of human value is derived from the Likert-Bowers model of the variables that determine "the effectiveness of a firm's human organization". A questionnaire based on the theoretical model called "survey of organizations" is designed to measure the "organizational climate".[149] The results of such a questionnaire may serve as a nonmonetary measure of human assets in terms of employee perceptions of the working atmosphere in the firm.

8.5 Conclusion

This chapter examines the nature and consequences of the concepts of fairness as fairness in presentation, fairness in distribution and fairness in disclosure to motivate the urgent calls for expanded disclosures and accounting innovations. Then innovations that may be viewed as future trends in accounting include

1. value added reporting,
2. employee reporting,
3. social accounting and reporting,
4. budgetary information disclosures,
5. cash-flow accounting and reporting, and
6. human-resource accounting.

Notes

1. Scott, D.R., "The Basis of Accounting Principles", *The Accounting Review* (December, 1941), p. 341.

2. Arthur Andersen & Co., *The Postulate of Accounting* (New York, 1960), p. 31.

3. Patillo, James W., *The Foundation of Financial Accounting* (Baton Rouge, LA: Louisiana State University Press, 1965), pp. 60–1.

4. Ibid.

5. Devine, C.T., "Research Methodology and Accounting Theory Formation", *The Accounting Review* (July, 1960), pp. 387–99.

6. Devine, Carl T., "The Rules of Conservatism Reexamined", *Journal of Accounting Research* (Autumn, 1963), pp. 129–30.

7. Chatfield, Michael, *A History of Accounting Thought* (Hinsdale, NJ: The Dryden Press, 1974), p. 275.

8. Skinner, R.M., *Accounting Principles: A Canadian Viewpoint* (Toronto: The Canadian Institute of Chartered Accountants, 1972), p. 33.

9. Lee, T.A., *Company Financial Reporting: Issues and Analysis* (London: Nelson, 1976), p. 61.

10. Flegm, E.H., *Accounting: How to Meet the Challenges of Relevance and Regulation* (New York: John Wiley & Sons, 1984), p. 47.

11. Leach, R., "The Birth of British Accounting Standards", in R. Leach and E. Stamp (eds.), *British Accounting Standards: The First Ten Years* (Cambridge: Woodhead-Faulkener, 1981), p. 7.

12. Chastney, J.G., *True and Fair View: History, Meaning and the Impact of the Fourth Directive,* Institute of Chartered Accountants in England and Wales Research Committee Occasional Paper No. 6 (London: Institute of Chartered Accountants in England and Wales, 1975).

13. Carpenter, David, "Some Approaches to a 'True and Fair View': A Review", *Irish Accounting Review* (Spring, 1944), pp. 49–64.

14. Rutherford, B.A., "True and Fair View Doctrine: A Search for Explication", *Journal of Business Finance Accounting* (Winter, 1985), pp. 483–94.

15. Walton, P.J., "True and Fair View in British Accounting", *European Accounting Review* (2, 1, 1993), p. 49.

16. Lee, T.A., *Modern Financial Accounting*, 3rd edn (Walton-on-Thames, Surrey: Nelson, 1981), p. 270.

17. Lee, T.A., *Company Auditing*, 2nd edn (Wokingham, Berkshire: Van Nostrand Reinhold for the Institute of Chartered Accountants of Scotland, 1981), p. 50.

18. European Community Commission, *Fourth Directive* (ECC: Brussels, 1978).

19. Alexander, David, "European True and Fair View?" *European Accounting Review* (2, 1, 1993), pp. 59–80.

20. Boys, P.G., and Rutherford, B.A., "The Most Universal Quality: Some Nineteenth Century Audit Reports", *Accounting History* (September, 1982), p. 13.

21. Nobes, C.W., and Parker, R.H., "'True and Fair': A Survey of UK Financial Directors", *Journal of Business Finance and Accounting* (April, 1981), pp. 359–76.

22. Houghton, K.A., "True and Fair View: An Empirical Study of Connotative Meaning", *Accounting, Organizations and Society* (12, 2, 1987), pp. 143–52.

23. Nobes, C.W., and Parker, R.H., "'True and Fair': UK Auditors' Views", op. cit., pp. 349–62.

24. Ibid.

25. Williams, Paul F., "The Legitimate Concern with Fairness", *Accounting, Organizations and Society* (12, 1987), pp. 169–92.

26. Ibid., p. 185.

27. Pallot, June, "The Legitimate Concern with Fairness: A Comment", *Accounting, Organizations, and Society* (16, 1991), pp. 201–8.

28. Pallot, June, "The Nature of Public Assets: A Response to Rawls", *Accounting Horizons* (June, 1990), pp. 79–85.

29. Chen, R., "Social and Financial Stewardship", *The Accounting Review* (July, 1975), pp. 533–4.

30. Pallot, "The Legitimate Concern with Fairness", p. 206.

31. Scott, D.R., "The Basic Accounting Principles", *The Accounting Review* (December, 1941), p. 248.

32. Belkaoui, Ahmed, *Socio-Economic Accounting* (Westport, CT: Greenwood Press, 1973).

33. Schreuder, H., and Ramanathan, K.V., "Accounting and Corporative Accountability: An Extended Comment", *Accounting, Organizations and Society* (Fall, 1984), p. 407.

34. Cooper, D.J., and Sherer, M.J., "The Value of Corporate Accounting Reports: Arguments for a Political Economy of Accounting", *Accounting, Organizations, and Society* (Fall, 1984), pp. 207–32.

35. Jensen, N.C., and Meckling, W.H., "Theory of the Firm: Managerial and Ownership Structure", *Journal of Financial Economics* (October, 1976), pp. 305–62.

36. Watts, A.L., and Zimmerman, J.L., "Towards a Positive Theory of the Determination of Accounting Standards", *The Accounting Review* (January, 1978), pp. 112–34.

37. Rawls, J.A., *A Theory of Justice* (Cambridge, MA: Harvard University Press, 1971).

38. Ibid., p. 67.

39. Ibid., pp. 62–3.

40. Ibid., p. 250.

41. Ibid., p. 83.

42. Ibid., p. 64.

43. Barry, Brian, *The Liberal Theory of Justice* (Oxford: Oxford University Press, 1973).

44. Phillips, Derek L., *Toward a Just Social Order* (Princeton, NJ: Princeton University Press, 1986), p. 354.

45. Gerwith, A., *Reason and Morality* (Chicago: University of Chicago Press, 1978), p. 313.

46. Williams, Paul F., "The Legitimate Concern with Fairness", op. cit., p. 184.

47. Nozick, R., *Anarchy, State, and Utopia* (New York: Basic Books, 1974).

48. Ibid., p. 156.

49. Ibid., pp. 159–60.

50. Ibid., p. 160.

51. Ibid., pp. 149–50.

52. Phillips, Derek L., *Toward a Just Social Order*, op. cit., p. 348.

53. Williams, Paul F., *The Legitimate Concern with Fairness*, op. cit., p. 184.

54. Ibid., p. 181.

55. Gerwith, A., *Reason and Morality*, op. cit.

56. Ibid., p. 48.

57. Ibid., p. 153.

58. Ibid., pp. 313–14.

59. Ibid., pp. 137–48.

60. Ibid., p. 150.

61. Bedford, N.M., *Extensions in Accounting Disclosure* (Englewood Cliffs, NJ: Prentice-Hall, 1973).

62. Ibid., p. 19.

63. Ibid., p. 40.

64. Ibid., p. 23.

65. Ibid., p. 144.

66. Lev, Baruch, "Toward a Theory of Equitable and Efficient Accounting Policy", *The Accounting Review* (January, 1988), pp. 1–22.

67. Ibid., p. 13.

68. Friedman, D., "Many; Few; One: Social Harmony and the Shrunken Choice Set", *American Economic Review* (March, 1980), p. 231.

69. Gaa, James C., "User Primacy in Corporate Financial Reporting: A Social Contract Approach", *The Accounting Review* (July, 1986), p. 435.

70. American Accounting Association, *Report of the Committee on the Social Consequences of Accounting Information* (Sarasota, FL: AAA, 1977), p. 248.

71. American Institute of Certified Public Accountants, *Objectives of Financial Statements* (New York: AICPA, 1973), p. 17.

72. Financial Accounting Standards Board, Statement of Financial Accounting Concepts No. 1: *Objectives of Financial Reporting of Business Enterprises* (Stamford, CT: FASB, 1978), vii.

73. Gaa, James C., "User Primacy in Corporate Financial Reporting", op. cit., p. 435.

74. AICPA, Special Committee on Financial Reporting, *Improving Business Reporting – A Customer Focus* (New York: AICPA, 1994), p. 9.

75. Wallman, Steven M., "The Future of Accounting and Disclosure in an Evolving World: The Need for Dramatic Change", *Accounting Horizons* (September, 1999), p. 84.

76. "SEC Commissioner Proposes Multilayered Reporting Model", *Journal of Accounting* (May, 1996), pp. 14–15.

77. Financial Accounting Standards Board Concepts Statement No. 5, *Recognition and Measurement in Financial Statements of Business Enterprises* (Stamford, CT: FASB), paragraph 9.

78. Ibid., paragraph 9.

79. Johnson, L. Todd, "Research on Disclosure", *Accounting Horizons* (March, 1992), p. 102.

80. Barth, Mary E., and Murphy, C.M., "Required Financial Statement Disclosures: Purposes, Subject, Number and Trends", *Accounting Horizons* (December, 1994), p. 4.

81. Ibid., p. 1.

82. Riahi-Belkaoui, Ahmed, "Earnings-Returns Relation Versus Net Value Added-Returns Relation: The Case for Nonlinear Specification," *Advances in Quantitative Analysis of Finance and Accounting* (Forthcoming); Riahi-Belkaoui, Ahmed, and Fekrat, Ali, "The Magic in Value Added: Merits of Derived Accounting Indicator Numbers", *Managerial Finance* (20, 9, 1994), pp. 16–26; Riahi-Belkaoui, Ahmed, and Picur, Ronald D., "Explaining Market Relations Earnings Versus Value Added Data", *Managerial Finance* (20, 9, 1994), pp. 44–55; Riahi-Belkaoui, Ahmed, "The Information Content of Value-Added, Earnings and Cash Flows: US Evidence", *The International Journal of Accounting* (28, 1, 1993), pp. 140–6.

83. Accounting Standards Steering Committee, *The Corporate Report* (London Accounting Standards Steering Committee, 1975), p. 200.

84. Ibid.

85. Ibid., pp. 88–91.

86. Stamp, Edward, *Corporate Reporting: Its Future Evolution* (Toronto: Canadian Institute of Chartered Accountants, 1980).

87. Taylor, Dennis, Webb, Laurie, and McGinley, Les, "Annual Reports to Employees: The Challenge to the Corporate Accountant", *Chartered Accountant in Australia* (May, 1979), p. 33.

88. Lewis, N.R., Parker, L.D., and Sutcliffe, E., "Financial Reporting to Employees: The Pattern of Development 1919 to 1979", *Accounting, Organizations and Society* (June, 1984), p. 278.

89. Ibid., p. 281.

90. Ibid.

91. Taylor, Webb, and McGinley, "Annual Reports to Employees: The Challenge to the Corporate Accountant", op. cit., p. 55.

92. Ibid., p. 36.

93. Foley, B.I., and Maunders, K.T., *Accounting Information Disclosure and Collective Bargaining* (London: Macmillan, 1977), pp. 27–34.

94. See Belkaoui, Ahmed, *A Socio-Economic Accounting* (Westport, CT: Quorum Books, 1984).

95. Mathews, M.R., "A Suggested Classification for Social Accounting Research", *Journal of Accounting and Public Policy* (3, 1984), pp. 199–222.

96. Ramanathan, K.V., "Toward a Theory of Corporate Social Accounting", *The Accounting Review* (July, 1976), p. 518.

97. Gray, R., Owen, D., and Maunders, K., "Corporate Social Reporting: Emerging Trends in Accountability and the Social Contract", *Accounting, Auditing and Accountability* (1, 1, 1988), p. 8.

98. Ibid., p. 5.

99. Ibid., p. 13.

100. See Henriques, D.B., "Tracking Environmental Risk", *New York Times* (April 28, 1991), p. 13.

101. Rawls, I.A., *A Theory of Justice* (Cambridge, MA: Harvard University Press, 1971).

102. Nozick, R., *Anarchy, State, and Utopia* (New York: Basic Books, 1974).

103. Gerwith, A., *Reason and Morality* (Chicago: University of Chicago Press, 1978).

104. Epstein, Marc, "What Shareholders Really Want", *New York Times* (April 28, 1991), p. 13.

105. Ibid.

106. "Pollution Price Tag: 71 Billion Dollars", *US News and World Report* (August 17, 1970), p. 41.

107. American Accounting Association, "Report of the Committee on External Reporting", *The Accounting Review* (44, supplement, 1969), p. 41.

108. American Accounting Association, "Report of the Committee on Environmental Effects of Organization Behavior", *The Accounting Review* (44, supplement, 1969), p. 88.

109. Rockness, J., and Williams, P.E., "A Descriptive Study of Social Responsibility Mutual Funds", *Accounting, Organizations, and Society* (1988), pp. 397–411.

110. Bruyn, S.T, *The Field of Social Investment* (Cambridge: Cambridge University Press, 1987), p. 12.

111. *Objectives of Financial Statements*, Report of the Study Group on the Objectives of Financial Statements (New York: AICPA, 1973), p. 13.

112. *The City Code on Takeovers and Mergers* (Great Britain), revised February, 1972.

113. Ibid., Rule 16.

114. Ijiri, Yuji, "Improving Reliability of Publicly Reported Corporate Financial Forecasts", in P. Prakash and A. Rappaport (eds.), *Public Reporting of Corporate Financial Forecasts*, (Chicago, IL: Commerce Clearing House, 1974), p. 169.

115. Sycamore, R.J., "Public: Disclosure of Earnings Forecasts by Companies", *The Chartered Accountant Magazine* (May, 1974), pp. 72–5.

116. Daily, R.A., "The Feasibility of Reporting Forecasted Information", *The Accounting Review* (October, 1971), pp. 686–92.

117. McDonald, Daniel L., "An Empirical Examination of the Reliability of Published Predictions of Future Earnings", *The Accounting Review* (July, 1973), pp. 502–59.

118. Ijiri, Yuji, "Improving Reliability of Publicly Reported Corporate Financial Forecasts", op. cit., p. 163.

119. Mautz, Robert K., "A View from the Public Accounting Profession", in E. Prakash and A. Rappaport (eds.), *Public Reporting of Corporate Financial Forecasts*, p. 102.

120. Ibid., p. 110.

121. Gross, M., *Financial and Accounting Guide for Nonprofit Organizations* (New York: The Ronald Press, 1972).

122. Hicks, B.E., *The Cash-Flow Basis of Accounting*, Working Paper No. 13 (Sudbury, Ontario: Laurentian University, 1980).

123. Hawkins, D., and Campbell, W., *Equity Valuation: Models, Analysis, and Implications* (New York: Financial Executives Institute, 1978).

124. Thomas, A.L., *The Allocation Problem in Financial Accounting Theory*, Accounting Research Study No. 3 (Sarasota, FL: American Accounting Association, 1969); *The Allocation Problem: Part Two*, Accounting Research Study No. 9 (Sarasota, FL: American Accounting Association, 1974).

125. Hawkins, D., and Campbell, W., *Equity Valuation: Models, Analysis and Implications*, op. cit., p. 5.

126. Staubus, G.I., *A Theory of Accounting to Investors* (Berkeley, CA: University of California Press, 1961).

127. Revsine, L., *Replacement-Cost Accounting* (Englewood Cliffs, NJ: Prentice-Hall, 1973).

128. Lee, T.A., "Reporting Cash Flows and Net Realizable Values", *Accounting and Business Research* (Spring, 1981), pp. 163–70.

129. Lawson, G.H., "Cash-Flow Accounting I & II", *The Accountant* (October 28– November 4, 1971), pp. 586–9.

130. Lee, T.A., "A Case for Cash-Flow Accounting", *Journal of Business Finance* (Issue 3, 1972), pp. 27–36.

131. Ashton, R.H., "Cash-Flow Accounting: A Review and a Critique", *Journal of Business Finance and Accounting and Reporting* (Winter, 1976), pp. 63–81.

132. Lee, T.A., "Cash-Flow Accounting and Reporting", in T.A. Lee (ed.), *Developments in Financial Reporting* (Oxford: Philip Allan, 1981), pp. 148–70.

133. Govindarajan, V., "The Objectives of Financial Statements: An Empirical Study of the Use of Cash Flow and Earnings by Security Analysis", *Accounting, Organizations and Society* (December, 1980), p. 392.

134. "Report of the Committee on Human-Resource Accounting", *Committee Report*, supplement to Vol. 48, *The Accounting Review* (1973), p. 169.

135. Woodruff, R.L., "Human-Resource Accounting", *The Canadian Chartered Accountant Magazine* (September, 1970), p. 27; Alexander, M.O., "Investments in People", *The Canadian Chartered Accountant Magazine* (July, 1971), pp. 38–45; Flamholtz, E., "Human-Resource Accounting: Measuring Positional Replacement Costs", *Human Resource Management* (Spring, 1973), pp. 8–16.

136. Elias, M.S., "The Effects of Human-Asset Statements on the Investment Decision: An Experiment", Empirical Research in Accounting: Selected Studies, supplement to Vol. 10, *Journal of Accounting Research* (1972), pp. 215–40.

137. Woodruff, R.L., "Human-Resource Accounting", op. cit., p. 2.

138. Flamholtz, E., "Toward a Theory of Human-Resource Value in Formal Organizations", *The Accounting Review* (October, 1972), pp. 666–78; Likert, R., and Bowers, D.G., "Improving the Accuracy of P/L Reports by Estimating the Change in Dollar Value of the Human Organization", *Michigan Business Review* (March, 1973), pp. 15–24.

139. Likert, R., and Bowers, D.G., "Improving the Accuracy of P/L Reports by Estimating the Change in Dollar Value of the Human Organization", op. cit., p. 15.

140. Ibid., p. 17.

141. Glautier, N.W.E., and Underdown, B., "Problems and Prospects of Accounting for Human Assets", *Management Accounting* (March, 1973), p. 99.

142. Flamholtz, E., *Human-Resource Accounting* (Los Angeles, CA: Dickenson Publishing, 1974), p. 190.

143. Hekimian, J.S., and Jones, J.G., "Put People on Your Balance Sheet", *Harvard Business Review* (January/February, 1967), p. 108.

144. Likert, R., and Bowers, D.G., "Organizational Theory and Human-Resource Accounting", *American Psychologist* (24, 6, September, 1969), p. 588.

145. Hekimian, J.S., and Jones, J.G., "Put People on Your Balance Sheet", op. cit., pp. 108–9.

146. Elovitz, D., "From the Thoughtful Businessman", *Harvard Business Review* (May/ June, 1967), p. 59.

147. Lev, B., and Schwartz, A., "On the Use of the Economic Concept of Human Capital in Financial Statements", *The Accounting Review* (January, 1971), p. 105.

148. Hermanson, R.H., "Accounting for Human Assets", Occasional Paper No. 14 (East Lansing, MI: Bureau of Business and Economic Research, Graduate School of Business Administration, Michigan State University, 1964).

149. Taylor, J.C., and Bowers, D.G., *The Survey of Organizations* (Ann Arbor, MI: Institute for Social Research, 1972).

References

Fairness in accounting

Alexander, David, "A European True and Fair View?" *European Accounting Review* (2, 1, 1993), pp. 59–80.

Carpenter, David, "Some Approaches to a 'True and Fair View': A Review", *Irish Accounting Review* (Spring, 1994), pp. 15–64.

Monti-Belkaoui, Janice, and Riahi-Belkaoui, Ahmed, *Fairness in Accounting* (Westport, CT: Greenwood Publishing, 1996).

Nobes, C.W., and Parker, R.H., "'True and Fair': A Survey of UK Financial Directors", *Journal of Business Finance and Accounting* (April, 1981), pp. 359–76.

Ordelheide, D., "True and Fair View: A European and German Perspective", *European Accounting Review* (2, 1, 1993), pp. 81–90.

Parker, R.H., and Nobes, C.W., "'True and Fair': UK Auditors' View", *Accounting and Business Research* (Autumn, 1991), pp. 349–62.

Rutherford, B.A., "The True and Fair View Doctrine: A Search for Explanation", *Journal of Business Finance and Accounting* (Winter, 1985), pp. 483–94.

Van Hulle, K., "Truth and Untruth about True and Fair", *European Accounting Review* (2, 1, 1993), pp. 99–104.

Walton, P.J., "The True and Fair View in British Accounting", *European Accounting Review* (2, 1, 1993), p. 49.

William, Paul F., "The Legitimate Concern with Fairness", *Accounting, Organizations and Society* (March, 1987), pp. 165–89.

Calls for expanded disclosures

American Institute of Certified Public Accountants, Special Committee on Financial Reporting, *Improving Business Reporting – A Customer Focus* (New York: AICPA, 1994).

Barth, Mary E., and Murphy, Christine M., "Required Financial Statement Disclosures: Purposes, Subject, Number and Trends", *Accounting Horizons* (December, 1994), pp. 1–22.

Bedford, N.M., *Extensions in Accounting Disclosures* (Englewood Cliffs, NJ: Prentice-Hall, 1973).

Elliott, Robert K., and Jacobson, Peter D., "Costs and Benefits of Business Information Disclosure", *Accounting Horizons* (December, 1994), pp. 80–96.

Gaa, James, "User Primacy in Corporate Financial Reporting: A Social Contract Approach", *The Accounting Review* (July, 1986), pp. 455–6.

Johnson., L. Todd, "Research on Disclosure", *Accounting Horizons* (March, 1992), pp. 101–5.

Lev, Baruch, "Toward a Theory of Equitable and Efficient Accounting Policy", *The Accounting Review* (January, 1988), pp. 1–22.

Value added reporting

American Accounting Association, Committee on Accounting and Auditing Measurement. 1989–90, *Accounting Horizons* (September, 1991), pp. 81–105.

Accounting Standards Steering Committee, *The Corporate Report* (London: Accounting Standards Steering Committee, 1975).

Askren, Barbara J., Bannister, J.W., and Pavlik, E., "The Impact of Performance Plan Adoption on Value Added and Earnings", *Managerial Finance* (20, 9, 1994), pp. 27–43.

Bannister, James W., and Riahi-Belkaoui, Ahmed, "Value Added and Corporate Control in the US", *Journal of International Financial Management and Accounting* (Autumn, 1991), pp. 241–57.

Bao, Ben-Hsien, and Bao, Da-Hsien, "An Empirical Investigation of the Association: Between Productivity and Firm Value", *Journal of Business Finance and Accounting* (Winter, 1989), pp. 699–718.

Bao, Ben-Hsien, and Bao, Da-Hsien, "The Time Series Behavior and Predictive Ability Results of Value Added Data", *Journal of Business Finance and Accounting* (April, 1996), pp. 449–60.

Burchell, Stuart, Clubb, Colin, and Hopwood, Anthony, "Accounting and its Social Context: Towards a History of Value Added in the United Kingdom", *Accounting, Organizations and Society* (10, 1985), pp. 381–413.

Cox, Bernard, *Value Added: An Application for the Accountant Concerned with Industry* (London: Heinemann, 1978).

Cruns, R.P., "Added-Value: The Roots Run Deep Into Colonial and Early America", *Accounting Historian Journal* (Fall, 1982), pp. 25–42.

Deegan, C., and Hallinan, A., "The Voluntary Presentation of Value Added Statements in Australia: A Political Cost Perspective", *Accounting and Finance* (May, 1991), pp. 1–29.

Gilchrist, R.R., *Managing for Profit: The Value Added Concept* (London: Allen and Unwin, 1971).

Gray, Sidney, and Maunders, K.T, "Recent Developments in Value Added Disclosures", *Certified Accountant* (August, 1979), pp. 255–6.

Gray, Sidney, *Value Added Reporting: Uses and Measurement* (London: Association of Certified Accountants, 1980).

Haller, A., *Wersehopfungsrechnung. Ein Instrument Steigerung der Aussagefahigkeit von Unternehmensabschlussen im Internationalen Kontext* (Stuttgart: SchatYer-Poeschel Verlag, 1997).

Harris, G.J., "Value Added Statements", *The Australian Accountant* (May, 1982), pp. 261–4.

Litzenberger, R.H., and Rao, C.W., "Estimates of the Marginal Rate of Time Preference and Average Risk Aversion of Investors in Electric Utility Shares: 1960–66", *Bell Journal of Economies and Management Science* (Spring, 1976), pp. 265–77.

McLeay, Stuart, "Value Added: A Comparative Study", *Accounting, Organizations and Society* (8, 1, 1984) pp. 31–56.

McSweeney, Brendan, "Irish Answer to Value Added Reports", in Frederick K. Choi and Gerhard G. Mueller (eds.), *Frontiers of International Accounting: An Anthology* (Ann Arbor, MI: UMI Research Press, 1985), pp. 225–45.

Meek, Gary K., and Gray, Sidney J., "The Value Added Statement: An Innovation for the US Companies", *Accounting Horizons* (June, 1988), pp. 73–81.

Morley, M.Y., "The Value Added Statement: A British Innovation", *The Chartered Accountant Magazine* (May, 1978), pp. 31–4.

Morley, M.F., "The Value Added Statement in Britain", *The Accounting Review* (May, 1979), pp. 618–89.

Morley, Michael F., "Value Added Reporting", in T.A. Lee (ed.), *Developments on Financial Reporting* (London: Philip Allan, 1981), pp. 251–69.

Morley, Michael E., *The Value Added Statement* (London: Gee and Co. for the Institute of Chartered Accountants of Scotland, 1978).

Pendrill, David, "Introducing a Newcomer: The Value Added Statement", *Accountancy* (September, 1981), pp. 121–2.

Rahman, M. Zubaidur, "The Local Value Added Statement: A Reporting Requirement for Multinationals in Developing Host Countries", *International Journal of Accounting* (February 2, 1990), pp. 87–98.

Renshall, M., Allan, R., and Nicholson, K., *Added Value in External Financial Reporting* (London: Institute of Chartered Accountants in England and Wales, 1979).

Riahi-Belkaoui, Ahmed, *Handbook of Management Control Systems* (Westport, CT: Greenwood Publishing, 1986).

Riahi-Belkaoui, Ahmed, *Value Added Reporting: The Lessons for US* (Westport, CT: Greenwood Publishing, 1992).

Riahi-Belkaoui, Ahmed, "The Information Content of Value Added. Earnings and Cash Flows: US Evidence", *The International Journal of Accounting* (28 & 2, 1993), pp. 140–6.

Riahi-Belkaoui, Ahmed, *Performance Results of Value Added Reporting* (Westport, CT: Greenwood Publishing, 1996).

Riahi-Belkaoui, Ahmed, "Earnings-Return versus Net Value-Added Returns Relation: The Case for Nonlinear Specification", *Advances in Quantitative Analysis in Finance and Accounting* (4, 1996), pp. 175–85.

Riahi-Belkaoui, Ahmed, "Multidivisional Structure and Productivity: The Contingency of Diversification Strategy", *Journal of Business Finance and Accounting* (June, 1997), pp. 201–214.

Riahi-Belkaoui, Ahmed, "Performance Plan Adoption and Performance: The Contingency of Ownership Structure", *Managerial Finance* (23, 5, 1997), pp. 18–27.

Riahi-Belkaoui, Ahmed, "An Empirical Case for Value Added Reporting in the United States", *Indian Journal of Accounting* (Forthcoming).

Riahi-Belkaoui, Ahmed, and Bannister, J.W., "Multidivisional Structure and Capital Structure: The Contingency of Diversification Strategy", *Managerial Decision Economics* (15, 1994), pp. 267–76.

Riahi-Belkaoui, Ahmed, and Fekrat, Ali, "The Magic in Value Added: Merits of Derived Accounting Indicator Numbers", *Managerial Finance* (20, 9, 1994), pp. 3–15.

Riahi-Belkaoui, Ahmed, and Pavlik, Ellen, "Asset Management Performance and Reputation Building for Large US Firms", *British Journal of Management* (2, 1991), pp. 231–8.

Riahi-Belkaoui, Ahmed, and Pavlik, Ellen, "The Effect of Ownership Structure on Value Added Performance", *Managerial Finance* (20, 9, 1994), pp. 16–26.

Riahi-Belkaoui, Ahmed, and Picur, Ronald D., "Explaining Market Returns: Earnings versus Value Added Data", *Managerial Finance* (20, 9, 1994), pp. 44–55.

Rutherford, B.A., "Value Added as a Focus of Attention for Financial Reporting: Some Conceptual Problems", *Accounting and Business Research* (Summer, 1972), pp. 215–20.

Rutherford, B.A., "Easing the CCA Transition in Value Added Statements", *Accountancy* (May, 1983), pp. 121–2.

Rutherford, B.A., "Five Fallacies About Value Added", *Management Accountant* (September, 1981), pp. 31–3.

Rutherford, B.A., "Published Statements of Value Added: A Survey of Three Years' Experience", *Accounting and Business Review* (Winter, 1980), pp. 15–28.

Rutherford, B.A., "Value Added as a Focus of Attention for Financial Reporting: Some Conceptual Problems", *Accounting and Business Research* (Summer, 1972), pp. 215–20.

Sinha, Gokul, *Value Added Income* (Calcutta: Book World, 1983).

Human resource accounting

Acland, D., "The Effects of Behavioral Indicators on Investor Decisions: An Exploratory Study", *Accounting, Organizations and Society* (I, 8, 1976), pp. 133–42.

Alexander, M.O., "An Accountant's View of the Human Resource", *The Personnel Administrator* (November–December, 1971), pp. 9–15.

American Accounting Association, *Report of the Committee on Accounting for Human Resources Committee Reports*, Supplement to *The Accounting Review* (48, 1975), pp. 169–85.

American Accounting Association, *Report of the Committee on Accounting for Human Resource. Committee* Reports, Supplement to *The Accounting Review* (49, 1974), pp. 115–26.

Ansari, S.L., and Flamholtz, D.T., "Management Science and the Development of Human Resource Accounting", *The Accounting Historian's Journal* (Fall, 1978), pp. 11–55.

Becker, S., *Human Capital* (New York: National Bureau of Economic Research, 1962).

Biagioni, L.F., and Ogan, P., "Human Resource Accounting for Professional Sports Teams", *Management Accounting* (November, 1977), pp. 25–9.

Brummet, R.L., Flamholtz, E.G., and Pyle, W.C., "Human Resource Measurement: A Challenge for Accountants", *The Accounting Review* (April, 1968), pp. 217–24.

Cannon, J.A., "Applying the Human Resource Accounting Framework to an International Airline", *Accounting, Organizations, and Society* (I, 8, 1976), pp. 255–63.

Caplan, E.H., and Landekick, S., *Human Resource Accounting: Past, Present, and Future* (New York: National Association of Accountants, 1974).

Carper, W.B., and Posey, M., "The Validity of Selected Surrogate Measures of Human Resource Value: A Field Study", *Accounting, Organizations and Society* (I, 8, 1976), pp. 145–52.

Conger, Jay A., and Kanungo, Rabindra N., "The Empowerment Process: Integrating Theory and Practice", *Academy of Management Review* (15, 1988), pp. 471–82.

Dermer, J., and Siegel, J.E, "The Role of Behavioral Measures in Accounting for Human Resources", *The Accounting Review* (January, 1974), pp. 88–97.

Dittman, D.A., Juris, H.A., and Revsine, L., "On the Existence of Unrecorded Human Assets: An Economic Perspective", *Journal of Accounting Research* (Spring, 1976), pp. 49–65.

Dittman, D.A., Juris, H.A., and Revsine, L., "Unrecorded Human Assets: A Survey of Accounting Firms' Training Programs", *The Accounting Review* (April, 1980), pp. 640–8.

Elias, N., "The Effects of Human Assets Statements on the Investment Decision: An Experiment", *Empirical Research in Accounting: Selected Studies* (1972), pp. 215–55.

Elliott, Robert K., "The Third Wave Breaks on the Shores of Accounting", *Accounting Horizons* (December, 1991), pp. 61–131.

Flamholtz, E., "The Theory and Measurement of an Individual's Value to an Organization", Ph.D. dissertation, University of Michigan, 1969.

Flamholtz, E., "A Model for Human Resource Valuation: A Stochastic Process with Service Rewards", *The Accounting Review* (April, 1971), pp. 255–67.

Flamholtz, E., "Assessing the Validity of a Theory of Human Resource Value: A Field Study", *Empirical Research in Accounting: Selected Studies* (1972), pp. 241–66.

Flamholtz, E., *Human Resource Accounting* (Encino, CA: Dickenson, 1974).

Flamholtz, E., "Human Resource Accounting: Measuring Potential Replacement Costs", *Human Resource Management* (Spring, 1975), pp. 8–16.

Flamholtz, E., "The Impact of Human Resource Valuation on Management Decisions: A Laboratory Experiment", *Accounting, Organizations, and Society* (I, 8, 1976), pp. 155–65.

Flamholtz, E., "Towards a Psycho-technical Systems Paradigm of Organizational Measurement", *Decision Sciences* (January, 1979), pp. 71–84.

Flamholtz, E., "The Process of Measurement in Managerial Accounting: A Psycho-technical Systems Perspective", *Accounting, Organizations and Society* (5, 8, 1980), pp. 31–42.

Flamholtz, E., *Human Resource Accounting* (San Francisco: Jossey-Bass, 1985).

Flamholtz, E., "Valuation of Human Assets in a Securities Brokerage Firm; An Empirical Study", *Accounting, Organizations and Society* (12, 7, 1987), pp. 509–18.

Flamholtz, E., and Coff, R., "Valuing Human Resources in Buying Service Companies", *Mergers and Acquisitions* (January–February, 1989), pp. 40–4.

Flamholtz, E., and Geis, G., "The Development and Implementation of a Replacement Cost Model for Measuring Human Capital: A Field Study", *Personnel Review* (UK) (15, 2, 1984), pp. 25–55.

Flamholtz, E., Geis, G., and Perle, R.J., "A Markovian Model for the Valuation of Human Assets Acquired by an Organizational Purchase", *Interfaces* (November–December, 1984), pp. 11–15.

Flamholtz, E., and Kaumeyer, R.A., Jr., "Human Resource Replacement Cost Information and Personnel Decisions: A Field Study", *Human Resource Planning* (Fall, 1980), pp. 111–38.

Flamholtz, E., and Lundy, T., "Human Resource Accounting for CPA Firms", *CPA Journal* (45, October, 1975), pp. 45–51.

Flamholtz, E., Bell, Oliver, J., and Teague, R., "Subjective Information Valuation and Decision-Making", Paper presented at the American Accounting Association Annual Meeting, Atlanta, Georgia, 1976.

Flamholtz, E., and Searfoss, D.G., "Developing an Integrated System", in *Human Resource Accounting* (San Francisco: Jossey-Bass, 1985), pp. 346–355.

Flamholtz, E., and Wollman, J.B., "The Development and Implementation of the Stochastic Rewards Model for Human Resource Valuation in a Human Capital Intensive Firm", Paper presented at the XXIII International Meeting of the Institute of Management Sciences, Athens, Greece, 1977.

Frantzreb, R.B., Landau, L.L.T., and Lundberg, D.E., "The Valuation of Human Resources", *Business Horizons* (June, 1974), pp. 73–80.

Friedman, A., and Lev, B., "A Surrogate Measure for the Firm's Investment in Human Resources", *Journal of Accounting Research* (Autumn, 1974), pp. 235–50.

Gambling, T.E., "A System Dynamic Approach to HRA", *The Accounting Review* (July, 1974), pp. 538–46.

Harrell, A.M., and Klick, H.D., "Comparing the Impact of Monetary and Nonmonetary Human Asset Measures on Executive Decision-Making", *Accounting, Organizations and Society* (5, 12, 1980), pp. 393–400.

Jaggi, B., and Lau, S., "Toward a Model for Human Resource Valuation", *The Accounting Review* (April, 1974), pp. 321–9.

Lau, A.H., and Lau, H., "Some Proposed Approaches for Writing Off Capitalized Human Resource Assets", *Journal of Accounting Research* (Spring, 1978), pp. 80–102.

Ogan, P., "Application of a Human Resource Value Model: A Field Study", *Accounting, Organizations and Society* (1, 8, 1976), pp. 195–218.

Riahi-Belkaoui, Ahmed, and Monti-Belkaoui, Janice, *Human Resource Valuation* (Westport, CT: Greenwood Publishing, 1995).

Schwan, E.S., "The Effects of Human Resource Accounting Data on Financial Decisions: An Empirical Test", *Accounting, Organizations and Society* (I, 8, 1976), pp. 219–37.

Tsaklanganos, A.A., "Human Resource Accounting: The Measure of a Person", *CA Magazine* (May, 1980), pp. 44–8.

Woodruff, R.L., IT "Human Resource Accounting", *Canadian Chartered Accountant* (September, 1970), pp. 2–7.

Employee reporting

Bougen, P., and Odgen, S., "Power in Organizations: Some Implications for the Use of Accounting in Industrial Relations", *Managerial Finance* (1981), pp. 22–6.

Burchell, S., Clubb, C., Hopwood, A.G., Hughes, J., and Nahapiet, J., "The Roles of Accounting in Organizations and Society", *Accounting, Organizations and Society* (5, 1980), pp. 5–28.

Cooper, D., and Essex, S., "Accounting Information and Employee Decision Making", *Accounting, Organizations, and Society* (1977), pp. 201–17.

Craft, A., "Information Disclosure and the Role of the Accountant in Collective Bargaining", *Accounting, Organizations, and Society* (1981), pp. 97–107.

Craig, R., and Hussey, R., *Employee Reports: An Australian Study* (Sydney, Australia: Enterprise Australia, 1981).

Foley, B.J., and Maunders, K.T, *Accounting Information. Disclosure and Collective Bargaining* (London: Macmillan. 1977).

Gogarty, J.P., "What Employees Expect to be Told", *Management Accounting* (UK) (November, 1975), pp. 359–60.

Gospel, H., "The Disclosure of Information to Trade Unions: Approaches and Problems", *Industrial Relations Journal* (1978), pp. 18–26.

Granof, M.F., "Financial Evaluation of Labor Contracts", *Management Accounting* (July, 1973), p. 42.

Holmes, G., "How UK Companies Report", *Accountancy* (November, 1977), p. 66.

Hussey, R., "Developments in Employee Reporting", *Managerial Finance* (I, 1981), pp. 12–16.

Hussey, R., *Employees and the Employee Report* (London: Touche Ross, 1978).

Hussey, R., *Who Reads Employee Reports?* (Oxford: Touche Ross, 1974).

Hussey, R., and Craig, R.J., *Keeping Employees Informed* (Sydney, Australia: Butterworth, 1982).

Institute of Chartered Accountants in England and Wales, *The Reporting of Company Financial Results to Employees* (London, 1976).

Tack, H.H., "The Accountant's Role in Labor Relations", *Management Accounting* (October, 1973), p. 60.

Jackson-Cox, J., Thirkell, J.E., and McQueeney, J., "The Disclosure of Company Information to Trade Unions: The Relevance of the ACAS Code of Practice on Disclosure", *Accounting, Organizations and Society* (June, 1984), pp. 253–73.

Jenkins, C., "A Trade Unionist's Viewpoint on Financial Information Requirement", *Management Accounting* (November, 1975), p. 359.

Jones, D.M.C., "Designing Accounts to Inform More Effectively", *Management Accounting* (November, 1975), p. 359.

Lau, C.T., and Nelson, M., *Accounting Implications of Collective Bargaining* (Ontario: The Society of Management Accountants in Canada, 1981).

Lewis, N.R., Parker, L.D., and Sutcliffe, P., "Financial Reporting to Employees: The Pattern of Development 1919 to 1979", *Accounting, Organizations, and Society* (June, 1984), pp. 275–85.

Lewis, N.R., Parker, L.D., and Sutcliffe, P., "Financial Reporting to Employees; Towards a Research Framework", *Accounting and Business Research* (Summer, 1984), pp. 229–39.

Martin, R., "Providing an Employee Report", *Management Accounting* (September, 1977), pp. 341–8.

Maunders, K.T., "Employee Reporting", in Thomas A. Lee (ed.), *Development in Financial Reporting* (London: Philip Allan, 1981), pp. 171–95.

Maunders, K.T., and Foley, B.J., "Accounting Information, Employees and Collective Bargaining", *Journal of Business Finance and Accounting* (Spring, 1974), pp. 109–27.

Maunders, K.T., and Foley, B.J., "How Much Should We Tell Trade Unions?", *Accounting Age* (February 22, 1974), pp. 340–6.

Miller, J., "Financial Information for Employees", *Accounting* (May 29, 1975), p. 690.

Ogden, S., and Bougen, P., "A Radical Perspective on the Disclosure of Information to Trade Unions", *Accounting, Organizations and Society* (10, 2, 1985), pp. 211–24.

Owen, D.L., and Lloyd, A.J., "The Use of Financial Information by Trade Union Negotiators in Plant Level Collective Bargaining", *Accounting, Organizations and Society* (10, 1985), pp. 329–550.

Palmer, J.R., *The Use of Accounting Information in Labor Negotiations* (New York: National Association of Accountants, 1977).

Parker, L.D., "Financial Reporting to Corporate Employees: A Growing Practice in Australia", *Chartered Accountant in Australia* (March, 1977), pp. 5–9.

Pfeffer, J., "Power and Resource Allocation in Organizations", in B. Staw and G. Salancik (eds.), *New Directions in Organizational Behavior* (Chicago: St. Clair Press, 1977), pp. 12–52.

Social accounting

Belkaoui, A., *Socio-Economic Accounting* (Westport, CT: Quorum Books, 1984).

Belkaoui, A., and Karpik, P., "Determinants of the Corporate Decision to Disclose Social Information", *Accounting, Auditing and Accountability Journal* (2, 1989), pp. 36–11.

Boal, K.B., and Peery, N., "The Cognitive Structure of Corporate Social Responsibility", *Journal of Management* (11, 5, 1985), pp. 71–82.

Bruyn, S.T., *The Field of Social Investment* (Cambridge: Cambridge University Press, 1987).

Carroll, A.B., "A Three-Dimensional Conceptual Model of Corporate Social Performance", *Academy of Management Review* (4, 1979), pp. 479–505.

Davis, K., "The Case For and Against Business Assumptions of Social Responsibilities", *Academy of Management Journal* (16, 1975), pp. 512–22.

Post, J.E., *Corporate Behavior and Social Change* (Reston, VA: Reston Publishing, 1978).

Preston, C.E., and Post, I.E., *Private Management and Public Policy: The Principle of Public Responsibility* (Englewood Cliffs, NJ: Prentice-Hall, 1975).

Riahi-Belkaoui, Ahmed, *Corporate Social Awareness and Empirical Outcomes* (Westport, CT: Greenwood Publishing, 1999).

Public reporting of corporate financial forecasts

Abdel-Khalik, A.R., and Thompson, R., "Research on Earnings Forecasts: The State of the Art", *Accounting Journal* (Winter, 1977–8), pp. 180–217.

Abdelsamad, M.H., and Gilbreath, G.H., "Publication of Earnings Forecasts: A Report of Financial Executives Opinions", *Managerial Planning* (January–February, 1978), pp. 26–50.

American Institute of Certified Public Accountants, *Presentation and Disclosure of Financial Forecasts* (New York: AICPA, 1975).

Asebrook, R., and Carmichael, D., "Reporting on Forecasts: A Survey of Attitudes", *Journal of Accounting* (August, 1975), pp. 38–18.

Backer, A., "Reporting Profit Expectations", *Management Accounting* (February, 1972), pp. 55–7.

Barefield, R.M., and Comiskey, E., "The Accuracy of Analysts' Forecasts of Earnings Per Share", *Journal of Business Research* (July, 1975), pp. 241–52.

Barnes, A., Sadan, S., and Schiff M., "Afraid of Publishing Forecasts", *Financial Executive* (November, 1977), pp. 52–8.

Cash-flow accounting

American Accounting Association, Committee on External Reporting, "An Evaluation of External Reporting Practices", a Report of the 1966–1968 Committee on External Reporting, *The Accounting Review* (Supplement, 1969), pp. 79–125.

Ashton, R.H., "Cash-Flow Accounting: A Review and a Critique", *Journal of Business Finance and Accounting* (Winter, 1976), pp. 63–81.

Barlev, B., and Levy, H., "On the Variability of Accounting Income Numbers", *Journal of Accounting Research* (Autumn, 1979), pp. 505–15.

Belkaoui, A., "Accrual Accounting and Cash Accounting: Relative Merits of Derived Accounting Indicator Numbers", *Accounting and Business Research* (Summer, 1985), pp. 299–312.

Climo, T., "Cash-Flow Statements for Investors", *Journal of Business Finance and Accounting* (Autumn, 1976), pp. 5–16.

Research perspectives in accounting

9

9.1 Introduction

The previous chapters have covered the different perspectives/visions in accounting knowledge, research, paradigms and standard-setting. They show the richness and diversity of the approaches used in the study and research of accounting topics. This richness and diversity calls for different perspectives in the methodologies to be used and different visions in the types of researchers attracted to accounting research.

9.2 Perspectives on accounting researchers

9.2.1 Accounting knowledge acquisition

Kolb *et al.* proposed an interesting model of human learning,[1] portrayed in Exhibit 9.1. Basically we start acquiring knowledge through our concrete experiences. The uniqueness of some events, rituals or phenomena leads us to increase our observations and reflections on what is happening, teaching us, if we are sufficiently motivated, to generate hypotheses in the form of abstract concepts and generalizations. This moves us to test the hypotheses, to understand the implications of the concepts in new situations and in the process to refine our knowledge. This is exactly the process that explains accounting knowledge acquisition, moving from particular facts (observed or discovered) to particular hypotheses (construction of the mind) to general theories (other constructions of the mind) to general and observed or discovered laws.[2] This model, however, does not make a distinction between the knowledge acquisition process (method), the methodology (dictating the method), and the epistemology (dictating the methodology). The relationships between epistemology (why of why of how), methodology (why of how), method (how) and knowledge are shown in Exhibit 9.2. Notice that knowledge is of three types:[3,4,5]

1. knowledge-that or factual knowledge,[6]
2. knowledge-of or knowledge by acquaintance or knowledge by experience,[7] and
3. knowledge-how.

The Kolb *et al.* model was used by Roy Payne to illustrate its role in the knowledge acquisition process.[8] It is illustrated in Exhibit 9.3. The first stage, from experiencing to observing and reflecting, generates a "knowledge-of" or personal knowledge. The second stage, from observing and reflecting to abstract theorizing, generates a "knowledge-that". The methodology we use to move from abstract reasoning to testing and experimentation generates a "knowledge-how". The final stage, from testing and experimentation to experiencing, generates a practical "knowledge-how". It is a total process going from information, science, methodology and wisdom. Payne summarizes as follows:

> In summary, knowledge is of several types: "knowledge-how: practical" and "knowledge-of" lie within the individual. "Knowledge-that" and "knowledge-how: scientific/philosophical" are extra-individual. Since knowledge depends on individual

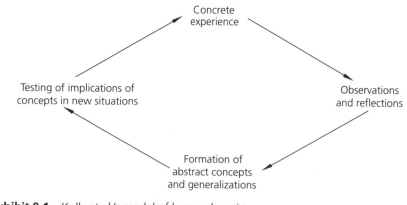

Exhibit 9.1 Kolb *et al.*'s model of human learning

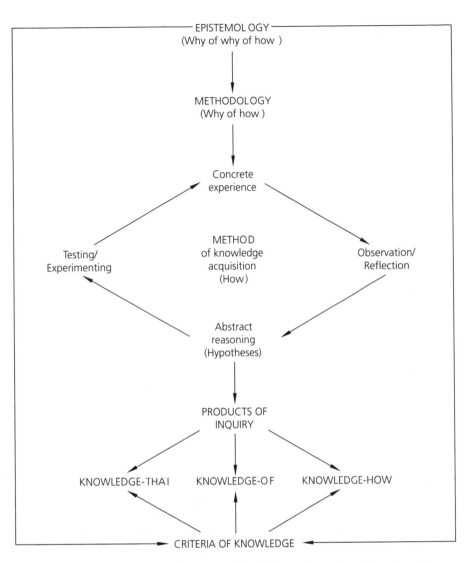

Source: Reprinted from Roy L. Payne, "The Nature of Knowledge and Organizational Psychology", in Nigel Nicholson and Toby D. Wall (eds.), *The Theory and Practice of Organizational Psychology* (1982), p. 61, by permission of the publisher Academic Press Limited, London.

Exhibit 9.2 The relationship between epistemology, methodology, methods and knowledge

learners, however, it is obvious that all types of knowledge are necessary to the successful working of the knowledge process. Furthermore, each type of knowledge has a different time-orientation reflecting its different roles in the knowledge process.[9]

9.2.2 Classification of accounting researchers

The variety of knowledge and the knowledge acquisition process lead to the need to classify scientists in general and accounting researchers in particular. Various frameworks are possible for the classification of researchers in general, including the typologies of Liam Hudson,[10] Gerald Gordon,[11] Mitroff's survey of the Apollo Scientists,[12,13] Abraham Maslow[14] and C.G. Jung.[15] It is, however, the typology of C.G. Jung that seems the most

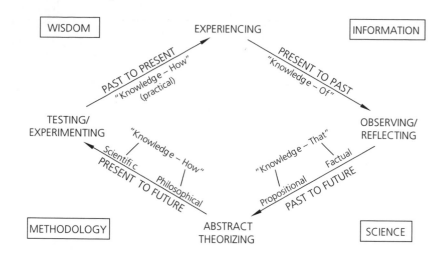

Source: Reprinted form Roy L. Payne, "The Nature of Knowledge and Organizational Psychology", in Nigel Nicholson and Toby D. Walls (eds.), *The Theory and Practice of Organizational Psychology* (1982), p. 43, by permission of the publisher Academic Press Limited, London.

Exhibit 9.3 Forms of knowledge and the learning cycle

useful in classifying scientists in general[16] and accounting researchers in particular.[17] Basically, Jung classified individuals by the way they receive information either by sensation or intuition and the way they reach decisions either by thinking or feeling. Here are the definitions of these components of the Jungian dimensions:

> Sensation involves receiving information through the senses, focusing on detail, emphasizing the here and now and the practical. Intuition, in contrast, involves input of information through the imagination, emphasizing the whole or Gestalt, dwelling in idealism, in hypothetical possibilities, and taking an interest in the long term. ... Thinking is concerned with the use of reasoning which is impersonal and formal to develop explanations in scientific, technical and theoretical terms. Feeling, on the other hand, relates to the reaching of decisions on the basis of highly valued judgments and focusing on human values, moral and ethical issues.[18]

The combination of the two dimensions, as shown in Exhibit 9.4, results in four personality types:

1. Sensing-thinking (Sts);
2. Sensing-feeling (Sfs);
3. Feeling-intuition (Ifs); and
4. Thinking-intuition (Its).

This typology was used by Mitroff and Kilman[19] to produce a classification of researchers:

- the Abstract Scientist (AS);
- the Conceptual Theorist (CT);
- the Conceptual Humanist (CH); and
- the Particular Humanist (PH).

The Abstract Scientist, a sensing-thinking person, is motivated by the conduct of inquiry along a precise methodology and logic, with a focus on certainty, accuracy and reliability,

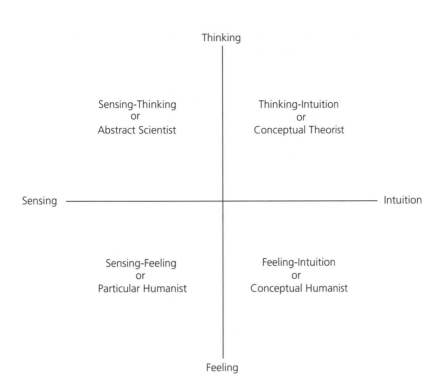

Exhibit 9.4   Jungian typology of researchers

and a reliance on a simple, well-defined consistent paradigm. As stated by Mitroff and Kilman:

> To know is to be certain about something. Certainty is defined by the ability to "phrase" or enumerate the components of an object, event, person, or situation in a precise accurate, and reliable fashion. Therefore knowledge is synonymous with precision, accuracy, and reliability. Any endeavor that cannot be subjected to this formula or line of reasoning is either suppressed, devalued, or set aside as not worth knowing or capable of being known.[20]

The Conceptual Theorist, a thinking-intuition person, attempts to generate multiple explanations or hypotheses for phenomena with a focus on discovery rather than testing. As stated by Mitroff and Kilman:

> Whereas the AS attempts to find the single schema that best represents the world, the CT is interested in exploring, creating, and inventing multiple possible and hypothetical representations of the world – even hypothetical worlds themselves. Further, the CT's emphasis is on the large-scale differences between these different representations rather than the details of any single schema. A potential danger for the AS is getting bogged down in infinite details; a potential danger for the CT is ignoring them altogether for the sake of comprehensiveness. ASs tend to suffer from "hardening of the categories"; CTs tend to suffer from "loosening of the wholes".[21]

The Particular Humanist, a sensing-feeling person, is concerned with the uniqueness of particular individual human beings. Everyone is a unique means rather than an abstract, theoretical end.

The Conceptual Humanist, an intuition-feeling person, focuses on human welfare directing his or her personal conceptual inquiry toward the general human good.

9.3 Perspectives on accounting methodologies: ideography versus nomothesis

The widely accepted view of the role of accounting research is that it functions to

> Establish general laws covering the behavior of empirical events or objects with which the science is concerned, and thereby enable us to connect together our knowledge of separately known events and to make reliable predictions of events yet unknown.[22]

To accomplish the above function, the natural science model, including careful sampling, accurate measurement, and good design and analysis of theory-supported hypotheses, is generally adopted as the model supporting good research.[23] This now has met with objection, leading to the ideographic versus nomothetic methodology debate. Allport first made the distinction between the two methodologies as follows:

> The nomothesis approach … seeks only laws and employs only those procedures admitted by the exact science. Psychology in the main has been striving to make itself a completely nomothetic discipline. The ideographic sciences … endeavor to understand some particular event in nature or in society. A psychology of individuality would be essentially ideographic.[24]

The debate persisted over the years, sometimes with other labels such as "qualitative versus quantitative research" or "inquiry from the inside versus inquiry from the outside" or "subjective versus objective research". The difference between nomothesis and ideography stems from differences in the underlying assumptions of social science knowledge. The subjective approach to social science features a nominalism assumption for ontology, an antipositivism assumption for epistemology, a voluntarism assumption of human nature and finally, an ideographic assumption for methodology. However, the objective approach features a realistic ontology, a positivist epistemology, a deterministic assumption of human nature, and nomothetic methodology.[25] In fact, Burrell and Morgan gave an exhaustive definition of both nomothesis and ideography. The ideographic approach

> is based on the view that one can only understand the social world by obtaining first-hand knowledge of the subject under investigation. It thus places considerable stress upon getting close to one's subject and … emphasizes the analysis in the subjective accounts which one generates by "getting inside" situations and involving oneself in the everyday flow of life, the detailed analysis of the insights generated by such encounters with one's subject and the insights revealed in impressionistic accounts found in diaries, biographies and journalistic records.[26]

On the other hand, the nomothetic approach is

> Basing research on protocol and technique. It is epitomized in the approach and methods employed in the natural sciences. … It is preoccupied with the construction of scientific tests and the use of quantitative techniques for the analysis of data. Surveys, questionnaires, personality tests and standardized research instruments of all kinds are prominent among the tools, which comprise nomothetic methodology.[27]

The approach – nomothesis versus ideography, or inquiry from the outside versus inquiry from the inside – differs in terms of the mode of inquiry, the type of organizational action, the type of organizational inquiry and the role of the researcher as shown in Exhibit 9.5, and in terms of a number of analytic dimensions as shown in Exhibit 9.6.[28] One noticeable difference in Exhibit 9.6 is associated with different types of knowledge. The ideographic method is interested in the knowledge of the particular as a condition for praxis, which is "a knowledge of how to act appropriately in a variety of particular situations".[29] The nomothetic method is interested in the development of universal knowledge theory.[30]

The difference between the two modes of inquiry is best translated into other languages by the use of two separate verbs to distinguish the two ways of knowing: knowledge about and acquaintance with. The French use *savoir and connaitre*; the Germans use *wissen and kennen*; and in Latin it is *seire and nosere*.

Although both approaches have been debated in the literature, it is not an exaggeration to state that nomothesis has dominated accounting research with its search for general laws, universal variables and a large number of subjects. The concern has been for methodological precision, rigor and credibility, even if often irrelevant to the reality of organizations and accounting. Accounting researchers should pay attention to more objections raised against natural science in particular and nomothesis in general. For example, Orlando Behling raised five key objections to the use of the natural science model used in social science research and applicable to accounting research, namely:

1. *Uniqueness.* Each organization, group and person differs to some degree from all others. The development of precise general laws in organizational behavior and organization theory is thus impossible.

2. *Instability.* The phenomena of interest to researchers in organizational behavior and organization theory are transitory. Not only do the "facts" of social events change with time, but the "laws" governing them change as well. Natural science research is poorly equipped to capture the fleeting phenomena.

| | MODE OF INQUIRY | |
Dimension of difference	From the Outside	From the Inside
Researcher's relationship to setting	Detachment, neutrality	"Being there", immersion
Validation basis	Measurement and logic	Experimental
Researcher's role	Onlooker	Actor
Source of categories	A priori	Interactively emergent
Aim of inquiry	Universality and generalizability	Situational relevance
Type of knowledge acquired	Universal, nomothetic: theoria	Particular, ideographic: praxis
Nature of data and meaning	Factual, context free	Interpreted, contextually embedded

Source: Reprinted with permission of Academy of Management, P.O. Box 3020, Briar Cliff Manor, NY 10510–8020. R. Evered and M.R. Louis, "Alternative Perspectives in Organizational Sciences: Inquiry from the Inside and Inquiry from the Outside" (Exhibit), *Academy of Management Review* (June, 1981), p. 388. Reproduced by permission of the publisher via Copyright Clearance Center, Inc.

Exhibit 9.5 Alternative modes of inquiry

Primary purpose of knowledge-yielding activity

Mode	Organizational action	Organizational inquiry	Role of researcher
From the inside	Copying	Situational learning	Organizational actor
	Action taking	Action research	
	Managing	Clinical practice	Participant observer
	Surviving	Case research	
			Unobtrusive observer
			Empiricist
	Organizational design	Traditional	Data analyst
	and engineering	positivistic science	
	Controlled		Rationalistic
	experimentation		model builder
From the outside	Social technology		

Source: Reprinted with permission of Academy of Management, P.O. Box 3020, Briar Cliff Manor, NY 10510–8020. R. Evered and M.R. Louis, "Alternative Perspectives in Organizational Sciences: Inquiry from the Inside and Inquiry from the Outside" (Exhibit), *Academy of Management Review* (June, 1981), p. 389. Reproduced by permission of the publisher via Copyright Clearance Center, Inc.

Exhibit 9.6   Difference between the two models of inquiry

3. *Sensitivity.* Unlike chemical compounds and other things of interest to natural science researchers, the people who make up organizations, and thus organizations themselves, may behave differently if they become aware of research hypotheses about them.

4. *Lack of realism.* Manipulating and controlling variables in organizational research change the phenomena under study. Researchers thus cannot generalize from their studies because the phenomena observed inevitably differ from their real-world counterparts.

5. *Epistemological differences.* Although understanding cause and effect through natural science research is an appropriate way of "knowing" about physical phenomena, a different kind of "knowledge" not tapped by this approach is more important in organizational behavior and organizational theory.

Luthans and Davis questioned the "sameness assumption" implied by nomothesis, namely, the selective examination of many subjects under the theoretical assumption that there are more similarities than differences among individuals.[32] Based on an interactive theoretic assumption of behavior–person–environment, of real people interacting in real organizations, ideography is suggested as a useful approach using intensive single-case experimental designs and direct observational measures.[33] Luthans and Davis stated:

> Central to an ideographic approach to interactive organizational behavior studies in a natural setting that intends to examine and make conclusions and test specific hypotheses are intensive single case experimental designs and direct methods such as systematic participant observations. When understood and on close examination, it turns out that these designs and methods hold up as well (and some ideographic researchers would argue better) to the same evaluative criteria for scientific research that currently are being used by nomothetically-based researchers.[34]

Among the qualitative or ideographic methodologies used, ethnography and phenomenology have gained a solid place. *Ethnography* is used by anthropologists immersing themselves in other people's realities. It has reached the level of paradigm:

Paradigmatic ethnography begins when the observer, trained in or familiar with the anthropological approach, gets off the boat, train, plane, subway or bus prepared for a lengthy stay with a suitcase full of blank note books, a tape recorder, and a camera. Paradigmatic ethnography ends when the masses of data that have been recorded, filed, stored, checked, and rechecked are organized according to one of several interpretive styles and published for a scholarly or general audience.[35]

Accounting researchers interested in the ethnographic method would have to have a lengthy, continuous first-hand involvement in the organizational setting under study. They would require field observations to examine the deep structure as well as the surface behavior of those in it. As suggested by John Van Maanen, they would need to:

1. separate the first-order concepts or facts of an ethnographic investigation and second-order concepts or theories used by the analyst to organize and explain these facts;

2. distinguish between presentational data that document "the running stream of spontaneous conversations and activities engaged in and observed by the ethnographer while in the field" and presentational data that "concern those appearances that informants strive to maintain (or enhance) in the eyes of the field worker, outsiders and strangers in general, work colleagues, close and intimate associates, and to varying degrees themselves"; and

3. continuously assess the believability of the talk-based information to uncover lies, areas of ignorance, and the various taken-for-granted assumptions.[36]

Phenomenology goes beyond participant observation and ethnography by emphasizing the search for reality as it is "given" in the structure of consciousness universal to humankind. Herbert Spiegelberg described the following seven steps in phenomenology to guide the researcher:

1. To investigate particular phenomena.
2. To investigate general essences.
3. To grasp essential relationships among essences.
4. To watch modes of appearances.
5. To watch the constitution of phenomena in consciousness.
6. To suspend belief in the existence of phenomena.
7. To interpret the meaning of phenomena.[37]

Although the debate of ideography versus nomothesis will go on in various social science literatures, there is an established school of thought that recommends the use of multiple methods. It is generally described as one of convergent methodology, multimethod/multitrait, convergent validation, or what has been called "triangulation".[38] In fact, the originator of the debate, Allport, proposed that the ideographic and nomothetic methods were "overlapping and contributing to one another".[39] The use of both methods can (1) lead to more confidence in the results, (2) help to uncover the deviant or off-quadrant dimension of a phenomenon, (3) lead to a synthesis or integration of theories, and (4) serve as a critical test.[40]

A thread linking all of these benefits is the important part played by qualitative method in triangulation. The research is likely to sustain a profitable closeness to situation, which allows greater sensitivity to the multiple sources of data. Qualitative data and analysis function as the glue that cements the interpretation of multimethod results. In one respect, qualitative data are used as a critical counter point to quantitative method. In another respect, the analysis benefits from the perceptions drawn from personal experiences and first-hand observations. Thus enters the artful researcher who uses the qualitative data to enrich and enlighten the portrait.[41]

What all of this implies for research practice is an eventual choice between the following three options: [42]

1. Pursue both nomothetic and ideographic research and the aggregate.
2. Alternate between both nomothetic and ideographic research, running back and forth between the two methods to capitalize on the strengths of one method in certain cases and overcome the deficiencies of the other method in some cases.
3. Develop a new science described eloquently as follows:

> The new science (human action science) that is gradually emerging is likely to be more actor based, experimentally rooted, praxis-oriented, and self-reflective than the current image of (positivistic, objective) science. It is likely to incorporate both the American "pragmatic" thinking of Pierce, James, Dewey and Mead and the German "critical" thinking of Marx, Dilthey, Husserl, Weber, Heidegger, Gadamer, and Habermas. It will probably develop for the inside and bridge toward the precision and generalizability of inquiry from the outside.[43]

9.4 Perspectives on accounting knowledge

The section draws on Pepper's *World Hypotheses* framework[44] to provide four different approaches to obtaining and classifying formal knowledge in accounting. These approaches are formism, mechanism, contextualism and organicism. They provide a better appreciation of the nature of competing knowledge claims made in accounting research, as well as enriching and extending our understanding of accounting in practice.

9.4.1 Stephen Pepper's "world hypotheses"

Knowledge is the result of a constant cognitive refinement: the criticism and improvement of common-sense claims, referring to common-sense knowledge as *dubitanda* – claims to be doubted. The cognitive refinement is accomplished by:

1. *multiplicative corroboration*, a confirmation of phenomena by various subjects, and
2. *structural corroboration*, the use of theories and hypotheses about the world and their confirmation by empirical data.

Pepper uses the example of the claim that a chair is very strong where multiplicative corroboration consists of having many persons sit upon it and structural corroboration consists of developing a theory of what is required of a chair to be strong. Structural corroboration is achieved by constructing a chair that conforms to the theory's hypothesis. Pepper distinguishes four hypotheses to be adequate structural hypotheses. They are epistemologically incommensurate in the sense that one cannot be used to reject another one and they cannot form an overall hypothesis. They are the four world hypotheses of formism, mechanism, contextualism and organicism. The reduction of the multitude of hypotheses to four world hypotheses is possible through a theory of the origin of world hypotheses, called the "root metaphor theory".

Two sets of assumptions concerning the logical structure of the social world can be used to distinguish between the four hypotheses. They are shown in Exhibit 9.7. A first dimension distinguishes between the analytical and synthetic theories. A second dimension distinguishes between dispersive and integrative theories. Basically analytic theories do not recognize and interpret synthesis, so that complexes or contexts are derivative and not an essential part of the organization. Synthetic theories are instead complexes or contexts so that analysis becomes derivative. Dispersive theories focus on interpretation of facts that are retrieved one by one from a universe of facts, rather loosely scattered about and not necessarily determining one another to any considerable degree. As a result of the use of these two dimensions, the four world hypotheses can be characterized as follows:

1. Formism includes analytic and dispersive theories,
2. mechanism includes analytic and integrative theories,
3. contextualism includes synthetic and dispersive theories, and
4. organicism includes synthetic and integrative theories.

1. Formism

Formism relates philosophically to "realism" and "platonic idealism", with exponents like Plato and Aristotle. It includes both analytic and dispersive theories. Its root metaphor is *similarity*. This assumes that formism focuses on phenomena – objects, events, processes – that are taken one by one from whatever source, attempts to identify similarities or differences through a mere description, and accepts the results of the description. The central activity is description on the basis of similarities, without concern for the sources of the similarities. The description in formism rests on three categories: (1) characters, (2) particulars, and (3) participation. If we state that "this is accounting", "this" is an uncharacterized

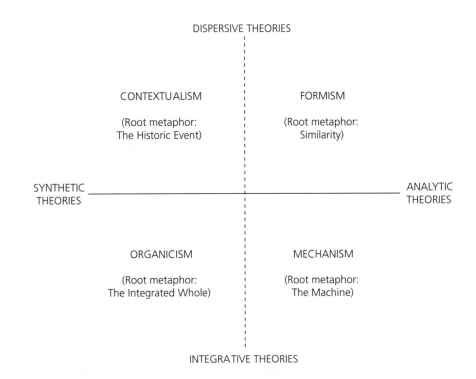

Exhibit 9.7 World hypotheses

particular; "accounting" is the unparticularization of a character, and "is" the participation of one in the other to produce the object. Formism is therefore a particularization of a character or the characterization of a particular. The set of particulars or norms that participate in one or more characters is a class. For example, cash, accounts receivables, short-term inventories and short-term investments which are liquid constitute the class of current assets. The classes can of course be classified in various ways.

What appears in formism is that truth is the degree of similarity of a description to its object of reference. It is a truth theory based on *correspondence.* It does not include statements of empirical uniformities, as they are only half truths where full truths are descriptions that correspond accurately to facts that have occurred and with laws that necessarily hold. As stated by Pepper:

> Empirical uniformities are signs of human ignorance. For if we knew the whole truth about them, we should know the law or the combinations of law which made their regularity necessary, or we should know that they were not necessary but were mere historical coincidences which have been mistakenly generalized and which cannot be relied upon for scientific predictions.[45]

2. Mechanism

Mechanism relates philosophically to the naturalism or materialism of Democrites, Lucretius, Galileo, Descartes, Hobbes, Locke, Berkeley, Hume, and Reichenbach. As shown in Exhibit 9.7, mechanism includes both analytic and integrative theories. Its root metaphor is a machine. Like formism, it is an analytical theory focusing on discrete elements rather than complexes or contexts. Unlike formism, however, it is integrative in the sense that the world is well-ordered and the facts occur in a determinate order and where, if enough were known, they could be predicted, or at least described, as being necessarily just what they are. Six features characterize the mechanistic type of knowledge:

1. Like a machine, the object of study is composed of parts having specified locations.

2. The parts can be expressed in a quantitative form, corresponding to the primary qualities of the machine.

3. A lawful relationship between the parts of a study object can be described by functional equations or statistical correlations. This is the statement of the interrelationships among the parts of the machine.

4. In addition to the primary qualities, there are other characteristics that can be expressed quantitatively, although not directly relevant to the object of study: They are the secondary qualities.

5. The secondary qualities are also related by some principle to the object of study because "if there were to be a complete description of the machine we should want to find out and describe just what the principle was which kept certain secondary qualities attached to certain parts of the machine".[46]

6. Secondary laws characterize the stable relationship between the secondary qualities.

The truth theory of mechanism is whether the machine works, which is measured by workability, which comes down to whether or not one's knowledge allows one to predict the outcomes of any casual adjustments made in the system.

3. Contextualism

Contextualism relates to the pragmatism of Pierce, James, Bergson, Dewey, and Mead. It includes both synthetic and dispersive theories. Its root metaphor is the *historic event* or the act in context. Unlike formism, contextualism is synthetic, in that it focuses on a pattern, a gestalt as the object of study rather than on disparate facts. Like formism, contextualism is dispersive in that the focus is on the interpretation of facts retrieved one by one from a universe of facts. These facts are characterized by continuously changing patterns, making change and novelty the fundamental contextualistic categories. With the historical event as the root metaphor, every event is subject to change and novelty and is characterized at a given time quality and texture. Quality is characterized by the spread of an event, its change and its degree of fusion. Texture is characterized by its strands, its context and its references. Basically, quality refers to the intuited wholeness of an event whose texture is in the details and relations making up the event. The truth theory of contextualism is operational in terms of *qualitative confirmation and pragmatic working*. Only verbs should be used in the language of contextualism – doing, enduring, enjoying, etc. The act and its setting are crucial. "These acts or events are intrinsically complex, composed of interconnected activities with continuously changing patterns. They are like incidents in the plot of a novel or a drama. They are literally the incidents of life."[47]

4. Organicism

Organicism relates to the absolute or objective idealism of Schelling, Hegel, Green, Bradley, Bosanquet, and Royce. Its root metaphor is the integrated whole or harmonious unity in terms of timeliness and enduring structures. Like mechanism, it is integrated in the sense that the world is composed of well-ordered and integrated facts that can be described as well as predicted. Like contextualism it is synthetic, focusing on the gestalt as the object of study rather than disparate facts. Everything is considered to be coherent and well integrated with seven features: (1) fragments of experience appearing with (2) nexuses or connections which spontaneously lead as a result of the aggravation of (3) traditions, gaps, opposition, or counteractions to resolutions in (4) an organic whole (5) implicit in the fragments and (6) transcend the previous contradictions by means of a coherent totality, which (7) economizes, saves, preserves all the original fragments of experience without any loss. Basically, organicism is concerned with the determination of an organic whole from connected and integrated fragments, in a kind of synthesis that recognizes the contradictions and integrates them in a more complete *holon*. The key is integration and comprehension culminating in a *telos* that is an ultimate, most inclusive structure. The truth theory of organicism is coherence as based on determinateness and absoluteness. In other words, organicism proposes the existence of degrees of truth dependent on the amount of facts known, and when all facts are known, as in principle they can be, then absolute truth has been obtained.[48]

9.4.2 Formism in accounting

Formism in accounting consists of searching for similarities and differences between different objects of study without any concern for potential relationships between them. It may be argued that all of the technical knowledge in accounting used in the teaching of accounting and included in standard textbooks is inescapably formistic to a great extent. The general rules, models and algorithms used to explain accounting phenomena and to help in the conduct of accounting practice are discrete objects of study, which can be compared in terms of the extent of similarities and differences between them. This aspect of the field of accounting is characterized by a relentless classification methodology. Every aspect of the accounting knowledge is subject to typologies that are assumed to reflect the world as it is or as it should be. The inquiry of researchers in formism is focused on the taxonomic character of the object of study rather than the causes of similarities and differences. Formism fits well in accounting practice where categorization is tantamount to reaching solutions. It is essentially the particularization of an accounting character or the characterization of an accounting particular. It is a constant search for a "holy grail" of accounting just as it is in such fields as zoology, botany and chemistry. The objects of study are assumed to contain certain systematic, observer-independent similarities, and the task of the accounting researcher is to find out what they are.

The formists in accounting usually find the identification of similarities and differences between objects of study not enough to depict the accounting reality, and call for a relationship between practice and research in accounting. The explicit search for causes is not, however, the realm of formism in accounting. It is more the realm of mechanism.

9.4.3 Mechanism in accounting

Mechanism in accounting consists of not only looking for similarities and differences between objects of study but also and mainly for quantitative relationships that allow both description and prediction. Mechanism in accounting is also the search for empirical regularities between different phenomena through various forms of statistical correlation. The object of study is viewed as multidimensional as a machine. We need to know the parts as well as the principles and relationships between the parts. That calls for operationalization of the discrete dimensions and description of the order that keeps them related. Most of empirical research in accounting, or so called mainstream research, is inescapably mechanistic to a great extent. Market research, behavioral research, positive accounting research, event prediction studies and most correlation-based studies in mainstream accounting research reflect the analytical bent of mechanism by focusing on discrete phenomena, not complexes or contexts, and the integrative bent of mechanism by looking at the world as well ordered with specific relationships that can be described and qualified. The result is less than perfect because of:

1. unsatisfactory level of correlation coefficients;
2. lack of control for alternative explanations;
3. unrepresentative samples; and
4. endless but "disguised" replications.

Mechanism in accounting focuses on obtaining an ever more exhaustive description and finer representation in order to delineate an abbreviated representation of the logic linking the parts of the accounting research object. The abbreviation has become the end product of mechanism in accounting. The Ohlson[49] and Feltham–Ohlson[50] equity valuation models are a good example of an abbreviation that maps book value and abnormal earnings into equity value. The focus on the empirical validations of these models is to explain increasingly higher percentages of variances over time.

Another problem with mechanism in accounting is the implied assumption that:

(a) measures are invariant, and
(b) the relationships between measures are invariant.

Studies in the positive theory of accounting account for so little of the variance in the dependent variables that their methodology cannot be regarded as the sole way of researching the role of accounting in organizations. Reliance on larger samples and more complex statistical methods points more to the poverty of the effort and to the small effects studied.

Similar remarks about mechanism have been made in organizational behavior and organizational psychology. But the real failure of mechanism results from the inordinately high amount of data required to guarantee the predictive power of a mechanistic type of knowledge, and the failure to transfer the knowledge easily to the actual world.

All this is contributing to friction within academic establishments with the prospects of decreasing interdisciplinary relationships and a decline in the production of useful formal accounting knowledge. In the process the scientific establishments in accounting may have created for themselves a self-made prison. They would resist any appeal to escape from their man-made trap because it runs counter to organized beliefs and values.

They rather control and engage in the production of their brand of accounting formal knowledge. Their monopoly of that brand of knowledge allows them to exclude others and/or to admit selectively only those they can reproduce. In the process their brand of accounting knowledge suffers a professional deformation because it is merely used to preserve their power and status, control entry into their field, and counteract other paradigms aiming for primacy in the field. The concerns of these accounting academic elites are protection, discipline, and punishment. The production of accounting knowledge is never separate from the exercise of power. One result of this situation is the constraining ideological influence on the production of accounting knowledge.

9.4.4 Contextualism in accounting

Contextualism in accounting focuses on the interpretation of independent facts drawn from a universe of facts under a specific context that would create a pattern or gestalt. The facts within each pattern are assumed to be subject to change and novelty. In addition, they are distinguishable by their quality and texture. Because of the notion of change the analysis under a specific context takes the ontological assumption that the social world or the accounting world is incessantly on the move. The fundamental difference between contextualism and formism in accounting is that the facts are now aggregated into specific contexts. Therefore, it may be argued that any new accounting technical knowledge that is accumulated for specific contexts constitute a good example of contextualism in accounting. Examples of the new contexts include:

● economic events, such as bankruptcy, takeover, bond ratings;
● industry classification;
● temporal classification, such as before and after a major political, economic or social event.

Every aspect of accounting knowledge can be classified under a grouping characterized by a specific context. One may consider the cases of accounting techniques and the body of knowledge classified by industry. Their study is confined to a particular industry at a time. The reduction of the analysis from all the facts to a few facts pertinent to a particular context gives accounting and management studies, with a focus on the creation of narratives, and stories for the interpretation of a unique episode are clear examples of contextualism. In addition, most of the professional accounting written in lay language attempts to provide "how to" solutions in specific contexts to the general public and executives interested by specific accounting problems in specific contexts. Contextualism appears to be more helpful to the practice of accounting than formism by working for specific gestalt in accounting where it can pinpoint "what is useful" and "what is not useful", and identify the working of specific organizational cultures in accounting. For example, a contextualist approach to behavioral accounting would require a focus on acts and events rather than the contrived experiments, unless the experiments are studied as events.

Contextualism in accounting research relies on an analysis of only facts of direct verification, facts which are specific to a given situation, such as a given industry. As such the end result may be limited in scope. And any attempt at indirect verification, which is equivalent to admitting that the world has a determinate structure, calls for reliance on other world hypotheses. That is a serious dilemma for contextualism in accounting, which is either to accept specificity or acknowledge the constant changes in contexts.

9.4.5 Organicism in accounting

Those adopting organicism in accounting are focusing on specific gestalt as objects of study, which are composed of well-ordered and integrated facts that can be described as well as predicted. Like mechanism in accounting, organicism seeks the determination of empirical regularities between different phenomena through various forms of statistical analysis. Unlike mechanism, the search of empirical regularities is reduced to specific contexts or gestalts. By doing so, organicism avoids most of the limitations of mechanism in accounting by integrating the research and findings around a specific context. For example, if the specific context is bankruptcy, mechanism will focus on generic models of bankruptcy while organicism will focus on specific models of bankruptcy in a specific context such as a specific industry, a specific period of time, a specific country, etc. ... Organicism in accounting is viewed as an important factor of future accounting research. As stated by Beaver:

> A second factor is the emphasis on contextual rather than generic research. In part, it is implicit in the first factor where there is an emphasis on institutional richness, which tends to lead to specific contexts. The value of generic studies is diminishing because prior research has reaped much of those gains and has already addressed the basic, first order question, e.g., is there a statistical relation between returns and earnings changes? However, as the questions become more demanding or the effects are of a second order, there is an increased premium of increasing the power of the tests. This often dictates particular samples and specific reporting issues. In a related view, the contextual investigations will often require the collection of distinctive databases.[51]

Organicism in accounting will depend indeed on the availability of original databases, the focus on specific contexts that will recognize the particularity of data and harmonize them in a more complete accounting *holon*, providing as a result more comprehensive and underlying structures. Organicism in accounting needs also to identify sequential steps that culminate in a *telos*, an overall exhaustive structure. What may appear as disparate accounting events will then be connected in a meaningful harmony through a higher synthesis, explication of anomalies and focus on comprehensiveness and underlying structures. The end result is a coherent and well-integrated accounting world.

9.5 Perspectives on accounting research

Accounting research is eclectic and diverse. To the novice it may appear that accounting researchers are muddling through in their search of topics, methodology and type of discourse. The reality is much different. Like every other social science, accounting conducts its research based upon assumptions about the nature of social science and the nature of society. An approach that has been applied by Burrell and Morgan to organizational analysis can be used to differentiate between four visions of research in accounting – the functionalist view, the interpretive view, the radical humanist view, and the radical structuralist view.[52] In this section they are explicated and applied to accounting research.

9.5.1 Burrell and Morgan's framework

1. The nature of social science

Four assumptions about the nature of social science are examined as they relate to ontology, epistemology, human nature and methodology. These assumptions also can be thought of in terms of the subjective–objective dimension.

First, the ontological assumption, concerning the very essence of the accounting phenomenon, involves nominalism–realism differences. The debate is whether the social world external to the individual cognition is a compound of pure names, concepts and labels that give a structure to reality as in nominalism, or whether it is a compound of real, factual and tangible structures as in realism.

Second, the epistemological debate, concerning the grounds of knowledge and the nature of knowledge, involves the antipositivism–positivism debate. This debate focuses on the utility of a search for laws or underlying regularities in the field of social affairs. Positivism supports the utility. Antipositivism refutes it and argues for individual participation as a condition of understanding the social world.

Third, the human–nature debate, concerning the relationship between human beings and their environment, involves the voluntarism–determinism debate. This debate focuses on whether humans and their activities are determined by the situation or environment as in determinism, or are the result of their free will as in voluntarism.

Fourth, the methodology debate, concerning the methods used to investigate and learn about the social world, involves the ideographic–nomothetic debate. This debate focuses on whether the methodology involves the analysis of the subjective accounts obtained by participating or getting inside the situation as in the ideographic method, or whether it involves a rigorous and scientific testing of hypotheses as in the nomothetic method.

2. The nature of society

One assumption about the nature of society is made – namely, the order–conflict debate or, more precisely, the regulation–radical change debate. *The sociology of regulation* attempts to explain society by focusing on its unity and cohesiveness and the need for regulation. *The sociology of radical change*, in contrast, seeks to explain society by focusing on radical change, deep-seated structural conflict, modes of domination, and the structural contradictions of modern society. As highlighted by Burrell and Morgan, the sociology of regulation is concerned with status quo, social order, consensus, social integration and cohesion, solidarity, need satisfaction, and actuality, whereas the sociology of radical change is concerned with radical change, structural conflict, models of domination, contradiction, emancipation, deprivation, and potentiality.

3. The framework for analysis of research

As described earlier, any social science discipline, including accounting, can be analyzed along metatheoretical assumptions about the nature of science, the subjective–objective dimension, and about the nature of society, the dimension of regulation–radical change. Using these two dimensions, Burrell and Morgan were able to develop a coherent scheme for the analysis of social theory in general and organizational analysis in particular.[53] The scheme consists of four distinct paradigms labeled as (1) the radical humanist, characterized by the radical change and subjective dimensions; (2) the radical structuralist, characterized by the radical change and objective dimensions; (3) the interpretive, characterized by the subjective and regulation dimensions; and (4) the functionalist, characterized by the objective and regulation dimensions. The framework is illustrated in Exhibit 9.8. It constitutes four views of reality to be used in analyzing a wide range of social theories including accounting. As Burrell and Morgan stated:

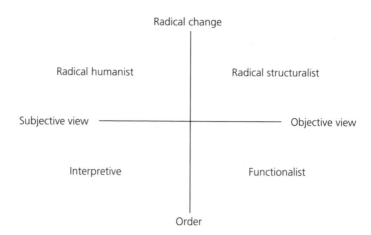

Exhibit 9.8   Four views for the analysis of social theory

> Given the cross linkages between rival intellectual traditions, it becomes clear to us that our two sets of assumptions could be counter-posed to produce an analytical scheme for studying social theories in general ... we found that we possessed an extremely powerful tool for negotiating our way through different subject areas, and one which made sense of a great deal of the confusion which characterizes much contemporary debate within the social sciences.[54]

For example, the framework was used by Morgan to examine how organizational theory is influenced by its own assumptions through references to paradigms, metaphors and puzzle-solving behavior.

9.5.2 The functionalist view in accounting

The functional view in accounting focuses on explaining the social order, in which accounting plays a role, from a realist, positivist, determinist and nomothetic standpoint. It is concerned with effective regulation on the basis of objective evidence.

The functionalist paradigm in accounting views accounting phenomena as concrete real-world relations possessing regularities and causal relationships that are amenable to scientific explanation and prediction.

In addition, the social order, as defined by extant structures of market and firm, is taken for granted, and no reference to domination or conflict is made. Both views of accounting phenomena and the social world are used to develop theories assumed to be value free rather than historically relative.

As in structural functionalism, the functionalist paradigm in accounting focuses on establishing the functions of accounting needed for an efficient operation of organizations. These functions are the "functional prerequisites" or "functional imperatives" of adaptation, goal attainment, integration, and latency or pattern maintenance. To serve these imperatives, the structures or elements of accounting are defined.

As in system theory, the functionalist paradigm in accounting focuses on both the search for analogical representation of the accounting system and a system analysis.

Interactionism with its focus on human association and interactions is expressed in the form of behavioral accounting.

Objectivism with its commitment to the models and methods used in the natural sciences is the predominant avenue in accounting theorizing and research. In fact, abstract empiricism as a label fits perfectly most of the published empirical accounting research. There is a definite urge to develop rigorous models of the accounting phenomena in the absence of confounding variables and a methodological reliance on hypothetic-deductive methods.

The functionalist view in accounting characterizes what is generally considered as mainstream accounting research. Its dominant assumptions include the following: "Theory is separate from observations that may be used to verify or falsify a theory. Hypothetic-deductive account of scientific explanation is accepted. Quantitative methods of data analysis and collection which allows generalization are favored."[55]

9.5.3 The interpretive view in accounting

The interpretive view in accounting would focus on explaining the social order from a nomalist, antipositivist, voluntarist and ideological standpoint. In accounting it would aim to understand the subjective experience of individuals involved in the preparation, communication, verification, or use of accounting information. Hermeneutics applied in accounting focus on the study of the accounting objectification, like accounting institutions, accounting texts, accounting literature, accounting languages, and accounting ideologies, using the method of *verstehen*.

Phenomenology, if applied to accounting, would attempt to make explicit the "essences" that cannot be revealed by ordinary positivist observations. The interpretive paradigm in accounting, although in its infancy, has focused on (1) the ability of information to "construct reality",[56] (2) the role of accounting as a "linguistic" tool,[57] and (3) other roles and images that accounting may take.[58]

To the interpretists, accounting is no more than names, concepts and labels used to construct social reality. It can be understood only from the point of view of those directly involved in its preparation, communication, or use. Methodologically, ideographic methods rather than hypothetic-deductive methods are needed to reenact the actor's definition of the problem.

Therefore the dominant assumptions of the interpretive view in accounting should be:

A. Beliefs About Knowledge

Scientific explanations of human intention sought. Their adequacy is assessed via the criteria of logical consistency, subjective interpretation, and agreements with actors' common-sense interpretation.

B. Beliefs About Physical and Social Reality

Social reality is emergent, subjectively created, and objectified through human interaction. All actions have meaning and intention that are retrospectively endowed and that are grounded in social and historical practices. Social order is assured. Conflict is mediated through common schemes of social meaning.

C. Relationship Between Theory and Practice

Theory seeks to explain action and to understand how social order is produced and reproduced.[59]

Although the interpretive paradigm is not predominant in accounting, it suffers from three major limitations: (1) it assumes that a "quasidivine" observer can understand social action through sheer subjectivity and without interference; (2) it creates the illusion of pure theory by using a monological line of reasoning; and (3) it fails to be an inquiry of change.[60]

9.5.4 The radical humanist view in accounting

The radical humanist view in accounting would focus on explaining the social order from a nominalist, voluntarist, and ideographic perspective and places emphasis on forms of radical change. It respects any research that reduces philosophical critique to some normative methodology. In the form of critical theory it requires two forms of analysis: "(a) a toxonomic analysis of the ontological, epistemological, and methodological concerns underlying organization science; and (b) a critique (based on this analysis) of the dynamic interplay between organizational research, theory and practice."[61] It will expand its epistemic critique to include: "(a) a discussion of the limitation of alternative modes of inquiry; (b) an analysis of the relationship between the community of organizational researchers and organizational practitioners and members; and (c) the acknowledgment of the practical aim of any particular mode of research".[62]

Critical theory in accounting will assume that theories, bodies of knowledge, and facts are mere reflections of a realistic worldview. It will view accountants, accountors, and accountees as prisoners of a mode of consciousness that is shaped and controlled through ideological processes. All aspects of accounting will be scrutinized for their alienating properties. In short, accounting will be viewed as creating a "psychic prison" where organizational realities become confirming and dominating. The argument is that accounting systems encourage and sustain alienation and conflict. This view would suggest that accounting should help people realize their potential by helping them realize their needs, or would direct it to avenues in line with Habermas' concern with communicative competence and Gramsci's and Lukacs' concern with ideology and false consciousness.[63]

Gramsci, in particular, addressed the problem of false consciousness by examining the position of intellectuals in contemporary society. Although he argued that all humans are intellectual beings, not everyone under capitalism performs intellectual functions. He further distinguished between traditional intellectuals, who historically have been autonomous of class interests, and organic intellectuals, who are ideologically aligned with class interests. In contemporary capitalism most intellectuals are organically tied to the bourgeoisie. Because of the ideological hegemony of capitalism, few intellectuals articulate the interests of the subordinate class. This type of radical humanist interpretation applied to the field of accounting suggest that until an "organic" elite of accountants emerge who are not tied ideologically to the capitalist class, the discipline of accounting will continue to reproduce the interests and ideology of capitalism. Classical or functionalist accountants, however, will be very quick to accuse the humanist of being partisan and nonacademic. As Burrell and Morgan discussed, humanists are often labeled as "radicals hellbent upon fanning the flames of revolutionary consciousness, or as mindless existentialists who will not or cannot adjust to the world of everyday 'reality' and accept the inevitable march of 'progress'".[64]

9.5.5 The radical structuralist view in accounting

The radical stucturalist view in accounting would challenge the social order from a realist, positivist, deterministic, and nomothetic standpoint. It would seek radical change, emancipation, and potentionality using an anaylsis emphasizing structural conflict, modes of domination, contradiction, and deprivation. This paradigm would generate accounting theories based upon metaphors such as the instrument of domination, schismatic system and catastrophe.

The role of accounting in Weber's classic analyses of bureaucracy as a mode of domination, in Robert Michels' analysis of the "iron law of oligarchy", and in Marxists' analyses of organization will emerge as a powerful instrument of domination to be understood as an essential part of a wider process of domination within society as a whole. As stated by David Cooper:

> From the point of view of these radical structuralists, organizations are instruments of social forces concerned to maintain the division of labour and distribution of wealth and power in society. To these researchers, whose perspective seems almost completely missing in current accounting research, there is an actuality of organization that includes sexual and racial discrimination, patterns of social stratification and unequal distributions of wealth, power and rewards. ... The failure to acknowledge these characteristics and consider the relationship of accounting practices to them seems a curious omission for studies that explicitly seek to account for accounting.[65]

Structuralist accountants will hold an objective view of the social world but focus on contradictions and crisis tendencies created by the accounting process. Unlike the radical humanists with their emphasis on superstructural phenomena such as ideology and distorted consciousness, the radical structuralists in accounting will focus on the link between accounting and economic and political relations of domination.

Marxist structuralists such as Althusser and Nicos Poulantzas have stressed the relative autonomy of political and ideological structures from the underlying economic base as a connection to the overly deterministic models of classical Marxists. With respect to the accounting enterprise, this approach would focus on the relative independence of accounting practices, policies, and theories from overt, economic and political forces. The development of accounting could be seen as a *sui generis* process, defined from within. A similar agenda for accounting within the radical structuralist school has been eloquently stated as follows:

> Radical theories may also be applied to more specific accounting questions: What underlies major shifts in the regulatory practices of the state and how much importance should accountants attribute to these changes? What determines the state's level of autonomy vis-à-vis advantaged and disadvantaged groups and, in this regard, how much credence may be attached to the view of writers, such as Benson, that disclosure regulations are captive of vested interest? Does the degree of state autonomy vary across regulatory spheres of interests? What stance should the accounting profession take in relation to the "contested terrain" of state regulation? Who are the sides in the struggle for control over the state's regulatory apparatus, and how should accountants choose a side to support? The continued dominance of neoclassical thought serves to exclude such questions from the accounting research agenda. This situation will persist as long as academic accounting falls short of the scholarly ideal that everything should be open for discussion in an intellectual community.[66]

9.6 Intellectual foundations in accounting

9.6.1 Marginal-economics-based accounting

The neoclassical marginal economics has had a paramount influence on accounting practice, theory, and research. Various recurring themes are good evidence of such influence.

Accounting's commitment to marginalism is best illustrated by two enduring emphases, namely, on individualism and on preserving objectivity and independence. The first emphasis included both a view of the sovereignty of the individual owners, which ignored the separation of ownership and management, and a view that explicitly recognizes the separation of ownership and management but also considers the firm as a "legal" person having the right to maintain command over a given level of resources.[67] The second emphasis put the accountant in the position of historian and accounting in the position of an impartial record of historical exchanges with objectivity as a paramount objective.

Both emphases improved constraints on the practice and teachings of accounting. As noticed by Anthony Tinker and his associates, the first emphasis preempted questions about the class affiliations of individuals and the part played by accountants in class conflicts, and the second emphasis led to shunning subjective questions of value and confirming accounting data to objective market prices.[68] The motivation behind the role of historian is explained as follows:

> This image of the accountant – often as a disinterested, innocuous "historian" – stems from the desire to deny the responsibility that accountants bear for shaping subjective expectations which, in turn, affect decisions about resources allocation and the distribution of income between and within classes. This attachment to historical facts provides a veneer of pseudo-objectivity that allows accountants to claim that they merely record – not partake in – social conflicts.[69]

Marginal economics and conventional accounting as based on its related economic value and profit are linked to the worth of future consumption possibilities as assessed by the present value of their cash-flow streams. This has constituted appealing reasons for valuing some of the accounting assets on the basis of the present-value concept and for comparing projects on the basis of their present values. Tinker, however, showed that in comparing alternative capital investment projects, marginal-economics-based accounting does not yield a unique solution.[70]

The comparison depends on the choice of the interest rate. The most desirable project for a society can be ascertained only for a given interest rate, which works well for a given firm using its cost of capital as the interest rate. However, given the difference in the cost of capital between firms, the calculations are indeterminate. This argues for using a given market rate of interest to conclude that one project is socially preferable to another. This solution, however, is challenged by what are known as the Cambridge Controversies. Basically, it is pointed out that the marginalist explanation is tautological. It is summarized as follows:

> We begin by asking how the rate of profit is determined and the answer is with reference to the quantity of capital and its marginal revenue product. We then ask how these are determined and the reply is by assuming a division of future income and discounting the returns to capital with the market rate of interest. All that has been said is that the market rate of interest is a function of the market rate of interest (and an assumed income distribution).[71]

Similarly, D.J. Cooper pointed out that the market rate of interest depends upon the supply and demand for monetary capital, which, in turn, depends upon the market rate of interest.[72] In short, marginal economics is shown as either tautological or indeterminate.

9.6.2 Political-economy accounting

Political-economy accounting was spurred by the limitations of marginal economics and the merits of political economy. For example, unlike marginalism, political economy recognizes two dimensions of capital: one as (physical) instruments of production and one as man's relationship to man in a social organization.[73] Different kinds of society (feudal, slave, capitalist, and so on) exist and are characterized by different social institutions (e.g., legal, state, educational, religious, law and order, political-government administration). In each of these societies exist contradicting groups with different powers striving for dominance, which may lead to forms of exploitation, alienation, and inequalities. Therefore, unlike the situation in marginalism, here accounting is to serve an ideological role in legitimizing the ideology of the basic organizing principle and in mystifying relationships amongst classes in society and reinforcing unequal power distributions.[74] Accounting as an ideology is within the realm of the political-economy accounting.

As another example, the research based on marginalism and assessing the usefulness of corporate reports for users has implications only for the private value of information with a bias for the shareholder and manager classes in society and is therefore not helpful in either the design or choice of alternative accounting reports aimed at informing the social welfare. The impact of corporate accounting reports on social welfare is also within the realm of the political-economy accounting.

What is political-economy accounting besides its alleged interest in ideology and social welfare? It is an alternative accounting approach aimed at looking at the accounting functions within the broader structural and institutional environment in which it operates. A good definition is as follows:

> A Political Economy of Accounting (PEA) is thus a normative, descriptive and critical approach to accounting research. It provides a broader, more holistic, framework for analyzing and understanding the value of accounting reports within the economy as a whole. A PEA approach attempts to explicate and interpret the role of accounting reports in the distribution of income, wealth, and power in society. In so doing, a PEA approach models the institutional structure of society that helps fashion this role and provides a framework for examining novel sets of institutions, accountings and accounting reports.[75]

In fact, D.J. Cooper and M.J. Sherer presented three features of the political-economy accounting:[76]

1. It should recognize power and conflict in society and consequently should focus on the effects of accounting reports on the distinction of income, wealth, and power in society. This feature contradicts directly the pluralist concept in favor of the views that either society is controlled by a well-defined elite or there is continuous societal conflict between essentially antagonistic classes.[77]

2. It should recognize the specific historical and institutional environment of the society in which it operates, namely, that (a) the economy is dominated by large corporations, (b) disequilibrium is a permanent feature of the economy, and (c) the state plays a paramount role in managing the economy, in failing to control its spending levels, in protecting commercial interests and large firms, in preserving social harmony and its own legitimacy, and at the same time in intervening in the determination of accounting policies.

3. It should adopt a more emancipated view of human motivation and the role of accounting. Accounting should be recognized as an influencing agent causing either motivation or even alienation at work and the pursuit of self-interest and playing a socially active rather than passive function.[78] For example:

> In the same way as the medical profession may have a legitimate concern with housing, social conditions and public health of the community, so the

accounting profession may have legitimate concerns in relation to its immediate environment (e.g. the commercial and financial sectors of the economy). Attempts to resolve technical issues without consideration of this environment may result in an imperfect and incomplete resolution due to the acceptance of current institutions and practices.[79]

9.6.3 Business disciplines-based accounting

To raise the stature and respectability of accounting, various proposals were made to both accounting and to various business disciplines. The effort was generally aimed at adaptation of accounting to a changing social and economic environment. Some of these proposals include:[80]

(a) a link with mathematics;[81,82]

(b) a focus on decision theory;[83]

(c) a reference to the elements of formal measurement theory;[84]

(d) a stress on the capital market setting, paralleling modern finance;[85]

(e) a role for the information economics approach;[86,87]

(f) a concern for the implications of probabilistic choice models, which incorporate mathematical psychology, for the theory of accounting information choice and use;[88]

(g) a foundation based on a positive theory of accounting;[89]

(h) a theory of accounting based on contract theory;[90]

(i) a multidimensional approach that will borrow or rely on well-known contributions to business such as

- bounded rationality;[91]
- dividend irrelevancy theorem;[92]
- organizational theory of the firm;[93]
- rational expectations;[94,95]
- statistical auditing;[96]
- linguistic relativism;[97]
- dual labor economics.[98]

9.7 Conclusions

This chapter covered the different perspectives on accounting researchers, on accounting methodologies, on accounting knowledge, on accounting research and on the intellectual foundations of accounting. What is obvious from the content of this chapter is that accounting is a full-fledged social science.

Notes

1. Kolb, D.A., Rubin, I.M., and McIntyre, J.M., *Organizational Psychology: An Experimental Approach* (Englewood Cliffs, NJ: Prentice-Hall, 1974).

2. Payne, Roy L., "The Nature of Knowledge and Organizational Psychology", in Nigel Nicholson and Toby D. Wall (eds.), *The Theory and Practice of Organizational Psychology* (London: Academic Press, 1982), pp. 37–67.

3. Pears, D., *What is Knowledge?* (New York: Harper and Row, 1971).

4. Hamlyn, D.W., *The Theory of Knowledge* (London: Macmillan, 1971).

5. Hospers, J., *An Introduction to Philosophical Analysis* (Englewood Cliffs, NJ: Prentice-Hall, 1967).

6. Phillips, D., *Abandoning Method* (San Francisco: Jossey-Bass, 1973).

7. Russell, B., *The Problems of Philosophy* (London: Butterworth, 1912).

8. Payne, Roy L., "The Nature of Knowledge and Organizational Psychology", op. cit.

9. Ibid., p. 46.

10. Hudson, L., *Contrary Imaginations* (New York: Scholar Books, 1966).

11. Gordon, G., "A Contingency Model for the Design of Problem Solving Research Programs: A Perspective or Diffusion Research", *Milbank Memorial Fund Quarterly* (Spring, 1974), pp. 185–220.

12. Mitroff, I.I., "Norms and Counter-Norms in a Select Group of the Apollo Moon Scientists: A Case Study of the Ambivalence of Scientist", *American Sociological Review* (1973–4), pp. 579–95.

13. Mitroff, I.I., *The Subjective Side of Science: An Inquiry into the Psychology of the Apollo Moon Scientists* (Amsterdam: Elsevier, 1974).

14. Maslow, A.H., *The Psychology of Science* (New York: Harper & Row; 1966).

15. Jung, C.G., *Collected Works, Vol. 6, Psychological Types* (Princeton, NJ: Princeton University Press, 1971).

16. Mitroff, I.I., and Kilman, R.H., *Methodological Approaches to Social Science* (San Francisco: Jossey-Bass, 1978).

17. Choudhury, Nandan, "Starting Out in Management Accounting Research", *Accounting and Business Research* (Summer, 1967), pp. 205–20.

18. Ibid., p. 206.

19. Mitroff, I.I., and Kilman, R.H., *Methodological Approaches to Social Science*, op. cit.

20. Ibid., p. 33.

21. Ibid., p. 68.

22. Braithwaite, R., *Scientific Explanation* (Cambridge: Cambridge University Press, 1973), p. 1.

23. Cole, T.D., and Campbell, D.T., "The Design and Conduct of Quasi-Experiments and True Experiments in Field Settings", in M.D. Dunnette (ed.), *Handbook of Industrial and Organizational Psychology* (Chicago: Rand McNally, 1976).

24. Allport, Gordon W., *Personality: A Psychological Interpretation* (New York: Henry Holt, 1937), p. 22.

25. Burrell, G., and Morgan, G., *Sociological Paradigms and Organizational Analysis* (London: Heinemann, 1979).

26. Ibid., p. 6.

27. Ibid., pp. 6–7.

28. Evered, R., and Louis, M.R., "Alternative Perspectives in the Organizational Sciences: Inquiry from the Inside and Inquiry from the Outside", *Academy of Management Review* (6 , 1981), pp. 385–95.

29. Ibid., p. 390.

30. Habermas, J., *Knowledge and Human Interest* (Boston: Beacon Press, 1971).

31. Behling, Orlando, "The Case for the Natural Science Model for Research in Organizational Behavior and Organizational Theory", *Academy of Management Review* (5, 1980), pp. 484–5.

32. Luthans, F., and Davis, T.R., "An Ideographic Approach to Organizational Behavior Research: The Use of A Single Case Experimental Designs and Direct Measures", *Academy of Management Review* (3, 1982), p. 382.

33. Ibid., p. 380.

34. Ibid.

35. Sanday, Peggy Reeves, "The Ethnographic Paradigm(s)", *Administrative Science Quarterly* (December, 1979), p. 525.

36. Van Maanen, John, "The Fact of Fiction in Organizational Ethnography", *Administrative Science Quarterly* (December, 1979), pp. 539–50.

37. Spiegelberg, H., "The Essentials of the Phenomenological Method", in *The Phenomenological Movement: A Historical Introduction*, 2nd edn (The Hague: Martinus Nijhoff, 1965), pp. 655–7.

38. Campbell, O.T., and Fiske, D.W, "Convergent and Discriminant Validation by the Multitrait-Multimethod Matrix", *Psychological Bulletin* (56, 1959), pp. 81–105.

39. Allport, *Personality*, op. cit., p. 22.

40. Jick, Todd D., "Rising Qualitative and Quantitative Methods: Triangulation in Action", *Administrative Science Quarterly* (December, 1979), p. 605.

41. Ibid.

42. Evered, R., and Louis, M.R., "Alternative Perspectives in the Organizational Sciences", op. cit., pp. 392–4.

43. Ibid., p. 394.

44. Pepper, S.C., *World Hypothesis* (Berkeley: University of California Press, 1992).

45. Ibid., p. 183.

46. Ibid., p. 193.

47. Ibid., p. 233.

48. Payne, R., "The Nature of Knowledge and Organizational Psychology", in N. Nicholson and T. Wall (eds.), *Theory and Method in Organizational Psychology* (NY: Academic Press, 1982), p. 52.

49. Ohlson, J.A., "Earnings, Book Values, and Dividends in Equity Valuation", *Contemporary Accounting Research* (Spring, 1995), pp. 685–731.

50. Feltham, G.A., and Ohlson, J.A., "Valuation and Clean Surplus Accounting for Operating and Financing Activities", *Contemporary Accounting Research* (Spring, 1995), pp. 685–731.

51. Beaver, W.H., "Directions in Accounting Research: Near and Far", *Accounting Horizons* (June, 1996), p. 122.

52. Burrell, Gibson, and Morgan, Gareth, *Sociological Paradigms and Organizational Analysis: Elements of the Sociology of Corporate Life* (London: Heinemann, 1979).

53. Ibid., p. 22.

54. Ibid., p. xiii.

55. Wai Fong, Chua, "Radical Development in Accounting Thought", *The Accounting Review* (October, 1986), p. 611.

56. Boland, R.J., and Pondy L.R., "Accounting in Organizations: A Union of Natural and Rational Perspectives", *Accounting, Organizations, and Society* (5, 1980), pp. 223–34; Burchell, S. *et al.*, "The Roles of Accounting in Organizations and Society", *Accounting, Organizations and Society* (5, 1980), pp. 5–27; Colville, I., "Reconstructing 'Behavioral Accounting'", *Accounting, Organizations, and Society* (2/3, 1983), pp. 269–86; Tomkins, C., and Groves, R., "The Everyday Accountant and Researching His Reality", *Accounting, Organizations and Society* (4, 1983), pp. 361–74.

57. Belkaoui, Ahmed, "Linguistic Relativity in Accounting", *Accounting, Organizations and Society* (October, 1978), pp. 97–104.

58. Hayes, D.C., "Accounting for Accounting: A Study about Managerial Accounting", *Accounting, Organizations and Society* (2/3, 1983), pp. 241–50.

59. Wai Fong, Chua, "Radical Development in Accounting", op. cit., p. 615.

60. Steffy, Brian D., and Grimes, Andrew J., "A Critical Theory of Organization Science", *Academy of Management Review* (11, 2, 1986), pp. 322–36.

61. Ibid., p. 324.

62. Ibid., p. 325.

63. Habermas, J., *Toward a Rational Society*, trans. J.J. Shapiro (Boston: Beacon Press, 1970); Gramsci, A., *Selections from the Prison Notebooks of Antonio Gramsci*, Quinton Hoare and Geoffrey Nowell-Smith (eds.) (London: Lawrence and Wishart, 1971); Lukacs, G., *History and Class Consciousness* (London: Merlin Press, 1973).

64. Burrell, G., and Morgan, G., *Sociological Paradigms and Organizational Analysis: Elements of the Sociology of Corporate Life*, op. cit., p. 307.

65. Cooper, David, "Tidiness, Muddle, and Things: Commonalities and Divergencies in Two Approaches to Management Accounting Research", *Accounting, Organizations and Society* (8, 1983), p. 277.

66. Tinker, Anthony, "Theories of the State and the State of Accounting: Economic Reductionism and Political Voluntarism in Accounting Regulation Theory", *Journal of Accounting and Public Policy* (Spring, 1984), p. 71.

67. For the first review, see Sprague, Charles E., *Accounting Principles for Business Enterprises*, Accounting Research Study No. 3 (New York: American Institute of Certified Public Accountants, 1963); Hatfield, Henry Rand, *Modern Accounting: Its Principles and Some of Its Problems* (New York: D. Appleton, 1909); Canning, John, *The Economics of Accountancy* (New York: Ronald Press, 1929). For the second review, see Paton, William, and Stevenson, Russell, *Principles of Accounting* (New York: Macmillan, 1918); idem., *Accounting Theory* (New York: Ronald Press, 1922); Sweeney, Henry W., "Maintenance of Capital", *Accounting Review* (December 1930), pp. 277–87.

68. Tinker, Anthony M., Merino, Barbara D., and Neimark, Marilyn Dale, "The Normative Origins of Positive Theories: Ideology and Accounting Thought", *Accounting, Organizations and Society* (May, 1982), p. 188.

69. Ibid., p. 188.

70. Tinker, Anthony M., "Towards a Political Economy of Accounting: An Empirical Illustration of the Cambridge Controversies", *Accounting, Organizations and Society* (June, 1980), p. 150.

71. Ibid., pp. 151–2.

72. Cooper, D.J., "Discussion of Towards a Political Economy of Accounting", *Accounting, Organizations, and Society* (June, 1980), pp. 161–6.

73. Tinker, "Towards a Political Economy of Accounting", p. 153.

74. Burchell *et al.*, "The Roles of Accounting in Organizations and Society", pp. 5–27.

75. Cooper, D.J., and Sherer, M.J., "The Value of Corporate Accounting Reports: Arguments for a Political Economy of Accounting", *Accounting, Organizations and Society* (June, 1984), p. 222.

76. Ibid., p. 218–19.

77. Stanworth, P., and Giddens, A. (eds.), *Elites and Power in British Society* (Cambridge: Cambridge University Press, 1974); Miliband, R., *The State in Capitalist Society* (London: Weidenfeld and Nicolson, 1969).

78. Cherns, A.B., "Alienation and Accountancy", *Accounting, Organizations and Society* (1978), pp. 105–14; Peasnell, K.V., "Statement of Accounting Theory and Theory Acceptance", *Accounting and Business Research* (Summer, 1978), pp. 217–25.

79. Cooper and Sherer, "The Value of Corporate Accounting Reports", p. 219.

80. Demski, Joel S., Fellingham, John C., Ijiri, Yuji, and Sunder, Shyam, "Some Thoughts in the Intellectual Foundations of Accounting", *Accounting Horizons* (16, 2, 2002), pp. 157–68.

81. Ijiri, Y., *The Foundations of Accounting Measurement: A Mathematical, Economic, and Behavioral Inquiry* (Houston, TX: Scholars Book Co.).

82. Mattessich, R., *Accounting and Analytical Methods* (Homewood, IL: Irwin, 1964).

83. Sterling, R.R., *Theory of Accounting and Control* (Cincinnati, OH: Thomson Press, 1997).

84. Mock, T.J., *Measurement and Accounting Information Criteria* (Sarasota, FL: American Accounting Association, 1976).

85. Gonedes, N., and Dopuch, N., "Capital Market Equilibrium, Information-Production and Selecting Accounting Techniques: Theoretical Framework and Review of Empirical Work", *Journal of Accounting Research* (12, Supplement, 1974), pp. 48–169.

86. Demski, J.S., and Feltham, G.A., *Cost Determination: A Conceptual Approach,* 1st edn (Ames, IA: Iowa State University Press, 1976).

87. Christensen, J., and Demski, J.S., *Accounting Theory An Information Content Perspective* (New York: McGraw-Hill/Irwin, 2002).

88. Hilton, R., *Probabilistic Choice Models and Information* (Sarasota, FL: American Accounting Association; 1985).

89. Watts, R., and Zimmerman, J., *Positive Accounting Theory* (Englewood Cliffs, NJ: Prentice-Hall, 1986).

90. Sunder, R., *Theory of Accounting and Control* (Cincinnati, OH: Thompson Press, 1997).

91. Simon, H.A., *Administrative Behavior: A Study of Decision-Making Processes in Administrative Organizations* (New York: Macmillan Co, 1947).

92. Miller, M.H., and Modiglian, F., "The Cost of Capital, Corporation Finance, and the Theory of Investment", *American Economic Review* (48, June, 1958), pp. 261–97.

93. Cyert, R., and March, J.M., *A Behavioral Theory of the Firm* (Maldon, MA: Blackwell Publishers, 1963).

94. Lucas, R., "Expectations and the Neutrality of Money", *Journal of Economic Theory* (4, 1972), pp. 103–24.

95. Muth, J., "Rational Expectations and the Theory of Price Movements", *Econometrica* (29, 1961), pp. 315–35.

96. Cyert, R., and Trueblood, R.M., *Sampling Technique in Accounting* (New York: Prentice-Hall, 1957).

97. Riahi-Belkaoui, Ahmed, *The Linguistic Shaping of Accounting* (Westport, CT: Greenwood Press, 1995).

98. Riahi-Belkaoui, Ahmed, *Accounting in the Dual Economy* (Westport, CT: Greenwood Press, 1991).

References

American Accounting Association, Committee on Concepts and Standards for External Financial Reports, *Statement on Accounting Theory and Theory Acceptance* (Sarasota, FL, 1977).

Beaver, W.H., "Directions in Accounting Research: Near and Far", *Accounting Horizons* (June, 1996), pp. 113–24.

Belkaoui, A., *Conceptual Foundations of Management Accounting* (Reading, MA: Addison-Wesley, 1930).

Belkaoui, A., "Linguistic Relativity in Accounting", *Accounting, Organizations and Society* (October, 1978), pp. 97–104.

Belkaoui, A., "A Test of the Linguistic Relativity in Accounting", *Canadian Journal of Administrative Sciences* (December, 1984), pp. 238–55.

Bernard, V.L., "Cross-Sectional Dependence and Problems in Inference in Market-Based Accounting Research", *Journal of Accounting Research* (4, 1987), pp. 75–8.

Burrell, G., and Morgan, G., *Sociological Paradigms and Organizational Analysis* (Aldershot: Gower, 1979).

Burrell, Gibson, and Morgan, Gareth, *Sociological Paradigms and Organizational Analysis: Elements of the Sociology of Corporate Life* (London: Heinemann, 1979).

Burtt, E.A., "The Status of 'World Hypothesis'", *Philosophical Review* (1943) LIT, pp. 590–601.

Chua, Wai Fong, "Radical Development in Accounting Thought", *The Accounting Review*, (October, 1986), pp. 601–32.

Cohen, J., *Power Statistics for Behavioral Sciences* (New York: Wiley, 1978).

Cooper, D.J., "Tidiness, Muddle and Things: Commonalities and Divergences in Two Approaches to Management Accounting Research", *Accounting, Organizations and Society* (1983), pp. 213, 269–86.

Feltham, G.A., and Ohlson, J.A., "Valuation and Clean Surplus Accounting for Operating and Financial Activities", *Contemporary Accounting Research* (Spring, 1995), pp. 689–731.

Foucault, M., "Orders of Discourse", *Social Science Information* (10, 1971), pp. 7–30.

Herbst, P.G., *Behaviorial Worlds: The Study of Single Cases* (London: Tavistock, 1970).

Hopper, T., and Powell, A., "Making Sense of Research into the Organizational and Social Aspects of Management Accounting: A Review of its Underlying Assumptions", *Journal of Management Studies* (September, 1985), pp. 429–65.

Lee, T., "Education, Practice and Research in Accounting: Gaps, Closed Loops, Bridges and Magic Accounting", *Accounting and Business Research* (Summer, 1989), pp. 237–53.

Magee, B., *Popper* (London: Fontana, 1973).

Mattessich, Richard, *Critique of Accounting – Examination of the Foundations and Normative Structure of Accounting* (Westport, CT: Greenwood Publishing, 1995).

Ohlson, J.A., "Earnings, Book Values, and Dividends in Equity Valuation", *Contemporary Accounting Research* (Spring, 1995), pp. 661–87.

Payne, R., "Truisms in Organizational Behavior", *Interpersonal Development* (6, 1975/76), pp. 203–20.

Payen, R., "The Nature of Knowledge and Organizational Psychology", in N. Nicholson and T. Wall (eds.), *Theory and Method in Organizational Psychology* (New York: Academic Press, 1982), pp. 37–67.

Pepper, S.C., *Concept and Quality* (Chicago: Open Court, 1966).

Pepper, S.C., *World Hypothesis: A Study in Evidence* (Berkeley: University of California Press, 1942).

Riahi-Belkaoui, A., *Accounting, A Multi Paradigmatic Science* (Westport, CT: Greenwood Publishing, 1996).

Riahi-Belkaoui, A., *Research Perspectives in Accounting* (Westport, CT: Greenwood Publishing, 1997).

Sarbin, T., "Contextualism: A World View for Modern Psychology", in *Nebraska Symposium, on Motivation* (Lincoln: University of Nebraska Press, 1977).

Spencer, L., and Dale, A., "Integration and Regulation in Organizations: A Contextual Approach", *Sociological Review* (27, 1979), pp. 679–702.

Tsoukas, H., "Introduction: From Social Engineering to Reflective Action in Organizational Behavior", in H. Tsoukas (ed.), *New Thinking in Organizational Behavior* (Oxford: Butterworth/Heinemann, 1994), pp. 1–21.

Watts, R.L., and Zimmerman, J.L., "Positive Accounting Theory: A Ten Year Perspective", *The Accounting Review* (1, 1990), pp. 112–34.

Webster, J., and Starbuck, W., "Theory Building in Industrial and Organizational Behavior", in H. Tsoukas (ed.), *New Thinking in Organizational Behavior* (Oxford: Butterworth/Heinemann, 1988), pp. 1–21.

Wells, M.C., "Revolution in Accounting Thought", *The Accounting Review* (July, 1976), pp. 250–78.

Accounting: a multiple paradigm science

10

10.1 Introduction

The History of thought and culture is, as Hegel showed with great brilliance, a changing pattern of great liberating ideas which inevitably turn into suffocating straitjackets, and so stimulate their own destruction by new emancipatory, and at the same time, enslaving conceptions. The first step to understand men is the bringing to consciousness of the model or models that dominate and penetrate their thought and action. Like all attempts to make men aware of the categories in which they think, it is a difficult and sometimes painful activity, likely to produce deeply disquieting results. The second task is to analyze the model itself, and this commits the analyst to accepting or modifying or rejecting it and in the last case, to providing a more adequate one in its place.[1]

Not long ago, contempt for accounting existed within and without the university. Fortunately, the situation has changed. Various surveys of research findings attest to the academic status of accounting.[2] Accounting researchers have employed different method- ologies and theories to examine all possible issues of interest in the field. Initially, in the early 1970s, such *a priori* research was criticized as theoretically deficient, or of doubtful value.[3] In 1970, Gonedes and Dopuch contended that an *a priori* model that justified the superiority of the set of accounting procedures is not possible. Fortunately Wells, in a seminal article in 1976, defended *a priori* research as a necessary step in a revolution in accounting thought.[4]

Wells proceeded to show that events in accounting seem to follow the pattern of successful revolution Kuhn describes, and thus that the discipline of accounting is emerging from a state of crisis. Briefly stated, Kuhn's thesis is that a science is dominated by a specific paradigm at any given point. Anomalies and a crisis stage may follow, ending in a revolution in which the reigning paradigm is replaced by a new, dominant paradigm. Central to Kuhn's revolutionary pattern is the definition of a "paradigm". Assuming for the time being that such a definition is possible, the next step is to identify the paradigms in accounting. This step was taken in 1977 by the American Accounting Association with the publication of its *Statement on Accounting Theory and Theory Acceptance* (SOATATA).[5] This statement considers developments in accounting thought from a "philosophy of science" perspective – that is, in terms of Kuhn's ideas about how progress occurs in science. SOATATA identifies three dominant theoretical approaches:

1. The "classical" (true-income/inductive) approach, used by both the "normative deductionists" and the "positive, inductive writers".

2. The "decision-usefulness" approach, used by those who stress decision models and focus on decision-makers (behavioral accounting and market-level research).

3. The "information/economics" approach, with a distinction made between the "single-individual case" and the "multi-individual case".

One of the arguments made in the AAA *Statement*, which is of great relevance to this study, is that the increasing varieties of accounting theories and approaches suggest the existence of several competing paradigms. The statement even suggests what these competing paradigms might be:

> For example, one paradigm, which could be labeled the "anthropological approach", specifies the professional practices of accountants as the empirical domain of accounting. Following this paradigm, accounting theory is formulated as a rationalization of, and by drawing inference from, extant accounting practices. Another paradigm rests largely on the behavior of stock markets to provide the empirical domain over which accounting a theory is constructed and applied. Still another general view of accounting specifies the decision processes of individuals and/or extant decision theories as the empirical domain of accounting theory. This tripartite categorization can be further expanded to incorporate both the ideal income approach and the information/economics approach, each of which suggests a somewhat unique empirical domain of accounting.[6]

First, if the application of Kuhn's concept to Wells' interpretations is accepted, accounting qualifies as a science. Second, if SOATATA's suggestions are accepted, accounting is a *multiple-paradigm science*. Two issues emerge from the acceptance of both Wells' and SOATATA's suggestions. First, to offset the confusion between theories and paradigms, an adequate definition of a "paradigm" must:

1. categorize theories as mere components of paradigms, and
2. differentiate between competing paradigms – two of the limitations of Wells' and SOATATA's suggestions.

Second, accounting, like most sciences, lacks a single comprehensive paradigm; thus, competing accounting paradigms should be properly identified and delineated to achieve a proper conception of the state of accounting.

10.2 The concept of a paradigm

10.2.1 Revolutionary changes, theories and the punctuated equilibrium paradigm

How do disciplines change? The question has been debated for a long time. Darwinism with its notion of incremental, cumulative change is far from being adequate for explaining changes in the disciplines and growth of knowledge. Instead natural historians like Niles Eldredge and Stephen Gould[7] propose a different notion of evolution known as punctuated equilibrium: an alternative between long periods with stable infrastructures and incremental adaptation and brief periods of revolutionary upheaval. Basically, "lineages exist in essentially static form (equilibrium) over most of their histories and new species arise abruptly, through sudden, revolutionary 'punctuations' of rapid change (at which point – as in the Darwinian model – environmental selection determines the fate of new variations)".[8] As Exhibit 10.1 shows, the punctuated equilibrium model has been described in six theories, including individuals, groups, organizations, scientific fields, biological species, and grand theory. Exhibit 10.2 shows how punctuated equilibrium models differ from traditional counterparts. For each theory the punctuated equilibrium offers three main components: deep structure, equilibrium periods and revolutionary periods. The interest in this

Commonalities:

During equilibrium periods, systems maintain and carry out the choices of their deep structure. Systems make adjustments that preserve the deep structure against internal and external perturbations, and move incrementally along paths built into the deep structure. Pursuit of stable deep structure choices may result in behavior that is turbulent on the surface.

Individuals: Levinson

Structure-Building Periods: The primary task is to build a life structure: a man must make certain key choices, form a structure around them, and pursue his goals and values within this structure. To say that a period is stable in this sense is not … to say that it is tranquil. … The task of … building a structure is often stressful … and may involve many kinds of change. Each stable period … has distinctive tasks and character according to where it is in the life cycle. (1978: 49) [Such periods] ordinarily last 5 to 7 years, 10 at most. (1986: 7)

Groups: Gersick (1988)

Project groups' lives unfold in two main phases, separated by a transition period halfway between the group's beginning and its expected deadline. Within phases, groups approach their work using stable frameworks of assumptions, premises, and behavior patterns. As frameworks vary, specific activities and efficacy vary from group to group. During a phase, groups accumulate more or less work, learning, and experience within the boundaries of their framework, but (even when hampered by it), they do not change their fundamental approach to their task.

Organizations: Tushman & Romanelli (1985)

Convergent Periods: Relatively long time spans of incremental change and adaptation which elaborate structure, systems, controls, and resources toward increased coalignment, [which] may or may not be associated with effective performance. (: 173) [They are] characterized by duration, strategic orientation, [and] turbulence. … (: 179) During [these] periods … inertia increases and competitive vigilance decreases: structure frequently drives strategy. (: 215) Scientific Fields: Kuhn (1970)

Normal Science is directed to the articulation of those phenomena and theories that the paradigm already supplies. (: 24) Three classes of problems – determination of significant fact, matching of facts with theory, and articulation of theory – exhaust … the literature of normal science, both empirical and theoretical. … Work under that paradigm can be conducted in no other way, and to desert the paradigm is to cease practicing the science it defines. (: 34)

Biological Species: Gould (1980)

Phyletic transformation [is] minor adjustment within populations [which is] sequential and adaptive. (: 15) [It is a mode of evolution in which] an entire population changes from one state to another. [This] yields no increase in diversity, only a transformation of one thing into another. Since extinction (by extirpation, not by evolution into something else) is so common, a biota with [only this, and] no mechanism for increasing diversity would soon be wiped out. (: 180) Grand Theory: Prigogine & Stengers (1984); Haken (1981)

In *stable regions*, deterministic laws dominate. (: 169) All individual initiative is doomed to insignificance. … (: 206)

Under given external conditions, the individual parts of the system have … stable configurations … or oscillations. … [If] small perturbations [are] imposed upon the system … the individual parts of the system relax to their former state once the perturbation is removed, or they change their behavior only slightly when the perturbation persists. (: 17)

Exhibit 10.1 Concepts of equilibrium periods in six theories

Commonalities:

Deep structure is a network of fundamental, interdependent "choices," of the basic configuration into which a system's units are organized, and the activities that maintain both this configuration and the system's resource exchange with the environment. Deep structure in human systems is largely implicit.

Individuals: Levinson (1986: 6)

Life Structure: The underlying pattern or design of a person's life at a given time. ... The life structure [answers the questions]: "What is my life like now? What are the most important parts of my life, and how are they interrelated? Where do I invest most of my time and energy?" The primary components of a life structure are the person's relationships with various others in the external world.

Groups: Gersick (see 1988: 17, 21)

Framework: A set of givens about the group's situation and how it will behave that form a stable platform from which the group operates. Frameworks may be partly explicit but are primarily implicit. They are integrated webs of performance strategies, interaction patterns, assumptions about and approaches toward a group's task and outside context.

Organizations: Tushman & Romanelli (1985: 176)

Strategic Orientation: Answers the question: What is it that is being converged upon? While [it] may or may not be explicit, it can be described by [five facets]: (1) core beliefs and values regarding the organization, its employees and its environment; (2) products, markets, technology and competitive timing; (3) the distribution of power; (4) the organization's structure; and (5) the nature, type and pervasiveness of control systems.

Scientific Fields: Kuhn (1970)

Paradigm: Universally recognized scientific achievements that for a time provide model problems and solutions to a community of practitioners. (: viii) [Paradigms indicate] what a datum [is], what instruments might be used to retrieve it, and what concepts [are] relevant to its interpretation. (: 122) [However, scientists] are little better than laymen at characterizing the established bases of their field. ... Such abstractions show mainly through their ability to do successful research. (: 47)

Biological Species: Gould (1989); Wake, Roth, & Wake (1983: 218–219)*

Genetic Programs: Stasis is ... an active feature of organisms and populations ... based largely on complex epistasis in genetic programs, and the resilient and limited geometries of developmental sequences. (: 124)

[Living systems require very specific internal processes.] The ... conditions governing each internal process are provided by preceding processes within the system, [constituting a network of] circular interaction: [the activity of each element affects all]. Each ... change of the system must remain within the ... limits of the process of circular production and maintenance of the elements, or the system itself will decompose. No element can interact with the environment independently ... and no independent change (evolution) of single elements can take place. ... The same is true for the "activity" of the genes: they never "express" themselves in a direct, linear way. Thus organisms have evolved as systems resistant to change, even genetic change. Grand Theory: Haken (1981: 17)

Order Parameters: Collective modes ... which define the order of the overall system. ... Order parameters ... may be material, such as the amplitude of a physical wave, [or] immaterial, such as ideas or symbols. ... Once ... established, they prescribe the actions of the subsystems ... at the microscopic level.

*The Wake *et al.* excerpt is from an article recommended by S.J. Gould (personal communication). It explains and expands on the excerpt from Gould.

Source: Reprinted with permission of Academy of Management, P.O. Box 3020, Briar Cliff Manor, NY 10510–8020. Connie J.G. Gersick, "Revolutionary Change Theories: A Multilevel Exploration of the Punctuated Equilibrium Paradigm", *Academy of Management Review* (16, 1, 1991), p.15. Reproduced by permission of the publisher via Copyright Clearance Center Inc.

Exhibit 10.2 Concepts of deep structure in six theories

chapter is with the application of the punctuated equilibrium paradigm to scientific fields in general and accounting in particular.

10.2.2 Kuhn's general theory of scientific revolutions

A theory of scientific revolutions will focus on the progress of knowledge and the motivation of such progress. Thomas Kuhn's works focused on the progress of knowledge in a particular discipline of normal science.[9] This thesis of scientific revolutions rests on the concept of paradigm. After criticisms were raised about the different and inconsistent uses of the term, Kuhn refined it for the second edition of his book:

> In much of the book the term "paradigm" is used in two different senses. On the one hand, it stands for the entire constellation of beliefs, values, techniques that are shared by the members of a given community. On the other hand it denotes one sort of element in that constellation, the concrete puzzle-solutions which, employed as models or examples, can replace explicit rules as a basis for the solution of the remaining puzzles of normal science.[10]

These paradigms do not remain forever dominant. Anomalies are first recognized. The anomaly is incorrigible. A period of insecurity and crisis arises with the dispute between those who see the anomaly as a counter-example and those who do not:

> Normal science repeatedly goes astray. And when it does – when, that is, the profession can no longer evade anomalies that subvert the existing tradition of scientific practice – then begins the extraordinary investigation that leads the profession at last to a new set of commitments, a new basis for the practice of science.[11]

The crisis continues with the emergence of alternative sets and ideas and clear identification of schools of thoughts. What actually goes on in the crisis period is not well known. H. Gilman McCann suggested the following characteristic levels of theoretical and quantitative work associated with the initial and final periods of a normal science:

1. The level of theoretical work will rise as the revolution develops. The rise is composed of (a) an increase in the level of theoretical work among followers of the given paradigm and (b) an initially high level of theoretical work by the followers of the new paradigm, followed by a decline once the success of the new paradigm is assured.

2. The shift to the new paradigm will occur earlier among theoretical papers than among others.

3. The level of quantitative work will rise as the revolution develops. The rise is composed of (a) an increase, possibly followed by a decline, in the level of work among the followers of the given paradigm and (b) an initially high level of quantitative work among supporters of the new paradigm, possibly followed by a decline as the new paradigm succeeds and the new problems come to light.

4. The shift to the new paradigm will occur earlier among quantitative papers than among others.

5. The rise in the level of quantitative work will be most pronounced among theoretical papers.

6. There will be an increase in the number of authors as the revolution develops.

7. There will be an increase in the productivity of authors as the revolution progresses.

8. The shift to the new paradigm will occur earlier among papers of younger authors than among papers of older ones.

9. The supporters of the new paradigm will be younger than the defenders of the old one.

10. There will be few neutral papers.

11. The proportion of citations to authors supporting the new paradigm will increase during the revolution.[12]

All laws and propositions become subject to empirical testimony. The final rejection of one paradigm for another does not, however, rest exclusively on the empirical evidence. Nonlogical factors, including metaphysical views, philosophical positions, ethnocentrism, nationalism, the social characteristics of the scientific community, may have a bearing on the decisions.[13] Domination of the new paradigm is accompanied by recognition bestowed on its proponents. It is this recognition, rather than money or power, which will become the motivating factor for researchers in a given paradigm and in a given scientific community. Basically, researchers will exchange social recognition for information. As stated by Hagstrom: "Manuscripts submitted to scientific periodicals are often called 'contributions' and they are, in fact, gifts".[14]

> In general, the acceptance of a gift by an individual or a community implies a kind of recognition of the status of the donor and the existence of certain kinds of reciprocal rights in science, the acceptance by scientific journals of contributed manuscripts establishes the donor's status as a scientist – indeed, status as a scientist can be achieved only by much gift-giving – and it assures him of prestige within the scientific community.[15]

Although it may be difficult to disagree with the notion that recognition is the primary motivation for research in any discipline, it is tempting to argue that the driving force is the satisfaction of a job well done. Merton argued the case as follows:

> Recognition of originality becomes socially validated testimony that one has successfully lived up to the most exacting requirements of one's role as a scientist. The self-image of the individual scientist will also depend greatly on the appraisal by his scientific peers of the extent to which he has lived up to this exacting and crucially important aspect of his role.[16]

> There is nevertheless, a gem of psychological truth in the suspicion enveloping the drive for recognition in science. Any intrinsic reward – fame, money, position – is morally ambiguous and potentially subversive of cultural esteemed values: for as rewards are meted out, they can displace the original motive: concern with recognition can displace concern with advancing knowledge.[17]

With recognition as either a goal or a sign of a job well done, the researchers in the dominant paradigm, and the other still struggling paradigms ("the resisters") communicate their information either in formal channels of communication for institutional recognition or indirect communication for elementary recognition.

10.2.3 Ritzer's visions of multiple paradigms applied to accounting

Central to the general theory of scientific revolutions is the proper definition of the concept of a paradigm. Kuhn's use of the term is different and inconsistent. The narrow definition provided in the epilogue to the second edition of his book was still found vague. It did not alleviate the major criticisms directed toward Kuhn's change of view that paradigms rise and fall as a result of political factors to the view that one paradigm wins over another for good reasons, including "accuracy, scope, simplicity, fruitfulness, and the like".[18] George Ritzer, for example, argued in favor of the first view and maintained that the emergence of a paradigm is essentially a political phenomenon.[19] He stated:

> One paradigm wins out over another because its supporters have more *power* than those who support competing paradigms and *not* necessarily because their paradigm is "better" than its competitors. For example, the paradigm whose supporters control the most important journals in a field and thereby determine what will be published is more likely to gain pre-eminence than paradigms whose adherents lack access to prestigious outlets for their works. Similarly, positions of leadership in a field are likely to be given to supporters of the dominant paradigm and gives them a platform to enunciate their position with a significant amount of legitimacy. Supporters of paradigms that are seeking to gain hegemony within a field are obviously at a disadvantage, since they lack the power outlined above. Nevertheless, they can, by waging a political battle of their own, overthrow a dominant paradigm and gain that position for themselves.[20]

Few were in agreement with Ritzer's arguments about the first view and also argued that the reasons advanced in the second view are paradigm-dependent. With the view that paradigms are politics-dependent, Ritzer offered the following definition of a paradigm:

> A paradigm is a fundamental image of the subject matter within a science. It serves to define what should be asked, and what rules should be followed in interpreting the answer obtained. The paradigm is the broadest unit of consensus within a science and serves to differentiate one scientific community (or subcommunity) from another. It subsumes, defines, and interrelates the exemplars, theories, methods, and instruments that exist within it.[21]

The basic components of a paradigm emerge from Ritzer's definition:

1. an *exemplar*, or a piece of work that stands as a model for those who work within the paradigm;
2. an *image* of the subject matter;
3. *theories*; and
4. *methods* and instruments.

This chapter uses Ritzer's definition to analyze scientific communities or subcommunities in accounting with the assumptions that:

1. accounting lacks a single comprehensive paradigm and is a multiple-paradigm science; and
2. each of these accounting paradigms is striving for acceptance, even domination within the discipline.

Although stated in terms of competing paradigms, the following statement could be used to argue for competing paradigms:

> While the value of the prediction of a theory to users influences its uses, it does not solely determine its success. Because the costs of errors and the implementation vary,

several theories about the phenomena can exist simultaneously for predictive purposes. However, only one will be generally accepted by theorists. In accepting one theory over another, theorists will be influenced by the intuitive appeal of the theory's explanation for phenomena and the range of phenomena it can explain and predict as well as by the usefulness of the predictions to users.[22]

Following suggestions made by the 1977 American Accounting Association's publication of its *Statement of Accounting Theory and Theory Acceptance*, the following paradigms were suggested: [23]

1. the anthropological/inductive paradigm;
2. the true-income/deductive paradigm;
3. the decision-usefulness/decision-model paradigm;
4. the decision-usefulness/decision-maker/aggregate-market-behavior paradigm;
5. the decision-usefulness/decision-maker/individual-user paradigm;
6. the information/economics paradigm.

Paradigms 1–5 are examined next with a particular focus on the four components of exemplar, image theories, and methods.

10.3 The anthropological/inductive paradigm

10.3.1 Exemplars

Several studies qualify as exemplars of the *anthropological/inductive paradigm* – namely, the works of Gilman, Hatfield, Ijiri, Littleton, and Paton.[24] The authors of these studies share a concern for a *descriptive-inductive* approach to the construction of an accounting theory and a belief in the value of *extant accounting practices*. For example, Ijiri considers the primary concern of accounting to be the functioning of accountability relationships among interested parties. The objective measurement is the economic performance of the firm. On the basis of discussions concerning research methodology and the role of logic in theory construction and policy formulation in accounting, Ijiri presents *accountability* as a descriptive theory of accounting:

> What we are emphasizing here is that current accounting practice can be better interpreted if we view accountability as the underlying goal. We are also suggesting that unless accounting is viewed in this manner, much of the current practice would appear to be inconsistent and irrational.[25]

In defense of his paradigm refuting the criticisms of advocates of current-cost and current-value accounting, Ijiri also presents an axiomatic model of existing accounting practice that evaluates the significance of historical cost in terms of accountability and decision-making.

Littleton arrives at his accounting principles from observations of accounting practice that evaluate the significance of historical cost in terms of accountability and decision-making.

> Teachers of bookkeeping and later of accounting and auditing found it necessary to supplement the accumulated rules and descriptions of procedure with explanations and justifications. This was done in order that study should be something more than

the memorizing of rules. Hence, it is appropriate to say that both the methods of practice and the explanations of theory were inductively derived out of experience.[26]

Good theory is practice-created and, moreover, is practice conditioning. Finally, whenever evidence of integration among accounting ideas is found, it will strengthen the conviction that accounting contains the possibility of being built into a system of coordinated explanations and justifications of what accounting is and what it can become.[27]

Two other studies by Gordon and by Watts and Zimmerman[28] qualify as exemplars of the anthropological/inductive paradigm. Both studies argue that management will select the accounting rule that will tend to smooth income and the rate of growth in income. Gordon theorizes on *income smoothing* as follows:

Proposition 1: The criterion a corporate management uses in selecting among accounting principles is the maximization of its utility or welfare. ...

Proposition 2: The ability of a management increases with

1. its job security,
2. the level and rate of growth in the management's income, and
3. the level and rate of growth in the corporation size. ...

Proposition 3: The achievement of the management goals stated in Proposition 2 is dependent in part on the satisfaction of stockholders with the corporation's performance; that is, other things the same, the happier the stockholders, the greater the job security, income, etc., of the management. ...

Proposition 4: Stockholders' satisfaction with a corporation increases with the average rate of growth in the corporation's income (or the average rate of return on its capital) and stability of its income. This proposition is as readily verified as Proposition 2.

Theorem: Given that the above four propositions are accepted or found to be true, it follows that a management would within the limits of its power, that is, the latitude allowed by accounting rules,

1. smooth reported income, and
2. smooth the rate of growth income.

By "smooth the rate of growth in income", we mean the following: If the rate of growth is high, accounting practices that reduce it should be adopted, and vice versa.[29]

Several empirical tests in the income-smoothing literature leave Gordon's model unconfirmed. Also, Gordon's assumptions that shareholder satisfaction is solely a positive function of income and that increases in stock prices always follow increases in accounting income have been more seriously contested. To avoid the pitfalls that may exist in Gordon's model, Watts and Zimmerman attempt to provide a positive theory of accounting by exploring the factors influencing management's attitudes regarding accounting standards.[30] At the outset, Watts and Zimmerman assume that the management's utility is a *positive* function of the expected compensation of future periods and a *negative* function of the dispersion of future compensation. Their analysis shows that the choice of accounting standards can affect a firm's cash flow through taxes, regulation, political costs, information-production costs, and management-compensation plans:

The first four factors increase managerial wealth by increasing the cash flows, and, hence, the share price. The last factor can increase managerial wealth by altering the terms of the incentive compensation.[31]

10.3.2 Image of the subject matter

To those who adopt the anthropological/inductive paradigm, the basic subject matter is:

1. existing accounting practices, and
2. management's attitudes toward those practices.

Proponents of this view argue in general either that the techniques may be derived and justified on the basis of their tested use or that management plays a central role in determining techniques to be implemented. Consequently, the accounting-research objective associated with the anthropological/inductive paradigm is to understand, explain and predict existing accounting practices. For example, Ijiri views the mission of this paradigmatic approach as follows:

> This type of inductive reasoning to derive goals implicit in the behavior of an existing system is not intended to be pro-establishment to promote the maintenance of the status quo. The purpose of such exercise is to highlight where changes are most needed and where they are feasible. Changes suggested as a result of such a study have a much better chance of actually being implemented.[32]

10.3.3 Theories

Four theories may be considered to be part of the anthropological/inductive paradigm:

1. information economics;[33]
2. the analytical/agency model;[34]
3. the income smoothing/earnings management hypotheses;[35] and
4. the positive theory of accounting.[36]

10.3.4 Methods

Those who adopt the anthropological/inductive paradigm tend to employ one of three techniques:

1. techniques used in income smoothing research;[37]
2. techniques used in earnings management research;[38] and
3. techniques used in positive theory research.[39]

10.4 The true-income/deductive paradigm

10.4.1 Exemplars

Studies that qualify as exemplars of the *true-income/deductive paradigm* are the works of Alexander, Canning, Edwards and Bell, MacNeal, Moonitz, Paton, Sprouse and Moonitz, and Sweeney.[40] These authors share a concern for a normative-deductive approach to the construction of an accounting theory and, with the exception of Alexander, a belief that, ideally, income measured using a single valuation base would meet the needs of all users.

These researchers are also in complete agreement that current price information is more useful than conventional historical-cost information is to users in making economic decisions. Paton, for example, refutes the propriety theory of accounts view by restating the theory of accounting in a way that is consistent with the conditions and needs of the business enterprise as a distinct entity or personality. According to Paton, accounting plays a significant and relevant role in the firm and in society:

> If the tendencies of the economic process as evidenced in market prices are to be reflected rationally in the decisions of business managers, efficient machinery for the recording and interpreting of such statistics must be available; and a sound accounting scheme represents an essential part of such a mechanism. ...
>
> To put the matter in very general terms, accounting, insofar as it contributes to render effective the control of the price system in its direction of economic activity contributes to general productive efficiency and has a clear-cut social significance, a value to the industrial community as a whole.[41]

Paton's theory of the accounting system consists of a logical discussion and justification of the accounting structure in terms of the fundamental classes of accounts; the proprietorship and liabilities; the property and equity accounts; the types of transactions; the expense, revenue and supplementary accounts; the account classification; the periodic analysis; and the concepts of debit and credit. Paton states:

> The liberal view that, ideally, all bona fide value changes in either direction, from whatever cause, should be reflected in the accounts has been adopted without argument. To show that all possible types of situations and transactions can be handled in a rational manner in accordance with the principles enunciated is a chief reason for this attitude.[42]

10.4.2 Image of the subject matter

To those who adopt the true-income/deductive paradigm, the basic subject matter is:

1. the construction of an accounting theory on the basis of logical and normative reasoning and conceptual rigor; and
2. a concept of ideal income based on some other method than the historical-cost method.

MacNeal argues for an ideal-income concept as follows:

> There is one correct definition of profits in an accounting sense. A "profit" is an increase in net wealth. A "loss" is decrease in net wealth. This is an economist's definition. It is terse, obvious, and mathematically demonstrable.[43]

Alexander, who also argues for an ideal-income concept, states:

> We must find out whether economic income is an ideal from which accounting income differs only to the degree that the ideal is practically unattainable, or whether economic income is appropriate even if it could conveniently be measured.[44]

10.4.3 Theories

The theories that emerge from the true-income/deductive paradigm present alternatives to the historical-cost accounting system. In general, five theories or schools of thought may be identified:

1. price-level adjusted (or current-purchasing-power) accounting;[45]
2. replacement-cost accounting;[46]
3. deprival-value accounting;[47]
4. continuously contemporary (net-realizable-value) accounting;[48]
5. present-value accounting.[49]

Each of these theories presents alternative methods of asset valuation and income determination that allegedly overcome the defects of the historical-cost accounting system.

10.4.4 Methods

Those who accept the true-income/deductive paradigm generally employ analytic reasoning to justify the construction of an accounting theory or to argue the advantages of a particular asset-valuation/income-determination model other than historical-cost accounting. Advocates of this paradigm generally proceed from objectives and postulates about the environment to specific methods.

10.5 The decision-usefulness/decision-model paradigm

10.5.1 Exemplars

Chambers was one of the first to point to the *decision-usefulness/decision-model paradigm*:

> It is therefore a corollary of the assumption of rational management that there shall be an information-providing system; such a system is required both as a basis for decisions and a basis for reviewing the consequences of decisions. ... A formal information-providing system would conform with two general propositions.
>
> The first is a condition of all logical discourse. The system should be logically consistent; no rule or process can be permitted that is contrary to any other rule or process. ... The second proposition arises from the use of accounting statements as a basis for making decisions of practical consequence. The information yielded by any such system should be relevant to the kinds of decision the making of which it is expected to facilitate.[50]

Chambers does not pursue this view of the decision-usefulness/decision-model paradigm. He prefers to base an accounting theory on the usefulness of "current cash equivalents", rather than on the decision models of specific user groups. Similarly, May offers a list of uses of financial accounts without explicitly employing the decision-model approach to the formulation of an accounting theory.[51] According to May, financial accounts are used as:

1. a report of stewardship;
2. a basis of fiscal policy;
3. a criterion of the legality of dividends;
4. a guide to wise dividend activity;
5. a basis for the granting of credit;
6. information for prospective investors;
7. a guide to the value of investments already made;

8. an aid to government supervision;
9. a basis for price of rate regulations;
10. a basis for taxation.

In fact, the words of Beaver, Kennelly and Voss and of Sterling may be considered the true exemplars of the decision-usefulness/decision-model paradigm.[52] Beaver, Kennelly and Voss examine the origin of the *predictive-ability criterion*, its relationship to the facilitation of decision-making, and the potential difficulties, associated with its implementation. According to the predictive-ability criterion, alternative methods of accounting measurement are evaluated in terms of their ability to predict economic events:

> The measure with the greatest predictive power with respect to a given event is considered to be the "best" method for that particular purpose.[53]

The predictive-ability criterion is presented as a purposive criterion in the sense that accounting data ought to be evaluated in terms of their purpose or use, which is generally accepted in accounting to be the facilitation of decision-making. The predictive-ability criterion is assumed to be relevant, even when applied in conjunction with a low specification of the decision model:

> Because prediction is an inherent part of the decision process, knowledge of the predictive ability of alternative measures is a prerequisite to the use of the decision-making criterion. At the same time, it permits tentative conclusions regarding alternative measurements, subject to subsequent confirmation when the decision models eventually become specified. The use of predictive ability as a purposive criterion is more than merely consistent with accounting's decision-making orientation. It can provide a body of research that will bring accounting closer to its goal of evaluation in terms of a decision-making criterion.[54]

Sterling develops criteria to be used in evaluating the various measures of wealth and income. Given the conflicting viewpoints about the objectives of accounting reports, Sterling chooses *usefulness* as the overriding criterion of a measurement method, emphasizing its importance over such requirements as objectivity and verifiability.[55]

Owing to the diversity of decision-makers and the inherent economic and physical impossibility of providing all of the information that users want, Sterling opts for usefulness as the relevant criterion of decision models:

> The basis for selection that I prefer is to supply information for rational decision models. The modifier "rational" is defined to mean those decision models that are most likely to allow decision-makers to achieve their goals. ...[56]

> In summary, an accounting system should be designed to provide relevant information to rational decision models. The accounting system cannot supply all the information desired by all decision-makers and, therefore, we must decide to exclude some kinds of information and to include other kinds.

Restricting the decision models to rational ones permits the exclusion of a raft of data based on the whims of decision-makers. It permits us to concentrate on those kinds that have been demonstrated to be effective in achieving the decision-makers' goals.[57]

10.5.2 Image of the subject matter

To those who adopt the decision-usefulness/decision-model paradigm, the basic subject matter is the usefulness of accounting information to decision models. Information relevant to a decision model or criterion is determined and then implemented by choosing the best accounting alternative. *Usefulness* to a decision model is equated with relevance to a decision model. For example, Sterling states:

> If a property is specified by a decision model, then a measure of that property is relevant (to that decision model). If a property is not specified by a decision model, then a measure of property is irrelevant (to that decision model).[58]

10.5.3 Theories

Two kinds of theories may be included within the decision-usefulness/decision-model paradigm. The first type of theory deals with the different kinds of decision models associated with business decision-making (EOQ, PERT, linear programming, capital budgeting, buy versus lease, make or buy, and so on). The information requirements for most of these decision models are fairly well specified. The second kind of theory deals with the different economic events that may affect a going concern (bankruptcy, takeover, merger, bond ratings, and so on). Theories to link accounting information to these events are still lacking. Developing such theories is the primary objective of those working within the decision-usefulness/decision-model paradigm.

10.5.4 Methods

Those who accept the decision-usefulness/decision-model paradigm tend to rely on empirical techniques to determine the predictive ability of selected items of information. The general approach has been to use discriminant analysis to classify into one of several *a priori* groupings, dependent on a firm's individual financial characteristics.

10.6 The decision-usefulness/decision-maker/ aggregate-market-behavior paradigm

10.6.1 Exemplars

The exemplars of the decision-usefulness/decision-maker-behavior paradigm are the works of Gonedes and of Gonedes and Dopuch.[59] In his pioneering paper, Gonedes extended the interest in decision-usefulness from the individual-user response to the aggregate-market response. Arguing that market response (for example, anticipatory price responses) to accounting numbers should govern the evaluation of the informational content of these numbers and to the procedures used to produce them, Gonedes developed the aggregate-market paradigm which implies that accounting procedures numbers have informational content dictated by market responses. To the counterarguments (1) that the procedures used to produce the numbers may induce market inefficiencies and (2) that recipients may be conditioned to respond to accounting numbers in a particular manner, Gonedes argued that if both cases were true, the opportunity for those who possess this knowledge to earn an abnormal profit would provide a basis for the demise of the market paradigm within the context of an efficient capital market.

In their award-winning paper, Gonedes and Dopuch provided a theoretical framework for assessing the desirability and effects of alternative accounting procedures. Their approach relies on the use of prices of (rates of returns on) firms' ownership shares. Gonedes and Dopuch concluded that the price-domain analysis is sufficient for assessing the effects of alternative accounting procedures. This conclusion is based primarily on one case of market failure in which information of a public good nature cannot be excluded from nonpurchasers (the free-rider problem); in such a case, the prices of firms' shares cannot be used to assess the desirability of alternative accounting procedures or regulations.

Among the market-failure possibilities is the issue of adverse selection.[60] Another is the effect of information on the completeness of markets and efficient risk-sharing arrangements.[61] Gonedes and Dopuch also noted that some criticisms of work based on capital-market efficiency treat remarks on assessing effects if they were remarks on assessing desirability.

A contemporary piece of work by Beaver may also be viewed as an exemplar of the decision-usefulness/decision-maker/aggregate-market-behavior paradigm.[62] Beaver raised the issue of the importance of this relationship between accounting data and security behavior. He argued that it is inconceivable that optimal informational systems for investors can be selected without a knowledge of how accounting data are impounded in prices, because these prices determine wealth and wealth affects the multiperiod investment decisions of individuals.

10.6.2 Image of the subject matter

To those who adopt the decision-usefulness/decision-maker/aggregate-market-behavior paradigm, the basic subject matter is the aggregate-market response to accounting variables. These authors agree that, in general, decision-usefulness of accounting variables can be derived from aggregate-market-behavior, or, as presented by Gonedes and Dopuch, only the effects of alternative accounting procedures or speculations can be assessed from aggregate-market behavior. According to Gonedes and Dopuch, the selection of the accounting-information system is determined by aggregate-market behavior:

10.6.3 Theories

The relationship between aggregate-market behavior and accounting variables is based on the theory of capital-market efficiency. According to this theory, the market for securities is deemed efficient in that (1) market prices "fully reflect" all publicly available information and, by implication, that (2) market prices are unbiased and respond instantaneously to new information. The theory implies that on the average, the abnormal return (the return in excess of the equilibrium expected return) to be earned from employing a set of extant information in conjunction with any trading scheme is zero.[63] This change in information set will automatically result in new equilibrium. In fact the theories confirming the market behavior paradigm include:

1. the efficient market model;[64]
2. the efficient market hypothesis;[65]
3. the capital asset pricing model;[66]
4. the arbitrage pricing theory; and[67]
5. the equilibrium theory of option pricing.[68]

10.6.4 Methods

Those who accept the market paradigm rely on the following methods:

1. the market model;[69]
2. the beta estimation models;[70]
3. the event study methodology;
4. the Ohlson's valuation model;[71]
5. the price-level balance sheet evaluation models;[72]
6. the information content of earnings models; and[73]
7. the models of the relation between earnings and return.[74]

10.7 The decision-usefulness/decision-maker/ individual-user paradigm

10.7.1 Exemplars

The work of William Bruns may be considered the first exemplar of the decision-maker/ individual-user paradigm.[75] Bruns proposed hypotheses that relate the use of accounting information and the relevance of accounting information to the decision-maker's conception of accounting, and other available information to the effect of accounting information on decisions. These hypotheses are also developed in a model that identifies and relates some factors that may determine when decisions are affected by accounting systems and information. *Behavioral accounting research* is the study of how accounting functions and reports influence the behavior of accountants and nonaccountants.

10.7.2 Image of the subject matter

To those who adopt the decision-usefulness/decision-maker/individual-user paradigm, the basic subject matter is the individual-user response to accounting variables. Advocates of this paradigm argue that, in general, the decision-usefulness of accounting variables may be derived from human behavior. In other words, accounting is viewed as a behavioral process. The objective of behavioral accounting research is to understand, explain and predict human behavior within an accounting context. This paradigm is of interest to internal users of accounting, procedures and attesters of information, and the general public or its surrogates.

10.7.3 Theories

Much of the research associated with the decision-usefulness/decision-maker/individual-user paradigm has been conducted without benefit of the explicit formation of a theory. In general, the alternative to developing appropriate behavioral accounting theories has been to borrow from other disciplines. Most of the borrowed theories adequately explain and predict human behavior within an accounting context. These borrowed theories include:

1. cognitive relativism in accounting;[76]
2. cultural relativism in accounting;[77]
3. behavioral effects of accounting information;[78]
4. linguistic relativism in accounting;[79]
5. functional and data fixation hypotheses;[80]
6. information inductance hypotheses;[81]

7. organizational and budgetary slack hypotheses;[82]
8. contingency approaches to the design of accounting systems;[83]
9. participative budgeting and performance;[84]
10. human information processing models,[85] which include:
    (a) the lens model;[86]
    (b) the probalistic judgment model;[87]
    (c) the predecisional behavioral model;[88] and
    (d) the cognitive style approach.[89]

10.7.4 Models

Those accepting this paradigm tend to use all of the methods favored by behaviorists – observation techniques, interviews, and questionnaires, and experimentation is the preferred method. It is also a good starting point for further validation.

10.8 The information/economics paradigm

10.8.1 Exemplars

Exemplars of the information/economics paradigm are the words of Crandall, Feltham, and Feltham and Demski.[90] In his pioneering paper, Feltham provides a framework for determining the value of a change in the information decision (the decision-maker). The framework relies on the individual components that are required to compute the expected payoff (or utility) for a particular information system. The components are:

1. a set of possible actions at each period within a time horizon;
2. a payoff function over the events that occur during periods;
3. probabilistic relationships between past and future events;
4. events and signals from the information system, including past and future signals;
5. a set of decision rules as functions of the signals.

The framework states that the value of changing from one information system to another is equal to the difference between the expected payoffs of the two alternatives.

Crandall examines the usefulness of the information/economics paradigm to the future development of accounting theory and offers the "applied information economics" approach as a new mainstream accounting theory. Simply, this approach consists of recognizing explicitly each component of the information/economics model and broadening the scope of accounting design to include all of these components. Crandall defines the components as the "filter", the "model", the "channel", "decoding", and the "decision rule". The implications for the future development of accounting theory are stated as follows:

> The ideal for the development of accounting theory would be the development of a constructive theory of information economics where, in some significant areas of the model, one could develop algorithms that pointed out the theoretically "best" design of the system, given a set of assumptions ...[91]

> [The purpose is] to permit the construction and evaluation of information systems for the purpose of maximizing the utility to each user, subject to constraints as to the cost

of the system, the decision rules available, the state of the technology, and the feasibility of obtaining information from the real world.[92]

The third exemplar, Feltham and Demski's "The Use of Models in Information Evaluation", presents and discusses a model of information choice that views information evaluation in *cost–benefit terms* and as a *sequential process*. The entire process is summarized as follows:

> … specification of a particular information system results in a set of signals being supplied to the decision maker; the decision maker may then use the resulting information in selecting his or her action; and this action may determine, in part, the events x of the subsequent period. The information evaluation must predict the relationship between each of the above elements: the signal generation process, $\phi(y/\eta)$; $a(y/\eta)$; the decision maker's prediction- and action-choice process and the relationship between the actions selected and the events that will occur, $\phi(x/y, \eta/a)$; $w(x)$. In addition, the decision maker must predict the gross payoff he or she will derive from the events of the subsequent period, as well as the cost of operating the particular information system $w'(y, \eta)$.[93]

10.8.2 Image of the subject matter

To those who adapt the information/economics paradigm, the basic subject matter is:

1. information is an economic commodity, and
2. the acquisition of information amounts to a problem of economic choice.

The value of information is viewed in terms of a cost–benefit criterion within the formal structure of decision theory and economic theory. This is best stated as follows:

> … the case of the argument on behalf of accrual accounting rests on the premises that (1) reported income under accrual accounting conveys more information than a less ambitious cash flow-oriented accounting system would, (2) accrual accounting is the most efficient way to convey this additional information, and as a corollary, (3) the "value" of such additional information system exceeds its "cost".[94]

Accounting information is evaluated in terms of its ability to improve the quality of the optimal choice in a basic choice problem that must be resolved by an individual or a number of heterogeneous individuals. A single individual must select among different actions that have different possible outcomes. Assuming a consistent, rational-choice behavior governed by the *expected utility hypothesis*, the action with the highest expected payoff (or utility) is preferred by the individual. Information in this context is required to revise the probabilities of the original outcomes. Thus, the individual may face a two-stage process:

1. a first stage, during which the information system produces different signals; and
2. a second stage, during which the observance of a signal results in a revision of probabilities and choice of the conditional best action.

The information system with the highest expected utility is preferred. The information required for a systematic probability-revision (*Bayesian-version*) analysis in turn facilitates information analysis on the basis of the subjective, expected-utility maximization rule.

10.8.3 Theories

The information/economics paradigm draws on insights from the "theory of teams", developed by Marschak and Radner,[95] on statistical decision theory, and on the economic theory of choice. What results is a normative theory of information evaluation for the systematic analysis of information alternatives. Central to the information/economics paradigm is the traditional economic assumption of consistent, rational-choice behavior.

10.8.4 Methods

Those who accept the information/economics paradigm generally employ analytic reasoning based on statistical decision theory and the economic theory of choice. The approach consists of isolating the general relationships and effects of alternative scenarios and applying Bayesian-revision analysis and a cost–benefit criterion to analyze questions of accounting policy. The primary assumption of this approach is rationality.

10.9 The science of accounting

The situation in accounting research has drastically improved over the years. Witness the following description of the situation made on December 20, 1923, in an address to the American Association of University Instructors in Accounting by Henry Rand Hatfield:

> I am sure that all of our colleagues look upon accounting as an intruder, a Saul among the prophets, a pariah whose very presence detracts somewhat from the sanctity of the academic walls. It is true that we ourselves speak of the science of accounts, or the art of accounting, even of the philosophy of accounts. But accounting is, alas, only a pseudo-science unrecognized by J. McKeen Cattel; its products are displayed neither in the salon, nor in the national academy; we find it discussed by neither realist, idealist, or phenomenalist. The humanists look down on us as beings who dabble in the sordid figures of dollars and cents instead of toying with infinities and searching for the illusive soul of things; the scientists and technologists despise us as able only to record rather than perform deeds.[96]

Needless to say, the situation has changed in favor of a dynamic research agenda, as evidenced by the transformation of accounting into a full-fledged "normal science" with competing paradigms striving for dominance. Accounting research is grounded in a common set of assumptions about social science and society, and has generated a healthy debate about how to enrich and extend our understanding of accounting in practice. Mainstream accounting research sees a parallel between physical and social sciences and accounting, justifying in the process a hypothetic-deductive account of scientific explanation and the need for confirmation of hypotheses.[97]

The first question of whether accounting is a science has never been adequately answered. A good definition of a science, provided by Buzzell, is:

> a classified and systematized body of knowledge organized around one or more central theories and a number of general principles ... usually expressed in quantitative terms ... knowledge which permits the prediction and, under some circumstances, the control of future events.[98]

Accounting meets the above criteria. It has a distinct subject matter and includes underlying uniformities and regularities conducive to empirical relationships, authoritative generalizations, concepts, principle, laws and theories. It definitely can be considered a science. If one subscribes to the unity-of-science argument, a single scientific method is equally applicable to accounting and other sciences. As Carl Hempel observed:

> The thesis of methodological unity of science states, first of all, that, notwithstanding many differences in their techniques of investigation, all branches of empirical science test and support their statements in basically the same manner, namely by deriving from them implications that can be checked intersubjectively and by performing for those implications the appropriate experimental or observational tests. This, the unity of method thesis holds, is true also of psychology and the social and historical disciplines. In response to the claim that the scholar in these fields, in contrast to the social sciences, often must rely on empathy to establish his assertions, logical empiricist writers stressed that imaginative identification with a given person often may prove a useful heuristic aid to the investigator who seeks to guess at a hypothesis about that person's beliefs, hopes, fears and goals. But whether or not a hypothesis they arrived at is factually sound must be determined by reference to objective evidence: the investor's emphatic experience is logically irrelevant to it.[99]

There is therefore a common acceptance by all sciences of a methodology for the justification of knowledge. That methodology rests in determining whether a true value can, in principle, be assigned to a hypothesis – that is, whether it can be refuted, confirmed, falsified, or verified, respectively. *Confirmation* is the extent to which a hypothesis is capable of being shown to be empirically true. *Falsification* is the extent to which a hypothesis is capable of being shown to be empirically untrue, that is, failing to describe the real world accurately. Confirmation of hypotheses does not necessarily imply that they are falsifiable, and vice versa. In fact, hypotheses that are naturally grounded in theory can be either purely confirmable, purely refutable, or both confirmable and refutable. Purely confirmable hypotheses come from existential statements, that is, statements that propose the existence of some phenomenon. For example, the hypothesis "There are CPAs within public accounting firms who view inflation accounting as useless" is a purely confirmable hypothesis. *Purely refutable hypotheses* come from universal laws, that is, statements that take the form of universal generalized conditionals. An example of such a hypothesis is "All accountants are CPAs". If the hypothesis is stated as "There are accountants who are CPAs", it becomes an existential statement, which is purely confirmable. Therefore, it appears that universal laws are basically negative existential statements that are purely refutable or falsifiable.

Both confirmable and refutable hypotheses come from singular statements, that is, statements that refer only to specific phenomena that are bound in time and space. For example, the hypothesis "All individuals are tolerant of ambiguity" can be both confirmed and refuted. However, there are hypotheses that are neither strictly confirmable nor strictly refutable. They are hypotheses arising from statistical or tendency laws, that is, statements specifying a "loosely specified" statistical relationship between a phenomenon and a large number of variables. Most accounting hypotheses fall within this category, which makes them neither strictly confirmable nor strictly falsifiable. The market model, the accounting predictive models of economic events, the positive theory of accounting, the human information-processing models, and most empirical accounting research fit the description. If the data contradict the hypothesis derived from these theories or models, defenders can always claim different excuses, including contamination of the data, or small or biased sample size. The rhetoric of research plays a crucial role in challenging whatever results are provided by the data. Is this a cause for alarm, given that statistical laws abound in accounting research? Bunge suggested that this would be a mistake.

Some die-hard classical determinists claim that stochastic statements do not deserve the name of law and are to be regarded, at their best, as contemporary devices. This anachronistic view has no longer currency in physics, chemistry, and certain branches of biology (notably genetics), especially ever since these sciences found that all major laws within domains are stochastic laws deducible (at least in principle) from laws concerning single systems in conjunction with definite statistical hypotheses regarding, e.g., the compensation of random deviations. Yet the prejudice against stochastic laws still causes some harm in psychology and sociology, where it serves to attack the stochastic approach without compensating for its loss by a scientific study of individuals.[100]

The refutation or confirmation is done by repeated testimony and new evidences.

10.10 Deconstruction

Various accounting texts about specific accounting paradigms and/or theories claim that they should be privileged over other forms of accounting knowledge and discourses. The text is used to ensure the hegemony of the paradigm and of special interests, as well as the closure around knowledge production. A philosophical phrase, termed deconstruction, introduced by Derrida[101] is intended to subvert these attempts. Because knowledge production is grounded and experienced in language, deconstruction uses the author's own system of grounding to reveal how the text violates that system. As stated by Norris:

> Derrida refuses to grant philosophy the kind of privileged status it has always claimed as the sovereign dispenser of reason. Derrida confronts this claim to power on its own chosen ground. He argues that philosophers have been able to impose their various systems of thought only by ignoring, or suppressing, the disruptive effects of language. His aim is always to draw out these effects by a critical reading which fastens on, and skillfully enriches, the elements of metaphor and other figurative devices at work in the texts of philosophy.[102]

What deconstruction implies is an exegesis of the texts to illustrate the construction of meaning within texts and subvert the hegemonic authority of a text to indicate the "truth" emanating outside the text. As stated by Arrington and Francis:

> Deconstructive readings of texts reveal how unruly and unstable meaning is and efface the veil of linguistic law and order we place over texts.[103]

In fact, Arrington and Francis are the first to use deconstruction to show that positive theory and the empirical tradition are not entitled to the kind of epistemic privilege and authority they have for a good number of accounting researchers. Their choice of a good exemplar of positive theory to deconstruct was Jensen's "Organization Theory and Methodolody".[104] Deconstruction in accounting research calls for more attempts to reveal the hidden assumptions of accounting texts. It assumes that all accounting discourse, even all historical narrative, is essentially rhetoric. The accounting deconstructionist will criticize the accounting text through various techniques, including demythologizing, decanonizing, dephallicizing, or de-faming.

10.11 Academic accountants: a flawed universal class

One element in the new conflictual order is a new class of academic accountants. The proletariat as a universal class was best expressed by Marx and Engels' theory of the "universal class of the proletariat", refuting criticisms and doubts that the proletariat could develop consciousness that would be necessary to perform its function as a universal class.[105] Gouldner joins the critical group, arguing that the lowliest class never came to power and that throughout the world during the twentieth century, a new class of intellectuals had been emerging, looking like the universal class defined by Hegel[106] but not constituting a universal class. *The new class is thus a flawed universal class.*

He advanced two major propositions: first, the rise of a "new class" comprised of humanistic intellectuals and technical intelligentsia, whose universalism is badly flawed; and second, the growing dominance of this class, as a cultural bourgeoisie and having monopoly over cultural capital and professionalism from which it gains its power.

This new class includes both technical and human intellectuals. It forms one "speech community" sharing a "culture of critical discourse" (CCD). The culture of critical discourse is a concept derived from the different linguistic repertoires identified in sociolinguistics.[107] Its definition is similar. "The culture of critical discourse (CCD) is a historically evolved set of rules, a grammar of discourse, which (1) is conceived to justify its assertions, (2) whose mode of justification does not proceed by involving authorities and (3) prefers to elicit the *voluntary* consent of those addressed solely on the basis of arguments addressed." This is a culture of discourse in which there is nothing that speakers will on principle permanently refuse to discuss or make problematic; indeed, they are even willing to talk about the value of talk itself and its possible inferiority to silence or to practice.

This grammar is the deep structure of the common ideology shared by the new class. *The shared ideology of the intellectuals and intelligentsia is thus an ideology about discourse.* Apart from the underlying technical languages (or sociolects) spoken by specialized professions, intellectuals and intelligentsia are commonly committed to a culture of critical discourse. CCD is the latent but mobilizable infrastructure of modern "technical language".[108] CCD is the latent but mobilizable infrastructure of modern intellectuals as well as their linguistic culture.

This new class is flawed because it is considered elitist and self-seeking and uses its special knowledge to advance its own interests and power. It does not represent the universal interest. The new class is dominant because of its monopolistic access to cultural capital. Borrowing from Pierre Bourdieu's theory of cultural reproduction,[109] Gouldner suggests that the new class uses cultural reproduction to maintain its interest and power just as economic reproduction is used to serve the interest of the holders of economic capital. Therefore, members of the new class will develop in the process of "cultural capital accumulation" to further their particular interest and the interests of those who share their culture of critical discourse.

The new class relies on credentials in capitalizing culture and monitoring the supply of specifically trained labor. "Culture is transmitted through the education and socialization. Generally, it is known that those with more formal education have lifetime earnings in excess of those with less. This increased income reflects the capital value of increased education."[110] This gives them a privileged position in the labor market and the potential for a new dominant class position. The trend has started with the new class developing a high level of status consciousness to defend their privileges (e.g., academic freedom to publish, to review, to recruit, etc.).

Whether the supply of accounting research by academic accountants is in response to the demand for value free knowledge[111] or to the demands of the markets for excuses,[112] academic accountants are also motivated by self-interest and the pressing need to publish.[113] They have gained a power associated with their monopoly over the cultural accounting capital. The research findings have given them consulting and policy-making powers to advance their own interests rather than the universal interest. For a culture of critical discourse, they have developed their linguistic repertoires, which differentiate them from other accounting speech communities.[114,115,116] As a new class, academic accountants also rely on credentials as criteria for membership, including Ph.D. degrees and publications in the "right" journals.

According to Gouldner, "professionalism is one of the public ideologies of the New Class. [P]rofessionalism is a tacit claim of the New Class to technical and moral superiority over the old class ... professionalism tacitly deauthorized the old class".[117] Through the new professional role, the academic accountants claim their own cultural research domain, and in the process recieve a higher compensation from the market system for accepting the professional role.[118] "Intellectuals who are willing to behave like professionals are allowed to form a relatively autonomous stratum with particularistic interest. They can use the mechanisms of licensing and the professional associations to establish monopolies with their markets".[119] The fragmentation of the American Accounting Association with separate "cultural" sections evidences this phenomenon.[120]

The same fragmentation orients the accounting researcher more toward immediate political (actions) policy than toward "theoretical" formulations of problems with general significance. This new close relationship to the policy-maker, whether it is the FASB, the SEC, the AAA or any other institution, makes him/her a "bureaucratic" intellectual who exercises advisory and technical functions within a bureaucracy as opposed to those intellectuals who elect to stay unattached to a bureaucracy.[121,122]

The bureaucratic intellectual is reduced to being an "ideologue" because he/she subordinates or abandons the search for a universally comprehensive understanding of social, cultural and physical reality in favor of an immediately instrumental arbitration of competing policies or courses of action.[123] Such a role is unfortunate if one subscribes to the prevailing assumption that a "particularization" of intellectual activity that links or constrains academic inquiry to specific social interests or needs leads to a fall from the "sacred" and a descent into the dishonorable realm of "ideology".[124,125]

In addition, with the role of teachers involved in the process of creating formal knowledge as opposed to its mere transmission,[126,127,128,129] the intellectuals moved to a role of "rationalization". As Shils suggests, in all modern societies (both liberal and totalitarian) "the trend of the present century" has been to increase pressures toward internal homogeneity due to the "incorporation of intellectuals in organized societies".[130] Intellectuals serve to elaborate the underlying "laws" of national and social organization relevant to the routine development and application of scientific knowledge to economic production and its social organization.[131,132,133] The call came mostly from the state to assist in reorientating the underlying mass population and in developing policies to ameliorate and prevent disturbances.[134] As a result, intellectuals have typically labored under the patronage of ruling classes or in institutions controlled by them.[135] The accounting intellectuals fit the described scenarios as they strive to provide the right excuses and create a new but flawed universal class.

10.12 Conclusions

Accounting may be approached from the point of view of the "philosophy" of science. Research output in accounting is not considered to be of doubtful value or theoretically deficient. Rather, accounting research findings provide indications that accounting events follow the pattern of successful revolutions theorized by Kuhn. In this chapter we have adopted a definition of a "paradigm" that is relevant to accounting. The essential components of such a paradigm are exemplars, the image of the subject matter, theories and methods. Our definition helped us to identify and delineate the competing paradigms in the accounting field:

1. the anthropological/inductive paradigm;
2. the true-income/deductive paradigm;
3. the decision-usefulness/decision-model paradigm;
4. the decision-usefulness/decision-maker/aggregate-market-behavior paradigm;
5. the decision-usefulness/decision-maker/individual-user paradigm;
6. the information/economics paradigm.

Each of these paradigms is the object of investigation and research by established scientific communities; a paradigm creates a coherent, unified viewpoint – a kind of *Weltanschauung* – that determines the way in which members view accounting research, practice and even education. In the interests of continuity and progress within the accounting discipline, these paradigms should never be considered absolute and final truthful knowledge. Instead, they should be subjected to constant verification and testing in a search for possible anomalies.

Most scientists and philosophers hold the view that scientific knowledge can never be proved. Popper argues that although a theory cannot be proved "true" with finality, it can be proved "false" with finality.[136] Generally known as the notion of falsification, or the theory of refutability, Popper's theory holds that to be accredited as scientific, a theory is falsified. The type of falsification that comes closest to Kuhn's view is termed *sophistication falsification*, which Lakatos summarizes as "no experiment, experimental report, observational statement, or well-corroborated, low-level falsifying hypothesis alone can lead to falsification. There is no falsification before the emergence of a better theory."[137] A "better theory" is one that "offers any novel, excess information, compared with its predecessor", in which "some of the excess information is corroborated".[138] The difference between Popper's *naive falsification and the sophisticated falsification* is that the latter requires the existence of a better theory. Lakatos tells us that the sophisticated falsificationist:

> … makes unfalsifiable by fiat some (spatio-temporally) singular statements, which are distinguishable by the fact that there exists at the same time a "relevant technique" such that "anyone who has learned it" will be able to decide that the statement is "acceptable".
>
> … This decision is then followed by a second kind of decision concerning the separation of the set of accepted basic statements from the rest. … The methodological falsificationist realizes that in the "experimental techniques" of the scientist, fallible theories are involved, "in the light of which" he or she interprets the facts. In spite of this, the methodological falsification "applies" these theories – he or she regards them in the given context not as theories under test but as *unproblematic background knowledge* which we accept (tentatively) as unproblematic while we are testing the theory.
>
> … Furthermore, problematic theories may qualify now as "scientific": although they are not falsifiable, they can be made "falsifiable" by an additional (third type) decision that the scientist can make by specifying certain rejection rules that may make statistically interpreted evidence "inconsistent" with the probabilistic theory.[139]

This may be the attitude to adopt in dealing with the competing paradigms in accounting.

Notes

1. Berlin, I., "Does Political Theory Still Exist?", in P. Laslett and W.G. Runaiman (eds.), *Philosophy, Politics and Society*, *2nd Series* (Oxford: Basil Blackwell, 1962), p. 19.

2. "Accounting Research 1960–1970: A Critical Evaluation", Monograph No. 7, N. Dopuch and L. Revsine (eds.) (Urbana, IL: Center for International Education and Research in Accounting, University of Illinois, 1973); Gonedes, N.J., and Dopuch, N., "Capital-Market Equilibrium, Information Production, and Selecting Accounting Techniques: Theoretical Framework and Review of Empirical Work", in *Studies on Financial Accounting Objectives*: *1974*, supplement to Vol. 12, *Journal of Accounting Research* (1974), pp. 48–129; A.R. Abdel-Khalik and T.F. Keller (eds.), *The Impact of Accounting Research in Financial Accounting and Disclosure of Accounting Practice*, (Durham, NC: Duke University Press, 1978).

3. Kuhn, Thomas S., "The Structure of Scientific Revolutions", *International Encyclopedia of Unified Science*, Second Enlarged Edition (Chicago: University of Chicago Press, 1970), pp. 10–15; Nelson, Carl L., "A Priori Research in Accounting", in N. Dopuch and L. Revsine (eds.), *Accounting Research 1960–1970: A Critical Evaluation*, Monograph No. 7 (Urbana, IL: Center for International Education and Research in Accounting, University of Illinois, 1973), pp. 3–18; Gonedes, N.J., and Dopuch, N., "Capital-Market Equilibrium, Information Production, and Selecting Accounting Techniques: Theoretical Framework and Review of Empirical Work", op. cit., p. 32.

4. Wells, M.C., "A Revolution in Accounting Thought", *The Accounting Review* (July, 1976), pp. 471–82.

5. American Accounting Association, Committee on Concepts and Standards for External Financial Reports, *Statement on Accounting Theory Acceptance* (Sarasota, FL: American Accounting Association, 1977).

6. Ibid., p. 47.

7. Eldredge, N., and Gould, S., "Punctuated Equilibrium: An Alternative to Phyletic Gradualism", in T.J. Schoff (ed.), *Models in Paleobiology* (San Francisco: Freeman, Cooper & Co., 1972), pp. 82–115.

8. Gersick, Connie J.G., "Revolutionary Change Theories: A Multilevel Exploration of the Punctuated Equilibrium Paradigm", *Academy of Management Review* (16, 1991), pp. 10–36.

9. Kuhn, T.S., *The Structure of Scientific Revolution* (Chicago: University of Chicago Press, 1962 [1st edn.], 1970 [2nd edn.]).

10. Ibid., 2nd edn., p. 175.

11. Ibid., 1st edn., p. 6.

12. McCann, H. Gilman, *Chemistry Transformed: The Paradigmatic Shift from Phlogiston to Oxygen* (Norwood, NJ: Ablex Publishing Corporation, 1978), p. 21.

13. Ibid., p. 13

14. Hagstrom, W.O., *The Scientific Community* (New York: Basic Books, 1965), p. 17.

15. Ibid., p. 13.

16. Merton, R.K., "Priorities in Scientific Discovery: A Chapter in the Sociology of Science", *American Sociological Review* (22, 1957), p. 640.

17. Merton, R.K., "Behavior Patterns of Scientists", *American Scientists* (57, 1969), pp. 17–18.

18. Kuhn, Thomas S., "Reflections on my Critics", in I. Lakatos and A. Musgrave (eds.), *Criticism and the Growth of Knowledge* (Cambridge University Press, 1970), pp. 231–78.

19. Ritzer, George, "Sociology: A Multi-Paradigm Science", *American Sociologist* (August, 1975), pp. 15–17.

20. Ibid., p. 15.

21. Ibid., p. 157

22. Watts, Ross L., and Zimmerman, J.L., *Positive Accounting Theory* (Englewood Cliffs, NJ: Prentice Hall, 1986), p. 12.

23. American Accounting Association, Committee on Concepts and Standards for External Financial Reports, *Statement of Accounting Theory and Theory Acceptance* (Sarasota, FL: American Accounting Association, 1977).

24. Hatfield, Henry Rand, *Accounting* (New York: D. Appleton & Company, 1927); Gilman, S., *Accounting Concepts of Profit* (New York: The Ronald Press, 1939); Paton, W.A., and Littleton, A.C., "An Introduction to Corporate Accounting Standards", Monograph No. 3 (Sarasota, FL: American Accounting Association, 1953); Ijiri, Yuji, "Theory of Accounting Measurement", *Studies in Accounting Research*, No. 10 (Sarasota, FL: American Accounting Association, 1975).

25. Ijiri, Yuji, "Theory of Accounting Measurement", op. cit., p. 37.

26. Littleton, A.C., "Structure of Accounting Theory", Monograph No. 5 (Sarasota, FL: American Accounting Association, 1953), p. 185.

27. Ibid., p. 31.

28. Gordon, M.J., "Postulates, Principles, and Research in Accounting", *The Accounting Review* (April, 1964), pp. 251–63; Watts, R.L., and Zimmerman, J.L., "Towards a Positive Theory of the Determination of Accounting Standards", *The Accounting Review* (January, 1968), pp. 112–34.

29. Gordon, M.J., "Postulates, Principles, and Research in Accounting", op. cit., pp. 261–2.

30. Watts, R.L., and Zimmerman, J.L., "Toward a Positive Theory of the Determination of Accounting Standards", op. cit., p. 14.

31. Ibid., p. 14.

32. Ijiri, Yuji, "Theory of Accounting Measurement", op. cit., p. 28.

33. Feltham, Gerald A., and Demski, Joel S., "The Use of Models in Information Evaluation", *The Accounting Review* (July, 1969), pp. 457–66.

34. Baiman, Stanley, "Agency Research in Managerial Accounting: A Survey", *Journal of Accounting Literature* (Spring, 1982), p. 159.

35. Beidleman, C.R., "Income Smoothing: The Role of Management", *The Accounting Review* (October, 1973), p. 653.

36. Watts, R.L., and Zimmerman, J.L., *Positive Accounting Theory*, op. cit.

37. Belkaoui, A., and Picur, R.D., "The Smoothing of Income Numbers: Some Empirical Evidence on Systematic Differences between Core and Periphery Industrial Sectors", *The Journal of Business Finance and Accounting* (Winter, 1984), pp. 527–46.

38. Dechow, P.H., Sloan, R.G., and Sweeney, A.P., "Detecting Earnings Management", *The Accounting Review* (April, 1995), pp.193–226.

39. Watts, R.L., and Zimmerman, J.L., *Positive Accounting Theory*, op. cit.

40. Paton, W.A., *Accounting Theory* (New York: Ronald Press, 1922); Canning, J.B., *The Economics of Accountancy* (New York: Ronald Press, 1929); Sweeney, Henry W., *Stabilized Accounting* (New York: Harper & Row, 1936); MacNeal, Kenneth, *Truth in Accounting* (Philadelphia: University of Pennsylvania Press, 1939); Alexander, Sidney S., "Income Measurement in a Dynamic Economy", *Five Monographs on Business Income* (New York: The Study Group on Business Income, The American Institute of Certified Public Accountants, 1950). *See also*: Edwards, E.O., and Bell, P.W., *The Theory and Measurement of Business Income* (Berkeley: University of California Press, 1961); Moonitz, Maurice, Accounting Research Study No. 1, *The Basic Postulates of Accounting* (New York: American Institute of Certified Public Accountants, 1961); Alexander, Sidney S., "Income Measurement in a Dynamic Economy", (rev.) David Solomons, in W.T. Baxter and Sidney Davidson (eds.), *Studies in Accounting Theory*

(Homewood, IL: Richard D. Irwin, 1962); Sprouse, R.T., and Moonitz, Maurice, Accounting Research Study No. 3, *A Tentative Set of Broad Accounting Principles for Business Enterprises* (New York: American Institute of Certified Public Accountants, 1962).

41. Paton, W.A., *Accounting Theory*, op. cit., p. 295.

42. Ibid., pp. 8–9.

43. MacNeal, Kenneth, *Truth in Accounting*, op. cit., p. 295.

44. Alexander, Sidney S., "Income Measurement in a Dynamic Economy", op. cit., p. 159.

45. Jones, Ralph Coughenour, *The Effects of Price-Level Changes* (Saratosa, FL: American Accounting Association, 1956); Mason, Perry, *Price-Level Changes and Financial Statements* (Sarasota, FL: American Association, 1971).

46. Edwards, E.O., and Bell, P.W., *The Theory and Measurement of Business Income;* Matthews, Russel L., "Price-Level Accounting and Useless Information", *Journal of Accounting Research* (Spring, 1965), pp. 133–55; Gynther, R.S., *Accounting for Price-Level Changes: Theory and Procedures* (New York: Pergamon, 1966); Revsine, L., *Replacement-Cost Accounting* (Englewood Cliffs, NJ: Prentice-Hall, 1973).

47. Baxter, W.T., "Accounting Values: Sale Price Versus Replacement Cost", *Journal of Accounting Research* (Autumn, 1967), pp. 208–14; Wright, F.K., "A Theory of Financial Accounting", *Journal of Business Finance* (Autumn, 1970), pp. 51–69; Stamp, Edward, "Income and Value Determination and Changing Price Levels: An Essay Toward a Theory", *The Accountant's Magazine* (June, 1971), pp. 277–92; Whittington, Geoffrey, "Asset Valuation, Income Measurement, and Accounting Income", *Accounting Business and Research* (Spring, 1974), pp. 96–101.

48. Chambers, R.J., *Accounting, Evaluation, and Economic Behavior* (Englewood Cliffs, NJ: Prentice-Hall, 1966); Sterling, Robert R., "On Theory Construction and Verification", *The Accounting Review* (January, 1971), pp. 12–29.

49. Solomons, David, "Economic and Accounting Concepts of Income", *The Accounting Review* (July, 1961), pp. 374–83; Lemke, Kenneth W., "Asset Valuation and Income Theory", *The Accounting Review* (January, 1966), pp. 33–41.

50. Chambers, R.J., "Blueprint for a Theory of Accounting", *Accounting Research* (January, 1955), pp. 21–2.

51. May, G.O., *Financial Accounting* (New York: Macmillan, 1943), p. 19.

52. Beaver, W.H., Kennelly, J.W., and Voss, W.M., "Predictive Ability as a Criterion for the Evaluation of Accounting Data", *The Accounting Review* (October, 1968), pp. 675–83; Sterling, Robert R., "Decision-Oriented Financial Accounting", *Accounting and Business Research* (Summer, 1972), pp. 198–208.

53. Beaver, W.H., Kennelly, J.W., and Voss, W.M., "Predictive Ability as a Criterion for the Evaluation of Accounting Data", op. cit., p. 675.

54. Ibid., p. 680.

55. Sterling, Robert R., "Decision-Oriented Financial Accounting", op. cit., p. 198.

56. Ibid., p. 199.

57. Ibid., p. 201.

58. Ibid., p. 199.

59. Gonedes, N.J., "Efficient Capital Markets and External Accounting", *The Accounting Review* (January, 1972); Gonedes, N.J., and Dopuch, N., "Capital-Market Equilibrium, Information Production and Selecting Accounting Techniques: Theoretical Frameworks and Review of Empirical Work", *Studies in Financial Accounting Objectives*: 1974, Supplement to *Journal of Accounting Research* (12, 1974), pp. 48–125.

60. Spence, M., "Job-Market Signaling", *Quarterly Journal of Economics* (August, 1973), pp. 356–75.

61. Rodner, Roy, "Competitive Equilibrium Under Uncertainty", *Econometrica* (January, 1968), pp. 60–85.

62. Beaver, W.H., "The Behavior of Security Prices and its Implications for Accounting Research (Methods)", in *Report of the Committee on Research Methodology in Accounting*, Supplement to *The Accounting Review* (47, 1972), pp. 407–37.

63. Fama, E.F., "The Behavior of Stock Markets Prices", *Journal of Business* (January, 1965), pp. 34–105.

64. Beaver, W.H., "Market Efficiency", *The Accounting Review* (January, 1981), p. 28.

65. Fama, E.F., "Efficient Capital Markets: A Review of Theory and Empirical Work", *Journal of Finance* (May, 1970), pp. 383–417.

66. Sharpe, W.F., "Capital-Asset Pricing – A Theory of Market Equilibrium under Conditions of Risk", *Journal of Finance* (September, 1964), pp. 425–42.

67. Ross, A.S., "The Arbitrage Theory of Capital Asset Pricing", *Journal of Economic Theory* (December, 1976), pp. 341–60.

68. Black, F., and Scholes, M., "The Pricing of Options and Corporate Liabilities", *Journal of Political Economy* (May/June, 1973), pp. 637–54.

69. Sharpe, W.F., "A Simplified Model of Portfolio Approach", *Management Science* (January, 1963), pp. 277–93.

70. Chen, S.N., and Lee, C.F., "Bayesian and Mixed Estimation of Time-Varying Betas", *Journal of Economics and Business* (December, 1982), pp. 291–301.

71. Ohlson, J., "Earnings, Book Values, and Dividends in Security Valuation", Working Paper, Columbia University, 1991.

72. Barth, M., "Relative Measurements Errors Among Alternative Pension Asset and Liability Measures", *The Accounting Review* (July, 1991), pp. 433–63.

73. Collins, D.W., and Kothari, S.E., "An Analysis of Intertemporal and Cross-Sectional Determinants of Earning Response Coefficients", *Journal of Accounting and Economics* (11, 1989), pp. 143–81.

74. Easton, P.D., and Harris, T.S., "Earnings as an Explanatory Variable for Returns", *Journal of Accounting Research* (Spring, 1991), pp. 19–36.

75. Bruns, William J., Jr., "Accounting Information and Decision Making: Some Behavioral Hypotheses", *The Accounting Review* (July, 1968), pp. 469–80.

76. Gibbins, Michael, "Propositions about the Psychology of Professional Judgment in Public Accounting", *Journal of Accounting Research* (Spring, 1984), pp. 103–25.

77. Riahi-Belkaoui, Ahmed, *The Cultural Shaping of Accounting* (Westport, CT: Greenwood Press, 1995).

78. Dyckman, T.R., Gibbons, M., and Swieringa, R.J., "Experimental and Survey Research in Financial Accounting: A Review and Evaluation", in A.R. Abdel Khalik and T.F. Keller (eds.), *The Impact of Accounting Research in Financial Accounting and Disclosure on Accounting Practice* (Durham, NC: Duke University Press, 1978), pp. 48–89.

79. Riahi-Belkaoui, Ahmed, *The Linguistic Shaping of Accounting* (Westport, CT: Greenwood Press, 1996).

80. Riahi-Belkaoui, Ahmed, "Actual Accounting, Modified Cash Basis of Accounting and the Loan Decision: An Experiment in Functional Fixation", *Managerial Finance* (18, 5, 1992), pp. 3–13.

81. Prakash, P., and Rappaport, A., "Information Inductance and Its Significance for Accounting", *Accounting, Organization, and Society* (December, 1982), p. 233.

82. Riahi-Belkaoui, Ahmed, *Organization and Budgetary Slack* (Westport, CT: Greenwood Press, 1994).

83. Otley, D.T., "The Contingency Theory of Management Accounting: Achievement and Prognosis", *Accounting, Organizations, and Society* (December, 1980), pp. 413–28.

84. Riahi-Belkaoui, Ahmed, "The Effects of Goal Setting and Task Uncertainty on Task Outcomes", *Management Accounting Research* (June, 1990), pp. 41–60.

85. Riahi-Belkaoui, Ahmed, *Human Information Processing* (Westport, CT: Greenwood Press, 1989).

86. Brunswick, E., *The Conceptual Framework of Psychology* (Chicago, IL: University of Chicago Press, 1952).

87. Edwards, W., "Conservatism in Human Information Processing", in B. Kleinmutz (ed.), *Formal Representation of Human Judgment* (New York: Wiley, 1968).

88. Payne, J.N., Braunstein, M.L., and Caroll, J.S., "Exploring Predecisional Behavior: An Alternative Approach to Decision Research", *Organizational Behavior and Human Performance* (February, 1978), pp. 14–44.

89. Huysman, J.H.B., "The Effectiveness of Cognitive Style Constraint in Implementing Operations Research Proposals", *Management Science* (September, 1970), pp. 94–5.

90. Feltham, Gerald A., "The Value of Information", *The Accounting Review* (October, 1968), pp. 684–96; Crandall, Robert H., "Information Economics and Its Implications for the Further Development of Accounting Theory", *The Accounting Review* (July, 1969), pp. 457–66; Feltham, Gerald A., and Demski, Joel S., "The Use of Models in Information Evaluation", *The Accounting Review* (July, 1969), pp. 457–66.

91. Crandall, Robert H., "Information Economics and Its Implications for the Further Development of Accounting Theory", op. cit., p. 464.

92. Ibid., p. 458.

93. Feltham, Gerald A., and Demski, Joel S., "The Use of Models in Information Evaluation", op. cit., p. 626.

94. Beaver, William, and Demski, Joel, S., "The Nature of Income Measurement", *The Accounting Review* (January, 1979), p. 43.

95. Marschak, Jacob, and Radner, Roy, *Economic Theory of Teams* (New Haven, CT: Yale University Press, 1972).

96. Hatfield, H.R., "A Historical Defense of Bookkeeping", *Journal of Accounting* (April, 1924), pp. 241–53.

97. Riahi-Belkaoui, Ahmed, *Inquiry and Accounting: Alternative Methods and Research Perspective* (Westport, CT: Quorum Books, 1987).

98. Buzzell, Robert D., "Is Marketing a Science?" *Harvard Business Review* (January–February, 1963), p. 37.

99. Hempel, C.G., "Logical Positivism and the Social Sciences", in P. Achinstein and S.F. Barker (eds.), *Legacy of Logical Positivism* (Baltimore, MD: Johns Hopkins University of Chicago Press, 1969), p. 151.

100. Bunge, Marie, *Scientific Research I: The Search for System* (New York: Spring, 1967), p. 336.

101. Derrida, J., *Writing and Difference* (trans. A. Boss) (Chicago, IL: The University of Chicago Press, 1978).

102. Norris, C., *Deconstruction: Theory and Practice* (New York: Methuen, 1982), pp. 18–19.

103. Arrington, C. Edward, and Francis, Jere R., "Letting the Cat Out of the Bag: Deconstruction, Privilege and Accounting Research", *Accounting, Organization and Society* (January, 1989), p. 7.

104. Jensen, Michael, "Organization Theory and Methodology", *The Accounting Review* (April, 1983), pp. 319–39.

105. Engels, F., and Marx, K., 'The Holy Family', in R. Naum and F. Engels (eds.), *Collected Works*, Vol. 4 (New York: International Publishers, 1975), p. 86.

106. Hegel, G.W.F., *Hegel's Philosophy of the Right*, trans. T.M. Knox (Oxford: Clarendon Press, 1942), pp. 131–4.

107. Bernstein, B., "Social Class, Language and Socialization", in F.A. Sebeok (ed.), *Current Trends in Linguistics* (The Hague: Monton, 1974).

108. Gouldner, A., "The New Class Project, I", *Theory and Society* (6, 1978), pp. 176–7.

109. Bourdieu, P., *Reproduction in Education, Society and Culture* (Beverley Hills, CA: Sage, 1977).

110. Gouldner, A.W., *The Future of the Intellectuals and the Rise of the New Class* (New York: Continuum Publishing, 1979), p. 26.

111. Peasnell, K.V., and Williams, D.J., "Ersatz Academics and Scholar-Saints: The Supply of Financial Accounting Research", *Abacus* (September, 1986), pp. 121–35.

112. Watts, R.L., and Zimmerman, J.L., "The Demand for and Supply of Accounting Theories: The Market for Excuses", *The Accounting Review* (April, 1979).

113. Orleans, H., *The Effects of Federal Programs on Higher Education* (Washington, DC: The Brookings Institution, 1962).

114. Haried, A.A., "The Semantic Dimensions of Financial Statements", *Journal of Accounting Research* (Autumn, 1980), pp. 632–74.

115. Belkaoui, A., "Linguistic Relativity in Accounting", *Accounting, Organizations and Society* (October, 1978), pp. 97–100.

116. Belkaoui, A., "The Interprofessional Linguistic Communication of Accounting Concepts: An Experiment in Sociolingusitics", *Journal of Accounting Research* (Autumn, 1980), pp. 362–74.

117. Gouldner, A.W., *The Future of the Intellectuals and the Rise of the New Class* (New York: Continuum Publishing, 1979), p. 26.

118. Lewis, M.T, Lin, W.T., and Williams, D.Z., "The Economic Status of Accounting Educators: An Empirical Study", in B. Schwartz, (ed.), *Advances in Accounting*, Vol. 1 (Greenwich, CT: JAI Press, 1984), pp. 127–44.

119. Szelenyi, I., "Gouldner's Theory of Intellectuals as a Flawed Universal Class", *Theory and Society* (11, 1982), pp. 779–98.

120. Belkaoui, A., and Chan, J., "Professional Value System of Academic Accountants", in M. Neimark (ed.), *Advances in Public Interest Accounting*, Vol. 2 (Greenwich, CT: JAI Press, 1987).

121. Merton, R.K., *Social Theory and Social Structure* (New York: Free Press, 1968), p. 265.

122. Nettl, J.P., "Power and the Intellectuals", in C.C. O'Brien and W.D. Vanech (eds.), *Power and Consciousness* (New York: New York University Press, 1969), pp. 53–124.

123. Barrow, C.W., "Intellectuals in Contemporary Social Theory: A Radical Critique", *Sociological Inquiry* (Fall, 1987), pp. 415–30.

124. Ashcraft, R., "Political Theory and the Problem of Ideology", *Journal of Politics* (August, 1980), pp. 687–705.

125. Ashcraft, R., "The Ideological and Sociological Interpretation of Intellectual Phenomena", in K.H. Wolff (ed.), *From Karl Mannheim* (Oxford University Press, 1971), pp. 116–31.

126. Aron, R., *The Option of the Intellectuals* (New York: W.W. Norton, 1962).

127. Shils, E., *The Intellectuals and The Powers* (Chicago, IL: University of Chicago Press, 1972), pp. 206–9.

128. Lipset, S.M., and Dobson, R.B., "The Intellectual as Critic and Rebel", *Daedalus* (101, Summer, 1972), pp. 137–98.

129. Berger, P.L., "The Socialist Myth", *Public Interest* (44, Summer, 1976), p. 5.

130. Berger, P.L., *The Constitution of Society* (Chicago, IL: University of Chicago Press, 1972), p. 191.

131. Machlup, F., *The Production and Distribution of Knowledge in the United States* (Princeton, NJ: Princeton University Press, 1962).

132. Price, D.K., *The Scientific Estate* (Boston, MA: Harvard University Press, 1965).

133. Galbraith, J.K., *The New Industrial State* (New York: Houghton-Mifflin, 1978), pp. 292–301.

134. Habermas, J., *Toward a Rational Society* (Boston, MA: Beacon Press, 1970), pp. 62–80.

135. Parsons, T., "The Intellectual: A Social Role Category", in *On Intellectuals* (New York: Doubleday, 1970), p. 14.

136. Popper, Karl, *Conjecture and Refutations* (London: Basic Books, 1963).

137. Lakatos, Imre, "Falsification and the Methodology of Scientific Research", in Imre Lakatos and Alan Musgrave (eds.), *Criticism and the Growth of Knowledge* (Cambridge: Cambridge University Press, 1970), p. 119.

138. Ibid., p. 120.

139. Ibid., pp. 106–9.

References

American Accounting Association, Committee on Concepts and Standards for External Financial Reports, *Statement on Accounting Theory and Theory Acceptance* (Sarasota, FL: American Accounting Association, 1977).

Arrington, C.E., and Francis, J.R., "Letting the Cat Out of The Bag: Deconstruction, Privilege, and Accounting Research", *Accounting, Organizations and Society* (January, 1985), pp. 1–88.

Belkaoui, Ahmed, *Socio-Economic Accounting* (Westport, CT: Quorum Books, 1984).

Belkaoui, Ahmed, *Public Policy and The Problems and Practices of Accounting* (Westport, CT: Quorum Books, 1985).

Belkaoui, Ahmed, *The Coming Crisis in Accounting* (Westport, CT: Quorum Books, 1989).

Burrell, G., and Morgan, G., *Sociological Paradigms and Organizational Analysis* (London: Heinemann, 1979).

Chau, Wia Fong, "Radical Developments in Accounting Thought", *The Accounting Review* (October, 1986), pp. 601–32.

Chau, Wia Fong, "Interpretive Sociology and Management Accounting Research – A Critical Review", *Accounting, Auditing and Accountability* (1, 2, 1988), pp. 59–79.

Cooper, D.J., and Sherer, M.J., "The Value of Corporate Accounting Reports: Arguments for a Political Economy of Accounting", *Accounting, Organizations and Society* (1984), pp. 207–32.

Danos, Paul, "A Revolution in Accounting Thought? A Comment", *The Accounting Review* (July, 1977), pp. 746–7.

Derrida, J., *Writing and Difference* (trans. A. Bass) (Chicago: The University of Chicago Press, 1978).

Hakansson, Nils H., "Where We Are in Accounting: A Review of Statement on Accounting Theory and Theory Acceptance", *The Accounting Review* (July, 1978), pp. 717–25.

Hopwood, A.G., "On Trying to Study Accounting in The Contexts in Which it Operates", *Accounting, Organizations, and Society* (1983), pp. 361–74.

Hunt, Herbert G., III, and Hogler, Raymond L., "Agency Theory as Ideology: A Comparative Analysis Based on Critical Legal Theory and Radical Accounting", *Accounting, Organizations and Society* (August, 1990), pp. 437–54.

Kuhn, Thomas S., "The Structure of Scientific Revolutions", in *International Encyclopedia of Unified Science,* Second Enlarged Edition (Chicago: University of Chicago Press, 1970).

Laughlin, Richard C., "Accounting Systems in Organizational Contexts: A Case for Critical Theory", *Accounting, Organizations and Society* (October, 1987), pp. 479–507.

Peasnell, K.V., "Statement on Accounting Theory and Theory Acceptance: A Review Article", *Accounting and Business Research* (Summer, 1978), pp. 217–25.

Riahi-Belkaoui, Ahmed, *Socio-Economy Accounting* (Westport, CT: Greenwood Publishing, 1984).

Riahi-Belkaoui, Ahmed, *Inquiry and Accounting: Alternative Methods and Research Perspectives* (Westport, CT: Greenwood Publishing, 1987).

Riahi-Belkaoui, Ahmed, *The Coming Crisis in Accounting* (Westport, CT: Greenwood Publishing, 1989).

Riahi-Belkaoui, Ahmed, *Behavioral Accounting* (Westport, CT: Greenwood Publishing, 1989).

Riahi-Belkaoui, Ahmed, *Human Information Processing* (Westport, CT: Greenwood Publishing, 1989).

Riahi-Belkaoui, Ahmed, *Morality in Accounting* (Westport, CT: Greenwood Publishing, 1992).

Riahi-Belkaoui, Ahmed, *Accounting: A Multiple Paradigm Science* (Westport, CT: Greenwood Publishing, 1996).

Riahi-Belkaoui, Ahmed, *Fairness in Accounting* (Westport, CT: Greenwood Publishing, 1996).

Riahi-Belkaoui, Ahmed, *Research Perspectives in Accounting* (Westport, CT: Greenwood Publishing, 1997).

Riahi-Belkaoui, Ahmed, *Financial Analysis and the Predictability of Important Economic Events* (Westport, CT: Greenwood Publishing, 1998).

Riahi-Belkaoui, Ahmed, *Capital Structure: Determination, Evaluation and Accounting* (Westport, CT: Greenwood Publishing, 1999).

Riahi-Belkaoui, Ahmed, *Corporate Social Awareness and Financial Outcomes* (Westport, CT: Greenwood Publishing, 1999).

The events and behavioral approaches

In previous chapters, we stated that accounting theory arises from the need to provide a rationale for what accountants are expected to do and that, to be complete, the construction of an accounting theory should be followed by theory verification. We also presented the traditional and regulatory approaches to the formation of an accounting framework characterized, in general, by a rigorous process of verification. Because an accounting theory should result from both processes, new approaches have been developed or revised, the aims of which are not yet generally accepted by the various interest groups or by the accounting profession in particular. They represent new streams of accounting research that use both conceptual and empirical reasoning to formulate and verify a conceptual accounting framework. Among the new approaches, we may distinguish the events approach, the behavioral approach, the human information processing approach, the predictive approach, and the positive approach.

Each of these approaches has generated new methodologies and interest and has employed unique ways of looking at accounting problems. Because the interests and the methodologies are unique, each approach has acquired the attributes of a distinct paradigm, causing accounting to become a multiparadigmatic science in a constant state of crisis. Each theorist, dissatisfied with competing paradigms, will use a particular approach to provide a theoretical framework for the accounting field.

Our purpose in this chapter and the following chapter is first to elaborate on each of the new approaches, emphasizing the contribution of each approach to accounting theory construction, and then to explain the resulting paradigmatic status of accounting. This chapter will examine the events, behavioral and human information processing approaches, the following chapter will cover the predictive and positive approaches.

11.1 The events approach

11.1.1 The nature of the events approach

The events approach was first explicitly stated after a divergence of opinion among the members of the Committee of the American Accounting Association, which issued *A Statement of Basic Accounting Theory* in 1966. The majority of the Committee members favored the *value approach* to accounting. Only one member, George Sorter, favored the events approach.[1]

The value school

The value school, also called the user-need school, considers that needs of users are known sufficiently to allow the deduction of an accounting theory that provides optimal input to the specified decision models. Input values cannot be optimal for all uses, and an exhaustive list of all normative and descriptive models is lacking. Furthermore, the conventional accounting model, based on the value approach, suffers from the following weaknesses.

- Its dimensions are limited. Most accounting measurements are expressed in monetary terms – a practice that precludes maintenance and use of productivity, performance, reliability, and other multidimensional data.

- Its classification schemes are not always appropriate. The chart of accounts for a particular enterprise represents all of the categories into which information concerning economic affairs may be placed. This will often lead to data being left out, or classified in a manner that hides its nature from nonaccountants.

- Its aggregation level for information is too high. Accounting data is used by a wide variety of decision-makers, each needing different degrees of quantity, aggregation and focus, depending on their personalities, decision styles and conceptual structures. Therefore, information concerning economic events and objects should be kept in as elementary a form as possible to be aggregated by the eventual user.

- Its degree of integration with the other functional areas of an enterprise is too restricted. Information concerning the same set of phenomena will often be maintained separately by accountants and nonaccountants, thus leading to inconsistency as well as information gaps and overlaps.[2]

The events approach

The events approach, on the contrary, suggests that the purpose of accounting is "to provide information about relevant economic events that might be useful in a variety of decision models".[3] It is up to the accountant to provide information about the events and leave to the user the task of fitting the events to their decision models, it is up to the user to aggregate and assign weights and values to the data generated by the event in conformity with his or her own utility function. The user, rather than the accountant, transforms the event into accounting information suitable to the user's own individual decision model. As a result, the contents of the accounting reports reflect observations of the real world, rather than the "wishful inferences of devious managers whose 'use' of alternative accounting techniques is manipulative rather than informative".[4]

"Event" refers to any action that may be portrayed by one or more basic dimensions or attributes. According to Johnson, "event" means "feasible observations of specified characteristics of an action in regard to which a reporter could say I foresaw that and saw it happen myself".[5]

Thus, the characteristics of an event may be directly observed and are of economic significance to the user. Given the number of characteristics and the number of events susceptible to observation that might be relevant to the decision models of all types of users, the events approach suggests a tremendous expansion of the accounting data presented in financial reports. Characteristics of an event other than monetary values may have to be disclosed. The events approach also assumes that the level of aggregation and evaluation of accounting data are decided by the user, given the user's loss function. If the user aggregates and evaluates data on events at this time, then measurement errors, biases and information losses generated by the accountant's attempt to match, assign weights, generate values and aggregate information into the financial statements can be avoided.

11.1.2 Financial statements and the events approach

What would be the consequence of the events approach to conventional annual reports?

In the value approach, the balance sheet is perceived as an indicator of the financial position of the firm at a given point in time. In the events approach, the balance sheet is perceived as an indirect communication of all accounting events relevant to the firm since its inception. Sorter proposes the following operational definition for the construction of a balance sheet when the events approach is employed: "A balance sheet should be constructed [in such a way] as to maximize the reconstructibility of the events to be aggregated."[6] Sorter's definition implies that all aggregated figures in the balance sheet may be disaggregated to show all the events that have occurred since the inception of the firm.

In the value approach, the income statement is perceived as an indicator of the financial performance of the firm for a given period. In the events approach, the income statement is perceived as a direct communication of the operating events that occur during a given period. Sorter proposes the following operational rule when the events approach is employed: "Each event should be described in a manner facilitating the forecasting of the same event in a future time period given exogeneous changes."[7]

In the value approach, the statement of cash flows is perceived as an expression of the changes in cash. In the events approach, however, it is better perceived as an expression of financial and investment events. In other words, an event's relevance rather than its output on cash flow determines the reporting of an event in the statement of cash flows.

11.1.3 The normative events theory of accounting

The normative events theory of accounting has been tentatively summarized as follows:

In order for interested persons (shareholders, employees, managers, suppliers, customers, government agencies, and charitable institutions) to better forecast the future of social organizations (households, businesses, governments, and philanthropies), the most relevant attributes (characteristics) of the crucial events (internal, environmental and transactional) which affect the organization are aggregated (temporally and sectionally) for periodic publication free of inferential bias.[8]

Thus, the objective of the normative events theory of accounting is to maximize the forecasting accuracy of accounting reports by focusing on the most relevant attributes of events crucial to the users. The theory calls for:

1. an explicit taxonomy of real events, which the accountant is to report;
2. more effective classification schemes, with particular reference to labels that make it possible to associate observations of particular events with other related events;
3. the structuring of an events-based accounting information system.[9]

11.1.4 Events-based accounting information systems

One way to meet the objective of the normative events theory of accounting is to integrate the events approach with database approaches to information management that assume that an enterprise creates a centrally managed database to be shared among a wide range of users with highly diverse needs. Such accounting system included hierarchical models,[10] network models,[11] relational models,[12] entity relationship models[13] and REA accounting models.[14]

1. The hierarchical model is based on the idea of an events-accounting information system that allows users to make inquiries of a database. The components of such a system include:
   (a) A mass database that contains a record of all events in some generalized format.
   (b) A user-defined structure that provides each user with his or her own conceptual structure (and aggregation levels) of the events.
   (c) User-defined functions, or operations, for manipulating the data.[15]
2. The network model is based on the concept of multidimensional accounting presented by Ijiri[16] and Charnes, Colantoni and Cooper.[17] It uses as input the initially unstructured database and a collection of queries or data requests to develop a hierarchical data structure that will minimize the number of records to be accessed to answer the desired set of queries.[18]
3. The relational model is founded on the mathematical theory of relations. Basically, a database is considered to be a collection of time-varying relations of assorted degrees. Users interact with the model via a language meaningful to the particular user. Substantial work remains to be done to improve the applicability of the relational approach to accounting models.[19]
4. The entity-relationship model assumes that an accounting system is most naturally modeled in a database environment as a collection of real-world entities and relationships among these entities.[20] This model basically replaces the traditional chart of accounts and double-entry bookkeeping procedures by viewing entity-relationship in the form of entity tables and relationship tables. To construct such an accounting data model, the following steps are suggested:
   (a) Identify (1) the entity *sets*, such as classes of objects, agents and events that exist in the conceptual world, and (2) the *relationship sets* that connect these entities.

(b) Construct an entity-relationship (E-R) diagram that will exhibit the semantic nature of identified relationships.

(c) Define the characteristics of entity sets and relationship sets that will be of interest to users of particular systems, and specify mapping that will identify those characteristics.

(d) Organize the results of steps (a), (b) and (c) into entity-relationship tables, and identify a key (unique) characteristic for each entity-relationship set.[21]

5. The REA accounting model is a generalized entity-relationship representation of accounting phenomena with components that consist of sets representing economic resources, economic events and economic agents.[22]

11.1.5 Evaluation of the events approach

The events approach offers certain advantages and certain limitations. The advantages predominantly take the form of efforts to provide information about relevant economic events that might be useful to a variety of decision models. As a result, more information may be available to users who can then use their own utility function to determine the nature and level of aggregation of the information they need to make their particular decisions. The usefulness of the events approach may depend, however, on one or more of the following arguments:

1. The usefulness of the events approach may depend on the psychological type of the decision maker.[23] It has been shown, for example, that structured/aggregate reports are preferable for high-analytic decision-makers, but that database inquiry systems (the events approach) are preferable for low-analytic decision-makers.[24]

2. Information overload may result from the attempt to measure the relevant characteristics of all crucial events affecting the firm

3. An adequate criterion for the choice of the crucial events has not been developed.

4. Measuring all the characteristics of an events approach may prove to be difficult, given the state of the art in accounting.

5. More research may be needed to examine the impact of different design approaches to the events approach theory, such as the hierarchical, network, relational, entity-relationship and REA models.

11.2 The behavioral approach

11.2.1 The nature of the behavioral approach

Most traditional approaches to the construction of an accounting theory have failed to take into consideration user behavior in particular and behavioral assumptions in general.

In 1960, Devine made the following critical remark:

> Let us now turn to … the psychological reactions of those who consume accounting output or are caught in its threads of control. On balance, it seems fair to conclude that accountants seem to have waded through their relationships to the intricate psychological network of human activity with a heavy-handed crudity that is beyond belief. Some degree of crudity may be excused in a new discipline, but failure to recognize that much of what passes as accounting theory is hopelessly entwined with unsupported behavior assumptions is unforgivable.[25]

The behavioral approach to the formulation of accounting theory emphasizes the relevance to decision-making of the information being communicated (communication-decision orientation) and the individual and group behavior caused by the communication of the information (decision-maker orientation). Accounting is assumed to be action-oriented; its purpose is to influence action (behavior) directly through the informational content of the message conveyed and indirectly through the behavior of accountants. Because accounting is considered to be a behavioral process,[26] the behavioral approach to the formulation of an accounting theory applies behavioral science to accounting. The overall objective of this approach is similar to that of behavioral science. The American Accounting Association's Committee on Behavioral Science Content of the Accounting Curriculum provides the following view of the objective of behavioral science, which may also apply to behavioral accounting:

> The objective of behavioral science is to understand, explain, and predict human behavior – that is, to establish generalizations about human behavior that are supported by empirical evidence collected in an impersonal way by procedures that are completely open to review and replication and capable of verification by other interested scholars. Behavioral science thus represents the systematic observation of man's behavior for the purpose of experimentally confirming specific hypotheses by reference to observable changes in behavior.[27]

The behavioral approach to the formulation of an accounting theory is concerned with human behavior, as it relates to accounting information and problems. In this context, the choice of an accounting technique must be evaluated with reference to the objectives behavior of the users of financial information.

Although relatively new, the behavioral approach has generated an enthusiasm and a new impetus in accounting research that focuses on the behavioral structure within which accountants function. A new multidisciplinary area in the field of accounting has been conveniently labeled behavioral accounting. The basic objective of behavioral accounting is to explain and predict human behavior in all possible accounting contexts. Research studies in behavioral accounting have relied on experimental, field, or correlational techniques. Most studies have made little attempt to formulate a theoretical framework that would support the problems or hypotheses to be tested. Instead, the studies generally have focused on the behavioral effects of accounting information or on the problems of human information processing. The results of these kinds of studies may provide an understanding of the behavioral environment of accounting that may serve as a guide in formulating an accounting theory. We will examine each group of studies and then evaluate the behavioral accounting approach.

11.2.2 Behavioral effects of accounting information

That accounting information, in terms of its content and format, may have an impact on individual decision-making, although evident and easily accepted, suggests avenues of research for the improvement of accounting and reporting systems. Accordingly, research studies in this area have examined alternative reporting models and disclosure practices to assess the available choices in terms of relevance and impact on behavior. Because a general theoretical framework has not been established, however, it is difficult to classify these studies. Several writers have attempted to provide classification schemes.[28] A more recent and exhaustive attempt by Dyckman, Gibbins and Swieringa[29] will be used in this section to illustrate the nature of studies of the behavioral effects of accounting information.

We may divide these studies into five general classes:

1. the adequacy of disclosure,
2. the usefulness of financial statement data,
3. attitudes about corporate reporting practices,
4. materiality judgments, and
5. the decision effects of alternative accounting procedures.[30]

Three approaches were used to examine the *adequacy of disclosure*. The first approach examined the patterns of use of data from the viewpoint of resolving controversial issues concerning the inclusion of certain information.[31] The second approach examined the perceptions and attitudes of different interest groups.[32] The third approach examined the extent to which different information items were disclosed in annual reports and the determinants of any significant differences in the adequacy of financial disclosure among companies.[33] The research on disclosure adequacy and use showed a general acceptance of the adequacy of available financial statements, a general understanding and comprehension of these financial statements, and a recognition that the differences in disclosure adequacy among the financial statements are due to such variables as company size, profitability, and size and listing status of the auditing firm.

Two approaches were used to examine the *usefulness of financial statement data*. The first approach examined the relative importance of the investment analysis of different information items to both users and preparers of financial information.[34] The second approach examined the relevance of financial statements to decision-making, based on laboratory communication of financial statement data in terms of readability and meaning to users in general.[35,36] The overall conclusions of these studies were that (1) some consensus exists between users and preparers regarding the relative importance of the information items disclosed in financial statements, and (2) users do not rely solely on financial statements when making their decisions.

Two approaches were used to examine attitudes about *corporate reporting practices*. The first approach examined preferences for alternative accounting techniques.[37] The second approach examined attitudes about general reporting issues, such as how much information should be available, how much information is available, and the importance of certain items.[38] These research studies showed the extent to which some accounting techniques proposed by the authoritative bodies are accepted and brought to light some attitudinal differences among professional groups concerning reporting issues.

Two approaches were used to examine *materiality judgments*. The first approach examined the main factors that determine the collection, classification and summarization of accounting data.[39] The second approach focused on what items people consider to be material and sought to determine that degree of difference in accounting data that is required before the difference is perceived as material.[40] These studies indicated that several factors appear to affect materiality judgments and that these judgments differ among individuals.

Finally, the *decision effects of accounting procedures* were examined, primarily in the context of the use of different inventory techniques, price-level information, and nonaccounting information.[41] The results indicated that alternative accounting techniques may influence individual decisions, and that the extent of the influence may depend on the nature of the task, the characteristics of the users and the nature of the experimental environment.

11.2.3 Linguistic effects of accounting data and techniques

Linguistics and accounting have a great number of similarities. Jain, for example, considers accounting rules to be analogous to financial grammar and, based on this analogy, uses the effect of grammatical structure on the perceptions of listeners to support the hypothesis that accounting methods affect decision-making.[42] More formally, Belkaoui argues that accounting is a language and that according to the "Sapir-Whorf hypothesis" its lexical characteristics and grammatical rules will affect both the linguistic and the nonlinguistic behavior of users.[43] Four propositions are introduced, derived from the linguistic relativity paradigm to conceptually integrate the research findings on the impact of accounting information on the user's behavior:

- The users that make certain lexical distinctions in accounting are enabled to talk and/or solve problems that cannot be solved by users who do not.

- The users that make certain lexical distinctions in accounting are enabled to perform (nonlinguistic) tasks more rapidly or more completely than those users who do not.

- The users that possess the accounting (grammatical) rules are more predisposed to different managerial styles or emphases than those who do not.

- The accounting techniques may tend to facilitate or render more difficult various (nonlinguistic) managerial behaviors on the part of users.[44]

These propositions have been empirically tested and verified in two studies that emphasize the importance of linguistic considerations in the use of accounting information and in international standard-setting.[45,46]

Within the *linguistic relativism thesis*, the role of language is emphasized as a mediator and shaper of the environment; this would imply that accounting language may predispose "users" to a given method of perception and behavior. Furthermore, the affiliation of users with different professional organizations or communities that have distinct interaction networks may create different accounting language repertoires. Accountants from different professional groups may use different organizational constraints and objectives. At worst, a confounding lack of communication may emerge. Using the *sociolinguistic thesis*, Belkaoui empirically shows that various affiliations in accounting create different linguistic repertoires or codes for intragroup communications and/or intergroup communications.[47] The sociolinguistic construct is used to justify the possible lack of consensus on the meaning of the accounting concepts. As a result, specific issues identified as in need of further research include: (1) the presence and nature of the "institutional language" within each accounting professional group; (2) the presence of a professional-linked linguistic code in the accounting field that is composed of a "formal language" and a "public language"; and (3) the construction of a test to determine whether or not the public language is understood by users of formal data (such as students).[48]

Other studies have investigated the linguistic effects of accounting data and techniques without relying on the linguistic relativism thesis or the sociological thesis. Instead, these studies have focused on the differences between the intragroup and intergroup communication of accounting data and/or techniques among users and producers of accounting data. To prove that these differences exist, accounting researchers have relied on various techniques, including: the semantic differential technique,[49,50,51] the antecedent-consequent technique,[52] multidimensional scaling techniques,[53] and the Cloze procedure.[54]

11.2.4 Functional and data fixation

Functional fixation, as it is used in accounting, suggests that under certain circumstances a decision-maker may be unable to adjust his or her decision process to a change in the accounting process that supplied him or her with impact data. Borrowed from the psychological literature, the phenomenon has been used in a slightly different way by accounting researchers.

Functional fixation originated as a concept in psychology, arising from an investigation of the impact of past experience on human behavior. Dunker introduced the concept of the functional fixation to illustrate the negative role of past experiences.[55] He investigated the hypothesis that an individual's prior use of an object in a function dissimilar to that required in a present problem would serve to exhibit the discovery of an appropriate, novel use for the objects. This result supported the functional fixation hypothesis with regard to several common objects, for example, boxes, pliers, weights and paper clips.

Ijiri, Jaedicke and Knight viewed the decision process as being characterized by three factors: decision inputs, decision outputs and decision rules.[56] They then introduced the conditions under which a decision-maker cannot adjust his or her decision process to a change in the accounting process. They attributed the inability to adjust, if it existed, to the psychological factor of functional fixation. Thus, whereas psychologists are interested in functional fixation involving function or objects, accounting research, influenced by the Ijiri, Jaedicke and Knight exploration, is interested in functional fixation involving data. Therefore accounting research should consider two forms of the functional fixation hypothesis, one focusing on function and one focusing on output or data. There lies the main difference: in the case of functional fixation, psychologists used objects such as medallions, string and boxes to solve relatively simple tasks, whereas the data fixation experiments all used data to solve unstructured problems. One might assume correctly that most of the interest in psychology has been on functional fixation. The exceptions to this assumption were a psychological data fixation study by Knight[57] and two mixed data fixation/functional fixation studies in accounting by Barnes and Welb, and Riahi-Belkaoui.[58,59] Various concepts exist for both the functional and data fixation results in accounting, namely:

- *The conditioning hypotheses:* It may be that the subjects of the experiments, mostly accounting students, have been conditioned to react to some form of accounting outputs and have failed to adjust their decision processes in response to a "well-disclosed" accounting change. The conditioning phenomenon inhibits the subjects from adopting the correct behavior, which is to adjust to the accounting change, and has led them to act as they have been conditioned to act in their previous behaviors or socialization sessions. Thus, the conditioning phenomenon is a form of functional fixation, as the subjects are no longer able to discriminate.

- *Prospect theory and framing hypotheses:*[60] Framing occurs because the wording of a question has the potential to alter a subject's response. Functional fixation can be viewed as a result of the particular choice of framing options made by the subjects in the experiments. The formulation of the decision tasks as well as the nouns, habits and personal characteristics of the subjects affect the framing of the decision and lead to functional data fixation results.

- *Primacy versus recency ego involvement:*[61] In matters of ego involvement with an accounting technique just learned, subjects will give importance to what is perceived as relevant, significant, or meaningful. This would explain some of the data fixation findings where the subjects have reverted to the use of either the first learned method (primacy) or the second learned method (recency) as to the method more clear or basic to their ego involvement.

The question that remains is whether opportunities to learn eliminate fixation. Luft and Shield show[62] experimentally that when individuals use information on intangible expenditures to predict future profits, expensing (vs. capitalizing) the expenditures significantly reduces the accuracy consistency, consensus, and self-insight of individuals' subjective profit predictions. Basically, learning is shown not to be necessarily a quick remedy for fixation on accounting, because accounting affects the learning process itself.

11.2.5 Information inductance

The behavior of an individual is influenced by information in two ways: (1) through information use when acting as a recipient, and (2) through information inductance when acting as a sender. Although the impact on information use is generally known and accepted as part of the stimulus–response paradigm, the more recent phenomenon of information inductance or simple inductance, introduced in accounting by Prakash and Rappaport,[63] is intended to refer to the complex process whereby the behavior of an individual is affected by the information he or she is required to communicate. Information inductance results from the sender's tendencies to anticipate the possible use of information, the consequences of such use, and his or her reactions to these consequences. As stated by Prakash and Rappaport:

> An individual's anticipating the consequences of his or her communication might lead him or her – before any information is communicated and, hence, even before any consequences arise – to choose to alter the information, or his or her behavior, or even his or her objectives. This is the process of information inductance.[64]

Time factors seem to govern inductance as follows: First, communication of information that is either in fact a description of the sender's behavior, or is regarded as such by the information sender, or concerning which the information sender has some apprehension that it could be so regarded by the information recipient, will be strongly conducive to information inductance. Secondly, consequences that represent possible feedback effects on the information sender will be strongly conducive to information inductance. We go on to classify broadly the feedback effects to an information sender as arising from:

1. external evaluation of performance;
2. regulation and control of operations;
3. interaction with the decisions of other behavioral units; and
4. changes in the set of choices open to the information sender.[65]

Information inductance may be integrated to information use to provide an integrated theory of the impact of information involving both senders and users.

11.3 The human information processing approach

Interest in the human information processing approach arose from a desire to improve both the information set presented to users of financial data and the ability of users to use the information. Theories and models from human information processing in psychology provide a tool for transforming accounting issues into generic information processing issues. There are three main components of an information processing model – input, process and output. Studies of the information set *input (or cues)* focus on the variables that are likely to affect the way people process information for decision-making. The variables examined are:

1. the scaling characteristics of individual cues (level of measurement, discrete or continuous, deterministic or probabilistic);
2. the statistical properties of the information set (number of cues, distributional characteristics, inter-relationship of cues, underlying dimensionality);
3. the informational content or predictive significance (bias, reliability or form of relationship to criterion);

4. the method of presentation (format, sequence, level of aggregation); and

5. the context (physical viewing conditions, instructions, task characteristics and feedback).[66]

Studies of the process component focus on the variables affecting the decision-maker, such as:

1. characteristics of judgment (personal, task-related, human or mechanical, number of judges); and

2. characteristics of decision rules (form, cue usage, stability, and heuristics).[67]

Studies of the output component focus on variables related to the judgment, prediction or decision that are likely to affect the way the user processes the information. The variables examined include:

1. the qualities of the judgment (accuracy, speed, reliability in terms of consistency, consensus and convergence, response biases, and predictability); and

2. self-insight (subjective cue usage, perceived decision quality, and perceptions of characteristics of information sets).[68]

The varying emphasis on any of the three components of an information processing model led to the use of four different approaches:

1. the lens model approach,

2. probabilistic judgment,

3. predecisional behavior, and

4. the cognitive style approach

Each approach will be examined next.

11.3.1 The lens model

Brunswick's lens model allows explicit recognition of the interdependence of environmental and individual-specific variables.[69] It is used primarily to assess human judgmental situations in which people make judgments on the basis of a set of explicit cues from the environment. The model emphasizes the similarities between the environment and the subject response. As seen in Exhibit 11.1, the right side of the model describes the relationships between the subject responses or judgments (Y_s) and the level of (X_i) in terms of their correlation (r_i). The left side of the model describes the relationships between the actual criterion or event (Y_e) and the level of cues (X_i). The analysis relies on a *regression model* when the cues are continuous and on an *analysis of variance (ANOVA) model* when the cues take on categorical values. Other methods include conjoint measurement, multidimensional scaling techniques, and discriminant analysis.

Most accounting research using the lens model has been motivated by the need to build mathematical models that represent the relative importance of different information cues (often called "policy capturing"), and by the need to measure the accuracy of judgment and its consistency, consensus, and predictability.[70] Various accounting decision problems have been examined using the lens model. These include:

1. *policy-capturing studies*, which examine the relative importance of different cues in the judgment process and consensus among decision-makers;

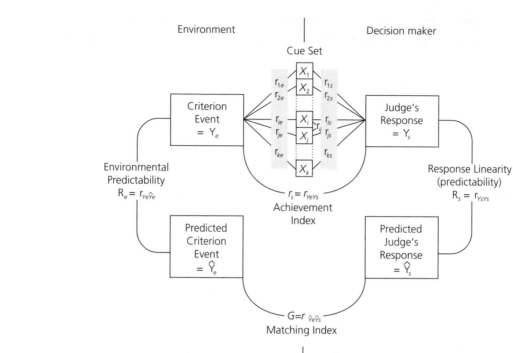

Exhibit 11.1 Brunswick's lens model

2. *accuracy of judgments* made on the basis of accounting cues; and

3. *effects of task characteristics on achievement and learning.*[71]

The policy-capturing research focused on issues related to between-judge consensus, the relative importance of cues, the functional form of the decision rule, and the judges' self-insight. Decision problems examined in the policy-capturing research included materiality judgments, internal control evaluation, reasonableness of forecasts, uncertainty disclosures, policy-making and loan classification.

The accuracy of judgments is very important to accountants. The research focused not only on judgmental accuracy but also on judgmental consistency consensus, and predictability. The decision problems examined in the accuracy of judgment research included bankruptcy prediction and stock recommendations and price predictions.

The effects of task characteristics on achievement and learning were examined in both the psychological and the accounting literature. In psychology, the problems examined included task predictability, the functional form of cue criterion relationships, the number of cues, cue validity distributions and inter-correlations, and feedback type. In accounting, the problems examined included the impact of accounting changes, feedback methods, the report format and cue presentation.

11.3.2 Probabilistic judgment

The probabilistic judgment approach, sometimes known as the *Bayesian approach*, focuses first on a comparison of intuitive probability judgments and the normative model. The normative model for probability revision, known as *Bayes' Theorem*, is used as the descriptive model of human information processing. Basically, the *a posteriori* probability form of Bayes' Theorem states that:

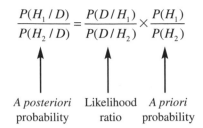

$$\frac{P(H_1/D)}{P(H_2/D)} = \frac{P(D/H_1)}{P(D/H_2)} \times \frac{P(H_1)}{P(H_2)}$$

A posteriori   Likelihood   *A priori*
probability   ratio   probability

where H_1, and H_2 are the alternative hypotheses and D is the datum.

The basic question examined in the early research in probabilistic judgment is whether probabilities are revised in the direction indicated by Bayes' Theorem.[72] The findings suggest that this occurs to a lesser extent than Bayes' Theorem would suggest. The phenomenon has been labeled *conservatism*. This shifted the focus of the research to finding the sources of the observed human information processing biases. Tversky and Kahneman reported that people rely on a number of heuristics to reduce the complex tasks of assessing probabilities and predicting values to simpler judgmental operations.[73] These heuristics include *representativeness*, *availability*, and *adjustment and anchoring*.

Representativeness refers to the heuristic people use when they assess the probability of an event on the basis of its degree of similarity, or representativeness, to the category of which it is perceived to be an example. *Availability* refers to the heuristic people use when they assess the probability of an event on the basis of the ease with which it comes to mind. Finally, *adjustment and anchoring* refer to the heuristic people use when they make estimates by starting with an initial value (anchoring) and then adjusting the value to yield the final answer.

The early literature of probabilistic judgment in accounting reached the same conclusion concerning the decision-makers' use of simplifying heuristics in their processing of information, with the difference that such use may be sensitive to task and situation variables. More current research has examined the choice of techniques used to elicit subjective probabilities and the departures from normative decision-making behavior.

Research on probability elicitation has attempted to assess the convergent validity of different elicitation techniques in auditing as well as their accuracy and their effect on audit decisions. No general conclusions can be derived at this stage of the research.

Research on the departures from normative decision-making behavior has focused on heuristics and biases – basically, representativeness in auditing, anchoring in auditing, anchoring in management control, and anchoring in financial analysis – and on the ability of decision-makers to perform the role of information evaluators. Little, however, is known about how the information processing capabilities of individuals interact with task structure to produce heuristics and biases.

11.3.3 Predecisional behavior

Most of the experiments based on the lens model or on probabilistic judgment involve highly repetitive situations in which the task is well defined, the subject is exposed to the right cues, and the possible responses are prespecified. These experiments fail to deal with the dynamics of problem definition, hypothesis formation and information search in less structured environments. In brief, they fail to explore the stages of predecisional behavior. Predecisional behavior is generally examined using *process-tracing methods*. The process-tracing method evolved from the theory of problem solving developed by Newell and Simon,[74] who argue that humans have a limited capacity to process information. They also suggest that humans have short-term memory with limited capacity and virtually unlimited long-term memory. As a result, humans tend to display satisficing rather than optimal responses, leading them to be adaptive. This adaptiveness, in turn, implies that the cognitive representation (nature and complexity) of the task determines the way in which the problems are solved, since the tasks tend to elicit and therefore control the behavioral responses of decision-makers.

Process tracers tend to rely on four methods:

1. eye movements;
2. information search behavior;
3. information cue attending or response time; and
4. verbal "think aloud" introspective protocols.[75]

Verbal protocol, the most frequently used technique in accounting, consists of asking subjects to "think aloud" into an audio or video recorder while performing a task. The protocols are then analyzed, using a particular coding strategy.

Given the potential reasonableness of the verbal protocol coding strategy employed by the researchers, Payne suggests the additional use of other data-collection methods so that the results of several methods can be compared to determine their convergence.[76] Joyce and Libby add the following disadvantages:

> Among the disadvantages are (1) the sheer volume of data collection in such studies, which limits the number of subjects that can be studied, and (2) the lack of objective coding techniques. This makes the analysis arduous and the communication of the results quite difficult. Reports of verbal protocol studies are usually quite long to read, even when the results from just a few subjects are presented.[77]

Very few accounting studies have relied on process tracing methods. Issues examined include the modeling of expert financial analysts, the general strategies used by managers in performance report evaluation, and audit decision-making. Although they are in the early stages of development, the accounting applications of the process tracing approaches are promising. Some of the potentials follow:

> For example, research examining the memory of experts might indicate explanations for differences between experts and novices demonstrated in prior research and might lead to the development of training aids. The role of cognitive representation in the choice of decision heuristics may provide insights into the methods for redesigning management reports or audit programs to lead to proper heuristic choices. Studies of the interaction of memory and information search lead to the development of decision aids to be used at these important stages in less structured accounting situations such as variance investigation and audit client screening.[78]

11.3.4 The cognitive style approach

The cognitive style approach focuses on the variables that are likely to have an impact on the quality of the judgments made by the decision-makers. "Cognitive style" is a hypothetical construct that is used to explain the mediation process between stimuli and responses. Five approaches to the studies of cognitive style in psychology have been reported: authoritarianism, dogmatism, cognitive complexity, integrative complexity and field dependence:[79]

1. *Authoritarianism* arose from the focus by Adorno and others on the relationship between personality, anti-democratic attitudes and behavior.[80] These researchers were primarily interested in individuals whose way of thinking made them susceptible to anti-democratic propaganda. Two of the behavioral correlates of authoritarianism – rigidity and intolerance of ambiguity – were reflections of an underlying cognitive style.

2. *Dogmatism* arose from Rokeach's efforts to develop a structurally based measure of authoritarianism to replace the content-based measure developed by Adorno and his colleagues.[81] Their interest was in developing a measure of cognitive style that would be independent of the content of thought.

3. *Cognitive complexity*, as introduced by Kelly[82] and Bieri,[83] focuses on the psychological dimensions that individuals use to structure their environments and to differentiate the behaviors of others. More cognitively complex individuals are assumed to have a greater number of available dimensions with which to construe the behavior of others than less cognitively complex persons. Decision-makers are also classified in terms of two cognitive styles: heuristic and analytic. Based on the terms used by Huysman,[84] they may be defined as follows:

   (a) *Analytic decision-makers* reduce problem situations to a more or less explicit, often quantitative, model on which they base decisions.
   (b) *Heuristic decision-makers* refer instead to common sense, intuition and unquantified feelings about future development as applied to the totality of the situation as an organic whole rather than to clearly identifiable parts.

4. *Integrative complexity*, as presented by Harvey and others[85] and later expanded by Schroeder and others,[86] results from the view that people engage in two activities in processing sensory input: differentiation and integration. *Differentiation* refers to the individual's ability to place stimuli along dimensions. *Integration* refers to the individual's ability to employ complex rules to combine these dimensions. A person engaging in less of both activities is said to be *concrete*, a person engaging in more of both activities is said to be *abstract*. The continuum from concrete to abstract is referred to as *integrative or conceptual complexity*.

   To the concept of integrative complexity is usually added the concept of environmental complexity and the level of information processing, as expressed by the *U-curve Hypothesis* depicted in Exhibit 11.2. As the level of environmental complexity increases, the level of information processing increases and reaches maximum level at an optimal level of environmental complexity beyond which it begins to decrease.[87] Schroeder and others extended the concept of the inverted U-shaped curve to the study of integrative complexity. The differences between the concrete and the abstract individual are also shown in Exhibit 11.2. The more abstract the individual, the higher the maximum level of information processing.

5. Finally, *field dependence*, as presented by Witkin and his associates, is a measure of extent of differentiation in the area of perception.[88] Field-dependent individuals tend to perceive the overall organization of a field and are relatively unable to perceive parts of the field as discrete. Field-independent individuals, however, tend to perceive parts of the field as discrete from the overall organization of the field, rather than fused with it.

Accounting studies based on these five approaches to cognitive style have focused on classifying users of information by their cognitive structure and on designing information

A. Propositions about the routine PJPA cycle
  A(1). *The judge's experience (accumulated learning)*
  P1: Experience produces structured judgment guides ("templates")
    C1(i): Template exists prior to event triggering its use
    C1(ii): Greater experience, more efficient memory use
    C1(iii): Template more complete for more common tasks
  P2: The templates are maintained in long-term memory
  P3: Templates' attributes are shaped by the environment
    C3(i): Some templates more ready for use than others
  A(2). *The triggering event (stimulus)*
  P4: The environment is subjectively perceived
    C4(i): Factors limiting perception also limit judgment
  P5: Templates are continuously updated
  A(3). *The judgment process*
  P6: Judgment is a continuous process
  P7: Judgment is an incremental process
    C7(i): Routine judgment responds to the short term
    C7(ii): Routine judgment avoids limits on future responses
  P8: Judgment is a conditional process
  P9: Judgment begins with a search for a template
    C9(i): Search-retrieval may use little information
  P10: Template selection depends on circumstantial fit
    C10(i): Routine template selection based on past learning
    C10(ii): Perception and search continue until template found
  P11: Routine judgment is not, and need not be, conscious
    C11(i): Explaining own judgment involves rationalization
    C11(ii): Own explanations correlate with common templates
  P12: The judgment environment is incompletely perceived
  P13: Personal characteristics affect template selection
  A(4). *The decision/action (response)*
  P14: Templates specify conscious response preferences
    C14(i): As outputs, preferences subject to imperfections
    C14(ii): Preferences based on past actions and learning
  P15: Preferences and actions are consciously bridged
  P16: The bridging process is instrumental, not probabilistic
    C16(i): Preferences, consequences instrumentally connected
  P17: The decision/action must be justifiable
    C17(i): Some information is to justify choice, not make it
    C17(ii): Justification includes some rationalization
  P18: Bridging evaluations tend to emphasize the downside

B. *Propositions about nonroutine PJPA*
  P19: Conscious judgment is a response to the circumstances
  P20: Conscious judgment strategies also guide judgment
    C20(i): Mental "red flags" prompt conscious intervention
    C20(ii): Complex responses need conscious implementation
  P21: Fully conscious professional judgment is infrequent

Source: Michael Gibbins, "Propositions about the Psychology of Professional Judgment in Public Accounting", *Journal of Accounting Research* (22, Spring, 1984), Table 1, "List of Propositions and Corollaries", p. 121. Reprinted with permission.

Exhibit 11.3 List of propositions and corollaries

Various concepts of culture exist in anthropology, suggesting different themes for accounting research.[105]

1. Following Malinowski's functionalism,[106] culture can be viewed as an instrument serving biological and psychological needs. Applying this definition to accounting research suggests the perception of accounting in each culture as a specific social instrument for task accomplishment and the analysis of cross-cultural or comparative accounting.

2. Following Radcliffe-Brown's structural functionalism,[107] culture can be viewed as an adaptive regulatory mechanism that unites individuals with social structures. Applying this definition to accounting research suggests the perception of accounting in each culture as an adaptive instrument existing by process of exchange with the environment and the analysis of an accounting culture.

3. Following Goodenough's ethnic science,[108] culture can be viewed as a system of shared cognition. The human mind thus generates culture by means of a finite number of rules. Applying this definition to accounting research suggests that accounting can be viewed as a system of knowledge that members of each culture share to varying degrees and the analysis of accounting as cognition.

4. Following Geertz's symbolic anthropology,[109] culture can be viewed as a system of shared symbols and meanings. Applying this definition to accounting research suggests that accounting can be viewed as a pattern of symbolic discourse or language and the analysis of accounting as language.

5. Following Levi-Strauss's structuralism,[110] culture can be viewed as a projection of the mind's universal unconscious infrastructure. Applying this definition to accounting suggests that accounting can be viewed in each culture as the manifestation of unconscious processes and the analysis of unconscious processes in accounting.

Applied to accounting, culture can be viewed as accounting's medium. Culture, in essence, determines the judgment/decision process in accounting. The model postulates that culture, through its components, elements, and dimensions, dictates the organizational structure adopted, the micro-organizational behavior, and the cognitive functioning of individuals in such a way as to ultimately affect their judgment/decision process when they are faced with an accounting and/or auditing phenomenon.[111] The definition of the components of culture is provided by Hofstede[112] as four dimensions that reflect the cultural orientations of a country and explain 50 percent of the differences in value systems among countries:

1. individualism versus collectivism;
2. large versus small power distance;
3. strong versus weak uncertainty avoidance; and
4. masculinity versus femininity.

These are defined next.

Individualism versus collectivism is a dimension that represents the degree of integration a society maintains among its members or the relationships between an individual and his or her fellow individuals. Although individualists are expected to take care of themselves and their immediate families only, collectivists are expected to remain emotionally integrated into in-groups that protect them in exchange for unquestioning loyalty.

Large versus small power distance represents the extent to which members of a society accept the unequal distribution of power in institutions and organizations. In large power distance societies, there is a tendency for people to accept a hierarchical order in which everyone has a place that needs no justification, whereas in small power distance societies people tend to live for equality and demand justification for any existing power inequalities.

Strong versus weak uncertainty avoidance is a dimension that represents the degree to which the members of a society feel uncomfortable with uncertainty and ambiguity. In strong uncertainty avoidance societies, people are intolerant of ambiguity and try to control it at all costs, whereas in weak uncertainty avoidance societies, people are more tolerant of ambiguity and tend to live with it.

Masculinity versus femininity is a dimension that represents the nature of the social division of sex roles. Masculine roles imply a preference for achievement, assertiveness, making money, sympathy for the strong, and the like. Feminine roles imply a preference for warm relationships, modesty, care for the weak, preservation of the environment, concern for the quality of life, and so on.

This cultural relativism model assumes that differences among these four dimensions create different cultural arenas that have the potential of dictating the organizational behavior that may shape the judgment decision process in accounting. The cultural relativism model calls for own-cross-cultural research in accounting. There are at least five basic possible approaches to cross-cultural research in accounting.[113]

1. Parochial studies is the approach comprising studies of the United States conducted by Americans.

2. Ethnocentric studies comprise studies that attempt to replicate American accounting research in foreign countries.

3. Polycentric studies comprise studies that describe accounting phenomena in foreign countries.

4. Comparative accounting studies focus on identifying the similarities in accounting phenomena in cultures around the world.

5. Culturally synergistic studies focus on creating universality in accounting while maintaining an appropriate level of cultural specificity.

Each of these types of research addresses a different set of accounting questions and is based on different sets of assumptions.

Cross-cultural research in accounting is needed for the reasons shown below:[114]

First, it would establish the boundary conditions for accounting models and theories.[115] The model proceeds with the testing of the validity of a model or theory in another culture to determine the cultural groups where the model or theory is valid and to specify the varieties for which the model is not valid in some cultural groups. Basically, the discovery of the limits of accounting theories is an important part of accounting research.

The second reason is to evaluate the impact of cultural and ecological factors on behavior in accounting.[116] Between-cultural-group mean comparisons are used to demonstrate cultural differences in the dependent variable. If these comparisons cannot be made because of the absence of score equivalence, then the strategy should be to test the universality of an accounting model or theory. Triandis, Malpass, and Davidson made a crucial distinction between cross-cultural research aimed at proving the cross-cultural generality of a relationship or phenomena and studies that attempt to show differences in the relationship of phenomena that depend on cultural factors as follows:

> The former study can be done with relatively loose methodology, since if the same finding is obtained in spite of differences in the stimuli, responses and people, it must be a strong finding. The latter requires extremely stringent controls and a multi-method approach, since there are many competing hypotheses that can account for

the observed differences. The best kind of study of the second type is more likely the one where the differences have been predicted on theoretical grounds.[117]

The third reason is that although variables are often generally confounded, the confounding is not complete, as a few cultunits may present deviant cases. "Cultunits" as the object of study of some cross-cultural psychologists were defined by Naroll as "people who are domestic speakers of a common district dialect language and who belong either to the same state or the same contact group".[118] As stated by Triandis:

> So, even if variables A and B are highly positively correlated, there are nevertheless a few cultunits that are high on A and low on B, and a few that are low on A and high on B. If we study the deviant cultunits we can establish whether relationships between dependent variables Y and the independent variables A and B are caused by A, caused by B, or caused by both A and B. This is information that is most valuable.[119]

The fourth reason is that cultures act as "natural grain-experiments" by being high or low on variables of particular interest.[120] For example, some cultures may focus on some aspects of accounting more than others. As a result, perceptual and decision styles may differ and can be traced to ecological differences.

The fifth reason is that cultures determine aspects of psychological functioning.[121] For example, some cultures may deem certain accounting functions to be useless or unnecessary for their particular context. As a result, those functions are not practiced because they are not rewarded. Triandis, Vassilion, Tanaka, and Shanmugam give the example of the low probability of the planning function in cultures where belief in the unpredictability of events is extremely high.[122] The study of behavior in cross-cultural accounting contexts needs to match the particular nature of the ecology with the particular nature of the participants.

The sixth reason is that the frequency of different accounting methods and behavior in different cultures need to be identified.

11.4 Evaluation of the behavioral approach

Most of the behavioral accounting research discussed in the preceding sections has attempted to establish generalizations about human behavior in relation to accounting information. The implicit objective of all these studies is to develop and verify the behavioral hypotheses relevant to accounting theory hypotheses on the adequacy of disclosure, the usefulness of financial statement data, attitudes about corporate reporting practices, materiality judgments, the decision effects of alternative accounting procedures, and the components of an information processing model (input, process and output). This implicit objective has not yet been reached, however, because most of the experimental and survey research in behavioral accounting suffers from a lack of theoretical and methodological rigor. Studies have examined the use of surrogates in behavioral accounting research without any conclusive results.

Similarly, viewing the experiment as a social contract implies a relationship between the subject and the experimenter: Some aspects of this relationship may threaten the validity of the experiment.

11.5 Conclusions

This chapter has elaborated on the meanings and important findings of event, behavioral and human information processing to the formulation of an accounting theory. Each of these approaches relies on different assumptions and on new methodologies and unique ways of looking at accounting problems and research questions. Each approach is beginning to take on the attributes of a distinctive paradigm, thereby causing accounting to become a multiparadigmatic science in which competing paradigms strive for dominance. In the next chapter, we will explain the impact of the predictive and positive approaches to the formulation of an accounting theory.

Notes

1. Sorter, G.H., "An 'Events' Approach to Basic Accounting Theory", *The Accounting Review* (January, 1969), pp. 12–19.
2. McCarthy, W.E., "Construction and Use of Integrated Accounting Systems with Entity Relationship Modeling", in P. Chen (ed.), *Entity-Relationship Approach to Systems Analysis and Design* (New York: North Holland Publishing Company, 1980), p. 628.
3. Sorter, G.H., "An 'Events' Approach to Basic Accounting Theory", op. cit., p. 13.
4. Johnson, O., "Towards an 'Events' Theory of Accounting", *The Accounting Review* (October, 1970), p. 649.
5. Ibid., pp. 643–4.
6. Sorter, G.H., "An 'Events' Approach to Basic Accounting Theory", op. cit., p. 15.
7. Ibid., p. 17.
8. Johnson, O., "Towards an 'Events' Theory of Accounting", op. cit., p. 65.
9. Wheeler, J.T., "Accounting Theory and Research in Perspective", *The Accounting Review* (January, 1970), p. 7.
10. Colantoni, C.S., Manes, R.E., and Whinston, A.B., "A Unified Approach to the Theory of Accounting and Information Systems", *The Accounting Review* (January, 1971), pp. 90–102; Lieberman, A.Z., and Whinston, A.B., "A Structuring of an Events-Accounting Information System", *The Accounting Review* (April, 1975), pp. 246–57.
11. Haseman, W.D., and Whinston, A.B., "Design of a Multidimensional Accounting System", *The Accounting Review* (January, 1976), pp. 65–79.
12. Everest, G.C., and Weber, R., "A Relational Approach to Accounting Models", *Accounting Review* (April, 1977), pp. 340–59.
13. McCarthy, W.E., "An Entity-Relationship View of Accounting Models", *The Accounting Review* (October, 1979), pp. 667–86.
14. McCarthy, W.E., "The REA Accounting Model: A Generalized Framework for Accounting Systems in a Shared Data Environment", *The Accounting Review* (July, 1982), pp. 554–78.
15. Lieberman, A.Z., and Whinston, A.B., "A Structuring of an Events-Accounting Information System", op. cit., p. 249.
16. Ijiri, Yuji, *The Foundations of Accounting Measurements* (Englewood Cliffs, NJ: Prentice-Hall, 1967), p. 110.
17. Charnes, A., Colantoni, C.S., and Cooper, W.W., "A Futurological Justification for Historical Cost and Multidimensional Accounting" (Pittsburgh, PA: Carnegie Mellon University School of Urban and Public Affairs, November, 1974).
18. Haseman, W.D., and Whinston, A.B., "Design of a Multidimensional Accounting System", op. cit., p. 79.
19. Everest, G.C., and Weber, R., "A Relational Approach to Accounting Models", op. cit., p. 359.
20. McCarthy, W.E., "An Entity-Relationship View of Accounting Models", op. cit., p. 667.
21. Chen, P., "The Entity-Relationship Model Toward a Unified View of Data", *ACM Transactions on Data-Base Systems* (March, 1976), pp. 9–36.

22. McCarthy, W.E., "The REA Accounting Model: A Generalized Framework for Accounting Systems in a Shared Data Environment", op. cit., p. 556.

23. Benbasat, I., and Dexter, A.S., "Value and Events Approaches to Accounting: An Experimental Evaluation", *The Accounting Review* (October, 1979), pp. 735–45.

24. The low/high analytic dimension is a psychological type variable whereby low analytic decision-makers tend to use hypothetical testing, feedback, and trial-and-error approaches to reach solutions, and high-analytic decision-makers tend to approach a problem by structuring it in terms of a planned method that may produce a likely solution. For more information, see Huysmans, J.H.B., "The Effectiveness of Cognitive Style Constraint in Implementing Operations Research Proposals", *Management Science* (September, 1970), pp. 92–104.

25. Devine, C.T., "Research Methodology and Accounting Theory Formation", *The Accounting Review* (July, 1960), pp. 387–99.

26. Report of The Committee on Behavioral Science "Content of the Accounting Curriculum", *The Accounting Review* (supplement, 1971), p. 247.

27. Ibid., p. 394.

28. Birnberg, J.G., and Nath, R., "Implications of Behavioral Science for Managerial Accounting", *The Accounting Review* (January, 1975), pp. 81–98; Hofstedt, T.R., "Some Behavioral Parameters of Financial Analysis", *The Accounting Review* (October, 1972), pp. 679–92; Rhode, J.G., "Behavioral Science Methodologies with Application for Accounting Research: References and Source Materials", Chapter 7 of "Report of the Committee on Research Methodology in Accounting", *The Accounting Review* (supplement, 1972), pp. 454–504.

29. Dyckman, T.R., Gibbins, M., and Swieringa, R.J., "Experimental and Survey Research in Financial Accounting: A Review and Evaluation", in A.R. Abdel-Khalik and T.F. Keller (eds.), *The Impact of Accounting Research in Financial Accounting and Disclosure on Accounting Practice* (Durham, NC: Duke University Press, 1978), pp. 48–89.

30. We will present a brief overview of the studies included in each class to provide an overview of the research topics and methodologies behavioral accountant researchers employ to conduct their inquiry. For a full examination of these studies, see Dyckman, Gibbins, and Swieringa's survey.

31. Horngren, Charles T., "Security Analysis and the Price Level", *The Accounting Review* (October, 1955), pp. 575–81, and "The Funds Statement and Its Use by Analysts", *Journal of Accountancy* (January, 1956), pp. 55–9.

32. Bradish, R.D., "Corporate Reporting and the Financial Analyst", *The Accounting Review* (October, 1965), pp. 757–66; Ecton, W.W., "Communication Through Accounting Bankers' Views", *Journal of Accountancy* (August, 1969), pp. 79–81.

33. Cerf, A.R., "Corporate Reporting and Investment Decisions" (Berkeley, CA: Institute of Business and Economic Research, 1961); Singhvi, S.S., and Desai, H.B., "An Empirical Analysis of the Quality of Corporate Financial Disclosure", *The Accounting Review* (January, 1971), pp. 129–38; Buzby, S.L., "Selected Items for Information and their Disclosure in Annual Reports", *The Accounting Review* (July, 1974), pp. 423–35; Belkaoui, A., and Kahl, A., "Corporate Financial Disclosure in Canada", *CCGAA Research Monograph No. 1* (Vancouver: Canadian Certified General Accountants Association, 1978).

34. Baker, H.K., and Haslem, J.A., "Information Needs of Individual Investors", *Journal of Accountancy* (November, 1973), pp. 64–9; Chandra, G., "A Study of the Consensus on Disclosure Among Public Accountants and Security Analysts", *The Accounting Review* (October, 1974), pp. 733–42; Belkaoui, A., Kahl, A., and Peyrard, J., "Information Needs of Financial Analysts: An International Comparison", *Journal of*

International Education and Research in Accounting (Fall, 1977), pp. 19–27; Belkaoui, A., "Consensus on Disclosure", *The Canadian Chartered Accountant Magazine* (June, 1979), pp. 44–6.

35. Falk, H., and Ophir, T., "The Effect of Risk on the Use of Financial Statements by Investment Decision Makers: A Case Study", *The Accounting Review* (April, 1973), pp. 323–8, and "The Influence of Differences in Accounting Policies on Investment Decision", *Journal of Accounting Research* (Spring, 1973), pp. 108–16; Libby, R., "Accounting Ratios and the Prediction of Failure: Some Behavioral Evidence", *Journal of Accounting Research* (Spring, 1975), pp. 150–61, and "The Use of Simulated Decision Makers in Information Evaluation", *The Accounting Review* (July, 1975), pp. 475–89.

36. Soper, F.J., and Dolphin, R., Jr., "Readability and Corporate Annual Reports", *The Accounting Review* (April, 1964), pp. 358–62; Smith, J.E., and Smith, N.P., "Readability: A Measure of the Performance of the Communication Function of Financial Reporting", *The Accounting Review* (July, 1971), pp. 552–61; Haried, A.A., "The Semantic Dimensions of Financial Statements", *Journal of Accounting Research* (Autumn, 1972), pp. 376–91, and "Measurement of Meaning in Financial Reports", *Journal of Accounting Research* (Spring, 1973), pp. 117–45; Oliver, B.L., "The Semantic Differential: A Device for Measuring the Interprofessional Communication of Selected Accounting Concepts", *Journal of Accounting Research* (Autumn, 1974), pp. 299–316; Belkaoui, A., "The Interprofessional Linguistic Communication of Accounting Concepts: An Experiment in Sociolinguistics", *Journal of Accounting Research* (Autumn, 1980), pp. 362–74.

37. Nelson, K., and Strawser, R.H., "A Note on APB Opinion No. 16", *Journal of Accounting Research* (Autumn, 1970), pp. 284–9; Brenner, V., and Shuey, R., "An Empirical Study of Support for APB Opinion No. 16", *Journal of Accounting Research* (Spring, 1972), pp. 200–8.

38. Copeland, R.M., Francia, A.J., and Strawser, R.H., "Students as Subjects in Behavioral Business Research", *The Accounting Review* (April, 1973), pp. 365–74; Godum, L.B., "CPA and User Opinions on Increased Corporate Disclosure", *The CPA Journal* (July, 1975), pp. 31–5.

39. Woolsey, S.M., "Materiality Survey", *Journal of Accountancy* (September, 1973), pp. 91–2; Patillo, James W., and Siebel, J.D., "Materiality in Financial Reporting", *Financial Executive* (October, 1973), pp. 27–8; Dyer, J., "A Search for Objective Materiality Norms in Accounting and Auditing", dissertation, University of Kentucky, 1973; Boatsman, J.A., and Robertson, J.C., "Policy-Capturing on Selected Materiality Judgments", *The Accounting Review* (April, 1974), pp. 342–52.

40. Rose, J., Beaver, W.H., Becker, S., and Sorter, G.H., "Toward an Empirical Measure of Materiality", supplement to Vol. 8, *Journal of Accounting Research* (1970), pp. 138–56; Dickhaut, J.W., and Eggleton, I.R.C., "An Examination of the Processes Underlying Comparative Judgments of Numerical Stimuli", *Journal of Accounting Research* (Spring, 1975), pp. 38–72.

41. Horngren, Charles T., "Security Analysts and the Price Level", *The Accounting Review* (October, 1955), pp. 575–81; Jensen, R.E., "An Experimental Design for the Study of Effects of Accounting Variations in Decision-Making", *Journal of Accounting Research* (Autumn, 1966), pp. 224–38; Livingstone, John L., "A Behavioral Study of Tax Allocation in Electric Utility Regulations", *The Accounting Review* (July, 1967), pp. 544–52; Khemakhem, Adbellatif, "A Simulation of Management-Decision Behavior: 'Funds' and Income", *The Accounting Review* (July, 1968), pp. 522–34; Dyckman, T.R., *Accounting Research Study* No. 1, "Investment Analysis and General Price-Level Adjustments: A Behavioral Study" (Sarasota, FL: American Accounting Association,

1969), and "On the Investment Decision," *The Accounting Review* (April, 1976), pp. 258–95; Barrett, M.E., "Accounting for Intercorporate Investments: A Behavioral Field Experiment", supplement to Vol. 9, *Journal of Accounting Research* (1971), pp. 50–92; Elias, N., "The Effects of Human Asset Statements on the Investment Decision: An Experiment", supplement to Vol. 10, *Journal of Accounting Research* (1972), pp. 215–40; Hofstedt, T.R., "Some Behavioral Parameters of Financial Analysis", pp. 679–92; Belkaoui, A., and Cousineau, A., "Accounting Information, Nonaccounting Information, and Common Stock Perception", *Journal of Business* (July, 1977), pp. 334–42.

42. Jain, Tribhowan, N., "Alternative Methods of Accounting and Decision Making: A Psycholinguistic Analysis", *The Accounting Review* (January, 1973), pp. 95–104.

43. Belkaoui, A., "Linguistic Relativity in Accounting", *Accounting, Organizations and Society* (October, 1978), pp. 97–104.

44. Ibid., p. 103.

45. Belkaoui, A., "The Impact of Socioeconomic Accounting Statements on the Investment Decision: An Empirical Study", *Accounting, Organizations and Society* (September, 1980), pp. 263–84.

46. Belkaoui, Janice, and Belkaoui, A., "Bilinguilism and the Perception of Professional Concepts", *Journal of Psychological Research* (12, 12, 1983), pp. 111–27.

47. Belkaoui, A., "The Interprofessional Linguistic Communication of Accounting Concepts: An Experiment in Sociolinguistics", op. cit., pp. 362–74.

48. Ibid., p. 371.

49. Haried, A.A., "The Semantic Dimensions of Financial Statements", op. cit., pp. 376–91.

50. Oliver, B.L., "The Semantic Differential: A Devise for Measuring the Interprofessional Communication of Selected Accounting Concepts", op. cit., pp. 299–316.

51. Flamholtz, E., and Cook, E., "Connotative Meaning and its Role in Accounting Change: A Field Study", *Accounting, Organizations and Society* (October, 1978), pp. 115–39.

52. Haried, A.A., "Measurement of Meaning in Financial Reports", *Journal of Accounting Research* (Spring, 1973), pp. 117–45.

53. Libby R., "Bankers' and Auditors' Perceptions of the Message communicated by the Audit Report," *Journal of Accounting Research* (Autumn, 1979), pp. 99–122.

54. Adelberg, A.H., "A Methodology for Measuring the Understandability of Financial Report Messages", *Journal of Accounting Research* (Autumn, 1979), pp. 565–92.

55. Dunker, K., "On Problem Solving", *Psychological Monographs* 58, no. 5 (1945).

56. Ijiri, Y., Jaedicke, R.K., and Knight, K.E., "The Effects of Accounting Alternatives on Management Decisions", in R.K. Jaedicke, Y. Ijiri and O. Nielsen (eds.), *Research in Accounting Measurement* (Sarasota, FL: American Accounting Association, 1966), pp. 186–99.

57. Knight, K.E., "Effect of Effort on Behavioral Rigidity in Luchins/Water Jar Task", *Journal of Abnormal and Social Psychology* (Fall, 1960), pp. 192–4.

58. Barnes, Paul, and Welb, John, "Management Information Changes and Functional Fixation: True Experimental Evidence from the Public Sector", *Accounting, Organizations and Society* (February, 1986), pp. 1–18.

59. Riahi-Belkaoui, Ahmed, "Accrual Accounting, Modified Cash Basis of Accounting and the Loan Decision: An Experiment in Functional Fixation", *Managerial Finance* (18, 5, 1992), pp. 3–13.

60. Kahneman, D., and Tversky, A., "Prospect Theory: An Analysis of Decision Under Risk", *Econometrica* (March, 1979), pp. 263–91.

61. Belkaoui, Ahmed, "Learning Order and the Acceptance of Accounting Techniques", *The Accounting Review* (October, 1975), pp. 897–9; Belkaoui, Ahmed, "The Primacy-Recency Effect, Ego Involvement and the Acceptance of Accounting Techniques", *The Accounting Review* (July, 1977), pp. 252–6.

62. Luft, Joan L., and Shields, Michael D., "Why Does Fixation Persists? Experimental Evidence in the Judgment Performance Effects of Expensing Intangibles", *The Accounting Review* (76, 4, October, 2001), pp. 561–88.

63. Prakash, P., and Rappaport, A., "Information Inductance and Its Significance for Accounting", *Accounting, Organizations and Society* (February, 1977), p. 298.

64. Ibid., p. 38.

65. Ibid., p. 38.

66. Libby, R., and Rappaport, A., "Human Information Processing Research in Accounting: The State of the Art in 1982", *Accounting, Organizations and Society* (December, 1982), p. 233.

67. Ibid., p. 233.

68. Ibid., p. 233.

69. Brunswick, E., *The Conceptual Framework of Psychology* (Chicago: University of Chicago Press, 1952).

70. Libby, R., and Lewis, B.L., "Human Information Processing Research in Accounting: The State of the Art in 1982", op. cit., p. 233.

71. Ibid., p. 234.

72. Edwards, W., "Conservatism in Human Information Processing", in B. Kleinmutz (ed.), *Formal Representations of Human Judgment* (New York: John Wiley & Sons, 1968).

73. Tversky, A., and Kahneman, D., "Judgment Under Uncertainty: Heuristics and Biases", *Science* (185, 1974), pp. 1125–31.

74. Newell, A., and Simon, H.A., *Human Problem Solving* (Englewood Cliffs, NJ: Prentice-Hall, 1972).

75. Payne, J.N., Braunstein, M.L., and Caroll, J.S., "Exploring Predecisional Behavior: An Alternative Approach to Decision Research", *Organizational Behavior and Human Performance* (February, 1978), pp. 17–44.

76. Ibid., pp. 17–44.

77. Joyce, E.J., and Libby R., "Behavioral Studies of Audit Decision Making", *Journal of Accounting Literature* (Spring, 1982), p. 115.

78. Libby, R., and Lewis, B.L., "Human Information Processing Research in Accounting: The State of the Art in 1982", op. cit., p. 279.

79. Goldstein, K.R., and Blackman, S., *Cognitive Style: Five Approaches and Relevant Research* (New York: John Wiley & Sons, 1978), pp. 12–13.

80. Adomo, T.W., Frenkel-Brunswick, E., Levinston, D.J., and Sanford, R.N., *The Authoritarian Personality* (New York: Harper & Row, 1950).

81. Rokeach, M., *The Open and Closed Mind* (New York: Basic Books, 1960).

82. Kelly, G.A., *The Psychology of Personal Constructs* (New York: W.W. Norton, 1955).

83. Bieri, J., "Cognitive Complexity and Personality Development", in O.J. Harvey (ed.), *Experience, Structure, and Adaptability* (New York: Springer Publishing, 1966).

84. Huysman, J.H.B., "The Effectiveness of the Cognitive Style Constraint in Implementing operations Research Proposals", *Management Science* (September, 1970), pp. 94–5.

85. Harvey, O.J., Hunt, D.E., and Schroeder, H.M., *Conceptual Systems and Personality Organizations* (New York: John Wiley & Sons, 1961).

86. Schroeder H.M., Driver, M.J., and Streufert, S., *Human Information Processing* (New York: Holt, Rinehart & Winston, 1967).

87. Ibid., p. 37.

88. Witkin, H.A., Dyks, R.B., Faterson, H.F., Goodenough, D.R., and Karyn, S.A., *Psychological Differentiation* (New York: John Wiley & Sons, 1962).

89. Walter, W.S., and Felix, W.L., Jr., "The Auditor and Learning from Experience: Some Conjectures", *Accounting, Organizations and Society* (June, 1984).

90. Chase, W.G., and Simon, H.A., "Perception in Chen", *Cognitive Psychology* (4, 1973), pp. 55–87.

91. Chiesi, H.L., Spilich, G.J., and Von, J.F., "Acquisition of Domain-Related Information in Relation to High and Low Domain Knowledge", *Journal of Verbal Learning and Verbal Behavior* (18, 1979), pp. 257–73.

92. Halpern, A.R., and Bowa, H.G., "Musical Expertise and Melodic Structure in Memory for Musical Notation", *American Journal of Psychology* (95, 1982), pp. 31–50.

93. Schneiderman, B., "Exploratory Experiments in Programmer Behavior", *International Journal of Computer and Information Science* (5, 1976), pp. 123–43.

94. Adelson, B., "Problem Solving and the Development of Abstract Categories in Programming Languages", *Memory and Cognition* (9, 1981), pp. 922–33.

95. Adelson, B., "When Novices Surpass Experts: The Difficulty of a Task May Increase with Expertise", *Journal of Experimental Psychology: Learning, Memory and Cognition* (10, 1984), pp. 483–95.

96. Weber, R., "Some Characteristics of the Free Recall of Computer Control by EDP Auditor", *Journal of Accounting Research* (Spring, 1980), pp. 914–41.

97. Gibbins, Michael, "Proposition about the Psychology of Professional Judgment in Public Accounting", *Journal of Accounting Research* (Spring, 1984), pp. 103–25.

98. Gibbins, Michael, "Knowledge Structures and Experienced Auditor Judgment", in Andrew Bailly (ed.), *Auditor Probability to the Year 2000: 1987 Proceeding of the Arthur Young Conference* (Reston, VA: Arthur Young, 1988), p. 57.

99. Ibid., pp. 51–73.

100. Gibbins, M., and Emby, C., "Evidence on the Nature of Professional Judgment in Public Accounting", in A.R. Abdel-Khalik and I. Solomon (eds.), *Auditing Research Symposium 1984* (Champaign: University of Illinois at Urbana/Champaign, 1985).

101. Emby, C., and Gibbins, M., "Good Judgment in Public Accounting: Quality and Justification", *Contemporary Accounting Research* (Spring, 1988), pp. 287–313.

102. Similar models have been proposed for the performance appraisal process. See, for example, De Nisi, A.S., Cafferty, T.P., and Meglinio, B.M., "A Cognitive View of the Performance Appraisal Loan. A Model and Research Proportion", *Organizational Behavior and Human Performance* (33, 1984), pp. 360–96; Feidman, J.M., "Beyond Attribution Theory: Cognitive Process in Performance Appraisal", *Journal of Applied Psychology* (66, 2, 1981), pp. 127–48.

103. Riahi-Belkaoui, Ahmed, "A Model About the Psychology of Judgment in Accounting", *The Middle East Business and Economic Review* (4, 29, 1992), pp, 25–31.

104. Riahi-Belkaoui, Ahmed, *The Cultural Shaping of Accounting* (Westport, CT: Greenwood Publishing, 1895).

105. Smircich, Linda, "Concepts of Culture and Organizational Analysis", *Administrative Science Quarterly* (28, 1983), pp. 339–58.

106. Malinowski, Bronislaw, *A Scientific Theory of Culture* (Chapel Hill: University of North Carolina Press, 1944).

107. Radcliffe-Brown, A.R., *Structure and Function in Primitive Society* (New York: Free Press, 1968).

108. Goodenough, Ward H., *Culture, Language and Society* (Reading, MA: Addison-Wesley, 1971).

109. Geertz, Clifford, *The Interpretation of Cultures* (New York: Basic Books, 1973).

110. Levi-Strauss, Claude, *Structural Anthropology* (Chicago: University of Chicago Press, 1983).

111. Riahi-Belkaoui, Ahmed, *The Cultural Shaping of Accounting*, op. cit.

112. Hofstedt, Geert, *Culture's Consequences: International Difference in W-Related Values* (Beverly Hills, CA: Sage, 1980).

113. Adler, Nancy J., "Understanding the Ways of Understanding: Cross-Cultural Management Methodology Reviewed", in R. Farmer (ed.), *Advances in International Comparative Management*, Vol. I (Greenwich, CT: JAI Press, 1984), pp. 31–67.

114. Riahi-Belkaoui, Ahmed, Perochon, Claude, Mathews, M.A., Bemardi, Bruno, and El-Adly, Youssef A., "Report of the Cultural Studies and Accounting Research Committee of the International Accounting Section, American Accounting Association, 1988–1989", *Advances in International Accounting* (4, 1991), pp. 175–98.

115. Wilier, D., *Scientific Sociology: Theory and Method* (Englewood Cliffs, NJ: Prentice-Hall, 1967).

116. Strodtbeck, E.L., "Considerations of Metamethod in Cross-Cultural Studies", *American Anthropologist* Pt. 2 (1969), pp. 66–123.

117. Triandis, Harry C., Malpass, Roy S., and Davidson, Andrew R., "Cross-Cultural Psychology", in B.J. Siegel (ed.), *Biennial Review of Anthropology 1971* (Stanford, CA: Stanford University Press, 1972), p. 8.

118. Naroll, R., "The Culture-Bearing Unit in Cross-Cultural Surveys", in R. Naroll and R. Cohen (eds.), *Handbook of Methods in Cultural Anthropology* (New York: Columbia University Press, 1970–3), p. 248.

119. Triandis, H.C., "Introduction to Cross-Cultural Psychology", in H.C. Triandis and W.W. Lambert (eds.), *Handbook of Cross-Cultural Psychology* (New York: Allyn and Bacon, 1980), p. 2.

120. Ibid., p. 4.

121. Ibid.

122. Triandis, H.C., Vassilion, V., Tanaka, Y., and Shanmugam, A.V., *The Analysis of Subjective Culture* (New York: Wiley, 1972).

References

The events approach

Benbasat, I., and Dexter, A.S., "Value and Events Approaches to Accounting: An Experimental Evaluation", *The Accounting Review* (October, 1979), pp. 735–99.

Calantoni, C.S., Manes, R.E., and Whinston, A.B., "A Unified Approach to the Theory of Accounting and Information Systems", *The Accounting Review* (January, 1971), pp. 90–102.

Chen, P. (ed.), *Entity-Relationship Approach to Information Modeling and Analysis* (ER Institute, 1981).

Chen, P. (ed.), *Entity-Relationship Approach to Systems Analysis and Design* (New York: North Holland Publishing Company, 1980).

Everest, G.C., and Weber, R., "A Relational Approach to Accounting Models", *The Accounting Review* (April, 1977), pp. 340–59.

Haseman W.D., and Whinston, A.B., "Design of a Multidimensional Accounting System", *The Accounting Review* (January, 1976), pp. 65–79.

Johnson, O., "Toward an 'Events' Theory of Accounting", *The Accounting Review* (October, 1970), pp. 641–53.

Lieberman A.Z., and Whinston, A.B., "A Structuring of an Events-Accounting Information System", *The Accounting Review* (April, 1975), pp. 246–58.

McCarthy, W.E., "An Entity-Relationship View of Accounting Models", *The Accounting Review* (October, 1979), pp. 667–86.

McCarthy, W.E., "The REA Accounting Model; A Generalized Framework for Accounting Systems in a Shared Data Environment", *The Accounting Review* (July, 1982), pp. 554–78.

McCarthy, W.E., "A Relational Model for Events-Based Accounting Systems", dissertation, University of Massachusetts, 1978.

Sorter, G.H., "An 'Events' Approach to Basic Accounting Theory", *The Accounting Review* (January, 1969), pp. 12–19.

Behavioral effects of accounting information

Dyckman, T.R., Gibbins, M., and Swieringa, R.J., "Experimental and Survey Research in Financial Accounting: A Review and Evaluation", in A.R. Abdel-Khalik and T.F. Keller (eds.), *The Impact of Accounting Research in Financial Accounting and Disclosure on Accounting Practice* (Durham, NC: Duke University Press, 1978), pp. 48–89.

Rhode, J.G., "Behavioral Science Methodologies with Application for Accounting Research: References and Source Materials", Chapter 7 of "Report of the Committee on Research Methodology in Accounting", *The Accounting Review* (supplement, 1972), pp. 454–504.

Linguistic effects of accounting data and techniques

Adelberg, A.H., "An Empirical Evaluation of the Communication of Authoritative Pronouncements in Accounting", *Accounting and Finance* (November, 1982), pp. 73–94.

Adelberg, A.H., "A Methodology for Measuring the Understandability of Financial Report Messages", *Journal of Accounting Research* (Autumn, 1979), pp. 565–92.

Belkaoui, A., "The Impact of Socioeconomic Accounting Statements on the Investment Decision: An Empirical Study", *Accounting, Organizations and Society* (September, 1980), pp. 263–84.

Belkaoui, A., "The Interprofessional Linguistic Communication of Accounting Concepts: An Experiment in Sociolinguistics", *Journal of Accounting Research* (Autumn, 1980), pp. 362–74.

Belkaoui A., "Linguistic Relativity in Accounting", *Accounting, Organizations and Society* (October, 1978), pp. 97–104.

Belkaoui, Janice, and Belkaoui, A., "Bilingualism and the Perception of Professional Concepts", *Journal of Psycholinguistic Research* (12, 12, 1983), pp. 111–27.

Belkaoui., A., and Cousineau, A., "Accounting Information, Nonaccounting Information, and Common Stock Perception", *Journal of Business* (July, 1977), pp. 334–42.

Flamholtz, E., and Cook, E., "Connotative Meaning and its Role in Accounting Change: A Field Study", *Accounting, Organizations and Society* (October, 1978), pp. 115–39.

Haried, A.A., "Measurement of Meaning in Financial Reports", *Journal of Accounting Research* (Spring, 1973), pp. 117–45.

Haried, A.A., "The Semantic Dimensions of Financial Statements", *Journal of Accounting Research* (Autumn, 1972), pp. 376–91.

Jain, Tribhowan N., "Alternative Methods of Accounting and Decision Making: A Psycholinguistic Analysis", *The Accounting Review* (January, 1973), pp. 95–104.

Li, D., "The Semantic Aspect of Communication Theory and Accounting", *Journal of Accounting Research* (Autumn, 1963), pp. 102–7.

Libby, R., "Bankers' and Auditors' Perceptions of the Message Communicated by the Audit Report", *Journal of Accounting Research* (Spring, 1979), pp. 99–122.

Oliver, B.L., "The Semantic Differential: A Device for Measuring the Interprofessional Communication of Selected Accounting Concepts", *Journal of Accounting Research* (Autumn, 1974), pp. 299–316.

Functional fixation hypothesis

Ashton, R.H., "Cognitive Changes Induced by Accounting Changes: Experimental Evidence on the Functional Fixation Hypothesis", *Studies on Human Information Processing in Accounting 1976*, supplement to Vol. 14, *Journal of Accounting Research* (1976), pp. 1–17.

Ijiri, Yuji, Jaedicke, R.K., and Knight, K.E., "The Effects of Accounting Alternatives of Management Decisions", in R.K. Jaedicke, Yuji Ijiri, and O. Nielsen (eds.), *Research in Accounting Measurement* (New York: American Accounting Association, 1966), pp. 186–99.

Information inductance

Prakash, E., and Rappaport, A., "Information Inductance and its Significance for Accounting", *Accounting, Organizations, and Society* (February, 1977), pp. 29–38.

Human information processing

Belkaoui, A., "Judgment Related Issues in Performance Evaluation", *Journal of Business Finance and Accounting* (Winter, 1982), pp. 489–500.

Brunswick, E., *The Conceptual Framework of Psychology* (Chicago: University of Chicago Press, 1952).

Einhorn, H.J., "A Synthesis: Accounting and Behavioral Science", *Studies on Human Information Processing in Accounting*, supplement to Vol. 14, *Journal of Accounting Research* (1976), pp. 196–206.

Einhorn, H.J., and Hogarth, R.M., "Behavioral Decision Theory: Processes of Judgment and Choice", *Journal of Accounting Research* (Spring, 1981), pp. 1–31.

Joyce, E.J., and Libby, R., "Behavioral Studies of Audit Decision Making", *Journal of Accounting Literature* (Spring, 1982), pp. 103–23.

Libby, R., *Accounting and Human Information Processing: Theory and Applications* (Englewood Cliffs, NJ: Prentice-Hall, 1981).

Libby, R., and Lewis, B.L., "Human Information Processing Research in Accounting: The State of the Art", *Accounting, Organizations, and Society* (September, 1977), pp. 245–68.

Libby, R., and Lewis, B.L., "Human Information Processing Research in Accounting: The State of the Art in 1982", *Accounting, Organizations and Society* (December, 1982), pp. 231–86.

Schroeder, H.M., Driver, M.J., and Streufert, S., *Human Information Processing* (New York: Holt, Rinehart & Winston, 1967).

Snowball, D., "On the Integration of Accounting Research on Human Information Processing", *Accounting and Business Research* (Summer, 1980), pp. 307–18.

Wright, W.F., "Comparison of the Lens and Subjective Probability Paradigms for Financial Research Purposes", *Accounting, Organizations and Society* (February, 1982), pp. 65–75.

The lens model in accounting research

Abdel-Khalik, A.R., and El-Sheshai, K., "Information Choice and Utilization in an Experiment on Default Prediction", *Journal of Accounting Research* (Autumn, 1980), pp. 325–42.

Ashton, R.H., "A Descriptive Study of Information Evaluation", *Journal of Accounting Research* (Spring, 1981), pp. 42–61.

Ashton, R.H., and Brown, P.R., "Descriptive Modeling of Auditor's Internal Control Judgments: Replication and Extensions", *Journal of Accounting Research* (Spring, 1980), pp. 1–15.

Belkaoui, A., "Diagnostic and Redundant Information: The Effects on the Quality of Loan Officers' Predictions of Bankruptcy in Terms of Accuracy, Calibration, and Decision Time", *Accounting and Business Research* (Summer, 1984), pp. 249–56.

Brown, P.R., "A Descriptive Analysis of Select Input Bases of the Financial Accounting Standards Board", *Journal of Accounting Research* (Spring, 1981), pp. 62–85.

Danos, P., and Imhoff, E.A., "Auditor Review of Financial Forecasts: An Analysis of Factors Affecting Reasonableness of Judgments", *The Accounting Review* (January, 1982), pp. 39–54.

Ebert, R.J., and Kruse, T.E., "Bootstrapping the Security Analyst", *Journal of Applied Psychology* (February, 1978), pp. 110–19.

Gibbs, T.E., and Schroeder, R.G., "Evaluating the Competence of Internal Audit Departments", in *Symposium on Audit Research III* (Urbana, IL; University of Illinois, 1979).

Hamilton, R.E., and Wright, W.F., "The Evaluation of Internal Controls Over Payroll" (unpublished manuscript, University of Minnesota, 1977).

Harrell, A.M., "The Decision-Making Behavior of Air Force Officers and the Management Control Process", *The Accounting Review* (October, 1977), pp. 833–41.

Harrell, A.M., and Klick, H.D., "Comparing the Impact of Monetary and Nonmonetary Human Asset Measures on Executive Decision Making", *Accounting, Organizations and Society* (December, 1980), pp. 393–400.

Holt, R.N., and Carroll, R.J., "Classification of Commercial Bank Loans Through Policy Capturing", *Accounting, Organizations and Society* (September, 1980), pp. 285–96.

Kessler, L., and Ashton, R.H., "Feedback and Prediction Achievement in Financial Analysis", *Journal of Accounting Research* (Spring, 1981), pp. 146–62.

Libby, R., "Bankers' and Auditors' Perceptions of the Message Communicated by the Audit Report", *Journal of Accounting Research* (Spring, 1979), pp. 99–122.

Libby, R., "The Impact of Uncertainty Reporting on the Loan Decision", *Studies in Auditing Selections from the Research Opportunities in Auditing Program*, supplement to *Journal of Accounting Research* (1979), pp. 35–57.

Mock, T.J., and Turner, J.L., "The Effect of Changes in Internal Controls on Audit Programs", in T.J. Burns (ed.), *Behavioral Experiments in Accounting*, Vol. II (Columbus: Ohio State University, 1979).

Moriarity, S., "Communicating Financial Information Through Multidimensional Graphics", *Journal of Accounting Research* (Spring, 1979), pp. 205–23.

Moriarity, S., and Barren, F.H., "Modeling the Materiality Judgments of Audit Partners", *Journal of Accounting Research* (Autumn, 1976), pp. 320–41.

Rockness, H.O., and Nikolai, L.A., "An Assessment of APB Voting Patterns", *Journal of Accounting Research* (Spring, 1977), pp. 154–67.

Schultz, J.J., and Gustavson, S.G., "Actuaries' Perceptions of Variables Affecting the Independent Auditor's Legal Liability", *The Accounting Review* (July, 1978), pp. 626–41.

Swieringa, R.J., Dyckman, T.R., and Hoskin, R.E., "Empirical Evidence About the Effects of an Accounting Change on Information Processing", in T.J. Burns (ed.), *Behavior Exponents in Accounting*, Vol. II (Columbus: Ohio State University, 1979).

Zimmer, I., "A Lens Study of the Prediction of Corporate Failure by Bank Loan Officers", *Journal of Accounting Research* (Autumn, 1980), pp. 629–36.

The probabilistic judgment model in accounting research

Biddle, G.C., and Joyce, E.J., "Heuristics and Biases: Some Implications for Probabilistic Inference in Auditing", in *Symposium on Auditing Research*, Vol. IV (Urbana: University of Illinois, 1981).

Chesley, G.R., "Subjective Probability Elicitation: Congruity of Datum and Response Mode", *Journal of Accounting Research* (Spring, 1977), pp. 1–11.

Chesley, G.R., "Subjective Probability Elicitation Techniques: A Performance Comparison", *Journal of Accounting Research* (Autumn, 1978), pp. 225–41.

Corless, J., "Assessing Prior Distributions for Applying Bayesian Statistics in Auditing", *The Accounting Review* (July, 1972), pp. 556–66.

Crosby, M., "Bayesian Statistics in Auditing: A Comparison of Probability Elicitation Techniques", *The Accounting Review* (April, 1981), pp. 355–65.

Crosby, M., "Implications of Prior Probability Elicitation on Auditor Sample Size Decisions", *Journal of Accounting Research* (Autumn, 1980), pp. 585–93.

Felix, W.L., "Evidence on Alternative Means of Assessing Prior Probability Distributions for Audit Decision Making", *The Accounting Review* (October, 1976), pp. 800–7.

Hirsch, M., "Disaggregated Probabilistic Accounting Information: The Effect of Sequential Events on Expected Value Maximization Decisions", *Journal of Accounting Research* (Autumn, 1978), pp. 256–69.

Joyce, E.J., and Biddle, G.C., "Anchoring and Adjustment in Probabilistic Inference in Auditing", *Journal of Accounting Research* (Spring, 1981), pp. 120–45.

Joyce, E.J., and Biddle, G.C., "Are Auditors' Judgments Sufficiently Regressive?" *Journal of Accounting Research* (Autumn, 1981), pp. 323–49.

Lewis, B.L., "Expert Judgment in Auditing: An Expected Utility Approach", *Journal of Accounting Research* (Autumn, 1980), pp. 594–602.

Magee, R.P., and Dickhaut, J.W., "Effect of Compensation Plans on Heuristics in Cost Variance Investigations", *Journal of Accounting Research* (Autumn, 1978), pp. 294–314.

Newton, L.K., "The Risk Factor in Materiality Decisions", *The Accounting Review* (January, 1977), pp. 97–108.

Snowball, D., and Brown, C., "Decision Making Involving Sequential Events: Some Effects of Disaggregated Data and Disposition Toward Risk", *Decision Sciences* (October, 1979), pp. 527–46.

Uecker, W.C., "The Effects of Knowledge of the User's Decision Model in Simplified Informatics Evaluation", *Journal of Accounting Research* (Spring, 1980), pp. 191–213.

Ward, B.H., "An Investigation of the Materiality Construct in Auditing", *Journal of Accounting Research* (Spring, 1976), pp. 138–52.

Wright, W.F., "Accuracy of Subjective Probabilities for a Financial Variable", in T.J. Burns (ed.), *Behavioral Experiments in Accounting*, Vol. II (Columbus: Ohio State University, 1979).

Predecisional behavior approach in accounting research

Biggs, S.F., "An Empirical Investigation of the Information Process Underlying Four Models of Choice Behavior", in T.J. Burns (ed.), *Behavioral Experiments in Accounting*, Vol. II (Columbus: Ohio State University, 1979).

Shields, M.D., "Effects of Information Supply and Demand on judgment Accuracy: Evidence from Corporate Managers", *The Accounting Review* (April, 1983), pp. 284–303.

Shields, M.D., "Some Effects of Information Load on Search Patterns Used to Analyze Performance Reports", *Accounting, Organizations and Society* (December, 1980), pp. 429–42.

Stephens, R.G., "Accounting Disclosures for User Decision Processes", in Yuji Ijiri and A.B. Whinston (eds.), *Quantitative Planning and Control* (New York: Academic Press, 1979), pp. 291–309.

Weber, R., "Some Characteristics of the Free Recall of Computer Controls by EDP Auditors", *Journal of Accounting Research* (Spring, 1980), pp. 214–41.

The cognitive style model in accounting research

Belkaoui, A., "How Receptive Are Accountants to Innovation? Personality Can Hinder Progress", *The Canadian Chartered Accountant Magazine* (May, 1982), pp. 469.

Belkaoui, A., "Relationship Between Self-Disclosure Style and Responsibility Accounting", *Accounting, Organizations and Society* (December, 1981), pp. 281–90.

Benbasat, I., and Dexter, A.S., "Value and Events Approaches to Accounting: An Experimental Evaluation", *The Accounting Review* (October, 1979), pp. 735–49.

Casey C.J., "Variation in Accounting Information Load: the Effect on Loan Officers Prediction of Bankruptcy", *The Accounting Review* (January, 1980), pp. 36–49.

Vasarhelyi, M., "Man-Machine Planning Systems: A Cognitive Style Examination of Interactive Decision Making", *Journal of Accounting Research* (Spring, 1977), pp. 138–53.

Weber, R., "Some Characteristics of the Free Recall of Computer Controls by EDP Auditors", *Journal of Accounting Research* (Spring, 1980), pp. 214–41.

Wisk, E.J., "A Test of Differential Performance Peaking for a Disembedding Task", *Journal of Accounting Research* (Spring, 1979), pp. 286–94.

The predictive approach

12

This chapter presents the predictive and positive approaches to the formulation of an accounting theory. Both of these approaches are emerging and popular paradigms striving for dominance in the accounting literature. In what follows, the contributions and findings of each approach, as well as the limitations recognized in the literature, will be examined.

12.1 The nature of the predictive approach

The predictive approach arose from the need to solve the difficult problem of evaluating alternative methods of accounting measurement alternatives. The predictive approach to the formulation of an accounting theory utilizes the criterion of predictive ability in which the choice among different accounting options depends on the ability of particular methods to predict events that are of interest to users. More specifically, "the measure with the greatest predictive power with respect to a given event is considered to be the 'best' method for that particular purpose".[1]

The criterion of predictive ability follows from the emphasis on relevance as the primary criterion of financial reporting.[2] Relevance connotes a concern with information about future events. Relevant data, therefore, are characterized by an ability to predict future events.

The criterion of predictive ability is also well accepted in the natural and physical sciences as a method of choosing among competing hypotheses. Beaver and others,[3] by showing that alternative accounting measures have the properties of competing hypotheses, have rationalized the use of predictive ability in accounting. An obvious advantage of the predictive approach is that it allows us to evaluate alternative accounting measurements empirically and to make a clear choice on the basis of a discriminator criterion.

Predictive ability is also a purposive criterion that can easily be related to one purpose of gathering accounting data, the facilitation of decision-making. The accounting literature has always held that accounting data must facilitate decision-making. As soon as the "facilitation of decision-making" is introduced, however, two problems arise. First, it is difficult to identify and define all the decision models employed by accounting information users, because most of the models are descriptive rather than normative. Second, even when the decision model is well defined, a criterion for the choice of relevant information is missing. Intended to resolve this second problem, the criterion of predictive ability allows us to determine which accounting measure produces the better decisions. Let us note here the fundamental distinction between prediction and decision. It is possible to predict without making a decision, but it is not possible to make a decision without a prediction.

It appears then that the predictive method may suffer from a failure to identify and define the decision models of users and types of events that ought to be predicted. Even if a given theoretical structure were developed to identify items or events that ought to be predicted, the problem remains of specifying a theory that will link those events to the accounting measures in terms of an explanatory and predictive relationship. A growing body of empirical accounting research has evolved from the predictive approach. Two streams may be identified. One is concerned with the ability of accounting data to explain and predict economic events; the other is concerned with the ability of accounting data to explain and predict market reaction to disclosure.

12.2 Prediction of an economic event

One general objective of accounting is to provide information that can be used to predict business events. In the perspective of the predictive approach to the formulation of an accounting theory, alternative accounting measurements should be evaluated on the basis of their ability to predict economic or business events. In general, the predictive value criterion is a probability relationship between economic events of interest to the decision-maker and relevant predictor variables derived in part from accounting information.

12.2.1 Time-series analysis

Time-series analysis is a structural methodological approach by which temporal statistical dependencies in a data set may be examined.[4] Past values of a single data set are used to give clues regarding future realizations of the same data set. Time-series analysis research focuses mainly in:

1. time-series properties of reported earnings, and

2. prediction issues in time-series analysis.

Each is examined next.

Time-series properties of reported earnings

Knowledge of the properties of reported earnings may enhance their information content predictive ability and feedback value. The application of statistical procedures to the study of the time-series properties of accounting variables stems from the thesis that accounting variables can best be described as random variables. The research has examined both the behaviors of reported earnings and models that describe quarterly earnings:[5]

1. With respect to the *annual-earnings series*, findings present a *moving-average process*, a *submartingale*, or one of two processes: *martingale* or *moving averages regressive*. What results is a continuous debate over which time-series model(s) should be applied to observed accounting numbers. Fortunately, a new line of research may provide some closure on the debate. It consists of first modeling the observed time-series and then using the method to test the fit of the derived models.[6,7] In any case, this type of research would be of more use and more interest to policy-makers if it was applied to determine the effect of accounting policy changes on probabilistic models of earnings behavior.[8]

2. With respect to the *quarterly-earnings series*, findings seem to show that the quarterly-earnings process is not totally random in character. It appears to follow an *autoregressive process* characterized by seasonal and quarter-to-quarter components.[9,10]

Predicting future accounting earnings

The reported earnings number is an aggregate number in two dimensions: one dimension is temporal, in that annual earnings are an aggregate of four individual quarterly earnings; one dimension is compositional, in that annual earnings are an aggregate of *time-equivalent* subseries, much as sales and cost of goods sold.[11] Accounting time-series-based research has considered the predictive ability of past annual earnings, past quarterly earnings, and earnings components:

1. With respect to the use of *past annual earnings* to predict future earnings, studies show that sophisticated autoregressive (or moving average) processes developed using Box and Jenkins procedures do not appear to forecast significantly better than the random-walk model.[12,13]

2. With respect to the use of *past quarterly earnings* to predict future earnings, studies show a better predictive ability of the models of quarterly earnings compared with annual models and more comprehensive Box and Jenkins' "individually identified" models.[14]

3. With respect to the use of *earnings components* to predict future earnings, evidence is in favor of good forecasting ability of disaggregated sales and earnings data,[15] but this is not demonstrated for models based on components such as interest expense,

depreciation expense and operating income before depreciation.[16] More work needs to be done before closure on the subject.

12.2.2 Distress prediction

The most relevant applications of the predictive approach are attempts made to seek empirically validated characteristics that distinguish financially distressed from non-distressed firms. Both univariate and multivariate models have been used to help an auditor determine when a firm is approaching default. Scott provides the following brief overview of the process:

> Most bankruptcy-prediction models are derived using a paired-sample technique. Part of the sample contains data from firms that eventually failed; the other part contains contemporaneous data from firms that did not fail. A number of plausible and traditional financial ratios are calculated from financial statements that were published before failure. Next, the researcher searches for a formula based either on a single ratio or a combination of ratios, that best discriminates between firms that eventually failed and firms that remained solvent. A careful researcher also tests the resulting formula both on the original sample and a holdout sample, that was not used to derive the formula.[17]

In Beaver's univariate study,[18] which tested a set of accounting ratios to predict corporate failure, the most noticeable result was the superior predictive ability of cash flow to total debt ratios, followed by net income to total assets. Among the multivariate studies, Altman's use of a multiple discriminant analysis for the prediction of corporate failure resulted in a discriminant model that contained five variables:

X_1 = networking capital/total assets;
X_2 = retained earnings/total assets;
X_3 = earnings before interest and taxes/total assets;
X_4 = market value of equity/book value of total liabilities;
X_5 = sales/total assets.[19]

Altman's estimated discriminant function is:

$$Z = 0.12X_1 1 + 0.14X_2 + 0.33X_3 + 0.006X_4 + 0.999X_5$$

The main findings are:

(a) firms with Z scores greater than 2.99 fell within the non-bankrupt group, while all those with Z scores less than 1.81 went bankrupt within the following year;

(b) a Z score of 2.675 minimized the total number of firms misclassified by the models.

A logit model was proposed by Ohlson to examine the effects of four basic factors on the probability of bankruptcy: the size of the firm, measures of the firm's financial structure, measures of performance, and measures of current liquidity.[20] The following nine financial ratios were chosen as independent variables to represent the four factors.

1. SIZE = total assets/GNP price-level index;
2. TLTA = total liabilities/total assets;
3. WCTA = working capital/total assets;
4. CLCA = current liabilities/current assets;

5. OENEG = one if total liabilities exceeds total assets, else zero;
6. NITA = net income/total assets;
7. FUTL = funds provided by operations/total liabilities;
8. INTWO = one if net income was negative for the last two years, else zero;
9. CHIN = $(NI_t - NI_{t-1} / |NI_t| + |NI_{t-1}|)$, where NI, is the net income for the most recent year. The denominator is a level indicator and CHIN is a measure of change in net income.

Three models are provided:

A. Model 1 predicts bankruptcy within one year. It is expressed as follows:
   Model 1: $-1.32 - 0.407$ SIZE $+ 6.03$ TLTA $- 1.43$ WCTA $+ 0.0757$ CLCA $- 2.37$ NITA $- 1.83$ FUTL $+ 0.285$ 1NTWO $+ 1.72$ OENEG $- 5.21$ CHIN

B. Model 2 predicts bankruptcy within two years given that the firm does not fail in the first year. It is expressed as follows:
   Model 2: $-1.84 - 0.519$ SIZE $+ 4.76$ TLTA $+ 1.71$ WCTA $+ 0.297$ CLCA $- 2.74$ NITA $- 2.18$ FUTL $+ 0.780$ INTWO $- 1.98$ OENEG $- 0.4218$ CHIN

C. Model 3 predicts bankruptcy within one or two years. It is expressed as follows:
   Model 3: $-1.13 - 0.478$ SIZE $+ 5.29$ TLTA $- 0.990$ WCTA $+ 0.062$ CLCA $- 4.62$ NITA $- 2.25$ FUTL $+ 0.521$ INTWO $- 1.91$ OENEG $- 0.212$ CHIN

The major limitation of the research and distress prediction arises from the absence of an articulated economic theory of financial distress. Witness the following statement made by Ohlson:

> This paper presents some empirical results of a study predicting corporate failure as evidenced by the event of bankruptcy. ... One might ask a basic and possibly embarrassing question: Why forecast bankruptcy? This is a difficult question, and no answer or justification is given here. ... Most of the analysis should simply be viewed as descriptive statistics which may, to some extent, include estimated prediction error-rates and no "theories" of bankruptcy or usefulness of financial ratios are tested.[21]

Despite the absence of an economic theory of distress, the discriminant analysis based models can be very helpful in a variety of practical decision contexts. For example, "(i) they can process information quicker and at a lower cost than do individual loan officers and bank examiners, (ii) they can process information in a more consistent manner, and (iii) they can facilitate decisions about loss function being made at more senior levels of management".[22]

Various limitations are associated with research on corporate distress prediction.[23] The first limitation arises from the absence of a general economic theory of financial distress that can be used to specify the variables to be included in the models.

A second limitation relates to the different definition of the event of interest. All of the studies examined observable events, such as legal bankruptcy, loan default and omission of preferred dividend rather than financial distress *per se*. Finally, the results of the superior predictive ability of some accounting ratios may not be generalized to permit the formulation of an accounting theory based on consistent predictors of corporate failure.

12.2.3 Prediction of bond premiums and bond ratings

The following four factors are assumed to create bond risks and consequently to affect the yields to maturity of bonds:

1. default risk: the inability of a firm to meet part or all bond interest and principal payments;

2. marketability risk: the possibility of learning to dispose of the bonds at a loss;

3. purchasing-power risk: the loss incurred by bondholders due to changes in the general price level;

4. interest-rate risk: the effect of unexpected changes in the interest rates on the market value of bonds.

Fisher examined the power of a four-factor model to explain differences in the risk premiums of industrial corporate bonds.[24] The following four variables are included in the model:

1. earnings variability, measured as the coefficient of variation on after-tax earnings of the most recent nine years;

2. solvency, or reliability in meeting obligations, measured as the length of time since the latest of the following events occurred: the firm was founded, the firm emerged from bankruptcy, or a compromise was made in which creditors settled for less than 100 percent of their claims;

3. capital structure, measured by the market value of the firm's equity/par value of its debt;

4. total value of the market value of the firm's bonds.

The first three variables represent different proxies for default risk; the fourth variable represents a proxy for marketable risk. The four variables account for 75 percent of the variation in the risk premiums on bonds.

The bonds ratings issued by the three rating agencies in the United States (Fitch Investors' Service, Moody's Investors' Service and Standard & Poor's Corporation) are judgments about the investment quality of long-term obligations. Each rating is an aggregation of default probability. Despite the claims by these agencies that their ratings cannot be empirically explained and predicted, various studies have attempted to develop models to predict the rating categories assigned to industrial bonds,[25] electric utility bonds,[26] and general-obligation municipal bonds.[27]

All of these studies tried in the first stage to develop a bond-ratings model from an experimental sample of bond ratings on the basis of a selected list of accounting and financial variables, using either regression, dichotomous probability function, or multiple discriminant or multivariate probit analysis. In the second stage, the obtained model was applied to a holdout sample to test the predictive ability of the model. Despite the general success of such models, some unresolved problems may limit their usefulness.

1. With one exception, these models suffer from the lack of an explicit and testable statement of what a bond rating represents and the absence of an economic rationale for the variables included.

2. None of these models account for possible differences in the accounting treatments used by individual companies.

3. The studies among the regression models treat the dependent variable as if it were on an interval scale. In other words, the assumption is that the risk differential between an AAA and an AA bond is the same as the risk differential between a BB bond and a B bond.

4. With one exception, all the studies confused *ex-ante* predictive power with *ex-post* discrimination. When a given discriminant model is developed on the basis of a

sample A_1 and tested on a time coincident sample A_2, the authors claim predictive success but actually demonstrate only *ex-post* discriminant success. Testing on A_2 implies only that the inference about the importance of the independent variables in the discriminant function is warranted. Prediction requires intertemporal validation. *Ex-ante* prediction means using the discriminant model developed based on the basis of A_2, from time dimension t_1, on a sample B from time dimension $t + 1$.[28]

Various recent bond-rating models have shown the importance of profit-based measures as well as other measures of financial fitness in the explanation and prediction of bond ratings. For example, Belkaoui developed a discriminant-analysis-based bond-rating model based on the following variables:

x_1 = total assets;
x_2 = total debt;
x_3 = long-term debt/total invested capital;
x_4 = short-term debt/total invested capital;
x_5 = current assets/current liabilities;
x_6 = fixed charge coverage ratio;
x_7 = five-year cash flow divided by a five-year sum of (1) capital expenditure, (2) change in inventories during most recent five years, and (3) common dividends;
x_8 = stock price/common equity per share; and
x_9 = subordination (0–1 dummy variable), 1 if the bond being rated is subordinated.[29]

Six discriminant functions are proposed to explain or predict bond ratings, including the following for an AAA rating:

$$Z = -31.6004 + 0.000737x_1 + 0.000119x_2 + 0.44234x_3 + 0.62823x_4 + 7.26898x_5 + 0.68425x_6 + 0.06102x_7 + 0.01802x_8 + 10.26302x_9$$

For an AA rating:
$$Z = -26.0425 + 0.000431x_1 - 0.000174x_2 + 0.49299x_3 + 0.67906x_4 + 6.80279x_5 + 0.54641x_6 + 0.06600x_7 + 0.01687x_8 + 9.7664x_9$$

For an A rating:
$$Z = -26.1304 + 0.00269x_1 - 0.000149x_2 + 0.58069x_3 + 0.60516x_4 + 7.83642x_5 + 0.4885x_6 + 0.06777x_7 + 0.00809x_8 + 8.18782x_9$$

For a BBB rating:
$$Z = -29.3824 + 0.000250x_1 - 0.000233x_2 + 0.71530x_3 + 0.79864x_4 + 8.5763x_5 + 0.50766x_6 + 0.0711x_7 + 0.00235x_8 + 4.27079x_9$$

For a BB rating:
$$Z = -31.3397 + 0.000265x_1 - 0.000295x_2 + 0.76589x_3 + 0.80544x_4 + 9.15411x_5 + 0.48010x_6 + 0.05952x_7 + 0.00705x_8 + 1.69732x_9$$

For a B rating:
$$Z = -34.8229 + 0.000242x_1 - 0.000357x_2 + 0.85499x_3 + 0.84459x_4 + 9.24043x_5 + 0.49208x_6 + 0.06970x_7 + 0.00099x_8 - 1.73660x_9$$

The classification method consists simply of using the discriminant functions on new data as follows. For each firm that needs to be classified into a bond-rating category, compute the classification score for each rating category from the discriminant function coefficient (multiply the data by the coefficients and add the constant term). The firm is then classified into the group for which the classification score is the highest.

12.2.4 Corporate restructuring behavior

The prominence of takeovers all over the world has prompted several studies. Marris's study of managerial capitalism showed that the companies acquired are those that are undervalued by the market.[30] Similarly, Gort supported a related hypothesis that the level of takeover activity varies with the degree of share undervaluation in the market.[31] This type of analysis relies heavily on a meaningful share price valuation model. More explicitly, the parameters measuring the relationship between the market prices of shares and relevant factors should be reasonably constant. Bonford found that the market will sometimes attach different weights to those factors.[32] Similarly, Tzoannos and Samuels, in experimenting with a number of valuation models, found that the variables, whether explaining earning yield or dividend yield, were not significant.[33] Thus the type of analysis based on share valuation might lack external validity.

Because of the difficulties of appraising the "true" value of a share, most of the other studies have attempted to identify the financial characteristics of the acquired firms. Accordingly, Chambers examined the undervaluation of net assets as a result of conservative accounting policies.[34] The undervaluation of net assets was seen as a key factor for predicting takeovers. These findings were later contested by Taussig and Hayes based on the absence of a control group in the Chambers study.[35] They rejected the hypothesis of a statistically significant relationship between understated asset values and the possibility of a takeover. Both studies were univariate, however, and considered only voluntary mergers. The first limitation with regard to the univariate nature of the analysis was corrected by Vance.[36] The second limitation was first corrected by various studies that considered companies acquired through voluntary mergers in England and the United States.[37,38,39]

In fact, the corporate restructuring internationally also included mergers, consolidations, divestitures, going private transactions, leverage buyouts (LBOs), and spinoffs, aimed at either (a) maximizing the market value of equities held by existing shareholders or (b) maximizing the welfare of existing management.[40,41] The modes of takeovers, however, are most often the subject of empirical analysis. The analyses taking place in the US context include several studies.[42,43,44,45,46]

Palepu's multivariate logit model was based on the following ten variables:

x_1 = average excess security return per day over the prior four years;

x_2 = average market adjusted security return per day over the prior four years;

x_3 = 0/1 dummy variable with 1 for low growth/high liquidity/low leverage combinations and 0 for all other combinations and high growth/low liquidity/high leverage combinations and 0 for all other combinations;

x_4 = average annual sales growth rate over the prior three years;

x_5 = ratio of net liquid assets to total assets averaged over the prior three years;

x_6 = ratio of long-term debt to total equity averaged over the prior three years;

x_7 = 0/1 dummy variable with 1 if there is at least one acquisition in a firm's four-digit SIC industry in the prior year;

x_8 = net book assets of firm ($ millions);

x_9 = ratio of firm's market price to book value of common equity in the prior year;

x_{10} = ratio of firm's market price to earnings at end of the prior fiscal year.

A likelihood of 9.93 percent to 12.45 percent was obtained. The Meeks study focused on the profitability of mergers of UK firms in the 1964–1972 period. The acquiring firms were examined using a standardized profitability measure E, called "the profitability of the amalgamation (standardized for industry and year) less three-year average premerger profitability of the amalgamation (similarly standardized)".[47] An average decline was reported, leading the author to title the study *Disappointing Marriage: A Study of the*

Gains from Mergers. Studies of mergers in Belgium, the Federal Republic of Germany, France, the Netherlands, Sweden, the United Kingdom and the United States show little improvement in profitability as measured by accounting profitability measures. As concluded by D.C. Mueller:

> No consistent pattern of either improved or deteriorated profitability can be claimed across the seven countries. Mergers would appear to result in a slight improvement here, a slight worsening of performance there. If a generalization is to be drawn, it would have to be that mergers have hit modest effects, up or down, on the profitability of the merging firms in the three to five years following merger. An economic efficiency gain from the merger would appear too small.[48]

In the context of the United Kingdom, Paul Barnes estimated the following discriminant function:

$$Z = -1.91218 - 1.61605x_1 + 4.99448x_2 + 1.11363x_3 - 0.70484x_4 - 0.11345x_5$$

where

x_1 = quick assets/current liabilities;
x_2 = current assets/current liabilities;
x_3 = pretax profit margin;
x_4 = net profit margin; and
x_5 = return on shareholders' equity.

The model was able to predict accurately 74.3 percent of a holdout sample.[49] Belkaoui's study focused on predicting Canadian takeovers on the basis of linear combination of sixteen ratios:

x_1 = cash flow/net worth;
x_2 = cash flow/total assets;
x_3 = net income/net worth;
x_4 = net income/total assets;
x_5 = long term debt + preferred stock/total assets;
x_6 = current assets/total assets;
x_7 = cash/total assets;
x_8 = working capital/total assets;
x_9 = quick assets/total assets;
x_{10} = current assets/total liabilities;
x_{11} = quick assets/current liabilities;
x_{12} = cash/current liabilities;
x_{13} = current assets/sales;
x_{14} = quick assets/sales;
x_{15} = working capital/sales; and
x_{16} = cash/sales.[50]

Five discriminant functions were produced for each of the five years preceding the takeover of Canadian firms.

Corporate restructuring behavior includes such mechanisms as mergers, consolidations, acquisitions, divestitures, going private, leverage buyouts and spinoffs. They are undertaken to either (a) maximize the market value of equities held by existing shareholders or (b) maximize the welfare of existing management. Research focused on the characteristics of acquired and nonacquired firms, and covered two areas: (a) *ex-post* classificatory analysis and (b) *ex-ante* predictive analysis, using either univariate or multivariate models.

All the studies point to the relevance of various accounting ratios in classifying or predicting takeovers. The limitations of these studies are similar to those advanced in the case of distress prediction.

12.2.5 Credit and bank lending decisions

Trade and bank lending decisions constitute another example of economic events that may be explained and/or predicted based on accounting and other financial information.

Various organizations, such as Dun & Bradstreet, Inc., the National Credit Office, the National Association of Credit Management, Robert Morris Associates, and various industry trade associations engage in some form of trade-credit analysis. From the perspective of the predictive approach, the research consists of replicating or predicting the credit evaluation or change therein based on accounting and other financial information. For example, Ewert evaluates, with some success, the extent to which financial ratios can be used to differentiate good from bad accounts, where bad accounts are either placed in collection or written off as uncollectable.[51] On the other hand, Backer and Gosman have had less success in predicting the firms that would be likely to be downgraded by Dun & Bradstreet on the basis of financial ratios.[52]

The bank lending decision has also been the subject of empirical and predictive research. Three areas of research can be identified. The first area deals with efforts to simulate aspects of a bank's investment and lending processes. The investment decision is the subject of simulation analysis by Clarkson[53] and Cohen, Gilmore and Singer.[54] The results imply that financial information plays a major role in the decision.

The second area deals with prediction of the loan classification decision. With minor success, Orgler uses a multiple regression model to replicate the Federal Deposit Insurance Corporation's classification of bank loans into "criticized" and "uncriticized" categories.[55] However, Dietrich and Kaplan have been more successful in using a statistical "logit" model to explain and predict four classes of loans from "current/in good standing" to "doubtful".[56]

The third area deals with the estimation and prediction of commercial bank financial distress. Studies have examined the feasibility of predicting bank financial distress based on accounting data. Sinkey has been able to predict a large proportion of failures based on a model that includes two variables: (a) operating expenses to operating income and (b) investments to assets.[57] Similarly, Pettaway and Sinkey have continued the same line of research using both market- and accounting-based screening models.[58] The accounting screen has been found to provide valuable lead time that regulators can use to carry out their statutory responsibilities more effectively.

12.2.6 Forecasting financial statement information

Because security analysts and most forecasting agencies focus on the US environment, management accountants and financial managers of multinational corporations (MNCs) may have to rely on their own efforts to forecast other companies' earnings and to provide forecasts of their own earnings. Their choice of techniques may be mechanical or nonmechanical and univariate or multivariate. Mechanical univariate forecasting approaches include moving average models and Box–Jenkins univariate models. Mechanical multivariate forecasting models include regression models, Box–Jenkins transfer function models, and econometric models. Finally, nonmechanical models include univariate models such as visual curve extrapolation and multivariate models such as security analyst approaches. These forecasts can be evaluated in terms of either dispersion or bias. Dispersion of forecast errors is generally measured by the mean square error (MSE) as follows:

$$MSE = 1/n \, (ax_{it} - fx_{it})^2$$

where

ax_{it} = actual value of the variable in period t for firm i,
fx_{it} = forecasted value of the variable in period t for firm i, and
n = number of forecasts examined.

Bias is measured by the expected value of the error (EVE):

$$EVE = 1/n \, (ax_{it} - fx_{it})$$

Earnings forecasts are becoming increasingly popular and important to an efficient functioning of capital markets. These forecasts are assumed to be particularly useful to users of accounting information. Earnings forecasts may be provided by analysts, management or statistical models. The relevance of these forecasts rests to a great extent on their reasonable accuracy; the investors in particular and the capital markets in general would have no confidence in inaccurate earnings forecasts, and consequently would not utilize them. An important question centers then on the predictive accuracy of each type of forecasts. Accordingly, various studies have examined the research question, "Are forecasts of earnings by analysts or management superior to statistical models?"

At this stage of the research, there seems to be a disagreement as to whether earnings forecasts made by analysts and/or management are more accurate than forecasts based on a statistical analysis of the pattern in historical annual earnings and quarterly earnings time-series models. In addition, industry variables seem to "make a difference" in the ability to forecast a firm's earnings. It is too early to have closure on the subject. Various issues remain unanswered, and the research to date suffers from various limitations. Abdel-Khalik and Thompson identify the following unanswered issues: "the relevance of forecasted data, the value of nonaccounting information in forecasting, the randomness of earnings time series, the cost of alternative forecasting procedures, and the respective motives of management and security analysts in making forecasts".[59]

Similarly, Griffin identifies the following caveats of the research:

> First, the results are typically based on an "average" firm or a firm at the median position in a cross section. Such average results may have application in specific contexts. Second, analysis by industry, size, risk, and other possible explanatory variables has received only scant attention so far in developing statistical models. Third, most studies use rather naive models and thus do not recognize recent research on the properties of accounting earnings. This suggests that they are potentially biased in favor of the superiority of the published forecasts.
>
> Finally, the finding that managers and analysts have about the same degree of forecasting success is probably not unreasonable given the present institutional setting. Company investor-relations programs and analysts' period meetings with management suggest that, insofar as the earnings forecast is concerned, the overlap of information accessible to management and analysts is considerable.[60]

Contemporary research provides ample evidence that analysts appear to *under-react* to prior returns and prior earnings. Explanations for this phenomenon included (a) the positive effect of predominantly prior permanent earnings, (b) the positive effect of the forecast horizon, (c) the positive effect of firm size, the extent to which other analysts following the same firm have serially correlated forecast errors, and the extent to which seasonal random walk forecast errors for the firm are serially correlated, and (d) the negative impact of the analyst's experience.

Findings on bias in forecast earnings and/or decrease in forecasting accuracy abound. They include:

1. Findings on bias in forecasting earnings and/or decrease in forecasting accuracy in complex firm environments such as (a) firm's cost structure, strikes, start-up and break-in problems with new products and processes; (b) low quality management discussion and analysis; (c) uncertainty about firm's future economic performance; (d) differential information; (e) auditor conservatism; (f) large capitalization firms; (g) optimism concerning the future of negative earnings firms; (h) level of industry diversification; (i) future earnings uncertainty; (j) degree of corporate seasonality; (k) earnings variability; (l) earnings management; and (m) business risk, financial risk and information availability.

2. Findings on bias in forecasting earnings and/or decrease in forecasting accuracy in specific international and country contexts.

3. Findings in difficulty of forecasting earnings of multinational firms due to specific international problems such as cultural, transaction, economic, translation and political risk exposures.

12.3 Prediction of market reaction: market-based research in accounting

12.3.1 Capital markets and external accounting

According to one interpretation of the predictive approach, the observations of capital market reaction may be used as a guide for evaluating and choosing among various accounting measurements. For example, Gonedes contends that:

> Observations of market reactions of recipients of accounting outputs should govern evaluations of the actual information content of accounting numbers produced via a given set of procedures and the informational content of accounting numbers produced via an alternative procedures.[61]

Beaver and Dukes favor the predictive approach when they state that:

> The method which produces earnings numbers having the highest association with security prices is the most consistent with the information that results in an efficient determination of security prices. ... It is the method that ought to be reported.[62]

In other words, the predictive approach favors the adoption of the accounting numbers that have the highest association with market prices. It calls for an evaluation of the usefulness of accounting numbers that are transmitted to capital-market transactions viewed as an aggregate. In this case, "aggregate" means the focus is on the reaction of the securities market rather than on the individual investors making up the market.

The roles of the securities market and of information in the securities market justify the use of the prediction of market reaction in the formulation of an accounting theory. The role of the securities market is to provide an orderly exchange market whereby investors may exchange claims to present and future consumption on a continuous basis. The role of the information is twofold:

(1) to aid in establishing a set of security prices, such that there exists an optimal allocation of securities among investors, and (2) to aid the individual investor, who faces a given set of prices, in the selection of an optimal portfolio of securities.[63]

Thus, the relevance of accounting information and the choice of accounting measurement procedures may be examined in terms of market reactions. The predictive approach is based on the theory and evidence of the efficient market model.

12.3.2 The efficient market model

It is generally assumed that the securities market is efficient. A perfectly efficient market is in continuous equilibrium, so that the intrinsic values of securities vibrate randomly and market prices always equal underlying intrinsic values at every instant in time.[64] "Intrinsic value" is generally regarded as what the price ought to be and what price would be given by other individuals who possessed the same information and competence as the person making the estimate.[65]

Various definitions of market efficiency need to be examined.

1. One definition, suggests Fama, is that in an efficient market, prices "fully reflect" the information available and, by implication, prices react instantaneously and without bias to new information.[66] A mathematical formulation of this definition, called the expected-return model or fair-game model, is also suggested by Fama:

$$Z_{j,t+1} = r_{j,t+1} - E(r_{j,t+1} \varphi_t)$$
$$E(Z_{j,t+1} \varphi_t) = 0$$

where:

$r_{j,t+1}$ = the realized return on security j in period $t+1$ (where "return" is defined as percentage change in security price adjusted for dividends received);

$E(Z_{j,t+1} \varphi_t)$ = the expected return on security j in period t+1, conditional on φ_t;

φ_t = the information set assumed to be fully reflected in prices in period t;

$Z_{j,t+1}$ = abnormal return on security j in period t + 1.

In other words, the rate-of-return series $(r_{j,t+1})$ is "a fair game" relative to the information series (φ_t).

Fama's definition has been criticized for being tautological (in that it merely implies that the expected deviation of a realization from its expected value is zero), for not being empirically testable unless some equilibrium model of security returns is specified, for failing to give a clear meaning to the term "information set", and for requiring prices to exist in an imaginary "as if" economy and the information set to be available in that "as if" economy.[67,68]

2. The second definition is based on some form of a model derived from the theory of rational expectations, whereby correct expectations are formed on the basis of all the available information, including prices. A behavioral process is generated whereby more informed individuals reveal information to less informed individuals through their trading actions or exchange of information. As a result, the rational expectations model that is derived produces prices that do not fully reveal everything.[69] Information is not free, and efficiency, in the strong sense, does not exist unless there is a decrease in the cost of information.

3. A third definition, proposed by Beaver, makes the distinction between market efficiency with respect to a signal (such as a particular type of accounting change)

and with respect to an information system (such as all published accounting information).[70] Signal efficiency (or y-efficiency) and information system efficiency (or η-efficiency), respectively, are defined as follows:

- y-efficiency: A securities market is efficient with respect to a signal Y_t' if and only if the configuration of security prices $\{P_{jt}\}$ is the same as it would be in an otherwise identical economy (with an identical configuration of preferences and endowments), except that every individual receives Y_t' as well as Y_{it}.
- η-efficiency: A securities market is efficient with respect to η_t' if y-efficiency holds for every signal (Y') from η_t'.[71]

More recently, Malkiel has proposed the following explicit definition:

> A Capital market is said to be efficient if it fully and correctly reflects all the relevant information in determining stock prices. Formally, the market is said to be efficient with respect to some information set ... if security prices would be unaffected by revealing that information to all participants. Moreover, efficiency with respect to an information set ... implies that is impossible to make economic profits by trading on the basis of [that information set].[72]

The first sentence is similar to Fama's definition. The second sentence implies that efficiency can only be tested by revealing information and measuring the market reaction. No market reaction following the release of the information implies efficiency. This test is only possible in a laboratory setting.

The third sentence implies that the efficiency can be evaluated by the profits that can be made on the information, which is the approach used in all empirical work on efficiency. One limitation of the approach is the inability to observe the information used in the trading strategies.

Market efficiency does not imply that security price should be smooth rather than random. As stated by Black:[73]

> A perfect market for stock is one in which there are no profits to be made by people who have no special information about the company, and in which it is difficult even for people who do have special information to make profits, because the price adjusts so rapidly as the information becomes available ... Thus we would like to see *randomness* in the prices of successive transactions rather than great continuity ... Randomness means a series of small upward movements (or small downward movements) is very unlikely. If the price is going to move up it should move up all at once, rather than in a series of small steps ... Large price movements are desirable, so long as they are consistently followed by price movements in the opposite directions.

Similarly, the discounted present value model of a security price is consistent with randomness in security prices, as shown by the "law of iterated expectations".[74]

Let us assume that

$$P_t = E[V^*/I_t] = E_t V^*$$

where P_t is a security price at time t, expressed as a rational expectation of a "fundamental value" V^*, conditional on information I_t available at time t. Similarly, the equation for one period ahead would be

$$P_{t+1} = E[V^*/I_{t+1}] = E_{t+1} V^*$$

The expectation of a change in the price over the next period follows:

$$E_t[P_{t+1} - P_t] = E_t[E_{t+1}[V^*] - E_t[V^*]] = 0$$

Given that $I_t C I_{t+1}$. It follows that by the law of iterated expectations that $E_t [E_{t+1} [V^*]] = E_t [V^*]$. The information set I_t does not allow the forecast of the realized changes in prices.[75]

12.3.3 The efficient market hypothesis

By defining the information set (φ) in three different ways, Fama distinguishes three levels of market efficiency: the weak, the semi-strong, and the strong forms.[76]

The weak form of the efficient market hypothesis

The weak form of the efficient market hypothesis states that the equilibrium expected returns (prices) "fully reflect" the sequence of past returns (prices). In other words, historical price and volume data for securities contain no information that may be used to earn profit superior to a simple "buy-and-hold" strategy. The weak form of the hypothesis began with the theory that price changes follow a true "random walk" (with an expected value of zero). This school of thought is challenged by "technical analysts" or "chartists", who believe that their rules, based on past information, can earn greater-than-normal profits. Filter rules, serial correlation and run tests have tested the weak efficient market hypothesis. The results support the hypothesis, particularly for returns longer than a day.

Technical analysis has been defined as follows:

> Technical analysis is the science of recording, usually in graphic form, the actual history of trading (price changes, volumes by transactions, etc.) in a certain stock or in "the averages" and then deducing from that pictured history the probable future trend.[77]

It is the search for regularities – often in the form of geometric patterns such as *double bottoms*, *head-and shoulders*, and *support* and *resistance levels* – that are assumed to be useful for predicting future price movements. Most researchers perceive technical analysis as a "black sheep" and as "voodoo"-based analysis. Yet, it persists in the marketplace and is gaining growing interest in the academic community.

The semi-strong form of the efficient market hypothesis

The semi-strong form of the efficient market hypothesis states that the equilibrium expected return (prices) "fully reflect" all publicly available information. In other words, no trading rule based on available information may be used to earn an excess return. The semi-strong form of the hypothesis is relevant to accounting because publicly available information includes financial statements. Tests of the semi-strong hypothesis have been concerned with the speed with which prices adjust to specific kinds of events. Some of the events examined have been stock splits, announcements of annual earnings, large secondary offerings of common stocks, new issues of stocks, announcements of changes in the discount rate and stock dividends.

The results again support the efficient market hypothesis in so far as prices adjust rather quickly after the first public announcement of information. The list of events examined is not exhaustive and further empirical research is warranted to prove this hypothesis, which is of extreme importance to accounting.

The strong form of the efficient market hypothesis

The strong form of the efficient market hypothesis states that the equilibrium expected returns (prices) "fully reflect" all information (not just publicly available information). In other words, no trading rule based on any information, including inside information, may be used to earn an excess return.

Evidence on the strong form of the efficient market hypothesis is not conclusive. Although Jensen[78] has been able to show that mutual funds do not exhibit any consistent superior performance over time (given presumed access to special information), Niederhoffer and Osborne[79] argue that superior returns are possible (given access to the specialists' books).

12.3.4 The capital-asset pricing model

The efficient market hypothesis requires the use of "expected returns" and assumes that securities are properly priced. A theory is needed to specify the relationship between the expected returns and the prices of the individual stock in question. One such theory is Sharpe, Lintner and Mossin's capital-asset pricing model,[80] which relates asset returns to asset risk as follows:

$$E(R_{it}) = R_{ft} + [E(R_{mt}) - R_{ft}]\, \beta$$

where:

$E(R_{it})$	= the expected return of security i in period t.
R_{ft}	= the return on a riskless asset in period t.
$E(R_{mt})$	= the expected return on the market portfolio in period t.
$\sigma(R_{it}, R_{mt})$	= the covariance between R_{it} and $R_{mt.}$
$\sigma(R_{mt})$	= the variance of the return on the market portfolio.

$$\beta = \frac{\sigma(R_{it}, R_{mt})}{\sigma^2(R_{mt})} \quad = \text{risk coefficient.}$$

Given certain assumptions, the capital-asset pricing model asserts that there is a linear relationship between an individual security and its systematic risk.

12.3.5 The arbitrage pricing theory (APT)

APT assumes that security returns are related to an unknown number of unknown factors. It is more general than the CAPM in that it allows for multiple risk factors. A multifactor model will be as follows:

$$R_i = a_i + b_{i1}F_1 + b_{i2}F_2 + \dots + b_{ij}F_3 + e_I$$

The securities will be priced as follows:

$$E(r_i) = R_j + Y_1 b_{i1} + Y_2 b_{i2} + \dots + b_{ij} Y_j$$

where:

R_f = returns on riskless asset
b_{ij} = sensitivity of security i to factor j, and
Y_j = security return premium (i.e., in excess of R_f per unit of security to factor j).

That is to say, the security expected returns are linearly related to the securities of the pervasive factors, with a common intercept equal to the riskless rate of interest.[81] The approaches were used for the identification of the factors. One approach relied on macro-economic and financial market variables that are assumed to capture the systematic risks of the economy. A second approach relied on characteristics of firms that are likely to explain differential sensitivity to the systematic risks before forming portfolios of stocks on the characteristics. Various studies attempted to identify the factors. Chen, Roll and Ross identified the following four factors:

1. growth rate in industrial production;
2. rate of inflation (both expected and unexpected);
3. spread between long-term and short-term interest rates; and
4. spread between low-grade and high-grade bonds.[82]

In addition to the last three factors. Berry, Burmeister and McElroy identified the two factors of the growth rate in aggregate sales in the economy and the rate of return on the Standard & Poor's (S&P) 500.[83] Finally, Salomon Brothers used the following five factors in their fundamental factor model:

1. rate of inflation (both expected and unexpected);
2. growth rate in gross national product;
3. rate of interest;
4. rate of change in oil prices; and
5. rate of growth in defense spending.[84]

An extensive empirical evidence, based on the second approach, shows that differences across stocks in observable characteristics are systematically associated with differences in average future returns.[85]

12.3.6 Equilibrium theory of option pricing

Options give one party right to buy (call option or put option) a specific number of shares of a specific company from the option writer at a specific price at any time up to and including a specific date. An equilibrium pricing of valuing (call) options was proposed by Black and Scholes[86] under the following formula:

$$V_c = N(d_1)P_s - \frac{E}{C^{RT}} N(d_2),$$

$$d_1 = \frac{In(P_s / E) + (R + 0.5\sigma^2)T}{\sigma\sqrt{T}}$$

$$d_2 = \frac{In(P_s / E) + (R + 0.5\sigma^2)T}{\sigma\sqrt{T}}$$

$$= d_1 - \sigma\sqrt{T}$$

where:

P_s = current market price of the underlying stock,
E = exercise price of the option,
R = continuously compounded risk-free rate of return expressed on an annual basis,
T = time remaining before expiration, expressed as a fraction of a year, and
σ = risk of the underlying common stock, measured by the standard deviation of the continuously compounded annual rate of return on the stock.

12.3.7 The market model

The capital-asset pricing model does not lend itself to an easy test of the efficient market hypothesis. Instead the Markovitz[87] and Sharpe[88] market model is used for this purpose. The model defines the stochastic process generating security price as:

$$R_{it} = \alpha_{it} + \beta_{it}.R_{it} + U_{it}$$

where:

$E(M_{it}) = 0,$
$\sigma(R_{mt}, M_{it}) = 0,$
$\sigma(M_{mt}, M_{it}) = 0,$
R_{it} = the return of security i in period $t,$
α_i, β_i = the intercept and the slope of the linear relationship between R_{it} and R_{mt}
R_{mt} = the market factor in period $t,$ and
M_{it} = the stochastic portion of the individualistic component of $R_{it}.$

The market model asserts that the return of each security is linearly related to the market return. More specifically, it states that the total return R_{it} can be separated into a systematic component $B_i R_{mt}$ which reflects the extent of common movement of the return of security in conjunction with the average return on all securities in the market. The systematic risk B_i reflects the response of security i to economy-wide events reflected in the market factor, and M_{ij} reflects the response of the class of events having an impact on security i only. Thus, the isolation of the individualistic component of security i, or M_{it}, enables an evaluation of the effect of specific information items or measurements. The model has been used in most studies evaluating the relation between market return and accounting return. To estimate the parameters α and β researchers have generally relied on the ordinary least-squares approach (or the generalized least-squares approach), which assumes that the market model parameters are consistent during the event period. There is, however, evidence of changes in both parameters in response to various economic events. Some studies relied on Ibbotson's[89] returns across times and securities (RATS) procedure to account for the variables of the regression parameters. The method proceeds with the estimation of the pooled cross-sectional coverage beta for each event date. Other methods call for using the switching regression involved, the Kalman filter model,[90] and the random coefficient model,[91] and the Bayesian random coefficient model (BERAB).[92] For example, the Bayesian estimates for random X and B (BERAB) at time t are:

$$\alpha_{Bt} = \alpha_0 + \frac{(R_t - \alpha_0 - \beta_0 R_{mt})(\sigma_u^2 + \sigma_{uv} R_{mt})}{(\sigma_\epsilon^2 + \sigma_u^2 + \sigma_v^2 R_{mv}^2 + 2\sigma_{uv} R_{mt})'}$$

$$\beta_{Bt} = \beta_0 + \frac{(R_t - \alpha_0 - \beta_0 R_{mt})(\sigma_u^2 + \sigma_{uv} R_{mt})}{(\sigma_\epsilon^2 + \sigma_u^2 + \sigma_v^2 R_{mv}^2 + 2\sigma_{uv} R_{mt})}$$

A description of BERAB follows:

> The Bayesian analysis suggests that the degree of belief we currently hold concerning any proposition depends on the information currently available to us. As the information about a proposition changes, our belief or probability is revised, representing learning behavior. In this scheme, the initial information based on previous observations is expressed as a prior probability distribution concerning the proposition, and new data is expressed as a likelihood function. Then the prior probability density and the likelihood function are combined by Bayes' theorem to yield a posterior probability density function. The posterior density combines both the sample and prior information. It characterizes the revision that has occurred because of the sample data and is the basis for subsequent decision-making.[93]

12.3.8 Beta estimation

The estimation of systematic risk or beta is essentially needed for studies examining the market impact of accounting information, and the association of beta with accounting-based indicators. Because of the potential econometric problem of error in the market model estimates various necessary corrections have been proposed.

First, the generalized Scholes–Williams correction provides the following estimator:[94]

$$B_I = (B_{i+1} + B_i^u + B_i^{-1})/1 + 2P_1$$

where:

B^{+1}, B^0, B^{-1} = leading, contemporaneous, and lagged betas, and
P_1 = first-order serial correlation of the index.

Cohen, Hawawini, Mayer, Schwartz and Whitcomb[95] suggest a generalized form of this estimator:

$$\beta_i = (\sum_{+n=1}^{+N} \beta_i^{+n} + \beta_i^0 + \sum_{-n=1}^{-N} \beta_i^{-n})/1 + \sum_{+n=1}^{+N} \beta_i^{-n} 2P_{+n}$$

where:

$+N$ = number of leads in the estimator, and
$-N$ = number of lags in the estimator.

Second, Vasicek's Bayesian correction[96] provides the following estimator:

$$B_i = (Bp/S^{2p} + B^B/S^{B2}(/(1/S^{2p} + 1/S^{2B}),$$

where:

Bp = best prior estimate,
S^{2p} = estimated variance of the estimate,
B^B = unweighted market average of betas, and
S^{2B} = estimated variance of market betas.

A typical application of these corrections is provided in Karpik and Belkaoui.[97]

12.3.9 Event-study methodology

The effect of an economic event on the value of a firm can be ascertained by the event-study analysis, assuming that the effect of an event will be reflected immediately in asset prices. Seven steps are required in an event study as follows:[98]

1. *Event definition*: The event of interest and the period of interest or event window need to be identified. For most earnings announcement using daily data, the event window is the day of the announcement and the day after the announcement.

2. *Selection criteria:* The firms to be included in the study need to conform to selection criteria prior to inclusion.

3. *Normal and abnormal returns:* The abnormal return is computed as the difference between the actual ex-post return of the security and the normal return of the firm over the event window. It may be expressed for each firm i and event date t as:

$$\epsilon_{it}^* = R_{it} - E[R_{it}/X_t]$$

where ϵ_{it}^*, R_{it} and $E(R_{it})$ are the abnormal, actual and normal returns respectively, for time t, given X_t as the conditioning information for the normal performance model.

The four models of normal return used are as follows:

(a) The abnormal return (AR) for security i at day t is calculated using the following procedures. Under the market model, the abnormal return is calculated as:

$$AR_{it} = R_{it} - \beta_0 - \beta_1 R_{mt} \tag{1}$$

Where R_{it} is the daily return of security at i at day t. R_{mt} is the return on the CRSP Equal-Weighted Index, CRSP Value-Weighted Index, MSCI World Index, or MSCI Country Index. β_0 and β_1 are ordinary least squares estimates.

(b) Under the two-index market model, the abnormal return is computed as:

$$AR_{it} = R_{it} - \beta_0 - \beta_1 R_{at} - \beta_2 R_{bt} \tag{2}$$

Where R_{at} is return on the CRSP Equal-Weighted Index, CRSP Value-Weighted Index, MSCI World Index, or MSCI Country Index. R_{bt} is return on the MSCI Country Index. β_0, β_1 and β_2 are ordinary least squares estimates.

(c) Under the market-adjusted model, the abnormal return is:

$$AR_{it} = R_{it} - R_{mt} \tag{3}$$

(d) Under the mean-adjusted model, the abnormal return is given by:

$$AR_{it} = R_{it} - MR_i \tag{4}$$

where MR_i is the average daily stock return of security i during the estimation period.

4. *Estimation procedure:* The period prior to the event is used as the estimation window for estimating the parameters of the model.

5. *Testing procedure:* Both the null hypothesis and the techniques for aggregating the abnormal returns of firms are designed.

6. *Empirical results:* The empirical results are presented and analyzed.

7. *Interpretation and conclusions:* The effect of the economic event on the value of the firms examined is subject to competing explanations.

An example of the design of an event study follows:

The event-study methodology uses the announcement date as day 0. It is well documented in event-study literature that most abnormal returns occur during the day -1 to $+1$ period. Thus our example of an analysis is focused on this three-day interval. The OLS procedure is used first to estimate the normal return:

$$R_{it} = \alpha_j + \beta_j (R_{mt}) + e_{jt}$$

where:

R_{it} = the rate of return on security j at time t,
α_j = the intercept term for security j's equation,
β_j = the regression coefficient of the market return at time t,
R_{mt} = the return on the CRSP value-weighted index at time t,
e_{jt} = the error term for security j at time t.

The parameter estimates α_j and β_j are determined from the daily returns during the 200-day regression period from day -240 to day -41.

The daily abnormal return (prediction error) is the difference between the forecast and the actual rate of return:

$$AR_{jt} = R_{jt} - (\alpha_j + \beta_j R_{mt})$$

Prediction errors are cumulated for an interval of three days. This cumulative abnormal return (CAR) is defined as:

$$\text{CAR} = \sum_{t=T_{1j}}^{T_{2j}} \text{AR}_j$$

T_{1j} and T_{2j} represent the days between which the CAR is calculated. For a sample of n securities, the abnormal return or the mean cumulative abnormal return (MCAR) is:

$$\text{MCAR} = \frac{1}{n} \sum_{j=1}^{n} \text{CAR}$$

In this example, we concentrate on a three-day announcement interval (day –1 to day 1) for the regression analysis. The event-study literature has shown that such a short interval will capture a major part of the total stock price effects.

Test statistics needed to determine whether MCAR is statistically different from zero are obtained by first standardizing the AR by its estimated standard deviation S_{jt}

$$\text{SAR}_{jt} = \text{AR}_{jt} / S_{jt}$$

where S_{jt} is the estimated standard error of the regression forecast error, and SAR_{jt} is the standardized prediction error, the test statistic for the abnormal return for security at time t. To test the returns over time, the SARs are cumulated and divided by the square root of the number of days in the test interval ($t = T, \ldots, T$) as follows:

$$\text{MSCAR}_j = \sum \text{SAR}_{jt} / T_{2j} - T_{1j} + 1)^{1/2}$$

Finally, the test statistic for a sample of n securities is:

$$Z = \sum_{j=1}^{n} \text{MSCAR}_j / n^{1/2}$$

Each SAR_{it} is assumed to have a unit normal distribution in the absence of abnormal performance. Under this assumption, Z is also distributed as unit normal.

Two interesting results emerged from the literature:

1. One first interesting result of the event-study type of research is the phenomenon of post-earnings-announcement drift. Various studies reported that even after earnings are announced, estimated cumulative "abnormal" returns continue to drift up for "good news" firms and down for "bad news" firms. Explanations offered for the phenomenon include.

   (a) the market's failure to fully reflect the attributes of the stochastic process underlying earnings,
   (b) transaction costs
   (c) investor sophistication, and
   (d) analyst experience.

   Multinationality may be leading cause of the post-earnings-announcement drift in abnormal returns. The idea that the drift may be negatively related to the level of multinationality can be supported by various findings, including:

(a) Drift is inversely related to size and bigger multinationality is characteristic of large firms.

(b) Drift is a result of the misperception of the earnings process by the holdings of unsophisticated investors and high multinationality firms are largely sought by sophisticated investors in general and fund managers who specialize in large capitalization stocks.

(c) Drift is inversely related to share price and annual trading volume as proxy for the inverse of direct and indirect cost of trading and the growth of institutional holdings in large multinational firms.

(d) Findings consistent with investors anchoring on the more efficient and more accurate earnings expectations of high multinationality firms, mitigating any resulting post-earnings-announcement drift.

2. One second interesting result of the event-study type is the evidence of increasing usefulness of earnings announcements from over-time increase in the absolute or squared abnormal stock returns or abnormal trading volume at earnings announcement dates. Four plausible explanations include:

(a) the likelihood that the absolute abnormal returns to earnings announcements are significantly positively correlated with the absolute abnormal returns to analysts reports,

(b) the impact of over-time increases in the amount of unexpected earnings new,

(c) the impact of over-time increases in investors' reaction to a unit of unexpected earnings news, and

(d) the impact of over-time increases of additional firm disclosures made concurrently with earnings.

12.3.10 Residual income valuation (RIV)

Dating back to 1938 in an article by Preinreich,[99] the RIV rests on the hypothesis that asset prices represent the present value of all future dividends (PVED):

$$P_t = \sum_{\tau=1}^{a} R^\tau E_t(d_{t+\tau})(PVED)$$

where P_t is market price of equity at date t, d_t symbolizes dividends (or net cash payments) received at the end of period t, R is unity plus the discount rate r, and E_t is the expectation operator based on the information set at date t.

The process of going from PVED to RIV rests on two assumptions:

1. The accounting system is assumed to satisfy a clean surplus relation (CSR):

$$b_t = b_{t-1} + x_t - d_t$$

where b_t is the book value of equity at date t, and x_t is the earnings in period ending at date t.

2. A regularity condition is assumed whereby the book value of equity grows at a rate less than k, that is

$$R^{-\tau} E_t(b_t + \tau) \xrightarrow{\tau \to \infty} 0$$

On the basis of the two assumptions, PVED is restated as function of book value and discounted expected abnormal earnings.[100]

$$P_t = b_t + \sum_{\tau=1}^{\infty} R^{-\tau} E_t(x_{t+\tau}^a)(RIV)$$

where $x_t^a = x_t - r \times b_{t-1}$

12.3.11 Feltham–Ohlson's model (FO)

Developed by both Ohlson[101] and Feltham and Ohlson,[102] the FO model relates a firm's market value to basic accounting data and "other" kinds of information. The model rests on the following notations:

oa_t = operating assets (net of operating liabilities)
ox_t = operating earnings
fa_t = financial assets (net of financial liabilities)
i_t = income due to financial activities
b_t = $fa_t + oa_t$ = book value
x_t = $i_t + ox_t$ = net earnings
P_t = market value
d_t = net dividends
c_t = (free) cash flows
R_t = discount rate
x_t^a = $x_t - (R-1)b_{t-1}$ = residual earnings
ox_t^a = $ox_t - (R-1)oa_{t-1}$ = residual operating earnings.

Four assumptions are made:[103]

1. P_t equals PVED:

$$P_t = \sum_{\tau-1}^{\infty} R^{-\tau} E_t[\tilde{d}_{t+\tau}].$$

2. Clean surplus accounting:

$fa_t = fa_{t-1} + i_t - d_t + c_t^1$
$oa_t = oa_{t-1} + ox_t - c_t.$

3. Net interest relation:

$i_t = (R-1)fa_{t-1}$

4. Linear information dynamics:

$$o\tilde{x}_{t+1}^a = \omega_{11}ox_t^a + \omega_{12}oa_t + v_{1t} + \tilde{\varepsilon}_{1t+1},$$
$$o\tilde{a}_{t+1} = \omega_{22}oa_t + v_{2t} + \tilde{\varepsilon}_{2t+1},$$
$$\tilde{v}_{1t+1} = \gamma_1 v_{1t} + \tilde{\varepsilon}_{3t+1},$$
$$\tilde{v}_{2t+1} = \gamma_2 v_{2t} + \tilde{\varepsilon}_{4t+1},$$

where v_{kt} represents "other" information relevant in the forecasting of future abnormal earnings. The parameters (ω_{11}, ω_{12}, ω_{22}, γ_1, γ_2) satisfy the regularity conditions

$$\omega_{11} \in [0,1], \ \omega_{22} \in [1,R], \ \omega_{12} \geq 0, \text{ and } \gamma_k \in [0,1], k = 1, 2.$$

Based on these assumptions the following model is proposed:

$$P_t = b_t + \alpha_1 ox_t^a + \alpha_2 oa_t + \beta_1 v_{1t} + \beta_2 v_{2t}^1$$

where

$$\alpha_1 = \omega_{11} / (R - \omega_{11}) \geq 0,$$
$$\alpha_2 = \omega_{12} R / (R - \omega_{11}) (R - \omega_{22}) \geq 0,$$
$$\beta_1 = R / (R - \omega_{11}) (R - \gamma_1) > 0,$$
$$\beta_2 = \alpha_2 / (R - \gamma_2) \geq 0.$$

With $\omega_{12} > 0$, conservatism is implied. As stated by Liu and Ohlson:

> Conservative accounting is necessary and sufficient to ensure the relevance of the second and fourth dynamic equation. These two equations determine the long and short run expected growth in (net) operating assets. Growth is "good" in that α_2 increases as ω_{22} increases, and β_2 increases as either ω_{22} or γ_2 increases. The reason for these relations is subtle but intuitive: Conservative accounting implies that a firm (on average) will look profitable (i.e. ox_t^a is typically positive), and hence a firm is "rewarded" for high growth in its size as measured by net operating assets. Imparting a slightly different perspective, growth combined with conservative accounting makes it more difficult to recognize high earnings and hence the earnings/accruals are of better quality compared to unbiased accounting.[104]

In an expanded model, the market value of the firm's equity is a linear and stochastic function of the book value of equity, current earnings, current dividends, and a variable representing other value relevant factors. It is stated as follows:

$$P_t = k (\varphi x_t - d_t) + (1 - k)y_t + \alpha_2 v_t$$

where:

P_t = market value or price of the firm at date t
k = $R_{jw} / (1 + R - w)$
R_t = the risk-free interest rate
w = persistence parameter for abnormal earnings (x^a) : $x_{t+1}^a + wx_t^a + e_{1,t+1}$
φ = $(R_f + 1) / R_f$
x_t = earnings for period t–1 to t
d_t = dividends paid at date t less new capital contributions for period t–1 to t
y_t = net book value at date t
α_2 = $(R_f + 1) / (R_f + 1 - w) (R_f + 1 - y)$
v_t = a variable summarizing other information that influences the prediction of future expected abnormal earnings, and
y = persistence parameter for v_t : $v_{t+1} = yv_t + e_{2,t+1}$

While the above models suggest that equity value is a linear additive function of both earnings and book value, that is, a weighted average of both earnings and book value, Burgstahler and Dichev[105] suggested that equity value is instead a convex function of both earnings and book value, where the function depends on the relative values of earnings and book value. In other words, the firm's value is a combination of its recursion value and adaptation value. Recursion value is the value resulting from the discounting of the stream of future earnings under the assumption that the firm continues to apply its current business technology to resources. Adaptation value is the value of the firm's resources independent of the firm's current business technology. The recursion value reflected by earnings determines the value of a successful firm that will continue its current operations. The adaptation value reflected by book value determines the value of an unsuccessful firm that will find alternative use of its resources. The earnings to book value ratio is the measure of the degree of success. It is implied that the value of high earnings to book value ratio firms is determined by earnings, the value of the earnings to book value ratio firms is determined by book value, while the value of the medium earnings to book value ratio firm is determined by both earnings and book value. What results is a valuation model that is a piece-wise form of the earnings and book value. The valuation models that can be used to test the piece-wise business model can be specified as follows:

$$V_t / B_{t-1} = b_1 + b_2 E_t / B_{t-1} + \epsilon \tag{1}$$
$$V_t / B_{t-1} = b_1 + b_2 D_M + b_3 D_H + b_4 E_t / B_{t-1} + b_5 D_M E_t / B_{t-1} + b_6 D_H E_t / B_{t-1} + \epsilon \tag{2}$$
$$V_t / B_t = b_1 + b_2 B_{t-1} / E_t + \epsilon \tag{3}$$
$$V_t / B_t = b_2 + b_2 D_M + b_3 D_H + b_4 B_{t-1} / E_t + b_5 D_M B_{t-1} / E_t + b_6 D_H B t_{-1} / E_t + \epsilon \tag{4}$$

where:

V_t is price per share at the end of the year t
E_t is earnings per share in year t
B_t is book value per share at the end of year t
D_H is a dummy variable (in equation (2), it is 1 for high earnings to book ratio firms, and equals 0 otherwise, and in equation (4), it equals 1 for high book to earnings ratio firms, and equals 0 otherwise)
D_M is a dummy variable (in equation (2), it equals 1 for medium earnings to book ratio firms, and equals 0 otherwise, and in equation (4), it equals 1 for medium book to earnings ratio firms, and equals 0 otherwise).

Equation (1) states that firm value is a simple linear function of earnings. Equation (2) states that firm value is a piece-wise function of earnings. It assumes that market value is an increasing convex function of expected earnings, for a given adaptation value. Equation (3) states that firm value is a simple linear function of book value. It assumes that market value is an increasing, convex function of adaptation value, for a given expected earnings.

12.3.12 Price-level balance sheet valuation models

These models focus on the relation between equity values and book values. In general, the relation is stated as follows:

MVE = MVA+MVL+MVC+GW

where:

MVE = market value of equity;
MVA = market value of separable assets other than the component whose incremental association is being assessed;
MVL = market value of separable liabilities other than the component whose incremental association is being assessed (liabilities are assumed to be negative values);
MVC = market value of the balance sheet component whose incremental value is being assessed;
GW = goodwill.

12.3.13 Information content of earnings

The information content of earnings is generally tested by the relationship between security returns and unexpected earnings. It is inferred by the significance of the slope coefficient (b) and the explanatory power of a cross-sectional over-time estimated model of the following form:

$$CAR_{it} = a + bUX_{it} + e_{it}$$

where:

CAR_{it} = cumulative abnormal return for security i over period t,
UX_{it} = unexpected earnings (preferably scaled), and
b = earnings response coefficient (ERC).

UX is measured either (a) using a random walk model as a proxy for the market earnings expectation as of the beginning of the year or (b) unexpected earnings using more sophisticated time-series models.

12.3.14 Models of the relation between earnings and returns

Two models of relation between earnings and returns have been used in research. The first model, model A, bases the returns and earnings association on a book valuation model. It is derived as follows: First, the price and book value as measures of the "stock" value of the shareholders' equity are related as follows:

$$P_{jt} = BV_{jt} + U_{jt} \tag{1}$$

where P_{jt} is the price per share of firm j at time t and BV_{jt} is the book value per share of firm j at time t.

Second, the accounting earnings and security returns as measures of the "flow" value or changes in value of the shareholders' equity can be derived by taking first differences of the variables in equation (1) as follows:

$$\Delta P_{jt} = \Delta BV_{jt} + U_{jt} \tag{2}$$

where:

$$\Delta BV_{jt} = A_{jt} - d_{jt} \tag{3}$$

A_{jt} = accounting earnings of firm j over the time period $t-1$ to t, and
d_{jt} = the dividend of firm j over time period $t-1$ to t.

Third, the relations between earnings and returns is obtained by substituting equation (3) into equation (2) and dividing by P_{jt-1} as follows:

$$R_{jt} = A_{jt} / P_{jt-1} + U_{jt} \tag{4}$$

where:

$$R_{jt} = (\Delta P_{jt} + d_{jt}) / P_{jt-1}$$

Equation (4) shows that if stock price and book value are related, then earnings divided by beginnings-of-period price (earnings level divided by beginnings-of-period price) allows us to explain returns.

The second model, model B, bases the returns and earnings association on an earnings valuation model. It is derived as follows: First, an earnings valuation model expresses price (including dividend) as a multiple of earnings as follows:

$$P_{jt} + d_{jt} = \sigma A_{jt} + V_{jt}$$

Second, changes in both sides of the equation coupled with division by beginning-of-period price yields the second model as follows:

$$R_{jt} = \sigma (\Delta A_{jt} / P_{jt}) + V_{jt}$$

12.3.15 Earnings persistence

Accounting researchers have relied on time-series models to obtain measures of earnings persistence and to form earnings expectations. Whether analysts, managers and investors rely on time-series models to form earnings expectations, it is still appropriate to investigate what economic characteristics cause earnings to behave in a persistent fashion. It is also appropriate to examine persistence measures derived from alternative time-series models that provide the best associations.

With regard to the choice of potential economic characteristics, a more robust and clean test is needed to identify a measure of firm complexity that can proxy for most variables found to be potential determinants of earnings persistence.

With regard to the time-series model that can provide the best association between persistence and diversification strategy, a higher-order autoregressive, integrated, moving average (ARIMA) model is expected to provide a far higher association.

This inquiry is related to prior work investigating the economic criterion for the choice of a specific time-series model. Lev[106] investigated the question of whether inter-firm differences in first- and second-order autocorrelation coefficients of earnings changes, return on equity changes, and sales can be explained by the firm's economic environment. His findings indicate that autocorrelation and variability of earnings over equity changes are systematically associated with the following factors: the type of product, the height of industry barriers to entry (a surrogate for the degree of completion), the degree of capital intensity (operating leverage), and firm size. Relying on the same economic characteristics, Baginski et al.[107] investigated whether persistence, estimated from time series, captures the joint effect of these economic variables and whether differenced, higher-order ARIMA model measures of persistence do so to a great extent. Their findings, which replicated the significant impact of the economic characteristics on persistence, showed that differenced, higher-order ARIMA models used to measure earnings persistence yield higher adjusted R^2s (in the 10–12 percent range) than lower-order ARIMA models: (2,1,0) and (4,1,0) yield adjusted R^2 of 10.3 percent and 12.5 percent respectively. Persistence measures from higher-order ARIMA models reflect the economic characteristics that give rise to earnings persistence. AlNajjar et al.[108] tested the relationship between multinationality and earnings persistence produced by ARIMA models. When higher-order ARIMA models were used, their results showed earnings persistence to be positively related to size and negatively related to multinationality.

Earnings persistence is generally measured by estimating an ARIMA true series earnings process. It measures the impact of a current shock on the whole stream of future realizations of the earnings series. A formula adapted from Flavin[109] and Kormendi and Lipe[110] indicates that for a given ARIMA (p, d, q) model specification, persistence is a function of the autoregressive and moving-average parameters as follows:

$$PER = \frac{1-\sum_{i=1}^{q} B^i \theta_i}{(1-B)^d (1-\sum_{j=1}^{p} B^j \varphi_j)} - 1$$

where:

$B = 1/(1+r)$ where r is the appropriate rate for discounting expected future earnings.
r is set at .10, providing similar results with $r = .04$ and .20.
θ_i = moving-average parameter of order i.
d = level of consecutive differencing.
φ_j = autoregressive parameter of order j.

12.3.16 Corporate valuation models[111]

All the corporate valuation models rely on data emanating from the economic balance sheet as it differentiates between core operations, non-operating assets, debt claims, other capital claims, and common equity claims. Basically, core operations relate to those assets and liabilities which are central to the cash-generating ability of the firm. The other assets and liabilities are termed non-operating net assets. Debt claims result from different forms of borrowing to include long-term debt, capitalized assets, short-term debt, current maturities of long-term debt and notes payable. Other capital claims consists of preferred stock, employee stock options, warrants and minority interest. The residual claim of the common shareholders is referred to as a common equity claim. Basically, the economic balance sheet can be expressed as:

$$\text{CORE} + \text{NONOP} = \text{DEBT} + \text{OCAP} + \text{COMEQUITY}$$

Where CORE is the value of core operations, NONOP is the value of non-operating net assets, DEBT is the value of debt claims, OCAP is the value of other capital claims, and COMEQUITY is the value of common equity.

The corporate valuation models rely also on two types of cash flows: (a) free cash flows generated by core assets and (b) non-operating cash flows generated by non-operating net assets. Cash flows are distributed to (a) debt claims, (b) other capital claims, and (c) common equity claims.

Four corporate valuation models are generally used to estimate COMEQUITY by estimating the values of the other economic balance sheet items. These models are (a) the flows to equity model, (b) the free cash-flow model, (c) the adjusted present value model, and (d) the residual income model. They are explained next.

1. The dividend discount model computes the value of a security as the present value of the security's expected future cash flows discounted at the cost of common equity. Basically:

$$\text{COMEQUITY} = \text{PV (DIVIDENDS)}$$

2. The flows to equity model computes the value of a security as the present value of the cash flows available to equity holders at the cost of common equity after serving both debt claims and other capital claims. Basically:

$$\text{COMEQUITY} = \text{PV (Free cash flow + Non-operating cash flow − Debt service −}$$
$$\text{Other capital cash flow)}$$

3. The free cash-flow model computes the value of a security as the present value of free cash flows at the firm's weighted-average cost of capital, plus the fair value of the non-operating net assets, minus the fair value of debt and other capital claims. Basically:

$$\text{COMEQUITY} = \text{PV (Free cash flows) + Non-operating net assets − Debt claims −}$$
$$\text{Other capital claims.}$$

4. The adjusted present value model highlights the value created by using leverage. It computes the value of a security as the present value of free cash flows at an unlevered cost of capital (the hypothetical cost of equity the firm would have if it had no leverage) plus the value of leverage (the amount by which the value of the core operations is higher in the free cash-flow model due to the use of a lower discount rate), plus the fair value of non-operating net assets, minus the fair value of debt and other capital claims. Basically:

$$\text{COMEQUITY} = \text{PV (Free cash flows at unlevered cost of equity) + Value of}$$
$$\text{leverage + Non-operating net assets − Debt claims − Other capital claims.}$$

5. The residual income model computes the value of a security as the current book value of equity (BV_o) plus the present value of future residual income at the cost of equity (K_e). In other words:

$$COMEQUITY = BV_o + PV \text{ (residual income stream)}$$

Given that the residual income is equal net income (NI) less base income, where base income equals the cost of equity multiplied by the book value of equity at the beginning of the period, the value of a security is:

$$COMEQUITY = BV_o + \sum_{t=1}^{a} \frac{NI_t - K_e . BV_{t-1}}{(1 + K_e)^t}$$

At the operating level, the residual income model is expressed as:

$$COMEQUITY = OPNA_o + \sum_{t=1}^{a} \frac{NOPAT_t - K_e . OPNA_{t-1}}{(1 + K_e)^t} + NONOP - DEBT - OCAP$$

where:

$OPNA_o$ = book value of core assets at the valuation date;
$NOPAT_t$ = net operating profit after tax;
K_e = weighted-average cost of capital;
$OPNA_{t-1}$ = book value of core operations at the beginning of the period;
NONOP = fair value of non-operating net assets;
DEBT = fair value of debt claims;
OCAP = fair value of other capital claims.

12.3.17 Evaluation of market-based research in accounting

Using theory and evidence regarding the efficient market hypothesis and the methodologies provided mainly by the capital-asset pricing model, portfolio theory and the market model, the predictive approach proceeds with the evaluation of accounting numbers and techniques on the basis of capital market reactions. The available evidence for market-based research accounting can be classified in the following categories:

1. information content studies;
2. difference in discretionary accounting techniques;
3. consequences of regulation;
4. impact on related disciplines.

A. Information content studies

The interest in these studies is with the marginal information contribution of accounting signals to the determination of security-return behavior. The approach used is to examine whether the announcement of some event results in a change in the characteristics of the stock-return distributions (i.e., mean or variance). The impetus was created by the famous Ball and Brown study[112] in which unexpected earning changes were found to be correlated with residual stock returns. These results are consistent with the hypothesis that accounting information – especially earnings – conveys information in the sense of leading to changes in equilibrium prices held with the following situations: (a) changes in the earnings-expectation models from a random-walk generating process to more complex models, (b) examining both the magnitude and the sign of the unexpected earnings, (c) using a methodology focusing on another property of the return distribution – the variance of residual returns, (d) analyzing trading rather than price changes, and (e) examining the impact of some non-earnings financial variables.

B. Voluntary differences and changes in accounting techniques

The interest in these studies is in the impact of the differences and changes on investors. The issue is whether the market is "sophisticated enough" not to be "fooled" by cosmetic accounting differences or accounting changes. If the investors are not able to "see through" the veil of accounting practices, the phenomenon is labeled as a *functional fixation* or *naive investor* hypothesis. The functional fixation or naive investor hypothesis assumes that a sufficient number of investors are unable to perceive the cosmetic nature of certain accounting changes, or are "fixated" on the bottom figure of net income. The efficient market hypothesis stipulates instead that rational investors should see through the veil of accounting practices, packaging of information and forms of disclosure. In addition, an *extended functional fixation* hypothesis assumes that when responding to accounting data, sometimes the price of a firm's stock is set by a sophisticated marginal investor, and sometimes it is set by an unsophisticated marginal investor.

Research on the subject has distinguished between accounting differences or changes having cash-flow consequences and those having no cash-flow consequences.

1. Research on the impact of accounting cross-sectional differences having no direct cash-flow effects showed investors' ability to adjust for the differences in a few well-known and clearly disclosed accounting techniques.

2. Research on the impact of accounting changes having no direct cash-flow (tax) effects showed both cases where (a) investors reacted rationally to changes in accounting techniques and (b) investors did not "see through" the veil of accounting practices.

3. Research on the impact of accounting changes having substantive direct cash-flow effects showed results that are generally inconsistent with investor rationality. For example, with respect to the market reaction to the adoption of LIFO, most of the studies show a negative market reaction. In this case, it is also very tempting to rely on a naive investor hypothesis or a functional fixation hypothesis as an explanation. As will be suggested later, various methodological limitations need to be corrected, and future research may he needed to provide additional insights into the nature of the market response to LIFO adoption.

C. The market impact of accounting regulation

The interest in these studies is with the market effects of accounting regulation. Concerted research effects in this area have focused on line-of-business, oil and gas accounting, and replacement costs, to name only a few. The main evidence is that concerted and direct research effects in this area seem to create convergent results. For example:

1. mandated line-of-business information has affected investor assessment of the return distributions of multiproduct firms;

2. the FASB and SEC regulations on the "full cost"/"successful-effects" issue are associated with statistically significant stock price reactions of oil and gas stocks;

3. price-adjusted estimates of earnings as well as replacement cost data did not generate any noticeable market reaction.

One consequence of this research is the increased demand for these studies by policy-makers, aware of the relevance of research to the consequences of their decisions. The research, however, has failed to answer fundamental questions:

The cynic is still tempted to say "so what?" to the many identified consequences of regulations. The key question still open can be stated as follows: How do we identify a successful or effective regulation? A corollary is: What market variables are potentially relevant and why? ... Formal theoretical analysis has the advantage of guiding research toward variables that bear directly on the impact of regulation. This is not to suggest that the identification of such variables would lead to a direct or easy resolution of policy, issues just that the variables researched would be more relevant.[113]

D. Impact on related disciplines

The interest is with the contribution of market-based research in accounting to accounting and related disciplines. We will evaluate the research in terms of the implications of the evidence for financial reporting and in terms of the adequacy of the methodology used.

A. Implications of the evidence for financial reporting. The findings identified earlier are not trivial. They have important implications for corporate financial reporting and planning. For example, Copeland uses the empirical evidence on the effect of various accounting changes in efficient capital markets to suggest the following implications for corporate financial reporting and planning:

1. Relevant new information, which will affect the future cash flows of the firm, should be announced as soon as it becomes available, so that shareholders can use it without the (presumably greater) expense of discovering it from alternative sources.

2. The most important information is forward-looking. Old news is no news. Shareholders are interested in information that can be presented in the President's letter or in an unaudited section of the annual report: information such as how much new investment is planned; what is the expected rate of return; how long will the expected rate be favorable; how much new equity will be issued; what is the firm's target capital structure; what are its plans and policies with respect to repurchasing its own common stock; and what is its dividend policy?

3. It does not matter whether cash-flow effects are reported in the balance sheet, in the income statement, or in footnotes; the market can evaluate the news as long as it is publicly available, whatever form it may take.

4. The market reacts to the cash-flow impact of management decisions, not to the effect on reported earnings per share. Companies should never seek to increase earnings per share if cash flow will decline as a result.

5. The Securities and Exchange Commission (SEC) should conduct a thorough cost–benefit analysis of all proposed changes in disclosure requirements. It can be aided in its efforts by academic studies, which, in some cases, have already demonstrated that certain types of disclosure are irrelevant.[114]

Above all, most of the evidence cited earlier seems to imply that capital markets are reasonably efficient handlers of accounting information and may be used to evaluate published numbers. This optimism is not, however, generally shared.

First, the efficient market hypothesis has been contested by Gonedes and Dopuch on the grounds that stock-price associations are not sufficient grounds on which to evaluate alternative information systems, and that social-welfare considerations are needed.[115] More specifically, Gonedes and Dopuch have identified two assertions used in the predictive approach for the evaluation of alternative accounting procedures:

1. Capital-market efficiency, taken by itself, provides justification for using prices of (or rates of return on) firms' ownership shares in assessing the desirability of alternative accounting procedures or regulations.

2. Capital-market efficiency, taken by itself, provides justification for using prices of (or rates of return on) firms' ownership shares in assessing the effects of alternative accounting procedures or regulations.[116]

Gonedes and Dopuch argue that the contemporary institutional setting allows a "free-rider" effect that makes the desirability assertion (1) logically invalid, although they consider the effects assertion (2) to be valid.

Second, the efficient market hypothesis and the empirical evidence supporting it are silent concerning the "optimal" amount of information. This point in particular is recognized in the SEC's Sommer Report (after its chairman, Al Sommer, Jr.) as follows:

> The "efficient market hypothesis" – which asserts that the current price of a security reflects all publicly available information – even if valid, does not negate the necessity of a mandatory disclosure system. This theory is concerned with how the market reacts to disclosed information and is silent as to the optimum amount of information required or whether that optimum should be achieved on a mandatory or voluntary basis; market forces alone are insufficient to cause all material information to be disclosed. …[117]

Third, a qualifier has been omitted in all of the studies cited earlier. The qualifier is whether the firm's decision-making is unchanged as a result of the accounting change, because market efficiency may be implied only if both no change in stock prices and the firm's decision-making are observed. This point is emphasized as follows:

> If the accounting change triggered a revision of the decision-making process which would, if extrapolated, alter the anticipated performance of the entity, and if the stock price remained unchanged, then market inefficiency would be the conclusion.[118]

Fourth, finding what information is used and should be provided to investors may be difficult. Published numbers are not the only source of information in terms of content and quality, and the task may be too complex for regulators and researchers to solve.

> Fifth, most of the empirical research cited suffers from the absence of a theory "to predict who should be better or worse off by accounting policy changes and which changes, if any, might include changes in management behavior to offset the effect of an accounting policy change …".[119]

Sixth, some major arguments exist against the use of the predictive approach with capital markets. For example, it has been argued that users individually or in aggregate react because they have been conditioned to react to accounting data, rather than because the data have any informational content. Accordingly, observations of users' reaction should not guide the formulation of an accounting theory. Sterling contends that:

> If the response of receivers to accounting stimuli is to be taken as evidence that certain kinds of accounting practices are justified, then we must not overlook the possibility that those responses were conditioned. Accounting reports have been issued for a long time, and their issuance has been accompanied by a rather impressive ceremony performed by the managers and accountants who issue them.

The receivers are likely to have gained the impression that they ought to react and have noted that others react, and thereby have become conditioned to react.[120]

It may also be argued that the recipients of accounting information react when they should not react or do not react the way they should.

B. Adequacy of the methodology used. Most of the empirical evidence on the information content of financial accounting numbers rests on research designs and methodological assumptions, which are frequently the subject of critical assessment.[121]

1. *Anomalous evidence regarding market efficiency:* There are a number of scattered pieces of anomalous evidence regarding market efficiency. Ball, who examined evidence showing that, post-announcement, risk-adjusted abnormal returns are systematically nonzero in the period following earnings announcements, argues that the anomalous evidence is due to inadequacies in the two-parameter, capital-asset pricing model used to adjust for risk differentials and to market inefficiencies.[122]

   Watts, however, examined evidence on systematic abnormal returns after quarterly earnings announcements to determine whether they emanate from market inefficiencies or deficiencies in the asset-pricing model.[123] The results show the abnormal returns to be due to market inefficiencies, and not to asset-pricing model inefficiencies. As a result, some accounting studies were based on dependent variables other than the change in security price, or some variant such as yield, volatility, or security beta. An analysis of trading volume is recommended when the theory suggests that the disclosure change may cause a change in the level of consensus. Other suggested dependent variables are a change in the variance–covariance structure, when it is deemed that the disclosure changes affect the risk levels of firms, and the use of systematic risk. Newer methodologies have also been proposed; these include the use of option prices and the use of intraday stock prices.[124]

2. *Self-selection bias and omitted variables:* One objective of the research design in capital market studies is to determine whether the observed market reaction is due to the variables being examined and to ensure that the reaction is caused by the variable of interest, and not by some other variable. This is basically a control problem.

   Hence, most studies evaluating the impact of accounting changes have shown an earnings bias, meaning that the changes in reported earnings of the firms are negatively related to the income effect of the accounting change.[125] This creates a systematic self-selection bias, given that a systematic characteristic of all these firms also affects market performance. This self-selection bias is in fact the result of a failure to account for other omitted variables that have an impact on market reaction. The impact of omitted variables should be thoroughly addressed in capital-market studies.

3. *Confounding effects:* A confounding effect arises with the release of other unrelated and relevant informational items by some of the test firms during the time period of interest. Thus effect can pose a serious threat to the internal validity of the study. Five alternative approaches to controlling for unrelated information events have been proposed:

   (a) Alternative 1: Retain all firms in the sample, and partition the firms into various event combination categories.

   (b) Alternative 2: Delete firms experiencing other events in the time period from the sample.

(c) Alternative 3: Retain all firms in the sample, but delete an "appropriate" time-period for each announcement.

(d) Alternative 4: Retain all firms in the sample, explicitly estimate the capital market efficiency of other events, and subtract this estimate from the observed return for the sample.

(e) Alternative 5: Retain all firms in the sample, and assume that the net position of other events is minimal.[126]

4. *The timing of capital-market impact:* The choice of the most appropriate time to investigate the market reaction to an event is crucial to the interpretation of the results of a study. Although the date of public disclosure is the most evident and popular, the problem remains that the reaction may be anticipated or delayed, depending on the nature of the accounting issue being investigated. For instance, Foster refers to the fact that a policy process occurs in conjunction with many accounting issues, during which the following information can be disseminated to the market:

(a) Information relating to the policy decision itself.

(b) Information relating to the information that firms will release in compliance with a specific decision.

(c) Information relating to the actions that management will take in response to a specific decision.[127]

Given this complex situation, the researcher must determine which event or set of events is the relevant one to examine.

5. *The choice of control group:* The most effective research design used in capital-market studies of accounting policy decision is the pre-test/post-test control group design, in which

Group A: $O_1 \chi O_2$
Group B: $O_3 O_4$

where O_1 is the capital-market reaction observation at point i and χ is the experimental effect expressed as either (1) the announcement of a policy decision by a standard-setting body, or (2) the firm's disclosure of the "mandated" informational items. Although laboratory experimentation dictates a random assignment of firms to O_2 and O_4 samples, capital-market studies rely on self-selection, given the impossibility of random assignment. A self-selection bias is created in that the differences between O_2 and O_4 may not be due to the impact of χ but to differences between the samples. To alleviate the self-selection problem, Foster provided the two tests as interval validity checks:

(a) A firm profile analysis.

(b) A nontreatment period, security-return analysis.[128]

6. *Behavioral finance:* A new theory in finance is challenging the concept of market efficiency, arguing that stock prices adjust slowly to information, so that one must examine returns over long horizons to get a full view of market inefficiency. DeBondt and Thaler[129] examined the long-term returns of stocks and noticed that past winners tend to be future losers and vice versa. The long-term returns reversals are attributed to investor overreaction.

Another behavioral model proposed by Barberis, Shleifer and Vishny (BSV)[130] relies on two judgment biases from cognitive psychology: (a) the representativeness bias of Kahneman and Tversky[131] which maintains that people give too much weight to recent patterns in the data and too little to the properties of the population that generates the data, and (b) the conservatism of Edwards[132] that shows the slow updating of models in the face of new evidence. The BSV model is explained as follows:

In the model of stock prices proposed by BSV to capture the two judgment biases, earnings are a random walk, but investors falsely perceive that there are two earnings regimes. In regime A, which investors assume is more likely, earnings are mean-reverting. When investors decide regime A holds, a stock's price under-reacts to a change in earnings because investors mistakenly think the change is likely to be temporary. When this expectation is not confirmed by later earnings, stock prices show a delayed response to earlier earnings. In regime B, which investors think is less likely, a run of earnings changes of the same sign leads investors to perceive that a firm's earnings are trending. Once investors are convinced that the trending regime B holds, they incorrectly extrapolate the trend and the stock price overreacts. Because earnings are a random walk, the overreaction is exposed by future earnings, leading to reversal of long-term returns.[133]

A third behavioral model proposed by Daniel, Hieshleifer and Subrahmanyam[134] (DHS) attempts to explain how the judgment biases of investors can produce overreaction to some extent and underreaction to others. The DHS model is explained as follows:

The DHS model has different behavioral foundations than the BSV model. In DHS there are informed and uninformed investors. The uninformed are not subject to judgment biases. But stock prices are determined by the informed investors, and they are subject to two biases, overconfidence and biased self-attribution. Overconfidence leads them to exaggerate the precision of their private signals about value, especially when the public signals contradict their private signals. Overreaction to private information and underreaction to public information tend to produce short-term continuation of stock returns but long-term reversals as public information eventually overwhelms the behavioral biases.[135]

7. *Chaos theory*: Based on the capital assets pricing model (CAPM), modern profitability theory (MPT) and the efficient market hypothesis (EMH), the capital market research (CMR) paradigms in accounting provide the framework for testing the analysis of accounting information. Witness the following statement:

The link provided by capital market theories connects the accounting information system to its function in capital markets. Information has a dual role in these markets. First, it aids in establishing a set of equilibrium security prices that affects the allocation of "real" resources and the productive decisions implemented by firms. Second, it enables individuals to exchange claims to present and future consumption across different states, thereby attaining both preferred patterns of lifetime consumption and the sharing of social risks. This explicit conceptualization of the role of information in capital markets appears to provide the elusive operational framework for the systematic analysis of alternative accounting information systems.[136]

However, theories of complexity and chaos, with a wide-ranging new vision of the relationship between order and disorder, pose a new challenge to CMR. Based on Mandelbrot's[137] early studies on fractal theory, Peters[138] offered the following proposal for a fractal market hypothesis (FMH).

Markets exist to provide a stable, liquid environment for trading. Investors wish to get a good price, but that would not necessarily be a "fair" price in the economic sense. ... Markets remain stable when many investors participate and have many different investment horizons. When a five-minute trader experiences a six-sigma event, an investor with a longer investment horizon must step in and stabilize the market. The investor will do so because, within his or her investment horizon, the five-minute trader's six-sigma event is not unusual. As long as another investor has a longer trading horizon than the investor in crisis, the market will stabilize itself. For this reason, investors must share the same risk levels (once an adjustment is made for the scale of the investment horizon), and the shared risk explains why the frequency distribution of returns looks the same at different investment horizons. We call this proposal the *Fractal Market Hypothesis* because of this self-similar statistical structure.[139]

Similarly, researchers at the Santa Fe Institute (SFI) are examining financial markets as complex adaptive systems generating results that are also contradictory to the traditional CMR paradigm, but appear to be quite congruent with actual stock price behavior. The end results of both the FMH and the SFI's work are summarized as follows:

> Both the FMH and the preliminary results of the SFI's stock market simulations point to the likelihood that heterogeneous expectations and various forms of "crowd behavior" produce stock price behavior that contradicts the assumptions of the financial economics paradigm. They both point out to the occurrence of price bubbles (persistent moves away from underlying fundamental values) and market crashes, implying that prices do not consistently tend to adjust instantaneously to new information. In fact, much of the price movement in the stock market appears to be generated by the market itself. In sum, both the FMH and the SFI's preliminary simulation results tend to undermine the validity of MPT, the CAPM, and the EMH itself.[140]

The new views of stock price behavior generated by chaos theory and complexity theory suggest that some investors and traders may use accounting information and some may not. In fact, they suggest that some individuals may even use accounting information during certain periods but may employ technical (non-fundamentalist) approaches at other times. It would seem, therefore, that if academic accountants wish to study the way financial accounting information is actually used, they would be well advised to follow the lead of many management accounting researchers and explore the potential of qualitative research and field work techniques to study the use of financial accounting information in the contexts in which it is actually constructed and used.[141]

12.3.18 Incomplete revelation hypothesis (IRH)

One wonders how useful is the efficient market hypothesis (EMH) that prices under-react to large earnings changes, ratios of prices to fundamentals, and other statistics derived from fundamental accounting analyses. Are the known evidences of mispricing statistical errors derived from fundamental accounting analyses? Are these evidences of mispricing statistical flukes resulting from fishing expeditions? To answer these concerns and questions, Bloomfield offered an alternative to the efficient market hypothesis called the "incomplete revelation hypothesis" (IRH).[142] Based on the "noisy rational expectations" models, the IRH identifies "noise traders" as agents that collect information about the value of an asset but elect to trade only randomly and sometimes irrationally. The end result is that the noise keeps prices in the market from revealing information completely.[143] Given the amount of data released by firms, translating these data into useful statistics can create a "trading interest" derived as "the additional shares traders are willing to trade for given deviations of market price from the value indicated by the statistic in question".[144] This allows the formulation of IRH as follows:

> Statistics that are more costly to extract from public data are less completely revealed by market prices. This association is driven by the following causal chain:
>
> • Statistics that are more costly to extract from publicly available information drive less trading interest.
>
> • Statistics that drive less trading interest are less completely revealed by market prices.[145]

Therefore what determines market reactions are the statistics that are more easily extracted from public data and the investors' attraction to these statistics.

12.4 Conclusions

The new approaches to the formulation of an accounting theory differ from the traditional approaches in terms of their novelty, their less general acceptance, and their reliance on verification. They present innovative and more empirically oriented methods of resolving accounting issues. The influence of the new approaches is manifested in the accounting literature of the last decade.

Notes

1. Beaver, W.H., Kennelly, J.W., and Voss, W.M., "Predictive Ability as a Criterion for the Evaluation of Accounting Data", *The Accounting Review* (October, 1968), p. 675.
2. *A Statement of Basic Accounting Theory*, Chapter 3 (New York: American Accounting Association, 1966).
3. Beaver, W.H., Kennelly, J.W., and Voss, W.M., "Predictive Ability as a Criterion for the Evaluation of Accounting Data", p. 676.
4. Ibid.
5. Ibid.
6. Cogger, K., "A Time-Series Analytic Approach to Aggregation Issues in Accounting Data", *Journal of Accounting Research* (Autumn, 1981), pp. 285–98.
7. Dharan, B.C., "Identification and Estimation Issues for a Causal Earnings Mode", *Journal of Accounting Research* (Spring, 1983), pp. 18–41.
8. Dopuch, N., and Watts, R.L., "Using Time-Series Models to Assess the Significance of Accounting Changes", *Journal of Accounting Research* (Spring, 1972), pp. 180–94.
9. Foster, G., "Quarterly Accounting Data: Time-Series Properties and Predictive Ability Results", *The Accounting Review* (January, 1977), pp. 1–21.
10. Griffin, P.A., "The Time-Series Behavior of Quarterly Earnings: Preliminary Evidence", *Journal of Accounting Research* (Spring, 1977), pp. 71–83.
11. Ball, Ray, and Foster, George, "Corporate Financing Reporting: A Methodological Review of Empirical Research", *Studies on Current Research Methodologies in Accounting: A Critical Evaluation*, supplement to Vol. 20, *Journal of Accounting Research* (1982), p. 209.
12. Watts, R.L., and Leftwich, R.W., "The Time-Series of Annual Accounting Earnings", *Journal of Accounting Research* (Autumn, 1977), pp. 253–71.
13. Albrecht, W.S., Lookabill, L.L., and McKeown, J.C., "The Time-Series Properties of Annual Accounting Earnings", *Journal of Accounting Research* (Autumn, 1977), pp. 226–44.

14. Collins, W.A., and Hopwood, W.S., "A Multivariate Analysis of Annual Earnings Forecasts Generated from Quarterly Forecasts of Financial Analysis and Univariate Time-Series Models", *Journal of Accounting Research* (Autumn, 1980), pp. 390–406.

15. Collins, D.W., "Predicting Earnings with Subentity Data: Some Further Evidence", *Journal of Accounting Research* (Spring, 1976), pp. 163–77.

16. Manegold, J.G., "Time-Series Properties of Earnings: A Comparison of Extrapolative and Component Models", *Journal of Accounting Research* (Autumn, 1981), pp. 360–73.

17. Scott, J., "The Probability of Bankruptcy: A Comparison of Empirical Predictions and Theoretical Models", *Journal of Banking and Finance* (September, 1981), p. 320.

18. Beaver, W.H., "Financial Ratios and Predictors of Failure", *Empirical Research in Accounting: Selected Studies*, supplement to Vol. 4, *Journal of Accounting Research* (1966), pp. 71–111.

19. Altman, E.I., "Predicting Railroad Bankruptcies in America", *Bell Journal of Economics and Management Science* (Spring, 1973), pp. 184–211.

20. Ohlson, J.A., "Financial Ratios and Probabilistic Prediction of Bankruptcy", *Journal of Accounting Research* (Spring, 1980), pp. 109–31.

21. Ibid.

22. Ball, R., and Foster, G., "Corporate Financial Reporting: A Methodological Review of Empirical Research", *Journal of Accounting Research* (20, supplement, 1982), p. 218.

23. Jones, Frederick L., "Current Techniques in Bankruptcy Predictions", *Journal of Accounting Literature* (6, 1987), pp. 131–64.

24. Fisher, L., "Determinants of Risk Premium on Corporate Bonds", *Journal of Political Economy* (June, 1959), pp. 217–37.

25. Horrigan, J.O., "The Determination of Long-Term Credit Standing with Financial Ratios", *Empirical Research in Accounting: Selected Studies*, supplement to Vol. 4, *Journal of Accounting Research* (1966), pp. 44–62; Pinches, G.E., and Mingo, K.A., "A Multivariate Analysis of Industrial Bond Ratings", *Journal of Finance* (March, 1973), pp. 1–18; Belkaoui, A., "Industrial Bond Ratings: A Discriminant Analysis Approach", *Financial Management* (Autumn, 1980), pp. 44–51; Belkaoui, A., *Industrial Bonds and the Rating Process* (Westport, CT: Greenwood Press, 1984).

26. Altman, E.I., and Katz, S., "Statistical Bond-Rating Classification Using Financial and Accounting Data", in M. Schiff and G.H. Sorter (eds.), *Proceedings of the Conference on Topical Research in Accounting* (New York: New York University Press, 1976), pp. 205–39.

27. Horton, J.J., "Statistical Classification of Municipal Bonds", *Journal of Bank Research* (Autumn, 1970), pp. 29–40.

28. Belkaoui, A., *Industrial Bonds and the Rating Process*, op. cit.

29. Ibid.

30. Marris, R.N., *The Economic Theory of Managerial Capitalism* (New York: Macmillan, 1964).

31. Gort, Michael, "An Economic Disturbance Theory of Mergers", *Quarterly Journal of Economics* (November, 1969), pp. 624–43.

32. Bonford, M.D., "Changes in the Evaluation of Equities", *The Investment Analyst* (December, 1968), pp. 62–75.

33. Tzoannos, J.T., and Samuels, J.M., "Mergers and Takeovers: The Financial Characteristics of Companies Involved", *Journal of Business Finance* (July, 1972), pp. 5–16.

34. Chambers, R.J., "Finance Information and the Securities Market", *Abacus* (September, 1965), pp. 4–30.

35. Taussig, R.A., and Hayes, S.L., III, "Cash Takeovers and Accounting Valuation", *The Accounting Review* (January, 1968), pp. 68–72.

36. Vance, J.S., "Is Your Company a Takeover Target?" *Harvard Business Review* (May–June, 1969), pp. 93–102.

37. Monroe, R.J., and Sinkowitz, M.A., "Investment Characteristics of Conglomerate Targets: A Discriminant Analysis", *Southern Journal of Business* (November, 1971), pp. 59–81.

38. Single, A., "Takeovers, Economic Natural Selection, and the Theory of the Firm: Evidence from the Post-War United Kingdom Experience", *The Economic Journal* (September, 1975), pp. 497–515.

39. Stevens, D.L., "Financial Characteristics of Merged Firms: A Multivariate Analysis", *Journal of Financial and Quantitative Analysis* (March, 1973), pp. 149–58.

40. Baker, J.K., Miller, T.O., and Rarnsberger, B.J., "A Typology of Merger Motives", *Akron Business and Economic Review* (Winter, 1981), pp. 24–5.

41. Schipper, K., and Smith, A., "Effects of Recontracting on Shareholder Wealth: The Case of Voluntary Spin-Offs", *Journal of Financial Economics* (December, 1983), pp. 43–67.

42. Boisjoly, R.E., and Corsi, T.M., "A Profile of Motor Carrier Acquisitions, 1976 to 1978", *Akron, Business and Economic Review* (Summer, 1982), pp. 30–5.

43. Harris, R.S., Stewart, J.E., Guilkey, D.K., and Carleton, W.T., "Characteristics of Acquired Firms: Fixed and Random Coefficients Probits Analyses", *Southern Economic Journal* (July, 1982), pp. 164–84.

44. Rege, W.P., "Accounting Ratios to Locate Takeovers Targets", *Journal of Business Finance and Accounting* (Autumn, 1984), pp. 302–11.

45. Dietrich, J.K., and Sorensen, E., "An Application of Logit Analysis to Prediction of Merger Targets", *Journal of Business Research* (September, 1984), pp. 393–402.

46. Palepu, K., "Predicting Takeover Targets: A Methodological and Empirical Analysis", *Journal of Accounting and Economics* (March, 1986), pp. 3–35.

47. Meeks, G., *Disappointing Marriage: A Study of the Gains from Mergers* (Cambridge: Cambridge University Press, 1977).

48. Mueller, D.C., "A Cross-National Comparison of the Results", in D.C. Mueller (ed.), *The Determinants and Effects of Mergers* (Cambridge, MA: Oegeschlager, Gann & Hain, 1980).

49. Barnes, Paul, "The Prediction of Takeover Targets in the UK by Means of Multiple Discriminant Analysis", *Journal of Business Finance and Accounting* (Spring, 1990), pp. 73–84.

50. Belkaoui, Ahmed, "Financial Ratios as Predictors of Canadian Takeovers", *Journal of Business Finance and Accounting* (5, Spring, 1978), pp. 93–101.

51. Ewert, D.C., *Trade Credit Management: Selection of Accounts Receivable Using a Statistical Model,* Research Monograph No. 79 (Atlanta: Georgia State University, 1980).

52. Backer, Morton, and Gosman, M.L., *Financial Reporting and Business Liquidity* (New York: National Association of Accountants, 1987).

53. Clarkson, G.P.E., *Portfolio Selection: A Simulation of Trust Investment* (Englewood Cliffs, NJ: Prentice-Hall, 1962).

54. Cohen, K.J., Gilmore, T.C., and Singer, F.A., "Bank Procedures for Analyzing Business Loan Applications", in K.J. Cohen and F.S. Hammer (eds.), *Analytical Methods in Banking* (Homewood, IL: Richard D. Irwin, 1966).

55. Orgler, Yuie E., "A Credit-Scoring Model for Commercial Loans", *Journal of Money, Credit and Banking* (2, November, 1970), pp. 435–45.

56. Dietrich, J.R., and Kaplan, Robert S., "Empirical Analysis of Commercial Loan Classification Decisions", *The Accounting Review* (January, 1982), pp. 18–38.

57. Sinkey, J.F., Jr., "A Multivariate Statistical Analysis of the Characteristics of Problem Banks", *Journal of Finance* (March, 1975), pp. 21–36.

58. Pettaway, R.H., and Sinkey, J.F., Jr., "Establishing On-Site Bank Examination Priorities: An Early-Warning System Using Accounting and Market Information", *Journal of Finance* (March, 1980), pp. 137–50.

59. Abdel-Khalik, A.R., and Thompson, R.B., "Research on Earnings Forecasts: The State of the Art", *The Accounting Journal* (Winter, 1977–78), p. 192.

60. Griffin, P.A., *Usefulness to Investors and Creditors of Information Provided by Financial Reporting: A Review of Empirical Accounting Research*, Research Report (Stamford, CT: Financial Accounting Standards Board, 1982), p. 83.

61. Gonedes, N.J., "Efficient Capital Markets and External Accounting", *The Accounting Review* (January, 1972), p. 12.

62. Beaver, W.H., and Dukes, R.E., "Inter-period Tax Allocation, Earnings Expectations, and the Behavior of Security Prices", *The Accounting Review* (April, 1972), p. 321.

63. Beaver, W.H., "The Behavior of Security Prices and Its Implications for Accounting Research (Methods)", *The Accounting Review* (April, 1972), p. 408.

64. Samuelson, P., "Proof That Properly Discounted Present Values of Assets Vibrate Randomly", *Bell Journal of Economics and Management Science* (Autumn, 1973), pp. 369–74.

65. Lorie, J., and Hamilton, M., *The Stock Market: Theories and Evidence* (Homewood, IL: Richard D. Irwin, 1973).

66. Fama, E.F., "Efficient Capital Markets: A Review of Theory and Empirical Work", *Journal of Finance* (May, 1970), pp. 383–417.

67. Verrecchia, R.E., "Consensus Beliefs, Information Acquisition, and Market Information Efficiency", *The American Economic Review* (December, 1980), pp. 874–84.

68. Rubinstein, M., "Securities Market Efficiency in an Arrow-Debreu Economy", *American Economic Review* (December, 1975), pp. 812–24.

69. Grossman, S.J., and Stiglitz, J.E., "Information and Competitive Price Systems", *The American Economic Review* (May, 1976), pp. 246–53.

70. Beaver, W.H., "Market Efficiency", *The Accounting Review* (January, 1981), p. 28.

71. Ibid.

72. Malkiel, B., "Efficient Market Hypotheses", in P. Newman, M. Milgate and J. Eatwell (eds.), *New Palgrave Dictionary of Money and Finance* (London, UK: Macmillan, 1992).

73. Black, F., "Toward a Fully Automated Stock Exchange", *Financial Analysts Journal* (July–August, 1971), pp. 29–44.

74. Leroy, S., "Risk Aversion and the Martingale Property of Stock Returns", *Journal of Economic Literature* (27, 1989), pp. 1583–621.

75. Campbell, John Y., Lo, Andrew W., and Mackinlay, A. Craig, *The Econometrics of Financial Markets* (Princeton, NJ: Princeton University Press, 1997).

76. Fama, E.F., "Efficient Capital Markets: A Review of Theory and Empirical Work", op. cit., p. 383.

77. Edwards, R., and Magee, J., *Technical Analysis of Stock Trends* (Boston: John Magee, 1966).

78. Jensen, M.C., "Risk, the Pricing of Capital Assets, and the Evaluation of Investment Portfolios", *Journal of Business* (April, 1969), p. 170.

79. Niederhoffer, V., and Osborne, M.F.M., "Market Making and Reversal on the Stock Exchange", *Journal of the American Statistical Association* (December, 1966), pp. 897–916.

80. Sharpe, W.F., "Capital-Asset Prices: A Theory of Market Equilibrium Under Conditions of Risk", *Journal of Finance* (September, 1974), pp. 425–42; Lintner, J., "The Valuation of Risky Assets and the Selection of Risky Investment in Stock Portfolios and Capital Budgets", *Review of Economics and Statistics* (February, 1965),

pp. 13–37, Mossin, J., "Equilibrium in a Capital-Asset Market", *Economica* (October, 1966), pp. 768–83.

81. Ross, S.A., "The Arbitrage Theory of Capital Asset Pricing", *Journal of Economic Theory* (December, 1976), pp. 341–60.

82. Chen, Nai-Fu, Roll, Richard, and Ross, Stephen A., "Economic Forces and the Stock Market", *Journal of Business* (July, 1986), pp. 383–403.

83. Berry, Michael A., Burmeister, Edwin, and McElroy, Marjorie B., "Sorting Out Risks Using; Known APT Factors", *Financial Analysts Journal* (March–April, 1988), pp. 29–42.

84. Sharpe, William F., Alexander, Gordon J., and Bailey, Jeffrey V., *Investments* (Englewood Cliffs, NJ: Prentice-Hall, 1995), p. 337.

85. Fama, E., and French, K., "Common Risk Factors in the Returns on Stocks and Bonds", *Journal of Financial Economics* (33, 1993), pp. 3–56.

86. Black, F., and Scholes, M., "The Pricing of Options and Corporate Liabilities", *Journal of Political Economy* (May–June, 1973), pp. 637–54.

87. Markovitz, J., "Portfolio Selection", *Journal of Finance* (March, 1952), pp. 77–9.

88. Sharpe, W.F., "A Simplified Model of Portfolio Analysis", *Management Science* (January, 1963), pp. 277–93.

89. Ibbotson, R.G., "Price Performance of Common Stock New Issues", *Journal of Financial Economics* (September, 1975), pp. 235–72.

90. Sarris, A.H., "Kalman Filter Models: A Bayesian Approach to Estimation of Time Varying Regression Coefficient", *Annuals of the Economic and Social Measurement* (Fall, 1973), pp. 501–23.

91. Chen, S.N., and Lee, C.F., "Bayesian and Mixed Estimators of Time Varying Betas", *Journal of Economics and Business* (December, 1982), pp. 91–301.

92. Ahn, Byungjun, and Sung, Hyun Mo, "The Bayesian Random Coefficient Market Model in Event Studies: The Case of Earnings Announcements", *Journal of Business Finance and Accounting* (September, 1995), pp. 907–22.

93. Ibid., p. 910.

94. Scholes, M., and Williams, J., "Estimating Betas from Non-synchronous Data", *Journal of Financial Economics* (December, 1977), pp. 309–28.

95. Cohen, K., Hawawini, G., Mayer, S., Schwartz, R., and Whitcomb, D., "Friction in the Trading Process and the Estimation of Systematic Risk", *Journal of Financial Economics* (August, 1983), pp. 263–70.

96. Vasicek, O., "A Note on Using Cross-Sectional Information in Bayesian Estimation of Security Betas", *Journal of Finance* (December, 1973), pp. 1233–9.

97. Karpik, P., and Belkaoui, A., "The Relative Relationship Between Systematic Risk and Value Added Variables", *Journal of International Financial Management and Accounting* (Autumn, 1989), pp. 259–76.

98. Campbell, John Y., Lo, Andrew W., and Mackinlay, A. Craig, *The Econometrics of Financial Markets* (Princeton, NJ: Princeton University Press), 1997, pp. 151–2.

99. Preinreich, G.A.D., "Annual Survey of Economic Theory: The Theory of Depreciation", *Econometrica* (6, 1938), pp. 219–41.

100. Lo, Kin, and Lys, Thomas, "The Ohlson Model: Contribution to Valuation Theory, Limitations, and Empirical Applications", *Journal of Accounting, Auditing and Finance* (Summer, 2000), pp. 337–67.

101. Ohlson, J., "Earnings, Book Values, and Dividends in Equity Valuation", *Contemporary Accounting Research* (Spring, 1995), pp. 661–87.

102. Feltham, G., and Ohlson, J.A., "Valuation and Clean Surplus Accounting for Operating and Financial Activities", *Contemporary Accounting Research* (Spring, 1995), pp. 689–731.

103. Liu, Jing, and Ohlson, James A., "The Feltham–Ohlson (1995) Model: Empirical Implications", *Journal of Accounting Auditing and Finance* (Summer, 2000), pp. 331–7.

104. Ibid., p. 324.

105. Burgstahler, David C., and Dichev, Ilia A., "Earnings, Adaptations and Equity Value", *The Accounting Review* (April, 1997), pp. 197–216.

106. Lev, B., "Some Economic Determinants of Time-Series Properties of Earnings", *Journal of Accounting and Economics* (5, 1983), pp. 31–48.

107. Baginski, S.P., Lorek, K.S., Willinger, G.L., and Branson, B.C., "The Relationship between Economic Characteristics and Alternative Annual Earnings Persistence Measures", *The Accounting Review* (74, 1999), pp. 105–20.

108. AlNajjar, Fouad, and Riahi-Belakoui, Ahmed, "Multinationality as a Determinant of Earnings Persistence", *Managerial Finance* (3, 2002), pp. 83–96.

109. Flavin, M., "The Adjustment of Consumption to Changing Expectations about Future Income", *Journal of Political Economy* (89, 1981), pp. 974–1009.

110. Kormendi, R., and Lipe, R., "Earnings Innovation, Earnings Persistence, and Stock Returns", *Journal of Business* (60, 1987), pp. 323–45.

111. For an in-depth review of corporate valuation models, see Soffer, Leonard C., and Soffer, Robin J. *Financial Statement Analysis: A Valuation Approach* (Upper Saddle River, NJ: Prentice-Hall, 2002).

112. Ball, R.J., and Brown, P., "An Empirical Evaluation of Accounting Income Number", *Journal of Accounting Research* (Autumn, 1968), pp. 103–26.

113. Lev, B., and Ohlson, J.A., "Market-Based Empirical Research in Accounting: A Review, Interpretation, and Extension", op. cit., p. 283.

114. Copeland, R.M., "Efficient Capital Markets: Evidence and Implications for Financial Reporting", *Journal of Accounting, Auditing, and Finance* (Winter, 1981), p. 47.

115. Gonedes, N.I., and Dopuch, N., "Capital-Market Equilibrium Information, Production and Selecting Accounting Techniques: Theoretical Framework and Review of Empirical Work", *Studies on Financial Accounting Objectives: 1974,* supplement to Vol. 12, *Journal of Accounting Research* (1974), pp. 48–129.

116. Ibid., p. 50.

117. *Report of the Advisory Committee on Corporate Disclosure to the Securities and Exchange Commission* (Washington, DC: US Government Printing Office, November, 1977, D-6).

118. Greer, W.R., Jr., and Morrissev, L.E., Jr., "Accounting Rule-Making in a World of Efficient Markets", *Journal of Accounting, Auditing and Finance* (Winter, 1981), p. 56.

119. Griffin, P.A., *Usefulness to Investors and Creditors of Information Provided by Financial Reporting: A Review of Empirical Accounting Research* (Stamford, CT: Financial Accounting Standards Board, 1982), p. 15.

120. Sterling, Robert R., "On Theory Construction and Verification", *The Accounting Review* (July, 1970), p. 453.

121. Many of the methodological issues covered in this section are also discussed in the following manuscripts: Abdel-Khalik, A.R., and Ayjinka, Bipin B., *Empirical Research in Accounting: A Methodological Viewpoint* (Sarasota, FL: American Accounting Association, 1979); Foster, G., "Accounting Policy Decisions and Capital-Market Research", *Journal of Accounting and Economics* (March, 1980), pp. 19–61; Ricks, W., "Market Assessment of Alternative Accounting Methods: A Review of the Empirical Evidence", *Journal of Accounting Literature* (Spring, 1982), pp. 59–99.

122. Ball, R., "Anomalies in Relationships Between Securities' Yields and Yield-Surrogates", *Journal of Financial Economics* (June/September, 1978), pp. 103–26.

123. Watts, R.L., "Systematic 'Abnormal' Returns After Quarterly-Earnings Announcements", *Journal of Financial Economics* (June/September, 1978), pp. 127–50.

124. Patell, J.M., and Wolfson, M.A., "Anticipated Information Releases Reflected in Call-Option Prices", *Journal of Accounting and Economics* (August, 1979), pp. 117–40.

125. Bremster, W.G., "The Earnings Characteristics of Firms Reporting Discretionary Accounting Changes", *The Accounting Review* (July, 1975), pp. 563–73.

126. Foster, G., "Accounting Policy Decisions and Capital-Market Research", op. cit., pp. 55–6.

127. Ibid., p. 39.

128. Ibid., pp. 47–8.

129. DeBondt, W., and Thaler, R., "Does the Stock Market Overact?" *Journal of Finance* (40, 1985), pp. 793–805.

130. Barberis, N., Shleifer, A., and Vishny R., "A Model of Investor Sentinent", *Journal of Financial Economics* (49, 1998), pp. 307–43.

131. Kahneman, D., and Tversky, A., "Intuitive Predictions: Biases and Connective Procedures." Reprinted in Kahneman, D., Slovic, A., and Tversky, A., *Judgment Under Uncertainty: Hemistics and Biases* (Cambridge, UK: Cambridge University Press, 1982).

132. Edwards, W., "Conservatism in Human Information Processing", in Kleimmantz, B. (ed.), *Formal Representation of Human Judgment* (New York: Wiley, 1968).

133. Fama, Eugene, F., "Market Efficiency Long-Term Returns, and Behavioral Finance", *Journal of Financial Economics* (49, 1998), pp. 283–306.

134. Daniel, K., Hieshleifer, D., and Subrahmanyam, A., "A Theory of Overconfidence, Self-Attribution, and Security Market Under- or Over-Reactions", Unpublished paper, University of Michigan, 1997.

135. Fama, Eugene F., "Market Efficiency Long-Term Returns, and Behavioral Finance", op. cit., p. 289.

136. Lev, L., and Ohlson, J., "Market-Based Empirical Research in Accounting: A Review Interpretation, and Extension", *Journal of Accounting Research* (20, 1982) Supplement, pp. 249–322.

137. Mandelbrot, B., *The Fractal Geometry of Nature* (New York: W.H. Freeman and Company, 1983).

138. Peters, E., *Fractal Market Analysis: Applying Chaos Theory to Investment and Economics* (New York: John Wiley and Sons, 1994).

139. Ibid., pp. 45–6.

140. Mouck, T., "Capital Market Research and Real World Complexity: The Emerging Challenge of Chaos Theory", *Accounting, Organizations and Society* (23, 2, 1998), p. 211.

141. Ibid., p. 111.

142. Bloomfield, Robert J., "The 'Incomplete Revelation Hypothesis' and Financial Reporting", *Accounting Horizons* (September, 2002), pp. 233–43.

143. Ibid., p. 235.

144. Ibid., p. 235.

145. Ibid., p. 235.

References

Barberis, N., Shleifer, A., and Vishny, R., "A Model of Investor Sentinent", *Journal of Financial Economics* (49, 1998), pp. 307–43.

DeBondt, W., and Thaler, R., "Financial Decision-Making in Market and Firms: A Behavioral Perspective", in R. Jarrow *et al.* (eds.), *Handbooks in OR and MS*, Vol. 9 (Elsevier, Amsterdam, 1995), pp. 385–412.

Fama, Eugene F., "Market Efficiency, Long-Term Returns, and Behavioral Finance", *Journal of Financial Economics* (49, 1998), pp. 283–306.

Lev, B., "On the Usefulness of Earnings and Earnings Research: Lessons and Directions from Two Decades of Empirical Research", *Journal of Accounting Research* (27, 1989), Supplement, pp. 153–92.

Lev, B., and Ohlson, J., "Market Based Empirical Research Accounting: A Review, Interpretation, and Extension", *Journal of Accounting Research* (20, 1982), Supplement, pp. 349–72.

Mouck, T., "Capital Markets and Real World Complexity: The Emerging Challenge of Chaos Theory", *Accounting, Organizations and Society* (23, 2, 1998), pp. 189–215.

Peters, E., *Fractal Market Analysis: Applying Chaos Theory to Investment and Economics* (New York: John Wiley and Sons, 1994).

Riahi-Belkaoui, Ahmed, *Financial Analysis and the Predictability of Important Economic Events* (Westport, CT: Greenwood Publishing, 1998).

Riahi-Belkaoui, Ahmed, *Capital Structure: Determination, Evaluation and Accounting* (Westport, CT: Greenwood Publishing, 1998).

Riahi-Belkaoui, Ahmed, *Earnings Measurements, Determination, Management and Usefulness* (Westport, CT: Greenwood Publishing, 1999).

The positive approach, income smoothing and earnings management

13

13.1 The positive approach

To those who adopt the anthropological/inductive positive paradigm, the basic subject matter is:

1. existing accounting practices, and
2. management's attitudes toward those practices.

Proponents of this view argue, in general, either that the techniques can be derived and justified on the basis of their tested use or that management plays a central role in determining the techniques to be implemented. Consequently, the accounting-research objective associated with the anthropological/inductive paradigm is to understand, explain and predict existing accounting practices. For example, Ijiri views the mission of this paradigmatic approach as follows:

> This type of inductive reasoning to derive goals implicit in the behavior of an existing system is not intended to be pre-established to promote the maintenance of the status quo. The purpose of such exercise is to highlight where changes are most needed and where they are feasible. Changes suggested as a result of such a study have a much better chance of actually being implemented.[1]

13.1.1 The information/economics paradigm

Exemplars of the information/economics paradigm are the works of Crandall, Feltham, and Feltham and Demski.[2] In his pioneering paper, Feltham provided a framework for determining the value of a change in the information system from the viewpoint of the individual making an informational decision (the decision-maker). The framework relies on the individual components that are required to compute the expected payoff (or utility) for a particular information system. The components are:

1. a set of possible actions at each period within a time horizon;
2. a payoff function over the events that occur during the periods;
3. probabilistic relationships between past and future events;
4. events and signals from the information system, including past and future signals; and
5. a set of decision rules as functions of the signals.

The framework states that the value of changing from one information system to another is equal to the difference between the expected payoffs of the two alternatives.

Crandall examined the usefulness of the information/economics paradigm to the future development of accounting theory and offered the applied-information-economics approach as a new mainstream accounting theory. Simply, this approach consists of recognizing explicitly each component of the information/economics model and broadening the scope of accounting design to include all of these components.

The third exemplar, Feltham and Demski's "The Use of Models in Information Evaluation", presents and discusses a model of information choice that views information evaluation in cost–benefit terms and as a sequential process. The entire process is summarized as follows:

> Specification of a particular information system n results in a set of signals being supplied to the decision maker; the decision maker may then use the resulting information in selecting his or her action a; and this action may determine, in part, the events × of the subsequent period. The information evaluation must predict the relationship between each of the above elements: the signal generation process, o (y/n); the decision maker's prediction- and action-choice process, a (y/n); and the relationship between the actions selected and the events that will occur, o (x/y, n, a). In addition, the decision maker must predict the gross payoff w(x) he or she will derive from the events of the subsequent period, as well as the cost of operating the particular information system w[1] (y, n).[3]

To those who adopt information/economics, the basic subject matter is (1) information is an economic commodity and (2) the acquisition of information amounts to a problem of economic choice. The value of information is viewed in terms of a cost–benefit criterion within the formal structure of decision theory and economic theory. Accounting information is evaluated in terms of its ability to improve the quality of the optimal choice in a basic-choice problem that must be resolved by an individual or a number of heterogeneous individuals. A single individual must select among different actions that have different possible outcomes. Assuming consistent, rational-choice behavior governed by the expected-utility hypothesis, the action with the highest expected payoff (or utility) is preferred by the individual. Information in this context is required to revise the probabilities of the original outcomes. Thus the individual may face a two-stage process: a first stage, during which the information system produces different signals, and a second stage, during which the observance of a signal results in a revision of probabilities and a choice of the conditional best action. The information system with the highest expected utility is preferred. The information required for a systematic probability-revision (Bayesian-revision) analysis, in turn, facilitates informational analysis on the basis of the subjective, expected-utility-maximization rule.

The information/economics paradigm draws its insight from various disciplines, including decision theory, game theory, information theory and economics. Some of the analytical models proposed include the decision-theory model, the syndicate-theory model, the information-evaluation decision-maker model, the team-theory model, and the demand-revelation model. Each of these frameworks, relying on a model of the firm, derives the demand for managerial accounting information. The usefulness of each model is based on the degree of congruence between the derived demand and the four observed uses of managerial accounting information, which are the belief-revision use, the performance-evaluation use (including b_1 the motivational use and b_2), and the risk-sharing use.

1. The *decision-theory model*, as proposed by Feltham, presents a framework for determining the value of a change in an information system as the difference between the expected payoff of two alternative systems.[4] Its usefulness is limited to belief revision because it does not include performance evaluation.

2. The *syndicate-theory model* includes multiperson firms jointly choosing a set of actions in the presence of a sharing rule for the resulting uncertainty outcome. Exemplars include papers by Wilson, Demski and Swieringa, and Demski.[5] The situation in this model is explained as follows:

   > Each individual is interested in maximizing his own expected utility through the choice of the action and the sharing rule. The belief revision demand for information can again be derived. In addition, the choice of the action and the sharing rule will have an important effect on the total risk borne by the Syndicate and how that risk is allocated among its members. Since the sharing rule can be based only on jointly observed information, the Syndicate Theory model can be used to derive the risk-sharing use of information. The motivational use of information is still ignored because all a motivational problems are assumed away. In particular, all information is assumed to be publicly available and the action is assumed to be jointly chosen and implemented.[6]

3. The *informational-evaluation-decision-maker model* keeps the multiperson characteristics and includes an owner or information evaluator delegating the action choice to one or more agents. Exemplars include the book by Demski and Feltham.[7] The situation in the model is evaluated as follows: "Since these models do not

explicitly state the agent's utility function, the reader does not know whether the agent is assumed to act in his own best interest. Therefore, any motivational implications derived from these models are suspect."[8]

4. The *team-theory model* includes a multiperson context and a sharing rule as in the syndicate-theory model.[9] The individuals are assumed to act in their own best interests using information available only to them and keeping the welfare of the team in mind. The situation in this model is evaluated as follows:

> The problem for the team is to choose the individual decision rule in order to maximize the team's welfare in the presence of decentralized information. Clearly, the belief revision use of information can be derived from the Team Model, but there is no motivational role for information in the Team Model since all individuals are assumed to have the same preferences. Each team member will therefore implement whichever decision rule is given to him. Further, the assumption of identical preferences implies that technological constraints are the only impediments to the full sharing and utilization of the privately acquired information. That is, when information can be transmitted in a Team setting, it is assumed to be transmitted honestly. In a more realistic setting, self-interest as well as technology may prevent the full and honest communication of information within the firm.[10]

5. The *demand-revelation model* is similar to the team-theory model with the additional issue of how to induce agents to reveal their private information honestly and to use it to maximize the profits of the organization. Exemplars are provided in the articles by Loeb, Groves, and Groves and Loeb.[11] The usefulness of the model is achieved by meeting both the belief-revision use and the motivational use.

13.1.2 The analytical-agency paradigm

Two types of paradigms characterize the agency paradigm: an analytical or principal–agent paradigm, which is essentially mathematical, and a positive-agency paradigm, which is essentially empirical. The tension between them is evident in the following observations:

> two almost entirely separate and valuable literatures that nominally address the same problem. ... Each of the agency literatures has its strong and weak points, and on occasion a tension has surfaced between them. ... Part is due to the "tyranny of journalism" that develops when mathematically inclined scholars take the attitude that if analytical language is not mathematics, it isn't rigorous, and if a problem cannot be solved with the use of mathematics, the effort should be abandoned. Part is due to the belief that the lack of the use of mathematics in the positive agency literature results in ex post facto theorizing that assumes the hypotheses will not be rejected. ... However, some believe that so little is put in the current principal–agent models that there is little hope of producing results that will explain much of the rich variety of observed contracting practices ... on the other hand, the methods of the positive agency literature justifiably seem unconstrained, and often perilously close to tautological to some.[12]

The analytical-agency paradigm traces its origin to the exemplar provided by Coase's seminal paper, which first referred to the nature of firm and the relationships of principal and agent.[13] He also put an emphasis on voluntary contracts that arise among various organizational parties as the efficient solution to these conflicts of interest. The analytical-agency paradigm evolved then to a view of the firm as a "nexus of contracts" with the statement by Jensen and Meckling that firms are "legal fictions which serve as a nexus for a set of contracting relationships among individuals."[14] E. Fama expanded this "nexus of contracts" view to include both capital markets and markets for managerial behavior.[15]

The agency relationship is said to exist when a contract between a person(s), a principal, and another persons(s), an agent, to perform some service on the principal's behalf involves a delegation of the decision-making authority to the agent.[16] Both principal and agent are assumed to be motivated solely by self-interest, that is, to maximize their subjective utility, but also to be aware of their common interest. As Fama noted: "In effect, the firm is viewed as a team of individuals whose members act from self-interest but realize that their destinies depend to some extent on the survival of the team in its competition with other teams."[17] The agent is striving to maximize the contractual fee he receives subject to the necessary effort levels. The principal is striving to maximize the returns from the use of his resources subject to the fee payable to the agent. These conflicts of interest are assumed to be brought into equilibrium by the agreed-on contracts. The contracts engage the members to agree to a set of cooperative behaviors, given implied self-interest motives.[18] Two reasons may lead to the divergence between self-interest and cooperative behavior, adverse selection and moral hazard, which are information-based problems.

Adverse selection, as an information problem, arises when the agent uses private information that cannot be verified by the principal to implement successfully an input-action rule different from that desired by the principal and thereby rendering the principal incapable of determining if the agent made the appropriate choice. The *moral-hazard* problem, as an *expost* information problem, arises when there are motivational problems and conflicts as a result of basing contracts on imperfect surrogates of behavior. Consider both the case of fire insurance and the problem in the Prisoner's Dilemma. As Arrow observed, "The outbreak of a fire may be due to a contribution of exogenous circumstances and individual choice, such as carelessness or, in the extreme case, arson. Hence, a fire insurance policy creates an incentive for an individual to change his behavior and ceases to be a pure insurance against an uncontrollable event."[19] Then, as Stanley Baiman observed, "The problem in the Prisoner's Dilemma presents a moral hazard: Both individuals would be better off if neither confessed. But such behavior is not enforceable because the two prisoners cannot write an enforceable contract between themselves based on their confessing behavior."[20]

The basic agency problem is enriched by different options concerning:

1. The initial distribution of information and beliefs (the basic agency problem assumes that neither individual has private precontract information, that is, no asymmetry of precontract information exists).

2. The description of the number of periods (the basic agency problem assumes a one-period world).

3. The description of the firms production function in terms of
   (a) the amount of capital supplied by the principal;
   (b) the agent's level of effort;
   (c) an exogenously determined, uncertain-state realization (weather, machine breakdown, competitors' behavior, and so on), which affects the agent's productivity.

4. The description of the feasible set of actions from which the agent chooses.

5. The description of the labor and capital markets.

6. The description of the feasible set of information system.

7. The description of the legal system that specifies the type of behavior that can be legally enforced and what is admissible evidence.

8. The description of the feasible set of payment schedules (the basic agency model assumes that the principal chooses the payment schedule and the monitoring system to reward and motivate the agent).

9. The description of the solution to the basic agency model. It consists of

   (a) the employment contract, which incorporates …
      i   the payment schedule for the agent;
      ii the information system choices …;
      iii specification of how the agent promises to act;
   (b) the agent's actual action.[21]

10. The role of self-interest.

11. The solution concept and the nature of optimality.

13.1.3 Positive theory of accounting

The call for a positive approach to accounting came when Jensen charged that "research in accounting has been (with one or two notable exceptions) unscientific … because the focus of this research has been overwhelmingly normative and definitional".[22] Jensen then called for "the development of a positive theory of accounting which will explain why accounting is what it is, why accountants do what they do, and what effects these phenomena have on people and resource utilization".[23] The basic message, later to become known as "the Rochester School of Accounting", is that most accounting theories are unscientific because they are normative and should be replaced by positive theories that explain actual accounting practices in terms of management's voluntary choice of accounting procedures and how the regulated standards have changed over time.

The major thrust of the positive approach to accounting is to explain and predict management's choice of standards by analyzing the costs and benefits of particular financial disclosures in relation to various individuals and to the allocation of resources within the economy. The positive theory is based on the propositions that managers, shareholders, and regulators/politicians are rational and that they attempt to maximize their utility, which is directly related to their compensation and, hence, to their wealth. The choice of an accounting policy by any of these groups rests on a comparison of the relative costs and benefits of alternative accounting procedures in such a way as to maximize their utility. For example, it is hypothesized that management considers the effects of the reported accounting of numbers on tax regulation, political costs, management compensation, information production costs, and restrictions found in bond-indenture provisions. Similar hypotheses may be related to standard-setters, academicians, auditors and others. In fact, the central ideal of the positive approach is to develop hypotheses about factors that influence the world of accounting practices and to test the validity of these hypotheses empirically:

1. To enhance the reliability of prediction based on the observed smoothed series of accounting numbers along a trend considered best or normal by management.

2. To reduce the uncertainty resulting from the fluctuations of income numbers in general and the reduction of systematic risk in particular by reducing the covariance of the firm's returns with the market returns.

Unlike the income-smoothing hypothesis, positive theories in accounting assume that the stock price depends on cash flows rather than on reported earnings. Furthermore, given an efficient market, two firms with identical cash-flow distributions are valued the same way despite the use of different accounting procedures. The central problem in positive theories is to determine how accounting procedures affect cash flows and, therefore, management's utility functions to obtain an insight into the factors that influence a manager's choice of accounting procedures. Resolution of the problem is guided by the following theoretical assumptions:

1. The agency theory may have originated with the emphasis on voluntary contracts that arise among various organizational parties as the efficient solution to these conflicts of interest. The theory evolves to a view of the firm as a "nexus of contracts" with the statement by Jensen and Meckling that firms are "legal fictions which serve as a nexus for a set of contracting relationships among individuals".[24] Fama expanded this "nexus of contracts" view to include both capital markets and markets for managerial labor.[25]

2. Given this "nexus of contracts" perspective of the firm, the contracting cost theory views the role of accounting information as the monitoring and enforcing of these contracts to reduce the agency costs of certain conflicts of interest. One possible conflict may be the conflict of interest between bondholders and stockholders of firms with debts outstanding; in such instances, decisions favorable to stockholders are not necessarily in the best interests of bondholders. This may require that lending agreements define the measurement rules to calculate accounting numbers for the purposes of restrictive covenants. Other possible agreements that may require the use of accounting numbers from audited financial statements to monitor the covenants of the agreements include management-compensation contracts and corporate by-laws. Thus the contracting cost theory assumes that accounting methods are selected as part of the wealth-maximizing process.[26]

The extent to which the accounting choice affects the contracting wealth depends on the relative magnitudes of the contracting costs. These contracting costs include:

(a) transaction costs (e.g. brokerage fees);

(b) agency costs (e.g. monitoring costs, bonding costs and residual loss from dysfunctional decisions);

(c) information costs (e.g. the costs of becoming informed);

(d) renegotiation costs (e.g. the costs of rewriting existing contracts when they are considered obsolete by some unpredictable event);

(e) bankruptcy costs (e.g. the legal costs of bankruptcy and the costs of dysfunctional decisions).

Both propositions imply that management is selecting the choice of the optimal accounting procedures for a given purpose. The central problem of the positive approach rests in determining what factors are likely to affect the optimum choice, guided by the assumption of agency and contracting cost theories.[27]

The accounting choice rests on variables representing the management's incentives to choose accounting methods under bonus plans, debt contracts and the political process. As a result, three hypotheses are generated: the bonus plan hypothesis; the debt equity hypothesis; and the political costs hypothesis. These hypotheses are generally stated in terms of the opportunistic behavior of managers. They are as follows:

1. *The bonus plan hypothesis* maintains that managers of firms with bonus plans are more likely to use accounting methods that increase current period reported income. The rationale is that such action may increase the percent value of bonuses if there are no adjustments for the method chosen.

2. *The debt equity hypothesis* maintains that the higher the firms debt/equity, which is equivalent to the closer (i.e. "tighter") the firm is to the constraints in the debt covenants and the greater the probability of a covenant violation and of incurrence of technical default costs, the more likely managers are to use accounting methods that increase income.

3. *The political cost hypothesis* maintains that large firms rather than small firms are more likely to use accounting choices that reduce reported profits.

The positive approach to accounting is generally drawn from a well-known essay in which Friedman argues "for distinguishing positive economics sharply from normative economics."[28] In fact, Friedman credits his distinction between "positive" and "normative" science to Keynes, who wrote:

> [A] positive science may be defined as a body of systematized knowledge concerning what is a normative or regulative science as a body of systematized knowledge relating to criteria of what ought to be, and concerned, therefore, with the ideal as distinguished from actual.[29]

The call for a positive approach to accounting came when Jensen charged that:

> ... research in accounting has been (with one or two notable exceptions) unscientific ... because the focus of this research has been overwhelmingly normative and definitional.[30]

Jensen then called for:

> ... the development of a positive theory of accounting which will explain why accounting is what it is, why accountants do what they do, and what effects these phenomena have on people and resource utilization.[31]

The basic message, later to become known as "the Rochester School of Accounting", is that most accounting theories are "unscientific" because they are "normative" and should be replaced by "positive" theories that explain actual accounting practices in terms of management's voluntary choice of accounting procedures and how the regulated standards have changed over time.

13.1.4 Evaluation of the positive approach

The positive approach looks into "why" accounting practices and/or theories have developed in the way they have in order to explain and/or predict accounting events. As such, the positive approach seeks to determine the various factors that may influence rational factors in the accounting field. It basically attempts to determine a theory that explains observed phenomena. The positive approach is generally differentiated from the normative approach, which seeks to determine a theory that explains "what should be" rather than "what is". The positive approach seemed to generate considerable optimism among its advocates, as the following statement attests:

> There is virtually an unlimited supply of interesting positive research questions that can be addressed with our existing methodology due to the rate at which the SEC and FASB continue to promulgate standards. Furthermore, this research is of interest not only to academics in accounting, finance, and economics, but to our students and the accounting profession (even though the profession may find some of the results disturbing).[32]

This optimism is not naturally shared by everybody. One striking criticism of the positive approach was based on four points: [33]

- The Rochester School's assertion that the kind of "positive" research they are undertaking is a prerequisite for normative accounting theory is based on a confusion of phenomenal domains at the different levels (accounting entities versus accountants), and is mistaken.

- The concept of "positive theory" is drawn from an obsolete philosophy of science and is, in any case, a misnomer, because the theories of empirical science make no positive statement of "what is".

- Although a theory may be used merely for prediction even if it is known to be false, an explanatory theory of the type sought by the Rochester School, or one that is to be used to test normative proposals, ought not to be known to be false. The method of analysis, which reasons backward from the phenomena to the premises which are acceptable on the basis of independent evidence, is the appropriate method for constructing explanatory theories.

- Contrary to the empirical method of subjecting theories to severe attempts to falsify them, the Rochester School introduces ad hoc arguments to excuse the failure of their theories. [34]

Another criticism is based on the argument that positive or "empirical" theories are also normative and value-laden because they usually mark a conservative ideology in their accounting-policy implications. [35]

The most striking criticism of positive accounting theory (PAT) comes from Sterling with his comments that (a) the two pillars of value-free study and accounting practices are insubstantial, (b) the economic and scientific support of the theory is mistaken and (c) the accomplishments have been nil. [36] His conclusion is not to be missed. He states:

> … I recommend that accountants adopt the weaker, shamelessly stolen, "Sterling's scalpel" which is that any accounting concept that does not have a common-sense core that you can explain to yourself should be discarded. I am confident that a careful application of that criterion in accounting will result in PAT becoming a cottage industry and displace it as the current dominant fad, as well as provide protection from future fads. [37]

13.2 Income smoothing hypothesis

13.2.1 Nature of income smoothing

Income smoothing may be viewed as the deliberate normalization of income in order to reach a desired trend or level. As far back as 1953, Heyworth observed "… more of the accounting techniques which may be applied to affect the assignment of net income successive accounting periods … for smoothing or leveling the amplitude of periodic net income fluctuations". [38] What followed were arguments made by Monsen and Downs [39] and Gordon [40] that corporate managers may be motivated to smooth their own income (or security), with the assumption that stability in income and rate of growth will be preferred over higher average income streams with greater variability. More specifically, Gordon theorized on income smoothing as follows:

> *Proposition 1:* The criterion a corporate management uses in selecting among accounting principles is the maximization of its utility or welfare.

Proposition 2: The utility of management increases with (1) its job security, (2) the level and rate of growth in the management's income, and (3) the level and rate of growth in the corporation's size.

Proposition 3: The achievement of the management goals stated in Proposition 2 is dependent in part on the satisfaction of stockholders with the corporation's performance; that is, other things being equal, the happier the stockholders, the greater the job security, income, etc., of the management.

Proposition 4: Stockholders' satisfaction with a corporation increases with the average rate of growth in the corporation's income (or the average rate of return on its capital) and the stability of its income. This proposition is as readily verified as Proposition 2.

Theorem: Given that the above four propositions are accepted or found to be true, it follows that management would within the limits of its power, that is, the latitude allowed by accounting rules, to (1) smooth reported income, and (2) smooth the rate of growth in income. By "smooth the rate of growth in income", we mean the following: if the rate of growth is high, accounting practices that reduce it should be adopted, and vice versa.[41]

The best definition of income smoothing was provided by Beidleman as follows:

> Smoothing of reported earnings may be defined as the intentional dampening or fluctuations about some level of earnings that is currently considered to be normal for a firm. In this sense smoothing represents an attempt on the part of the firm's management to reduce abnormal variations in earnings to the extent allowed under sound accounting and management principles.[42]

Given the above definition, what need to be explicated are the motivation of smoothing, the dimensions of smoothing and the instruments of smoothing.

13.2.2 Motivations of smoothing

As early as 1953, Heyworth claimed that motivations behind smoothing include the improvements of relations with creditors, investors and workers, as well as dampening of business cycles through psychological processes.[43] Gordon proposed that:

1. The criterion a corporate management uses in selecting among accounting principles is to maximize its utility or welfare.
2. The same utility is a function of job security, the level and rate of growth of salary and the level and growth rate in the firm's size.
3. Satisfaction of shareholders with the corporation's performance enhances the status and rewards of managers.
4. The same satisfaction depends on the rate of growth and stability of the firm's income.[44]

These propositions culminate the need to smooth, as explained in the following theorem:

> Given that the above four propositions are accepted or found to be true, it follows that a management should within the limits of its power, i.e., the latitude allowed by accounting rules, (1) smooth reported income and (2) smooth the rate of growth in income. By smoothing the rate of growth in income we mean the following: If the rate of growth is high, accounting practices which reduce it should be adopted and vice versa.[45]

Beidleman considers two reasons for management to smooth reported earnings.[46] The first argument rests on the assumption that a stable earnings stream is capable of supporting a higher level of dividends than a more variable earnings stream, having a favorable effect in the value of the firm's shares as overall riskiness of the firm is reduced. He states:

> To the extent that the observed variability about a trend of reported earnings influences investors' subjective expectations for possible outcomes of future earnings and dividends, management might be able favorably to influence the value of the firm's shares by smoothing earning.[47]

The second argument attributes to smoothing the ability to counter the cyclical nature of reported earnings and likely reduce the correlation of a firm's expected returns with returns on the market portfolio. He states:

> To the degree that auto-normalization of earnings is successful, and that the reduced covariance of returns with the market is recognized by investors and incorporated into their evaluation process, smoothing will have added beneficial effects in share values.[48]

It results from the need felt by management to neutralize environmental uncertainty and dampen the wide fluctuations in the operating performance of the firm subject to an intermittent cycle of good and bad times. To do so, management may resort to organizational slack behavior,[49] budgetary slack behavior,[50] or risk-avoiding behavior.[51] Each of these behaviors necessitates decisions affecting the incurrence and/or allocation of discretionary expenses (costs) which result in income smoothing.

In addition to these behaviors intended to neutralize environmental uncertainty, it is also possible to identify organizational characterizations that differentiate among different firms in their extent of smoothing. For example, Kamin and Ronen[52] examined the effects of the separation of ownership and control on income smoothing, under the hypothesis that management controlled firms are more likely to be engaged in smoothing as a manifestation of managerial discretion and budgetary slack. Their results confirmed that income smoothing is higher among management controlled firms with high barriers to entry.

Management was also assigned to circumvent news of the constraints of generally accepted accounting principles by attempting to smooth income numbers so as to convey their expectations of future cash flows, enhancing in the process the apparent reliability of predictions based on the observed smoothed series of numbers.[53] Three constraints are presumed to lead managers to smooth:

1. the competitive market mechanisms, which reduce the options available to management;
2. the management compensation scheme, which is linked directly to the firm's performance; and
3. the threat of management displacement.

This smoothing is not limited to high management and external accounting. It is also presumed to be used by lower-level management and internal accounting in the form of organizational slack and slack budgeting.[54]

13.2.3 The smoothing object

Basically the smoothing object should be based on the most visible and used financial indication, which is the profit. Because income smoothing is not a visible phenomenon, the literature speculates on various expressions of profit as the most likely to be the object of smoothing. These expressions include (a) net income based indicators, generally before extraordinary items and before or after tax, (b) earnings per share based indicators, generally before extraordinary gains and losses and adjusted for stock splits and dividends. The researchers choose net income or earnings per share based indicators as the object of smoothing because of the belief that management's long-term concern is with the net income and users have a kind of functional fixation on the bottom figure, whether it is income or earnings per share. This is a simplistic reasoning as management may find it necessary and practical to smooth sales and fixed sales commitments have only the flexibility of smoothing expenses. Similarly, a firm with a good control on its expenses may find it more practical to smooth its sales revenues.

13.2.4 The dimensions of smoothing

The dimensions of smoothing are basically the means used to accomplish the smoothing of income numbers. Dascher and Malcolm distinguished between real smoothing and artificial smoothing as follows:

> Real smoothing refers to the actual transaction that is undertaken or not undertaken on the basis of its smoothing effect on income, whereas artificial smoothing refers to accounting procedures which are implemented to shift costs and/or revenues from one period to another.[55]

Both types of smoothing may be indistinguishable. For example, the amount of reported expenses may be lower or higher than previous periods because of either deliberate actions on the level of the expenses (real smoothing) or the reporting methods (artificial smoothing). For both types, an operational test proposed is to fit a curve to a stream of income calculated two ways:

(a) excluding a possible manipulative variable, and

(b) including it.[56]

Artificial smoothing was also considered by Copeland and defined as follows:

> Income smoothing involves the repetitive selection of accounting measurement or reporting rules in a particular pattern, the effect of which is to report the stream of income with a smaller variation from trend than would otherwise have appeared.[57]

Besides real and artificial smoothing, other dimensions of smoothing were considered in the literature. A popular classification adds a third smoothing dimension, namely classificatory smoothing. Barnea *et al.* distinguished between three smoothing dimensions, as follows:

1. *Smoothing through events' occurrence and/or recognition:* Management can time actual transactions so that their effects on reported income would tend to dampen its variations over time. Mostly, the planned timing of events' occurrences (e.g. research and development) would be a function of the accounting rules governing the accounting recognition of the events.

2. *Smoothing through allocation over time:* Given the occurrence and the recognition of an event, management has more discretionary control over the determination over the periods to be affected by the events' quantification.

3. *Smoothing through classification (hence classifactory smoothing):* When income statement statistics other than net income (net of all revenues and expenses) are the object of smoothing, management can classify intra-income statement items to reduce variations over time in that statistic.[58]

Basically, real smoothing corresponded to the smoothing through events' occurrence and/or recognition, while artificial smoothing corresponded to the smoothing through the allocation over time.

13.2.5 The smoothing variables

The smoothing devices or instruments are the variables used to smooth the chosen performance indicator. Copeland suggested the following five conditions necessary for a smoothing instrument:

A. Once used, it must not commit the firm to any particular future action.
B. It must be based upon the exercise of professional judgment and be considered within the domain of "Generally Accepted Accounting Principles".
C. It must lead to material shifts relative to year-to-year differences in income.
D. It must not require a "real" transaction with second parties, but only a reclassification of internal account balances.
E. It must be used, singularly or in conjunction with other practices, over consecutive periods of time.[59]

Beidleman suggested two different and less restrictive criteria:

1. It must permit management to reduce the variability in reported earnings as it strives to achieve its long-run earnings (growth) objective.

2. Once used, it should not commit the firm to any particular action.[60]

Examples of smoothing instruments used include:

1. Switch from accelerated to straight-line depreciation.[61]
2. Choice of cost or equity method.[62]
3. Pension costs.[63]
4. Dividend income.[64]
5. Gains and losses on sale of securities.[65]
6. Investments tax credit.[66]

13.2.6 Research findings on income smoothing

1. Sector and country analysis

It is possible to identify organizational characterizations, sector classifications and country classifications that differentiate among different firms in their extent of smoothing.

1. With respect to the organizational characterizations, Kamin and Ronen[67] examined the effects of the separation of ownership and control on income smoothing under the hypothesis that management-controlled firms are more likely to be engaged in smoothing as a manifestation of managerial discretion and budgetary slack. Their results confirmed that a majority of the firms examined behave as if they were smoothers and a particularly strong majority is included among management-controlled firms with high barriers to entry.

2. With respect to sectorial classifications, Belkaoui and Picur[68] tested the effects of a dual economy in income smoothing behavior. The main hypothesis was that a higher degree of smoothing of income numbers will be exhibited by firms in the periphery sector than firms in the core sector as a reaction to differences in the opportunity structures, experiences, and environmental uncertainty. Their results indicated that a majority of US firms may be resorting to income smoothing with a higher number included among firms in the periphery sector. However, using an income variability method of analysis, those results could not be replicated methods using a US sample[69] or a Canadian sample.[70] In a Finnish context, Kinunem et al.[71] found that one sector firms may have more opportunities and more predisposition to income smoothing behavior than firms operating in the more peripheral sector of the Finnish economy. The following explanation is provided for the Finnish results:

> As an explanation for these findings, it can be argued that compared with the periphery sector, Finnish accounting rules provide the sector firms more opportunities to exploit certain earnings management instruments (such as accounting for depreciation of fixed assets, untaxed reserves, pension liabilities, exchange losses and R&D costs). Furthermore, because these firms sell their products in highly competitive international markets, and are very much dependent on those markets, they presumably face a higher degree of environmental uncertainty than firms in the periphery sector. Therefore, the core sector firms are more apt to income smoothing in the conventional sense.[72]

3. With regard to country classifications excluding the US, the evidence shows a certain degree of income smoothing in Japan,[73,74] the UK,[75,76] Canada,[77,78] France,[79] and Singapore.[80]

2. Job security and anticipatory smoothing

The general idea behind income smoothing is that the manager may take actions that increase reported income when income is low and take actions that decrease reported income when income is high. This is possible through either the flexibility allowed within generally accepted accounting principles or deliberate changes in operations. We may ask about the motivations of managers engaged in income smoothing. Fudenberg and Tirole[81] analytically show that income smoothing to increase job security arises in equilibrium if the following assumptions hold:

1. Managers enjoy nonmonetary private benefits (incumbency rents) from running the firm.

2. The firm is not committed to long-term incentive contracts, which result in managers' dismissal in case of poor performance.

3. This is information decay in the sense that current earnings are more important than previous earnings in management's performance evaluation.

Because of these assumptions, managers will in good times save for bad times. In other words:

> First, when current earnings are relatively low, but expected future earnings are relatively high, managers will make accounting choices that increase current period discretionary accruals. In effect, managers in this setting are "borrowing" earnings from the future. Second, when current earnings are relatively high, but expected future earnings are relatively low, managers will make accounting choices that decrease current year discretionary accruals. Managers are effectively "saving" current earnings for possible use in the future.[82]

DeFond and Park[83] investigated the intuition derived from the Fudenberg–Tirole model by examining the effects of current relative premanaged earnings and expected future relative earnings on the behavior of discretionary accruals. Their evidence suggests that when current earnings are "poor" and expected future earnings are "good", managers "borrow" earnings from the future for use in the current period. Conversely, when current earnings are "good" and expected future earnings are "poor", managers "save" current earnings for possible use in the future. These findings that managers of firms experiencing poor (good) performance in the current period and expecting good (poor) performance in the next period choose income-increasing (income-decreasing) discretionary accruals in order to reduce the threat of being dismissed did not directly examine the link between job security and income smoothing. Accordingly, Ahmed et al.[84] hypothesized that the extent of income smoothing varies directly with managers' job security concern as proxied by the degree of competition in the firm's product markets, product durability, and capital intensity. Basically, the argument is that managers of firms in more competitive industries, durable goods industries, and capital-intensive businesses are likely to have greater job security concerns than managers of other firms, and therefore are more likely to engage in a greater extent of income smoothing. The results were consistent with the predictions. Using a different methodology, Elgers et al.[85] were able to provide results indicating that patterns in measured discretionary accruals and relative earnings performance are consistent with the theory that managers smooth earnings based on both current-year's results and expected next-year results, a phenomenon better labeled as "anticipatory income smoothing".

3. Stockholders' wealth and income smoothing

The only literature in income smoothing maintained and/or established a positive relationship between income smoothing and shareholders' wealth. The statements and/or findings are as follows:

1. Stockholder satisfaction is bound to increase with the rate of growth in a firm's income and the stability of its income.[86]

2. The possibility that analysts may become more enthusiastic about self-smoothers increases the interest in the firm's market shares and may have a favorable effect on share value and cost of capital.[87]

3. Income variability may be shown to be significantly correlated with both overall and systematic risk measures.[88]

4. Smoothing may imply a direct, cause–effect relationship between earnings fluctuations and market risk.[89]

5. By allowing management to select alternative accounting techniques owners can capitalize upon managers' expertise.[90]

6. Smooth income reduces the probability of financial ratio covenants leading to a reduction in the cost of default and renegotiation.[91,92]

7. Firms that do not smooth have higher unexpected returns from earnings surprises than firms that smooth income.[93]

8. Institutional investors avoid firms that exhibit large variations in earnings. A smoother income stream is preferred.[94]

Other analyses of the impact of income smoothing on stockholders' wealth were more market based. Michelson et al.[95] found lower returns, lower risk and larger firm sizes for smoothing firms. Wang and Williams[96] found that firms with a smooth income series were less risky and had a market response four times as large as that for the other firms. This favorable impact of smoothing is evaluated as follows:

Contrary to the widespread view that managers engage in income smoothing to increase their own welfare at the expense of stockholders, this study documents consistent evidence indicating that accounting income smoothing can be beneficial to the firm's stockholders and prospective investors. Specifically, the analysis demonstrated that income smoothing may enhance the informational value of earnings and reduce the riskiness of the firm.[97]

Chaney et al.[98] present evidence that managers smooth income around their arrangements of the firm's permanent earnings. Income smoothing becomes a long-term strategy to communicate a firm's permanent earnings using discretionary accruals to remove (or offset) a portion of the transitory component of reported earnings. The evidence shows that (a) if the current year's income before discretionary accruals is lower than last year's reported earnings, discretionary accruals will be positive, and (b) if the current year's income before discretionary accruals is already higher than last year's reported earnings, discretionary accruals will be negative. They conclude as follows:

> We suggest that smoothing income around the managers' assessment of the firm's permanent earnings enhances the market's perception of the firm whose earnings are being managed. When firms consistently manage earnings to present a smooth pattern of profits to market participants, they avoid the dips in earnings (and related reputation effects) that may follow periods of over-reported earnings. We hypothesize and present evidence that earnings response coefficients, which reflect the relation between unexpected earnings and market returns, as well as the perceived reliability of reported earnings, are higher for firms that engage consistently in income smoothing.[99]

Finally, Chaney and Lewis[100] investigated income smoothing and underperformance in initial public offerings. They found a positive association between a proxy for income smoothing and firm performance, in the sense that (a) firms that perform well tend to report earnings with less variability relative to cash from operations compared to other firms, and (b) the earnings response coefficient is greater for firms that are able to smooth earnings relative to cash flows. The result is interpreted as being totally consistent with the hypothesis that the market is better able to assess the information content of earnings for firms with smoother earnings.

13.3 Earnings management

13.3.1 Earnings management as accrual management

Basically, the operational definition of earnings management is the potential use of accrual management with the intent of obtaining some private gain. The following relationships are central to an understanding of earnings management as accrual management.

1. Total accruals = Reported Net Income – Cash flows from operations.
2. Total accruals = Non discretionary accruals + Discretionary accruals.

The general approach for estimating discretionary accruals is to regress total accruals on variables that proxy for normal accruals. Unexpected accruals or discretionary accruals are considered to be the unexplained (the residual) components of total accruals.

In addition to the use of unexpected accruals and discretionary accruals as a proxy for earnings management, many studies provided evidence on which specific accruals or accounting methods are used for earnings management. Examples of specific accruals that have been proven to be used for earnings management include:

1. depreciation estimates and bad debts provisions surrounding initial public offers;[101]
2. loan loss reserves of banks[102] and claim loss reserves of insurers;[103]
3. deferred tax valuation allowances.[104]

13.3.2 Accruals models

Discretionary accrual models involve first the computation of total accruals. Therefore total accruals models are presented first, followed by discretionary accrual models.

a. Total accruals models

Two models are generally used for the computation of accruals, namely the balance sheet approach and the cash flow approach.

The balance sheet approach for the computation of total accruals, TA, is as follows:

$$TA_t = \Delta CA_t - \Delta Cash_t - \Delta CL_t + \Delta DCL_t - DEP_t$$

where ΔCA_t is the change in the current assets in year t (Compustat # 4); $\Delta Cash_t$ is the change in cash and cash equivalent in year t (Compustat # 1); ΔCL_t is the change in current liabilities in year t (Compustat # 5); ΔDCL_t is the change in debt included in current liabilities in year t (Compustat # 34); and DEP_t is the depreciation and amortization expense in year t (Compustat # 14). Based on the findings that studies relying on the traditional balance sheet approach to the measurement of total accruals suffer from potential contamination from measurement of total accruals, Collins and Hribar[105] suggested a straightforward approach that computes total accruals as the difference between net income and operating cash flow (taken from the cash flow statement).

b. Discretionary accruals models

Six competing discretionary accruals models are considered in the literature. They are as follows:

1. **The De Angelo Model**

   The discretionary portion of accruals in the De Angelo Model[106] is the difference between total accruals in the event year t scaled by total assets (A_{t-1}) and nondiscretionary accruals (NDA_t). The measure of nondiscretionary accruals (NDA_t) rests on last period's total accruals (TA_{t-1}) scaled by lagged total assets (A_{t-2}); in other words:

   $$NDA_t = T_{At-1} / A_{t-2}$$

2. **The Healy Model**

   In the Healy Model,[107] the nondiscretionary accruals (NDA_t) are the mean of total accruals TA_t scaled by lagged total assets (A_{t-1}) from the estimation period. In other words:

   $$NDA_t = 1 / n \sum_\gamma (TA_\gamma / A_{\gamma-1})$$

   where NDA_t is nondiscretionary accruals in the year t scaled by lagged total assets; n is the number of years in the estimation period; and γ is a year subscript for years ($t-n, t-n+1, \ldots, t-1$) included in the estimation period. The discretionary portion is the difference between the total accruals in the event year scaled by A_{t-1} and NDA_t.

The main difference between the De Angelo model and the Healy model is that NDA follows a random walk process in the De Angelo model and a mean reverting process in the Healy model.

3. The Jones model

The main objective of the Jones model is to control for the effect of changes in the firm's circumstances on nondiscretionary accruals.[108] The nondiscretionary accruals in the event year are expressed as follows:

$$NDA_t = \alpha_1 (1 / A_{t-1}) + \alpha_2 (\Delta REV_t / A_{t-1}) + \alpha_3 (PPE_t / A_{t-1})$$

where: NDA_t is the nondiscretionary accruals in the year t scaled by lagged total assets; ΔREV_t is the revenue in the year t less revenues in year $t-1$; PPE_t is gross property plant and equipment at the end of the year t; A_{t-1} is total assets at the end of the year $t-1$; and α_1, α_2, α_3 are the firm-specific parameters.

The estimates of the firm-specific parameters are obtained by using the following model in the estimation period:

$$TA_t / A_{t-1} = \alpha_1 (1 / A_{t-1}) + \alpha_2 (\Delta REV_t / A_{t-1}) + \alpha_3 (PPE_t / A_{t-1}) + E_t$$

where α_1, α_2 and α_3 represent the OLS estimates of α_1, α_2 and α_3. The residual E_t represents the firm-specific discretionary portion of the total accruals.

The variations of the Jones model include:

(a) A model that expands the Jones model by adding lagged total accruals and lagged stock returns as two additional explanatory variables.[109]
(b) A model that replaces "changes in sales" in the Jones model by "change in cash sales".[110]

4. The modified Jones model

In order to eliminate the conjectured tending of the Jones model to measure discretionary accruals with error when discretion is exercised over revenue recognition, the modified model estimates nondiscretionary accruals during the event period (i.e. during periods in which earnings management is hypothesized) as follows:

$$NDA_t = \alpha_1 (1 / A_{t-1}) + \alpha_2 [(\Delta REV_t - \Delta REC_t) / A_{t-1}] + \alpha_3 (PPE_t / A_{t-1})$$

where ΔREC_t is net receivables in year t less net receivables in year $t-1$, and other variables areas in previous equation.

The estimates of α_1, α_2 and α_3 and nondiscretionary accruals are obtained from the original Jones model, not from the modified model, during the estimation period (in which no systematic earnings management is hypothesized). The difference between the two models is explicated as follows:

> Revenues are adjusted for the change in receivables in the event period. The original Jones model implicitly assumes that discretion is not exercised over revenue in either the estimation period or the event period. The modified version of the Jones model implicitly assumes all changes in the credit sales in the event period result from earnings management. This is based on the reasoning that is easier to manage earnings by exercising discretion over the recognition of revenue on credit sales than it to manage earnings by exercising discretion over the recognition of revenue on cash sales. If this modification is successful, then the estimate of earnings management should no longer be biased toward zero in samples where earnings management has taken place through the management of revenues.[111]

5. The Industry Model

The Industry Model relaxes the assumption that nondiscretionary accruals are constant over time. Rather than attempting a modeling of the determinants of nondiscretionary accruals directly, the Industry Model assumes that the variations in the determinants of nondiscretionary accruals are common across firms in the same industry. The model is expressed as follows:

$$NDA_t = \beta_1 + \beta_2 median;(TA_t/A_{t-1})$$

where NDA_t is measured by the Jones model and median; TA_t/A_{t-1} is the median value of total accruals in year t scaled by lagged total assets for all nonsample firms in the same two-digit standard industrial classification (SIC) industry (industry j). The firm-specific parameters β_1 and β_2 are obtained from an ordinary least squares regression in the observation in the estimation period. The ability of the Industry Model to mitigate measurement error in discretionary accruals hinges critically on the following two factors:

> First, the industry removes variation in nondiscretionary accruals that is common across firms in the same industry. If changes in nondiscretionary accruals largely reflect responses to changes in firm-specific circumstances, then the industry model will not extract all nondiscretionary accruals from the discretionary accrual proxy. Second, the industry removes variation in discretionary accruals that is correlated across firms in the same industry, potentially causing problem 2. The severity of this problem depends on the extent to which the earnings management stimulus is correlated across firms in the same industry.[112]

6. The Kang and Sivaramakrishnan model

The Kang and Sivaramakrishnan model[113] relies on an alternative approach which (a) estimates managed accruals using the level rather than change of current assets and current liabilities, (b) includes cost of goods sold as well as other expenses, and (c) does not require the regression to be uncontaminated. The model is expressed as follows.

$$AB_{i,t} = \phi_0 + \phi_1[\delta_{1,i}REV_{i,t}] + \phi_2[\delta_{2,i}EXP_{i,t}] + \phi_3[\delta_{3,i}GPPE_{i,t}] + u_{i,t}$$

$AB_{i,t}$ = accrual balance

$= AR_{i,t} = INV_{i,t} + OCA_{i,t} - CL_{i,t} - DEP_{i,t}$

$AR_{i,t}$ = receivables, excluding tax refunds;

$INV_{i,t}$ = inventory;

$OCA_{i,t}$ = other current assets than cash, receivables, and inventory;

$CL_{i,t}$ = current liabilities excluding taxes and current maturities of long term debt;

$DEP_{i,t}$ = depreciation and amortization;

$REV_{i,t}$ = net sales revenues;

$EXP_{i,t}$ = operating expenses (cost of goods sold, selling and administrative expenses before depreciation);

$GPPE_{i,t}$ = gross property plant and equipment;

$NTA_{i,t}$ = net total assets;

$$\delta_{1,i} = \frac{AR_{i,t}-1}{REV_{i,t}-1}$$

$$\delta_{2,i} = \frac{NV_{i,t-1} + OCA_{i,t-1} - CL_{i,t-1}}{EXP_{i,t-1}}$$

$$\delta_{3,i} = \frac{DEP_{i,t} - 1}{GPPE_{i,t-1}}$$

The parameters and δ_1, δ_2, and δ_3 are turnover ratios which accommodate firm–specificity and compensate for the fact that the equation is estimated from a pooled sample.

13.3.3 The mispricing of discretionary accruals

There is sufficient evidence showing that investors do correctly use available information in forecasting future earnings performance.[114,115,116] It reflects investors' naive fixation on reported earnings, rather than earnings ability to summarize value-relevant information. In fact, most analysts would argue that since investors tend to "fixate" on reported earnings, examining the accrual and the cash-flow components of current earnings can be used to detect mispriced securities, the reasoning being accrual and cash-flow components of earnings have different implications for the assessment of future earnings. Accordingly, Sloan[117] investigated whether stock prices reflect information about future earnings contained in the accrual and cash-flow components of current earnings. The persistence of earnings performance was found to depend on the relative magnitudes of the cash and accrual components of earnings.

However, stock prices acted as if investors failed to identify correctly the different properties of the two components of earnings. The market erroneously overestimates the persistence of the accruals component of accrual earnings while underestimating the persistence of the cash-flow component. Accruals also exhibit negative serial correlation or mean reversion tendencies. The end result is that the market responds as if surprised when seemingly predictable earnings reversal occurs in the following year. Similarly, Subramanyam[118] find that abnormal accruals are positively related to future profitability. Xie provides more evidence on the issue. Xie[119] estimated abnormal accruals after controlling for major unusual accruals and nonarticulation events (i.e., mergers, acquisitions and divestitures) and found that this refined measure of abnormal accruals, which isolates managerial discretion, is still overpriced. These results are consistent with DeFond and Park's[120] conclusion that the market overprices abnormal accruals because investors underanticipate the future reversal of these accruals.

13.3.4 Issues in earnings management

1. It is very easy to suspect that earnings management is intended to meet expectations of financial analysts or management (represented by public forecasts of earnings). In fact, there is evidence of (a) managers taking actions to manage earnings upward to avoid reporting earnings lower than analysts' forecast,[121] (b) financial analysts' stock recommendation (e.g., buy, hold and sell) as a good predictor of earnings management,[122] (c) firms in danger of falling short of a management earnings forecast using unexpected accruals to manage earnings upward,[123] and (d) firms with a high percentage of institutional ownership typically not cutting research and development spending to avoid a decline in reported earnings.[124]

2. There are good reasons to suspect that earnings management is intended to influence short-term price performance in various ways.

   (a) There is evidence of negative unexpected accruals (income-decreasing) prior to management buyout.[125]

   (b) There is evidence of positive (income-increasing) unexpected accruals prior to seasoned equity offering,[126] initial public offers[127,128] and stock-financed acquisitions.[129] A reversal of unexpected accruals seems to follow initial public offers and stock-financed acquisitions.

3. Earnings management is due and can persist because of asymmetric information, a condition caused by management knowing information that they are not willing to disclose. The persistence is due to blocked communication where the managers cannot communicate all their private information unless the principal contractually precommits not to use the information against the managers. Incentives for managers to reveal their private information truthfully, created by blocked communication, become a key for earnings management.

4. Earnings management takes place in the context of a feasible reporting set and a given set of contracts that determine sharing rules among stakeholders. Both contract sets are endogenous to the earnings management question. As the environment conditions change, both the reporting and contractual sets change also, leading to different forms of earnings management over time. For example, in environmental conditions where accounting data are used in compensation contracts, there is a strong incentive for managers to manage the data used in contracts. As a result, the contracting use leads to an internal or stewardships incentive for earnings management.[130]

5. Corporate strategies for earnings management follow one or more of three approaches: (1) choose from the flexible options available within GAAP, (2) rely on the subjective estimates and application choices available within the options, and (3) use asset acquisitions and dispositions and the timing for reporting them.[131] Note here that the choices made within GAAP constitute earnings management, while choices made outside GAAP constitute fraud. The court may be the one to decide in some cases whether some management reporting actions that are taken outside the bounds of GAAP are fraud or earnings management.[132]

6. The earnings game, or more precisely the quarterly earnings report game, may be a major reason for earnings management.[133] Management is tempted to issue an earnings report that satisfies Wall Street's expectations more than reflecting financial reality. DeGeorge *et al.*[134] found that quarterly earnings reports that meet analysts' expectations exactly or exceed them by just a penny per share happen more frequently than would be likely in a random statistical distribution, while reports that miss by just a penny occur far less frequently.

7. Earnings management is a result of attempts to exceed thresholds.[135] The three thresholds of importance to executives are:

   (a) to report positive profits, that is, report earnings that are above zero;

   (b) to sustain recent performance, that is, make at least last year's earnings; and

   (c) to meet analysts' expectations, particularly the analysts' consumes earnings forecast.[136]

Empirical explorations identified earnings management to exceed each of the three thresholds, with the positive profit threshold predominating.[137]

8. Earnings management may originate as a result of meeting covenants of implicit compensation contracts. Evidence in this thesis takes the following forms:

   (a) Divisional managers for a large multinational firm are likely to defer income when the earnings target in their bonus plan will not be met and when they are entitled to the maximum bonuses permitted under the plan.[138]

(b) Firms with caps in bonus are more likely to report accruals that defer income when that cap is reached than firms that have comparable performance but which have no bonus cap.[139]

(c) During a proxy contest, incumbent managers exercised accounting discretion to improve reported earnings.[140]

(d) CEOs in their final years in office reduced R&D spending, presumably to increase reported earnings.[141]

9. Earnings management arises from the threat of two forms of regulation: industry-specific regulation and antitrust regulation. The banking and insurance industries are good examples of the existence of regulatory monitoring that is tied to accounting data. As stated by Healy and Wahlen:

> Banking regulations require that banks satisfy certain capital adequacy requirements that are written in terms of accounting numbers. Insurance regulations require that insurers meet conditions for minimum financial health. Utilities have historically been rate-regulated and permitted to earn only a normal return in their invested assets. It is frequently asserted that such regulations create incentives to manage the income statement and the balance sheet variables of interest to regulators.[142]

There is in fact a lot of evidence supporting the above hypothesis. For example:

(a) Banks that are close to minimum capital requirements tend to overstate loan loss provisions, understate loan write-offs, and recognize abnormal gains on securities portfolios.[143,144,145,146]

(b) Financially weak property casualty insurers that risk regulatory attention tend to understate claim loss reserves[147] and engage in reinsurance transactions.[148]

10. Because of the need for government subsidies or protection as well as the fear of antitrust investigations or other political consequences, managers may resort to earnings management. There is a lot of evidence supporting this hypothesis. For example:

(a) Firms under investigation for antitrust violations reported income-decreasing abnormal accruals in the investigation years.[149,150]

(b) Firms in industries seeking import-relief tend to defer income in the year of application.[151]

(c) Firms in the cable television industry tend to defer earnings during the period of Congressional scrutiny.[152]

(d) Firms subject to price controls will adjust their discretionary accounting accruals downward to reduce net income and to increase the likelihood of approval of the requested price increase.[153]

(e) The magnitude of the discretionary component of the post-retirement obligation is negatively associated with the extent of the external regulations and auditor quality.[154]

(f) More unionized firms are more likely to use immediate recognition of Statement of Financial Accounting Standards No. 106 on Employer's Accounting for Postretirement Benefits Other than Pensions, which is consistent with incentives to reduce labor negotiation costs.[155]

11. Firm valuation is generally assumed to be one of the targets of earnings management. Various analytical models have tried to explicate that relationship. Gigler[156] considers the case of the firm whose trade-off, when determining which income figure to disclose, is between the cost of acquiring new capital and the cost of competition. An overstatement of disclosed income will occur if the reduced cost

of capital is longer than the increased cost of competition. The credibility of the disclosed income is possible because the firm incurs a proprietary cost by misrepresenting income. Chaney and Lewis[157] are concerned with an explanation for why corporate offices manage the disclosure of accounting information. They show that earnings management affects firm value when value-maximizing managers and investors are asymmetrically informed. Eilifsen *et al.*[158] add to the previous two models by showing that if taxable income is linked to accounting income, there will exist an automatic safeguard against manipulation of earnings, a claim also made Johansson and Ostman.[159]

12. Negative earnings surprises are generally more costly than negative forecast revisions. In addition, the magnitude of market response to earnings surprises seems to be greater for negative surprises than positive ones. It should not be surprising that managers may take action to avoid the negative earnings surprises. Two possible ways of achieving this goal are to either (1) manage earnings upward if unmanaged earnings fall short of expectations or (2) guide analysts' expectations downward to avoid overly optimistic forecasts.[160] Both actions entail costs. As stated by Matsumoto:

> Managing earnings is difficult because auditors and boards of directors scrutinize questionable accounting practices. Moreover, because accruals reverse in subsequent periods, managers are unlikely to be able to use abnormal accruals to continually increase earnings above expectations every period. Guiding analysts' forecasts downward requires revising current expectations downward if initial forecasts are too high, which could cause a negative stock price reaction at forecast revision date. Guiding expectations early on to keep them at a "beatable" level is also costly to the extent that it leads to lower stock prices for an extended period of time.[161]

Both mechanisms of managing earnings upwards or guiding analysts' forecast downward to avoid missing expectations at the earnings announcement are found to be higher for firms with higher transient institutional ownership, greater reliance on implicit claims with their stakeholders, and higher value relevance of earnings.

13.4 The paradigmatic status of accounting

13.4.1 Evolution or revolution in accounting?

In the last three chapters, we have presented an array of approaches used to formulate an accounting theory. Given the advantages and flaws of each approach, we may expect that the situation will lead to a fruitful debate and a unified theory of accounting. This view may be advanced by anyone who believes that progress in accounting will proceed through the accumulation of ideas or evolution. Such a view requires the acceptance of most proposed approaches as potential contributors to a final, unified, or comprehensive theory of accounting.

The prevailing and more logical view, however, is that accounting, like most social and natural sciences, progresses through revolution rather than evolution. The notion of revolution in accounting is taken from Kuhn's "The Structure of Scientific Revolutions"[162] and proposed, successively, in the American Accounting Association's Statement of Accounting Theory and Theory Acceptance.[163] Kuhn's model of revolution comprises the following steps:

1. A science at any given time is dominated by a specific paradigm.

2. The science goes through a period of accumulation of knowledge, during which researchers work on and expand the dominant paradigm; during this period, it is known as a normal science.

3. Anomalies may develop that cannot be explained by the existing paradigm.

4. A crisis stage is reached, beginning with the search for new paradigms and ending with a revolution and the overthrow of the dominant paradigm by a new reigning paradigm.

After using the term "paradigm" in at least twenty-one different ways and being criticized for vagueness, Kuhn offered the following definition:

> Paradigm: The concrete puzzle solutions which, when employed as models or examples, can replace explicit rules as a basis for the solution of the remaining puzzles of normal science.[164]

Given this narrow definition, Ritzer, in a pioneering article in sociology, offered a more operational definition:

> A Paradigm is a fundamental image of the subject matter within a science. It serves to define what should be studied, what questions should be asked, how they should be asked, and what rules should be followed in interpreting the answers obtained. The Paradigm is the broadest unit of consensus within a science and serves to differentiate one scientific community (or subcommunity) from another. It assumes, defines, and interrelates the exemplars, theories, methods, and instruments that exist within it.[165]

A paradigm, therefore, may be identified by three basic components: (1) a major article explicating the idea or exemplar, (2) theories, and (3) methods and techniques.

We may easily argue that accounting is currently in the crisis stage, given the general dissatisfaction with the old matching–attaching approach to the specification of content of the annual reports.

13.4.2 Accounting: a multiparadigmatic science

If accounting is in the crisis stage, then it may be possible to identify competing paradigms. In other words, accounting is a multiparadigmatic science, with each of its paradigms competing for hegemony within the discipline. Following Ritzer's definition of paradigm, each existing accounting paradigm will contain its own exemplar, theories, and methods. In other words, the approaches to the formulation of an accounting theory presented in the first chapters result from the attempt of each of the accounting paradigms to resolve accounting questions. More specifically, "each of the currently competing accounting paradigms tends to specify a different empirical domain over which an accounting theory ought to apply".[166]

An examination of the existing accounting literature allows us to identify the following basic accounting paradigms:

1. the anthropological paradigm, which specifies accounting practices as the domain of accounting;

2. the behavior-of-the-markets paradigm, which specifies the capital-market reaction as the domain of accounting;

3. the economic-event paradigm, which specifies the prediction of economic events as the domain of accounting;

4. the decision-process paradigm, which specifies the decision theories and the decision processes of individuals as the domain of accounting;

5. the ideal-income paradigm, which specifies the measurement of performance as the domain of accounting;

6. the information-economics paradigm, which specifies the evaluation of information as the domain of accounting;

7. the user-behavior paradigm, which specifies the information recipients' behavior as the domain of accounting.

13.5 Conclusions

The new approaches to the formulation of an accounting theory differ from the traditional approaches in terms of their novelty, their less general acceptance, and their reliance on verification. They present innovative and more empirically oriented methods of resolving accounting issues. The influence of the new approaches is manifested in the accounting literature of the last decade.

Notes

1. Ijiri, Yuji, *Theory of Accounting Measurement*, Studies in Accounting Research, No. 10 (Sarasota, FL: American Accounting Association, 1975), p. 78.

2. Feltham, Gerald A., "The Value of Information", *Accounting Review* (October, 1968), pp. 684–96; Crandall, Robert H., "Information Economics and Its Implications for the Further Development of Accounting Theory", *Accounting Review* (July, 1969), pp. 457–66; Feltham, Gerald A., and Demski, Joel S., "The Use of Models in Information Evaluation", *Accounting Review* (July, 1969), pp. 475–66.

3. Feltham, G.A., and Demski, J.S., "The Use of Models in Information Evaluation", op. cit., p. 626.

4. Feltham, G.A., "The Value of Information", op. cit., pp. 684–91.

5. Wilson, R.B., "The Theory of Syndicates", *Econometrica* (January, 1968), pp. 119–32; Demski, J.S., and Swieringa, R.J., "A Cooperative Formulation of the Audit Choice Problem", *Accounting Review* (July, 1974), pp. 506–13; Demski, J., "Uncertainty and Evaluation Based on Controllable Performance", *Journal of Accounting Research* (Autumn, 1976), pp. 23–5.

6. Baiman, Stanley, "Agency Research in Managerial Accounting: A Survey", *Journal of Accounting Literature* (Spring, 1982), p. 159.

7. Demski, J.S., and Feltham, Gerald A., *Cost Determination: A Conceptual Approach* (Ames: Iowa State University Press, 1977).

8. Baiman, S., "Agency Research in Managerial Accounting", op. cit., pp. 159–60.

9. Marschak, J., and Radnor, R., *Economic Theory of Games*, Aroles Foundation Monograph No. 22 (New Haven, CT: Yale University Press, 1972).

10. Baiman, S., "Agency Research in Managerial Accounting", op. cit.

11. Loeb, M., "Coordination and Information Incentive Problems in the Multidivisional Firm" (Ph.D. diss., Graduate School of Management, Northwestern University, May, 1975); Groves, T., "Information Incentives and the Internationalization of Production Externalities", in S. Liu (ed.), *Theory and Measurement of Economic Externalities* (New York: Academic Press, 1975); Groves, T., and Loeb, M., "Incentives in Divisionalized Firms", *Management Science* (March, 1979), pp. 221–30.

12. Jensen, M.C., and Meckling, J.W.H., "Theory of the Firm: Managerial Behavior, Agency Costs and Ownership Structure", *Journal of Financial Economics* (October, 1976), pp. 305–60.

13. Coase, R.J., "The Nature of the Firm", *Economica* (4, November, 1937), pp. 386–405.

14. Jensen, M.C., and Meckling, J.W.H., "Theory of the Firm: Managerial Behavior, Agency Costs and Ownership Structure", *Journal of Financial Economics* (October, 1976), pp. 305–60.
15. Fama, E.F., "Agency Problems and the Theory of the Firm", *Journal of Political Economy* (2, 1980), pp. 288–307.
16. Jensen, M.C., and Meckling, J.W.H., "Theory of the Firm", op. cit., p. 31.
17. Fama, E.F., "Agency Problems and the Theory of the Firm", op. cit., pp. 288–307.
18. Baiman, S., "Agency Research in Managerial Accounting", op. cit., p. 162.
19. Arrow, K.J., *Limits of Organization* (New York: Norton, 1974), pp. 35–6.
20. Baiman, S., "Agency Research in Managerial Accounting", op. cit., p. 163.
21. Ibid., pp. 165–72.
22. Jensen, M.C., "Reflections on the State of Accounting Research and the Regulation of Accounting", in *Stanford Lectures in Accounting* (Stanford, CA: Stanford University, 1976), p. 11.
23. Ibid., p. 13.
24. Jensen, M.C., and Meckling, J.W.H., "Theory of the Firm", op. cit., p. 31.
25. Fama, E.F., "Agency Problems and the Theory of the Firm", op. cit., pp. 288–307.
26. Zimmerman, Jerold L., "Research on Positive Theories of Financial Accounting", in John O. Mason, Jr. (ed.), *Accounting Research Convocation* (Birmingham, AL: School of Accountancy, The University of Alabama, November, 1982), p. 22.
27. Watts, Moss L., and Zimmerman, Jerold L., "Positive Accounting Theory: A Ten Years Perspective", in Stewart Jones, Claudio Romano and Ratnatunga Janek (eds,.) *Accounting Theory: The Contemporary Review* (Sydney, Australia: Harcourt, Brace and Jovanvich, 1995), p. 409.
28. Friedman, Milton, "The Methodology of Positive Economics", in *Essays in Positive Economics* (Chicago: University of Chicago Press, 1953), pp. 6–7.
29. Keynes, John Maynard, *The Scope and Method of Political Economy* (New York: Macmillan, 1981). pp. 34–5.
30. Jensen, M.C., "Reflections on the State of Accounting Research and the Regulation of Accounting", *Stanford Lectures in Accounting* (Stanford, CA: Stanford University, 1976).
31. Ibid., p. 13.
32. Zimmerman, J.L., "Positive Research in Accounting", in R.D. Nair and T.H. Williams (eds.), *Perspectives on Research: T. Beyer Consortium* (Madison: University of Wisconsin, 1980), pp. 107–28.
33. Christenson, C., "The Methodology of Positive Accounting", *The Accounting Review* (January, 1983), pp. 1–22.
34. Ibid., pp. 19–20.
35. Tinker, A.M., Merino, B.D., and Neimark, M.D., "The Normative Origins of Positive Theories: Ideology and Accounting Thought", *Accounting, Organizations and Society* (May, 1982), pp. 167–200.
36. Sterling, Robert R., "Positive Accounting: An Assessment," *Abacus* (26, 2, 1990), pp. 97–135.
37. Ibid., p. 133.
38. Heyworth, S.R., "Smoothing Periodic Income", *The Accounting Review* (January, 1953), p. 32.
39. Monsen, R.J., and Downs, A., "A Theory of Large Managerial Firms", *The Journal of Political Economy* (June, 1965).
40. Gordon, M.J., "Postulates, Principles, and Research in Accounting", *The Accounting Review* (April, 1964), pp. 251–63.
41. Ibid., pp. 261–2.

42. Beidleman, Carl R., "Income Smoothing: The Role of Management", *The Accounting Review* (October, 1973), p. 653.

43. Heyworth, S.R., "Periodic Income Smoothing", *The Accounting Review* (January, 1953), p. 34.

44. Gordon, M.J., "Postulates, Principles, and Research in Accounting", *The Accounting Review* (April, 1964), pp. 251–63.

45. Ibid.

46. Beidleman, Carl R., "Income Smoothing: The Role of Management", *The Accounting Review* (October, 1973), pp. 658–67.

47. Ibid., p. 654.

48. Ibid., p. 654.

49. Cyert, R.N., and March, J.G., *A Behavioral Theory of the Firm* (Englewood Cliffs, NJ: Prentice-Hall, 1967).

50. Schiff, M., and Levin, A.Y., "Where Traditional Budgeting Fails", *Financial Executive* (May, 1968), pp. 57–62.

51. Thompson, J.D., *Organizational in Action* (New York: McGraw Hill, 1967).

52. Kamin, J.Y., and Ronen, J., "The Smoothing of Income Numbers: Some Empirical Evidence in Systematic Differences Among Management-Controlled and Owner-Controlled Firms", *Accounting, Organizations and Society* (3, 2, 1978), pp. 141–53.

53. Barnea, A., Ronen, J., and Sadan, S., "Classificatory Smoothing of Income with Extraordinary Items", *The Accounting Review* (January, 1976), pp. 110–22.

54. Belkaoui, Ahmed, *Behavioral Accounting* (Westport, CT: Greenwood Press, 1989).

55. Dascher, Paul E., and Malcolm, Robert E., "A Note on Income Smoothing in the Chemical Industry", *Journal of Accounting Research* (Autumn, 1970), pp. 253–4.

56. Gordon, M.J., "Discussions of the Effects of Alternative Accounting Rules for Nonsubsidiary Investments", *Empirical Research in Accounting: Selected Studies*, 1966, supplement to Vol. 4, *Journal of Accounting Research* (1966), p. 223.

57. Copeland, R.M., "Income Smoothing, Empirical Research in Accounting: Selected Studies", supplement to Vol. VI, *Journal of Accounting Research* (1968), p. 101.

58. Barnea, A., Ronen, Joshua, and Sadan, Sincha, "Classificatory Smoothing of Income with Extraordinary Item", *The Accounting Review* (January, 1976), p. 111.

59. Copeland, R., "Income Smoothing", *Empirical Research in Accounting: Selected Studies* (1968), p. 102.

60. Beidleman, C., "Income Smoothing: The Role of Management", *The Accounting Review* (October, 1973), p. 658.

61. Archibald, T.R., "The Return to Straight-line Depreciation: An Analysis of a Research in Accounting Method", *Empirical Research in Accounting: Selected Studies* (1967), pp. 164–80.

62. Barefield, R.M., and Comiskey, E.E., "The Smoothing Hypothesis: An Alternative Test", *The Accounting Review* (April, 1972), pp. 291–8.

63. Beidleman, C., "Income Smoothing: The Role of Management", *The Accounting Review* (October, 1973), pp. 653–67.

64. Copeland, R., "Income Smoothing", *Empirical Research in Accounting: Selected Studies* (1968), pp. 101–16.

65. Dopuch, N., and Drake, D., "The Effect of Alternative Accounting Rules for Nonsubsidiary Investments", *Empirical Research in Accounting: Selected Studies* (1966), pp. 192–219.

66. Gordon, M.J., Horwitz, B.N., and Myers, P.T., "Accounting Measurement and Normal Growth of the Firm", in R.K. Jaedicke, Y. Ijiri and O.W. Nielson (eds.), *Research in Accounting Measurement* (Sarasota American Accounting Association, 1968), pp. 220–3.

67. Kamin, J.Y., and Ronen, J., "The Smoothing of Income Numbers: Some Empirical Evidence on Systematic Differences Among Management – Controlled and Owner-Controlled Focus", *Accounting, Organizations and Society* (3, 2, 1978), pp. 141–53.

68. Belkaoui, Ahmed, and Picur, Ronald D., "The Smoothing of Income Numbers: Some Empirical Evidence on the Systematic Differences Between Core and Periphery Industrial Sectors", *Journal of Business Finance and Accounting* (11, 4, 1984), pp. 527–45.

69. Albrecht, W.D., and Richardson, F.M., "Income Smoothing by Economic Sector", *Journal of Business Finance and Accounting* (Winter, 1990), pp. 713–30.

70. Breton, Gaetan, and Chenail, Jean Pierre, "Une Elide Empirique du Lissage des Benefices dans les Enterprises Canadiennes", *Comptabilité, Controle, Audit* (March, 1997), pp. 53–68.

71. Kinnunen, Juha, Kasanen, Eero, and Nisleanen, Jyrkir, "Earnings Management and the Economy Sector Hypothesis: Empirical Evidence on a Converse Relationship in the Finnish Case", *Journal of Business Finance and Accounting* (June, 1995), pp. 497–520.

72. Ibid., p. 501.

73. Genay, H., "Assessing the Condition of Japanese Banks: How Informative Are Accounting Earnings", *Economic Perspectives* (22, 4, 1998), pp. 12–34.

74. Sheikkoleslami, M., "The Impact of Foreign Stock Exchange Listing on Income Smoothing. Evidence from Japanese Firms", *International Journal of Management* (11, 2, 1994), pp. 737–42.

75. Bragshaw, R.E., and Elchni, A.E.K., "The Smoothing Hypothesis and the Role of Exchange Differences", *Journal of Business Finance and Accounting* (16, 5, 1989), pp. 621–33.

76. Beattie, V., Brown, S., Ewers, D., John, B., Manson, S., Thomas, D., and Turner, M., "Extraordinary Items and Income Smoothing: A Positive Accounting Approach", *Journal of Business Finance and Accounting* (21, 6, 1994), pp. 791–811.

77. Saudagaran, S.M., and Sepe, J.F., "Replication of Moses Income Smoothing Tests with Canadian and UK Data, A Note", *Journal of Business Finance and Accounting* (23, 8, 1996), pp. 1219–22.

78. Breton, G., and Chenail, J.P., "Une Etude Empirique", op. cit.

79. Chalayer, S., "Le Lissage des Resultats: Elements Enqlicatifs Avances des la Literature", *Comptabilité, Controle, Audit* (2, 1, 1995), pp. 89–104.

80. Ashani, N., Koh, H.C., Tan, S.L., and Wang, W.H., "Factors Affecting Income Smoothing Among Listed Companies in Singapore", *Accounting and Business Research* (24, 96, 1994), pp. 291–301.

81. Fudenberg, K., and Tirole, J., "A Theory of Income and Dividend Smoothing Based on Incumbency Results", *Journal of Political Economy* (103, 1995), pp. 75–93.

82. DeFond, Mark L., and Park, Chul W., "Smoothing Income in Anticipation of Future Earnings", *Journal of Accounting and Economics* (23, 1997), p. 1116.

83. Ibid., pp. 115–39.

84. Ahmed, A.S., Lobo, G.J., and Zhou, J., "Job Security and Income Smoothing: An Empirical Test of the Fudenberg and Tirole (1995) Model", Working Paper, Syracuse University, October, 2000.

85. Elgers, P.T., Pfeiffer, Jr., R.J., and Porter, S.L., "Anticipatory Income Smoothing: A Re-Examination", Working Paper, University of Massachusetts, February, 2000.

86. Gordon, M.J., "Postulates, Principles and Research in Accounting", *The Accounting Review* (April, 1964), p. 262.

87. Beidleman, C.R., "Income Smoothing: The Role of Management", *The Accounting Review* (October, 1973), pp. 655.

88. Lev., B., and Kunitzky, S., "On the Association Between Smoothing Measures and the Risk of Common Stock", *The Accounting Review* (April, 1974), p. 268.

89. Moses, O.D., "Income Smoothing and Incentives: Empirical Tests Using Accounting Changes", *The Accounting Review* (April, 1987), p. 366.

90. Demski, J.S., Patell, J.M., and Wolfson, M.A., "Decentralized Choice of Monitoring Systems", *The Accounting Review* (59, 1984), pp. 16–34.

91. Trueman, B., and Titman, S., "An Explanation for Accounting Income Smoothing", *Journal of Accounting Research*, Supplement to Vol. 26 (1988), pp. 27–39.

92. Beattie, V., Brown, S., Ewers, D., John, B., Manson, S., Thomas, D., and Turner, M., "Extraordinary Items and Income Smoothing: A Positive Accounting Approach", *Journal of Business Finance and Accounting* (21, 1994), pp. 791–811.

93. Booth, G.G., Kallanki, J., and Martikainem, T., "Post Announcement Drift and Income Smoothing; Finnish Evidence", *Journal of Business Finance and Accounting* (23, 1996), pp. 1197–211.

94. Badrinath, S.G., Gay, D., and Kale, J.P., "Patterns of Institutional Investment, Prudence and the Managerial 'Safety Net' Hypothesis", *Journal of Risk and Insurance* (56, 1989), pp. 605–29.

95. Michelson, S.E., Jordan-Wagner, J., and Wroton, C.W., "A Market Based Analysis of Income Smoothing", *Journal of Business Finance and Accounting* (22, 8, 1995), pp. 1179–93.

96. Wang, Z., and Williams, T.H., "Accounting Income Smoothing and Stockholder Wealth", *Journal of Applied Business Research* (10, 3, 1994), pp. 96–104.

97. Ibid., p. 102

98. Chaney, P.K., Jeter, D.C., and Lewis, C.M., "The Use of Accruals in Income Smoothing: A Permanent Earnings Hypothesis", *Advances in Quantitative Analysis of Finance and Accounting* (6, 1998), pp. 103–35.

99. Ibid., p. 131.

100. Chaney, Paul K., and Lewis, Craig M., "Income Smoothing and Underperformance in Initial Public Offerings", *Journal of Corporate Finance* (4, 1998), pp. 1–29.

101. Toeh, S.H., Wong, T.J., and Rao, G., "Are Accruals during Initial Public Offerings Opportunistic?" *Review of Accounting Studies* (3, 1998), pp. 173–208.

102. Liu, C., Ryan, S., and Wahlen, J., "Differential Valuation Implications of Loan Across Banks and Fiscal Quarters", *The Accounting Review* (January, 1997), pp. 133–46.

103. Petroni, K.R., "Optimistic Reporting in the Property Casualty Insurance Industry", *Journal of Accounting and Economics* (18, 1994), pp. 157–79.

104. Visvanathan, G., "Deferred Tax Valuation Allowances and Earnings Management", *Accrual of Financial Statement Analysis* (3, 1998), pp. 6–15.

105. Collins and Hribar, "Errors in Estimating Accruals; Implications for Empirical Research", Working paper, University of Iowa, 1999.

106. DeAngelo, L., "Accounting Numbers as Market Valuation Substitutes: A Study of Management Buyouts of Public Shareholders", *The Accounting Review* (62, 3, July, 1986) pp. 431–53.

107. Healey, P.M., "The effects of bonus schemes in accounting decisions", *Journal of Accounting and Economics* (7, 1989), pp. 85–107.

108. Jones, J., "Earnings Management during Import Relief Investigations", *Journal of Accounting Research* (29, 1991), pp. 193–228.

109. Beneish, R.D., "Detecting GAAP Violations: Implications for assessing earnings management among firms with extreme financial performance", *Journal of Accounting and Public Policy* (16, 1997), pp. 271–309.

110. Beneish, R.D., "Discussion of all Accruals during the Initial Public Offerings Opportunistic?" *Review of Accounting Studies* (3, 1998), pp. 209–21.

111. Dechow, Patricia M., Sloan, Richard G., and Sweeny, Amy P., "Detecting Earnings Management", *The Accounting Review* (70, 1995), p. 199.

112. Ibid., p. 42.

113. Kang, Sok-Hyon, and Sivaramakrishnan, K., "Issues in Testing Earnings Management and an Instrumental Variable Approach", *Journal of Accounting Research* (33, 1995), pp. 353–66.

114. Ou, J., and Penman, S., "Financial Statement Analysis and the Prediction of Stock Returns", *Journal of Accounting and Economics* (11, 1989), pp. 295–330.

115. Bernard, V., and Thomas, J., "Evidence that Stock Prices do not Fully Reflect the Implications of Current Earnings for Future Earnings", *Journal of Accounting and Economics* (13, 1990), pp. 305–40.

116. Maines, L.A., and Hand, J.R., "Individuals' Perceptions and Misperceptions of the Time Series Properties of Quarterly Earnings", *The Accounting Review* (July, 1996), pp. 317–36.

117. Sloan, R.G., "The Stock Prices fully Reflect Information in Accruals and Cash Flows about Future Earnings", *The Accounting Review* (3, 1996), pp. 289– 315.

118. Subramanyam, K.R., "The Pricing of Discretionary Accruals", *Journal of Accounting and Economics* (12, 1996), pp. 149–282.

119. Xie, H., "The Mispricing of Abnormal Accruals", *The Accounting Review* (76, 2001), pp. 357–73.

120. DeFond, M.L., and Park, C.W., "The Reversal of Abnormal Accruals and the Market Valuation of Earnings Surprises", *The Accounting Review* (July, 2001), pp. 145–76.

121. Burgstahler, D., and Eames, M., "Management of Earnings and Analyst Forecasts", Working paper, University of Management, 1998.

122. Abarbanell, J., and Lehavy, R., "Can Stock Recommendations Predict Earnings Management and Analyst's Earnings Forecast Errors?" Working paper, University of California at Berkeley, 1998.

123. Kaznik, R., "On the Association between Voluntary Disclosure and Earnings Management", *Journal of Accounting Research* (37, 1999), pp. 57–82.

124. Bushee, B., "The Influence of Institutional Investors on Myopic R&D Investment Behavior", *The Accounting Review* (3, 1998), pp. 305–33.

125. Perry, S., and Williams, T., "Earnings Management Preceding Management Buyout Offers", *Journal of Accounting and Economics* (15, 1992), pp. 157–79.

126. Teoh, S.H., Welch, I., and Wong, T.J., "Earnings Management and the Long Term Market Performance of Initial Public Offerings", *Journal of Finance* (December, 1998), pp. 1935–74.

127. Teoh, S.H., Welch, I., and Wong, T.J., "Earnings Management and the Post Issue Performance of Seasoned Equity Offerings", *Journal of Financial Economics* (October, 1998), pp. 63–99.

128. Teoh, S.H., Welch, I., Wong, T.J., and Rao, G., "Are Accruals during Initial Public Offerings Opportunistic?" *Review of Accounting Studies* (3, 1998), pp. 175–208.

129. Erickson, R., and Wang, S.W., "Earnings Management by Acquiring Firms in Stock for Stock Mergers", *Journal of Accounting and Economics* (97, 1999), pp. 149–76.

130. Dye, R., "Earnings Management in an Overlapping Generations Model", *Journal of Accounting Research* (26, 1998), pp. 195–235.

131. Brown, Paul R., "Earnings Management: A Subtle (and Troublesome) Twist to Earnings Quality," *The Journal of Financial Statement and Analysis* (Winter, 1999), p. 62.

132. Ibid.

133. Collingwood, Harris, "The Earnings Game", *Harvard Business Review* (June, 2001), pp. 65–74.

134. DeGeorge, Francois, Patel, Jayendra, and Zeckhauser, Richard, "Earnings Management to Exceed Thresholds", *Journal of Business* (72, 1999), pp. 1–33.

135. Ibid.

136. Ibid.

137. Ibid.

138. Guidry, F.A., Leone, A., and Rock, S., "Earnings-based Bonus Plans and Earnings Management by Business Unit Managers", *Journal of Accounting and Economics* (26, 1999), pp. 113–42.

139. Holhausen, R., Larker, D., and Sloan, R., "Annual Bonus Schemes and the Manipulation of Earnings", *Journal of Accounting and Economics* (19, 1995), pp. 29–74.

140. DeAngelo, L.E., "Managerial Competition, Information Costs, and Corporate Governance. The Use of Accounting Performance Measures in Proxy Contests", *Journal of Accounting and Economics* (17, 1994), pp. 133–43.

141. Dechow, P., and Sloan, R.G., "Executive Incentives and the Horizon Problem: An Empirical Investigation", *Journal of Accounting and Economics* (14, 1991), pp. 51–89.

142. Healy, Paul M., and Wahlen, James M., "A Review of the Earnings Management Literature and Its Implications for Standard Setting", *Accounting Horizons* (4, 1999), pp. 365–83.

143. Moyer, S., "Capital Adequacy Ratio Regulations and Accounting Choices in Commercial Banks", *Journal of Accounting and Economics* (12, 1990).

144. Scholes, M., Wilson, G.P., and Wolfson, M., "Tax Planning, Regulatory Capital Planning, and Financial Reporting Strategy for Commercial Banks", *Review of Financial Studies* (3, 1990), pp. 625–50.

145. Beatty, A., Chamberlain, S., and Maglilo, J., "Managing Financial Reports of Commercial Banks: The Influence of Taxes, Regulatory Capital and Earnings", *Journal of Accounting Research* (2, 1995), pp. 231–61.

146. Collins, J., Shackelford, D., and Wahlen, J., "Bank Differences in the Coordination of Regulatory Capital, Earnings and Taxes", *Journal of Accounting Research* (2, 1995), pp. 263–91.

147. Petroni, K.R., "Optimistic Reporting in the Property Casualty Insurance Industry", *Journal of Accounting and Economics* (15, 1992), pp. 485–508.

148. Adiel, R., "Reinsurance and the Management of Regulatory Ratios and Taxes in the Property – Casualty Insurance Industry", *Journal of Accounting and Economics* (1, 1996), pp. 207–40.

149. Cahan, S., "The Effect of Anti-trust Investigations on Discretionary Accruals: A Refined Test of the Political Cost Hypothesis", *The Accounting Review* (67, 1992), pp. 77–95.

150. Makar, Stephen, and Alam, Pervaiz, "Earnings Management and Antitrust Investigations: Political Costs over Business Cycles", *Journal of Business Finance and Accounting* (5, 1998), pp. 701–20.

151. Jones, J.J., "Earnings Management During Import Relief Investigations", *Journal of Accounting Research* (29, 1991), pp. 193–228.

152. Key, K.G., "Political Cost Incentives for Earnings Management in the Cable Television Industry", *Journal of Accounting and Economics* (3, 1997), pp. 309–37.

153. Lim, Stephen, and Matolcsy, Zoltan, "Earnings Management of Firms Subject to Produce Price Controls", *Accounting and Finance* (39, 1999), pp. 131–50.

154. Asthana, Sharad, "The Impact of Regulatory and Audit Environment on Managers' Discretionary Accounting Choices: The Case of SFAS No. 196", *Accounting for the Public Interest* (1, 2001), pp. 23–96.

155. D'Souza, Julia, Jacob, John, and Ramesh, K., "The Use of Accounting Flexibility to Reduce Labor Renegotiation Costs and Manage Earnings", *Journal of Accounting and Economics* (30, 2001), pp. 187–208.

156. Gigler, F., "Self-Enforcing Voluntary Disclosures", *Journal of Accounting Research* (32, 1994), pp. 224–40.

157. Chaney, P.K., and Lewis, C.M., "Earnings Management and Firm Valuation Under Asymmetric Information", *Journal of Corporate Finance* (1, 1995), pp. 319–45.

158. Eilifsen, A., Knivsfla, K.H., and Saettem, F., "Earnings Manipulation: Cost of Capital versus Tax", *The European Accounting Review* (8, 1999), pp. 481–91.

159. Johansson, S.E., and Ostman, L., *Accounting Theory – Integrating Behavior and Measurement* (London: Pitman, 1995), p. 201.

160. Matsumoto, Dawn A., "Management's Incentives to Avoid Negative Earnings Surprises", *The Accounting Review* (77, 3, July, 2002), pp. 483–514.

161. Ibid., p. 486.

162. Kuhn, Thomas S., "The Structure of Scientific Revolutions", op. cit., p. 105.

163. Committee on Concepts and Standards for External Financial Reports, *Statement on Accounting Theory and Theory Acceptance* (Sarasota, FL: American Accounting Association, 1977).

164. Kuhn, Thomas S., "The Structure of Scientific Revolutions", op. cit., p. 105.

165. Ritzer, G., "Sociology: A Multiparadigm Science", *The American Sociologist* (August, 1975).

166. *Statement of Accounting Theory and Theory Acceptance*, op. cit., p. 47.

References

Positive theory of accounting

Coase, R.J., "The Nature of the Firm", *Economica* (4, November, 1937), pp. 386–405.

Fama, E.E., "Agency Problems and the Theory of the Firm", *Journal of Political Economy* (2, 1980), pp. 288–307.

Freidman, Milton, "The Methodology of Positive Economics", in *Essays in Positive Economics* (Chicago: University of Chicago Press, 1953), pp. 6–7.

Jensen, M.C., and Meckling, J.W.H., "Theory of the Firm: Managerial Behavior, Agency Costs and Ownership Structure", *Journal of Financial Economics* (October, 1976), pp. 305–60.

Sterling, Robert R., "Positive Accounting: An Assessment", *Abacus* (26, 2, 1990), pp. 97–135.

Zimmerman, Jerold L., "Research on Positive Theories of Financial Accounting", in John O. Mason, Jr. (ed.), *Accounting Research Convocation* (Birmingham, AL: School of Accountancy, The University of Alabama, November, 1982).

Income smoothing

Albrecht, W.D., and Richardson, F.M., 'Income Smoothing by Economy Sector', *Journal of Business Finance and Accounting* (17, 5, Winter, 1990), pp. 713–30.

American Institute of Certified Public Accountants, *Report of the Study Group on the Objectives of Financial Statements*, New York AICPA (October, 1973)

Amihud, Y., Kamin, J., and Ronen, J., "Managerialism and Ownerism in Risk-Return Preferences", Ross Institute of Accounting Research (R.I.A.R) Working Paper 95–4, New York University, 1975.

Archibald. T.R., "The Return to Straight Line Depreciation: An Analysis of a Change in Accounting Method", *Empirical Research in Accounting: Selected Studies* (1967), pp. 164–80.

Barefield, R.M, and Comiskey, E.E., "The Smoothing Hypothesis: An Alternative Test", *The Accounting Review* (April, 1972), pp. 291–8.

Barnea, A., Ronen, J., and Sadan, S., "The Implementation of Accounting Objectives – An Application to Extraordinary Items", *The Accounting Review* (January, 1975), pp. 58–68.

Barnea, A., Ronen, J., and Sadan, S., "Classificatory Smoothing of Income with Extraordinary Items", *The Accounting Review* (January, 1976), pp. 110–22.

Baumol, W.J., *Business Behavior, Value and Growth*, 2nd edn (New York: Macmillan, 1959).

Biedleman, C., "Income Smooth: The Role of Management", *The Accounting Review* (October, 1973), pp. 653–67.

Beidelman, C.R., "Income Smoothing: The Role of Management", *The Accounting Review* (October, 1973), pp. 653–67.

Belkaoui, A., and Picur, R.D., "The Smoothing of Income Numbers: Some Empirical Evidence on Systematic Differences Between Core and Periphery Industrial Sector", *Journal of Business Finance and Accounting* (11, Winter, 1984), pp. 527–45.

Bernard, V.L., and Stober, R.S., "The Nature and Amount of Information Reflected In Cash Flows and Accruals", *The Accounting Review* (October, 1989), pp. 624–52.

Copeland, R.N., "Income Smoothing", *Journal of Accounting Research*, Supplement to Volume 6, *Empirical Research in Accounting: Selected Studies* (6, 1968), pp. 101–16.

Copeland, R., and Licastro, R., "A Note on Income Smoothing", *The Accounting Review* (July, 1968), pp. 540–5.

Copeland, R., and Wojdak, J., "Income Manipulation and the Purchase Pooling Choice", *Journal of Accounting Research* (Autumn, 1969), pp. 188–95.

Cushing, B.E., "An Empirical Study of Changes in Accounting Policy," *Journal of Accounting Research* (Autumn, 1969), pp. 196–203.

Cyert, R., and March, J., *A Behavioral Theory of the Firm* (Englewood Cliffs, NJ: Prentice-Hall, 1963).

Dascher, P.E., and Malcom, R.E., "A Note on Income Smoothing in the Chemical Industry", *Journal of Accounting Research* (Autumn, 1970), pp. 253–9.

Eckel, N., "The Smoothing Hypothesis Revisited", *Abacus* (June, 1981), pp. 28–40.

Gordon, M.J., "Postulates, Principles and Research in Accounting", *The Accounting Review* (April, 1964), pp. 251–63.

Gordon, M.J., Horwitz, B.N., and Meyers, P.T., "Accounting Measurement and Normal Growth of the Firm", in Jaedicke, Ijiri and Nielsen (eds.), *Research in Accounting Measurement* (Evanston, IL: A.A.A., 1966), pp. 221–31.

Hepworth, S.R., "Smoothing Periodic Income", *The Accounting Review* (January, 1953), pp. 32–9.

Hepworth, S.R., "Periodic Income Smoothing", *The Accounting Review* (January, 1953), p. 34.

Lambert, R., "Income Smoothing as Rational Equilibrium Behavior", *The Accounting Review* (October, 1984), pp. 604–18.

Horwitz, B.N., "Comments on Income Smoothing: A Review by J. Ronen, S. Sadan and C. Snow", *Accounting Journal* (Spring, 1977), pp. 27–9.

Imhoff, E.A., Jr., "Income Smoothing: An Analysis of Critical Issues", *Quarterly Review of Economics and Business* (Autumn, 1981), pp. 23–42.

_____, "Income Smoothing – A Case for Doubt", *Accounting Journal* (Spring, 1977), pp. 85–101.

Jeter, D.C., and Chaney, P.K., "An Empirical Investigation of Factors Affecting the Earnings Association Coefficient", *Journal of Business Finance and Accounting* (19, 6, November, 1992), pp. 839–63.

Jordan-Wagner, J., and Wootton, C.W., "An Analysis of Earnings in Oil Related Industries", *Petroleum Accounting and Financial Management Journal* (Spring, 1993), pp. 110–23.

Lev, B., and Kunitzky, S., "On the Association Between Smoothing Measures and the Risk of Common Stock", *The Accounting Review* (April, 1974), pp. 259–70.

Mason, R.D., and Lind, D.A. *Statistical Techniques in Business and Economics*, 8th edn (Homewood, IL: Irwin, 1993), pp. 136–7.

Moses, O.D., "Income Smoothing and Incentives: Empirical Tests Using Accounting Changes", *The Accounting Review* (April, 1987), pp. 358–77.

O'Hanlon, J., "The Relationship in Time Between Annual Accounting Returns and Annual Stock Market Returns in the UK", *Journal of Business Finance and Accounting* (18, 3, April, 1991), pp. 305–14.

Ronen, J., and Sadan, S., *Smoothing Income Numbers, Objectives, Means, and Implications* (Reading, MA: Addison-Wesley, 1981).

Ronen, J, and Sadan, S., "Smoothing Income Numbers", op. cit.

_____, "Classificatory Smoothing: Alternative Income Models", *Journal of Accounting Research* (Spring, 1975), pp. 133–49.

Strong, N., "Modeling Abnormal Returns: A Review Article", *Journal of Business Finance and Accounting* (19, 4, June, 1992), pp. 531–53.

Thorne, D., "The Information Content of the Trend Between Historic Cost Earnings and Current Cost Earnings (United States of America)", *Journal of Business Finance and Accounting* (18, 3, April, 1991), pp. 289–303.

Trueman B., and Titman, S., "An Explanation for Accounting Income Smoothing", *Journal of Accounting Research* (Supplement, 1988), pp. 127–39.

Zmijewski, M.E, and Hagerman, R.L., "An Income Strategy Approach to the Positive Theory of Accounting Standard Setting/Choice", *Journal of Accounting and Economics* (August, 1981), pp. 129–49.

Earnings management

Adiel, R., "Reinsurance and the Management of Regulatory Ratios and Taxes in the Property – Casualty Insurance Industry", *Journal of Accounting and Economics* (22, 1–3, 1996), pp. 207–40.

Ayers, B.C., "Deferred Tax Accounting under SFAS No. 109: An Empirical Investigation of its Incremental Value-Relevance Relative to APB No. 11", *The Accounting Review* (73, 2, 1998), pp. 195–212.

Beatty, A., Chamberlain, S., and Magliolo, J., "Managing Financial Reports of Commercial Banks: The Influence of Taxes, Regulatory Capital and Earnings", *Journal of Accounting Research* (33, 2, 1995), pp. 231–61.

Beaver, W., Eger, C., Ryan, S., and Wolfson, M., "Financial Reporting, Supplemental Disclosures and Bank Share Prices", *Journal of Accounting Research* (Autumn, 1989), pp. 157–78.

Healy, Paul M., and Wahlen, James M., "A Review of the Earnings Management Literature and its Implications for Standard Setting", *Accounting Horizons* (4, 1999), pp. 365–84.

____, and Engel, E., "Discretionary Behavior with respect to Allowances for Loan Losses and the Behavior of Security Prices", *Journal of Accounting and Economics* (22, 1996), pp. 177–206.

____, and McNichols, M., "The Characteristics and Valuation of Loss Reserves of Property-Casualty Insurers", Working paper, Stanford University, 1998.

Beneish, M.D., "Detecting GAAP Violation: Implications for Assessing Earnings Management among firms with Extreme Financial Performance", *Journal of Accounting and Public Policy* (16, 1997), pp. 271–309.

____ "Discussion of: Are Accruals During Initial Public Offerings Opportunistic?" *Review of Accounting Studies* (3, 1998), pp. 209–21.

Burgstahler, D., and Dichev, I., "Earnings Management to Avoid Earnings Decreases and Losses", *Journal of Accounting and Economics* (24, I, 1997), pp. 99–126.

____ and ____ "Incentives to Manage Earnings to Avoid Earnings Decreases and Losses: Evidence from Quarterly Earnings", Working paper. University of Washington, 1998.

____ and Eames, M., "Management of Earnings and Analysts Forecasts", Working paper, University of Washington, 1998.

Bushee, B., "The Influence of Institutional Investors on Myopic R&D Investment Behavior", *The Accounting Review* (73, 3, 1998), pp. 305–33.

Cahan, S., "The Effect of Antitrust Investigations on Discretionary Accruals: A Refined Test of the Political Cost Hypothesis", *The Accounting Review* (67, 1992), pp. 77–95.

Collins, J., Shackelford, D., and Wahlen, J., "Bank Differences in the Coordination of Regulatory Capital, Earnings and Taxes", *Journal of Accounting Research* (33, 2, 1995), pp. 263–91.

DeAngelo, E., DeAngelo, H., and Skinner, D., "Accounting Choices of Troubled Companies", *Journal of Accounting and Economics* (17, January, 1994), pp. 113–43.

DeAngelo, L.E., "Managerial Competition, Information Costs, and Corporate Governance: The Use of Accounting Performance Measures in Proxy Contests", *Journal of Accounting and Economics* (10, 1998), pp. 3–36.

Dechow, P., "Accounting Earnings and Cash Flows as Measures of Firm Performance: The Role of Accounting Accruals", *Journal of Accounting and Economics* (18, I, 1994), pp. 3–40.

___, and Sloan, R.G., "Executive Incentives and the Horizon Problem: An Empirical Investigation", *Journal of Accounting and Economics* (14, 1991), pp. 51–89.

___, ___, and Sweeney, A.P., "Causes and Consequences of Earnings Manipulation: An Analysis of Firms Subject to Enforcement Actions by the SEC", *Contemporary Accounting Research* (13, I, 1996), pp. 1–36.

Defeo, V., Lambert, R., and Larcker, D., "The Executive Compensation Effects of Equity-for-Debt Swaps", *The Accounting Review* (54, 1999), pp. 201–27.

DeFond, M.L., and Jiambalvo, J., "Debt Covenant Effects and the Manipulation of Accruals", *Journal of Accounting and Economics* (17, January, 1994), pp. 145–76.

DeGeorge, F., Patel, J., and Zeckhauser, R., "Earnings Management to Exceed Thresholds, Working paper, Boston University, 1998.

Dye, R., "Earnings Management in an Overlapping Generations Model", *Journal of Accounting Research* (1998), pp. 195–235.

Erickson, M., and Wang, S-W., "Earnings Management by Acquiring Firms in Stock for Stock Mergers", *Journal of Accounting and Economics* (27, April, 1999), pp. 149–76.

Foster, G., "Briloff and the Capital Market", *Journal of Accounting Research* (17, Spring, 1979), pp. 262–74.

Gaver, J., Gaver, K., and Austin, J., "Additional Evidence on Bonus Plans and Income Management", *Journal of Accounting and Economics* (18, 1995), pp. 3–28.

Guay, W.A., Kothari, S.P., and Watts, R.L., "A Market-Based Evaluation of Discretionary Accrual Models", *Journal of Accounting Research* (34, Supplement, 1996), pp. 83–105.

Current-value accounting

14

The theory and measurement of business income occupy a central place in the literature of financial and managerial accounting. Despite the proliferation of articles on its merits and measurement methods, however, the *income concept* remains the subject of different interpretations and schools of thought, each claiming practical or conceptual superiority to the others. Basically, four schools of thought exist concerning the better measurement of business income.

The *classical school* is characterized primarily by adherence to the unit-of-measure postulate and the historical-cost principle. Generally known as *historical cost accounting* or *conventional accounting*, the classical school regards "accounting income" as business income.

The *neoclassical school* is characterized primarily by its abandonment of the unit-of-measure postulate, its recognition of changes in the general price level, and its adherence to the historical-cost principle. Generally known as *general, price-level-adjusted historical cost-accounting*, the neoclassical school's concept of business income is the "general, price-level-adjusted accounting income".

The *radical school* is characterized by its choice of *current values* as the valuation base. This school is divided into two forms. In one form, the current-value-based financial statements are not adjusted for changes in the general price level. Generally known as *current-value accounting*, this school's concept of business income is "current income". In the second form of the radical school, the current-value-based financial statements are adjusted for changes in the general price level. Generally known as *general, price-level-adjusted current-value accounting*, this school's concept of business income is "adjusted current income".

In this chapter, our purposes are (1) to rationalize the existence of these four schools of thought by examining some of the features of the income concept in accounting and economics and introducing the concept of *capital maintenance*; and (2) to elaborate on the conceptual and operational problems associated with the implementation of current-value accounting. We will examine the other schools of thought in subsequent chapters.

14.1 The relevance of the income concept

Arguments in favor of measuring income could be extended *ad infinitum*. Income is a basic and important item of financial statements that has various uses in various contexts. Income is generally perceived as a basis for taxation, a determinant of dividend-payment policies, an investment and decision-making guide, and an element of prediction.

First, income is a basis for the *taxation* and *redistribution of wealth* among individuals. A version of income known as *taxable income* is computed according to rules specified by governmental fiscal legislation. However, two bases of taxation other than income have been suggested. The possession of *resources* may be a more equitable basis for taxing economic entities. It also may be argued that individuals should be taxed on the basis of their *expenditures* rather than on the basis of their income.[1]

Second, income is perceived as a guide to a firm's *dividend* and *retention policy*. The income that is recognized is an indicator of the maximum amount to be distributed as dividends and retained for expansion or reinvested in the firm. Owing to the differences between accrual accounting and cash accounting, however, a firm may recognize an amount of income and, at the same time, not possess the funds to pay dividends. Thus, the recognition of income *per se* does not guarantee that dividends will be paid. Liquidity and investment prospects are additional variables necessary for the determination of dividend policies.

Third, income is viewed as an *investment* and *decision-making guide* in general. It is generally hypothesized that investors seek to maximize the return on capital invested, commensurate with an acceptable degree of risk. For example, the American Accounting Association's Committee on External Reporting defined a normative stockholders' valuation model centering on (1) the future dividend-per-share flows to be derived from an investment, and (2) the risk associated with these flows.[2] The model is:

$$V_{ok} = \sum_{i=1}^{m} \frac{(a_{ik})(D_{ik})(m_{ik})}{\prod_{i=1}^{m}[1+\beta_j(m_{jk})]} + \frac{(I_{nk}-CG_{nk})(a_{nk})}{\prod_{i=1}^{m}[1+\beta_j(m_{jk})]} - I_o$$

where:

V_{ok} = the net subjective present value of the gain that can be obtained by an investor k at time period o from buying one share at the market price I_o.

D_{ik} = the expected value of cash flows (dividends per share) during each period i.

I_{nk} = the expected transaction price of the stock at period n as projected investor k, less commission and other direct outlays.

CG_{nk} = the expected capital-gains tax to be paid by the investor k when the securities are sold in period n.

β_j = the before-tax opportunity rate for a riskless investment. The rate may change over time j.

n_k = the discrete time period used by the investor.

a_{ik} = a "certainty equivalent" factor that adjusts the expected cash flows to a value such that a given investor is indifferent between D and a cash flow that is certain to be paid. This factor is determined by each investor's utility preference for risk.

$M_{ik} (m_{jk})$ = i the expected marginal tax rate for each cash flow for each investor k and for each time period i or j.

I_o = the transaction price at the time of decision.

The Committee on External Reporting also suggested that a firm's ability to pay dividends is a function of the following variables:

1. net cash flows from operations;
2. nonoperating cash flows;
3. cash flows from changes in the levels of investment by stockholders and creditors;
4. cash flows from investment in assets;
5. cash flows from priority claims;
6. cash flows from random events;
7. management attitudes regarding stocks of resources; and
8. cash dividend policy.[3]

It is doubtful, however, that accounting income could be used to predict most of these variables. In addition, there has been a gradual shift of emphasis from the income concept to a cash-flow concept. For example, the "Trueblood Report" expresses the following objective:

> An objective of financial statements is to provide information useful to investors and creditors for predicting, comparing and evaluating potential cash flows to them in terms of account, timing and related uncertainty.[4]

Fourth, income is perceived as a *predictive* device that aids in the prediction of future incomes and future economic events. In fact, past values of income, based on historical cost and on current value, have been found to be useful in predicting future values of both versions of income.[5] Income consists of both *operational* results or *ordinary income*, and *nonoperational* results or *extraordinary gains and losses*, the sum of which is equal to net income. Ordinary income is assumed to be current and repetitive; extraordinary gains and losses are not. Research findings show that, as a predictor of future earnings, ordinary income is superior to net income.[6] Because such findings imply that the behavior of net income may be erratic and of no use to investment decision-making, there is some reason to use a measure of income that is conducive to accurate predictions. In others words, *income smoothing* may be justified by the need for sound predictive ability and may be intended by management to show plausible forms of trends over time to outside users of financial statements.[7] Income smoothing has been defined as the "intentional dampening of fluctuations about some level of earnings that is currently considered to be normal for a firm".[8] This definition implies that a choice must be made among a number of accounting procedures and measurements to minimize the cyclical behavior of accounting income. Income smoothing is motivated by the desire to enhance the reliability of prediction based on income and to reduce the risk surrounding the accounting numbers.[9] A recent study focuses more precisely on the reduction of systematic risk through the impact of income smoothing on reducing the covariance of the firms returns with market returns.[10] Three smoothing dimensions may be identified (see section 13.2):

1. smoothing through the occurrence and/or recognition of events;
2. smoothing through allocation over time; and
3. smoothing through classification.[11]

The fifth way that income may be perceived is as a measure of efficiency. Income is both a measure of management's stewardship of an entity's resources and of management's efficiency in conducting the affairs of a firm. This concern is well expressed in the FASB Report of the Study Group on the Objectives of Financial Statements, which maintains that "an objective of financial statements is to supply information useful in judging management's ability to utilize enterprise resources effectively in achieving the primary enterprise goal" and "the earning process consists of effort and performance directed at reaching the primary enterprise goal of returning, over time, the maximum amount of cash to its owners".[12] Management's primary goal is assumed to be to maximize earnings per share. In fact, the *stockholders' welfare-maximization* (SWM) model may be challenged by the *management welfare-maximization* (MWM) model. The management welfare-maximization model implies that managers may try to increase their remunerations by maximizing sales or assets, the firm's rate of growth, or managerial utility.[13] As a result, Findlay and Whitmore contend the following with respect to earnings:

> SWM assumes that earnings are objectively determined to reveal the time position of the business to its owners and the capital market. ... MWM presumes management manipulation or avoidance within the legality of full disclosure in order to present the firm's operations in the most favorable light.[14]

Thus, management welfare-maximization casts doubt on income as a measure of efficiency.

In conclusion, income has a role to play in various areas, but its usefulness may be subject to number of limitations, as indicated by the five cases we have discussed here.

14.2 The traditional accounting concept of income

14.2.1 A description of accounting income

Accounting income is operationally defined as the difference between the *realized revenues* arising from the transactions of the period and the *corresponding historical costs*. This definition suggests five characteristics of accounting income:

1. Accounting income is based on the *actual transaction* entered into by the firm (primarily revenues arising from the sales of goods or services minus the costs necessary to achieve these sales). Conventionally, the accounting profession has employed a transaction approach to income measurement. The transactions may be external or internal. Explicit (external) transactions result from the acquisition by a firm of goods or services from other entities; implicit (internal) transactions result from the use or allocation of assets within a firm. External transactions are explicit because they are based on objective evidence; internal transactions are implicit because they are based on less objective evidence, such as the use and passage of time.

2. Accounting income is based on the *period postulate* and refers to the financial performance of the firm during a given period.

3. Accounting income is based on the *revenue principle* and requires the definition, measurement, and recognition of revenues. In general, the *realization principle* is the

test for the recognition of revenues and, consequently, for the recognition of income. Specific circumstances present exceptions, however, as suggested in Chapter 7.

4. Accounting income requires the measurement of expenses in terms of the *historical cost* to the enterprise, constituting a strict adherence to the cost principle. An asset is accounted for at its acquisition cost until a sale is realized, at which time any change in value is recognized. Thus, expenses are expired assets or expired acquisition costs.

5. Accounting income requires that the realized revenues of the period be related to appropriate or corresponding relevant costs. Accounting income, therefore, is based on the *matching principle*. Basically, certain costs or period costs are allocated to or matched with revenues and the other costs are reported and carried forward as assets. Costs allocated and matched with period revenues are assumed to have an expired service potential.

14.2.2 Advantages of accounting income

Among the important and most spirited defenders of accounting income are Ijiri, Kohler, Littleton, and Mautz.[15] We will discuss four of their principal arguments.

The first argument in favor of accounting income is that it has survived the test of time. Most users of accounting data believe that accounting income is useful and that it constitutes a determinant of the practices and thought patterns of decision-makers. To support this argument, Kohler states that:

> Accounting is what it is today not so much because of the desire of accountants as because of the influence of businessmen. If those who make management and investment decisions had not found financial reports based on historical cost useful over the years, changes in accounting would long since have been made.[16]

Second, because it is based on actual, factual transactions, accounting income is measured and reported objectively and is therefore basically verifiable. Objectivity is generally reinforced by the belief of advocates of the use of accounting income that accounting should report facts rather than values. As Kohler states, "accounting has never been a device for 'measuring (current) value', 'changes in value' or the present worth of an asset or asset group".[17]

Third, by relying on the realization principle for the recognition of revenue, accounting income meets the criterion of conservatism. In other words, reasonable caution is taken in the measurement and reporting of income by ignoring value changes and recognizing only realized gains.

Fourth, accounting income is considered useful for control purposes, especially in reporting on stewardship (management's use of resources entrusted to it). Accounting income conveys the background of the story of the way in which management has met its responsibilities.

14.2.3 Disadvantages of accounting income

In addition to being strongly defended, accounting income has also been severely criticized in the literature for its various limitations. Basically, the arguments against the use of accounting income question its relevance to decision-making. Let us examine some of these arguments.

One argument is that accounting income fails to recognize unrealized increases in values of assets held in a given period due to the application of the historical-cost and realization principles. This prevents useful information from being disclosed and permits the disclosure of a heterogeneous mix of gains from prior and current periods. The net result does not correspond effectively to the income of the current period.

A second argument is that the reliance of accounting income on the historical-cost principle makes comparability difficult, given the different acceptable methods of computing "cost" (for example, the different inventory costing methods) and the different acceptable methods of cost allocation deemed arbitrary and incorrigible.[18]

Third, reliance of accounting income on the realization principle, historical-cost principle, and conservatism may result in misleading and misunderstood data or data that is irrelevant to users. A case in point is the lack of usefulness of ratios based on financial statements prepared in conformity with these principles.

Reliance on the historical-cost principle may give users the impression that the balance sheet represents an approximation of value rather than merely a statement of unallocated cost balances. In addition, the emphasis on income determination has led to a resolution of controversial issues based on their impact on the income statement, thereby creating a mixture of items on the balance sheet that are quite hard to define (for example, deferred tax-allocation debits and credits).

14.3 The nature of the economic concept of income

The concept of income has always been an important point of interest to economists. Adam Smith was the first economist to define income as an *increase in wealth*.[19] Most classicists, Marshall in particular, followed Smith's concept of income and linked conceptualization to business practices.[20] For example, they separated fixed and circulating (working) capital, separated physical capital and income, and emphasized realization as a test of income recognition. Toward the end of the nineteenth century, the understanding that income is more than cash was expressed in Von Bohm Bawerk's theories on capital and income.[21] Von Bohm Bawerk attempted to develop a nonmonetary concept of income despite the monetary movement that dominated economic analysis at the time. At the beginning of the twentieth century, ideas concerning income advanced. Fisher, Lindahl and Hicks provided a major, new outlook on the nature of the economic concept of income. Fisher defined economic income as a series of events that corresponds to different states: the enjoyment of psychic income, the real income, and the money income.[22] *Psychic income* is the actual personal consumption of goods and services that produces a psychic enjoyment and satisfaction of wants. Psychic income is a psychological concept that cannot be measured directly, but it can be approximated by real income. *Real income* is an expression of the events that give rise to psychic enjoyments. Real income is best measured by the *cost of living*. In other words, the satisfaction created by the psychic enjoyment of profit is measured by the money payments made for the acquisition of goods and services before or after consumption. Thus, psychic income, real income, and the cost of living are three different stages of income. Finally, *money income* represents all the money received and intended to be used for consumption to meet the cost of living. Although psychic income is the most fundamental income level and money income is that stage of income most often referred to as "income", Fisher perceived real income to be the most practical for accountants.

Lindahl introduced the concept of income as *interest*, referring to the continuous appreciation of capital goods over time.[23] The differences between the interest and the consumption anticipated for a given period are perceived as saving. This idea led to the generally accepted concept of economic income as consumption plus saving expected to take place during a certain period, the saving being equal to the change in economic capital. This may be expressed by the identity:

$$Y_e = C + (K_t - K_{t-1})$$

where:

Y_e = economic income;
C = consumption;
K_t = capital as of period t;
K_{t-1} = capital as of period $t-1$.

Hicks used the concepts introduced by Fisher and Lindahl to develop a general theory of *economic income*,[24] which defined a person's personal income as "the maximum amount he can consume during a week and still expect to be as well-off at the end of the week as he was at the beginning".[25] This definition has become the basis of many discussions on the concept of income. One problem raised by such a definition, however, is the lack of consensus on the interpretation of the term "as well-off", or "welloffness". The most accepted interpretation is that of capital maintenance, in which case the "Hicksian" income is the maximum amount that may be consumed in a given period and still maintain the capital intact.

14.4 Concepts of capital maintenance

The concept of *capital maintenance* implies that income is recognized after capital has been maintained or costs have been recovered. *Return on capital* (income) is distinguished from *return of capital* (cost recovery). Two principal concepts of capital maintenance or cost recovery may be expressed both in terms of units of money (*financial capital*) and in terms of units of the same general purchasing power (*physical capital*). Thus we are provided with four concepts of capital maintenance:

1. money maintenance: financial capital measured in units of money;
2. general purchasing-power money maintenance: financial capital measured in units of the same purchasing power;
3. productive-capacity maintenance: physical capital measured in units of money;
4. general purchasing-power, productive-capacity maintenance: physical capital measured in units of the same purchasing power.

The first concept implies that the financial capital invested or reinvested by the owners is maintained. Under the money-maintenance concept, income is equal to the change in net assets adjusted for capital transactions expressed in terms of dollars. Conventional accounting, as it relies on historical cost for the valuation of assets and liabilities, conforms to the money-maintenance concept.

The second concept implies that the purchasing power of the financial capital invested or reinvested by the owner is maintained. Under the general purchasing-power, money-maintenance concept, income is equal to the change in net assets adjusted for capital transactions expressed in units of the same purchasing-power, money. General price-level adjusted, historical-cost financial statements conform to the general purchasing-power, money-maintenance concept.

The third concept implies that the physical productive capacity of the firm is maintained. Interpretations of the specific meaning of "productive capacity" differ. The *Sandilands Report* in the United Kingdom interpreted productive capacity as follows:

> What is meant by a company's "productive capacity" and how is it to be maintained intact? We have received various suggestions as to how this calculation should be made, which may be classified into three alternative definitions of productive capacity:

- Productive capacity should be defined as the *physical assets* possessed by the company, so that profit would be the amount that could be distributed after making sufficient provision to replace the physical assets held by the company as they are consumed or wear out.

- Productive capacity should be defined as the capacity to produce the same *volume* of goods and services [output] in the following year as could be produced in the current year.

- Productive capacity should be defined as the capacity to produce the same *value* of goods and services [output] in the following year as could be produced in the current year.[26]

Although the first definition of productive capacity in terms of the same assets does not take into account technological improvements, the last two definitions in terms of "same volume of output" and "same value of output" do allow technological improvements to be made. Productive-capacity maintenance is the concept of capital maintenance used in current-value accounting that discloses assets and liabilities in the financial statements at their current values.

Finally, the fourth concept of capital maintenance implies the maintenance of the physical productive capacity of the firm measured in units of the same purchasing power. General purchasing-power, productive-capacity maintenance is the concept of capital maintenance used in general price-level-adjusted, current-value accounting.

The following example illustrates the impact of each of the four concepts of capital maintenance on the income statement. Suppose that a given firm has $2,000 in net assets at the beginning and $3,000 in net assets at the end of a given period. Also assume that $2,500 in net assets are required to maintain the firm's actual physical productive capacity and that the general price level increased ten percent during the period. According to each of the concepts of capital maintenance, the firm's income would be:

1. Money maintenance:
   $3,000 – $2,000 = $1,000

2. General purchasing-power maintenance:
   $3,000 – [$2,000 + (0.10 × $2,000)] = $800

3. Productive-capacity maintenance:
   $3,000 – $2,500 = $500

4. General purchasing-power, productive-capacity maintenance:
   $3,000 – [$2,500 + (0.10 × $2,500)] = $250

The accounting income is therefore $1,000, the general price-level-adjusted accounting income is $800, the current-value-based income is $500, and the general price-level-adjusted, current-value-based income is $250. In the rest of this chapter, we will discuss current-value accounting; the other concepts will be presented in the following chapters.

14.5 Concepts of current value

The productive-capacity maintenance concept requires that the assets and liabilities of a firm be represented in terms of current values. Current value can be calculated on the basis of:

1. capitalization, or the present-value method;
2. current entry price;

3. current exit price; or

4. a combination of values derived from these three methods.

14.5.1 Capitalization

Under the *capitalization method* for calculating current value, the *capitalized value* or *present value* of an asset, group of assets, or total assets is the net amount of the discounted expected cash flows pertaining to the asset, group of assets, or total assets during their useful lives. To compute this capitalized value, four variables must be known:

1. the expected cash flows that may result from the use or disposal of the asset;

2. the timing of those expected cash flows;

3. the number of years of the asset's remaining life; and

4. the appropriate discount rate.

If these variables can be determined in an accurate and objective manner, the capitalization or present-value method can be expressed by:

$$P_0 = \sum_{j=1}^{n} \frac{R_j}{(1+i)^j}, P = \sum_{j=2}^{n} \frac{R_j}{(1+i)^{j-1}}, \text{and } I_1 = (P_1 - P_0) + R_j$$

where:

P_0 = the capitalized value or present value at time 0;
P_1 = the capitalized value or present value at time 1;
I_1 = income for the first year;
R_j = expected net cash flow in period j;
i = appropriate discount rate;
n = useful remaining life of the asset.

Whereas the accounting income based on historical data for a specified period may be labeled *ex-post income*, or *periodic income*, the present-value income is the *total pure-profit income* expected to be accrued up to the firm's planning horizon. It is an *ex-ante income*, or *economic income*, that reflects expectations about future cash flows. Such income may be computed when all the relevant variables are known with certainty as well as when all the relevant variables are probabilistic.

For example, assume that the following net cash flows are expected to result from the total assets of a firm with a remaining useful life of four years:

Year	0	1	2	3	4
Cash Flow	–	$7,000	$8,500	$10,000	$12,000

If the appropriate discount rate is assumed to be 5 percent, then the present value at the beginning of Year 1 will be $32,887, which (using present-value tables) is computed:

Capitalized Value at Beginning of Year 1			Capitalized Value at End of Year 1		
$7,000 × 0.9524 =	$6,667		$8,500 × 0.9524	=	$8,095
8,500 × 0.9071 =	7,710		10,000 × 0.9070	=	9,070
10,000 × 0.8638 =	8,638		12,000 × 0.8638	=	10,366
12,000 × 0.8227 =	9,872				
	$32,887				$27,531

The income for the first year can then be computed:

Expected cash flow from the use of the assets for Year 1	$7,000
+ Capitalized value of the total asset at the end of Year 1	27,531
= Total value of the firm at the end of Year 1	$34,531
– Capitalized value of the total assets at the beginning of Year 1	$32,887
= Income for the first year	$ 1,644

The present-value or economic income of $1,644 represents the real increase in the value of the firm in the first year. This value is equivalent to 5 percent of the starting capital of $32,887. Because most theorists define the discount rate as the *subjective rate* return, Edwards and Bell call the present-value or economic income the *subjective profit*.[27] Several appropriate discount rates, however, may be used to compute capitalized value:

1. the historical rate of discount;
2. the current rate of discount;
3. the average expected rate of discount;
4. the weighted-average cost of capital; and
5. the incremental borrowing rate.

The FASB appropriately defines these rates as follows:

> The *historical rate of discount* is the rate of return that is implicit in the amount of cash (or other consideration) paid to acquire an asset. More specifically, it is the rate of discount that, at the date of acquisition, causes the present value of the expected cash flows from an asset to be equal to the asset's historical cost.
> The *current rate of discount* is the rate of return implicit in the amount of cash (or other consideration) that would have to be paid if the same asset were acquired currently.
> The *average expected rate of discount* is the average rate of return that is expected to be earned on similar assets during some (usually long-term) future period …
> The *weighted-average cost of capital* is based on a particular structure, that is a particular ratio of long-term debt, preferred stockholders' equity, and common stockholders' equity …
> The *incremental borrowing rate* is the rate of interest that would have to be paid to obtain additional borrowed capital currently …[28]

The variables included in the capitalized-value formula are merely expectations that are subject to change. At the end of the first year, for example, suppose it is estimated that the expected cash flows will be $10,000 a year for the remaining three years, instead of $8,500, $10,000, and $12,000. The present-value income for the first year is found as follows:

Cash flow expected at the end of the first year	$7,000
+ Capitalized value at the end of Year 1 of expected cash flows of $10,000 a year for three years	27,232
= Total value of the firm at the end of Year 1	$34,232
– Capitalized value of the total assets at the beginning of Year 1	$32,887
= Income for the first year	$1,345

The new income for the year ($1,345) includes the following elements:

1. Anticipated economic income (0.05 × $32,887)	$1,644
2. Diminution in the capitalized value of the firm	(299)
3. Income for the year	$1,345

Although we consider the diminution in the capitalized value of the firm to be a loss in this analysis, another point of view considers it to be a mere adjustment of the original value of the firm due to changes in expectations. In other words, the capitalized value of the firm based on the new expectations would be $32,602, rather than $32,887.

Consequently, the new income for the year ($1,345) would then include the following elements:

1. Economic income (0.05 × $32,602) $1,630
2. Changes in the original value of the firm ($32,887 − $32,602)   (285)
3. Decrease in the capitalized value $1,345

The next question that arises pertains to the nature of the differences between the present-value or economic income and the accounting income. The economic income is an *ex-ante* income based on future cash-flow expectations; the accounting income is an *ex-post* or *periodic* income based on historical values. Solomons, in his revision of a work by Alexander, proposes the following distinction between economic income and accounting income:

Accounting income
+ Unrealized tangible asset changes
− Realized tangible asset changes that occurred in prior periods
+ Changes in the value of intangible assets
= Economic income[29]

Here, intangible assets refer not to the conventional intangible assets found on the balance sheet but to a concept called *subjective goodwill*, which arises from the use of expectations in the computation of economic income. Thus, in the previous example, the economic income for the four-year period is equal to $4,613, as shown in Table 14.1. Assuming an annual depreciation of $7,000, the accounting income is equal to $9,500. The difference between the economic income and the accounting income is $4,887, which is the subjective goodwill. A reconciliation is presented in Table 14.2.

Table 14.1 Computation of economic income

Year	(1) Capitalized value at the beginning of the year	(2) Capitalized value at the end of the year	(3) Expected cash flow for the year	(4) Economic profit (4) = (2) + (3) − (1)
	$	$	$	$
1	32,887	27,531	7,000	1,644
2	27,531	20,408	8,500	1,377
3	20,408	11,428.8	10,000	1,020.8
4	11,428.8	—	12,000	571.2
Total economic profit				4,613
Total cash flow			37,500	
Total depreciation expense (assumed)			28,000	
Accounting income			9,500	9,500
Subjective goodwill				4,887

Table 14.2 Reconciliation of the economic and accounting income

Year	Depreciation accounting $	Subjective goodwill $	Difference $
1	7,000	5,356	(1,644)
2	7,000	7,123	123
3	7,000	8,979.2	1,979.2
4	7,000	11,428.8	4,428.8
Total	28,000	32,887	4,887

The capitalized-value method is deemed useful for such long-term operating decisions as capital budgeting and product development. The options yielding the highest positive capitalized values are deemed to be the best methods. Capitalized values of long-term receivables and long-term payables are also used in financial statements, as shown by APB Opinion No. 21, *Interest on Receivables and Payables*.[30] The capitalized value is generally considered to be an ideal attribute of assets and liabilities, although it presents some conceptual and practical limitations. From a practical viewpoint, capitalized value suffers from the subjective nature of the expectations used for its computation. From a conceptual viewpoint, capitalized value suffers from:

1. the lack of an adequate adjustment for the risk preferences of all users;
2. the ignorance of the contribution of factors other than physical assets to the cash flows;
3. the difficulty of allocating total cash flows to the separate factors that comprised the contribution; and
4. the fact that the marginal present values of physical assets used jointly in operations cannot be added together to obtain the value of the firm.[31]

14.5.2 Current entry price

Interpretations of current entry prices

Current entry price represents the amount of cash or other consideration that would be required to obtain the same asset or its equivalent. The following interpretations of current entry price have been used.

Replacement cost-used is equal to the amount of cash or other consideration that would be needed to obtain an equivalent asset on the second-hand market having the same remaining useful life.

Reproduction cost is equal to the amount of cash or other consideration that would be needed to obtain an identical asset to the existing asset. Edwards and Bell focus on the replacement of an existing asset with an identical asset:

> It must be remembered that it is not the current cost of equivalent services provided by fixed assets over some time period which we wish to measure, but the current cost of using the particular fixed asset which the entrepreneur chooses to adopt and is still using. It is that particular decision that the entrepreneur wishes to evaluate on the basis of accounting data. It may well be that he then may wish to compare these data with opportunity cost data relating to selling and/or replacing the fixed asset, but in order to make this decision about the future, he must have information about the actual, present, and past.[32]

Whereas both replacement cost-used and reproduction cost emphasize the replacement of existing assets, *replacement cost-new* emphasizes the replacement of the productive capacity of assets. Replacement cost-new is equal to the amount of cash or other consideration needed to replace or reproduce the productive capacity of an asset with a new asset that reflects changes in technology. For example, Paton and Paton consider the alternative of replacing an existing asset with an asset of equivalent capacity:

> It should be understood that the significant replacement cost is the cost of providing the existing capacity to produce in terms of the most up-to-date methods available. Thus, it is largely a waste of time to estimate the cost of replacing an obsolete or semiobsolete plant unit literally in kind; such an estimate will never afford a basis for a sound appraisal of the property nor furnish a useful measure of current operating cost. The fact of interest is what it would cost to replace the capacity represented in the existing asset with a machine of modern design. To put the point in another way, cost of replacing in kind is a significant basis on which to measure the economic importance of property in use only in the case of standard, up-to-date facilities.[33]

The common characteristic of the three notions of current entry prices is that they all correspond to the costs of replacing or reproducing an asset held. The issue that remains to be solved is the choice of the method of measurement of current entry prices. The three most advocated methods use *quoted market prices*, *specific price indexes*, and *appraisals* or management estimates. The American Accounting Association Committee on Concepts and Standards has expressed the following order of preference:

> The current cost of obtaining the same or equivalent services should be the basis for valuation subsequent to acquisition, as well as at the date of acquisition. Where there is an established market for assets of like kind and condition, quoted market prices provide the most objective evidence of current cost. Such prices may be readily available for land, buildings, and certain types of standard equipment. Where there is no established market for assets of like kind and condition, current cost may be estimated by reference to the purchase price of assets which provide equivalent service capacity. The purchase price of such substitute assets should be adjusted for differences in operating characteristics such as cost, capacity, and quality. In other cases, adjustment of historical cost by the use of specific price indexes may provide acceptable approximations of current cost. Appraisals are acceptable only if they are based on the above methods of estimating costs.[34]

Accounting for holding gains and losses

The valuation of assets and liabilities at current entry prices gives rise to *holding gains and losses* as entry prices change during a period of time when they are held or owed by a firm. Holding gains and losses may be divided into two elements:

1. the realized holding gains and losses that correspond to the items sold or to the liabilities discharged; and
2. the non-realized holding gains and losses that correspond to the items still held or to the liabilities owed at the end of the reporting period.

These holding gains and losses may be classified as income when capital maintenance is viewed solely in money terms. They may also be classified as capital adjustments, because they measure the additional elements of income that must be retained to maintain the existing productive capacity. Thus, justification for the holding gains and losses on capital adjustment may be related to a particular definition of income.

Proponents of the capital-adjustment alternative favor a definition of income based on the preservation of physical capital. Such an approach would define the profit of an entity for a given period as the maximum amount that could be distributed and still maintain the operating capability at the level that existed at the beginning of the period. Because the changes in replacement cost cannot be distributed without impairing the operating capability of the entity, this approach dictates that replacement-cost changes be classified as capital adjustments.

Proponents of this alternative favor a definition of income based on the preservation of financial capital (the money-maintenance concept). Such an approach would define profit as the maximum amount that could be distributed and still maintain the financial capital invested at the level that existed at the beginning of the period. Such an approach dictates that replacement-cost changes be classified as holding gains and losses. The academic literature provides two alternative arguments in support of the holding-gains treatment. The first argument is that holding gains represent "realizable cost savings" in the sense that the entity is better off because it would now cost more to acquire the asset. The second argument is that replacement-cost changes may be viewed as "surrogates" for changes in net realizable value or capitalized value. Thus, the holding gains represent increases in the expected net receipts from using or selling the asset in the future.

The following two examples demonstrate the accounting treatments of holding gains and losses for inventories and depreciable assets.

Example 1: The accounting treatment of inventories at the current entry price and the corresponding holding gains and losses

Assume that a firm invests $6,000 in a new company on January 1. On the same date, it buys 1,000 pounds of coffee at $6.00 a pound. During the year, the firm sells 600 pounds of coffee at $10.00 per pound when the replacement cost is $8.00 per pound. The replacement cost of coffee at the end of the year is $9.00 per pound. The accounting entries are as follows:

	$	$
Merchandise Inventory (1,000 × $6.00)	6,000	
Cash		
(to record purchase of merchandise)		6,000
Cash	6,000	
Cost of Goods Sold (600 × $8.00)	4,800	
Sale (600 × $10.00)		6,000
Merchandise Inventory (600 × $8.00)		
(to record sale of merchandise)		4,800
Merchandise Inventory	2,400	
Realized Holding Gain [600 × ($8 – $6)]		1,200
Unrealized Holding Gain [400 × ($9 – $6)]		1,200
(to record holding gains)		

Example 2: The accounting treatment of non-current assets at the current entry price and the corresponding holding gains and losses

Assume that a firm purchases an asset with a four-year useful life for $2,000 and that its replacement cost increases $1,000 a year. The depreciation expenses must be determined on the basis of replacement cost. Most proponents of the replacement cost method agree on the need to include added amounts in current expenses as a "catch-up", "make-up" or "back-log" depreciation if the replacement costs continue to increase over the useful life of the asset. Determination of the "back-log" depreciation is shown in the following table:

Year	1 $	2 $	3 $	4 $
Year-end replacement cost	3,000	4,000	5,000	6,000
Depreciation expense based on replacement cost	750	1,000	1,250	1,500
Backlog depreciation		250	500	750
Opening accumulated depreciation		750	2,000	3,750
Adjusted accumulated depreciation	750	2,000	3,750	6,000

Thus, the accounting entries in each year would be:

	$	$
Year 1:		
Asset (replacement cost)	1,000	
Depreciation	750	
Holding Gain		1,000
Accumulated Depreciation		750
Year 2:		
Asset (replacement cost)	1,000	
Depreciation	1,000	
Backlog Depreciation	250	
Holding Gain		1,000
Accumulated Depreciation		1,250
Year 3:		
Asset (replacement cost)	1,000	
Depreciation	1,250	
Backlog Depreciation	500	
Holding Gain		1,000
Accumulated Depreciation		1,750
Year 4:		
Asset (replacement cost)	1,000	
Depreciation	1,500	
Backlog Depreciation	750	
Holding Gain		1,000
Accumulated Depreciation		2,250

If, however, we assume that the value of the asset increases uniformly over the year, then the depreciation expense should be computed on the basis of the average current entry price for the year. The entries for the first year result from the fact that depreciation expense is $625 (25 percent of the average asset value of $2,500) and that the holding gain will be $875 ($1,000 less one-half-year depreciation on the $1,000 increase). Accordingly, the entries for each year would be:

	$	$
Year 1:		
Asset (replacement cost)	1,000	
Depreciation	625	
Holding Gain		875
Accumulated Depreciation		750
Year 2:		
Asset (replacement cost)	1,000	
Depreciation (0.25 × $3,500)	875	
Holding Gain		625
Accumulated Depreciation		1,250
Year 3:		
Asset (replacement cost)	1,000	
Depreciation (0.25 × $4,500)	1,125	
Holding Gain		375
Accumulated Depreciation		1,750
Year 4:		
Asset (replacement cost)	1,000	
Depreciation (0.25 × $5,500)	1,375	
Holding Gain		125
Accumulated Depreciation		2,250

Three methods have been suggested to account for *backlog depreciation*:

1. charge or credit to retained earnings;
2. charge or credit to current income; and
3. adjust holding gains and losses by the amount of backlog depreciation.

The first method treats backlog depreciation as a prior-period adjustment, given that it represents the amount that should have been charged in previous periods for the replacement of the asset.

The second method treats backlog depreciation as an expense of the current period, given that income should be charged with all of the estimated costs of replacing assets.

The third method argues that the true holding gain or loss should reflect the age of the asset.

In fact, the three methods result from two fundamentally different interpretations of depreciation. One view is that depreciation should provide a reserve for the future replacement of assets, so that backlog depreciation should be treated according to either of the first two methods. The second view is that depreciation is a current cost of operations, so that backlog depreciation should be treated according to the third method.

Replacement-cost techniques applied

Exhibit 14.1 shows the Bhuller Corporation balance sheet on December 31, 19X6, and December 31, 19X7. The Bhuller Corporation's income statement appears in Exhibit 14.2.

The following additional information is available:

1. The firm uses the LIFO inventory method.
2. During 19X7, the replacement cost was $70,000 for the land and $80,000 for the plant.
3. The sales were made at the end of 19X7, when the replacement cost of inventory was $20 per unit.

| | December 31, 19X6 | | December 31, 19X7 | |
	Debit $	Credit $	Debit $	Credit $
Cash	10,000		30,000	
Accounts receivable	20,000		30,000	
Inventories	30,000	(3,000 units)	20,000	(2,000 units)
Land	40,000		40,000	
Plant (five-year life)	50,000		50,000	
Less: allowance for depreciation		10,000		20,000
Bonds (10% interest rate)		50,000		50,000
Common stock		50,000		50,000
Retained earnings		40,000		50,000
Total	150,000	150,000	170,000	170,000

Exhibit 14.1   Bhuller Corporation balance sheet

	$	$
Sales (5,000 units @ $40 per unit)		200,000
Cost of goods sold		
Beginning inventory (3,000 units @ $10 per unit)	30,000	
Purchases (4,000 units @ $12 per unit)	48,000	
Units available	78,000	
Ending inventory (2,000 units @ $10 per unit)	20,000	58,000
Gross margin		142,000
Operational expenses		
Depreciation	10,000	
Interest	5,000	
Other expenses	117,000	132,000
Net operating profit		10,000

Exhibit 14.2   Bhuller Corporation income statement

The income statement of the Bhuller Corporation for 19X7 under the current entry price is shown in Exhibit 14.3. Two items deserve explanation and further attention. First, the holding gain on plant was determined by the following entry:

	$	$
Plant	30,000	
Depreciation	13,000	
Accumulated Depreciation		22,000
Holding Gain		21,000

In other words, if the $30,000 increase in plant value is accrued uniformly over the year, the depreciation expense should be $13,000 (20 percent of the average asset value of $65,000). The holding gain is equal to $30,000 less the 1½ year depreciation on the $30,000.

Second, the operating profit before holding gains and losses and the realized holding gains and losses are both based on the realization concept. Consequently, their sum is equal to the accounting profit. The added advantage of employing the current entry price is the dichotomy between the results of (1) the operational decisions involving the production and sales of goods and services, and (2) the holding decisions involving holding assets over time in expectation of an increase in their replacement cost.

	$	$
Sales (5,000 units @ $40)		200,000
Cost of goods sold		
Beginning inventory (3,000 units @ $20)	60,000	
Purchases (4,000 units @ $20)	80,000	
Goods available	140,000	
Ending inventory (2,000 units @ $20)	40,000	100,000
Gross margin		100,000
Depreciation (0.20 × 80,000 + 50,000 ÷ 2)	13,000	
Interest	5,000	
Other expenses	117,000	135,000
Operating profit before		
Holding gains and losses		(35,000)
Realized holding gains		
1. On inventory		
a. Purchases:		
[4,000 units × ($20–$12)]	32,000	
b. Beginning inventory:		
[1,000 units × ($20–$10)]	10,000	
2. On depreciation: ($13,000–$10,000)	3,000	
		45,000
Unrealized holding gains		
1. On ending inventory:		
($20–$10) × (2,000 units)	20,000	
2. On plant	18,000	
3. On land: ($70,000–$40,000)	30,000	68,000
Net profit		78,000

Exhibit 14.3   Bhuller Corporation income statement for 19X7
Current-entry-price basis

The Bhuller Corporation balance sheet for 19X7, based on the current entry price, appears in Exhibit 14.4.

Evaluation of current-entry-price-based accounting

The primary advantage of *current-entry-price-based accounting* results from the breakdown and segregation of current-value income into current operating profit and holding gains and losses.

First, the dichotomy between current operating profit and holding gains and losses is useful in evaluating the past performance of managers. Current operating profit and holding gains and losses constitute the separate results of holding or investment decisions and production decisions, allowing a distinction to be made between the recurring and relatively controllable gains arising from production and the gains arising from factors that are independent of current and basic enterprise operations. Edwards and Bell state:

> These two kinds of gains are often the result of quite different sets of decisions. The
> business firm usually has considerable freedom in deciding what quantity of assets to

	$	$
Assets		
Cash		30,000
Accounts receivable		30,000
Inventories (2,000 units @ $20)		40,000
Land		70,000
Plant	80,000	
Less: Accumulated depreciation	(32,000)	48,000
Total assets		218,000
Equities		
Bonds		50,000
Common stock		50,000
Retained earnings		
Beginning balance		40,000
Operating profit		(35,000)
Realized holding gain		45,000
Unrealized holding gain		68,000
Total liabilities and equities		218,000

Exhibit 14.4 Bhuller Corporation balance sheet December 19X7
Current-entry-price basis

hold over time at any or all stages of the production process and what quantity of assets to commit to the production process itself. ... The difference between the forces motivating the business firm to make profit by one means rather than by another and the difference between the events on which the two methods of making profits depend require that the two kinds of gain be carefully separated if the two types of decisions involved are to be meaningfully evaluated.[35]

Second, the dichotomy between current operating profit and holding gains and losses is useful in making business decisions. Such a dichotomy allows the long-run profitability of the firm to be assessed, assuming the continuation of existing conditions. Because it is recurring and relatively controllable, the current operating profit may be used for predictive purposes.

Third, current operating profit corresponds to the income that contributes to the maintenance of physical productive capacity, that is, the maximum amount that the firm can distribute and maintain its physical productive capacity. As such, current operating profit has been appropriately labeled *distributable* or *sustainable income.*

An important characteristic of distributable income from operations is that it is sustainable. If the world does not change, the company maintains its physical capacity next year and will have the same amount of distributable income that it had this year.[36]

Fourth, the dichotomy between current operating profit and holding gains and losses provides important information that can be used to analyze and compare interperiod and intercompany performance gains.

Fifth, in addition to the dichotomy between current operating profit and holding gains and losses, the current-entry-price method allows the separation to be made between realized holding gains and losses and unrealized holding gains and losses. It represents an abandonment of the realization and conservatism principles, so that holding gains and losses are recognized as they are accrued rather than as they are realized.

The feasibility of financial statements based on replacement costs is apparently becoming more and more accepted. Revsine reports the results of efforts to prepare replacement-cost financial statements for an electronic equipment manufacturer:

Very few implementation problems were encountered during the course of the study. In those cases where data were initially absent, it was usually possible to reconstruct the missing information or to develop some surrogate approach. One might reasonably expect that even these occasional problems would diminish were market-based measures widely adopted for reporting purposes.

This study has indicated that the test company was already employing what is essentially a replacement-cost system for internal inventory accounting. This itself indicates the practicality of the replacement-cost inventory procedures more force-fully than any academic study ever could. ...

On the basis of these results, it would appear defensible to conclude that the data necessary to prepare replacement-cost financial statements were generally available. Thus, this case study did not disclose any obstacles which would impede the implementation of replacement-cost reports. Whether this conclusion can be generalized to other situations is a subject for future research.[37]

There are, however, some disadvantages to the current-entry-price system. Each claim about the benefits to be derived from dichotomizing current-value income into current operating profit and holding gains and losses has been contested.[38]

The current-entry-price system is based on the assumption that the firm is a going concern and that reliable current-entry-price data may be easily obtained. Both assumptions have been called "invalid" and "unnecessary".[39]

The current-entry-price system recognizes current value as a basis of valuation but does not account for changes in the general price level and gains and losses on holding monetary assets and liabilities.

Finally, there is the difficulty of correctly specifying what is meant by "current entry price". Is an asset held for use or sale to be replaced by an equivalent, identical, or new asset? A defensible argument may be made for each of the interpretations of current entry price, namely, replacement cost-used, reproduction cost, and replacement cost-new.

14.5.3 Current exit price

Interpretations of current exit prices

Current exit price represents the amount of cash for which an asset might be sold or a liability might be refinanced. The current exit price is generally agreed to correspond (1) to the selling price under conditions of orderly rather than forced liquidation, and (2) to the selling price at the time of measurement. In case the adjusted future selling price is of concern, the concept of *expected exit value*, or *net realizable value*, is employed instead. More specifically, expected exit value or net realizable value is the amount of cash for which an asset might be expected to be sold or a liability might be expected to be refinanced. Thus, expected exit value or net realizable value refers to the proceeds of expected future sales, whereas current exit price refers to the current selling price under conditions of orderly liquidation.

The concept of current exit price was introduced by MacNeal and was further developed by Sterling and Chambers.[40] In fact, another embracing term for current exit price – *current cash equivalent* – has been proposed by Chambers, who explains:

> At any *present-time*, all past prices are simply a matter of history. Only present prices have any bearing on the choice of an action. The price of a good ten years ago has no more relation to this question than the hypothetical price 20 years hence. As individual prices may change even over an interval when the general purchasing power of money does not, and as the general purchasing power of money may change even

though some individual prices do not, no useful inference may be drawn from past prices which has a necessary bearing on present capacity to operate in a market. Every measurement of a financial property for the purpose of choosing a course of action to buy, to hold, or to sell is a measurement at a point of time, in the circumstances of the time, and in the units of currency at that time, even if the measurement process itself takes some time.

Excluding all past prices, there are two prices which could be used to measure the monetary equivalent of any nonmonetary good in possession: the buying price and the selling price. But the buying price, or replacement price, does not indicate capacity, on the basis of present holdings, to go into a market with cash for the purpose of adapting oneself to contemporary conditions, whereas the selling price does. We propose, therefore, that the single financial property which is uniformly relevant at a point of time for all possible future actions in markets is the market selling price or realizable price of any or all goods held. Realizable price may be described as *current cash equivalent*. What men wish to know, for the purpose of adaptation, is the numerosity of the money tokens which could be substituted for particular objects and for collections of objects if money is required beyond the amount which one already holds.[41]

According to the current exit approach, all assets and liabilities are revalued at their net realizable values. Net realizable values are generally obtained from market quotations adjusted for estimated selling costs and therefore correspond to the quoted sales prices on the demand market, whereas current entry prices correspond to the quoted sales prices on the supply market. Whenever the net realizable value cannot be estimated directly from the demand market, two alternatives may be considered:

1. the use of specific sales price indices, computed either by external sources or internally by the firm; and
2. the use of appraisals by external appraisers or by management.

The primary characteristic of current-exit-price systems is the complete abandonment of the realization principle for the recognition of revenues. Valuing all nonmonetary assets at their current exit prices produces an immediate recognition of all gains. Thus, operating gains are recognized at the time of production, whereas holding gains and losses are recognized at the time of purchase and, consequently, whenever prices changes rather than at the time of sale. The critical event in the accounting cycle becomes the point of purchase or production rather than the point of sale.

Net realizable value techniques applied

Assume the same data given in Example 14.1, except that the current exit price of coffee at the end of the period is $12 per unit. The income statement, balance sheet, and relevant notes, based on the current exit price, are shown in Exhibits 14.5 and 14.6.

Evaluation of current-exit-price-based accounting

The use of current-value accounting based on current exit price presents advantages and disadvantages. First, we will discuss some of the advantages attributed to *current-exit-price-based accounting*.

First, the current exit price and the capitalized value of an asset provide different measures of the economic concept of *opportunity costs*. Thus, a firm's *opportunity cost* is either the cash value to be derived from the sale of the asset or the present value of the benefits to be derived from the use of the asset. Both values are relevant to making decisions

	$	$
Revenues		
Sales (600 lbs × $10)	6,000	
Inventory (400 lbs × $12)	4,800	
Total		10,800
Cost		
Cost of sales (600 lbs × $8)	4,800	
Inventory (400 lbs × $9)	3,600	8,400
Operating profit		2,400
Realized holding gains on sales [600 lbs × ($8 – $6)]		1,200
Unrealized holding gains on inventory		
[400 lbs × ($9 – $6)]		1,200
Current-exit-price income		4,800

Exhibit 14.5   Income statement. Current-exit-price basis

Assets	$	Liabilities and stockholders' equity	$
Cash	10,000	Share capital	10,000
Inventory[a]	4,800	Retained earnings	
		Realized[b]	2,400
		Unrealized[c]	2,400
	14,800		14,800

[a]Inventory at the end of the year is valued at the net realizable value at that time (400 lbs × $12 = 4,800).

[b]Realized retained earnings include:
  (1) Realized operating profit (sales – cost of goods sold = $6,000 – $4,800 = $1,200).
  (2) Realized holding gains on sales ($1,200)

[c]Unrealized retained earnings include:
  (1) Unrealized operating profit: revenues on inventory on hand – cost of inventories on hand = $4,800 – $3,600 = $1,200.
  (2) Unrealized holding gains on inventory ($1,200).

Exhibit 14.6   Balance sheet. Current-exit-price basis

concerning whether a firm should continue to use or to sell assets already in use and whether or not a firm should remain a going concern.

Second, current exit price provides relevant and necessary information on which to evaluate the financial adaptability and liquidity of a firm. Thus, a firm holding fairly liquid assets has a greater opportunity to adapt to changing economic conditions than a firm holding assets with little or no resale value. Third, current exit price provides a better guide for the evaluation of managers in their stewardship function because it reflects current sacrifices and other choices. Chambers states:

> As financial statements include in general terms the disposition of assets and increments in assets from time to time, they are regarded as the basis on which the performance of a company and its management may be judged. ... If the amounts of assets from time to time were stated on any basis other than their money equivalents,

there would be no firm and satisfactory basis for determining the use and dispositions of assets. Since all uses and dispositions in a period entail movements of money and money equivalents, financial statements based on the money equivalents of assets provided information on which periodical performance may fairly be judged.[42]

Fourth, the use of current exit price eliminates the need for arbitrary cost allocation on the basis of the estimated useful life of the asset. More explicitly, depreciation expense for a given year is the difference between the current exit price of the asset at the beginning and at the end of the period.

Finally, the feasibility of exit-price-based financial statements was becoming more accepted. For example, McKeown reports the results of efforts by an electronics manufacturer to prepare exit-price-based financial statements:

> Preparation of two exit-value balance sheets and an exit-value income statement for X Company demonstrated that, in this case, readily available market prices could be determined at very little cost for the land and building and most of the equipment. Market prices for the rest of the equipment (mainly metal furniture) were estimated, again at nominal cost, by use of general guidelines suggested by used-furniture dealers. A more accurate estimate for these items might have been obtained by employing an appraiser. However, the cost of appraisal of these items would have been significant (5 percent of the appraised value) and would probably be incurred every three or five years, if at all. This procedure of relatively infrequent appraisals should yield accurate estimates because, according to the used furniture dealers, the resale price is determined mainly by the type and quality of the asset rather than the age. Thus, barring major changes in the used-asset market, an appraisal of a particular item (possibly adjusted by a specific price index) should be valid for several years. Measurements of items other than fixed assets were readily computed at nominal cost. The only way management would have had any effect on the exit-value figures reported would have been solicitation of special offers for particular assets. Although this activity could be called manipulation, the economic fact remains that management could realize the offered amount. Further, the effect of these offers could easily be segregated. Other than the solicitation of special offers, management cannot manipulate exit value figures because the measurements are taken from the markets rather than management estimates. This provides less opportunity for manipulation of profit figures than is available under conventional accounting procedures (alternative depreciation methods, sale of particular fixed assets to realize an available gain or loss, etc.).
>
> The conclusion must be reached that critics of exit value who based their opposition on lack of feasibility of implementation will find no evidence to support their position in this case. Preparation of exit-value statements for X Company was possible at a reasonable cost.[43]

There are, however, some significant disadvantages to the current exit-price-based system that need to be mentioned.

First, the current-exit-price-based system is relevant only for assets that are expected to be sold for a determined market price. The current exit price may be easily determined for an asset for which a second-hand market exists. It may be more difficult to determine the current exit price of specialized, custom-designed plant and equipment that has little or no alternative use. Scrap values may be the only alternative measure for such assets.

Second, the current-exit-price-based system is not relevant for assets that the firm expects to use. The disclosure of the amount of cash that would be available if the firm sold such assets to move out of its industry and move into another one is not likely to be relevant to any user interested in the actual profitability of the firm in its present industry.

Third, the valuation of certain assets and liabilities at the current exit price has not yet been adequately resolved. On one hand, there is the general problem of valuation of intangibles and the specific problem of valuation of goodwill. Also, the absence of marketable value makes the determination of realizable value difficult. McKeown, however, has shown that the realizable values may be known or imputed.[44] On the other hand, there is the problem of valuation of liabilities. Should they be valued at their contractual amounts or at the amounts required to fund the liabilities? Chambers makes a strong case for valuing liabilities at their contractual amounts, pointing out that "at a given time, the issuer owes the bondholders the contractual amount of the bonds, whatever the price at which the bonds are traded".[45]

Fourth, the abandonment of the realization principle at the point of sale and the consequent assumption of liquidation of the firm's resources contradict the established assumption that the firm is a going concern.

Finally, the current-exit-price-based system does not take into account changes in the general price level.

14.5.4 Other interpretations of current values

Other proposals for the implementation of current-value accounting have been made. In this section, we will examine these proposals. For convenience, they will be grouped into the following categories:

1. essential versus nonessential assets;
2. the value to the firm;
3. SEC replacement-cost proposal;
4. the combination of values;
5. the concept of business income.

Essential versus nonessential assets

In October 1975, the Australian Institute of Chartered Accountants and the Australian Society of Accountants published an exposure draft advocating the disclosure of supplementary current-value-based financial statements by 1 July 1977. Although that deadline was postponed, the Australian Accounting Standards Committee published a preliminary exposure draft on *A Method of Current-Value Accounting* in June 1975. The exposure draft introduced a form of current-value accounting that uses different treatments for essential assets and nonessential assets. *Essential assets* are determined on the basis of "the expected role of particular assets on the entity's operations in the immediately foreseeable future that is, broadly speaking, continuing use or termination of use".[46] A *nonessential asset* is valued at its current-exit price; an essential asset is valued at its current entry price. The holding gains and losses on essential assets are credited or debited to a revaluation account; the holding gains and losses on nonessential assets are included in income. Liabilities are valued at their contractual amounts. This valuation of liabilities is also the position taken by Chambers, who contends that:

> No amount shall be shown as a liability unless it represents an amount owed to and legally recoverable by a creditor. Whether the due date is near or distant is immaterial.

Long-dated obligations may become due and payable if any circumstances threaten the security of creditors.[47]

The distinction between essential and nonessential assets represents a modification of the current-entry-price-based system to reflect economic realities. In other words, exit price is a preferred alternative for an asset that has no future use.

The value to the firm

In the United Kingdom, the "Report of the Inflation Accounting Committee", chaired by F.E.P. Sandilands, was issued in September 1975.[48] The "Sandilands Report" concludes that the following developments are necessary for changes in the laws of corporations:

1. The same unit of measure should be employed for all users.
2. The operating profit should be disclosed separately from the holding gains and losses.
3. The financial statements should include relevant information for assessing the liquidity of the company.

The most important recommendation of the "Sandilands Report", however, is the use of the *value to the firm* as a valuation base. Accounting based on the value to the firm is also described as *current-cost accounting* (CCA). According to this approach, assets are valued at an amount that represents the opportunity costs to the firm, that is, the maximum loss that might be incurred if the firm is deprived of these assets. Thus, the value to the firm in most cases will be measured by the replacement cost, given that the replacement cost represents the amount of cash necessary to obtain an equivalent or identical asset. If the replacement cost is greater than the net realizable value, the value to the firm will be:

1. the discounted cash-flow value if it is greater than net realizable value, given that it is preferable to use the asset than to sell it; and
2. the net realizable value if it is greater than the discounted cash flow, given that it is preferable to sell the asset than to use it.

The "Sandilands Report" also recommends that all holding gains and losses be excluded from current-cost profit, which leads to the following:

- All unrealized gains arising from the reevaluation of fixed assets (and stock, where applicable) should be shown in reevaluation reserves on the balance sheet.
- Realized holding gains arising on fixed assets should similarly be included in movements in balance sheet reserves.
- The cost of sales adjustment (where applicable) should be taken to a balance sheet "stock adjustment reserve", whether it is positive or negative.
- Extraordinary gains should be classed as "extraordinary items", which implies that they may be included in profit for the year, provided they are shown separately and distinguished from current-cost profit.
- Operating gains should be shown "above the line" in the profit-and-loss account (earnings statement) as current-cost profit for the year.[49]

The "Sandilands Report" also recommends that a "summary statement of total gains and losses for the year" appear immediately after the income statement. Such a summary statement might be:

	£	£
Current-Cost Profit After Tax (as shown in Profit-and-Loss Account)		XXX
Extraordinary Items After Tax		XXX
Net Profit After Tax and Extraordinary Items		XXX
Movements in Reevaluation Reserves Net of Tax		
Stock-Adjustment Reserve	XXX	
Reevaluation Reserves		
Gain or Loss Due to Changes in the Asset-Valuation Bases	XXX	
Other Gains or Losses	XXX	XXX
Total Gain (Loss) for the Year After Tax		XXX

SEC replacement-cost proposal

As a first step toward correcting some of the limitations of historical-cost accounting, the Securities and Exchange Commission cited replacement cost as the mandatory method of disclosure for large corporations. In March 1976, the SEC issued Accounting Series of Release No. 190, which called for supplementary disclosure of replacement-cost information by all SEC registrants with inventories, gross property, plant and equipment that aggregate more than $100 million and that make up more than ten percent of total assets.[50] Replacement cost is defined as the lowest amount that would have to be paid in the normal course of business to obtain a new piece of equipment operating at productive capacity. The regulation requires the designated firms:

1. to estimate the current replacement cost of inventories and productive capacity; and

2. to restate cost of goods sold and services, depreciation, depletion, and amortization for the two most recent full fiscal years on the basis of the replacement cost of equivalent productive capacity.

The SEC proposal was a timid attempt to show the impact of inflation on fixed assets and inventory, rather than on all monetary and nonmonetary assets. The SEC explicitly states its objectives in Regulation 210.3–17:

> The purpose of this rule is to provide information to investors which will assist them in obtaining an understanding of the current cost of operating the business, which cannot be obtained from historical-cost financial statements taken alone. A secondary purpose is to provide information which will enable investors to determine the current cost of inventories and productive feet capacity as a measure of the current economic investment in these assets existing at the balance sheet date.[51]

The combination of values

The *combination-of-values* approach avoids some of the disadvantages of the current-exit-price, current-entry-price, and capitalization methods. The Canadian Accounting Research Committee's preliminary position favors a combined use of current entry and current exit prices.[52] More specifically, the following values were advocated:

● Monetary assets should be shown at discounted cash flow, except for short-term items where the time-value-of-money effect is small ...

● Marketable securities should be valued at current exit prices with adjustments for selling costs ...

● In general, inventory items should be valued at current entry prices ...

● Normally, longer-term intercorporate investments should be valued at current entry prices ...

- Fixed assets should normally be valued at replacement cost-new (less applicable depreciation calculated on the basis of the estimated useful life of the assets held) ...

- In general, intangible values should be valued at current value ...

- Liabilities should be shown at the discounted value of future payments, except for short-term items when the time-value-of-money effect is small ...[53]

A similar combination-of-values approach has been proposed by Sprouse and Moonitz, except that they advocate common-dollar current-value statements.[54]

Although the combination-of-values approach may appear to be based on arbitrary rules, advocates of this approach have suggested specific decision rules for the choice of a valuation method based on the market opportunity costs of assets.[55]

The *opportunity cost of an action* is the value of the benefits foregone as a result of the choice of the proposed action rather than the best option.

The *opportunity cost of an asset* is indicated by one of the following decision rules:

1. If $C > \bar{R} > \underline{S}*$, use the asset until replacement is required.

2. If $C > S > \underline{R}$, use the asset until replacement is required.

3. If $R > C > \underline{S}$, use the asset but do not replace it.

4. If $S > \underline{C} > R$, sell the asset and replace it for resale rather than use.

5. If $S > \bar{R} > C*$, sell the asset and replace it for resale rather than use.

6. If $R* > \bar{S} > C$, sell the asset and do not replace it.

where:

C = the capitalized value of the asset.
R = the replacement cost of the asset (current entry price).
S = the net realizable value (current exit price).
$*$ = the opportunity cost.
$-$ = the nonrelevant value in the comparison.[56]

From these rules, we can state the following valuation bases:

1. Use the replacement cost of the assets for all situations in which the assets need to be replaced, as in (1), (2), (4) and (5).

2. Use the net realizable value of the assets for all situations in which the assets should be used but should not be replaced, as in (3), and should be sold and should not be replaced, as in (6).

If we add to these two rules a decision rule advocating the valuation of monetary assets and liabilities at their capitalized values, the resulting combination-of-values approach may be easily justified conceptually and practically.

The combination-of-values approach is deemed relevant within a particular set of financial statements by the FASB Study Group on the Objectives of Financial Statements:

> The Study Group believes that the objectives of financial statements can not be best served by the exclusive use of a single valuation basis. The objectives that prescribe statements of earnings and financial position are based on users' needs to predict, compare, and evaluate earning power. To satisfy these informational requirements, the Study Group concludes that different valuation bases are preferable for different assets and liabilities. That means that financial statements might contain data based on a combination of valuation bases. ... Current replacement cost may be the best

substitute for measuring the benefits of long-term assets held for use rather than sale. Current replacement cost may be particularly appropriate when significant price changes or technological developments have occurred since the assets were acquired. ... Exit value may be an appropriate substitute for measuring the potential benefit or sacrifice of assets and liabilities expected to he sold or discharged in a relatively short time.[57]

Edwards also argues for a combination-of-values approach:

A firm that values its assets at exit prices derived from markets in which the firm is normally a buyer reports unusual value to those which would obtain in a liquidation situation, at least so far as the assets being so valued are concerned. To employ such values when liquidation is not contemplated is surely misleading. ...

I am not convinced of the merit of adopting, as a normal basis for asset valuations in the going concern, exit prices in buyer markets. These are unusual values suitable for unusual situations. ...

The point at issue, of course, is not whether to value by current entry or exit prices, but when to shift from entry to exit values. ...

The principle ... that all assets and liabilities of the going concern should be valued at current prices except for those that the firm normally sells ... would come close to a rule of "replacement cost or net realizable value, whichever is higher" [except for] a firm which is temporarily selling at a loss.[58]

The concept of business income

Edwards and Bell have introduced the concept of *business income*, labeled *money income* by others.[59] To explain the components of business or money income, we will highlight the ways in which it differs from accounting income.

We have defined *accounting income* as the difference between the realized revenue arising from the transactions of the period and the corresponding historical costs. In presenting replacement-cost income, we also have shown that (1) *the current operating profit* (representing the difference between the realized revenues and the corresponding replacement costs) and (2) *the realized holding gains and losses* (representing the difference between the replacement costs of the units sold and the historical costs of the same units) constitute the two types of gains included in accounting income. The realized holding gains and losses also may be divided into two elements: (1) the holding gains and losses realized and accrued during the period, and (2) the holding gains and losses realized during the period but accrued during previous periods. More specifically, accounting income P_a may be expressed:

$$P_a = x + y + z$$

where:

x = current operating profit;
y = realized and accrued holding gains for the period;
z = realized holding gains for the period accrued during previous periods.

Business income differs from accounting income in two ways: (1) business income is based on replacement-cost valuation, and (2) business income recognizes only the gains accrued during the period. More specifically, business income comprises (1) the current operating profit x defined earlier, (2) the realized and accrued holding gains for the period y and (3) the unrealized holding gains and losses accrued during the period business income P_b may be expressed:

$$P_b = P_a - z + w$$

In other words, business income is equal to accounting income *less* realized holding gains for the period accrued during previous periods *plus* unrealized holding gains and losses.

14.6 Conclusions

The accounting model for current-value accounting discussed in this chapter is based on the interpretation of the "Hicksian" concept of capital maintenance, or physical productive-capacity maintenance. Four different concepts of current value have been proposed in the literature and in practice: the capitalized value, the current entry price, the current exit price, and a combination of these values. Each method provides definite advantages compared with historical-cost accounting. The major disadvantage of any current-value method, as well as of historical-cost accounting, is that none of these methods recognizes changes in the purchasing power of the dollar. Accordingly, in Chapter 15, we will focus on general price-level-adjusted historical-cost accounting; in Chapter 16, we will focus on general price-level-adjusted current-value accounting.

Notes

1. Kaldor, N., *An Expenditure Tax* (London: Allen & Unwin, 1955), pp. 54–78.
2. 1966–1968 Committee on External Reporting, *An Evaluation of External Report Practices* (Evanston, IL: American Accounting Association, 1969), p. 81.
3. Ibid., pp. 83–8.
4. Ibid., p. 81.
5. Werner, Frank, "A Study of the Predictive Significance of Two Incomes Measures", *Journal of Accounting Research* (Spring, 1969), pp. 123–33.
6. Ronen, J., and Sadan, S., "Extraordinary Items and the Predictive Ability of Income Number", Vincent C. Ross Institute of Accounting Research, *Working Paper* 74–3 (New York: New York University, 1974).
7. Beidleman, Carl R., "Income Smoothing; The Role of Management", *The Accounting Review* (October, 1973), pp. 653–67.
8. Ibid., p. 654.
9. Barnea, A., Ronen, J., and Sadan, S., "Classificatory Smoothing of Income with Extraordinary Items", *The Accounting Review* (January, 1976), pp. 110–22.
10. Beidleman, Carl R., "Income Smoothing: The Role of Management", p. 654.
11. Barnea, A., Ronen, J., and Sadan, S., "Classificatory Smoothing of Income with Extraordinary Items", op. cit., p. 111.
12. *Objectives of Financial Statements* (New York: American Institute of Certified Public Accountants, 1974), p. 26.
13. Papandreou, A., "Some Basic Issues in the Theory of the Firm", in B. Haley (ed.), *Survey of Contemporary Economics* (Homewood, IL: Richard D. Irwin, 1952), pp. 250–62; Baumol, W., *Business Behavior, Value, and Growth* (New York: Macmillan, 1959); Marris, R., *The Economic Theory of Managerial Capitalism* (London: Macmillan, 1964); Findlay, Chapman M., IL, and Whitmore, G.A., "Beyond Shareholder Wealth Maximization", *Financial Management* (Winter, 1974), pp. 25–35.
14. Ibid., p. 30.
15. Littleton, A.C., "The Significance of Invested Cost", *The Accounting Review* (April, 1952), pp. 167–73; Kohler, E.L, "Why Not Retain Historical Cost?" *Journal of*

Accountancy (October, 1943), pp. 35–41; Ijiri, Yuji, "A Defense of Historical-Cost Accounting", in Robert R. Sterling (ed.), *Asset Valuation and Income Determination* (Lawrence, KS: Scholars Book Co., 1971), pp. 1–14; Mautz, R.K., "A Few Words for Historical Cost", *Financial Executive* (January, 1973), pp. 93–8.

16. Kohler, E.L., "Why Not Retain Historical Cost?" op. cit., p. 36.

17. Ibid., p. 32.

18. Thomas, Arthur L., Accounting Research Study No. 3, "The Allocation Problem in Financial Accounting" (Evanston, IL: American Accounting Association, 1969), and Accounting Research Study No. 9, "The Allocation Problem: Part 2" (Sarasota, FL: American Accounting Association, 1974).

19. Smith, Adam, *An Enquiry into the Nature and Causes of the Wealth of Nations* (London: George Routledge, 1890).

20. Marshall, Alfred, *Principles of Economics*, 8th edn (London: Macmillan, 1947), Book II, Chs. 2, 4, Appendix E.

21. Von Bohm Bawerk, Eugene, *Positive Theory of Capital*, Vol. 88 of *Capital and Interest* (South Holland, IL: Libertarian Press, 1959), pp. 16–66.

22. Keynes, John Maynard, *The General Theory of Employment, Interest, and Money* (London: Macmillan, 1936), Ch. 6.

23. Fisher, Irving, *The Nature of Capital and Income* (New York: Macmillan, 1912), p. 38; Lindahl, E., *Die Gerechtigkeit der Besieuerung* (Lund, 1919), translated in R.A. Musgrave and A. Peacock, *Classics in the Theory of Public Finance* (New York: Macmillan, 1958),

24. Hicks, J.R., *Value and Capital*, 2nd edn (Oxford: Clarendon Press, 1946).

25. Ibid., p. 122.

26. Sandilands, F.E.P., *Inflation Accounting: Report of the Inflation Accounting Committee* (London: Her Majesty's Stationery Office, Cmmd, 6225, September, 1975), p. 35.

27. Edwards, E.O., and Bell, P.W., *The Theory and Measurement of Business Income* (Berkeley and Los Angeles: University of California Press, 1961), pp. 38–44.

28. FASB Discussion Memorandum, An Analysis of Issues Related to Conceptual Framework for Financial Accounting and Reporting: Elements of Financial Statements and Their Measurement (Stamford, CT: Financial Accounting Standards Board, December 2, 1976), pp. 206–8.

29. Alexander, Sidney S., "Income Measurement in a Dynamic Economy", rev. by David Solomons, in W.T. Baxter and Sidney Davidson (eds.), *Studies in Accounting Theory* (Homewood, IL: Richard D. Irwin, 1962), pp. 126–7.

30. APB Opinion No. 21, *Interest on Receivables and Payables* (New York: American Institute of Certified Public Accountants, 1972.)

31. Thomas, Arthur L., "Discounted Services Again: The Homogeneity Problem", *The Accounting Review* (January, 1964), pp. 1–11; Barton, A.D., An Analysis of Business Income Concepts, International Center for Research in Accounting, *Occasional Paper No. 7*, (Lancaster, England: University of Lancaster, 1975), p. 50.

32. Edwards, E.O., and Bell, P.W., *The Theory and Measurement of Business Income*, op. cit., p. 286.

33. Paton, W.A., and Paton, W.A., Jr., *Asset Accounting* (New York: Macmillan, 1952), p. 325.

34. Accounting for Land, Buildings, and Equipment, *The Accounting Review* (July, 1964), p. 696.

35. Edwards, E.O., and Bell, P.W., *The Theory and Measurement of Business Income*, op. cit., p. 73.

36. Vancil, Richard F., and Weil, Roman L., "Current Replacement-Cost Accounting Depreciable Assets, and Distributable Income", in *Replacement-Cost Accounting:*

Readings on Concepts, Uses, and Methods (Glen Ridge, NJ: Thomas Horton and Daughters, 1976), p. 58.

37. Revsine, L., "Replacement-Cost Accounting: A Theoretical Foundation", in J.J. Cramer, Jr., and G.H. Sorter (eds.), *Objectives of Financial Statements. Selected Papers*, *Vol. 2* (New York American Institute of Certified Public Accountants, 1974), pp. 241–44.

38. Drake, D.F., and Dopuch, N., "On the Case of Dichotomizing Income", *Journal of Accounting Research* (Autumn, 1965), pp. 192–205; Prakash, P., and Sunder, S., "The Case Against Separation of Current Operating Profit and Holding Gain", *The Accounting Review* (January, 1979), pp. 1–22.

39. Sterling, Robert R., "The Going Concern: An Examination", *The Accounting Review* (July, 1968), pp. 481–502.

40. Chambers, R.J., *Accounting, Evaluation, and Economic Behavior* (Englewood Cliffs, NJ: Prentice-Hall, 1966); MacNeal, Kenneth, *Truth in Accounting* (Lawrence, KS: Scholars Book Co., 1970); Sterling, Robert R., *Theory of the Measurement of Enterprise Income*, (Lawrence: University of Kansas Press, 1970).

41. Ibid., pp. 91–2.

42. Chambers, R.J., *Accounting for Inflation, Exposure Draft* (Sydney, Australia: University of Sydney, September, 1975), paragraph 20.

43. McKeown, James C., "Usefulness of Exit-Value Accounting Statements in Satisfying Accounting Objectives", in J.J. Cramer, Jr., and G.H. Sorter (eds.), *Objectives of Financial Statements: Selected Papers, Vol. 2* (New York: American Institute of Certified Public Accountants, 1973), p. 227.

44. McKeown, James C., "An Empirical Test of a Model Proposed by Chambers", *The Accounting Review* (January, 1971), pp. 12–29.

45. Chambers, R.J., "Continuously Contemporary Accounting", *Abacus* (September, 1970), pp. 643–7.

46. Australian Accounting Standards Committee, *A Method of Current-Value Accounting* (Sydney: Australian Institute of Chartered Accountants and Australian Society Accountants, June, 1975), paragraph 16.

47. Chambers, R.J., *Accounting for Inflation*, op. cit., paragraph 30.

48. Sandilands, F.E.P., Inflation Accounting: Report of the Inflation Accounting Committee.

49. Ibid., paragraph 621.

50. Accounting Series Release No. 190, *Notice of Adoption and Amendments to Regulation Requiring Disclosure of Certain Replacement-Cost Data* (Washington, DC: Securities Exchange Commission, 1976).

51. SEC Regulation 210.3–17, "Current Replacement-Cost Information, Statement Objectives" (Washington, DC: Securities and Exchange Commission, 1976).

52. Accounting Research Committee Discussion Paper, *Current-Value Accounting* (Toronto: Canadian Institute of Chartered Accountants, August, 1976), p. 28.

53. Ibid., pp. 66–8.

54. Sprouse, R.T., and Moonitz, Maurice, *Accounting Research Study* No. 3, "A Tentative Set of Accounting Principles for Business Enterprises" (New York: American Institute of Certified Public Accountants, 1962).

55. Barton, Allan, *An Analysis of Business Income Concepts*, pp. 45–6.

56. Ibid., p. 46.

57. *Objectives of Financial Statements*, op. cit., pp. 41–3.

58. Edwards, E.O., "The State of Current-Value Accounting", *The Accounting Review* (April, 1975), pp. 235–45.

59. Edwards, E.O., and Bell, P.W., *The Theory and Measurement of Business Income*; Parker, R.H., and Harcourt, C.G. (eds.), *Readings in the Concept and Measurement of Income* (New York: Cambridge University Press, 1969), pp. 17–18.

References

Historical cost

Anthony, R.N., "Case for Historical Costs", *Harvard Business Review* (November/December, 1976), pp. 69–79.

Ijiri, Yuji, "The Significance of Historical-Cost Valuation", in *The Foundation of Accounting Measurement* (Englewood Cliffs, NJ: Prentice-Hall, 1967), pp. 64–7.

Ijiri, Yuji, "A Defense of Historical-Cost Accounting", in Robert R. Sterling (ed.), *Asset Valuation and Income Determination* (Lawrence, KS: Scholars Book Co., 1971), pp. 1–14.

Ijiri, Yuji, *Research Monograph Report No. 1*, "Historical-Cost Accounting and its Rationality" (Vancouver: Canadian Certified General Accountants' Research Foundation, 1981).

Kohler, E.L., "Why Not Retain Historical Cost?", *Journal of Accountancy* (October, 1963), pp. 35–41.

Littleton, A.C., "The Significance of Invested Cost", *The Accounting Review* (April, 1952), pp. 167–73.

Mautz, R.K., "A Few Words for Historical Cost", *Financial Executive* (January, 1973), pp. 23–7, 93–8.

Capitalization

Alexander, Sidney S., "Income Measurement in a Dynamic Economy", rev. by David Solomons in W.T. Baxter and Sidney Davidson (eds.), *Studies in Accounting Theory* (Homewood, IL: Richard D. Irwin, 1962), pp. 126–200.

Barton, A.D., "Expectations and Achievements in Income Theory", *The Accounting Review* (October, 1974), pp. 664–81.

Bierman, H., Jr., and Davidson, Sidney, "The Income Concept – Value Increment or Earnings Predictor?" *The Accounting Review* (April, 1969), pp. 239–46.

Bromwich, M., "The Use of Recent Valuation Model in Published Accounting Reports", *The Accounting Review* (July, 1977), pp. 587–96.

Mattessich, R., "On the Perennial Misunderstanding of Asset Reassessment by Means of 'Present Values'", *Cost and Management* (March/April, 1970), pp. 29–31.

Parker, R.H., and Harcourt, G.C. (eds.), *Readings in the Concept and Measurement of Income* (New York: Cambridge University Press, 1969).

Schwader, K., "A Critique of Economic Income in an Accounting Concept", *Abacus* (August, 1967), pp. 23–35.

Shwayder, K., "The Capital-Maintenance Rule and the New Asset Valuation Rule", *The Accounting Review* (April, 1969), pp. 3–16.

Sterling, Robert R., and Lemke, K.W. (eds.), *Maintenance of Capital: Financial Versus Physical* (Lawrence, KS: Scholars Book Company, 1982).

Current entry price

Drake, D.R., and Dopuch, N., "On the Case of Dichotomizing Income", *Journal of Accounting Research* (Autumn, 1965), pp. 192–205.

Prakash, P., and Sunder, S., "The Case Against Separation of Current Operating Profit and Holding Gain", *The Accounting Review* (January, 1979), pp. 1–22.

Revsine, L., "Replacement-Cost Accounting", *Contemporary Topics in Accounting Series* (Englewood Cliffs, NJ: Prentice-Hall, 1973).

Rosenfield, P., "Current Replacement Value Accounting – A Dead-End", *Journal of Accountancy* (September, 1975), pp. 63–73.

Rosenfield, P., "Reporting Subjective Gains and Losses", *The Accounting Review* (October, 1969), pp. 788–97.

Stamp, Edward, "The Valuation of Assets", *TM Chartered Accountant Magazine* (November, 1975), pp. 67–9.

Current exit price

Bedford, N.M., and McKeown, James C., "Net Realizable Value and Replacement Cost", *The Accounting Review* (April, 1972), pp. 333–8.

Chambers, R.J., *Accounting, Evaluation, and Economic Behavior* (Englewood Cliffs, NJ: Prentice-Hall, 1966; reprinted Houston, TX: Scholars Book Co., 1974).

Chambers, R.J., *Accounting for Inflation: Exposure Draft* (Sydney, Australia: University of Sydney, August, 1975).

Chambers, R.J., *Accounting for Inflation: Markets and Problems* (Sydney, Australia: University of Sydney, August, 1975).

Chambers, R.J., "NOD, COG, and PuPu: See How Inflation Teases", *Journal of Accountancy* (February, 1975), pp. 56–62.

Staubus, G.J., "Current Cash Equivalent for Assets: A Dissent", *The Accounting Review* (October, 1967), pp. 650–61.

Sterling, Robert R., *Theory of the Measurement of Enterprise Income* (Lawrence, KS: University of Kansas Press, 1970).

General price-level accounting

In Chapter 14, we introduced the radical school of thought associated with the adoption of current-value accounting. We also established that a neoclassical school exists as a middle ground between the classical school of historical-cost accounting and the radical school of current-value accounting. This option consists of the restatement of historical-cost financial statements prepared in accordance with general purchasing power. Known as *general price-level accounting*, or *general price-level-adjusted, historical-cost accounting*, this school differs from current-value accounting and historical-cost accounting in its complete renunciation of the stable monetary unit postulate. Also, it should be emphasized at the outset that *general price-level accounting and current-value accounting are competing alternative measures for dealing with problems created by inflation*. General price-level accounting reflects changes in the general price level; current-value accounting reflects changes in the *specific* price level. In general price-level accounting, the *change* in the unit of measure is measured.

In this chapter, we will analyze the conceptual and operational features of general price-level accounting information and the means of providing such information.

15.1 General price-level restatement of historical-cost financial statements

Historical-cost accounting assumes either that the monetary unit is stable or that the changes in the value of the monetary unit are not material. It is well recognized, however, that the general purchasing power of the dollar has been continually declining. *General purchasing power*, which refers to the ability of the monetary unit to purchase goods or services, is inversely related to the price of the goods or services for which it may be exchanged. When the price of goods or services increases, the movement is referred to as *inflation*, which is also a decrease in the general purchasing power of money. When the price of goods or service decreases, the movement is referred to as *deflation*, which is also an increase in the general purchasing power of money. Because historical-cost accounting does not recognize these changes in the general purchasing power of money, the balance sheet contains diverse kinds of assets and liabilities that refer to different dates and that are expressed in changes in the purchasing power of the dollar. General price-level accounting corrects this situation by completely restating the historical-cost financial statements in a way that reflects changes in the purchasing power of the dollar.

Changes in the purchasing power of the dollar are measured by means of *index numbers*. A *price index* is the ratio of the average price of a group of goods or services on a given date and the average price of a similar group of goods or services on another given date, known as the *base year*, when the price index is equal to 100. Price indices that measure the changes in prices on a general basis reflect the purchasing power of the dollar. Such indices are used to restate the historical-cost based amounts on the financial statements in terms of units of purchasing power at a base year or at the end of the current period. So that inter-company comparisons will be meaningful, the established common date to which dollars are to be restated in terms of general purchasing power is the end of the current period.

To introduce the steps required in the preparation of general price-level statements, we will use a simplified model drawn from the discussion introduced by Chambers.[1] Assume that a firm's balance sheet may be divided into *monetary items* and *nonmonetary items*. At this level, *monetary items* may be defined as items for which amounts are fixed in terms of numbers of dollars by contract or otherwise, regardless of changes in price levels. For the period 0, the balance sheet equation, expressed in dollars at time 0, is:

$$M_0 + N_0 = R_0$$

where:

M_0 = net monetary items;
N_0 = net nonmonetary items;
R_0 = residual equity.

Let us also assume that there is a change in the general price level p. By definition, $p = (P_1/P_0) - 1$, where P_0 is the price index at time 0 and P_1 is the price index at time 1. The balance sheet equation at t_2 restated for the changes in the general price level, is:

$$M_0 (1 + p) + N_0 (1 + p) = R_0 (1 + p)$$

which is equivalent to

$$M_0 + M_{0p} + N_0 + N_{0p} = R_0 + R_{0p}$$

Given that, by definition, net monetary assets are expressed in fixed amounts of dollars, it is appropriate to remove $M_0 p$ from each side of the equation and to replace M_0 with M_1:

$$M_1 + (N_0 + N_0\text{p}) = (R_0 + R_{0p}) - M_{0p}$$

The last equation may be interpreted as follows:

1. M_1 represents the net monetary assets at t_1.
2. $N_0 + N_{0p}$ represents the general price-level restated nonmonetary assets at t_1.
3. $R_0 + R_{0p}$ represents the general price-level restated residual equity at t_1.
4. M_{0p} represents the gains or losses on monetary items. By definition M_0 is equal net monetary assets C_0 less monetary liabilities L_0.

The balance sheet equation at $t2$ may be restated:

$$C_1 + (N_0 + N_{0p}) - L_1 = (R_0 + R_{0p}) - (C_{0p} - L_{0p})$$

or:

$$C_1 + (N_0 + N_{0p}) - L_1 = (R_0 + R_{0p}) - C_{0p} + L_{0p}$$

Consequently L_{0p} represents the gain from the outstanding liabilities during the period and C_{0p} represents the loss resulting from holding monetary assets from t_0 to t_1.

From this simplified model, we can develop the methodology required for the restatement of historical-cost amounts in traditional financial statements into units of general purchasing power. The following steps are necessary:

1. Obtain the complete set of historical-cost financial statements.
2. Determine and obtain an acceptable general price-level index on which data on the index numbers are available to cover the life of the oldest item on the balance sheet.
3. Classify each item on the balance sheet as a monetary or a nonmonetary item.
4. Adjust the nonmonetary items by a conversion factor to reflect the current general purchasing power.
5. Calculate the general purchasing power (general price-level) gains or losses arising from holding monetary items.

With the exception of the first step, we will discuss each of these steps in the remainder of Chapter 15.

15.2 Adjusting specific items for general price-level changes

15.2.1 Treatment of monetary items

Calculation of the general price-level gain or loss

As previously stated, the amounts of monetary items are fixed in terms of number of dollars, by contract or otherwise, regardless of changes in the general or specific price levels. Although these amounts are fixed, the values of the monetary items in terms of purchasing power change. Holders of monetary items, therefore, gain or lose purchasing power because the general level of prices changes. Such gains and losses are called *general purchasing-power gains or losses*, or *general price-level gains* or *losses on monetary items*. More specifically, during periods of rising prices:

- monetary assets lose purchasing power, which is recognized by a general price-level loss; and
- monetary liabilities gain purchasing power, which is recognized by a general price-level gain.

During periods of decreasing prices:

- monetary assets gain purchasing power, which is recognized by a general price-level gain; and
- monetary liabilities lose purchasing power, which is recognized by a general price-level loss.

The general price-level gain or loss is calculated by:

1. Computing the net monetary asset position at the beginning of the period. For example, if cash and payables at the beginning of the period are $30,000 and $20,000, respectively, net monetary assets will be $10,000.

2. Restating the net monetary asset position at the beginning of the period in terms of the purchasing power of the dollar at the end of the period. If, for example, the general price-level index is 120 at the beginning of the period and 180 at the end of the period, then the net monetary asset position at the beginning of the period ($10,000) is restated as $15,000 [$10,000 × (180/120)].

3. Restating all of the monetary receipts for the year on a year-end basis and adding the result to the restated net monetary position at the beginning of the period (found in Step 2). Assuming that sales of $20,000 occur evenly during the year and that the average general price index is 150, the adjusted monetary receipts are restated as $24,000 [$20,000 × (180/150)]. This result is added to the $15,000 found in Step 2 to arrive at a total restated net increase in monetary items of $39,000.

4. Restating all of the monetary payments of the year on a year-end basis and deducting the result from the total restated net increase in monetary items found in Step 3. Assume that purchases and expenses of $15,000 also occur evenly during the year. The adjusted monetary payments are then restated as $18,000 ($15,000 × (180/150)). This result is deducted from the $39,000 found in Step 3 to yield the adjusted, computed net monetary asset position of $21,000 at the end of the period

5. Deducting the actual net monetary assets at the end of the period from the computed net monetary assets at the end of the period found in Step 4 to obtain a purchasing power gain of $6,000.

Using our example, these five steps may be summarized as follows:

	Monetary Items	
	Unadjusted	**Adjusted**
	$	**$**
Steps 1 and 2	10,000	15,000
Step 3	20,000	24,000
Total	30,000	39,000
Step 4	15,000	18,000
Total	15,000	21,000
Step 5		15,000
Purchasing power gain (or loss)		6,000

To summarize, general price-level gains or losses are computed by restating the monetary position at the beginning of the period and the net monetary transactions during the period as units of general purchasing power at the end of the period. The result is compared with actual net monetary position, and the difference is the general price-level gain or loss.

Treatment of the general price-level gain or loss

A lack of agreement exists on the nature of the general price-level gain or loss and its relevant accounting treatment. The following approaches have been suggested:

1. Accounting Research Study No. 6, APB Statement No. 3, and the FASB and the CICA Exposure Drafts on general price-level accounting take the position that the general price-level gain or loss should be included in current income.[2]
2. Only the general price-level loss should be included in current income; the general price-level gain should be treated as a capital item.
3. Both the general price-level gain and loss should be treated as capital items.
4. Both the general price-level gain and loss should be included in current income, with the exception of gains and losses related to long-term debt, which should not appear until they are realized through the redemption of the bonds.[3]
5. All price-level gains and losses should be included in current income, with the exception of gains and losses that arise from including monetary items in shareholders' equity (for example, preferred shares having monetary characteristics).

Despite the controversy generated by each of these different viewpoints, pronouncements of the various accounting bodies predominantly favor the first treatment. The AICPA first expressed this viewpoint in 1969 in APB Statement No. 3:

41 General price-level gains and losses on monetary items arise from changes in the general price level and are not related to subsequent events such as the receipt or payment of money. Consequently, the Board has concluded that these gains and losses should be recognized as part of the net income of the period in which the general price level changes.

42 A different viewpoint than that expressed in paragraph 41, held by a Board member, is that all of a monetary gain should not be recognized in the period of general price-level increase. Under this view, a portion of the gain on net monetary liabilities in a period of general price-level increase should be deferred to future periods as a reduction of the cost of nonmonetary assets, since the liabilities represent a source of funds for the financing of these assets. The proponent of this view believes that the gain from holding net monetary liabilities during inflation is not realized until the assets acquired from the funds borrowed are sold or consumed in operations. The Board does not agree with this view, however, because it believes that the gain accrues during the period of the general price level increase and is unrelated to the cost of nonmonetary assets.[4]

The conclusion reached by the APB was sustained by the FASB Exposure Draft on the subject, which stated:

48 The net gain or loss of general purchasing power that results from holding monetary assets and liabilities shall be included in determining net income in units of general purchasing power. No portion of the general purchasing-power gain or the loss shall be deferred to future periods.

77 General purchasing-power gains or losses on monetary assets and liabilities arise from changes in the general price level while the assets are held or the liabilities are owned. They are not related to subsequent events, such as the receipt or payment of money. Consequently, the Board concludes (paragraph 48) that those gains and losses should be recognized in determining general purchasing-power income in the period in which general price level changes.[5]

The same position was also reached by the Accounting Standards Steering Committee in the United Kingdom, which published a Provisional Statement of Standard Accounting Practice No. 7 in May 1974. The Committee justified its position as follows:

16 It has been argued that the gain on long-term borrowing should not be shown as profit in the supplementary statement because it might not be possible to distribute it without raising additional finance. This argument, however, confuses the measurement of profitability with the measurement of liquidity. Even in the absence of inflation, the whole of a company's profit may not be distributable without raising additional finance, for example, because it has been invested in, or earmarked for investment in nonliquid assets.

17 Moreover, it is inconsistent to exclude such gains when profit has been debited with the cost of borrowing (which must be assumed to reflect anticipation of inflation by the lender during the currency of the loan) and with depreciation on the converted cost of fixed assets.[6]

The Accounting Research Committee in Canada took a similar position.[7]

Thus, as a general rule, all price-level gains or losses are recognized in the general price-level income statement. The only exception, recommended in both the FASB and the Canadian positions, concerns gains or losses attributable to preferred shares (monetary preference shares) carried at an amount equal to their fixed redemption or liquidation price, which should be credited or charged to common shareholders' equity on the general price-level balance sheet.

15.2.2 Treatment of nonmonetary items and stockholders' equity

Nonmonetary items are restated in terms of the current general purchasing power by multiplying the cost of the item reported on the historical-cost-based financial statements by the following conversion factor:

$$\frac{\text{Current Year Index}}{\text{Index When Nonmonetary Item Was Acquired}}$$

For example, assume that a piece of equipment is acquired for $100,000 on December 31, 19X0, when the general price-level index is 120. The estimated useful life of the assets is four years. Further assume that the financial statements at the end of 19X2 are restated in terms of units of general purchasing power. If the current price index on December 31, 19X3 is 180, the adjustment of the equipment account will then be:

	Unadjusted Amount $	Conversion Factor $	Adjusted Amount $
Equipment	100,000	180/120	150,000
Accumulated Depreciation	50,000	180/120	75,000
Net Equipment	50,000		75,000

The restatement of stockholders' equity, with the exception of retained earnings, is similar to the restatement of nonmonetary items. The original invested capital is multiplied by the following conversion factor:

$$\frac{\text{Current Year Index}}{\text{Index When Capital Was Invested}}$$

Retained earnings, which cannot be adjusted by a single conversion factor, represent net income after dividends accumulated since the creation of the going concern. Retained earnings may be restated as follows:

1. The first time historical-cost financial statements are restated in terms of units of current general purchasing power, retained earnings may be determined simply as the residual after all other items in the balance sheet have been restated.

2. In the following periods, the end-of-period retained earnings in units of current general purchasing power may be determined by:

    (a) net income in units of current general purchasing power reported in the general price-level statement (including general price-level gains and losses on monetary items);
    (b) adjustments resulting from general price-level gains or losses on monetary share-holders' equity items.

An important difference is not apparent between general price-level accounting and current-value accounting. Under current-value accounting, an increase in the price of a nonmonetary item results in a holding gain. Under general price-level accounting, the adjustment of historical cost is simply a restatement of a nonmonetary item in terms of the current general purchasing power, and no gain or loss is recognized.

15.3 The monetary–nonmonetary distinction

It is important to distinguish between monetary and nonmonetary items, because different treatments are applied to the two types of items. *Nonmonetary items* must be translated into dollars of the same purchasing power at the end of the current period. *Monetary items*, on the other hand, are already stated in end-of-current-period dollars and gain or lose purchasing power as a result of changes in the general price level.

The distinction between monetary and nonmonetary items seems apparent. Monetary items gain or lose purchasing power; nonmonetary items do not. This line of reasoning is used in APB Statement No. 3 and reported by different researchers.[8] Determining monetary items according to expected effect (gain or loss of purchasing power) and then calculating the gain or loss is, however, circular reasoning. As Hendriksen points out, it "bases the classification on the assumed effect, rather than determining the effect from the classification and a change in the price level".[9]

What definition will allow monetary assets to be identified apart from their expected effects? Accounting Research Study No. 6 defined a monetary item in terms of *fixed claims* as an item "the amount of which is fixed by statute or contract and is therefore not affected by a change in the general price level".[10]

Because it does not specify *how* the amount is to be fixed, however, this definition is inadequate. Thus, to correct for this misspecification, the official definition adopted in the various pronouncements of the accounting bodies considers monetary items to be items the amounts of which *are fixed by contracts or otherwise fixed in terms of dollars* (or whatever is the domestic currency), *regardless of changes in specific prices or in the general price level*. This definition is general and applies to assets, liabilities and shareholders' equities that have the specified characteristics. Accordingly, monetary and nonmonetary items are identified and segregated as shown in Exhibit 15.1. Problem areas exist, however, because some assets and liabilities may exhibit characteristics of both monetary and nonmonetary items. Thus, various degrees of *fixity* are possible, as implied by the word "fixed" in the definition of a monetary item. Must a monetary item be a monetary item permanently? Because conditions may change, the price of a monetary item need not be fixed permanently. But what degree of fixity justifies classifying an item as monetary? The decision remains a matter of professional judgment, as the following problem areas indicate.

First, preferred shares are classified as nonmonetary items in APB Statement No. 3. The FASB Exposure Draft considers that:

> … preferred stock carried at an amount equal to its fixed liquidation or redemption price is monetary because the claim of the preferred stockholders on the assets of the enterprise is in a fixed number of dollars; preferred stock carried at less than its fixed liquidation or redemption price is nonmonetary, but becomes monetary when restated to an amount equal to its fixed liquidation or redemption price.[11]

The FASB Exposure Draft also recommends that:

> … gains or losses of general purchasing power that result from monetary stockholders' equity items (for example, preferred stock that is carried … at … fixed liquidation or redemption price) shall be charged or credited directly to common stockholders' equity in the general purchasing-using-power financial statements.[12]

Second, deferred income taxes are classified as nonmonetary items in APB Statement No. 3 on the basis that they are a cost-saving and are deferred as reductions of expenses in future periods. A similar classification is retained in the FASB Exposure Draft. The argument is that tax-allocation credits are classified as liabilities under the accrual method, whereas under the deferred method, these are credits simply treated as deferred credits representing savings to be amortized to income in future periods. It follows that deferred income taxes would be classified as nonmonetary items, given the adoption of the deferred method in the United States. On the other hand, the Canadian Institute of Chartered Accountants recommends that deferred income taxes be treated as monetary items, even though the deferred method is required in Canada. The *CICA Handbook* indicates that the deferral should be computed at current tax rates without subsequent adjustment of the accumulated tax-allocation debit or credit balances to reflect changes in the tax rates.[13] Consequently, deferred income taxes refer to fixed amounts of money and can be defined as monetary units. The FASB Exposure Draft *Constant Dollar Accounting* changed the classification of deferred income-tax items to monetary items. The FASB states its position as follows:

> Again, although the nonmonetary classification may be technically preferable, the monetary classification provides a more practical solution and identifies the effect of inflation with the period the inflation occurs, rather than with the period the deferred income tax item is reversed.[14]

Third, foreign currency on hand, claims to foreign currency, and obligations payable in foreign currency may be interpreted as either monetary or nonmonetary items. If they are perceived as commodities, they are nonmonetary items, because the prices of commodities may fluctuate. It they are perceived as similar to domestic-currency items, they are monetary items. A more logical viewpoint is to classify foreign-currency items as monetary it they are stated at the *closing* rate of exchange in the historical-cost financial statements

Assets	Monetary item	Nonmonetary item
Cash on hand and demand bank deposits (US dollars)	X	
Time deposits (US dollars)	X	
Foreign currency on hand and claims to foreign currency	X	
Marketable securities		
Stocks		X
Bonds (other than convertibles)	X	
Convertible bonds (until converted, these represent an entitlement to receive a fixed number of dollars)	X	
Accounts and notes receivable	X	
Allowance for doubtful accounts and notes receivable	X	
Inventories		
Produced under fixed contracts and accounted for at the contract price	X	
Other inventories		X
Loans to employees	X	
Prepaid insurance, advertising, rent, and other prepayments		X
Long-term receivables	X	
Refundable deposits	X	
Advances to unconsolidated subsidiaries	X	
Equity investment in unconsolidated subsidiaries or other investees		X
Pension, sinking, and other funds under an enterprise's control	X	X
Property, plant, and equipment		X
Accumulated depreciation of property, plant, and equipment		X
Cash-surrender value of life insurance	X	
Purchase commitments (portion paid on fixed-price contracts)		X
Advances to a supplier (not on contrail)	X	
Patents, trademarks, licenses, formulas		X
Goodwill		X
Other intangible assets and deferred charges		X
Liabilities		
Accounts and notes payable	X	
Accrued expenses payable (for example, wages)	X	
Accrued vacation pay (if it is to be paid at the wage rates as of the vacation dates and if those rates may vary)		X
Cash dividends payable	X	
Obligations payable in foreign currency	X	
Sales commitments (portion collected on fixed-price contracts)		X
Advances from customers (not on contract)	X	
Accrued losses of firm purchase commitments	X	
Deferred income		X
Refundable deposits	X	
Bonds payable and other long-term debts	X	
Unamortized premiums or discounts and prepaid interest on bonds and notes payable	X	
Convertible bonds	X	
Accrued pension obligations	X	X
Obligations under warranties		X
Deferred income-tax credits	X	
Deferred investment-tax credits		X
Preferred stock		
Carried at an amount equal to a fixed liquidation or redemption price	X	
Carried at an amount less than fixed liquidation or redemption price		X
Common stockholders' equity		X

Exhibit 15.1 Classification of items as monetary or nonmonetary

and as nonmonetary if they are stated at the *historical* rate of exchange in the historical-cost financial statements. The FASB Exposure Draft *Constant Dollar Accounting* classifies foreign currency on hand, claims to foreign currency, and obligations payable in foreign currency as monetary items. The FASB states its position as follows:

> Although the nonmonetary classification may be technically preferable and result in somewhat different disclosures, as a practical matter, the monetary classification produces essentially the same net effect on aggregate disclosure as restating those foreign-currency items as nonmonetary and then reducing them to their net realizable value. The monetary classification obviates that two-step procedure and is more understandable.[15]

Fourth, long-term debts in foreign currency also may be interpreted as either monetary or nonmonetary. Again, a logical alternative is to classify long-term debt in a foreign currency as monetary if it is stated at the closing rate of exchange and as nonmonetary if it is stated at the historical rate of exchange.

Fifth, convertible debt is perceived to have monetary and nonmonetary characteristics. Accounting Research Study No. 6 proposes that convertible debt be treated as monetary when the market price of shares is below the conversion price and as nonmonetary when the market price of shares is at or above the conversion price. Another, more accepted position is that convertible bonds should be treated as monetary debts, obligations to pay a fixed number of dollars until they are converted.

15.4 Price-level indices

A *price-level index* compares general or specific changes in price from one period to another. *A general price-level index* can be defined as a series of measurements, expressed as percentages, of the relationship between the average price of a group of goods and services on a succession of dates and the average price of a similar group of goods and services on a common date. The components of the series are called *price-index numbers*. A price index does not, however, measure the movement of the individual component prices, some of which move in one direction and some of which move in the opposite direction. Thus, the general price-level index is based on a large range of goods and services, whereas the specific price-level index refers to a particular good or industry. Because general price-level accounting reflects changes in the purchasing power of the dollar, a general price-level index must be employed to restate the historical-cost statements in terms of dollars of constant purchasing power.

15.4.1 Index formulas

The computations of a general price-level index differ according to the formula used to assign weights to prices. We will use the following symbols to represent the four basic formulas:

p = the price of the commodity or service;
q = the quantity of the commodity or service;
$p_0 q_0$ = the price and quantity of the commodity in the base period;
$p_n q_n$ = the price and quantity of the commodity in the current period;
$p_a q_a$ = the price and quantity of the commodity in some average period.

The *Laspeyres formula* assumes that the price index is a weighted sum of current-period prices divided by a weighted sum of base-period prices, where the weights are *base-period* quantities of commodities. Such an index, called a *Laspeyres index*, is computed:

$$I = \frac{\sum p_n q_0}{\sum p_0 q_0}$$

The *Paasche formula* assumes that the price index is a weighted sum of current-period prices divided by a weighted sum of base-period prices, where the weights are *current-period* quantities of commodities. Such an index, called a *Paasche index*, is computed:

$$I = \frac{\sum p_n q_n}{\sum p_0 q_n}$$

The *fixed-weighted formula* assumes that the price index is a weighted sum of current-period prices divided by a weighted sum of base-period prices, where the weights are *average-period* quantities of commodities. Such an index, called a *fixed-weighted index*, is computed:

$$I = \frac{\sum p_n q_a}{\sum p_0 q_a}$$

The *Fisher formula* assumes that the price index is a geometric average of Laspeyres and Paasche formulas. The *Fisher index* is computed:

$$I = \sqrt{\frac{\sum p_n q_n}{\sum p_0 q_n} + \frac{\sum p_n q_a}{\sum p_0 q_a}}$$

15.4.2 Choice of a general price-level index

General price-level accounting employs a conversion factor based on changes in the general price-level index to convert dollars on one date to the number of dollars having the same purchasing power on another date. An appropriate concept of purchasing power and an appropriate general price-level index must be chosen. Hendriksen presents different concepts of purchasing power, namely, general purchasing power of the dollar, purchasing power of the stockholders, investment purchasing power of the firm and specific replacement purchasing power.[16] The general purchasing power measured by a general price-level index reflects changes in the value of money and, consequently, is deemed most relevant for general price-level accounting. For example, APB Statement No. 3 states:

> The purpose of the general price-level restatement procedures is to restate historical-dollar financial statements for changes in the general purchasing power of the dollar, and this purpose can only be accomplished by using a general price-level index.[17]

Thus, the concept of general purchasing power implies the use of a general price-level index. In the United States, the Department of Commerce and the Department of Labor regularly maintain and publish general price indices. Among the most important are:

1. the *Consumer Price Index*, prepared by the Bureau of Labor Statistics of the US Department of Labor;
2. the *Wholesale Price Index*, prepared by the Bureau of Labor Statistics of the US Department of Labor;
3. the *Composite Construction-Cost Index*, prepared by the Construction Industry Division of the Business and Defense Service Administration of the US Department of Commerce;

4. the *GNP (Gross National Product) Implicit Price Deflator*, prepared by the Office of Business Economics of the US Department of Commerce.

The two price indices most commonly suggested for general price-level accounting are the *Consumer Price Index* (CPI) and the *GNP Implicit Price Deflator* (IPI). The CPI is a *base-weighted* index designed to measure price changes in a basket of retail goods and services acquired by middle-income families of specific size living in urban centers. The GNP Implicit Price Deflator is a *currently weighted* index designed to measure price changes in all goods and services produced in a given year. Both the CPI and the IPI have limitations. The base-weighted CPI fails to account for the substitution of relatively lower-priced goods that takes place when relative prices change. In other words, the CPI has an *upward bias*: it *overstates* the effect of changes in prices on the cost of living. On the other hand, the currently weighted IPI has a *downward bias*: it *understates* the price increase in the cost of living. For example, Rosen says that:

> In summary, when prices are rising, currently weighted indices may have a downward bias (that is, they tend to understate the percentage price increase) and base-weighted indices may have an upward bias (that is, they tend to overstate a percentage price increase).[18]

The IPI is considered to be a better currently compiled, general price-level index than the CPI. The IPI covers all goods and services produced in the economy, whereas the CPI covers only goods and services purchased by a "typical consumer". Thus, in terms of measuring the extent of overall price changes, the IPI is probably more relevant. Annual estimates are available from 1919, and quarterly estimates are available from 1947.

However, the FASB Exposure Draft *Constant Dollar Accounting* designates the *Consumer Price Index for All Urban Consumers* (CPI-U) rather than the GNP Implicit Price Deflator as an index of general purchasing power for two reasons. First, the CPI-U has two practical advantages: It is calculated more frequently (monthly instead of quarterly), and it is not revised after its initial publication. Second, the rates of change in the CPI-U and the GNP Implicit Price Deflator tend to be similar and, therefore, use of the CPI-U tends to produce a comparable result.[19]

15.5 A simplified illustration of general price-level indexing

The following simplified example briefly illustrates how general price-level, historical-cost financial statements can be prepared from historical-cost financial statements.

The Picur Company began business operations on December 31, 19X5, when the price level was 100 (base period). The comparative balance sheets for 19X5 and 19X6 are shown in Exhibit 15.2. The 19X6 income statement appears in Exhibit 15.3.

In addition to the balance sheets and the income statement, the following supplementary information is available:

1. The price deflator is:

    December 31,19X5 100
    December 31,19X6 180
    Average price index for 19X6 120

2. All revenues and costs were incurred evenly throughout the year, with the exception of the cost of goods sold and the depreciation expense.

	December 31, 19X5 Debit $	Credit $	December 31, 19X6 Debit $	Credit $
Monetary assets	30,000		60,000	
Inventories	30,000	(3,000 units)	20,000	(2,000 units)
Land	40,000		40,000	
Plant and equipment	50,000		50,000	
Accumulated depreciation	10,000			
Liabilities (1%)		50,000		50,000
Capital stock		100,000		100,000
Retained earnings				10,000
Total	150,000	150,000	170,000	170,000

Exhibit 15.2   The Picur Company. Comparative balance sheet as of December 31

	$	$
Sales (5,000 units @ $40)		200,000
Cost of goods sold		
Beginning inventory (3,000 units @ $10)	30,000	
Purchases (4,000 units @ $12)	48,000	
Units available	78,000	
Ending inventory (2,000 units @ $10)	20,000	58,000
Gross margin		142,000
Operational expenses		
Depreciation	10,000	
Interest	5,000	
Selling and administrative expenses	117,000	132,000
Net operating profit		10,000

Exhibit 15.3   The Picur Company. Income statement for the year ended
December 31, 19X6

3. The inventory purchases were made on a date when the price-level index was at 150.

4. A LIFO flow is assumed.

5. Depreciation for plant and equipment was accumulated by the straight-line method over a five-year life span.

The procedure for restating the historical-cost financial statements is:

1. Restate the 19X5 balance sheet to 19X6 price levels. (The 19X5 balance sheet for the Picur Company adjusted to 19X6 price levels is shown in Exhibit 15.4.)

2. Restate the 19X6 balance sheet to current 19X6 price levels. (The 19X6 adjusted balance sheet for Picur appears in Exhibit 15.5.) At this stage, there is no direct conversion factor for retained earnings. It is simply the amount required to achieve a balance between assets and equities.

3. Restate the 19X6 income statement to 19X6 price levels. (The 19X6 adjusted income statement for Picur is illustrated in Exhibit 15.6.)

4. Calculate the monetary gains or losses that result from changes in the general price level. (This computation is shown in Exhibit 15.7 for Picur.)

Assets	Unadjusted amount $	Conversion factor	Adjusted amount $
Monetary assets	60,000	180/180	60,000
Inventories	20,000	180/100	36,000
Land	40,000	180/100	72,000
Plant and equipment	50,000	180/100	90,000
Accumulated depreciation	(10,000)		(18,000)
Total	160,000		240,000
Equities			
Liabilities (10%)	50,000	180/180	50,000
Capital	100,000	180/100	180,000
Retained earnings	10,000		10,000
Total	160,000		240,000

Exhibit 15.4   The Picur Company. Balance sheet December 31, 19X6

Assets	Unadjusted amount $	Conversion factor	Adjusted amount $
Monetary assets	30,000	180/100	54,000
Inventories	30,000	180/100	54,000
Land	40,000	180/100	72,000
Plant and equipment	50,000	180/100	90,000
Accumulated depreciation	—		—
Total	150,000		270,000
Equities			
Liabilities (10%)	50,000	180/100	90,000
Capital	100,000	180/100	180,000
Retained earnings	—		—
Total	150,000		270,000

Exhibit 15.5   The Picur Company. Balance sheet December 31, 19X5

5. Prepare a reconciliation of retained earnings as follows:

	$
Retained earnings, January 1, 19X6	0
Add: Net profit	23,400
Less: General price-level loss	(13,400)
Retained earnings, January 1, 19X6	10,000

15.6 Evaluation of general price-level accounting

The controversy concerning the relevance of general price-level accounting has been an ongoing one. Some of the arguments in favor of and against general price-level accounting will be presented here as a reflection of the positions taken in the literature and in practice. The number and order of these presentations do not reflect on their relative merits.

Assets	Unadjusted amount $	Conversion factor	Adjusted amount $
Sales (5,000 units @ $40)	200,000	180/120	300,000
Cost of goods sold			
Beginning inventory (3,000 units @ $10)	30,000	180/100	54,000
Purchases (4,000 units @ $72)	48,000	180/150	57,600
Units available			111,600
Ending inventory (2,000 units @ $10)	20,000		36,000
Cost of goods sold	58,000		75,600
Gross margin	142,000		224,400
Operational expenses			
Depreciation	10,000	180/100	18,000
Interest	5,000	180/120	7,500
Selling and administrative expenses	117,000	180/120	175,500
Net operating profit	10,000		23,400

Exhibit 15.6 The Picur Company [December 31, 19X6]. Income statement adjusted to 19X6 price level

Assets	Unadjusted amount $	Conversion factor	Adjusted amount $
Net monetary assets on January 1, 19X6	(20,000)	180/100	(36,000)
Add: Monetary receipts during 19X6 sales	200,000	180/120	300,000
Net monetary items	180,000		264,000
Less: Monetary payments			
Purchases	48,000	180/150	57,600
Interest	5,000	180/120	7,500
Selling and administrative expenses	117,000	180/120	175,500
Total	170,000		240,600
Computed net monetary assets			
December 31, 19X6			23,400
Actual net monetary assets			
December 31, 19X6			(10,000)
Loss on monetary assets			13,400

Exhibit 15.7 The Picur Company. Monetary gains or losses on monetary items

15.6.1 Arguments in favor of general price-level accounting

A number of arguments have been advanced in favor of general price-level accounting. First, financial statements that are not adjusted for general price-level changes include diverse kinds of assets and claims expressed in dollars of different purchasing power. General price-level accounting is designed to express the level of changes in the price of these assets and in the purchasing power of the claims. General price-level statements present data expressed on the basis of a common denominator, the purchasing power of the dollar at the end of the period. Such statements facilitate comparisons between firms because a common unit of measure is used. The FASB states that:

> Changes in the purchasing power of the dollar affect individual enterprises differently, depending on the amount of the change and the age and composition of the enterprise's assets and equities. For example, during periods of inflation, those who hold monetary assets (cash and receivables in fixed dollar amounts) suffer a loss in purchasing power represented by those monetary assets. On the other hand, in periods of inflation, debtors gain because their liabilities are able to be repaid in dollars having less purchasing power. In periods of deflation, the reverse is true. Conventional financial statements do not report the effects of inflation or deflation on individual enterprises.[20]

The second argument in favor of general price-level accounting is that conventional historical-cost accounting does not measure income properly as a result of the matching of dollars of different "size" on the income statement. Expenses incurred in previous periods are set off against revenues that are usually expressed in current dollars. General price-level accounting provides a better matching of revenues and expenses because common dollars are used. A more realistic income relationship is therefore possible through the development of more logical dividend policies. The FASB states that:

> Investors and others often look to the income statement, or to ratios that are based in part on measures of income, for information about the ability of an enterprise to earn a return on its invested capital. In the conventional income statement, revenues are measured in dollars of current, or at least very recent, purchasing power whereas certain significant expense items are measured in dollars of different purchasing power of earlier periods. Depreciation and cost of goods sold are two of the most commonly cited examples, although the problem arises whenever amounts in the income statement represent expenditure of dollars of different purchasing power. In periods of inflation, depreciation and cost of goods sold tend to be understated in terms of the purchasing power sacrificed to acquire depreciable assets and inventory. Further, information stated in terms of current general purchasing power may indicate that an enterprise's income-tax and dividend payout rates are significantly different in terms of units of money and in units of general purchasing power.[21]

The third argument in favor of general price-level accounting is that it is relatively easy to apply. It merely replaced a "rubber dollar" with a "dated dollar".[22] General price-level accounting represents the least departure from generally accepted accounting principles. As a result, it may be relatively objective and verifiable. These characteristics may make it more acceptable to many firms than current-value accounting.

Fourth, general price-level accounting provides relevant information for management evaluation and use. Thus, the general price-level gains and losses resulting from holding monetary items reflect management's response to inflation. The restated nonmonetary items approximate the purchasing power needed to replace the assets. Finally, general price-level accounting presents the impact of general inflation on profit and provides more realistic returns on investment rates.

The staff of the Accounting Research Division of the AICPA argues the case for the preparation of price-level statements as a means for financial analysis as follows:

> If price-level changes can be measured in some satisfactory manner and if the effects of those changes can be properly disclosed, the inferences that can be drawn from

accounting data will be statistically more reliable. Specifically, for example, all the revenues and expenses in the earnings statement for any one year will be expressed in dollars of the same size and not in a mixture of dollars from different years. Similarly, the various balance sheet items will all be expressed in terms of a common dollar. Since both the results of operations and financial position will be stated in terms of the same "common dollar", a calculation of a rate of return on invested capital can be made in which both numerator and denominator are expressed in the same units.

Some inferences can be drawn in terms of the various groups interested in business activity. Investors and their representatives (for example, management, including the board of directors) can tell whether the capital invested in the business has been increased or decreased as the result of all the policies followed and all the financial events that have taken place bearing on the business entity. More specifically, management and owners can tell if the dividend policy actually followed in the past has resulted in distributions out of economic or business capital, and if not, what proportion of the earnings (adjusted for price-level changes) has in fact been distributed. With price-level adjusted data before them, the directors can tell if a proposed dividend will equal, exceed, or fall short of current earnings, or any other norm or standard they wish to use.

Owners, management, and government can tell if taxes levied on income were less than pre-tax earnings, and if so, to what extent, and if not, how much they exceeded pre-tax earnings. Creditors will be better informed as to the buffer or cushion behind their claims. In addition, employees, as well as investors, and management will have a more reliable gauge of the rate of return to date on the capital employed and will be able to use the information more intelligently to decide if the business entity has been profitable or not.

Financial statements fully adjusted for the effect of price-level changes will also reveal the losses or gains from holding or owning monetary items. All interested groups then have one important measure of the effect of a changing dollar on their positions as debtors or creditors.

Financial data adjusted for price-level effects provide a basis for a more intelligent, better informed allocation of resources, whether those resources are in the hands of individuals, of business entities, or of government.[23]

15.6.2 Arguments against general price-level accounting

A case against general price-level accounting may be based on the following arguments. First, most empirical studies indicate that the relevance of general price-level information is either weak[24] or not accepted.[25] Further research is warranted before any definite conclusions can be reached regarding the relevance of general price-level information and the ability to interpret it meaningfully.

Second, general price-level changes account only for changes in the general price level and do not account for changes in the specific price level. Thus, holding gains and losses on nonmonetary assets are not recognized. In addition, users of general price-level-adjusted data may believe that the restated values correspond to current values.

Third, the impact of inflation differs among firms. Capital-intensive firms may be affected by inflation more than firms that rely heavily on short-term assets. Similarly, high-leverage firms stand to gain from inflation. As a result, general price-level accounting may distort normal income. High-leverage companies will "look good" by showing high general price-level gains. Some of the general price-level gains and losses on monetary items, however, are unrealized and should be excluded from the financial statements and deferred to later periods.

Fourth, the costs of implementing general price-level accounting may exceed the benefits. Miller presents the following arguments:

- Companies may lose the ability to use LIFO for tax purposes.
- GPP [general purchasing power] may result in higher property tax assessments.
- Companies must roll forward (restate) prior years each time comparative statements are prepared.
- Companies must also provide replacement-cost information to the Securities and Exchange Commission (SEC).
- Investors may not attempt to understand the statements.
- There are better ways to disclose the effect of inflation on a specific company, its assets, its operations, and its future.[26]

Finally, some technical problems beset general price-level accounting. The first problem is related to the choice of an appropriate general price-level index. Of the two general indices suggested for use in price-level accounting – the Consumer Price Index and the GNP Implicit Price Deflator – it has been suggested that if price-level restatements are to be made, only the GNP Implicit Price Deflator is sufficiently representative of the entire economy. For this reason, this index is more appropriate for measuring fluctuations in the exchange value of the dollar. There is, however, a problem of timeliness. The GNP Implicit Price Deflator is only available quarterly; the Consumer Price Index is available monthly. If the GNP Implicit Price Deflator were adopted, it might be necessary to approximate its effects with the Consumer Price Index for periods when the GNP Implicit Price Deflator is not available. The FASB's decision to adopt the Consumer Price Index for All Urban Consumers has resolved this problem.

The second problem is that general price-level accounting requires assets and liabilities to be identified and classified as monetary or nonmonetary items. Although there is general agreement on how most items should be classified, some items are subject to different interpretations. Examples are deferred income taxes, preferred shares, foreign-currency items, and convertible debt.

The third technical problem is that general price-level accounting applies the accounting principles employed in conventional accounting. Only the unit of measurement is changed. Therefore, the restated cost of nonmonetary assets should not exceed the current value. For example, the lower-of-cost-or-market rule is applied, just as it is applied in historical-cost accounting. Inventories should not be restated at more than net realizable value. Paragraph 37 of APB Statement No. 3 recommends a write-down of restated cost to replacement cost only for nonmonetary assets that are stated at lower-of-cost-or-market, such as inventories or other current assets. It does not consider, however, the write-down of noncurrent assets to replacement costs. Accordingly, the FASB Discussion Memorandum on general price-level accounting poses the following questions:

> If the cost of a nonmonetary asset is to be restated upward for a decrease in the general purchasing power of the dollar and the restated amount would exceed replacement cost or some other defined amount, should the restated amount be limited to such a defined amount in general price-level financial statements? Further, if such a limit to restatement is required, should it be required for all nonmonetary assets or only for certain assets (for example only for inventory)?[27]

15.7 Conclusions

In this chapter and in Chapter 14, we have established that all the profit concepts are based on different notions of capital maintenance. Conventional accounting, because it relies on historical-cost accounting for the valuation of assets and liabilities, conforms to the money-maintenance concept. Current-value accounting, in which assets and liabilities are brought into the financial statements at their current value, conforms to the physical productive-capacity maintenance concept. Finally, general price-level accounting, because it relies on a general price-level restatement of historically based assets and liabilities, conforms to the general purchasing-power, money-maintenance concept.

Each of these accounting methods is based on certain principles and rules. Conventional accounting is based on generally accepted accounting principles in general and the historical-cost principle and stable monetary-unit postulate in particular. Conventional accounting recognizes neither changes in the general price level nor changes in the specific price level. Current-value accounting is characterized by the complete abandonment of the historical-cost principle and recognizes only changes in the specific price level. General price-level accounting is characterized by the abandonment of the stable monetary-unit postulate and recognizes only changes in the general price level. Each of these methods apparently attempts to correct some of the deficiencies of conventional historical-cost accounting but not all of them. Consequently, in Chapter 16 we will introduce another accounting valuation method based on a recognition of changes to both the general and the specific price levels.

Notes

1. Chambers, R.J., *Toward a General Theory of Accounting* (Adelaide, Australia: University of Adelaide, 1961), and *Accounting, Evolution, and Economic Behavior* (Englewood Cliffs, NJ: Prentice-Hall, 1965), pp. 223–7.

2. Accounting Research Study No. 6, *Reporting the Financial Effects of Price-Level Changes* (New York: American Institute of Certified Public Accountants, 1963), p. 13; APB Statement No. 3, *Financial Statements Restated for General Price-Level Changes* (New York: American Institute of Certified Public Accountants, June 1969), p. 8; FASB Exposure Draft, *Financial Reporting in Units of General Purchasing Power* (New York: Financial Accounting Standards Board, December 31, 1974), paragraph 30; FASB Exposure Draft, *Constant Dollar Accounting* (New York: Financial Accounting Standards Board, March 2, 1979), p. 3; *Accounting Research Committee, Accounting for Changes in the General Purchasing Power of Money* (Toronto: Canadian Institute of Chartered Accountants, July, 1975), p. 12.

3. Mason, Perry, *Price-Level Changes and Financial Statements Basic Concepts and Methods* (Columbus, OH: American Accounting Association, 1956), pp. 23–4.

4. APB Statement No. 3, op. cit., paragraphs 41, 42.

5. FASB Exposure Draft, *Financial Reporting in Units of General Purchasing Power*, op. cit., paragraphs 48, 77.

6. Accounting Standards Steering Committee, Provisional Statement of Standard Accounting Practice No. 7, *Accounting for Changes in the Purchasing Power of Money* (London: Her Majesty's Stationery Office, May, 1974), paragraphs 16, 17.

7. Accounting Research Committee, *Accounting for Changes in the General Purchasing Power of Money.*

8. Johnson, J.L., "The Monetary and Nonmonetary Distinction", *The Accounting Review* (October, 1965), pp. 281–3; Heath, L.C., "Distinguishing Between Monetary and

Nonmonetary Assets and Liabilities in General Price-Level Accounting", *The Accounting Review* (July, 1972), pp. 458–68; Boersema, J.M., "The Monetary-Nonmonetary Distinction in Accounting for Inflation", *Cost and Management* (May/June, 1975), pp. 6–11.

9. Hendriksen, E.S., *Accounting Theory* (Homewood, IL: Richard D. Irwin, 1970), p. 207.

10. Accounting Research Study No. 6, op. cit., p. 38.

11. ASB Exposure Draft, Financial Reporting in Units of General Purchasing Power, op. cit., p. 13.

12. Ibid., p. 14.

13. *CICA Handbook* (Toronto: Canadian Institute of Chartered Accountants, 1980), Section 3470.19.

14. FASB Exposure Draft, *Constant Dollar Accounting*, p. 5.

15. Ibid., p. 2.

16. Hendriksen, E.S., *Accounting Theory*, 3rd edn (Homewood, IL: Richard D. Irwin, 1977), pp. 231–6.

17. APB Statement No. 3, op. cit., p. 13.

18. Rosen, L.S., *Current-Value Accounting and Price-Level Restatements* (Toronto: Canadian Institute of Chartered Accountants, 1972), p. 40.

19. FASB Exposure Draft, *Constant Dollar Accounting*, op. cit., p. 2.

20. FASB Discussion Memorandum, *Reporting the Effects of General Price-Level Changes in Financial Statements* (Stamford, CT: Financial Accounting Standards Board, 1977), p. 8.

21. Ibid.

22. Miller, Elwood, L., "What's Wrong with Price-Level Accounting?" *Harvard Business Review* (November/December, 1978), p. 113.

23. Accounting Research Study No. 6, op. cit., pp. 14–16.

24. Dyckman, T.R., *Studies in Accounting Research* No. I, "Investment Analysis and General Price-Level Adjustments" (Evanston, IL: American Accounting Association, 1969), p. 17; Morris, R.C., "Evidence of the Impact of Inflation Accounting on Share Prices", *Accounting and Business Research* (Spring, 1975), p. 90; Peterson, Russel J., "A Portfolio Analysis of General Price-Level Restatement", *The Accounting Review* (July, 1975), p. 532.

25. Horngren, Charles T., "Security Analysts and the Price Level", *The Accounting Review* (October, 1955), pp. 575–81; Baker, M., *Financial Reporting for Security and Investment Decisions* (New York: National Association of Accountants, 1970).

26. Miller, Elwood L., "What's Wrong with Price-Level Accounting?", op. cit., p. 114.

27. FASB Discussion Memorandum, *Reporting the Effects of General Price-Level Changes in Financial Statements*, p. 11.

References

APB Statement No. 3, *Financial Statements Restated for General Price-Level Changes* (New York: American Institute of Certified Public Accountants, June, 1969).

Accounting Research Committee, *Accounting for Changes in the General Purchasing Power of Money* (Toronto: Canadian Institute of Chartered Accountants, July, 1975).

Accounting Research Study No. 6, *Reporting the Financial Effects of Price-Level Changes* (New York: American Institute of Certified Public Accountants, 1963).

Baker, M., *Financial Reporting for Security and Investment Decisions* (New York: National Association of Accountants, 1970).

Boersema, J.M., "The Monetary–Nonmonetary Distinction in Accounting for Inflation", *Cost and Management* (May/June, 1975), pp. 6–11.

Davidson, Sidney, Stickney, Clyde P., and Weil, Roman L., *Inflation Accounting: A Guide for the Accountant and the Financial Analyst* (New York: McGraw-Hill, 1976).

Davidson, Sidney, and Weil, Roman L., "Inflation Accounting", *Financial Analysts Journal* (January/February, 1975), pp. 27–31, 70–84.

Dyckman, T.R., *Studies in Accounting Research No. 1*, "Investment Analysis and General Price-Level Adjustments" (Evanston, IL: American Accounting Association, 1969).

FASB Exposure Draft, *Financial Reporting in Units of General Purchasing Power* (Stamford, CT: Financial Accounting Standards Board, December 31, 1974).

Heath, L.C., "Distinguishing Between Monetary and Nonmonetary Assets and Liabilities in General Price-Level Accounting" *The Accounting Review* (July, 1972), pp. 458–68.

Horngren, Charles T., "Security Analysts and the Price Level", *The Accounting Review* (October, 1955), pp. 575–81.

Johnson, G.L., "The Monetary and Nonmonetary Distinction", *The Accounting Review* (October, 1965), pp. 821–3.

Largay James, A., III., and Livingstone, John L., *Accounting for Changing Prices* (New York: John Wiley & Sons, 1976).

Mason, Perry, *Price-Level Changes and Financial Statements Basic Concepts and Methods* (Columbus, OH: American Accounting Association, 1956).

Miller, Elwood L., "What's Wrong with Price-Level Accounting?" *Harvard Business Review* (November/December, 1978), pp. 111–18.

Morris, R.C., "Evidence of the Impact of Inflation Accounting on Share Prices", *Accounting and Business Research* (Spring, 1975), pp. 87–95.

Peterson, Russel J., "A Portfolio Analysis of General Price-Level Restatement", *The Accounting Review* (July, 1975), pp. 525–32.

Rosen, L.S., *Current-Value Accounting and Price-Level Restatements* (Toronto: The Canadian Institute of Chartered Accountants, 1972).

Short, Daniel G., "The Impact of Price-Level Adjustment in the Context of Risk Assessment", *Journal of Accounting Research*, Supplement, *Studies for Changes in General and Specific Prices: Empirical Research and Public Policy Issues* (1978), pp. 259–72.

Stickney, Clyde P., "Adjustments for Changing Prices", in Sidney Davidson and Roman L. Weil (eds.), *Handbook of Modern Accounting*, 2nd edn., New York: McGraw-Hill, 1977.

Alternative asset-valuation and income-determination models

16

In Chapters 14 and 15, we established that income may be recognized only after "capital" has been kept intact. Consequently, income measurement depends on the particular concept of capital maintenance that is chosen. The various concepts of capital maintenance imply different ways of evaluating and measuring the elements of financial statements. Thus, both income determination and capital maintenance are defined in terms of the *asset-valuation* base used. A given asset-valuation base determines a particular concept of capital maintenance and a particular income concept. An asset-valuation base is a method of measuring the elements of financial statements, based on the selection of both an attribute of the elements to be measured and the unit of measure to be used in measuring that attribute. As we discussed in Chapters 14 and 15, four attributes may be measured and two units of measure may be used. The four attributes of all classes of assets and liabilities that may be measured are:

1. historical cost;
2. current entry price (for example, replacement cost);

3. current exit price (for example, net realizable value); and

4. capitalized or present value of expected cash flows.

The two units of measure that may be used are units of *money* and units of *purchasing power*. Combining the four attributes and the two units of measure yields the following eight alternative asset-valuation and income-determination models:

1. *Historical-cost accounting* measures historical cost in units of money.

2. *Replacement-cost accounting* measures replacement cost (that is, current and entry price) in units of money.

3. *Net-realizable-value accounting* measures net realizable value (that is, current exit price) in units or money.

4. *Present-value accounting* measures present value in units of money.

5. *General price-level accounting* measures historical cost in units of purchasing power.

6. *General price-level replacement-cost accounting* measures replacement cost in units of purchasing power.

7. *General price-level net-realizable-value accounting* measures net realizable value in units of purchasing power.

8. *General price-level present-value accounting* measures present value in units of purchasing power.

Each of these alternatives yields a different financial statement that imparts a different meaning and relevance to its users. In this chapter, we will evaluate these alternatives using a simplified example to enhance conceptual clarity and comparability among the approaches. The nature of the differences and the basis of comparison among the results of the various alternatives will also be highlighted.

16.1 The nature of the differences

The differences among the alternative asset-valuation and income-determination models arise from the different attributes to be measured and the units of measure to be used. We will examine each characteristic of the elements of the financial statements in the following sections.

16.1.1 Attributes to be measured

The attributes of assets and liabilities refer to what is being measured. First we will define the four attributes to be measured:

1. *Historical cost* refers to the amount of cash or cash-equivalent paid to acquire an asset, or the amount of cash-equivalent liability.

2. *Replacement cost* refers to the amount of cash or cash-equivalent that would be paid, to acquire an equivalent or the same asset currently, or that would be received to incur the same liability currently.

3. *Net realizable value* refers to the amount of cash or cash-equivalent that would be obtained by selling the asset currently, or that would be paid to redeem the liability currently.

4. *Present or capitalized value* refers to the present value of net cash flows expected to be received from the use of the asset, or the net outflows expected to be disbursed to redeem the liability.

We may classify these attributes in three ways:

1. These measures may be classified with respect to whether they focus on the past, present, or future. Historical-cost focuses on the past, replacement cost and net realizable value focus on the present, and present value focuses on the future.

2. These measures may be classified with respect to the kind of transactions from which they are derived. Historical cost and replacement cost concern the acquisition of assets, or the incurrence of liabilities; net realizable value and present value concern the disposition of assets, or the redemption of liabilities.

3. The third classification is with respect to the nature of the event that originates the measure. Historical cost is based on an actual event, present value is based on an expected event, and replacement cost and net realizable value are based on hypothetical events.

One question that we will examine in this chapter is: What attribute or attributes of the elements of financial statements should be measured in financial accounting or reporting?

16.1.2 Units of measure

Financial accounting measurements can be made in one of two units of measure: (1) units of money, or (2) units of general purchasing power. Similarly, each of the four attributes we have defined is measurable in either units of money or units of general purchasing power. In the United States and in most other countries, conventional financial statements are expressed in units of money. Given the continuous decline of the purchasing power of the dollar, however, another unit of measure – the unit of purchasing power – was often presented as a preferable alternative, because it recognized changes in the general price level.

Do not confuse the general price level with either the specific price level or the relative price level. A change in the general price level refers to changes in the prices of *all* goods and services throughout the economy; the reciprocal of such changes would be a change in the general purchasing power of the monetary unit. A change in the specific price level refers to a change in the price of a particular product or service. Current value accounting differs from historical-cost accounting in that the former recognizes changes in the specific price level on the basis of either replacement cost or net realizable value.

Finally, a change in the relative price level of a commodity refers to the part of the specific price change that remains after the effects of the general price-level change have been eliminated. Thus, if all prices increase by 32 percent and the price of a specific good increases by 10 percent, the relative price change is only 20 percent, or $(132/110) - 1$.

All three types of price changes may be incorporated in the asset-valuation and income-determination models. Note that both historical cost and current value are expressed in units of money and that general price-level restatements may be made for both.

Another question that we will examine in this chapter is: What unit of measure should be used to measure any particular attribute of the elements of financial statements?

16.2 Basis for comparison and evaluation

We have established that the alternative accounting models (historical-cost accounting, general price-level accounting, replacement-cost accounting, general price-level-adjusted replacement-cost accounting, net-realizable-value accounting, present-value accounting, and general price-level-adjusted present-value accounting) are based on a choice of one of four available attributes (historical cost, replacement cost, net realizable value, and present value) and one of two available units of measure (units of money and units of general purchasing power). Now, we will compare the models on the basis of whether they *avoid timing errors* and *avoid measuring-unit errors*, and we will evaluate them in terms of interpretability[1] and relevance.

Although theoretically considered the best accounting models, the present-value models will not be included in our comparison and evaluation due to their recognized practical deficiencies. First, present-value models require the estimation of future net cash receipts and the timing of those receipts, as well as the selection of the appropriate discount rates. Second, when applied to the valuation of individual assets, these models require the arbitrary allocation of estimated future net cash receipts and the timing of those receipts, as well as the selection of the appropriate discount rates. Third, when applied to the valuation of individual assets, present-value models require the arbitrary allocation of estimated future net cash receipts among the individual assets.[2] Owing to this lack of objectivity, present-value models have been largely rejected as impractical. In this chapter, we will compare and evaluate the remaining accounting models. The criteria for comparison and evaluation will be examined next.

16.2.1 Timing errors

The criteria for determining what attribute or attributes of the elements of financial statements should be measured in financial accounting and reporting should favor the attribute that avoids *timing errors*. Timing errors result when changes in value occur in a given period but are accounted for and reported in another period. A preferable attribute would be the recognition of changes in value in the same period that the changes occur. Ideally, "profit is attributable to the whole process of business activity".[3]

16.2.2 Measuring-unit errors

The criteria for determining what unit of measure should be applied to attributes of the elements of financial statements should favor the unit of measure that avoids *measuring-unit errors*. Measuring-unit errors occur when financial statements are not expressed in units of general purchasing power. A preferred measuring unit would recognize the general price-level changes in the financial statements.

16.2.3 Interpretability

Our first criterion for evaluation is the interpretability of the accounting model. In other words, the resulting statements should be understandable in terms of both meaning and use. According to Sterling:

> When an attribute involves an arithmetical calculation, the "empirical interpretation" of that attribute requires that it be placed in an "if … then …" statement.[4]

Thus, for an accounting model to be interpretable, it must be placed in an "if … then …" statement to convey to the user an understanding of its meaning as well as to demonstrate one of its uses. Given that we have two possible units of measure, the interpretation of the accounting models, by definition, will be one of the following:

1. If the accounting model measures any of the attributes in units of money, its results are expressed in the *number of dollars* (NOD) or, as Chambers refers to it, the *number of odd dollars* (NOOD).[5]

2. If the accounting model measures historical cost in units of general purchasing power, its results still are expressed in NOD.

3. If the accounting model measures current values in units of general purchasing power, its results are expressed in the *command of goods* (COG) or, as Chambers refers to it, the *command of goods in general* (COGG).[6]

16.2.4 Relevance

The second criterion for evaluation is the relevance of the accounting model. In other words, the resulting financial statements should be useful. Sterling defines relevance as follows:

> If a decision model specifies an attribute as an input or as a calculation, then that attribute is relevant to that decision model.[7]

Because decision models are not available or are not well specified, relevance focuses on what ought to be measured. For our purposes, the problem is to decide whether NOD or COG constitutes the relevant measure. From a normative point of view, the answer is straightforward. Because COG expresses changes in both the specific and general price levels, it should be considered the most relevant attribute. COG expresses the goods that could be commanded in either the input or the output market. Thus, COG can be defined, in terms of the input market, as price-level-adjusted replacement-cost or, in terms of the output market, as a price-level-adjusted net realizable value.

16.3 Illustration of the different accounting models

To illustrate the different accounting models, we will consider the simplified case of the DeCooning Company, which was formed January 1, 19X6, to distribute a new product called "Omega". Capital is composed of $3,000 equity and $3,000 liabilities that carry a 10 percent interest. On January 1, the DeCooning Company began operations by purchasing 600 units of Omega at $10 per unit. On May 1, the company sold 500 units at $15 per unit. Changes in the general and specific price levels for the year 19X6 are:

	January 1 $	May 1 $	December 31 $
Replacement cost	10	12	13
Net realizable value	0	15	17
General price-level index	100	130	156

A brief description of each accounting model follows, accompanied by illustrations using the given data.

16.3.1 Alternative accounting models expressed in units of money

To illustrate and isolate only the timing difference, first we will present the alternative accounting models that do *not* reflect changes in the general price level. These models are (1) historical-cost accounting, (2) replacement-cost accounting, and (3) net-realizable-value accounting. The income statements and the balance sheets for 19X6 under the three accounting models are shown in Exhibits 16.1 and 16.2 respectively.

	Historical cost $	Replacement cost $	Net realizable value $
Revenues	7,500[a]	7,500	9,200[b]
Cost of goods sold	5,000[c]	6,000[d]	7,300[e]
Gross margin	2,500	1,500	1,900
Interest (10%)	300	300	300
Operating income	2,200	1,200	1,600
Realized holding gains and losses (included above)		1,000[f]	1,000
Unrealized holding gains and losses (not applicable)		300[g]	300
General price-level gains and losses (not applicable)		(not applicable)	(not applicable)
Net income	2,200	2,500	2,900

[a] $500 \times \$15 = \$7,500$
[b] $7,500 + (\$17 \times 100) = \$9,200$
[c] $500 \times \$10 = \$5,000$
[d] $500 \times \$12 = \$6,000$
[e] $6,000 + (\$13 \times 100) = \$7,300$
[f] $500 (\$12 - \$10) = \$1,000$
[g] $100 (\$13 - \$10) = \$300$

Exhibit 16.1 DeCooning Company. Income statement for the year ended December 31, 19X6

	Historical cost $	Replacement cost $	Net realizable value $
Assets			
Cash	7,200	7,200	7,200
Inventory	1,000	1,300[a]	1,700[b]
Total assets	8,200	8,500	8,900
Equities			
Bonds (10%)	3,000	3,000	3,000
Capital	3,000	3,000	3,000
Retained earnings			
Realized	2,200	2,200[c]	2,200[c]
Unrealized	(not applicable)	300	700[d]
Total equities	8,200	8,500	8,900

[a] $100 \times \$13 = \$1,300$
[b] $100 \times \$17 = \$1,700$
[c] May be divided into current operating profit ($1,200) and realized holding gains and losses ($1,000)
[d] Unrealized operating gain $400 ($1,700 − $1,300) + unrealized holding gain $300

Exhibit 16.2 DeCooning Company. Balance sheet for the year ended December 31, 19X6

Historical-cost accounting

Historical-cost accounting, or *conventional accounting*, is characterized primarily by:

1. the use of historical cost as the attribute of the elements of financial statements;
2. the assumption of a stable monetary unit;
3. the matching principle; and
4. the realization principle.

Accordingly, *historical-cost income*, or *accounting income*, is the difference between realized revenues and their corresponding historical costs. As shown in Exhibit 16.1, accounting income is equal to $2,200. What does this figure represent to the DeCooning Company? Generally, it is perceived as a basis for the computation of taxes and dividends and for the evaluation of performance. Its possible use in various decision models results from the unconditional and long-standing acceptance of this version of income by the accounting profession and the business world. This attachment to accounting income may be explained primarily by the fact that it is objective, verifiable, practical and easy to understand. Accountants and business people may prefer accounting income over other measures of income due to its practical advantages and the concern that confusion could result from the adoption of another accounting model.

Despite these practical advantages, both timing and measuring-unit errors are reflected in DeCooning's accounting income figure of $2,200. First, the accounting income contains timing errors because this single figure (1) includes operating income and holding gains and losses that are recognized in the current period and that occurred in previous periods, and (2) omits the operating profit and holding gains and losses that occurred in the current period but that are recognizable in future periods. Second, the accounting income contains measuring-unit errors because (1) it does not take into account changes in the general price level that would have resulted in amounts expressed in units of general purchasing power, and (2) it does not take into account changes in the specific price level, because it relies on historical cost (rather than replacement cost of net realizable value) as the attribute of the elements of financial statements.

Then how should we evaluate historical-cost financial statements? First, they are *interpretable*. Historical-cost financial statements are based on the concept of money maintenance, and the attribute being expressed is the *number of dollars* (NOD). The balance sheet reports the stocks in NOD as of December 31, 19X6, and the income statement reports the change in NOD during the year.

Second, historical-cost financial statements are *not relevant because the command of goods* (COG) is not measured. A measure of COG reflects changes in both the specific price level and the general price level, and, as such, represents the ability to buy the amount of goods necessary for capital maintenance.

In summary, historical-cost financial statements:

1. contain timing errors;
2. contain measuring-unit errors;
3. are interpretable; and
4. are not relevant.

Replacement cost accounting

Replacement-cost accounting, as a particular case of current-entry-price-based accounting, is characterized primarily by:

1. the use of replacement cost as the attribute of the elements of financial statements;
2. the assumption of a stable monetary unit;
3. the realization principle;
4. the dichotomization of operating income and holding gains and losses; and
5. the dichotomization of realized and unrealized holding gains and losses.

Accordingly, *replacement-cost net income* is equal to the sum of replacement-cost operating income and holding gains and losses. *Replacement-cost operating income* is equal to the difference between realized revenues and their corresponding replacement costs. From Exhibit 16.1, the DeCooning Company's replacement-cost income of $2,500 is composed of (1) replacement-cost operating income of $1,200, (2) realized holding gains and losses of $1,000, and (3) unrealized holding gains and losses of $300.

What do these figures represent for DeCooning? The replacement-cost operating income of $1,200 represents the "distributable" income, or the maximum amount of dividends that DeCooning can pay and maintain its productive capacity. The realized holding gains and losses of $1,000 are an indicator of the efficiency of holding resources up to the point of sale. The realized holding gains and losses are an indicator of the efficiency of holding resources after the point of sale and may act as a predictor of future operating and holding performances.

In addition to these practical advantages, replacement-cost net income contains timing errors only on operating profit. It does, however, contain measuring-unit errors. First, the replacement-cost net income contains timing errors because (1) it omits the operating profit that occurred in the current period but that is realizable in future periods, (2) it includes the operating profit that is recognized in the current period but that occurred in previous periods, and (3) it includes holding gains and losses in the same period in which they occur. Second, the replacement-cost net income contains measuring-unit errors because (1) it does not take into account changes in the general price level that would have resulted in amounts expressed in units of general purchasing power and (2) it does take into account changes in the specific price level, because it relies on replacement-cost as the attribute of the elements of financial statements.

We may evaluate replacement-cost financial statements as follows. First, they are *interpretable*. Replacement-cost financial statements are based on the concept of productive-capacity maintenance, and the attribute being expressed is the number of dollars (NOD) in the income statement. The asset figures, however, are interpretable as measures of the command of goods (COG). The asset figures shown in Exhibit 16.2 are expressed in terms of the purchasing power of the dollar at the end of the year. They reflect changes in both the specific price level and the general price level and therefore represent the COG required for capital maintenance. Second, because COG is the relevant attribute, the replacement-cost net income is not relevant, even though the asset figures are relevant.

In summary, replacement-cost financial statements:

1. contain timing errors in operating profit;

2. contain measuring-unit errors;

3. are interpretable as NOD for income-statement figures and as COG for asset figures; and

4. provide relevant measures of COG only for asset figures.

Net-realizable-value accounting

Net-realizable-value accounting, as a particular case of current-exit-price-based accounting, is characterized primarily by:

1. the use of net realizable value as the attribute of the elements of financial statements;

2. the assumption of a stable monetary unit;

3. the abandonment of the realization principle; and

4. the dichotomization of operating income and holding gains and losses.

Accordingly, *net-realizable-value net income* is equal to the sum of net-realizable-value operating income and holding gains and losses. *Net-realizable-value operating income* is equal to the operating income on sales and the net operating income on inventory. Operating income on sales is equal to the difference between realized revenues and their corresponding replacement costs of the items sold. In Exhibit 16.1, the DeCooning Company's net-realizable-value net income of $2,900 is composed of (1) net-realizable-value operating income of $1,600, (2) realized holding gains and losses of $1,000, and (3) unrealized holding gains and losses of $300.

Note that the net-realizable-value operating income of $1,600 is composed of operating income on sales of $1,200 and operating income on inventory of $400. Thus, in Exhibit 16.2, unrealized retained earnings equal the sum of unrealized holding gains and losses of $300 and operating income on inventory of $400.

What do these figures represent for DeCooning? They are similar to the figures obtained with replacement-cost accounting, except for the operating income on inventory, which results from the abandonment of the realization principle and the recognition of revenues at the time of production and at the time of sale. Net-realizable-value net income is an indicator of the ability of the firm to liquidate and to adapt to new economic situations.

To these practical advantages, we may add that net-realizable-value net income contains no timing errors, but it does contain measuring-unit errors. First, the net-realizable-value net income does not contain any timing errors (as shown in Exhibit 16.3) because (1) it reports all operating profit and holding gains and losses in the same period in which they occur, and (2) it excludes all operating and holding gains and losses that occurred in previous periods. Second, the net-realizable-value net income contains measuring-unit errors because (1) it does not take into account changes in the general price level (if it had, it would have resulted in amounts expressed in units of general purchasing power), and (2) it does take into account changes in the specific price level because it relies on net realizable value as the attribute of the elements of financial statements.

We may evaluate net-realizable-value financial statements as follows. First, they are *interpretable*. Net-realizable-value financial statements are based on the concept of productive-capacity maintenance. The attribute being measured is expressed in NOD on the income statement and in COG on the balance sheet. Unlike replacement-cost accounting, under net-realizable-value accounting, asset figures are expressed as measures of COG in the output market rather than in the input market.

Second, because COG is the relevant attribute, net-realizable-value income is *not relevant*, although the asset figures are relevant. In summary, net-realizable-value financial statements:

1. contain no timing errors;
2. contain measuring-unit errors;
3. are interpretable as NOD for net income and as COG for asset figures; and
4. provide relevant measures of COG only for asset figures.

	Historical cost $		Replacement cost $		Net realizable value $	
Total operating and holding gains	Reported income	Error	Reported income	Error	Reported income	Error
$2,900	$2,200	$700	$2,500	$400	$2,900	0

Exhibit 16.3 DeCooning Company. Timing-error analysis for the year ended December 31, 19X6

16.3.2 Alternative accounting models expressed in units of general purchasing power

To illustrate both timing and measuring-unit errors in this section, we will present accounting models that reflect changes in the general price level. These models are:

1. general price-level-adjusted, historical-cost accounting;
2. general price-level-adjusted, replacement-cost accounting; and
3. general price-level-adjusted, net-realizable-value accounting.

Continuing with our example of the DeCooning Company, the income statement and the balance sheet for 19X6, under the three accounting models, appear in Exhibits 16.4 and 16.5, respectively. The general price-level gain or loss is shown in Exhibit 16.6.

General price-level-adjusted, historical-cost accounting

General price-level-adjusted, historical-cost accounting is characterized primarily by:

1. the use of historical cost as the attribute of the elements of financial statements;
2. the use of general purchasing power as the unit of measure;
3. the matching principle; and
4. the realization principle.

	Historical cost $	Replacement cost $	Net realizable value $
Revenues	9,000[a]	9,000	10,700[b]
Cost of goods sold	7,800[c]	7,200[d]	8,500[e]
Gross margin	1,200	1,800	2,200
Interest (10%)	300	300	300
Operating income	900	1,500	1,900
Real realized holding			
Gains and losses	(included above)	(600)[f]	(600)
Real unrealized holding			
Gains and losses	(not applicable)	(260)[g]	(260)
General price-level			
Gain or loss	180[h]	180	180
Net income	1,080	820	1,220

[a] $7,500 \times \dfrac{156}{130} = \$9,000$

[b] $\$9,000 + (\$17 \times 100 \text{ units}) = \$10,700$

[c] $\$5,000 \times \dfrac{156}{100} = \$7,800$

[d] $\$6,000 \times \dfrac{156}{130} = \$7,200$

[e] $\$7,200 + (\$13 \times 100 \text{ units}) = \$8,500$

[f] $[(\$12 \times \dfrac{156}{130}) - (\$10 \times 156)] \times \dfrac{500}{100} = (\$600)$

[g] $[\$13 - (\$10 \times \dfrac{156}{100})] \times 100 \text{ units} = (\$260)$

[h] See Exhibit 16.6

Exhibit 16.4 DeCooning Company. General price-level income statements for the year ended December 31, 19X6

	Historical cost $	Replacement cost $	Net realizable value $
Assets			
Cash	7,200	7,200	7,200
Inventory	1,560[a]	1,300	1,700
Total assets	8,760	8,500	8,900
Equities			
Bonds (10%)	3,000	3,000	3,000
Capital	4,680[b]	4,680	4,680
Retained earnings			
Realized	900	900	900
Unrealized	(not applicable)	(260)	140[c]
General price-level			
Gain or loss	180	180	180
Total equities	8,760	8,500	8,900

[a]$1,000 × $\frac{156}{100}$ = $1,560

[b]$3,000 × $\frac{156}{100}$ = $4,680

[c]Unrealized operating gain $400 ($1,700–$7,300) + Unrealized holding loss $260

Exhibit 16.5 DeCooning Company. General price-level balance sheets for the year ended December 31, 19X6

	Unadjusted amount $	Conversion factor $	Adjusted amount $
Net monetary assets on January 1, 19X5	3,000	156/100	4,680
Add: Monetary receipts during 19X6			
Sales	7,500	156/130	9,000
Net monetary items	10,500		13,680
Less: Monetary payments			
Purchases	6,000	156/100	9,360
Interest (10%)	300	156/156	300
Total	6,300		9,660
Computed net monetary assets, December 31, 19X6			4,020
Actual net monetary assets, December 31, 19X6			4,200
General price-level gain			180

Exhibit 16.6 DeCooning Company. General price-level gain or loss for the year ended December 31, 19X6

Accordingly, general price-level-adjusted, historical-cost income is the difference between realized revenues and their corresponding historical costs, both expressed in units of general purchasing power. In Exhibit 16.4, general price-level-adjusted, historical-cost income is equal to $1,080. Included in the $1,080 historical-cost income figure is a $180 general price-level gain, computed as shown in Exhibit 16.5. Again, what does the $1,080 figure represent to the DeCooning Company? It represents accounting income expressed in dollars that have the purchasing power of dollars at the end of 19X6. In addition to the practical advantages listed for accounting income, general price-level-adjusted, historical-cost income is expressed in units of general purchasing power. For these reasons, the use of such an accounting model may constitute a less radical change for those used to historical-cost income than any current-value accounting model.

Despite these practical advantages, the general price-level-adjusted, historical-cost income of $1,080 contains the same timing errors that historical-cost income contains. However, general price-level-adjusted, historical-cost income contains no measuring-unit errors, because it takes into account changes in the general price level. It does not, however, take into account changes in the specific price level, because it relies on historical cost, rather than replacement cost or net realizable value, as the attribute of the elements of financial statements. How should we evaluate the general price-level-adjusted, historical-cost financial statements presented in Exhibits 16.4 and 16.5? First, they are *interpretable*. General price-level-adjusted, historical-cost financial statements are based on the concept of purchasing-power money maintenance. The attribute being measured is NOD in some cases and COG in other cases. Hence, general price-level-adjusted, historical-cost income and balance sheet figures, with the exception of cash (and monetary assets and liabilities), may be interpreted as NOD measures. Only the cash figures (and monetary assets an liabilities) may be interpreted as COG measures. Second, only the cash figures (and monetary assets and liabilities) are *relevant*, because they are expressed as COG measures.

In summary, general price-level-adjusted, historical-cost financial statements:

1. contain timing errors;
2. contain no measuring-unit errors;
3. are interpretable; and
4. provide relevant measures of COG only for cash figures (and monetary assets and liabilities).

General price-level-adjusted, replacement-cost accounting

General price-level-adjusted, replacement-cost accounting is characterized primarily by:

1. the use of replacement cost as the attribute of the elements of financial statements;
2. the use of general purchasing power as the unit measure;
3. the realization principle;
4. the dichotomization of operating income and real realized holding gains and losses; and
5. the dichotomization of real realized and real unrealized holding gains and losses.

Accordingly, *general price-level-adjusted, replacement-cost income* is equal to the difference between realized revenues and their corresponding replacement costs, both expressed in units of general purchasing power. Similarly, general price-level-adjusted, replacement-cost financial statements eliminate "fictitious holding gains and losses" to arrive at "real holding gains and losses". Fictitious holding gains and losses represent the general price-level restatement that is required to maintain the general purchasing power of nonmonetary items. We can see from Exhibit 16.4 that general price-level replacement-cost income is equal to $820. Included in the $820 income figure is a $180 general price-level gain computed as shown in Exhibit 16.5. The $820 figure represents DeCooning's replacement-cost net income, expressed in units of general purchasing power at the end of 19X7. Such a measure of income has all of the advantages of replacement-cost accounting income and the added advantage of being expressed in units of general purchasing power.

For these reasons, general price-level-adjusted, replacement-cost accounting constitutes a net improvement over replacement-cost accounting, because this accounting model not only adopts replacement cost as the attribute of the elements cost financial statements but also employs a general purchasing power as the unit of measure. Despite these improvements, however, general price-level-adjusted, replacement-cost income contains the same timing errors that replacement-cost income contains. Second, general price-level-adjusted, replacement-cost income contains no measuring-unit error because it takes into account changes in the general price level. In addition, this measure of income takes into account changes in the specific price level, because it adopts. replacement cost as the attribute of the element of financial statements.

How should we evaluate the general price-level-adjusted, replacement-cost financial statements presented in Exhibits 16.4 and 16.5? First, they are *interpretable*. General price level-adjusted, replacement-cost financial statements are based on the concept of purchasing-power, productive-capacity maintenance. The figures on both the income statement and the balance sheet are expressed as COG measures. Second, general price-level-adjusted, replacement-cost financial statements are relevant, because they are expressed as COG measures. Note, however, that COG is in the input market, rather than the output market.

In summary, general price-level-adjusted, replacement-cost financial statements:

1. contain timing errors;
2. contain no measuring-unit errors;
3. are interpretable; and
4. provide relevant measures of COG in the input market.

General price-level-adjusted, net-realizable-value accounting

General price-level-adjusted, net-realizable-value accounting is characterized primarily by:

1. the use of net realizable value as the attribute of the elements of financial statements;
2. the use of general purchasing power as the unit of measure;
3. the abandonment of the realization principle;
4. the dichotomization of operating income and real holding gains and losses; and
5. the dichotomization of real realized and real unrealized gains and losses.

Accordingly, general price-level-adjusted, net-realizable-value net income is equal to the sum of net-realizable-value operating income and holding gains and losses, both expressed in units of general purchasing power. The general price-level-adjusted, net-realizable-value operating income is equal to the sum of operating income arising from sale and operating income on inventory, both expressed in units of general purchasing power. From Exhibit 16.4 the general price-level-adjusted, net-realizable-value net income of $1,220 is composed of (1) general price-level-adjusted, net-realizable-value operating income of $1,900, (2) real realized holding losses of ($600), (3) real unrealized holding losses of ($200), and (4) a general price-level gain of $180.

Again, the general price-level-adjusted, net-realizable-value operating income of $1,900 is composed of general price-level-adjusted, net-realizable-value operating income on sales of $1,500 and general price-level-adjusted, net-realizable-value operating income on inventory of $400.

In addition to the advantages of net-realizable-value net income, general price-level-adjusted, net-realizable-value net income is expressed in units of general purchasing power.

For these reasons, general price-level-adjusted, net-realizable-value accounting represents a net improvement on net-realizable-value accounting, because it not only adopts net realizable value as an attribute of the elements of financial statements but also employs general purchasing power as the unit of measure.

Thus, general price-level-adjusted, net-realizable-value income contains *no* timing errors (as explained in the discussion of net-realizable-value accounting) and *no* measuring-unit errors, because it is expressed in units of general purchasing power. How should we evaluate the general price-level-adjusted, net-realizable-value financial statements presented in Exhibits 16.4 and 16.5? First, they are *interpretable*. General price-level-adjusted, net-realizable-value financial statements are based on the concept of purchasing-power, productive-capacity maintenance. The figures on both the income statement and the balance sheet are expressed as COG measures. Second, these financial statements are *relevant*, because they are expressed as COG measures. Note, however, that COG is in the *output market* rather than the input market.

In summary, general price-level-adjusted, net-realizable-value financial statements:

1. contain no timing errors;
2. contain no measuring-unit errors;
3. are interpretable; and
4. provide relevant measures of COG in the output market.

Such statements, therefore, meet all of the criteria established for the comparison and evaluation of the alternative accounting models, as shown in Exhibit 16.7.

Accounting model	Timing error operating profit	Holding gains	Interpretation measuring-unit error	NOD	COG	Relevance
1. Historical-cost accounting	Yes	Yes	Yes	Yes	No	No
2. Replacement-cost accounting	Yes	Eliminated	Yes	Yes (income statement)	Yes (asset figures)	Yes (asset figures)
3. Net-realizable-value accounting	Eliminated	Eliminated	Yes	Yes (income statement)	Yes (monetary assets and liabilities)	Yes (monetary assets and liabilities)
4. General price-level-adjusted historical cost accounting	Yes	Yes	Eliminated	Yes	Yes	Yes
5. General price-level-adjusted replacement cost accounting	Yes	Eliminated	Eliminated	Eliminated	Yes	Yes
6. General price-level-adjusted net realizable-value accounting	Eliminated	Eliminated	Eliminated	Eliminated	Yes	Yes

Exhibit 16.7 Error-type analysis

16.4 Toward a solution to the problem of financial reporting and changing prices

16.4.1 Early attempts

Long recognized as a problem in the accounting literature, the issue of accounting for changing prices has been extensively studied by the various accounting standard-setting bodies. The AICPA Committee on Accounting Procedures in 1947, 1948, and 1953[8] and APB Opinion No. 6, entitled *Status of Accounting Research Bulletins*, all examined the problems related to changes in the general price level without success. These attempts were followed by the AICPA's publication of Accounting Research Study No. 6, *Reporting the Financial Effects of Price-Level Changes*, in 1963, and by APB Statement No. 3, *Financial Statements Restated for General Price-Level Changes*, in June 1969. Both documents recommended the supplemental disclosure of general price-level information without success. The Financial Accounting Standards Board approached the price-level issue at a time when inflation was a major concern in the economy. After issuing a Discussion Memorandum (*Reporting the Effects of General Price-Level Changes in Financial Statements*) on February 15, 1974, an Exposure Draft (*Financial Reporting in Units of General Purchasing Power*) on December 31, 1974, a Research Report (*Field Tests of Financial Reporting in Units of General Purchasing Power*) in May 1977, another Exposure Draft (*Financial Reporting and Changing Price*) on December 28, 1978, and a supplemental Exposure Draft to the 1974 proposed statement on general purchasing-power adjustments (*Constant Dollar Accounting*) on March 2, 1979, the Board issued FASB Statement No. 33, *Financial Reporting and Changing Prices*, in September 1979, calling for information on the effects of both general inflation and specific price changes.

16.4.2 Financial reporting and changing prices: a step forward

FASB Statement No. 33 is the result of years of attempts by the diverse standard-setting bodies to develop methods of reporting the effects of inflation on earnings and assets. In its deliberations, the FASB considered a variety of accounting systems,[9] which can be grouped under the following headings:

1. Measuring of inventory and property, plant, and equipment:
   (a) Historical cost.
   (b) Current reproduction cost.
   (c) Current replacement cost.
   (d) Net realizable value.
   (e) Net present value of expected future cash flows (value in use).
   (f) Recoverable amount.
   (g) Current cost.
   (h) Value of business (current cost of lower recoverable amount).

2. Concepts of capital maintenance:
   (a) Financial capital maintenance.
   (b) Physical capital maintenance (the maintenance of operating capacity).

3. Measuring units:
   (a) Measurements in nominal dollars.
   (b) Measurements in constant dollars.

This list suggests that the FASB examined all of the alternative asset-valuation and income-determination models presented in this chapter. The Board concluded, however, that supplementary information should be presented according to historical-cost/constant-dollar accounting and current-cost accounting. More specifically, the FASB now requires major companies to disclose the effects of both general inflation and specific price changes as supplementary information in their published annual reports. Major companies are defined as companies with assets of more than $1 billion (after deducting accumulated depreciation) or with inventory and property, plant, and equipment of more than $125 million (before deducting accumulated depreciation).

The requirements of FASB Statement No. 33 are outlined below. FASB Statement No. 33 has since been replaced by FASB Statement No. 89, on broadly similar lines. However, Statement No. 89 is optional, not a requirement.

1. *Constant-dollar disclosures (current year)*

   (a) Information on income from continuing operations for the current fiscal year, on a historical-cost/constant-dollar basis.

   (b) The general purchasing-power gain or loss on net monetary items for the current fiscal year. The general purchasing-power gain or loss on net monetary items shall *not* be included in income from continuing operations.

2. *Current-cost disclosures (current-year)*

   An enterprise is required to disclose:

   (a) Information on income from continuing operations for the current fiscal year, on a current-cost basis.

   (b) The current-cost amounts of inventory and property, plant, and equipment at the end of the current fiscal year.

   (c) Increases or decreases for the current fiscal year in the current-cost amounts of inventory and property, plant, and equipment, net of inflation. The increases or decreases in current-cost amounts shall *not* be included in income from continuing operations.

3. *Five-year summary data*

   (a) Net sales and other operating revenues.

   (b) Historical-cost/constant-dollar information:
       i   Income from continuing operations.
       ii   Income per common share from continuing operations.
       iii Net assets at fiscal year-end.

   (c) Current-cost information (except for individual years in which the information was excluded from the current-year disclosures):
       i   Income from continuing operations.
       ii   Income per common share from continuing operations.
       iii Net assets at fiscal year-end.
       iv   Increases or decreases for the current fiscal year in the current-cost amount.

   (d) Other information:
       i   General purchasing-power gain or loss on net monetary items.
       ii   Cash dividends declared per common share.
       iii Market price par common share at fiscal year-end.

4. *Limitation*

   Whenever the recoverable amount of an asset is less than either the constant-dollar value or the current-cost value, the recoverable amount should be used to value the asset. "Recoverable amount" means the current value of the net cash flow expected to be realized from the use or sale of the asset.

5. *Methodology*

   (a) The constant-dollar method should use the Consumer Price Index for All Urban Consumers.

   (b) The current-cost method may use internally or externally developed specific price indices or evidence such as vendor invoice prices or price lists to determine the current cost of an asset. The method selected should be based on availability and cost, and should be applied consistently.

   (c) The constant-dollar amounts should be based on average-for-the-year indices.

   (d) The current costs should be based on average current costs of the period for the restatement of items required to compute operating income (cost of goods sold, depreciation and depletion), and should be restated at end-of-period current costs, net of general inflation, for the measurement of increases or decreases in inventory, plant, property and equipment. The latter statement requires the use of year-end current costs restated in average-for-the-period constant dollars.[10]

FASB Statement No. 33 provided the following information to explain the minimum disclosure requirements for constant-dollar and current-cost data:

1. Income from continuing operations is income after applicable income taxes, excluding the results of discontinued operations, extraordinary items, and the cumulative effects of accounting changes. If none of the foregoing is present for a business enterprise, income from continuing operations is identical to net income.

2. The general purchasing-power gain or loss on net monetary items and the increase or decrease in current-cost amounts are excluded from income from continuing operations.

3. Current-cost information need not be disclosed if it is not materially different from constant-dollar information. The reasons for the omission of current-cost information must be disclosed in notes to the supplemental information.

4. Information relating to income from continuing operations may be presented either in the format of a conventional income statement or in a reconciliation format that discloses adjustments to income from continuing operations in the historical cost/nominal-dollar income statement.

5. The *average* Consumer Price Index for All Urban Consumers (CPI-U) is used by business enterprises that present only the minimum constant-dollar data for a fiscal year. If an enterprise presents comprehensive financial statements on a constant dollar basis, either the *average* or the *year-end* CPI-U may be used.

6. An enterprise that presents only the minimum data required by FASB Statement No. 33 need not restate any financial statement amounts other than inventories, plant assets, cost of goods sold, and depreciation, depletion, and amortization expense.

7. If the historical-cost/constant-dollar amounts or the current-cost amounts of inventories and plant assets exceed the recoverable amounts of those assets, all data required by FASB Statement No. 33 must be presented on the basis of the lower recoverable amounts. The recoverable amount of an asset *expected to be sold* is the net realizable value of the asset (expected sales proceeds less costs of completion and disposal). The recoverable amount of an asset *in continuing use* is its value in use (net present value of future cash inflows, including ultimate proceeds on disposal). Thus, *value in use* is synonymous with *direct valuation*.

8. The current costs of inventories, plant assets, cost of goods sold, and depreciation, depletion, and amortization expense may be determined by one of the following methods:

(a) Indexation by use of either externally or internally developed specific-price indices.

(b) Direct pricing by use of current invoice prices; vendor price lists, quotations, or estimates; or standard manufacturing costs that reflect current costs.[11]

Exhibits 16.8, 16.9 and 16.10 illustrate these FASB requirements. Thus, FASB Statement No. 33 required two supplemental income computations, one dealing with the effects of general inflation and the other with specific price changes. Both types of information were intended to help users make decisions about investment, lending and other matters in the following specific ways:

1. *Assessment of future cash flows*: Present financial statements include measurements expenses and assets at historical prices. When prices are changing, measurements that reflect current prices are likely to provide useful information for the assessment of future cash flows.

2. *Assessment of enterprise performance*: The worth of an enterprise can be increased as result of the prudent timing of asset purchases when prices are changing. The increase is one aspect of performance, even though it may be distinguished from operating performance. Measurements that reflect current prices can provide a basis for assessing the extent to which past decisions about the acquisition of assets have created opportunities for earning cash flows.

3. *Assessment of the erosion of operating capability*: An enterprise typically must hold minimum quantities of inventory, property, plant, equipment and other assets to maintain its ability to provide goods and services. When the prices of those assets are

	As reported in the primary statements	Adjusted for general inflation	Adjusted for changes in specific prices (current costs)
	$	$	$
Net sales and other operating revenues	500,000	500,000	500,000
Cost of goods sold	400,000	450,000	455,000
Depreciation and amortization expense	20,000	25,000	26,000
Other operating expenses	40,000	40,000	40,000
Interest expense	15,000	15,000	15,000
Provision for income taxes	20,000	20,000	20,000
Total expenses	495,000	550,000	556,000
Income (loss) from continuing operations	5,000	(50,000)	(56,000)
Gain from decline in general purchasing power of net amounts owned		5,000	5,000
Increase in specific prices (current costs) of inventories and property, plant, and equipment held during the year[a]			30,000
Effect of increase in general price level			20,000
Excess of increase in specific prices over increase in general price level			10,000

[a]As of December 31, 19X5, current cost of inventory is $55,000 and current cost of property, plant, and equipment, net of accumulated depreciation, is $80,000

Exhibit 16.8 Statement of income from continuing operations adjusted for changing prices for the year ended December 31, 19X6 (in thousands of average 19X5 dollars)

	Year ended December 31				
	19X1 $	19X2 $	19X3 $	19X4 $	19X5 $
Net sales and other operating revenues	350,000	400,000	420,000	450,000	500,000
Historical-cost information adjusted for general inflation					
Income (loss) from continuing operations				(29,000)	(20,000)
Income (loss) from continuing operations per common share				(2.0)	(2.0)
Net assets at year-end				100,000	120,000
Current-cost information					
Income (loss) from continuing operations				(10,000)	(26,000)
Income (loss) from continuing operations per common share				(1.00)	(2.6)
Excess of increase in specific prices over increase in general price-level				5,000	10,000
Net assets at year-end				120,000	130,000
Gain from decline in general purchasing power of net amounts owed				4,500	5,000
Cash dividends declared per common share	2.00	2.05	2.10	2.15	2.20
Market price per common share at year-end	40	30	45	40	39
Average consumer price	170.5	181.5	195.4	205.0	220.9

Exhibit 16.9 Five-year comparison of selected supplemental financial data adjusted for changing prices (in thousands of average 19X5 dollars)

	$	$
Income from continuing operations, as reported on the income statement		5,000
Adjustments to restate costs for the effect of general inflation		
Cost of goods sold	(50,000)	
Depreciation and amortization expense	(5,000)	(55,000)
Loss from continuing operations adjusted for general inflation		(50,000)
Adjustments to reflect the difference between general inflation and changes in specific prices (current costs)		
Cost of goods sold	(5,000)	
	(1,000)	(6,000)
Loss from continuing operations adjusted for changes in specific prices		(56,000)
Gain from decline in general purchasing power of net amounts owed		5,000
Increase in specific prices (current costs) of inventories and property, plant, and equipment held during the year[a]		30,000
Effect of increase in general price level		20,000
Excess of increase in specific prices over increase in general price level		10,000

[a]As of December 31,19X5, current cost of inventory is $55,000 and current cost of property, plant, and equipment, net of accumulated depreciation, is $80,000.

Exhibit 16.10 Statement of income from continuing operations adjusted for changing prices for the year ended December 31, 19X6 (in thousands of average 19X5 dollars)

increasing, larger amounts of money must be invested to maintain the previous levels of output. Information on the current prices of resources that are used to generate revenues can help users assess the extent to which and the manner in which operating capability has been maintained.

4. *Assessment of erosion of general purchasing power*: When general price-levels are increasing larger amounts of money are required to maintain a fixed amount of purchasing power. Investors typically are concerned with assessing whether or not an enterprise has maintained the purchasing power of its capital. Financial information that reflects changes in general purchasing power can help investors make that assessment.[12]

Obviously, because it required the presentation of both general price-level and specific price-level information, FASB Statement No. 33 was a step forward. It fell short, however, of a total solution, which would require the use of general price-level-restated, current-cost accounting in conjunction with general price-level-restated, replacement-cost cost accounting or with general price-level-restated, net-realizable-value accounting. Moreover, some of the specific requirements discussed in FASB Statement No. 33 did not pertain to most situations.[13]

16.5 Conclusions

Given the existence of four measurable attributes of the elements of financial statements and two units of measure in which to express these attributes, eight alternative asset-valuation and income-determination models exist:

1. historical-cost accounting;
2. replacement-cost accounting;
3. net-realizable-value accounting;
4. present-value accounting;
5. general price-level-adjusted, historical-cost accounting;
6. general price-level-adjusted, replacement-cost accounting;
7. general price-level-adjusted, net-realizable-value accounting;
8. general price-level-adjusted, present-value accounting.

In this chapter, we have compared and evaluated six of these models on the basis of four criteria: (1) the avoidance of timing errors, (2) the avoidance of measuring-unit errors, (3) their interpretability, and (4) their relevance as measures of command of goods (COG).

Although the present-value models are conceptually preferable, they were not included in our comparison and evaluation because their subjectivity and the uncertainty surrounding their use make their implementation currently impractical.

Our comparison of the remaining models revealed that the general price-level-adjusted, net-realizable-value accounting is the only model to meet each of the four criteria set forth in the chapter and therefore most closely represents a preferred-income position. FASB Statement No. 33, *Financial Reporting and Changing Prices*, and the later FASB Statement No. 89, fell short of adopting the solution and, instead, required the disclosure of supplemental information on the effects of both inflation and specific-price changes.

Notes

1. Sterling, Robert R., "Relevant Financial Reporting in an Age of Price Changes", *Journal of Accountancy* (February, 1975), pp. 42–51; Basu, S., and Hanna, J.R., *Inflation Accounting: Alternatives, Implementation Issues, and Some Empirical Evidence* (Hamilton, Ontario: The Society of Management Accountants of Canada, 1977).

2. Thomas, A.L., *The Allocation Problem in Accounting* (Sarasota, FL: American Accounting Association, 1969).

3. Sprouse, R.T., and Moonitz, Maurice, *A Tentative Set of Broad Accounting Principles for Business Enterprises*, Accounting Research Study No. 3 (New York: American Institute of Certified Public Accountants, 1962), p. 55.

4. Sterling, Robert R., "Relevant Financial Reporting in an Age of Price Changes", op. cit., p. 44.

5. Chambers, R.J., "NOD, COG, and PuPu: See How Inflation Teases!", *Journal of Accountancy* (September, 1975), p. 61.

6. Ibid., p. 61.

7. Sterling, Robert R., "Relevant Financial Reporting in an Age of Price Changes", op. cit., p. 46.

8. AICPA Committee on Accounting Procedures, Accounting Research Bulletin No. 33, *Depreciation and High Costs* (New York: American Institute of Certified Public Accountants, December, 1944); AICPA Committee on Accounting Procedures Accounting Research Bulletin No. 43, *Restatement and Revision of Accounting Research Bulletins*, Ch. 9, Section A (New York: American Institute of Certified Public Accountants, June, 1953).

9. FASB Statement No. 33, *Financial Reporting and Changing Prices* (Stamford, CT: Financial Accounting Standards Board, September, 1979), pp. 47–8.

10. Ibid., paragraphs 29, 30, 35, 51, and 52.

11. Ibid., paragraphs 9, 11, 12, 14, 17, 20, and 22.

12. Ibid., paragraph 12.

13. Several FASB pronouncements dealing with specific situations have been issued subsequent to FASB Statement No. 33. These include FASB Statement No. 39, *Financial Reporting and Changing Prices: Specialized Assets Mining and Oil and Gas* (October, 1980); FASB Statement No. 40, *Financial Reporting and Changing Prices: Specialized Assets Timberlands and Growing Timber* (November, 1980); FASB Statement No. 41, *Financial Reporting and Changing Prices: Specialized Assets Income-Producing Real Estate* (November, 1980); FASB No. 46, *Financial Reporting and Changing Prices: Specialized Assets-Motion Picture Films* (March, 1981); FASB Statement No. 89, *Financial Reporting and Changing Prices* (December, 1986).

References

Basu, S., and Hanna, J.R., *Inflation Accounting: Alternatives, Implementation Issues, and Some Empirical Evidence* (Hamilton, Ontario: The Society of Management Accountants of Canada, 1977).

Chambers, R.J., *Accounting, Evaluation, and Economic Behavior* (Englewood Cliffs, NJ: Prentice-Hall, 1966).

Chambers, R.J., "NOD, COG, and PuPu: See How Inflation Teases!", *Journal of Accountancy* (September, 1975), pp. 56–62.

Edwards, E.O., and Bell, P.W., *The Theory and Measurement of Business Income* (Berkeley: University of California Press, 1961).

Gynther, R.S., "Capital Maintenance, Price Changes, and Profit Determination", *The Accounting Review* (October, 1970), pp. 712–30.

Hanna, J.R., *Accounting-Income Models: An Application and Evaluation*. Special Study No. 8 (Toronto: The Society of Management Accountants of Canada, July, 1974).

Kerr, Jean St. G., "Three Concepts of Business Income", in Sidney Davidson *et al.* (eds.), *An Income Approach to Accounting Theory* (Englewood Cliffs, NJ: Prentice-Hall, 1964, pp. 40–8.

Louderback, J.G., "Projectability as a Criterion for Income Determination Methods", *The Accounting Review* (April, 1971), pp. 298–305.

Parker, P.W., and Gibbs, P.M.D., "Accounting for Inflation: Recent Proposals and Their Effects", *Journal of the Institute of Actuaries* (December, 1974), pp. 1–10.

Revsine, L., and Weygandt, J.J., "Accounting for Inflation: The Controversy", *Journal of Accountancy* (October, 1974), pp. 72–8.

Rosen, L.S., *Current-Value Accounting and Price-Level Restatements* (Toronto: Canadian Institute of Chartered Accountants, 1972).

Rosenfield, Paul, "Accounting for Inflation: A Field Test", *Journal of Accountancy* (June, 1969), pp. 45–50.

Rosenfield, Paul, "CPP Accounting: Relevance and Interpretability", *Journal of Accountancy* (August, 1975), pp. 52–60.

Rosenfield, Paul, "The Confusion Between General Price-Level Restatement and Current Value Accounting", *Journal of Accountancy* (October, 1972), pp. 63–8.

Sterling, Robert R., "Relevant Financial Reporting in an Age of Price Changes", *Journal of Accountancy* (February, 1975), pp. 42–51.

Sterling, Robert R., *Theory of Measurement of Enterprise Income* (Lawrence, KS: University Press of Kansas, 1970).

Wolk, H.I., "An Illustration of Four Price-Level Approaches to Income Measurement", in J. Don Edwards (ed.), *Accounting Education: Problems and Prospects* (Sarasota, FL: American Accounting Association, 1974), pp. 415–23.

Zeff, S.A., "Replacement Cost: Member of the Family Welcome Guest, or Intruder?" *The Accounting Review* (October, 1962), pp. 611–25.

Index